A Practical Guide To

Connecticut School Law

Fourth Edition

Thomas B. Mooney
Shipman & Goodwin LLP

NEW WITH THIS EDITION:

THIS FOURTH EDITION OF THE GUIDE COMES WITH A CD THAT SETS FORTH THE ENTIRE TEXT. HYPERLINKS (GREY IN THE HARD COPY, BLUE ON THE CD) ARE INCLUDED WHERE AVAILABLE, PROVIDING ACCESS THROUGH THE INTERNET TO THE SOURCE MATERIAL (STATUTES, CASES, RULINGS, ETC.). A NEW CD WILL BE AVAILABLE WHEN THE GENERAL STATUTES ARE UPDATED THROUGH 2005. PLEASE CONTACT CABE OR THE AUTHOR TO OBTAIN THE UPDATE OR IF YOUR CD IS LOST OR DAMAGED.

PUBLISHED BY:

CONNECTICUT ASSOCIATION OF BOARDS OF EDUCATION, INC.
81 WOLCOTT HILL ROAD
WETHERSFIELD, CT 06109-1242
(860) 571-7446

ISBN 0-9644680-4-2

385613 v.01

To Marlee, Emilee and Caroline
with love and thanks

THOMAS B. MOONEY is a partner in the Hartford law firm of Shipman & Goodwin LLP. Mr. Mooney attended Yale College, where he was elected to Phi Beta Kappa and graduated magna cum laude in 1973. Mr. Mooney attended Harvard Law School, graduating cum laude in 1976. Since that time, Mr. Mooney has been at Shipman & Goodwin LLP, where he chairs the firm's Education Practice Group, and he represents boards of education in Connecticut in all aspects of school law. Mr. Mooney also teaches school law courses at the University of Connecticut, where he is Adjunct Professor at the School of Law and Professor in Residence at the Neag School of Education.

Mr. Mooney has written on school law issues for a number of publications, including Education Week, The American School Boards Journal, School Law in Review, and the Connecticut Law Review. He has written about the misadventures of the Nutmeg Board of Education for the CABE Journal for the last twenty-four years. CABE published his collected columns, See You in Court! The Annals of the Nutmeg Board of Education, as well as the first edition of this Guide, in 1994. Mr. Mooney also writes "Legal Mailbag," a monthly question-and-answer column in the CAS Bulletin. In 2000, CABE conferred the Friend of Public Education Award upon Mr. Mooney for his many years of work on behalf of individual boards of education in general and for the work he has done on behalf of CABE. In 2001, the Connecticut Association of Schools presented Mr. Mooney with its Distinguished Friend of Education Award.

FOREWORD

Education of our youth is a fundamental responsibility of our society. As we seek to fulfill that responsibility, disputes are inevitable and arise with increasing frequency. The courts and the legislatures are constantly addressing the rights and responsibilities of all members of the school community: school boards, superintendents, administrators, teachers, support staff, parents and students. It is a struggle for all of us to keep up with new developments in the laws governing public education. The following review of Connecticut school law is offered as a guide to the various education law questions that arise most frequently. While lawyers may find it helpful, it is intended for anyone who is interested in the state and federal laws governing public elementary and secondary education.

Many people generously contributed to this Guide. I would like to thank my colleagues at Shipman & Goodwin LLP for their support and help in writing, editing and publishing this book. Harrison Burgess, our Librarian, was invaluable in finding cases and statutory materials, and in helping me with correct citation form. A number of lawyers at Shipman & Goodwin LLP kindly agreed to review and correct my work as well. I thank Christine Chinni, Rich Mills, Susan Freedman, Anne Littlefield, Craig Meuser, Henry Zaccardi, Andreana Bellach, Julie Fay, Elisa Bartlett, Rebecca Rudnick, Lisa Banatoski Mehta, Gabe Jiran, Catherine Intravia, Rita Graham, Linda Yoder, Saranne Murray, Brenda Eckert and Vaughan Finn and for their assistance in editing the Guide. In addition, I want to thank Dorothy Weiner, Karen Jones, Deanna Alvarez, Jeanne Swayner, Jessie Rodriguez, Margaret Poland-Steele, Gail Koval, and Carla Mitchell for their great help in getting this Fourth Edition ready for the publisher.

I wish to express special appreciation for three friends at our firm. For twenty-eight years, Brian Clemow has been my mentor, my partner and my friend. He introduced me to education law. Throughout the years, Brian has demonstrated the finest qualities of the legal profession—honesty, hard work, discipline, and dedication to the highest legal and ethical standards. I also want to thank my secretary Linda Badolato for her assistance throughout this revision. Linda works tirelessly (but somehow cheerfully) to keep me organized and to assure that our clients' needs are met. This Edition would not have been possible without her help and support. Finally, I wish to thank Patricia Vibert, my retired secretary, who for eighteen years made my problems her problems and is now enjoying some well-deserved rest and antiquing.

I wish also to thank others outside the firm who graciously agreed to review the Guide and improved my efforts immeasurably. Mark Stapleton, Ronald Harris, Theresa DeFrancis, Karen Flanagan, Katherine Nicoletti, Laura Anastasio and Robin Cecere, at the State Department of Education, Darlene Perez at the State Teachers Retirement Board, Mitchell Pearlman and Thomas Hennick at the Freedom of Information Commission, and Erik Bartlett at McGann, Bartlett & Brown all reviewed sections of the Guide. Their suggestions added substance in the areas of their expertise and helped assure that the Guide is readable and accurate.

This Guide grew out of my column, "See You in Court," which the Connecticut Association of Boards of Education has published for the last twenty-four years. I thank Bob Rader, Patrice McCarthy, Kelly Balser, Bonnie Carney and Toni Pepe for their help and support through the years.

Finally, I thank my parents, Tom and Daphne Mooney, and Marlee Denis Mooney, my wife of thirty-one years, for their love and support. Marlee is a saint to put up with me and the hours of a school board lawyer with patience and good humor. I dedicate this Guide to Marlee and our daughters Emilee and Caroline, the true loves of my life.

Thomas B. Mooney
Hartford, Connecticut
November 1, 2004
(860) 251-5710

CHAPTER FOUR
STUDENTS

TABLE OF CASES

INTRODUCTION

Our schools have always been subject to statutes and court rulings, but it has never been more difficult for school districts to keep up with their legal obligations. In recent years, there has been explosive growth in the various statutes, rules and regulations that govern school officials and their employees. Since education is fundamental to the welfare of our state and country, legislators are constantly passing new legislation affecting the schools. The General Assembly and the United States Congress enact new laws every year concerning the rights of students, parents, teachers, administrators and the public at large. At the same time, the courts are always defining and redefining statutory and constitutional rights. It is a tremendous challenge for anyone to keep up with developments in school law. This book is intended to help you understand the major provisions of Connecticut school law. The hope here is to provide practical guidance for all persons who are involved with or interested in the process of education, including school board members, superintendents, principals, teachers, parents and even students.

School law comes from a variety of sources. First, there is statutory law at both the state and federal level. In general, state statutes govern many issues of school district operation, such as board of education responsibilities, employment issues and the like. They are codified in the Connecticut General Statutes by Title, with education statutes set out in Title 10. That is why Connecticut education statutes always start out with the number 10, as in the Tenure Act, Connecticut General Statutes, § 10-151. Federal statutes address issues ranging from student records and special education to employment discrimination. They are also codified by title, and Title 20 of the United States Code contains many of the relevant statutes, such as IDEA, at 20 U.S.C. § 1400 *et seq.* The Latin "*et sequitur*" simply means "and following," *i.e.* the statutes start there and go on.

In establishing statutory rights, the General Assembly and the United States Congress often create administrative agencies that are responsible for administering and interpreting particular laws. These agencies generally adopt regulations that supplement the statutes. These regulations are binding upon persons subject to the jurisdiction of the agency. In addition, these agencies are often charged with the responsibility for hearing and adjudicating disputes based on the laws they administer. The Connecticut State Board of Education, the Connecticut State Board of Labor Relations, the Connecticut State Board of Mediation and Arbitration, the Connecticut Commission on Human Rights and Opportunities, the

Connecticut Freedom of Information Commission, and the United States Department of Education all regulate the conduct of school districts and their agents. State regulations track the statutory title that authorizes them, and thus the regulations affecting school districts usually start with 10, for Title 10, or with 31, for Title 31, Labor (*e.g.* Conn. St. Reg. § 10-145d-420).

Unfortunately, disputes arise over just what these statutes and regulations really mean. Sometimes, there is no state or federal agency directly involved, and any claims must go right to court. Where an agency is involved, however, persons with claims must first exhaust their administrative remedies before the courts will hear the claim. Once the responsible administrative agency has made a decision, it may then be appealed to court. The courts will interpret the statutes to provide clarification of the legal responsibilities of school officials.

In addition to issues involving statutory interpretation, the courts will decide other legal claims involving school districts in two other situations. First, claims may be based on common law principles, *i.e.*, court decisions that over time define rights and responsibilities not specifically set out in statute. Tort liability for negligence is an example of a common law claim. Second, claims may be based on the Connecticut Constitution or the United States Constitution. Since school districts are part of the "government," they are subject to constitutional requirements. The federal constitutional protections, such as free speech or due process, are well-known, and litigation over constitutional claims is common. The state constitution affords Connecticut residents additional protections, and it has served as the basis for various challenges affecting school districts, such as school funding and racial balance in the schools. Such claims must be made directly to the state or federal courts, which have the responsibility for interpreting the state and federal constitutions respectively.

Generally, there is provision for the appeal of court decisions. Both the federal and state judicial systems have three tiers. The first level of federal court is the federal district court. Some states are further divided into various districts, but in Connecticut there is just one district. The second level is the Court of Appeals. The country is divided into eleven circuits (and the District of Columbia Circuit), with a court of appeals for each circuit. Thus, we say that the Sixth Circuit or that the Second Circuit has issued a ruling, referring to the respective appellate court. The Second Circuit Court of Appeals covers Connecticut as well as Vermont and New York, and its decisions are binding in Connecticut.

Finally, the decisions of the courts of appeals may be appealed to the United States Supreme Court. However, the Court generally has discretion as to which cases to hear. Given the number of cases submitted to it, it will accept only a small fraction of the cases submitted, typically those that will make new law or resolve a dispute between circuits. When it declines to hear cases, the court denies "certiorari," a Latin word for "to be informed" that is used to mean permission to hear an appeal. When the Court declines to hear a case (*cert. denied*), as it often does, the lower court decision stands but we cannot assume that the Court agrees with it.

The Connecticut courts are organized in a similar fashion. The trial court in Connecticut is the Superior Court. Decisions of the Superior Court may generally be appealed to the Appellate Court. Cases decided by the Appellate Court may then be appealed to the Connecticut Supreme Court, though some cases may be certified directly to the Connecticut Supreme Court from the Superior Court. In rare cases involving questions of constitutional law, it is even possible to appeal a decision of the Connecticut Supreme Court to the United States Supreme Court.

School districts are confronted with legal requirements that can arise from each of these sources -- statutory law, administrative regulations, common law or constitutional law, each as interpreted by the state or federal courts. In the following, I have provided citations to the various statutes, regulations and court decisions to facilitate further review and research if desired. A table of cases is also provided for those situations in which the reader knows the name of a particular case and would like to do further reading. However, this book is not written solely for lawyers. This review of school law and related observations are intended to provide practical guidance and understanding to educators, school board members and parents concerning the laws affecting the schools in Connecticut.

A. The Role of Government in Education

Education in Connecticut is a right guaranteed by the Connecticut Constitution:

> There shall always be free public elementary and secondary schools in the state. The general assembly shall implement this principle by appropriate legislation.

Article Eighth, Section 1. The state has delegated this responsibility to local and regional boards of education through the general statutes. As creatures of statute, local and regional boards of education have only those powers that are granted to them by statute. However, school boards have significant discretion and authority within that statutory framework to provide for the education of children who reside within the school district.

In 1973, the United States Supreme Court ruled that education is not a right protected by the United States Constitution. *San Antonio School District v. Rodriguez*, 411 U.S. 1 (1973). In that case, the plaintiffs had challenged the Texas educational funding formula under the federal constitution. The Court dismissed their claim, however, because there is no express reference to education in the federal constitution. Accordingly, state constitutional and statutory law is the foundation for much of school law in Connecticut. Increasingly, however, the federal government is asserting a role in educational matters through the power of the purse. This federal role is described in Section A(2), below.

1. <u>The educational interests of the state</u>

Since education is a state responsibility under our Connecticut Constitution, local and regional boards of education act as agents for the State in implementing this responsibility – the "educational interests of the state." This concept has evolved significantly over the last thirty years through the seminal cases of *Horton v. Meskill* and *Sheff v. O'Neill.*

a. *Horton v. Meskill*

In 1974, the year after the *Rodriguez* case, Wesley Horton challenged the school funding statutes in state court, and the Connecticut Supreme Court decided this now-famous case in 1977. *Horton v. Meskill*, 172 Conn.

615 (1977). On behalf of his son, Barnaby Horton (then a first grade student in Canton and later a state representative representing Hartford), Mr. Horton claimed that the statutory formula for distributing state aid for education was inequitable, violating his son's right to education as guaranteed by the Connecticut Constitution. The court agreed. It ruled that the formula in place at the time was inequitable, and it directed the General Assembly to revise the funding formula. In its ruling, the court found that the Connecticut Constitution guarantees all Connecticut children "a substantially equal educational opportunity," and that the state is responsible for enacting appropriate legislation to assure that each child in Connecticut receives such an equal educational opportunity.

Following the court's decision in *Horton v. Meskill*, the General Assembly made significant changes in the statutes related to state funding for education. The legislature established a "minimum expenditure requirement" (commonly called the MER) to assure relatively equal funding of education, and it established a funding formula to provide for a "guaranteed tax base" (GTB) to help all school districts afford to fund education in compliance with the MER (discussed in greater detail at Section E(1)(a)). The plaintiffs in *Horton v. Meskill* later challenged subsequent changes in the formula that reduced aid to education, but the Connecticut Supreme Court rejected the challenge, holding that the General Assembly has some discretion in passing legislation concerning funding for education. *Horton v. Meskill (II)*, 195 Conn. 24 (1985). Over time, the GTB grant was replaced with the current program for state grants, Educational Cost Sharing (ECS), but the basic outline remains – state funding will vary with the financial capability of the local school district, but all districts must fund education at least at the MER level.

b. *Sheff v. O'Neill*

In 1989, a racially mixed group of eighteen schoolchildren residing in the city of Hartford and two neighboring suburban towns initiated a new legal challenge concerning education in Connecticut. They alleged that the racial and ethnic concentration of minorities in the Hartford schools violated their right under the state constitution to "a substantially equal educational opportunity." No federal remedy was available under the Equal Protection Clause of the U.S. Constitution, because there was no history of legally-sanctioned segregation in Connecticut. *See* Section F(11), below. The plaintiffs in *Sheff* focused, therefore, on the Connecticut Constitution. They claimed that the pattern of racial, ethnic and economic isolation in Hartford deprived students in Hartford of their right to a substantially equal educational opportunity. Plaintiffs did not allege that the state "intended" the concentration of minorities (over 90%) in the Hartford Public Schools. Rather, the plaintiffs argued that statutes providing that school district boundaries coincide with municipal boundaries perpetuate the effects of segregation. The Superior Court rejected that claim. The lower court found that the current pattern of racial separation among school districts was the result of living patterns, not any action by the state. It ruled that the significant differences in minority student populations therefore did not violate the Connecticut Constitution. *Sheff* v. *O'Neill,* 13 Conn. L. Rptr. No. 18, 533 (May 1, 1995).

In 1996, the Connecticut Supreme Court reversed. It held that funding alone does not guarantee equal educational opportunity, and that the racial and ethnic concentration of the Hartford schools violated the state Constitution. *Sheff v. O'Neill*, 238 Conn. 1 (1996). In finding for the plaintiffs, the Court considered the state's constitutional obligation to provide schoolchildren with a substantially equal educational opportunity under Article Eighth, Section 1, as well as the state constitutional guarantee that "[n]o person shall be denied the equal protection of the law nor be subjected to segregation or discrimination . . . because of . . . race." Article First, Section 20. The court decided that these two constitutional provisions must be read together, and it concluded that the existence of extreme racial and ethnic isolation deprived schoolchildren of a substantially equal educational opportunity. It then ordered the General Assembly to take appropriate remedial measures.

Characterizing the majority's opinion as result-driven, three dissenting justices hotly contested this analysis of the state constitutional provisions, the use of mastery scores for interdistrict analysis, and the finding of racial and ethnic isolation as the cause of poor academic performance. They argued that *de facto* segregation is not a constitutional violation and that the term "segregation" in the Connecticut Constitution meant intentional state action or *de jure* segregation. The dissent also argued that the poor academic performance noted by the majority was caused by poverty, and that it was inappropriate to compare performance across districts because such comparisons do not take into account important variables such as socioeconomic status, limited English proficiency, low birth-weight and "all of the other dismal factors associated with the concentration of poverty in the Hartford school district."

The majority found that the plaintiffs' claims had merit, but it did not specify a remedy; instead it referred the matter back to the General

Assembly for appropriate action. It noted, however, that "[e]very passing day denies these children their constitutional right to a substantially equal educational opportunity," and urged "the legislature and the executive branch to put the search for appropriate remedial measures at the top of their respective agendas." As described below, the General Assembly promptly adopted comprehensive legislation to address the mandates of the *Sheff* case, and those efforts continue.

c. Remedial efforts

The General Assembly enacted many remedial measures in 1997 promptly after *Sheff*. These measures do not rely on race-based school assignment to reduce racial, ethnic and economic isolation. Rather, the General Assembly addressed the problem in a number of other ways.

First, the General Assembly amended the definition of the "educational interests of the state" set out in Conn. Gen. Stat. § 10-4a to include the following statement:

> (3) in order to reduce racial, ethnic and economic isolation, each school district shall provide educational opportunities for its students to interact with students and teachers from other racial, ethnic and economic backgrounds and may provide such opportunities with students from other communities.

Conn. Gen. Stat. § 10-226h provides that local and regional boards of education may meet this new obligation by various methods: interdistrict magnet school programs; charter schools; interdistrict after-school, Saturday and summer programs and sister-school projects; intradistrict and interdistrict public school choice programs; interdistrict school building projects; interdistrict program collaboratives for students and staff minority staff recruitment; distance learning through the use of technology; and any other experience that increases awareness of the diversity of individuals and cultures.

In addition, districts must report to the appropriate regional educational service center on their efforts to reduce racial, ethnic and economic isolation every two years. These required reports are to include information on the number and duration of such programs, the number of students and staff, and evidence of progress over time in the reduction of racial, ethnic and economic isolation. In turn, regional educational service centers are obligated to report on these efforts to the Commissioner of Education, and the Commissioner of Education is obligated to report to the Governor and the General Assembly on these efforts, again every two years. The report from the Commissioner of Education is to include an analysis of the success of such programs and a recommendation for any statutory changes that would assist in the growth of such programs. Conn. Gen. Stat. § 10-226h.

Second, the General Assembly established a state-wide interdistrict public school choice program, OPEN Choice. Conn. Gen. Stat. § 10-266aa. This program is limited to the Hartford, New Haven, Bridgeport, and New London regions. In each case, students residing in any of these four cities may attend other school districts, and students in other towns in the region may elect to attend school in Hartford, New Haven, Bridgeport, or New London, respectively, subject to both space and to new rules to control the proportion of non-minority students from these cities.

Students participating in the OPEN Choice program may now attend school in the receiving school district from kindergarten through high school. The program is run on a space-available basis, and the state provides grants for tuition and for transportation. The sending school district is required to pay the special education costs in excess of the amount the receiving district receives from the state. Also, for purposes of state grant calculations, the statute provides that students participating in the program will count as one-half for both the sending and receiving school districts. *Id.*

The law directs regional educational service centers (RESCs) to assist districts in operating such programs. If a greater number of students wish to attend a district than space is available, attendance must be determined by use of a lottery designed to preserve or increase racial, ethnic and economic diversity. The statute provides, however, that preference shall be given to siblings and to students who attend a school that has lost accreditation or that has been designated a school in need of improvement under the No Child Left Behind Act, P.L. 110-107. The statute also provides that the admission policies must be consistent with Conn. Gen. Stat. § 10-15c, which prohibits discrimination on the basis of, *inter alia,* race, color, and national origin, and thereby may avoid the problems of race-based remedies under federal law, as well as the statutes concerning participation in the OPEN Choice program. Conn. Gen. Stat. § 10-266aa.

Third, the State Board of Education was required to establish a five-year implementation plan to achieve resource equity and equality of opportunity, increase student achievement, reduce racial, ethnic and economic isolation, improve effective instruction and encourage greater parental and community involvement in the schools of the state. Conn. Gen. Stat. § 10-4p. The statute required that this state plan include methods for significantly reducing disparities, provide for monitoring of the progress made, and include proposals for minority staff recruitment. These reports must include recommendations for changes in state law, budget proposals and administrative actions, and must describe the responsibility of local and regional boards of education.

Fourth, the General Assembly expanded the obligation of the State Board of Education to provide local and regional districts with a model program for the participation of parents in the schools. This program must include the participation of "the community" in the schools, and must provide for the establishment of "school-based teams" that include representation of parents, students, administrators, boards of education, community groups and other organizations. The expectations for such teams are set forth in Conn. Gen. Stat. § 10-4g. The State Board of Education is also required to develop a program to encourage local and regional boards of education to involve parents in the educational process and to increase community involvement in the schools, including providing opportunities for parents to meet with their children's teachers for the purpose of reviewing the curriculum and developing strategies for parents to assist actively in the educational process. *Id.*

Fifth, the General Assembly increased the number of state charter schools by changing the limitation from twelve local and twelve state charter schools to twenty-four charter schools overall, whether state or local. Also, the State Board of Education is required to consider the impact of a proposed charter school on the racial, ethnic and economic isolation of the student population. Admission criteria are to "promote a diverse student body" without, however, violating Conn. Gen. Stat. § 10-15c, which prohibits discrimination on the basis of race, color or national origin (among other things). Conn. Gen. Stat. § 10-66bb(c), (d).

Sixth, the statute expands the optional subjects for adult education courses to include adult literacy and parenting skills. Conn. Gen. Stat. § 10-69.

Seventh, local and regional boards of education are now required to adopt and implement written policies and procedures to "encourage parent-teacher communication." The statute does not address the potential labor relations issues related to the adoption of such policies. The statute sets out examples of policy provisions, however, providing that "[t]hese policies and procedures may include monthly newsletters, required regular contact with all parents, flexible parent-teacher conferences, drop-in hours for parents, home visits and the use of technology such as homework hot lines to allow parents to check on their children's assignments and students to get assistance if needed." Conn. Gen. Stat. § 10-221(f). Given this statute and the fact that the length and number of parent-teacher conferences are not mandatory subjects of bargaining (Conn. Gen. Stat. § 10-153d(b)), boards of education may unilaterally adopt such policies. If such policies impose a significant change in working conditions, however, negotiations may be required over the impact of such changes.

The federal No Child Left Behind Act, P.L. 110-107, imposes new requirements for school/parent communications. Section 1118 requires Title I schools to develop jointly with parents of students participating in Title I programs a written parent involvement policy regarding the school's Title I programs. This provision prescribes the elements that such a policy must include, including how parent involvement with Title I programs will be coordinated with other parent involvement strategies under other programs (*e.g.*, the requirement above for parent-teacher communication). Such policies must also describe how the school will involve parents in the joint development of its Title I plan (required by Section 1112) and in any school improvement plan as may be required by Section 1116 (if the school does not make "adequate annual process," as described in Chapter One, Section A(2)). This policy must be written in language parents can understand (in contrast to the No Child Left Behind Act, which is virtually incomprehensible). The required policy must include a "school-parent compact," outlining how parents, school staff and students will all share responsibility for improved student achievement. Each year, Title I schools are required to disseminate this policy, and must also convene an annual meeting for parents to involve them in the planning and review of programs funded by Title I.

Eighth, the General Assembly augmented statutory provisions for interdistrict magnet school programs. It clarified that two or more school districts may establish cooperative arrangements to operate interdistrict magnet programs (*see* discussion below at Section B(1)(c)), and that these cooperative arrangements may receive state funds for this purpose. Conn. Gen. Stat. § 10-264l. In considering applications for interdistrict magnet school programs, the Commissioner of Education must consider whether the program is likely to improve student performance and whether the program is likely to reduce racial, ethnic and economic isolation. Interdistrict magnet schools may not permit attendance of students from any one school district to exceed eighty percent of the students attending the school. For schools that begin operation after July 1, 2005, no participating district may have more than seventy-five percent of the total. In addition, such schools may not have a racial minority enrollment of less than twenty-five percent or more than seventy-five percent. *Id.*

Ninth, there are grants to local and regional boards of education to establish "lighthouse schools," *i.e.* a school in Hartford, New Haven or Bridgeport that has a specialized curriculum and is designed to promote public school choice within the district and with other districts. Conn. Gen. Stat. § 10-266cc.

Finally, the General Assembly amended Conn. Gen. Stat. § 10-220 in several respects. It amended the statute to require that boards of education adopt plans for minority recruitment of teachers. In addition, it addressed the issue of the physical condition of school facilities. Conn. Gen. Stat. § 10-220 sets out the basic responsibilities of local and regional boards of education, and, as amended, this statute now provides that all school boards must:

> provide an appropriate learning environment for its students which includes (1) adequate instructional books, supplies, materials, equipment, staffing, facilities and technology, (2) equitable allocation of resources among its schools, and (3) a safe school setting . . . .

Conn. Gen. Stat. § 10-220(a). School districts must report to the Commissioner annually on the condition of their facilities and the action taken to implement their long-term school building program. Finally, the strategic school profiles required each year must now include information on "(4) equitable allocation of resources among its schools and (5) reduction of racial, ethnic and economic isolation." Conn. Gen. Stat. § 10-220(c).

These legislative efforts leave intact the basic allocation of educational responsibility by town district lines in accordance with Conn. Gen. Stat. §10-240. The plaintiffs in *Sheff* have not been satisfied with the legislative response. They returned to court and claimed that these remedial efforts did not adequately address the issues raised in the *Sheff* case. In 1999, the Superior Court ruled against the plaintiffs. *Sheff v. O'Neill*, 45 Conn. Supp. 630 (1999). The court held that the State's efforts were appropriate, and that there had been insufficient time since P.A. 97-290 was enacted to determine whether these measures would be successful. *See also Yennie v. State of Connecticut*, 2002 Conn. Super. LEXIS 3886 (Conn. Super. Ct. 2002) (challenge to legislation disbanding State Board of Trustees for the Hartford Public Schools and returning control to Hartford residents dismissed as raising same issues as are being litigated in *Sheff*).

Local and regional school districts and the State Board of Education still have much work to do in implementing the *Sheff* mandate to reduce racial, ethnic and economic isolation. The *Sheff* plaintiffs and the State defendants reached a settlement in 2003 setting forth specific targets for measuring reduction in racial, ethnic and economic isolation, and the State has committed millions to building new interdistrict magnet schools. *See* OLR Research Report 2003-R-0112 (January 27, 2003). Absent a material breach of the settlement (which could result in earlier court action), the hiatus in the litigation was to have lasted until 2007, when plaintiffs would have been free to take further action to enforce *Sheff*. In August 2004, however, the plaintiffs were already back in court challenging the progress made as inadequate. It remains to be seen, however, whether the courts will agree.

d. Enforcing the "educational interests of the state"

Under our Connecticut Constitution, the state has the ultimate responsibility for assuring that all students in Connecticut receive a substantially equal educational opportunity. The statutes set out this responsibility by defining the educational interests of the state, and by imposing on local and regional boards of education the responsibility for implementing these interests. Conn. Gen. Stat. § 10-4a; Conn. Gen. Stat. § 10-220(a).

The "educational interests of the state" are defined as the concern that all students receive an equal educational opportunity, that school districts fund education at least at the level of the minimum expenditure requirement, that local and regional school districts provide educational opportunities for its students to interact with students and teachers from other racial, ethnic and economic backgrounds to reduce isolation on such bases, and that school districts comply with all statutes pertaining to education. Conn. Gen. Stat. § 10-4a. We see *Horton v. Meskill* in the reference to the obligation to finance education at the MER level, which was added to the statute in 1979. We see *Sheff v. O'Neill* in the reference to the duty to provide educational opportunities for students to interact with students from other racial, ethnic and economic backgrounds. The constitutional obligations announced in these cases are now core components of the educational interests of the state.

The State Board of Education may review whether a local or regional school district has implemented the educational interests of the state. Under Conn. Gen. Stat. § 10-4b, any resident of a school district or a parent of a student enrolled in that school district may file a written complaint with the State Board of Education, alleging the failure or inability of a school district to implement the educational interests of the state. In addition, the State Board of Education may itself initiate such a complaint. It is noteworthy that the educational interests of the state are not limited to constitutional concerns, but rather include "the concern of the state . . . that the mandates in the general statutes pertaining to education within the jurisdiction of the State Board of Education be implemented." Conn. Gen. Stat. § 10-4a. Accordingly, a 10-4b complaint may be filed when it is alleged that a school district is not meeting its statutory obligations.

If the State Board of Education finds that a complaint is "substantial," the Department must notify the local or regional board of education of the complaint. The Department then assigns an agent to investigate the complaint, and that agent has the power to compel disclosure of information by subpoena. If the investigation establishes that there is reasonable cause to believe that a local or regional board of education has failed or is unable to make reasonable provision to implement the educational interests of the state, or if a local governmental body, such as the town, is responsible for such failure or inability, the matter is referred to the State Board of Education for a hearing in accordance with provisions of the Uniform Administrative Procedures Act, Conn. Gen. Stat. § 4-166 *et seq.*

Both the local or regional board of education, and any responsible local governmental body (typically in funding disputes), are entitled to appear and be heard on the complaint. In addition, the State Board of Education has subpoena power to compel testimony and to obtain relevant documents concerning the matter. Conn. Gen. Stat. § 10-4b(a). After hearing the matter, the State Board of Education will decide the matter, and it may order the local or regional board of education, or any responsible local governmental body, to take remedial action. Conn. Gen. Stat. § 10-4b(b). If the local or regional board of education, or a responsible local governmental body, then fails to take appropriate remedial action, the State Board of Education may seek an order from the Superior Court to compel compliance with its remedial order. Conn. Gen. Stat. § 10-4b(c). *See, e.g., New Haven v. State Board of Education*, 228 Conn. 699 (1994).

e. Other litigation

Sheff has not been the only recent constitutional challenge to the State's actions in allocating educational responsibility to local and regional school districts. As a threshold matter, it is important to note that there is general rule prohibiting a town from suing the State on constitutional grounds, based on the principle that a creature of state legislation cannot sue its creator. *See, e.g., Berlin v. Santaguida*, 181 Conn. 421 (1980). If a municipal agency is already in court challenging a statute on other proper grounds, however, it may then also raise constitutional issues. *Donahue v. Southington*, 259 Conn. 783 (2002).

Johnson v. Rowland (Docket No. CV-98-0492103-S) was brought in Connecticut Superior Court in 1998, and it involved students living in some of the less affluent towns in Connecticut, including East Hartford, Seymour and Meriden. They claimed that the current formula for allocating state funds to support education denies them the "substantially equal educational opportunity" to which they are entitled under the Connecticut Constitution. After five years, plaintiffs withdrew the case, but it is likely that a new related challenge will be brought, raising the issue of whether state funding is "sufficient."

Even the statutes governing the operation of regional school districts have been challenged. In May 2000, property owners brought an action for declaratory judgment against the Region One Board of Education and the Attorney General. They claimed that the current method of funding regional school districts is inequitable. By statute, member towns are required to pay to support the regional school district based on their respective student populations. Conn. Gen. Stat. § 10-51(b). The equalized property value per student in Region One, however, ranges from $1,464.00 in Canaan to $5,910.00 in Salisbury. Plaintiffs claimed that the resulting disproportionate burden is "unreasonable and unconstitutional."

The Superior Court disagreed. *Seymour et al. v. Region One Board of Education*, 2001 Conn. Super. LEXIS 7 (Conn. Super. Ct. January 2, 2001). It ruled that the plaintiffs had raised political, rather than legal issues and dismissed the claims as not justiciable, *i.e.* a controversy subject to the jurisdiction of the court. Contributing to that result may have been the plaintiff's demand for relief – that the court order that costs be allocated among all residents of the district as a whole. Understandably, the Superior Court had no interest in writing legislation as requested by plaintiffs. The

Connecticut Supreme Court, however, reversed. *Seymour et al v. Region One Board of Education*, 261 Conn. 475 (2002). The court held that the claim was justiciable. If the court finds that the present statutory mechanism for allocating costs is so inequitable as to be unconstitutional, the court ruled, it could leave the remedy to the legislature, as the courts did in *Horton v. Meskill* and *Sheff v. O'Neill*. After a hearing, however, the Superior Court dismissed the plaintiffs' claims, finding that their status as taxpayers was insufficient, and that they did not prove any special injury to give them standing to challenge the statutory funding scheme. *Seymour v. Region One Board of Education*, 2003 Conn. Super. LEXIS 2637 (Conn. Super. Ct. 2003).

Finally, it bears remembering that the heart of *Horton* and *Sheff* is the simple statement in Article Eighth, Section 1 of our Connecticut Constitution:

> There shall always be free public elementary and secondary schools in the state. The general assembly shall implement this principle by appropriate legislation.

This short statement continues to present our courts with serious challenges.

2. <u>The new federal role in education</u>

Traditionally, education has been a local and state concern. Indeed, shortly after finding that an enforceable right to privacy can be found in the penumbra of the other rights guaranteed by the United States Constitution, the United States Supreme Court ruled, by contrast, that education is not a constitutional right, because the word "education" is not used in the Constitution. *San Antonio School District v. Rodriguez*, 411 U.S. 1 (1973).

Starting in the 1970s, however, the federal government has asserted greater control of education. In 1972, Congress enacted Title IX, prohibiting discrimination in programs receiving federal funds on the basis of gender. In 1973, Congress passed Section 504 of the Rehabilitation Act of 1973, prohibiting discrimination in programs receiving federal funds on the basis of disability. In 1974, Congress passed the Family Educational Rights and Privacy Act (FERPA), 20 U.S.C. § 1232g, which gives parents and students rights of access and confidentiality in school records. In 1975, Congress passed the Education for All Handicapped Children Act (now IDEA), requiring school districts that accept federal funds to assure that children with disabilities receive an appropriate educational program. Finally, in 1979, the United States Department of Education was established as a separate department of the federal government. In one decade, Congress thus revolutionized the federal role in education, and its efforts continue apace. Starting in 1997, Congress has been attempting to regulate use of the Internet, particularly in school. *See* Section F(15), below. Finally, in 2001 Congress enacted the No Child Left Behind Act, P.L. 107-110, which comprehensively amends the Elementary and Secondary Education Act.

The growing federal presence in regulating our schools is evident in various areas of school law, and each of the developments mentioned above are described in the applicable sections of this Guide. Here, we will briefly review the major provisions of the No Child Left Behind Act. This description of the No Child Left Behind Act (or NCLB) however, is simply an introduction to a complicated statute that is likely to bedevil school districts for years to come.

a. Testing and accountability

Section 1116 of the Act requires states to implement a state-wide accountability system to ensure that all school districts and each individual school (including charter schools) make adequate yearly progress ("AYP") toward having all students proficient in reading and mathematics by 2014. The State is responsible for measuring the progress of local school districts and their schools. The Act leaves it to each state to define what constitutes AYP. First, a state must establish a starting point for the percentage of students who should be at the proficient level. The state must then raise the bar incrementally in order to reach 100% of students performing at the proficient level by 2014.

Significantly, AYP is measured not only by district and by individual school, but the data must also be broken out by grade level and must be disaggregated for economically disadvantaged students, students from major ethnic and racial groups, students with disabilities, and students with limited English proficiency. Subject to a "safe harbor," each of these groups must achieve AYP or the school or school district will not. The safe harbor is that the subgroup or school will be deemed to have achieved AYP *if* (1) the percentage of students in the subgroup(s) or school not demonstrating proficiency has declined by at least ten percent, and (2) the subgroup or school meets other requirements (writing and/or high school graduation rates) as determined by the State. *See* Series 2002-2003, Circular Letter C-13 (September 5, 2002).

The Act identifies specific consequences for the failure to make AYP. If a school district as a whole fails to meet AYP for two consecutive years, the state must identify it as in need of improvement, and the district must develop a two-year District Improvement Plan. Similarly, if an individual school fails to meet AYP for two consecutive years, the State must identify it as a school in need of improvement and require that it develop a two-year School Improvement Plan. If the school receives Title I funds, students in the school will also be eligible to participate in a "public school choice" program to transfer to higher-performing schools in the district. The district (with State assistance) must provide technical assistance to the school as it implements its school improvement plan, and it must give parents of such students prompt notice of the schools designated for public school choice. According to the United States Department of Education, districts must comply with this requirement notwithstanding inadequate space or funding.

If a Title I school "in need of improvement" fails to meet AYP for a third consecutive year, in addition to offering students transfer and transportation (if eligible), the school must make supplemental education services available to all low-income students, with priority for low-achieving students, and the district must continue to provide technical assistance.

If a Title I school that is identified as a school in need of improvement fails to meet AYP for a fourth consecutive year, the school board must choose among one or more of the following interventions:

- Replace school staff;
- Implement a new curriculum;
- Decrease management authority at the school level;
- Appoint an outside expert to advise the school;
- Extend the school day or school year;
- Change the internal organizational structure of the school.

Finally, if a Title I school fails to meet AYP for a fifth consecutive year, the school board must restructure the school or school district using one or more of the following "alternative governance" structures:

- Reopen the school as a public charter school;
- Replace all or most of the school staff;
- State takeover (if permitted by law);
- Hire a private management contractor.

The implications of these provisions are profound, and many Connecticut schools have been identified as being in need of improvement, with many more to come.

b. Other major provisions

The No Child Left Behind Act imposes a host of other obligations, and the State Department of Education has provided helpful information on these requirements. *See, e.g.*, Series 2003-2004, Circular Letter C-17 (January 15, 2004) and Series 2003-2004, Circular Letter C-10 (October 29, 2003).

It is unlikely that parents will be able to bring private litigation to enforce NCLB obligations. In 2002, the United States Supreme Court dismissed a claim a student had brought under FERPA because the statute did not clearly confer a private right of action. *Gonzaga University v. Doe*, 536 U.S. 273 (2002). The district court in New York applied this analysis to an attempt to sue the New York City Board of Education under the No Child Left Behind Act, and it dismissed the action. *Association of Community Organizations for Reform Now v. New York City Department of Education*, 2003 WL 21471910 (S.D.N.Y. June 30, 2003). We can only hope that this approach will hold up.

Some of the more significant provisions of No Child Left Behind Act can be identified as follows.

- District and individual school "report cards" setting forth prescribed information concerning the school, student achievement and the staff – Section 1111.
- Equal access to public school facilities – *see* Chapter One, Section F(2)(e).
- Homeless education – *see* Chapter Four, Section A(1)(b)(7).
- Parent involvement policy – *see* Chapter One, Section F(1)(a)(3).
- Recruiter access to students and student recruiting information – *see* Chapter Four, Section D(2)(c).
- Parent access to information and student privacy – *see* Chapter Four, Section D(5).
- Student transfer from unsafe schools – *see* Chapter Four, Section A(1).
- Transfer of disciplinary records – *see* Chapter Four, Section D(4)(f).
- Participation in proportionate share of funding for children enrolled in private schools – Section 9501.
- School prayer certification – *see* Chapter Two, Section A(4).

- Qualifications for teachers and paraprofessionals – *see* Chapter Seven, Section C(5)(a).

B. The Board of Education

At the outset, the two terms, "school board" and "school district" must be distinguished. The statutes define the school district as the "town," and give "school districts" extensive authority, *e.g.*, to sue and be sued, to hold and convey property for school purposes, to build, equip, purchase and rent buildings for school purposes, to make major repairs to them and supply them with fuel, furniture and other "appendages," to lay taxes and borrow money for school purposes, and to employ teachers and a superintendent. Conn. Gen. Stat. § 10-240; Conn. Gen. Stat. § 10-241. From this archaic list of school district functions (what is an "appendage"?), we see that the operation of the schools is in many ways a town function. However, these same statutes provide that the town shall maintain the control of all the public schools within its limits "through its board of education." As other statutes make clear, some of these "school district" responsibilities relate to the town, such as the power to lay taxes or to approve school construction projects, and others relate exclusively to the board of education, such as the authority to hire teachers and a superintendent.

1. <u>Board organization</u>

The dual nature of the board of education as a town body as well as an agent of the state is evident in the statutes. Similarly, the courts have held that board of education members have a dual status, serving as town officers for some purposes, and serving as agents of the state implementing the educational interests of the state for other purposes. *Cheney v. Strasburger*, 168 Conn. 135 (1975).

Boards of education are typically subject to town control as to their number, election and other procedural matters. Individual towns have the responsibility to create their school boards and are left with the discretion to establish the number of board of education members. By ordinance, towns may establish boards of education with three, five, six, seven, eight, nine or twelve members. Conn. Gen. Stat. § 9-203; Conn. Gen. Stat. § 9-205. The statutes set out detailed provision for terms of office and how those terms are staggered. Conn. Gen. Stat. § 9-203 *et seq.* In addition, by charter, towns may establish boards of education of any number ranging from three to twelve members for terms of two, three, four or six years. Conn. Gen. Stat. § 10-206a. Regional boards of education must have at least five members.

Conn. Gen. Stat. § 10-46. Currently, membership on boards of education in Connecticut ranges from five to twelve, with nine being the most common number.

Board of education members in Connecticut may not be employed by the board of education on which they sit. Conn. Gen. Stat § 10-232. The statute provides that if a board member is employed in violation of this section, his or her office of board member automatically becomes vacant. This prohibition, however, deals only with employment of the board member directly, and it does not address issues of nepotism. There is no statutory prohibition against a relative of a board member, including husband, wife or child, from being employed by the board of education. In such cases, there may be a local ethics ordinance governing the actions of the board member, such as a requirement that the board member abstain from any vote on which he or she may have a personal interest.

Board of education employees may serve in another elective office for the same town. Conn. Gen. Stat. § 10-156e provides that "any employee of a local or regional board of education . . . shall have the right to serve on any governmental body of the town in which he resides except that no such employee shall serve on such employee's employing board of education."

By contrast, certain employees of the federal government and of certain agencies receiving federal funds may not engage in partisan political activities, including running for office in a partisan election. This prohibition, known as the Hatch Act, 5 U.S.C. § 7321 *et seq.*, was first passed in 1939, and was significantly amended in 1993. Given that such employees cannot run in a partisan election, they rarely serve on boards of education. Such persons may be appointed to serve on a board of education (presuming that the employee does not engage in prohibited partisan activities). If a member of a board of education is or becomes subject to the Act through new employment, however, the Hatch Act could prevent that board member from running for reelection.

a. Local boards of education

The statutes give the "school board" extensive authority independent of the town. The powers of the school board are separately set out in the statutes. Conn. Gen. Stat. § 10-220, for example, describes the basic charge of the board of education "to maintain good public elementary and secondary schools, implement the educational interests of the state as defined in Conn.

Gen. Stat. § 10-4a and provide such other educational activities as in its judgment will best serve the interests of the school district . . . ."

From these provisions, we see the dual role of board of education members. On the one hand, school board members are municipal officials serving their communities. On the other hand, they act as state agents with responsibility for implementing the educational interests of the state. This divided responsibility has led to some confusion and litigation. The Connecticut Supreme Court has ruled that charter provisions can be binding upon local boards of education as long as the provision is not "inconsistent with or inimical to the efficient operation of the district." *Local #1186, AFSCME v. New Britain Board of Education*, 182 Conn. 93 (1980). It can be difficult, however, to apply this rule to specific situations.

For example, the courts have split on whether local board members, as state officers as they implement the educational interests of the state, are subject to recall under municipal recall provisions. In *Mazzaferro v. Bravo*, No. CV-84-02243775 (Superior Court, June 13, 1984), for example, the Superior Court held that recall of board of education members was allowed under the Wallingford Charter. *See also Opinions of the Attorney General* 84-18 (February 10, 1984) (a local board of education member may be subject to a recall vote under applicable local charter provisions, if any, even if the recall election is held because of an educational decision). Subsequently, however, the Superior Court ruled that the charter provision in question in *Mazzaferro* was not authorized. *Mazzaferro v. Bravo*, No. CV-84-02243775 (Superior Court, August 1, 1985). *See also Sherman v. Kemish*, 29 Conn. Supp. 198, *motion denied*, 161 Conn. 564 (1971) (recall of school board member disallowed).

More generally, however, courts find charter provisions binding where they do not interfere with the board of education responsibility to provide for the education of resident children. For example, the courts have upheld charter provisions applying civil service requirements to non-certified employees of the board of education because they do not implicate the educational interests of the state, but rather are matters of "local concern." *Wallingford v. Wallingford Board of Education*, 152 Conn. 568 (1965). Similarly, the Superior Court upheld a charter provision in New Haven requiring City approval of Board of Education contracts in excess of one year. *New Haven Board of Education v. City of New Haven*, 1994 WL 700427 (Conn. Super. Ct. 1994).

Two interesting charter changes made in the Town of Naugatuck were the subject of litigation over six years involving two separate decisions by both the Appellate Court and the Connecticut Supreme Court. *See Board of Education v. Town and Borough of Naugatuck,* 257 Conn. 409 (2001) (dispute not moot). The first change made the Mayor a member of the Board of Education, and the second change provided for a separate vote on the board of education and town budgets. The Superior Court struck down both provisions. *Board of Education v. Town and Borough of Naugatuck*, 22 Conn. L. Rptr. No. 17, 567 (October 26, 1998). The Appellate Court, however, affirmed the provision making the Mayor a member of the board of education. The court reviewed the specific language of Conn. Gen. Stat. § 9-210, the statute that lists "incompatible offices," *i.e.* offices that the same person cannot hold because their responsibilities conflict. Since board of education member and mayor were not listed as incompatible, the court upheld the charter provision. *Board of Education v. Town and Borough of Naugatuck*, 70 Conn. App. 358 (2002). *See also Borer v. West Haven Board of Education*, No. CV020469040S, 2003 Conn. Super. LEXIS 1831 (Conn. Super. Ct. 2003) (mayor, as *ex officio* member of the Board of Education, may place motions on the floor and participate in related debate, notwithstanding provision that he is authorized to vote only to break a tie).

The Appellate Court agreed with the trial court and struck down the provision for a separate vote on the board of education budget. The Connecticut Supreme Court, however, reversed and held that a separate vote on the board of education is not inconsistent with the statutory provisions for funding education. *Board of Education v. Town and Borough of Naugatuck*, 268 Conn. 295 (2004). While education is a matter of state concern, the procedure for approving the related funding is, in the Court's view, a matter of local concern appropriately left to the voters in the school district.

b. Regional boards of education

The statutes also provide that towns can join together to operate their schools through a regional board of education. Conn. Gen. Stat. § 10-46. The interested towns first vote to join a regional study committee, which has the responsibility for studying the question of regionalization. This committee then submits a report to the towns participating in the study. Conn. Gen. Stat. § 10-43. If the committee recommends the creation of a regional school district and if that recommendation is accepted by the State Board of Education, the matter is submitted to the vote of the residents of the towns by referendum. If a majority votes in favor of the proposed regional school district in each of the participating towns, the new regional school district is created. Conn. Gen. Stat. § 10-45.

Some regional districts operate all the elementary and secondary schools for the participating towns. Other regional districts operate schools only at the secondary level. The grades to be served by the regional school district are set out in the regionalization plan, and the statutes also provide a process for the addition or withdrawal of grades after a district has been formed. Conn. Gen. Stat. § 10-47b.

Regional boards of education have the same authority and responsibility as local boards of education. Conn. Gen. Stat. § 10-47. In addition, the regional school district, acting through the regional board of education, has many of the same rights as do other school districts, such as purchasing real estate for school purposes and establishing the budget for the district. Once a budget is proposed, it is submitted to a regional district meeting for approval, and the approved budget is the district's appropriation for the year. The costs of operating the schools in the district are apportioned among the towns in the district in accordance with a statutory formula based on student enrollment. Conn. Gen. Stat. § 10-51.

Regional school districts are subject to the requirements of Conn. Gen. Stat. § 9-369b, which prohibits the expenditure of public funds to affect a referendum result. *See* Section E(6) below. The statutes also set forth a procedure for the dissolution of a regional school district. Conn. Gen. Stat. § 10-63c provides that, following a report by a committee formed to study the withdrawal of one or more towns from the regional school district, an affirmative vote of each member town is required for withdrawal of one or more towns from the district. As to regional school districts that do not contain a high school, however, the affirmative vote of *any* member town of the district is now sufficient to dissolve the district.

c. Cooperative arrangements

In addition to the formal process of regionalization, local and regional boards of education have an option of creating cooperative arrangements for specific educational activities and programs. Conn. Gen. Stat. § 10-158a provides extensive authority for boards of education to join together to establish programs, and some boards have used this statutory authority to establish interdistrict schools.

Conn. Gen. Stat. § 10-158a provides that two or more local or regional school boards can establish "cooperative arrangements to provide school accommodations, services, programs or activities to enable such boards to carry out the duties specified in the general statutes." Such cooperative arrangements are typically supervised through the creation and appointment of a committee, and the statute authorizes the participating boards of education to give such committees extensive powers, including the power to apply for and expend federal grants, to receive and disburse funds appropriated by the participating boards of education, to employ personnel, to enter into contracts, and otherwise to provide the specified programs, services and activities. Certified staff who are hired by such a cooperative arrangement may achieve tenure with the cooperative arrangement in the same manner as teachers employed by local and regional boards of education.

The statute even permits such cooperative arrangements to hold real and personal property in trust for the participating school districts, an authority that local boards of education do not have. Cooperative arrangements between districts may even provide for the construction of schools, but any such agreement must be for a period of not less than twenty years. Conn. Gen. Stat. § 10-35(b). If a cooperative arrangement receives a school building project grant from the State Department of Education, and the building is no longer used as an interdistrict magnet school facility, the Commissioner of Education must determine whether the title reverts to the state or whether the participating districts will reimburse the state for the difference between the funding received and the reimbursement that would have otherwise been provided. Conn. Gen. Stat. § 10-264h.

A participating board of education may withdraw from the cooperative arrangement only by first giving written notice of its intent to withdraw at least one year before the effective date of any such withdrawal. The remaining boards of education may continue with the cooperative arrangement, if feasible, and may continue to hold property previously purchased by the participating school boards in trust. When the cooperative arrangement is terminated, the property held by the cooperative arrangement must be returned to participating school districts in accordance with the trust agreement that the participating districts created when they created the cooperative arrangement. Conn. Gen. Stat. § 10-158a.

d. Regional educational service centers

Throughout Connecticut there are six regional educational service centers, ACES, CES, CREC, LEARN, EASTCONN and Education

Connection. These agencies, called RESCs, are created by statute, Conn. Gen. Stat. § 10-66a *et seq.*, and the statutes confer upon them extensive authority. A RESC has the authority typical of a municipality, including the authority to enter into contracts, to sue and be sued, to receive state and federal grants, to hold real and personal property, issue bonds and notes and "otherwise to provide the programs, services and activities agreed upon by the member boards of education." Conn. Gen. Stat. § 10-66c. Given its role as a state agent, courts have held that a RESC enjoys sovereign immunity for some purposes, including immunity under the Eleventh Amendment from Age Discrimination in Employment Act (ADEA) claims. *Brown v. Area Cooperative Educational Services*, 3:02 CV1218 (WWE) (D. Conn. 2003).

A RESC is governed by its board, which is composed of at least one member from each participating board of education selected by that board of education. The board may designate from its members an executive board and delegate powers to the executive board as it deems appropriate. Members of a RESC board may be appointed to serve in that capacity for up to four years at a time, and, like board of education members generally, they may not receive compensation for their services (although they too may be reimbursed for necessary expenses). Each RESC has an executive director, who serves as the executive agent of the board as does a superintendent for a local or regional board of education. Conn. Gen. Stat. § 10-66b.

Historically, RESCs provided special education and other services to member districts in a cost-effective way, given the economies of scale. More recently, however, the RESCs have provided a broader array of services, ranging from professional and technical assistance to the operation of interdistrict magnet schools. The statutes that apply to local and regional boards of education apply to regional educational service centers. Conn. Gen. Stat. § 10-66i. Their certified employees achieve tenure, and employees, both certified and non-certified, can unionize. Also, the superior court has held that Conn. Gen. Stat § 10-236a, which indemnifies board of education employees who are assaulted in the line of duty, also applies to RESC employees. *Fenton v. Area Cooperative Educational Services*, 2001 Conn. Super. LEXIS 232 (Conn. Super. Ct. January 22, 2001).

The General Assembly has looked increasingly to the RESCs to provide services to districts within their region. Under Conn. Gen. Stat. § 10-221d(b), for example, a RESC is responsible for arranging for the fingerprinting of candidates for employment if requested to do so by a local or regional board of education, and the RESCs have thus become a clearinghouse for such criminal records check information. Under Conn.

Gen. Stat. § 10-264i, the RESCs are approved transportation providers for interdistrict magnet schools. Similarly, RESCs have significant responsibilities under Conn. Gen. Stat. § 10-266aa in administering the interdistrict choice program that was implemented to reduce racial, ethnic and economic isolation among students in Connecticut, as required by *Sheff v. O'Neill*, 238 Conn. 1 (1996). Indeed, several of the RESCs operate magnet schools on behalf of boards of education acting alone or together with other boards of education in cooperative arrangements under Conn. Gen. Stat. § 10-158a or otherwise. Our understanding of the RESCs role in such situations as manager and/or the agent of the board(s) of education in operational issues is evolving. For example, some RESCs undertake the responsibility to conduct expulsion hearings in such situations, which appears to be authorized. *See* Conn. Gen. Stat. § 10-66i.

2. Board operation

Before they may take office, members of a board of education must take an oath as prescribed by statute. Conn. Gen. Stat. § 10-218a. Within one month of the date newly elected members take office, the members of the board of education are required hold an organizational meeting to elect from their members a chairperson and a secretary. Conn. Gen. Stat. § 10-218. If this election cannot be made because of a tie vote, or if a board of education fails to act within this time period, the town (through the town council or the selectmen) has the right to choose these officers. *Id.* In addition, when a seat on a board of education becomes vacant, the remaining members of the board have the authority to fill the vacancy until the next town election, unless the charter or a special act provides otherwise. Conn. Gen. Stat. § 10-219.

Though Section 10-219 requires that the vacancy be filled, it does not contain an express provision for the town to fill such a vacancy if the board does not act in a timely manner, as is the case with board officers under Section 10-218. However, Conn. Gen. Stat. § 7-107 provides that, where a town board or commission has the power by law to fill a vacancy but fails to do so within thirty days after it occurs, the board of selectmen or the chief executive officer of the town may appoint a qualified person to the vacancy until the next municipal election. This provision may permit town officials to make the appointment if the board of education fails to fill the vacancy within the specified thirty-day period.

The provisions are similar for regional boards of education. At the first meeting of a regional board of education, the members must establish a system of election for four-year terms that assures continuity of membership, including selection by lot of those members whose initial terms will be shorter to establish an appropriate rotation system. Conn. Gen. Stat. § 10-46(a). Vacancies on a regional board of education are to be filled by the respective town within thirty days of the vacancy, unless the board members are elected at large, in which case the vacancy is filled at a regional district meeting called within thirty days of the vacancy. Conn. Gen. Stat. § 10-46(b), (c). In the month following the last election of board members, the regional board of education must hold an organizational meeting, at which the board members elect a chairperson, a secretary, a treasurer and any other officer established by the board. In cases of a tie vote for any officer, ties are broken by lot. Conn. Gen. Stat. § 10-46(d).

a. Meetings

The chairperson is responsible for calling a meeting of the board at least once every six months and "whenever such chairperson deems it necessary." Conn. Gen. Stat. § 10-218. The chair must also call a meeting when requested to do so by at least three of the members, and, if no meeting is held within fourteen days after the request is made, any three members may themselves call the meeting. *Id.* Normally, the process for setting the agenda is described in board bylaws, which typically give that responsibility to the superintendent and/or the chairperson. However, if a minority of the board were ever stymied in an effort to get a matter on the agenda, those board members arguably could have the matter heard by invoking the procedure under Conn. Gen. Stat. § 10-218. Specifically, under that statute, they could request a meeting on a particular matter. If that request were refused, these members could then hold a meeting by providing the required notification to the other members in accordance with that statute.

The "meeting" is the way boards of education in Connecticut exercise their responsibilities. Outside of a meeting, members of a board of education have no special authority. However, despite this central role of the "meeting" in board of education operation, there is very little law guiding boards of education in how to conduct their meetings. One source of authority for board of education operation may be the town charter, but charter provisions usually simply set forth the number of board of education members and how they will be elected. By statute, however, regional boards of education are required to follow "standard parliamentary practice" in the election of officers, Conn. Gen. Stat. § 10-46(e), and more generally both local and regional boards of education typically operate in accordance with parliamentary procedure, as discussed in Section B(2)(b) below.

Most of the legal requirements for board of education meetings are imposed by the Freedom of Information Act (or FOIA), as discussed in Section D below. Posting, recording votes and keeping track of the reasons for executive sessions are all requirements contained in the FOIA. There are, however, no statutory requirements regarding how a quorum is established, how minutes should be maintained, etc. Usually boards of education adopt bylaws to direct them in their operation, and such bylaws can be very helpful in guiding board members in fulfilling their statutory duties. Given the important role such bylaws have in governing board of education procedures, typically bylaws can be amended only with prior notice and a two-thirds vote. *See* Robert's Rules of Order, Section 56.

In establishing bylaws and otherwise determining procedures for conducting meetings, boards of education have significant discretion. While the public may have the right to attend its meetings, for example, a board of education does not have to permit the public to participate in the meeting. Many boards of education provide through policy or bylaw that the public will have the right to make comments to the board, usually at the beginning of the meeting. However, there is no legal obligation to do so. While boards of education must hold their meetings in public, they are not public meetings.

If a board of education chooses to hear from the public (as is common), it must do so in a constitutional manner. Since a board of education meeting is considered a public forum, free speech requirements under the First Amendment apply to public statements at board meetings. Once a board of education has created a public forum, it may not pick and chose from among the speakers on the basis of the content of their speech. *City of Madison v. Wisconsin Employment Relations Commission*, 429 U.S. 167 (1976). To be sure, the board can limit comments to a particular topic, say on school overcrowding (and thus create a limited public forum), but even in that situation all must be free to speak to the issue without discrimination based on viewpoint.

Boards of education can also adopt reasonable restrictions as to time and manner of speech at their meetings. As long as such time limits are applied to all speakers equally, boards of education can require that speakers sign up to speak and can adopt a rule that each speaker will be allowed no more than, say, three or five minutes to address the board. Finally, the board, generally acting through its chair, can require that speakers adhere to reasonable standards of decorum. As provided in Robert's Rules of Order, the chair may require that speakers be courteous, avoid personal attacks, refrain from the use of vulgarity and the like. Again, such requirements must be imposed with an even hand, without regard to the content (as opposed to the manner) of the particular speech. No speaker at a meeting of a board of education, however, has a First Amendment right to be disruptive or rude.

Finally, under specific circumstances, the public may demand a hearing from a board of education. Conn. Gen. Stat. § 10-238 provides that a board of education must hold a hearing if it receives a petition signed by the greater of fifty electors or one percent of the electors in the town, such signatures to be verified by the town clerk. The hearing must be "on any question specified in such petition," and must be held within three weeks after receipt of the petition. While the statute provides that a hearing must be held, there is no requirement that the board members answer any questions or take action on any matters raised by the petition.

b. Parliamentary procedure

In conducting their meetings, most, if not all, boards of education in Connecticut follow Robert's Rules of Order, a guide to parliamentary procedure. Typically the board's bylaws specify that the procedure for meetings will be governed by Robert's Rules, but boards of education are free to adopt other rules of procedure or to adopt Robert's Rules except as otherwise specified. Robert's Rules addresses virtually any question that comes up in conducting board business, and an exhaustive review is not possible here. However, there are a few matters of parliamentary procedure that come up frequently and warrant discussion.

1. A majority vote

First, when boards of education act on a matter, a simple majority vote of those present and voting suffices to pass the measure. For example, a nine-member board of education would through its bylaws typically define a quorum as a majority, *i.e.* five. If a bare quorum is achieved at a meeting and two of the five members present abstain from a particular vote, for example, a measure could validly pass by a two-to-one majority. All members who are present count in establishing a quorum, and the majority of those present and voting in the example would be the two members voting in the affirmative.

2. Abstention

Members of a board of education may choose to abstain from voting on any topic. Under Robert's Rules, a board member cannot be compelled to vote on any subject, and he or she is free to decide whether or not to abstain in a particular case. Robert's Rules, Section 44. Moreover, under Robert's Rules, there is no requirement that a board member justify or otherwise explain his/her decision to abstain. *Id.* While abstentions are to be discouraged, particularly in a small deliberative body such as a school board, there are occasions when abstention is appropriate, as in conflict situations.

The impact of an abstention can vary depending on the situation. In most cases, there is no direct impact, because a motion will pass with a majority of those present and voting. In certain circumstances, however, abstention can affect the result and even prevent the board of education from taking action. *See* Robert's Rules, Section 44. A majority vote of *all* members of the board of education, for example, is necessary for the election of a superintendent. Conn. Gen. Stat. § 10-157. *See also* Conn. Gen. Stat. § 10-229. Abstaining in such cases is the equivalent of a negative vote on the proposed motion.

3. Review of prior action

Boards of education sometimes wish to revisit action already taken, because of new information, changed circumstances or an odd vote as described above. In such cases, board members must distinguish between two different procedures under Robert's Rules to review prior action.

The first method is a vote to reconsider. This procedure can be invoked only during the same session when the original action was taken, and therefore it is used infrequently. In addition, a motion to reconsider can only be made by a member who voted with the prevailing side on the earlier vote. If these requirements are met, a motion to reconsider is in order and can be passed by a majority vote.

More typically, the change of heart or of potential votes comes at a subsequent meeting of the board. In such cases, a vote to reconsider is not proper, and the appropriate motion would be one to rescind or amend. Such a motion can be made by any member of the board of education, whether or not he or she voted with the majority the first time. However, to avoid the possibility of surprise that the matter will come up again (as when the chief supporter is absent on vacation), Robert's Rules imposes special notification and/or voting procedures in such matters. To be valid, a motion to rescind will require one of the following: advance written notification of the substance of the motion, a two-thirds vote, or an affirmative vote of an absolute majority of the board (*e.g.*, five members of a nine member board).

4. The role of the chairperson

Questions sometimes arise concerning the role of the chairperson of the board. While it provides for the election of a chairperson and a secretary, Conn. Gen. Stat. § 10-218 does not describe the duties of either board officer in detail. Rather, it provides that the board of education "may prescribe their duties." Often boards address the responsibilities of their officers in the bylaws.

The most common issue that comes up concerning the role of the chairperson is whether s/he may and/or should vote. Under Robert's Rules, the general rule is that the chairperson may vote when his or her vote will affect the result. Such votes can operate in two ways. The vote of the chairperson can operate to break a tie. Alternatively, the vote of the chair can operate to create a tie. If that occurs, the motion is defeated, because it was not passed with a majority of those present and voting. Clearly, however, s/he may not vote twice, once to create the tie and again to break the tie. Robert's Rules, Section 43.

This provision from Robert's Rules has led to some debate about whether the chairperson should vote when his or her vote will not affect the result. Both under Robert's Rules and as a matter of public policy, the chairperson of a board of education should feel free to vote. There are some general remarks in Robert's Rules suggesting that the chairperson of an assembly should not vote when the vote will not affect the result, so as to preserve his or her neutrality on matters before the body whenever possible:

> If the presiding officer is a member of the assembly, however, the presiding officer has the same voting right as any other member. In an assembly (as distinguished from a small board or a committee), however—unless the vote is secret (that is, unless it is by ballot) — the chair protects his impartiality by exercising his voting right only when his vote would affect the outcome, in which case he can either vote and thereby change the result, or he can abstain.

Robert's Rules, Section 4. From this provision, we see that the role of the chair may be different in a small board, and there is not the same expectation that the chairperson will not vote. This distinction makes sense; in a nine member board, each vote is over ten percent of the board's authority, and the importance of each vote may well override any concern over the impartiality of the chairperson.

Robert's Rules recognizes that the unique characteristics of a small board affect the role of the chairperson. Robert's Rules provides that "[i]n a board meeting where there are not more than about a dozen members present, some of the formality that is necessary in a large assembly would hinder business." Section 48. Among the differences in accepted procedure in a small board is the role of the chairperson:

> — *The chairman can speak in discussion without rising or leaving the chair; and*, subject to rule or custom within the particular board (which should be uniformly followed regardless of how many members are present), *he usually can make motions and usually votes on all questions.*

Section 48 (emphasis added). While whether to vote remains the prerogative of the chairperson, these provisions of Robert's Rules and the public policy behind it demonstrate that it is perfectly appropriate for the chairperson of a board of education to vote on all matters pending before the board.

Two other responsibilities warrant brief mention. Robert's Rules, Section 49, describes appointment by the chairperson as the "ordinary procedure." Absent a provision to the contrary, therefore, the chairperson of a board of education that operates pursuant to Robert's Rules has the authority to appoint members to committees. Significantly, Robert's Rules also provides that, where the chairperson has the authority to appoint members to committee, he/she also has the authority to remove or replace committee members. *Id.*

Finally, while not strictly an issue of parliamentary procedure, it is customary that a board of education will speak through its chairperson. While all board members retain their First Amendment right of free speech, clear communication is facilitated when a board of education speaks with one voice.

5. Point of order

When the chairperson presides over a meeting, he or she does so on behalf of all members, and Robert's Rules assures that the will of the majority will prevail on matters of parliamentary procedure. If a board member believes that the chairperson has erred in action taken (or not taken, such as calling for a second), the board member should immediately raise a "point of order." The chairperson must immediately recognize the member raising the point of order. The member should state his or her objection to the procedures, and the chairperson must then rule on the objection. The matter is resolved if there is no further disagreement. If the member disagrees with the ruling of the chair, however, he or she may challenge the ruling by stating, "I appeal." If another member of the board seconds the appeal, the issue is submitted to the entire board for decision.

Procedural issues must be raised promptly when they occur. Robert's Rules is designed to assist deliberative bodies in making decisions in an efficient and final manner. If a point of order is not raised promptly, as for example the lack of a second before voting on a motion, it is deemed waived, and action taken will be valid notwithstanding the procedural flaw. This requirement prevents members from holding procedural objections in reserve for later use in attacking action taken by the body.

Points of order are not limited to situations of disagreement, and board members may assist the chair by raising points of order. If, for example, a member of the public is speaking and becomes abusive, any board member can raise a point of order to remind the chair of the need for order and decorum.

6. Parliamentarian

These issues are the most common issues that arise under Robert's Rules, but other potential issues are limited only by the human imagination. Boards of education are well-advised to adopt Robert's Rules to govern procedures. Also, it may be helpful to appoint a board member with a good mind for detail to serve the board as the parliamentarian. Armed with Robert's Rules and some study beforehand, that board member may be able to provide prompt guidance as issues of procedure arise from time to time.

C. The Superintendent

School boards in Connecticut act through the superintendent of schools. The statutes expressly provide that the superintendent is the "chief executive officer" of the board of education, and "shall have executive authority over the school system and the responsibility for its supervision." Conn. Gen. Stat. § 10-157(a). As such, he or she has the responsibility for the day-to-day operation of the school district. By contrast, board of education members possess no authority when away from a duly-called meeting, unless they are fulfilling a responsibility that the full board of education has delegated to them.

Given the central role superintendents of schools play in Connecticut, the statutes regulate their employment and authority. School districts are required to employ a superintendent of schools to supervise their schools. There is provision for the appointment of an acting superintendent when the superintendent has left the board's employment or is incapable of performing his or her duties. While appropriate certification is essential for the superintendent, as discussed below, an acting superintendent may be appointed without proper certification with the approval of the Commissioner of Education. However, such appointments cannot exceed ninety days, unless the Commissioner of Education extends that period "for good cause shown." Conn. Gen. Stat. § 10-157(b).

The board of education is responsible for interviewing candidates and employing the superintendent. Sometimes this process gets more attention in the press than either the board of education or the superintendent candidates would wish. This concern is addressed in the Freedom of Information Act (the FOIA). Generally, the FOIA requires public disclosure of board of education business. However, there are specific provisions regarding job interviews and related meetings for the purpose of filling the position of superintendent and other "executive-level employment position[s]." Meetings of a personnel search committee for executive level positions are excluded from the definition of a public "meeting" under the FOIA. Conn. Gen. Stat. § 1-200(2). A public agency can even name all of its members to such a committee. *Hackett and Norwich Bulletin v. Norwich City Council*, Docket #FIC 92-340 (June 23, 1993); *Steinmetz and The News-Times v. Danbury Board of Education*, Docket #FIC 2003-109 (September 24, 2003). The statute exempts such personnel search committees from the posting and public access requirements that normally apply to meetings. Also, while the names of persons attending an executive session must generally be included in the minutes, the law excludes from this requirement job applicants who attend for the purpose of an interview. Conn. Gen. Stat. § 1-231.

After making a decision, the board of education must vote to elect a new superintendent. Within seven days of the decision of the new superintendent to accept an offer of employment, the board of education must notify the Commissioner of Education of the name and address of the new superintendent. Then, before the superintendent may begin his or her duties, the board of education must receive confirmation from the

Commissioner of Education that the superintendent is properly certified for that position. Conn. Gen. Stat. § 10-157(a).

The election of the superintendent is subject to other specific rules as well. A majority of all of the members of the board of education is required for the election of a superintendent of schools. Upon the request of the superintendent, the board of education is required to provide him or her with a written contract of employment. At a minimum, that contract must include salary, employment benefits and the term of office of the superintendent. Conn. Gen. Stat. § 10-157(a).

The statutes also authorize boards of education to collaborate in the hiring of the superintendent. The statutes expressly authorize two or more towns, or a regional school district and one or more towns, jointly to form a committee to employ a superintendent. Such agreements must provide for the term of office for the superintendent, how he or she will be evaluated, how expenses (including salary) will be shared, how the joint committee will act to supervise the employment of the superintendent, and how his or her contract may be terminated. Once so employed, such a superintendent has statutory authority and responsibility over all districts participating in the cooperative arrangement. Conn. Gen. Stat. § 10-157a.

The statutes provide that superintendents may not be employed for more than a term of three years at any one time. Some superintendents have proposed a roll-over or "evergreen" provision in the board/superintendent contract. Such provisions state that, absent board of education action by a specific date, the contract will be automatically renewed for another year. Such provisions conflict with the requirement that a majority of all members of the board of education vote to elect the superintendent. As such, they are illegal and unenforceable. An appropriate way in which to address the legitimate concerns of a superintendent over his or her employment security is to make provision in the contract that the board of education must vote by a specific date on whether to extend the board/superintendent contract. Such a provision may require that, in effect, the board provide the superintendent at least one year's notice before the contract will expire.

The statute also requires that the board of education evaluate the superintendent at least annually. This provision is the only responsibility the board of education has for the direct evaluation of personnel. As the chief executive officer of the school district, the superintendent, not the board of education, is responsible for supervising and evaluating all other staff members. *See* Conn. Gen. Stat. § 10-151b (the superintendent is required to evaluate teachers, or to delegate that responsibility to others, in accordance with the provisions of the local teacher evaluation plan).

Boards of education are required "to evaluate the performance of the superintendent annually in accordance with guidelines and criteria mutually determined and agreed to by such board and such superintendent." Conn. Gen. Stat. § 10-157(a). The statutes do not tell us how to resolve any disputes between a board of education and a superintendent over the guidelines and criteria for evaluation. As a practical matter, however, the parties generally have little or no difficulty coming up with a mutually acceptable plan. Indeed, difficulty over the format of the evaluation does not bode well for the future relationship between board and superintendent.

The confidentiality of the superintendent's evaluation is an issue of concern. The General Assembly has provided that evaluations of "teachers" (all certified staff below the rank of superintendent) are confidential (except for records of "personal misconduct," as described in Section D, below). Conn. Gen. Stat. § 10-151c. However, there is no similar statute expressly protecting the evaluation of the superintendent from public disclosure.

Some years ago, the Connecticut Supreme Court ruled in *Chairman, Criminal Justice Commission v. Freedom of Information Commission*, 217 Conn. 193 (1991), that evaluations of public officials may be kept confidential because of the potential for personal embarrassment and an expectation of privacy (which could be augmented by contract provisions describing the parties' understanding that the evaluation would be confidential). However, the Connecticut Supreme Court subsequently adopted a new general test for confidentiality that subjects virtually all information related to public responsibilities to disclosure; *i.e.* the information must not relate to a matter of legitimate public concern, and its disclosure must be highly offensive to a reasonable person. *Perkins v. Freedom of Information Commission*, 228 Conn. 158 (1993); *Kureczka v. Freedom of Information Commission*, 228 Conn. 271 (1994).

The Connecticut Supreme Court did not overrule the *Chairman* case expressly, but it recently affirmed the *Perkins* rule. *See Pane v. City of Danbury*, 267 Conn. 669 (2004). Moreover, the Freedom of Information Commission and some lower courts have held superintendent evaluations to be subject to public disclosure. Therefore, unless there is statutory change permitting evaluation documents to be kept confidential, boards and superintendents should approach the evaluation process with the understanding that the superintendent evaluation document will be subject to public disclosure upon request.

In addition to the concern over the disclosure of the formal evaluation document, boards of education must also be aware of the possibility that the individual evaluations of the superintendent conducted by board members may be subject to public disclosure. In recent years, the Freedom of Information Commission has ruled on several occasions that such individual reports are part of the evaluation process and are therefore subject to public disclosure in the same manner as are the overall evaluation reports. *See, e.g., Conrad v. Hamden Board of Education*, Docket #FIC 94-154 (February 22, 1995); *Casey v. Darien Board of Education*, Docket #FIC 1997-068 (October 22, 1997), *reversed and remanded in Chairman, Board of Education of the Town of Darien v. Freedom of Information Commission*, 60 Conn. App. 584 (2000). Unless and until the law changes in this area, boards and superintendents must be aware of the possibility that even interim evaluation documents may be subject to public disclosure.

The statutes do not regulate the termination of the superintendent's contract. It is clear that superintendents do not achieve tenure in their positions. The Teacher Tenure Act covers certified staff below the rank of superintendent, but not the superintendent. *Cimochowski v. Hartford Public Schools*, 261 Conn. 287 (2002). Superintendents and boards of education therefore typically include in their written agreements a section governing termination of the contract.

Generally, there is provision for the superintendent to provide a specified period of notice if he or she wishes to resign. Also, there is usually provision for a board vote prior to contract expiration so that the superintendent knows whether the contract will be extended. Finally, board/superintendent contracts generally include provision for termination prior to contract expiration in specific circumstances, as they should. Often provision is made for termination for any of the grounds set out in the Tenure Act for terminating the contract of a teacher, except for elimination of position (which would not typically apply to the superintendent of schools). Such provisions must be negotiated between the board and the superintendent. Typically they include provision for notification that contract termination is under consideration, the right to a hearing before the board of education, the right to be represented by counsel (at individual expense) in any such hearing, and the right to a written decision. Happily, boards and superintendents are generally able to resolve differences without resort to such provisions, and such hearings are virtually unheard of in Connecticut.

D. Freedom of Information

Given the high level of public interest in the work of local or regional boards of education, freedom of information issues confront boards of education in Connecticut almost every day. The following discussion will not attempt to review all provisions of the Freedom of Information Act, but rather will provide an overview of the law and identify the areas of particular concern.

The Freedom of Information Act, Conn. Gen. Stat. § 1-200 *et seq.*, (FOIA) provides that the public will have access into the workings of public agencies. The law provides this access in two basic ways. First, the law states that the public shall have access to the meetings of public agencies, including boards of education, subject to narrow exceptions that are strictly construed. Second, the law provides that the public shall have access to records that are developed and/or maintained by public agencies.

Board of education members and school district personnel must understand both aspects of freedom of information law. The requirements of the law are enforced by the Freedom of Information Commission, the responsible state agency. The Freedom of Information Commission publishes its decisions, relevant legislation and other matters of interest on its website, http://www.state.ct.us/foi. When a member of the public feels that he or she has been denied his or her rights under the FOIA, he or she may file a complaint with the Commission. Complaints regarding a failure to respond to a request for documents may be filed after four business days without receiving a response to the request. More generally, complaints must be filed within thirty days of the denial of access to documents or to a public meeting. This time limitation is extended to thirty days from the time the complainant learned of a meeting, if it was not properly posted. Conn. Gen. Stat. § 1-206(b)(1). Once a complaint has been filed, a hearing is generally held (unless it is settled, as described below). The law provides, however, that the Commission may review the complaint, and construing it in favor of the complainant, dismiss the complaint because it does not allege a violation of the law, or the violation alleged is a harmless technical error that does not infringe on the complainant's rights. Conn. Gen. Stat. § 1-206(b)(4).

If the complaint is set down for hearing, it will be heard by a member of the Commission or a staff attorney serving as hearing officer. After hearing the complaint, the hearing officer will propose a decision for the consideration of the full Commission. A board of education has the right to defend itself at both proceedings, but the only opportunity to present evidence is at the initial hearing before the hearing officer. Once the full Commission has ruled on a complaint, either party may appeal that decision to Superior Court in accordance with the Uniform Administrative Procedures Act. Conn. Gen. Stat. § 4-166 *et seq*.

The Freedom of Information Commission has an ombudsman program that offers public agencies an opportunity to settle complaints informally even after they are filed. The Commission will appoint a member of the Commission staff to serve in this capacity, with the understanding that he or she will not later be involved in the case if it is not resolved. The ombudsman is available to discuss the merits of the case with both the complainant and the respondent, and the ombudsman will convey offers of settlement between the parties, and will often even propose a resolution to the complaint. Given the time, expense and risks of the hearing process, it is often worthwhile to seek resolution of complaints through this informal resolution process.

A fundamental principle of the Freedom of Information Act is that the public may attend meetings of a public agency, subject to limited exceptions. To understand this requirement, we must look at (1) the definition of a "public agency," (2) the definition of a "meeting" or "hearing or other proceeding," and (3) the rules for conducting a meeting, including executive session.

1. Public agency

The FOIA defines "public agency" broadly as "any executive, administrative or legislative office of the state or any political subdivision of the state and any state or town agency," including "school district" and "official." We all understand that boards of education are public agencies subject to the FOIA. "Officials" are also public agencies, though the term "official" is not self-defining. Given that the superintendent is elected pursuant to statute, it is a reasonable conclusion to find that he or she is an "official" under the law and thus a public agency subject to the FOIA, as described below. It is not clear, however, how far into the ranks of public employment the term "official" will be applied. Recently, the Commission found that an assistant superintendent is an "official" under the Act, and is thus subject to its provisions. *Hughes v. Superintendent of Schools et al.*, Docket #FIC 2001-557 (May 29, 2002).

Committees created by the board of education or by the superintendent (or any other "official") are also subject to the requirements of the FOIA. The law provides that committees of a board of education are "public agencies," and thus committee meetings must also comply with the FOIA. Notably, a committee "created by" a public agency is a public agency as well, even if no members of the agency are themselves members of the committee. Conn. Gen. Stat. § 1-200(1). For example, in *Wotjas v. Kelley*, Docket #FIC 1996-162 (May 14, 1997), the Commission held that "school-based improvement teams" created by a board of education were "committees" of the board subject to FOIA requirements. Similarly, in *Hughes v. Superintendent of Schools et al.*, Docket #FIC 2001-557 (May 29, 2002), the Commission held that a kindergarten review committee was a public agency because the creator of the committee, an assistant superintendent, was herself an official.

There is provision in the FOIA for exemption of a committee composed entirely of individuals who are not members of a public agency. The FOIA, however, will typically apply nonetheless because the Freedom of Information Commission will exempt such a committee from FOIA requirements only if it finds that the public interest in exempting the committee outweighs the public interest in having the committee comply with FOIA requirements, a difficult standard to meet. Conn. Gen. Stat. § 1-202. This broad definition of "committees" subject to the FOIA makes it imperative that boards of education provide in-service training to assure that persons serving on committees understand their obligations under the Freedom of Information Act.

2. Public meeting or "hearing or other proceeding"

When a particular gathering falls within the definition of a "meeting," the posting, access and other requirements under the FOIA (discussed below) are triggered. The basic rule is that there is a "meeting" of the board of education any time a quorum of the board of education convenes to discuss or act upon a matter over which the board of education has responsibility. Under this definition, a "workshop" in which no action is contemplated is still a "meeting," because the board of education will discuss matters over which it has responsibility. *Strilowich v. New Fairfield Public Schools*, Docket #FIC 2003-063 (December 10, 2003). In addition, a "meeting" occurs whenever there is a hearing or other proceeding of the board of education or of a "public official," whether or not the quorum requirement is met. Conn. Gen. Stat. § 1-200(2).

Significantly, with a multi-member public agency, the quorum need not be present at the same time and place, though of course that is the general procedure. The law provides that there may be a meeting of the public agency whenever there is communication by or to a quorum of the board, whether the communication is in person or by means of electronic equipment. Conn. Gen. Stat. § 1-200(2). Consequently, public agencies may not avoid the requirements of the FOIA by meeting with less than a quorum, if the goal is to communicate with the entire agency (or at least a quorum) on a particular topic. Also, meetings may be conducted by conference call or otherwise by electronic means under the FOIA. It is advisable, however, to address this issue through bylaw so that board members may make the policy decisions as to whether and under what circumstances board members may participate in a meeting by electronic means.

The law is still unfolding as to when electronic communication may be a "meeting" because it permits a quorum to discuss or act upon a matter within its responsibilities. The Freedom of Information proposed a declaratory ruling that sets out various hypothetical situations and gives public officials a lot to think about. Draft Declaratory Ruling # 94. In April 2004, at the recommendation of its Executive Director, however, the Commission declined to adopt a declaratory ruling on the subject. Report of Counsel, April 14, 2004. The Commission will continue to address these issues on a case-by-case basis, and it is important that public agencies take care not to make decisions through e-mail exchanges.

A meeting can involve more than one agency. The FOIA addresses this situation specifically. It provides that a meeting that is properly posted by one public agency (*e.g.* the board of finance) shall not be considered a meeting of another public agency (*e.g.* the board of education), even if a quorum of that other agency attends the meeting. Conn. Gen. Stat. § 1-200(2).

Any "hearing or other proceeding" of a public agency is also a meeting, even when it involves less than a quorum. When a public agency has delegated authority to a smaller number of members, their actions (*e.g.*, hearings, workshops) are likely to be considered a "proceeding" of the agency subject to the Freedom of Information Act. *Common Council of Middletown v. Freedom of Information Commission*, 16 Conn. L. Rptr. No. 5, 163 (April 1, 1996) (discussion among members of both parties but less than a quorum during a meeting recess constitutes "meeting" because group had implied authority to discuss matter on behalf of the public agency); *East Hartford*

Town Council v. Freedom of Information Commission, 2 Conn. Ops. 212 (February 26, 1996). If less than a quorum gathers on a less formal basis, however, no "proceeding" may occur, even if the group discusses matters within the agency's jurisdiction. *Windham v. Freedom of Information Commission*, 249 Conn. 291 (1999), *affirming*, 48 Conn. App. 529 (1998). *See also Dortenzio v. Freedom of Information Commission*, 48 Conn. App. 424 (1998) (predisciplinary conference held by police chief is not a "hearing or other proceeding" of a public agency).

Similarly, there can be questions concerning "meetings" conducted by a single-member public agency, such as the superintendent (who as an "official" serves as such). The superintendent is not subject to the provisions concerning multi-member agencies (relating to the convening of a quorum to discuss or act upon a matter within its jurisdiction), and thus typically the issue will be whether the event is a "hearing or other proceeding" of the official, *e.g.*, superintendent. The statute specifically excludes from the definition of "meeting" "an administrative or staff meeting of a single-member public agency." Conn. Gen. Stat. § 1-200(2). Accordingly, a superintendent's meeting with his/her staff is not a meeting under FOI, but the participation of outside parties can raise the issue.

The law excludes certain other situations from the definition of "meeting" under the FOIA as well. Any meeting of a personnel search committee (for an executive level position) is not a "meeting" under the law. Conn. Gen. Stat. § 1-200(2). This is true even if the public agency names all of its members to such a committee. *Hackett and Norwich Bulletin v. Norwich City Council*, Docket #FIC 92-340 (June 23, 1993). Similarly, a chance meeting or social gathering will not become a meeting of a board of education, even if a quorum of the board shows up at an event, provided that the gathering was neither planned nor intended for the purpose of discussing matters related to official business. *Id.* Of course, if board members seize the moment and conduct business (even by just discussing board issues), an illegal "meeting" will result.

A caucus of the members of a single political party falls outside the definition of a "meeting," even if those members would otherwise constitute a quorum of the board of education. Conn. Gen. Stat. § 1-200(3). If a caucus does constitute a quorum of the board of education, the exclusion from the definition of "meeting" under the FOIA may be lost if persons other than the board members themselves attend the caucus, such as the superintendent or even the local party chairman. *Betts v. Wilson*, Docket #FIC 1995-29 (November 8, 1995). However, members of a multi-member public agency who are not members of the same political party may register as a caucus (either "majority caucus" or "minority caucus"). This option was added in 2002, and it is not affected by party affiliation or by a change in party affiliation. The members of the proposed caucus, however, must register with the town clerk, and they may not be members of more than one caucus or realign into a different caucus during the remainder of their term of office. Conn. Gen. Stat. § 1-200(3).

Strategy or negotiations with respect to collective bargaining are subject to special rules. Meetings for that purpose are also excluded from the definition of "meeting." Conn. Gen. Stat. § 1-200(2). Boards of education can convene what is called a "non-meeting" to discuss negotiations strategy or to actually conduct labor negotiations without regard to the posting and other requirements of the FOIA. Moreover, there is another option for having a confidential discussion if the board is discussing confidential documents related to collective bargaining. "Records, reports and statements of strategy or negotiations with respect to collective bargaining" are exempt from disclosure under the FOIA, and the board may convene into executive session when they are discussed. Conn. Gen. Stat. § 1-200(6); Conn. Gen. Stat. § 1-225. If there are no such documents, however, the executive session privilege is not available, and any confidential strategy discussions should be held in a "non-meeting."

The Freedom of Information Act is "remedial legislation," *i.e.* legislation intended to implement a public policy decision, in this case the policy that the public should have access to the workings of government. As such, any exceptions to the general requirements of the FOIA will be construed narrowly to maximize public access to meetings of public agencies (or to public documents, as discussed below). This principle is evident in interpretations of what is or is not a "meeting." For example, a "retreat" for members of a board of education will be subject to the "meeting" requirements even if the board claims that the purpose of such a gathering is primarily social. That portion of the gathering in which matters related to official business are discussed, albeit informally, will be a "meeting" subject to all of the requirements of the Freedom of Information Act.

3. <u>"Meeting" requirements</u>

Once a convening of a quorum of the board of education falls within the definition of a meeting, the posting and access requirements of the Freedom of Information Act apply. There are three types of "meetings" under the FOIA, and each has unique posting requirements.

First, a regular meeting of a board of education is one that has been included in the listing of regular meetings posted with the town clerk no later than January 31 of each year. The agenda of a regular meeting must be filed in the "regular office or place of business" of the board of education at least twenty-four hours before the meeting convenes, and the posting must be available to the public. Generally, no business other than that listed on the posted agenda may be conducted at the meeting of the board of education. However, by a two-thirds vote, the members of the board of education may add an item to the agenda at a regular meeting. Conn. Gen. Stat. § 1-225(a).

Second, any meeting of the board of education that is not included on the list of regular meetings filed with the town clerk is a "special meeting." The posting requirements for a special meeting are similar to those for a regular meeting. Notice of the meeting, including the time and place of the meeting, as well as the business to be transacted, must be filed with the town clerk at least twenty-four hours before the meeting convenes. In addition, each member of the board of education is entitled to written notice delivered to his or her abode before the meeting, unless the member waives such notice or actually attends the meeting. Significantly, items cannot be added to the agenda of a special meeting. The board can address only such business as is included in the notice of the meeting. Conn. Gen. Stat. § 1-225(a).

The third type of "meeting" under the FOIA is an "emergency meeting." Such a meeting is similar to a special meeting, in that the board of education is not permitted to deal with any item not on the posted agenda for the meeting. The difference between a special meeting and an emergency meeting is that the notice of an emergency meeting need not be filed twenty-four hours before the meeting. In an emergency meeting, the board may go ahead and conduct business if and to the extent required by the emergency. However, in such cases the board of education must include in the minutes of the meeting a statement setting forth the nature of the emergency, and the minutes of the meeting must be filed with the town clerk within seventy-two hours of the meeting. Conn. Gen. Stat. § 1-225(a). While not required by the FOIA, boards of education that confront the need to convene an emergency meeting may be well-served to notify the regular members of the media who cover their meetings, to avoid a claim that the "emergency" was an attempt to circumvent the requirements of the law.

Regardless of the type of meeting, the agenda for the meeting must set forth the business to be transacted. Conn. Gen. Stat. § 1-225(d). There is no clear guidance in the statute as to the level of detail that is required in the agenda. As a practical matter, the agenda should be adequate to identify for the potentially interested members of the public the business to be transacted. *See Ramos v. Chairman, Planning & Zoning Commission, Town of Portland*, Docket #FIC 2003-025 (December 10, 2003). Standard phrases such as "Old Business" or "New Business" may be appropriate under Robert's Rules of Order, but they are not sufficiently descriptive of the business to be transacted for purposes of the FOIA. Similarly, inclusion of "executive session" on the agenda of a meeting is of no legal significance. As discussed below, a board of education may convene into executive session at any time if the subject matter falls within the executive session privilege. Conversely, if the matter to be discussed does not properly fall within the executive session privilege, including "Executive Session" on the agenda does not validate an otherwise inappropriate executive session.

The FOIA imposes further responsibilities when public meetings are held. Specifically, the Act requires that the votes of all members of the board be reduced to writing and be available for public inspection within forty-eight hours of the session, and that the minutes of special and emergency meetings be available within seven calendar days. These periods exclude Saturdays, Sundays and holidays when the board of education offices are closed. Conn. Gen. Stat. § 1-225(b). The minutes of the board meeting must also be available for public inspection within seven days of the session to which they refer, but weekends and holidays extend this period. *Id.*

The FOIA does not specify the format for minutes other than to require recording of votes and of persons present in executive session. To comply with these legal requirements and to serve as an appropriate repository of information, boards of education should, at a minimum, maintain minutes that include the following: (1) when the meeting was convened, (2) the members of the board who were present, (3) a short description of the business that was transacted, (4) a listing of any action taken by the board, specifying any votes taken and listing how each board member voted, (5) any executive sessions held, with a statement of the reason(s) for the executive session and who was in attendance (excluding persons attending for the purpose of a job interview), and (6) when the meeting was adjourned. Since board-appointed committees are public agencies, these requirements apply to such committees as well.

a. Rights of the public

Members of the public are free to attend board of education meetings, except for that portion properly designated as executive session, as described below. The right to attend a meeting is not limited to residents; anyone can attend a meeting. Also, public agencies cannot require that persons attending a meeting provide their name or any other information as a condition of attending the meeting. Conn. Gen. Stat. § 1-225(a).

In addition to attending, members of the public have the right to tape-record any meeting of a board of education (or any other public agency), and there is no requirement that any person making such a recording ask permission or even notify the board. In addition, the public (including the media) may broadcast and/ or photograph meetings of public agencies, including boards of education. Conn. Gen. Stat. § 1-226.

A board of education cannot prohibit such activities, though it may adopt rules in advance to govern recording, photographing and/or broadcasting its meetings. Even if the board has not adopted such rules, the statute provides that a photographer or broadcaster and its personnel, or any person recording the proceedings, is required to handle such activities "as inconspicuously as possible and in such manner as not to disturb the proceedings of the public agency." Conn. Gen. Stat. § 1-226. However, a board of education is well-advised to consider such matters in advance, because any such rules it would wish to make to regulate such activities must be prescribed prior to the meeting. *Id.*

Finally, a board of education can assure that its meetings are held without disruption from persons attending the meeting. The FOIA provides that the board can have removed from the meeting room persons who are willfully interrupting the meeting. In addition, the law provides that, where such removal does not make it possible to conduct the meeting in an orderly fashion, the members of the board can order the meeting room cleared and continue in session. However, duly accredited representatives of the press or other news media must be permitted to attend the session, unless they were participating in the disturbance. These provisions are rarely invoked, but in a compelling case, they may be used. Conn. Gen. Stat. § 1-232.

b. Executive session

Under circumstances narrowly prescribed by the Freedom of Information Act, a board of education may exclude the public from a portion of its meeting by calling an executive session. The FOIA provides that a public agency may hold an executive session by a two-thirds vote of the members present and voting. The law further provides that the board must state the reasons for the executive session. Conn. Gen. Stat. § 1-225(a). The statute does not give any guidance on how specifically the reasons must be stated (e.g. "personnel matters" vs. "consideration of a leave request from Mr. Smith"). However, the statute provides that the agency must state the reasons for the executive session, "as defined in said section [of the FOIA]." *Id.* The Freedom of Information Commission has interpreted this requirement, for example, to require reference to the specific litigation that the public agency is discussing. *Pirozzoli v. Inland Wetlands Commission, Town of Berlin*, Docket #FIC 2003-324 (March 24, 2004). One reasonable approach is to state the reasons for an executive session in a manner that identifies which of the five statutory reasons for executive session applies.

There are some procedural requirements to keep in mind with regard to executive session. Once in executive session, only discussion is permitted, and any votes must be taken in open session. Moreover, that discussion must be limited to topic privileged to the executive session, and board members should take care not to stray into topics that are not covered by the executive session privilege. If a board member raises an issue outside of the reason for the executive session, the other board members may simply remind the member of the proper scope of the executive session and refrain from further discussion. *Downes v. Board of Education, North Branford Public Schools*, Docket #FIC 2003-361 (April 14, 2004).

Finally, attendance in the executive session must be limited to the members of the board of education, and any other persons whose "testimony or opinion" is required, and only for the period their presence is necessary to present such information. The minutes of the executive session must list all persons who attend the executive session, except for the names of job applicants who attend for the purpose of being interviewed. Conn. Gen. Stat. § 1-231.

1. Personnel matters

The first subject that is proper for executive session is:

> Discussion concerning the appointment, employment, performance, evaluation, health or dismissal of a public officer or employee, provided that such individual may require that discussion be held at an open meeting.

Conn. Gen. Stat. § 1-200(6). This provision is probably violated more frequently than any other provision of the Freedom of Information Act. The key provision here is that the individual who is the subject of the discussion may require that the discussion as to him or her be held in public. All too often boards convene in executive session and let the discussion stray to a particular individual's performance or employment. If that individual has not been given prior notice and an opportunity to require that the discussion be held in open session, the board has violated his or her rights.

Such violations can be costly; one district neglected to inform a teacher that it would deliberate on a nonrenewal recommendation in executive session, and the Freedom of Information Commission later nullified the board's vote of nonrenewal. *Minneman v. Acting Superintendent of Norwich Public Schools and Norwich Board of Education,* Docket #FIC 88-94 (July 13, 1988). However, the employee has only the right to require that such discussion take place in open session, and he or she may not demand to attend the executive session.

This provision only relates to discussion of individual board members or employees. Sometimes boards of education wish to discuss budget matters or similar matters in executive session, because the decision to be made could affect staffing and ultimately result in layoffs. However, there is no executive session privilege for budget discussions, and the potential impact on personnel does not justify an executive session. Moreover, the privilege extends only to discussion; any action on personnel matters must be taken through a vote in open session.

Finally, this executive session privilege can also apply to discussion concerning the appointment, performance or evaluation of board members themselves. *Danbury Board of Education v. Freedom of Information Commission*, 213 Conn. 216 (1989). The provision refers to discussion concerning public officers or employees, and board of education members are clearly public officers. Conn. Gen. Stat. § 1-200(6). Moreover, this privilege applies to the discussion of appointments of members to serve on an interim basis. *Id.*, *Royce v. Freedom of Information Commission*, 29 Conn. L. Rptr. No. 18, 688 (July 30, 2001). Since the privilege relates to individuals, executive session is not appropriate for a discussion of the performance of the board as a whole. The performance of one or more individual board members may be discussed in executive session, provided that the member or members to be discussed are given the opportunity to require that discussion as to him or her be held in open session.

2. Pending claims and litigation

The second subject that is privileged to executive session is:

> Strategy and negotiations with respect to pending claims or pending litigation to which the public agency or a member thereof, because of his conduct as a member of such agency, is a party until such litigation or claim has been finally adjudicated or otherwise settled.

Conn. Gen. Stat. § 1-200(8). Before a public agency can discuss a "pending claim" in executive session, it must have received written notice of the claim. Similarly, before a public agency can rely upon the executive session privilege for "pending litigation" (1) it must have been served with papers, or (2) must have received a written demand which asserts the intent to institute an action if relief is not granted, or (3) must wish to discuss action to enforce or implement legal relief or a legal right. Conn. Gen. Stat. § 1-200(9). These limitations assure that public agencies do not adopt an overly broad view of pending claims and litigation and use executive session anytime they are confronted with a sensitive or difficult situation. There is, however, some flexibility in properly discussing "pending claims and litigation." In *Fuhrman v. Freedom of Information Commission*, 243 Conn. 427 (1997), the Connecticut Supreme Court held that a municipality was within its rights to discuss in executive session the hiring of a lobbyist, certain consultant reports and the costs related to possible legal action as part of a discussion on "strategy" with regard to pending litigation.

3. Security devices and real estate

The third and fourth reasons for executive session are rarely the subject of dispute. The FOIA permits public agencies to convene into executive session to consider security strategy or the deployment of security personnel or devices. Conn. Gen. Stat. § 1-200(6). The law also permits executive session discussion concerning the acquisition of real estate, when publicity regarding the acquisition could cause the price to increase. This privilege terminates when all of the property has been acquired, or the proceedings to acquire such property have been terminated. Conn. Gen. Stat. § 1-200(6).

4. Confidential documents

The final reason for which boards of education may convene into executive session is:

> Discussion of any matter which would result in the disclosure of public records or the information contained therein described in subsection (b) of section 1-210.

Conn. Gen. Stat. § 1-200(6). As discussed in Section D(2)(c)(1) below, Conn. Gen. Stat. § 1-210(b) sets out a list of a number of different types of documents that are exempt from disclosure. When a board of education is discussing information that is contained in such confidential records, it may rely on this provision to hold such discussion in executive session. It is important to note that a document must exist to permit such executive session discussion.

a. Student records

Boards of education rely upon the privilege to discuss confidential student records in executive session quite frequently, perhaps even more than they realize. There is no express executive session privilege to discuss specific students or to consider student disciplinary matters. The FOIA has long been interpreted, however, to mean that student records are considered confidential (as required by law) as "personnel or medical files and similar files the disclosure of which constitutes an invasion of personal privacy." Conn. Gen. Stat. § 1-210(b)(1). The law was clarified in 1997, and it now expressly provides that information contained in student records that is privileged from disclosure under Family Educational Rights and Privacy Act (FERPA), 20 U.S. C. § 1232g, is confidential under Conn. Gen. Stat. § 1-210(b)(17). As such, expulsion hearings and other discussion of such confidential information (*i.e.* personally identifiable student information) may be discussed in executive session.

This exemption does not excuse compliance with FOIA. Boards of education (or committees or hearing officers) should still conduct such hearings in accordance with FOIA, albeit limiting discussion of all personally identifiable information to executive session. *Gulash v. Board of Education, Trumbull Public Schools*, Docket # FIC 2000-158 (November 29, 2000). Any such executive session, however, must be posted, and it is not permissible simply to hold student disciplinary hearings without any public posting. *Id.*

b. Attorney-client privilege

There is no general executive session privilege for discussions with the board's lawyer. Earlier in the history of the Freedom of Information Act, some courts held that the common law rule that the attorney-client relationship is confidential could justify executive session discussion between a public agency and its lawyer. However, the General Assembly amended the law, and now it is clear that executive session may not include matters otherwise privileged by the attorney-client relationship unless the executive session is for a purpose expressly permitted under the FOIA. Conn. Gen. Stat. § 1-232(b).

Despite this amendment, the privilege to discuss confidential documents in executive session may come into play and provide a basis on which to conduct executive session discussion of confidential legal matters. Conn. Gen. Stat. § 1-210(b)(10) identifies as confidential "communications privileged by the attorney-client privilege." If the board's lawyer presents the board with a written opinion, the board may discuss the privileged information contained in that opinion in executive session.

The Connecticut Supreme Court has addressed the scope of the attorney-client privilege under the FOIA. In *Shew v. Freedom of Information Commission*, 245 Conn. 149 (1998), the court considered a situation in which the Town of Rocky Hill hired a lawyer to investigate the possible abuse of authority by a former police chief. The lawyer's investigation included interviews with witnesses and rendering legal advice. The court adopted a test previously announced by the Appellate Court in *Shew v. Freedom of Information Commission,* 44 Conn. App. 611 (1997), that communications between town employees and legal counsel for the town are privileged if (1) the lawyer is acting in a professional capacity, (2) the communications are made to the lawyer by current employees, (3) the communications are related to the legal advice sought by the town, and (4) the communications are made in confidence.

In 1999, the General Assembly codified this rule by enacting Conn Gen. Stat. § 52-146r, which provides in relevant part, "In any civil or criminal case or proceeding or in any legislative or administrative proceeding, all confidential communications shall be privileged and a government attorney shall not disclose any such communications unless an authorized representative of the public agency consents to waive the privilege and allow such disclosure." The statute defines a "government attorney" as a lawyer who is either employed or retained by a public agency. In 2002, the Connecticut Supreme Court ruled that this statute codified the existing attorney-client privilege. *Maxwell v. Freedom of Information Commission*, 260 Conn. 143 (2002).

This privilege is limited, and not every communication between a lawyer and public agency is subject to the privilege. Most important, the communication must be confidential. Some communications are by their nature not confidential. In the *Maxwell* case, for example, the Connecticut Supreme Court let stand a decision of the Freedom of Information Commission directing the disclosure of invoices from the town attorney to the town. Thus, legal invoices will be subject to disclosure unless the board of education (or other public agency) can demonstrate that the documents contain confidential information related to the advice it sought. Similarly, if the board of education receives an opinion which it then shares with an adverse party or anyone else outside of the agency, the information is no longer confidential. It would not therefore be proper to discuss in executive session the matters set forth in now-public attorney-client communication. The attorney-client privilege is not waived, however, any time any information from the agency's lawyer is disclosed. *McLaughlin v. Freedom of Information Commission*, 83 Conn. App. 190 (2004). The question is whether the information was provided in confidence. If so, the attorney-client privilege applies, and the written opinion can be discussed in executive session.

5. Collective bargaining issues

There is no separate executive session privilege for collective bargaining. If the board wishes to discuss confidential documents related to collective bargaining strategy, it may do so in executive session. However, if a board of education wishes to discuss "records, reports and statement of strategy or negotiations with respect to collective bargaining" in executive session, such documents must exist. Conn. Gen. Stat. § 1-210(b)(9). Without such documents, such strategy discussions (or negotiations themselves) must be held as a "non-meeting," as described below.

Collective bargaining is excluded from the definition of a "meeting" under the FOIA. Consequently, collective bargaining sessions are not typically held in an executive session, but rather are held outside the scope of the Freedom of Information Act, as a "non-meeting." Such sessions may be held at any time without posting, and related strategy sessions or board updates are often held either before the start or after the end of a regular or special meeting, again without posting.

While there has been no dispute over the ability of boards of education to conduct negotiations or discuss negotiations strategy without triggering the FOIA requirements for meetings, the courts have had to clarify whether and to what extent other meetings relating to collective bargaining are subject to the FOIA.

In *Bloomfield Board of Education v. Frahm*, 35 Conn. App. 384 (1994), the appellate court found that a written statement of grievance was not a record relating to collective bargaining strategy and, as such, was subject to public disclosure. Grievance responses, however, may be considered statements of strategy with regard to collective bargaining, and as such are protected from disclosure as confidential documents under Conn. Gen. Stat. § 1-210(b)(9). Once a grievance is finally resolved, however, it is likely that all related records will be subject to disclosure, because they no longer contain "strategy" with respect to collective bargaining.

Grievance hearings are subject to special rules. The Connecticut Supreme Court has held that holding grievance hearings is part of the duty to bargain in good faith. *Waterbury Teachers Association v. Freedom of Information Commission*, 42 Conn. App. 700 (1996). Given the broad definition of the duty to bargain in good faith, one could logically argue that the entire grievance hearing process should be exempt from FOIA requirements as a continuation of the negotiations process. In 1997, however, the Connecticut Supreme Court reversed the Appellate Court on this issue, and held that the evidentiary portions of grievance hearings held by a public agency such as a board of education are subject to the requirements of the Freedom of Information Act. *Waterbury Teachers Association v. Freedom of Information Commission*, 240 Conn. 835 (1997).

In the *Waterbury Teachers Association* case, the Connecticut Supreme Court held that grievance hearings, in their entirety, are *not* outside the scope of the FOIA as "strategy or negotiations with respect to collective bargaining." In the Court's view, the first portion of the hearing, during which evidence is presented, is not "strategy or negotiations with respect to collective bargaining," and is thus a proceeding of a public agency under the FOIA. Unless some other FOIA exemption applies (such as that permitting executive session for discussion concerning individual personnel matters), that portion of the hearing devoted to "receiving testimony and evidence from witnesses" must be held in open session. Discussion thereafter concerning appropriate remedies and settlements, however, may be closed to the public, because such matters relate to "strategy or negotiations with respect to collective bargaining" and as such are not covered by the FOIA. *Borer v. Personnel & Negotiations Committee, Milford Public Schools*, Docket #FIC 1999-611 (May 24, 2000).

The Connecticut Supreme Court had previously reached a similar conclusion regarding interest arbitration hearings. In *Glastonbury Education Association v. Freedom of Information Commission,* 234 Conn. 704 (1995), it ruled that those portions of the binding arbitration hearing process that do not involve "strategy and negotiations with respect to collective bargaining" are subject to Freedom of Information meeting requirements. The Court failed, however, to give arbitrators and parties any meaningful guidance on when and how to make parts of the binding interest arbitration process open to the public. Based on the further analysis of this issue in the *Waterbury* case, however, it appears that the presentation of evidence concerning ability to pay and the issues in dispute are subject to Freedom of Information Act requirements.

By contrast, grievance arbitration proceedings before the State Board of Mediation and Arbitration are confidential. *State Board of Labor Relations v. Freedom of Information Commission*, 244 Conn. 487 (1998). Such proceedings at the SBMA are not subject to the FOIA because information it receives concerning a labor dispute is confidential by statute. Conn. Gen. Stat. § 31-100.

Finally, the Appellate Court has ruled that a meeting of the municipal legislative body to consider whether to vote to reject a teacher interest arbitration award involves "strategy or negotiations with respect to collective bargaining." Accordingly, such meetings are exempt from the requirements of FOIA. *Presnick v. Freedom of Information Commission*, 53 Conn. App. 162 (1999).

6. Other negotiations

While the FOIA does permit executive session discussion of documents related to "strategy or negotiations related to collective bargaining," there is no similar express provision for confidential discussion of strategy or negotiations with regard to business contracts. Conn. Gen. Stat. § 1-210(b)(7), however, includes in the list of documents exempt from disclosure the following: "The contents of real estate appraisals, engineering or feasibility estimates and *evaluations made for or by an agency relative to* the acquisition of property or to *prospective public supply and construction contracts* [until such transaction(s) are complete]." (Emphasis added). In addition, the Appellate Court affirmed a ruling that proposed contracts for a project that the University of Connecticut ultimately dropped were exempt from disclosure as preliminary drafts. *Coalition to Save Horsebarn Hill v. Freedom of Information Commission*, 3 Conn. App. 89 (2002). It appears therefore that a public agency can discuss confidential information contained in proposed contracts in executive session.

This provision of the law is not clear, and debate can even occur over what is a "public supply and construction contract" and whether the discussion of same would result in the disclosure of information contained in confidential documents. Unfortunately, unless and until the General Assembly, the Commission, and/or the courts clarify this matter, there is uncertainty over the scope of this provision. Consequently, it may be advisable to have negotiations on such matters handled as a staff function, outside the requirements of the Act.

4. Public records

Another basic requirement of the Freedom of Information Act is that the public have access to public records or files developed or maintained by public agencies, including boards of education. In brief, the law provides that any person may have prompt access to inspect public records during regular business hours, and that the public agency must provide copies of any such documents promptly upon request, unless the records requested are exempt from disclosure under the FOIA.

a. Defining "public records"

The definition of "public records or files" is very broad. It includes:

> any recorded data or information relating to the conduct of the public's business prepared, owned, used, received or retained by a public agency, whether such data or information be handwritten, typed, tape-recorded, printed, photocopied, photographed or recorded by any other method.

Conn. Gen. Stat. § 1-200(5). From this definition, we see that any recorded information will fall within the definition of "public records." This includes e-mail messages. *Goodenow and the Record-Journal v. Superintendent, Wallingford Public Schools*, Docket #FIC 2003-170 (October 22, 2003). It even includes voice mail messages. Here, it is important to differentiate between what is or is not a "public record" and how long it must be maintained. As described below, specific rules guide public agencies in the retention of public records. Even a transitory record that need not be retained (such as a voice mail message), however, is a record subject to disclosure as long as it exists.

The board of education or its agents do not have to create the record for it to become a "public record." Once a document is received or maintained by the board, it is a public record. For example, letters of complaint from parents against a teacher are "received" and "retained." As such, they are public records. Finally, documents may be considered public records, even if others have received the documents as the agent of the public agency, rather than the agency itself. In *First Selectman, Town of Columbia v. Freedom of Information Commission*, No. CV000501055, 2000 Conn. Super. LEXIS 3200 (Conn. Super. Ct. November 28, 2000), the Superior Court held that transcripts and other documents received by the Town's attorneys were public records under the FOIA.

There are limits to the scope of "public records" for purposes of the Freedom of Information Act. The critical fact is that the record must be "prepared, owned, used, received or retained by a public agency." Under certain conditions, documents used personally by employees of a public agency are not public documents. Specifically, if a document created by the employee is neither required to be maintained nor is shared with the public agency, it is not a "public record." *Fromer v. Freedom of Information Commission*, 2004 Conn. Super. LEXIS 2036 (Conn. Super. Ct. 2004) (instructors at the University of Connecticut are not "public agencies" and their Power Point presentations are not public documents); *Edelman v. Windham Public Schools*, Docket #FIC 1999-408 (March 22, 2000) (lesson plans are not public documents). These decisions are significant because once a document is characterized as a public record, it is subject to record retention requirements, as set forth below.

b. Records retention

1. General considerations

Public records are subject to protection against destruction. Unauthorized destruction of a public record is a Class A misdemeanor, and each violation of this provision is a separate offense. Public records are to be retained in accordance with a records retention schedule of the Public Records Administrator. The Public Records Administrator has published records retention schedules that set out detailed requirements for retaining records. Different schedules apply to different public agencies, and even within the schedule for records retention that applies to school districts, there is wide variation on the retention period, ranging from no requirement for disciplinary records concerning detentions to permanent retention for physicians' standing orders. Record Retention Schedules for Towns, Municipalities and Boards of Education.

The law further provides that, once records have been retained in accordance with that schedule, the agency holding those records must petition the Public Records Administrator for permission to destroy the record, which is generally granted without further inquiry.

2. Tape-recording, voice-mail and e-mail

As technology advances, it is a challenge to comply with record retention requirements. A voice mail message, or even an answering machine, for example, will create a "record," at least within the broad statutory definition. Nonetheless, public agencies are not required to retain voice mail messages or tapes of answering machines. Conn. Gen. Stat. § 1-213(b)(3). Tapes of board of education meetings, however, stand on a different footing. The law provides that such tape-recorded records be maintained for a period of at least six months after the official minutes are approved, unless there is a known need to maintain such records longer. State of Connecticut, Record Retention Schedules Pursuant to C.G.S. Sections 11-8 and 11-8a, Schedule M1.

In 1998, the Public Records Administrator issued a Management and Retention Guide for Electronic and Voice Mail. *General Letter 98-1* (Public Records Administrator, June 1, 1998). She stated that the records created by voice mail and answering machines are considered to be "transitory in nature, and may be deleted at will." She clarified, however, that there are times that the content could later be used as evidence (*e.g.*, bomb threat), and they should be retained for the same period that would apply to a written record of the same nature. While that remains good advice, the Freedom of Information Act was subsequently amended in 2004 to provide that it should not be construed to require retention or transcription of voice mail messages. Conn. Gen. Stat. § 1-213(b)(3).

The Public Records Administrator also addressed the issue of e-mail. Boards of education (and other public agencies) are responsible for establishing guidelines for which of the following three categories apply to various e-mail messages received and sent:

Transitory	No retention requirement (may be deleted at will)

Less than permanent	Follow retention period for equivalent hard copy records as specified in an approved retention schedule (may be deleted only after making hard copy or retaining in accordance with schedule and receiving signed approval from the Public Records Administrator)
Permanent	Must be retained permanently (may be deleted when information is retained in the form of a hard-copy printout or approved microfilm)

Determination of the appropriate category for such records should be based on function and common sense. Junk e-mail, or a casual communication between coworkers, for example, would be transitory. If technology advances so that parents register children or provide emergency student information by e-mail, for example, such e-mail records should be retained for the same period as such records would be retained in hard copy (unless they are converted to hard copy).

c. Exemptions from disclosure

While documents and other records maintained by a school board are "public records," they are not necessarily subject to public disclosure. The FOIA recognizes two kinds of exemptions to the disclosure of public records.

The first kind of exemption is mandatory and requires confidentiality by virtue of federal law or state statute. Conn. Gen. Stat. § 1-210(a). For example, certain teacher evaluation documents are exempt from disclosure under Conn. Gen. Stat. § 10-151c unless the teacher authorizes the disclosure. Similarly, records of the investigation of ethics complaints are exempt by statute unless the subject of the complaint requests that the records be made public. Conn. Gen. Stat. § 1-82a. Records of child abuse are exempt from disclosure under Conn. Gen. Stat. § 17a-28 and Conn. Gen. Stat. § 17a-101k. *See Town of Groton v. Freedom of Information Commission*, 29 Conn. L. Rptr. No. 7, 243 (May 14, 2001); *Carroll v. Casey Family Services, Inc.*, No. CV020077308S, 2002 Conn. Super LEXIS 1943 (Conn. Super. Ct. 2002); *Losacano v. Town of Plainfield*, 2003 Conn. Super. LEXIS 1643 (Conn. Super. Ct. May 23, 2003). Notably, Conn. Gen. Stat. § 17a-101k refers to such records, "wherever located," and therefore a copy of an abuse report maintained by a school district is exempt from disclosure as well. *See State of*

Connecticut, Department of Public Health v. Freedom of Information Commission, No. CV 98 0492649 (Conn. Super. Ct. October 12, 1999). The courts, however, have inherent power to review a situation and order the release of such records where appropriate. *In re Anastasia C.*, 31 Conn. L. Rptr. No. 9, 333 (Conn. Super. Ct. March 11, 2002).

The second kind of exemption is permissive, and it is found in the FOIA itself. Conn. Gen. Stat. § 1-210(b). The FOIA does not require that any documents be kept confidential, but it does give public agencies the right to maintain certain documents as exempt from public disclosure.

1. Exemptions under the statute

Documents that are permissively exempt from disclosure are listed in Conn. Gen. Stat. § 1-210(b). Disclosure of some such documents might otherwise violate the law, such as personally identifiable student records that are confidential under the Family Educational Rights and Privacy Act (FERPA), 20 U.S.C. § 1232g. Significantly, however, the Freedom of Information Act does not require that any documents be kept confidential. Rather, it simply provides exemptions from disclosure. Moreover, the Commission and the courts have construed these exemptions narrowly in light of the general public policy in favor of disclosure of public records. While the full list of exemptions is beyond our scope here, the following are the exemptions that are most significant to boards of education:

- Preliminary drafts or notes, provided the public agency has determined that the public interest in withholding such documents clearly outweighs the public interest in disclosure. Conn. Gen. Stat. § 1-210(b)(1). This provision permitted the University of Connecticut to keep confidential documents related to a cancelled construction project with Pfizer. *Coalition to Save Horsebarn Hill v. Freedom of Information Commission*, 3 Conn. App. 89 (2002). However, any memoranda or letters, advisory opinions, recommendations or any report that is part of the process of governmental decision-making is not a preliminary draft exempt from disclosure. Conn. Gen. Stat. § 1-210(e)(1).

- Personnel or medical files and similar files the disclosure of which would constitute an invasion of personal privacy. Special rules pertain to such documents, as discussed below.

- Test questions, scoring keys and other examination data used to administer a licensing examination, examination for employment or academic examinations.

- Records and reports relating to strategy concerning pending claims or pending litigation until the matter is finally adjudicated.

- Records, reports and statements of strategy or negotiations with respect to collective bargaining. As discussed above, written statements of grievance are not exempt from disclosure under this provision, but responses are, at least until the matter has been finally resolved.

- Records, tax returns, reports and statements exempted by federal or state law.

- Communications privileged by the attorney-client relationship. This exemption is significant. As discussed above, oral communications between a board of education and its lawyer are not automatically privileged to executive session, and one of the listed purposes for executive session must apply to confer the privilege of confidentiality upon that discussion. Conn. Gen. Stat. § 1-232(b). If the discussion would result in the disclosure of information contained in a document privileged by the attorney-client privilege, however, the discussion may be held in executive session. Conn. Gen. Stat. § 1-200(6); Conn. Gen. Stat. § 1-210(b)(9). A written communication between client and counsel, therefore, may permit the board to discuss confidential legal matters discussed in that communication in executive session.

- Names and addresses of students enrolled in any public school or college without the consent of each student. This exemption can extend to the names and addresses of parents when disclosure of that information can result in the disclosure of the names or addresses of students. *Hartford Board of Education v. Freedom of Information Commission*, 3 Conn. Ops. 153 (February 10, 1997). *See also Paulsen v. Superintendent, Bethel Public Schools*, Docket #FIC 2002-206 (February 26, 2003).

- Records that contain personally identifiable student information and thus are confidential in accordance with the Family Educational Rights and Privacy Act (FERPA), 20 U.S.C. § 1232g.

- Records pertaining to government-owned or leased property (*e.g.*, emergency plans, operational specifications, engineering and architectural drawings) when there are reasonable grounds to believe that disclosure may result in a safety risk. The General Assembly expanded this exemption in 2002 to include documents related to buildings owned by agents of local government.

- Records that would disclose the residential, work or school address of any participant in the address confidentiality program established by the Secretary of State under P.A. 03-200 for "any person who has been a victim of family violence, injury or risk of injury to a child, sexual assault or stalking, and who wishes to keep such person's residential address confidential because of safety concerns."

See Conn. Gen. Stat. § 1-210(b) for the complete list of exempt documents.

2. Personnel files

There are special rules that apply to requests for disclosure of information contained in personnel files. Before addressing the applicable rules under the FOIA, some general comments about personnel files may be helpful. First, it is important to recognize that the personnel file is not a geographic location, but rather a category of information. The state law on personnel files does not apply to public agencies, presumably because its provisions for disclosure were unnecessary for public agencies, given access rights previously set forth in the FOIA. This statute, however, provides helpful guidance in defining the personnel file. Conn. Gen. Stat. § 31-128a defines the "personnel file" as "papers, documents and reports, *including electronic mail and facsimiles*, pertaining to a particular employee that are used or have been used by an employer to determine such employee's eligibility for employment, promotion, additional compensation, transfer, termination, disciplinary or other adverse personnel action including employee evaluations or reports relating to such employee's character, credit and work habits." (Emphasis added). Significantly, this definition relates to categories of documents, not to a physical location.

Second, it is advisable to maintain personnel files in a way that protects legitimate confidentiality issues. Under Conn. Gen. Stat. § 31-128c, a private employer is obligated to keep medical records separate from other personnel file records. While this statutory requirement is not applicable to public agencies, it suggests an appropriate practice. Similarly, Conn. Gen. Stat. § 31-51i(f) requires that criminal history record information concerning applicants or employees be accessible only to persons in the personnel or similar department of an employer, and general disclosure of that information may violate the rights of the applicant or employee. Accordingly, it is advisable to segregate confidential records within the personnel file or otherwise. The challenge is to devise a system for protecting such information while still assuring that it is accessible when needed.

Irrespective of how personnel file information is maintained, it is often the subject of requests for disclosure. Some believe that any information contained in a personnel file is automatically exempt from disclosure. That is not the case. Salary information, job applications for successful candidates and attendance information, for example, have all been held to be public information. Conversely, social security numbers, tax deductions, unlisted telephone numbers and family status have been held to be personal and confidential.

Statutory exemptions apply to certain personnel file information. Already mentioned above are the provisions for confidentiality in Conn. Gen. Stat. § 10-151c ("records of teacher performance and evaluation") and Conn. Gen. Stat. § 1-82a (records related to ethics complaints). The identity of a sexual harassment complainant in an internal investigation by a public agency is similarly exempt from disclosure. Conn. Gen. Stat. § 46a-70(d). Conn. Gen. Stat. § 31-51i provides that criminal conviction information on an employment application shall not be disclosed except to the personnel department. In addition, the Freedom of Information Act itself provides that the home addresses of certain public employees, including municipal police or firefighters, judges and prosecutors (but not, unfortunately, the high school principal) need not be disclosed. Conn. Gen. Stat. § 1-217. When a public agency receives a request for such information, it should notify the subject of the records that such information has been requested in accordance with the procedures under Conn. Gen. Stat. § 1-214, described below.

When a public agency receives a request for information that is not exempt by statute from disclosure, it must decide whether the information is part of "personnel or medical files and similar files the disclosure of which would constitute an invasion of personal privacy." Disclosure of such records will be considered an invasion of privacy (and thus exempt from disclosure under the FOIA) only if the information sought does not pertain to a legitimate matter of public concern and disclosure of the information would be highly offensive to a reasonable person. *Perkins v. Freedom of Information*

Commission, 228 Conn. 158 (1993); *Kureczka v. Freedom of Information Commission*, 228 Conn. 271 (1994); *Pane v. City of Danbury*, 267 Conn. 669 (2004).

When a request is made for material in a personnel file, the custodian of the records must first determine whether disclosure of the requested documents would legally constitute an invasion of privacy, applying the rules described above. If it would not, the material must be disclosed. The board of education may, but is not required to notify the subject of the request in such cases, and it may not delay in the disclosure of the information. Conn. Gen. Stat. § 1-214(b).

If the board reasonably believes that disclosure would be an invasion of privacy, it must immediately notify in writing the employee in question (unless such notice would be impractical because of the number of employees concerned) and his or her bargaining representative, if any. If the employee does not file a written objection to the proposed disclosure of the requested records within seven business days of receipt, or if the board does not receive any such written objection within nine business days if there is no evidence of receipt, the requested documents must be disclosed. Any written objection must be on a form prescribed by the board of education, and the employee or his or her bargaining representative must state that, under penalties for false statements, there is good ground for the objection and it is not interposed for the purpose of delay. Conn. Gen. Stat. § 1-214.

If the employee or official objects to disclosure in such cases, the documents may not be disclosed. If access to requested documents in a personnel file is denied in accordance with this procedure, the requesting party may then appeal to the Freedom of Information Commission, which will decide the matter and which may order disclosure after hearing. *Id.* The law is clear, however, that the burden of proving the exemption falls to the party objecting to the disclosure of the information. *Director, Retirement & Benefits Services Division v. Freedom of Information Commission*, 256 Conn. 764 (2001).

Disclosure of documents in the personnel file is an invasion of privacy only if (1) the information does not pertain to legitimate matters of public concern, and (2) its disclosure would be highly offensive to a reasonable person. Both tests must be met, and if there is public interest in the information, the information must be disclosed. We must ask, therefore, in what information does the public have a legitimate concern and/or when is the release of information highly offensive?

The general rule is that strictly personal information need not be disclosed if the employee objects pursuant to the procedure described above. Typical of such information is the names of beneficiaries, spouses, or children; social security numbers, personal bank/financial and mortgage account information, unlisted home telephone numbers and employee tax withholding information. *See Jerr v. Freedom of Information Commission*, No. CV0504546S, 2001 Conn. Super. LEXIS 2238 (Conn. Super. Ct. August 6, 2001). Similarly, there is no public interest in information concerning the purely private affairs of a public employee (*e.g.*, marriage troubles). *Henderson v. State of Connecticut Department of Public Safety*, Docket #FIC 2003-074 (December 10, 2003).

The Connecticut Supreme Court has provided guidance to define the ambit of matters that are "of legitimate public concern." A complaint against a state trooper alleging an improper relationship with complainant's wife is not such a matter, because the allegation does not relate to the trooper's job performance. *Department of Public Safety v. Freedom of Information Commission*, 242 Conn. 79 (1997). Also, the identity and home address of a complainant in a sexual harassment investigation, as well as sexually explicit information, are exempt, because such information is not a legitimate matter of public concern and its disclosure would be highly offensive to a reasonable person. *Rocque v. Freedom of Information Commission*, 255 Conn. 651 (2001). *See also* Conn. Gen. Stat. § 46a-70(d). Similarly, addresses of employees who have taken significant steps to maintain the confidentiality of such information may also be exempt from disclosure. *West Hartford v. Freedom of Information Commission*, 218 Conn. 256 (1991); *Director, Retirement & Benefits Services Division v. Freedom of Information Commission*, 256 Conn. 764 (2001).

Job applicants have a legitimate interest in the confidentiality of personally identifiable information in their application, as reflected in Conn. Gen. Stat. § 1-231, which exempts the names of persons attending job interviews from disclosure. *See also* Conn. Gen. Stat. § 1-213(b)(2). The Freedom of Information Commission has recognized this interest, and it has ruled that a public agency may redact any personally identifiable information concerning unsuccessful applicants for employment. *Parsons v. Mayor, City of Groton*, Docket #FIC 2003-142 (November 12, 2003).

Employee evaluations stand on a different footing. The Freedom of Information Commission and the lower courts have held that evaluation information concerning public employees is not confidential because the information is a matter of legitimate public concern, and its disclosure is not highly offensive to a reasonable person. *See, e.g., First Selectman, Town of Ridgefield v. Freedom of Information Commission*, 60 Conn. App. 64 (2000) (evaluations of police officers are not exempt from disclosure). In reaching this conclusion, courts have relied on *Perkins* and *Kureczka*. Application of these cases to issues of employee evaluation is questionable. The Connecticut Supreme Court has not expressly overruled its prior decision in *Chairman, Criminal Justice Commission v. Freedom of Information Commission*, 217 Conn. 193 (1991), which held that evaluations of public officials may be kept confidential because of the potential for personal embarrassment and an expectation of privacy. *See also Town of Somers v. Freedom of Information Commission*, 210 Conn. 590 (1989) (enactment of Section 10-151c, discussed below, clarified prior law). Unless and until the Connecticut Supreme Court clarifies this issue, however, public employers and employees should anticipate that disclosure of their evaluations may be ordered.

By contrast, teacher evaluation records (other than records of misconduct, as discussed below) are exempt pursuant to a special statutory provision unique to teachers. Conn. Gen. Stat. § 10-151c provides that records of teacher performance and evaluation maintained by local and regional boards of education "shall not be deemed to be public records and shall not be subject to the provisions of section 1-210." Accordingly, a board of education may decline requests for disclosure of records of "teacher performance and evaluation" without following the procedures that apply to other documents contained in a personnel file. The law defines "teacher" as the term is defined in the Tenure Act, and therefore the scope of the law includes all certified employees of a board of education below the rank of superintendent.

Clearly, records developed in connection with teacher evaluation pursuant to the local teacher evaluation plan are exempt. *Town of Somers v. Freedom of Information Commission*, 210 Conn. 590 (1989) ("goals and objectives" exempt from disclosure). Many other records concerning a teacher's employment, however, are not exempt from disclosure. Letters of parent complaint, for example, are not, because parents do not have the responsibility for evaluating teacher performance. Also, the Commission has ruled in several cases that formal discipline, such as a written reprimand, is not a record of teacher performance and evaluation. *See Carpenter v. Freedom of Information Commission*, 59 Conn. App. 20 (2000), *cert. denied*, 254 Conn. 933 (2000) (teacher reprimand for inappropriate computer use held to be a public document not exempt under Section 10-151c).

This ruling was codified by the General Assembly in 2002. Now, Conn. Gen. Stat. § 10-151c expressly states that "records of the personal misconduct of a teacher shall be deemed to be public records" which therefore are subject to disclosure without the consent of the teacher. In 2004, the Appellate Court interpreted Conn. Gen. Stat. § 10-151c as amended, and it affirmed a decision of the Freedom of Information Commission ordering disclosure of a "last chance agreement," which set forth the discipline of the teacher for showing an inappropriate video in class. The court rejected the teacher's claim that, since the record related to his decision to show a movie in class, it was perforce a confidential record of teacher performance, and it ruled that discipline records must be disclosed. *Wiese v. Freedom of Information Commission*, 82 Conn. App. 604 (2004).

Finally, this law does not prevent disclosure of records of teacher performance and evaluation. It expressly provides that a teacher may consent to the disclosure of such evaluation information, as long as such consent is provided in writing. Also, a separate consent is required for each request for disclosure of such records. Conn. Gen. Stat. § 10-151c.

d. Inspection of public records

Under the Freedom of Information Act, the public has the right of access to public records, unless the records are exempt from disclosure as set forth above. The law provides that members of the public have the right "to inspect such records promptly during regular office or business hours." Conn. Gen. Stat. § 1-210(a). The law does not define "promptly," but the Freedom of Information Commission has acknowledged that public agencies must supervise the inspection of public records, given their responsibility for maintaining such records safely. Consequently, public agencies are not required to drop everything when a request to inspect records is made. Rather, compliance with the legal requirement of "prompt" access will depend upon the particular facts and the specific request. For example, if the request is to inspect the minutes of a recent meeting, it is fair to expect almost immediate access. In contrast, if the request is to inspect purchase orders from the 1995-96 school year, taking some reasonable time to track down the records and to schedule the inspection will likely be considered "prompt" under the law.

Three points should be made concerning the right to inspect (and copy, as discussed below) a public record. First, this right exists without regard to the reason for the request. It would be improper, therefore, to condition access to public records on a "good reason." Second, anyone can exercise this right without condition. While asking a person's name may be considered good manners in some quarters, the right of access does not depend upon disclosing one's name. Third, even an adverse party in litigation is entitled to access to documents under the FOIA, unless they are somehow otherwise exempt from disclosure. *Hartford Police Department v. Freedom of Information Commission*, 252 Conn. 377 (2000).

The right to inspect public records is not a right to require that a public agency create a record. In responding to requests from the public, public agencies do not have to create new documents that set out information in a format requested by an outside party. Similarly, public agencies are not required to conduct research. If a person requests the average salary of coaches in the district, for example, and the district does not maintain that information, it may simply say that it has no documents that are responsive to the request. The courts have distinguished, however, between research, on the one hand, and searching for records that exist, on the other. In *Wildin v. Freedom of Information Commission*, 56 Conn. App. 683 (2000), the Appellate Court held that a request for existing documents must be granted, notwithstanding the fact that it entailed a burdensome search of the files. Similarly, public agencies must comply with requests for records, even if the same person has requested the same records previously. *Mayor, City of Torrington v. Freedom of Information Commission*, 31 Conn. L. Rptr. No. 15, 552 (April 22, 2002).

The law provides that a person making a request for access to records is generally entitled to a response within four business days of the request, and it further provides that a failure to respond within the four-day period may be deemed to be a denial of access, which the person can then appeal to the Freedom of Information Commission. Some public agencies have inferred from this provision that they automatically have four days to respond to a request. That is incorrect. The law requires "prompt" access, and if a record is readily available for inspection or copying, it is a violation of the law to make the person requesting the record wait four days. Conversely, if a response will take more than four days, *e.g.*, retrieving purchase orders from 1989, it is appropriate to respond within the four business days with a good faith estimate of the time it will take to respond "promptly" to the request.

A common example of the right to "prompt" access is the sending of the board packet. Understandably, superintendents and boards of education would prefer to make the contents of the board packet public first when it is discussed at an open board meeting. However, except to the extent that the packet contains documents that are exempt from disclosure under Conn. Gen.

Stat. § 1-210(b), a member of the public has the right to inspect and receive a copy of the materials as soon as they are sent out to board members.

e. Copies of public records

In addition to the right to inspect public records, members of the public have the right to receive copies of such records, unless the requested record is exempt from disclosure under Conn. Gen. Stat. § 1-210(b). Conn. Gen. Stat. § 1-212(a). Again, the statute provides that such copies shall be provided "promptly," and what constitutes "prompt" provision of a copy will depend upon the scope and nature of the request. The law also provides that a request for a copy of a public record shall be made in writing. *Id.*

Boards of education (and other public agencies) may charge a fee for any requested record. The FOIA provides that agencies may charge up to fifty cents per page for copies of records (though state agencies may only charge twenty-five cents per page). When it is anticipated that the charges for the requested records will equal or exceed ten dollars, the agency may require payment in advance before making and providing the copies. When the requested record is not a document, for example a tape recording of a board of education meeting, the public agency may charge the actual cost of making or obtaining the copy. Conn. Gen. Stat. § 1-212.

There is provision in the FOIA for the waiver of charges for copies. Public agencies may not charge for copies under the following circumstances: (1) the requesting party is indigent, (2) the public agency has determined that the requested records are exempt from disclosure, (3) in the judgment of the agency, compliance with the request will benefit the general welfare, or (4) the person requesting the record is an elected official and the official obtains the record from an agency of the political subdivision (*e.g.*, town board of education) in which the official serves, provided that s/he certifies that the record pertains to her/his official duties.

With advances in technology come new issues, and in 2002, the General Assembly amended the law concerning access to public documents. Specifically, Conn. Gen. Stat. § 1-210(a) and new Conn. Gen. Stat. § 1-212(g) now expressly provide that members of the public may copy documents on their own with a hand-held scanner, rather than ask the public agency to make copies. The public agency may charge up to $10.00 each time the individual copies records with a hand-held scanner, and the process may not leave a mark or impression on the documents and may not interfere unreasonably with the operation of the public agency. *Id.* This amendment reverses a Superior Court decision in which the court vacated the order of the Commission ordering the City of Hartford to permit a title examiner to scan public records. *Office of the Municipal Clerk, City of Hartford v. Freedom of Information Commission*, 7 Conn. Ops. 538 (April 16, 2001).

There are special rules that govern information contained on computer files. Conn. Gen. Stat.§ 1-211 provides that the right of access to public records includes access to information that is contained in computer files, unless that information is otherwise exempt. Upon request by a member of the public, the board of education (or any other public agency) must provide a copy of the information that is contained in the computer files. The copy is to be made on paper, disk, tape or any other electronic storage device or medium, as requested by the member of the public, if the board can reasonably make such a copy or have such a copy made. *Id.*

The board may charge no more than its actual cost in providing the record, including either (1) the hourly wage rate of employees for time spent in producing the computer copy and the cost of the diskette or other storage medium on which the copy is provided, or (2) the cost of retaining an outside party to make the copy, if necessary. Conn. Gen. Stat. § 1-212. Except for computer time charges if the agency uses an outside agency for computer storage, public agencies (including boards of education) may not charge for the cost of finding the information in the first place. Conn. Gen. Stat. §§ 1-211, Conn. Gen. Stat. § 1-212(b).

The scope of this provision was illustrated in a case decided by the Connecticut Supreme Court in 2002. The Hartford Courant Company had requested copies of certain conviction records maintained by the Department of Public Safety, and it offered to pay for the cost of an electronic copy in accordance with Conn. Gen. Stat. § 1-212. The Department responded, however, that it would provide such copies in accordance with Conn. Gen. Stat. § 29-11(c), at a total cost of $20,375,000.00 The Courant appealed without success to the Freedom of Information Commission and to Superior Court, but the Connecticut Supreme Court saw the matter differently. The Court held that Conn. Gen. Stat. § 1-212 controlled, notwithstanding Conn. Gen. Stat.§ 29-11(c), which provides that the Department of Public Safety may charge $25 to respond to a request concerning conviction information. Moreover, the Court interpreted Conn. Gen. Stat. § 1-212 to mean that a public agency may be required to develop a software program to provide computer-stored information pursuant to a Freedom of Information request (provided, of course, that the requesting party pays for the related costs). In reaching this conclusion, the Court relied on the language of Conn. Gen. Stat.

§ 1-212(b), which provides that in responding to request for such information public agencies may charge an "amount equal to the hourly salary attributed to all agency employees engaged in providing the requested computer-stored public record, *including their time performing the formatting or programming functions necessary to provide the copy as requested.*" (Emphasis added by the Court). *Hartford Courant Company v. Freedom of Information Commission*, 262 Conn. 86 (2002).

E. Board Finances

A board of education in Connecticut has dual status. For some purposes, it is an agency of the town, and it is thus subject to charter requirements concerning election, civil service and other matters. As regards the provision of educational services, however, a board of education may act independently of town control. Education in Connecticut is a state responsibility, and the General Assembly has delegated that responsibility to each local or regional board of education. As school boards carry out that responsibility, they act as agents of the state. The challenge, of course, is to determine when a school board may act independently and when it is subject to charter provisions and other town controls.

1. The school budget

School spending is perhaps the clearest example of the independent authority of boards of education. Conn. Gen. Stat. § 10-222 sets out the procedure for adopting a budget. The local board of education must prepare an itemized estimate of the expenses for operating the schools in the coming year. That estimate is then presented to the municipality on the budget submission date. The municipality is charged with the responsibility for considering the request in light of the other municipal needs. The municipality then sets the budget in accordance with its local procedures, *i.e.* through action of the legislative body, the town meeting or referendum.

Once the municipality has made its appropriation to the board of education, the board of education may expend those funds in its discretion. In exercising that discretion, the board of education may transfer funds from one line item to another, provided that the total expenditure does not exceed the amount of the appropriation and other funds received for school purposes. *See* Section E(3).

There will often be tension between the board of education and the municipal body making appropriations, because these two agents of local government may have different priorities and responsibilities. As we all know, budget time can be brutal, and board of education budget requests are often cut during the budget process. From time to time, local boards of education have claimed that the local finance authority has not appropriated funds sufficient for the operation of the schools. However, it is very difficult for a board of education to challenge such decisions. The courts have recognized that the local fiscal authority has a job to do, and the courts will not often overrule decisions made by the local fiscal authority, which must consider not only the requests by the board of education, but also the other financial demands on a municipality. *See, e.g., Fowler v. Enfield*, 138 Conn. 521 (1952). Generally, a school board must make do with the appropriation it receives from the municipality.

a. The "minimum expenditure requirement"

The broad discretion of local officials in passing on a school budget is subject to a major limitation—the minimum expenditure requirement. For twenty-five years, the Connecticut courts have wrestled with the state constitutional requirement that all children in Connecticut have "equal opportunity to receive a suitable program of educational experiences." Conn. Gen. Stat. § 10-4a. This requirement resulted from the leading case on school funding, *Horton v. Meskill*, 172 Conn. 615 (1977), which held that gross disparities among school districts in funding education caused by the state system of financing education primarily through real estate taxation were unconstitutional. *See* discussion above at Section A(1). To remedy the problem, the General Assembly adopted a funding program with strings attached. While the details change from time to time (and the formula for state funding changes almost every year), a constant has been the "minimum expenditure requirement" or MER, which is the minimum amount that must be spent annually on each student in the town.

State funds are distributed in accordance with a formula that differentiates among districts on the basis of their need. The theory is that the state funds will help equalize the burden of funding education among the economically diverse school districts in Connecticut. Reflecting that goal, the original grant was called the Guaranteed Tax Base (GTB) grant, and over time the program evolved into the current Educational Cost Sharing (or ECS) program. Under Conn. Gen. Stat. § 10-262i(c), towns are required to expend all ECS funds for educational purposes. Moreover, the statute provides that districts may not use increases in ECS funding to supplant local expenditures for education, although we have no judicial guidance on what would or would not be considered supplanting. In any event, districts that do not spend at least at the MER level are in violation of their duty to implement the educational interests of the state, an obligation that will be enforced in court if necessary. *New Haven v. State Board of Education*, 228 Conn. 699 (1994).

This requirement does limit the discretion of some local municipal officials in appropriating funds for educational purposes. Where school spending is at or near the MER, local officials do not have much if any discretion, and sufficient funds must be appropriated to meet the MER. At the end of the fiscal year, each district must report on spending for the year. Where a district has spent less than the MER, the State Board of Education can withhold grant funds in the amount of two times the shortfall in the second fiscal year following. Alternatively, the district may avoid such a forfeiture of state grant funds if it agrees to spend an equal amount above and beyond the then-applicable MER in that second fiscal year following. Conn. Gen. Stat. § 10-262j. In either event, a failure to meet the MER is serious.

The MER requirement can limit the discretion of the local fiscal authority even where the total appropriation could be sufficient. Under Conn. Gen. Stat. § 10-262f(20), some expenditures may not be counted toward the minimum expenditure requirement, such as expenditures for special education, transportation, adult education, and health and welfare services for children in non-public schools. *See New Haven v. State Board of Education*, 228 Conn. 699 (1994) (failure to meet the MER because of excluded expenditures not excused, even when the overall appropriation would otherwise have met MER).

b. Contingent appropriations

Everyone has an opinion on how to run the schools, and local municipal officials are no exception. Towns have tried various ways to dictate how local boards of education should expend funds appropriated to them, but school boards continue to be able to exercise their independent discretion in deciding upon school expenditures. Conn. Gen. Stat. § 10-222.

The leading case concerning the autonomy of local boards of education is *Ellington Board of Education v. Board of Finance of the Town of Ellington*, 151 Conn. 1 (1963). There, the Board of Education concluded that it needed additional teaching positions, but the Town identified a roof repair as a greater priority. In considering the itemized estimate of the Board of Education, the Town did not appropriate funds for the new positions. However, it did place some $47,000 in a contingency fund, which the Board of

Education could use if, and only if, it decided to repair the roof. The Board of Education sued, claiming that the Town had overstepped its authority in seeking to dictate priorities to the Board of Education. The Connecticut Supreme Court agreed. It held that the responsibility of the Town was limited to determining the overall amount of money reasonably necessary to operate the schools for the coming year. Since the Town had determined that the $47,000 was available and necessary for school purposes, the court ordered that these funds be released to the Board of Education without restriction.

In 1996, the Connecticut Supreme Court clarified and limited its ruling in *Ellington*. The court held that boards of education may not unilaterally transfer funds from one line item to another in a separate capital budget for school purposes. *Board of Education v. City of New Haven*, 237 Conn. 169 (1996). There, the New Haven Board of Education, citing its discretion under the *Ellington* case, sought to reallocate funds in the annual capital budget without obtaining the City's approval for the transfer. The court considered Conn. Gen. Stat. § 10-240, which provides that the municipality is the school district. It also considered Conn. Gen. Stat. § 10-241, which sets out school district responsibilities. Without differentiation, this statute lists some responsibilities that are exercised by the municipality (*e.g.*, laying taxes to support education) and others that are exercised by the board of education (*e.g.*, hiring teachers). Interpreting this statute, the Court held that the municipality shares responsibility with the board of education for providing for the capital needs of a school district. The board of education, therefore, may not unilaterally transfer funds from a separate capital account and expend them for a purpose other than that for which the funds were appropriated. The Court did not overrule *Ellington*. Rather, it distinguished between the operating budget of a board of education and a shared capital budget. Boards of education continue to have discretion over the operating budget under Conn. Gen. Stat. § 10-222, but they may not exercise the same unilateral control over capital budgets (even for educational facilities).

The issue of capital budgets has also arisen with regional school districts, which have more fiscal autonomy than local boards of education. *See* discussion below, at Section E(2).

c. Funds received from other sources

Generally, the board of education cannot receive funds independently of the town, and it may spend only those funds that are appropriated by the municipality for that particular year. However, there are various exceptions, as discussed below.

In certain situations, the municipality must credit the board of education expenditure account for specified special education expenditures it makes during the course of the year. Boards of education are eligible for funding on a current fiscal year basis for certain expenses that are difficult to budget, *i.e.* for the costs of educational placements made by the state (*e.g.*, by the Department of Children and Families) beyond one time the average per pupil cost. Conn. Gen. Stat. § 10-76d(e)(5). Local and regional school districts are also eligible for current reimbursement for the cost of "catastrophic" expenses for a single student, otherwise known as "excess costs," which are defined as more than five times the average per pupil costs. Conn. Gen. Stat. § 10-76g(b). The General Assembly reduced the base amount to four and one-half times the average per pupil costs, supposedly starting July 1, 2005. A similar change was enacted for 2003 and then delayed for two years. Moreover, the statute was amended to provide that funding will be reduced proportionately when available funds are insufficient, and districts have thus not even received full funding at the higher "five times level."

When the state pays such reimbursement, the town treasurer is required to credit the board's expenditure account in the amount of the state funds that are attributable to expenses beyond the board's itemized budget estimate. Conn. Gen. Stat. § 10-76d(e)(5); Conn. Gen. Stat. § 10-76g(b). This obligation to credit state funds received to the board of education expenditure account is limited to the amount by which the expenditures exceeded the budgeted estimates of such expenditures. This limitation makes sense, because there would be no reason to credit the board's account for funds it had already included in its budget. Given this limitation, however, it is important that the board of education clearly set out its budget estimates for such expenditures and that it carefully document expenditures. Conn. Gen. Stat. § 10-76g(b) provides that the town treasurer must credit the board's expenditure account "no later than thirty days after receipt by the treasurer of necessary documentation from the board of education . . . ." It is advisable, therefore, to seek agreement with the town treasurer in advance over the type of documentation he or she will require.

While credit for excess special education costs is typically the most significant source of credit, the statutes include other provisions for credit to the board of education expenditure account. When school districts receive funds from students or parents due to lost, damaged or stolen textbooks, library materials or other educational materials, or when the district receives insurance proceeds from such lost or damaged educational materials, the town is required to credit such funds as an additional appropriation to the board of education. Conn. Gen. Stat. § 10-222a. Also, amounts received by a board of education from outside groups in payment for custodial and other costs related to using school facilities are deemed appropriated to the board of education, though such appropriation may be net of any expenses incurred by the town in providing such custodial services. *Id.*

School districts may also receive "any donation or gift of personal property to be used for the educational benefit of students," and such funds may be maintained (and carried over from year to year) in a school activity fund authorized by Conn. Gen. Stat. § 10-237(c). While the tax consequences of any such gift are the donor's problem, it may be helpful to note that the value of the gift may be considered a "charitable contribution" which is a deductible expense as long as the gift is (1) acknowledged in writing before the donor's tax return is due ("substantiation" requirement) and (2) made for a purely public purpose. Internal Revenue Code § 170(c)(1).

The statute does not address the mechanics of receiving and accepting a gift of money. If the personal property is, say, a car to be used in the auto shop, the gift can simply be accepted and used. Since board of education accounts are operated by the municipality, a cash contribution would generally be processed through the town accounts, but the disposition of such funds would be up to the board of education. Alternatively, the board of education could maintain and use such donations through a school activity fund, as described in Section E(4) below.

Acceptance of gifts can raise policy issues, particularly if such gifts have strings attached or if the gift benefits a single school. Boards are well-advised therefore to adopt policies concerning the acceptance of gifts. Also, while it is not the board's concern, gifts may not be tax-deductible if they are given only for a specified purpose that serves the donor's personal interests. Boards of education, therefore, must be cautious about making any representation as to whether gifts will or will not be taxable.

d. Expenditures before budget adoption

On occasion, it is impossible for a municipality to approve a budget before the start of the fiscal year. Towns may borrow money in anticipation of taxes, and life goes on while the budget wars rage. However, this situation poses problems for boards of education because they can generally spend only those funds that are appropriated to them.

The General Assembly addressed this problem in the statutes governing municipal finance without specific reference to boards of education. Conn. Gen. Stat. § 7-405 provides that, if no budget has been adopted at the beginning of a specific fiscal year, necessary expenditures may be made for the first ninety days as authorized by the budget-making body. If no budget has been adopted at the end of that ninety-day period, the budget-making body may authorize payment of expenses in successive monthly periods within the limits of line-item appropriations from the prior fiscal year. This procedure does not expressly state how board of education expenses should be handled, and the law is especially unclear with regard to the first ninety days. However, a reasonable approach most consistent with the statute is that the board of education will be authorized to expend amounts monthly equal to the pro rata appropriation from the prior year. For this purpose, the entire board of education budget is one "line item."

2. Regional boards of education

The budget process for regional boards of education is different from that of local boards. A regional board of education has fiscal autonomy. The regional board owns property, may borrow money, may issue debt and may otherwise exercise many of the powers that a municipality holds as the "local school district." The regional district may invest funds held, and any interest from such investments must be used to reduce the net expenses otherwise chargeable to the member towns.

The statutes prescribe the budget process for regional school districts. Conn. Gen. Stat. § 10-51. The regional board must present its budget to the public not less than two weeks before the annual meeting. After that public hearing, the board of education prepares an annual budget, which must include a statement of (1) estimated receipts and expenditures for the next fiscal year, (2) estimated receipts and expenditures for the current fiscal year, (3) estimated surplus or deficit in operating funds at the end of the current fiscal year, (4) bonded or other debt, (5) estimated per pupil expenditures for the current and next fiscal year, and (6) other relevant information. *Id.*

The budget is accepted or rejected at the annual district meeting. The board can require that the vote on the budget be by ballot or by voting machine on the day following the district meeting. Also, two hundred voters can petition the board at least three days before the meeting and require that the vote be by ballot or machine on the day following the district meeting. Significantly, the budget is adopted by a majority vote of all of the electors in the constituent towns. A majority vote against the budget in one town will not defeat the budget if an overall majority vote supports passage. *Id.*

If the budget is defeated, the regional board of education must call another district meeting to consider the same or an amended budget no sooner than one week nor later than four weeks after the first vote. The board must follow this process until the budget is approved. Conn. Gen. Stat. § 10-51. As with other municipal budget referenda, an automatic recount is required when the difference between yes and no votes in the vote on the budget for a regional school district is less than two thousand votes and is less than one-half of one percent. Conn. Gen. Stat. § 9-370a.

Conn. Gen. Stat. § 7-405(b) provides a mechanism for the continued operation of a regional school district if no budget has been passed at the start of the new fiscal year. This statute provides that the disbursing officer for each member town of the regional school district must provide funds to such district in an amount equal to the total of the town's appropriation to the district for the previous fiscal year and the town's proportionate share of any increment in debt service over the previous fiscal year, until the regional school district budget is approved. The member towns are then credited for any such expenditures in implementing the new budget.

Once the budget is passed, the board must then estimate the share of net expenses of operating the district to be paid by each member town. Conn. Gen. Stat. § 10-51(b) defines "net expenses" as "estimated expenditures, including estimated capital expenditures, less estimated receipts as presented in a regional school district budget." In 2001, the General Assembly clarified the term "net expenses" by adding the reference to capital expenditures. The expenses for operating the district are allocated among the member towns on the basis of the respective student populations from each town.

Regional school districts have flexibility in how they may bill the member towns. For example, the Attorney General has opined that Regional School District No. 12 may bill each of the member towns monthly for the projected gross operating budget and then offset these charges as other funds are received. Since the end result is that the towns are billed no more than the net operating expenses, this procedure is permissible. *Opinion to Sergi, Opinions of the Attorney General* # 1997-011 (April 9, 1997).

At the end of the year, any appropriation that has not been expended must be used to reduce the net expenses chargeable to the member towns in the following year. Conn. Gen. Stat. § 10-51(c). There is no general authority for regional school districts to hold a surplus or a reserve fund. *See Opinion to Sergi*, *Opinions of the Attorney General* # 2003-010 (May 30, 2003). However, the board may create a capital reserve fund to finance a specific capital improvement or the acquisition of a specific piece of equipment. No annual appropriation to such a reserve fund, however, may exceed one percent of the district budget. Conn. Gen. Stat. § 10-51(d).

Regional districts are permitted generally to transfer from one line item in the budget to another, but an issue arose when one regional school district transferred surplus funds to a capital carry-over account at the end of the year. Since the courts have not addressed the issue, we do not have a definitive ruling on this point, but in 1997 the Attorney General opined that such transfers are not permitted. *Opinion to Sergi, Opinions of the Attorney General* # 1997-011 (April 9, 1997). The Attorney General concluded that the statutory process for funding a capital carry-over account through the annual appropriation under Conn. Gen. Stat. § 10-51(d) is the exclusive method for transferring funds to such an account. In any event, the statutes also authorize regional boards of education to finance capital projects and equipment through the bonding authorization process. Conn. Gen. Stat. § 10-56. Moreover, the addition in 2001 of "capital expenditures" to "net expenses" in Conn. Gen. Stat. § 10-51(b) may reduce the importance of the capital carry-over account, if any.

Like local boards of education, a regional board of education must maintain its expenses within the limits of the approved budget. Should additional expenditures be necessary, the regional board must submit a supplementary budget, following the procedures that apply to the annual budget. However, it is possible that the district will operate in deficit in a given year due to unforeseen circumstances or unanticipated costs. Any deficit must be addressed in establishing the budget for the next year. Conn. Gen. Stat. § 10-51(a).

3. Payment of school expenses

Once an appropriation is made, the board of education has autonomy over how it expends those funds. Conn. Gen. Stat. § 10-222 expressly provides:

> The money appropriated by any municipality for the maintenance of public schools shall be expended by and in the discretion of the board of education. Any such board may transfer any unexpended or uncontracted-for portion of any appropriation for school purposes to any other item of such itemized estimate.

As the fiscal year progresses, a board of education may reorder its priorities, and transfer funds from one account to another, provided that total expenditures do not exceed the amount appropriated. The board of education is generally responsible for making such transfers, but it may delegate limited authority to others. Conn. Gen. Stat. § 10-222 provides that boards of education may authorize designated personnel (presumably the superintendent) to "make limited transfers under emergency circumstances if the urgent need for the transfer prevents the board from meeting in a timely fashion to consider such transfer." The statute further provides that the transfer must be announced at the next regularly scheduled meeting of the board of education.

Given that line-item transfers are a board of education responsibility, it is advisable to adopt policies concerning line item transfers. Without such a delegation to the superintendent or other appropriate person, presumably transfers now may not be made by anyone other than the board of education. Also, boards should carefully define "line item" in adopting such policies. This term is not defined in the statute, and in preparing its budget the board of education can determine how detailed the line items in its budget are to be. By adopting broad categories (*e.g.*, personnel, insurance, instructional supplies) as the line items, with more specific breakdowns within the line items, boards of education may reduce the frequency with which transfers (and the concomitant board action or announcement) are necessary.

Some municipal requirements may potentially affect the rights of boards of education in making expenditure decisions. For example, some municipalities have charter provisions or other requirements that all contracts over a certain limit go out to bid. Since a board of education has dual status as a town agency and an agent of the state, it is not always clear which town requirements apply. However, as a general rule, provisions that would restrict the board of education in deciding how to expend its appropriation, such as bid requirements or approval from a municipal purchasing agent, will not be enforceable. Where goods or services are put out to bid, however, the board of education may reserve to itself the right to choose the bidder in its discretion. A bid decision may be challenged only on the basis of fraud, corruption or favoritism. *Spiniello Construction Co. v. Manchester*, 189 Conn. 539 (1983). However, school construction contracts must be put out to bid and awarded to the "lowest responsible bidder" to be eligible for state-reimbursement. Conn. Gen. Stat. § 10-287(b).

The *New Haven Board of Education* case, discussed above at Section E(1)(b), clarified that municipalities may control expenditures made from a separate capital budget, even if the appropriation to that budget is made for educational facilities under the control of the board of education. Reallocation of such funds, therefore, is a joint responsibility of the town and the school board.

Despite its independence in how funds for education will be spent, the board of education is not independent of the town in spending such funds. The board of education "account" is a town account. Conn. Gen. Stat. § 10-248 provides that the town treasurer shall pay the expenses of maintaining the public schools. Significantly, the town treasurer does not exercise any discretion in this regard; within the limit of the appropriation, such expenses "shall be incurred with the approval of the board of education." The statute further provides that payments will be made on orders drawn by the board of education, which are to be signed by persons authorized by the board, by bylaw or special vote. If such authority is not otherwise delegated, such orders are to be signed by the board member who is designated to serve as secretary of the board. *Id.*

The appropriation made to the board of education is carried as a town account, and boards of education may not carry funds over from one year to the next. With cooperation between the board of education and the town, a school district can create a contingency fund, an escrow fund or some other creature of municipal finance which will carry over from one fiscal year to another. Such funds may be appropriate in a variety of situations, as for example when the budget contains funds for a retroactive labor settlement which is not resolved at the end of the fiscal year. However, funds typically revert to the town at the end of the fiscal year because the board of education has no general means to hold funds from one year to the next. In a given year, a board of education may expend only the amount appropriated to it (plus such other funds as are received for school purposes).

4. <u>School activity funds</u>

While the appropriation to the board of education is typically held in the general fund by the municipality, the statutes also provide for separate school funds. Local and regional boards of education are authorized by Conn. Gen. Stat. § 10-237 to create and maintain "a school activity fund" for purposes specified in the statute. Such a fund may handle the finances of that part of the school lunch program and any driver education program not provided by town appropriations. In addition, such a fund may handle funds of schools and school organizations as the board of education determines to be desirable, and the fund can include gifts and donations.

In contrast to the appropriation to the board of education, which is made on an annual basis, such school activity funds carry over from year to year. The statute provides that the board of education must designate one of its members or some other person to serve as treasurer for the fund. This treasurer must be bonded and can even earn a salary. Each school fund and school organization fund is to be kept separate, and the control of any school fund or school organization fund remains in the name of the respective school or organization. Finally, the statute provides that any such school activity funds shall be considered town accounts and must be audited by the town auditor on the same basis as other town accounts.

5. Deficits

Local school districts operate on an annual funding basis, and local boards of education have no authority to operate in a deficit. In fact, school board members or school officials who authorize expenditures in excess of the appropriation to the board of education theoretically face personal liability for such expenditures. Conn. Gen. Stat. § 7-349. There are no reported cases, however, of personal liability for authorizing in good faith expenditures that create a deficit.

Section 10-222 provides a procedure (but no clear answer) for school boards that face a deficit because of unanticipated expenses. The statute provides that where additional funds are needed, the chair of the board of education must notify the chair of the board of finance or other appropriating authority. The board of education must then submit a request for additional funds in the same manner as other town boards or departments. The law further provides that no additional funds shall be expended unless the requested supplemental appropriation is granted.

The General Assembly added these provisions to the law in 1982, after several school districts ran out of money and threatened to close school early. The unanswered question is what to do when additional expenditures are unavoidable but no supplemental appropriation is made. If it is absolutely impossible to keep expenditures within the appropriation, the board members must first follow the outlined procedures. If no appropriation is made, it may be necessary to seek protection through the courts. However, it is clear that the courts will be loath to get involved in such matters, which will be viewed as essentially political disputes. Consequently, every effort must be made to make any possible cuts to bring the projected expenditures back within the appropriation.

6. Referendum

Many town charters provide that the board of education budget will be submitted to referendum, either upon petition or in the normal course. Where approval of the board of education budget requires a referendum, school board members and other school officials are free to express their own views, but they must take care not to expend public funds to influence any person to vote for approval of the budget or any other referendum question.

Actions of boards of education are not subject to review by referendum except as provided by law. For example, some years ago the Town of Milford sought to hold an "advisory referendum" posing the question, "Are you in favor of the Board of Education entering into a busing contract presently known as Project Concern for the forthcoming year, 1969-1970?" The Superior Court, however, enjoined the Town from conducting the referendum because the matter was for the Board of Education to decide:

> When a question such as this, whether or not the contract for busing should be entered into, presents itself, and no provision exists for its submission to referendum, the expense of submitting it to the voters, even on a "straw vote" basis, as here, would constitute a misapplication and waste of public funds.

Murray v. Egan, 28 Conn. Supp. 204, 208-09 (1969). It is appropriate, therefore, to conduct referenda only in accordance with law.

When referenda are held, it is important to avoid any expenditure of public funds to advocate a referendum result. Conn. Gen. Stat. § 9-369b prohibits any such expenditures of public funds to influence a vote on a referendum question. The scope of this prohibition is very broad, and it applies to both local and regional school districts. The statute clearly prohibits a board of education from paying for posters or an advertisement urging approval of the board's budget in a pending referendum vote.

However, the law also prohibits indirect expenditures. The State Elections Enforcement Commission, the agency responsible for administering this statute, has, for example, repeatedly held that it is a violation of this law to permit students to act as couriers for information advocating approval of a referendum question, because such delivery would be the functional equivalent of the cost of postage. This prohibition applies whether the material is prepared by the school district or by a third party, such as the PTO.

Using equipment or supplies to produce materials advocating approval of a referendum question is similarly prohibited. This prohibition extends to such use even if the party advocating a referendum result reimburses the district for the use of the equipment. School officials granting permission for such improper activities can be personally liable for the value of the facilities or equipment used. School facilities, however, can be made available to parties advocating a referendum result if they are made available to all interested parties on a non-discriminatory basis.

The prohibition against expending public funds to advocate a referendum result applies once a referendum has been scheduled. Significantly, prohibited advocacy is not limited to direct statements, such as "Vote Yes." The Commission will look at such materials as a whole to determine whether they are neutral and factual, or whether they cross the line and constitute advocacy materials. If they do constitute advocacy, expenditure of public funds on their preparation and/or dissemination will be a violation of the law.

In this technological age, it is important to be vigilant against making such indirect expenditures. While advocacy material may generally be posted on the school district website, it must be removed once the referendum is "pending." *Avalon Bay, Communities, Inc. v. Gulbin*, File No. 2001-186 (St. Elec. Enf. Com. March 27, 2002); *In the Matter of Matthew Paulsen, Bethel*, File. No. 2003-152A (St. Elec. Enf. Com. 2003). The same analysis applies to a "link" to such material. Also, when students expressed support for a referendum on a publicly-funded cable access program, a violation of the prohibition was found. *In the Matter of Daniel Bernier, Killingly*, File No. 97-219 (St. Elec. Enf. Com. 1997). *Compare In the Matter of Paul Benyeda, Montville*, File No. 2002-149 (St. Elec. Enf. Com. 2002) (mayor did not violate prohibition by making advocacy statements on his own time on cable access program that was not publicly funded). A related question is whether a board of education can maintain its practice of broadcasting and re-broadcasting its meetings while a referendum is pending, even if advocacy statements are made. While it does not appear that the Commission has addressed this issue, the answer appears to be a qualified yes. It is important to maintain the established practice with regard to such broadcasts. Any special re-broadcast may be seen as an expenditure to advocate a referendum result.

The State Elections Enforcement Commission has provided guidance concerning these prohibitions in a short flyer. This helpful, concise summary is available at http://www.seec.state.ct.us/, and it addresses the questions most frequently raised concerning Conn. Gen. Stat. § 9-369b. For example, it specifies that "a notice limited to the time, place and question to be voted upon may be sent home to parents via children in school," but it states that "children in school may not be used as couriers of information that advocates a position on a referendum." It also defines "advocacy" broadly:

> A communication advocates a position on a referendum when in part, or taken as a whole, it urges the listener or reader to vote in a particular manner. The style, tenor and timing of a communication are factors which are considered by the Commission when reviewing alleged improprieties of Section 9-369b.

In *Sweetman v. State Elections Enforcement Commission*, 249 Conn. 296 (1999), the Connecticut Supreme Court confirmed that this statement is a proper description of the legal standard. Moreover, it applied this standard to the communication at issue in that case, and held that the communication violated the law because the content would encourage a reader to vote in favor of the referendum, even though the specific words, "Vote Yes" were not included.

The law sets forth three "safe harbors," *i.e.* situations where public funds may be expended concerning a referendum result without violating the law. First, a public official may expend public funds to prepare a written, printed or typed summary of his or her views and to distribute that summary to the news media. Significantly, the official may express support for or opposition to the referendum in such a statement. Such a summary may also be provided to members of the public upon their request, but public funds may not be expended on a general distribution of such a summary to the public. Conn. Gen. Stat. § 9-369b(a).

Second, by vote of the legislative body, a town may authorize the preparation and printing of concise explanatory texts concerning referenda proposals. If the legislative body is the town meeting, the board of selectmen may authorize such explanatory texts. The town clerk is responsible for preparing the text, and it is subject to the approval of the municipal attorney to assure that the text does not advocate either the approval or disapproval of the question. This option is also available to a regional school district. The regional board of education may vote to approve an explanatory text, and the secretary of the board is responsible for preparing the text and otherwise fulfilling the duties of the town clerk, and the text must be approved by legal counsel for the board.

The statute also empowers the legislative body of the municipality or regional board of education to authorize "the preparation and printing of materials concerning any such proposal or question in addition to the explanatory text." Conn. Gen. Stat. § 9-369b(a). Such materials are subject to the approval of the municipal attorney, and like the explanatory text must be neutral and advocate neither approval nor disapproval of the referendum question. *Id.*

Third, a municipality may provide by ordinance for the preparation and printing of "concise summaries of arguments in favor of, and arguments opposed to, local proposals or questions approved for submission to the electors of a municipality at a referendum." Any such ordinance must provide for the establishment of a committee to prepare such summaries, and the members of the committee must represent the various viewpoints concerning such referendum questions. When such summaries are prepared, they must then be approved by vote of the town's legislative body, and are to be posted and distributed in the same manner as are explanatory texts prepared by the town clerk for referendum questions. Conn. Gen. Stat. § 9-369b(d). Interestingly, however, when it extended the provisions for explanatory texts to regional school districts in 2004, the General Assembly did not take similar action with regard to this provision.

Though the law does not expressly so state, it is important to keep in mind that school board members and school officials retain their right under the First Amendment to speak out in favor of the proposed school budget or other referendum question. The prohibition applies only to the expenditure of public funds. School officials can certainly advocate for a referendum result at meetings of the board of education. In addition, since board of education members do not receive a salary, their devoting their time to such advocacy would not be considered an expenditure. Other school officials may speak out as well, as long as they do so voluntarily on their own time, so that the value of their salary will not be an imputed expenditure to advocate a referendum result.

Finally, the General Assembly has granted special status to challenges to referenda. A person claiming that (1) he or she is aggrieved by a decision of an election official, (2) votes were miscounted in certifying a referendum result, or (3) there was a violation of certain laws concerning referenda may petition a judge of the Superior Court for expedited relief, and the judge must act, before or after the referendum, on a tight timetable in hearing the matter and issuing a decision. P.A. 04-117, Section 4.

In any event, the prohibitions in the law must be taken seriously. The law provides that persons violating its provisions are subject to a fine not to exceed twice the amount of the illegal expenditure or $1,000, whichever is greater. Moreover, the law specifically prohibits a school board or other public agency from reimbursing a public employee or officer for any such fine imposed. Normally, public officials and employees are indemnified for claims made against them for their actions in fulfilling their responsibilities. For fines imposed for violations of Conn. Gen. Stat. § 9-369b, however, one is personally liable.

F. Board Responsibilities

As the agents responsible for providing education to resident children, local and regional boards of education have many and varied responsibilities. Many of those responsibilities are set forth in Conn. Gen. Stat. § 10-220, "Duties of boards of education." The statute begins with the following broad statement:

> Each local or regional board of education shall maintain good public elementary and secondary schools, implement the educational interests of the state as defined in section 10-4a and provide such other educational activities as in its judgment will best serve the interests of the school district.

This and other statutes impose various responsibilities on boards of education. The following will review the most significant responsibilities.

1. Rules, policies and procedures

Boards of education are charged with the responsibility for prescribing rules for the management, studies, classification and discipline of the public schools. Conn. Gen. Stat. § 10-221. In many cases, the determination of what policies and procedures to have in place is up to the board of education. However, in recent years the General Assembly has intervened with increasing frequency into school affairs, imposing upon boards of education the responsibility for adopting a growing list of required policies and procedures.

a. Required policies and procedures

1. Policies regarding students

The General Assembly has long required that school districts inform parents and students at least annually of policies governing student conduct and discipline. Conn. Gen. Stat. § 10-233e. Since 1984, districts have been required to adopt and implement written policies concerning homework, attendance, promotion and retention. Conn. Gen. Stat. § 10-221(b). Since 1987, districts have been responsible for adopting and implementing policies concerning the use, sale or possession of alcohol or controlled drugs, including a process for cooperation with appropriate agencies and law enforcement officials. Conn. Gen. Stat. § 10-221(d).

Since 1990, school districts have had the duty to adopt a written policy and procedures for dealing with youth suicide prevention and youth suicide attempts, Conn. Gen. Stat. § 10-221(e), as well as a written policy regarding the reporting by school employees of suspected child abuse. Conn. Gen. Stat. § 17a-101i(e). Since 1991, school districts have been obligated to adopt and implement policies and procedures concerning truants and habitual truants enrolled in the public schools. Conn. Gen. Stat. § 10-198a. *See* Chapter Four, Section B(2)(b).

Boards of education are required to have developed and to implement a three-year plan to improve reading skills of students in grades kindergarten through three. Conn. Gen. Stat. § 10-221h. The State Department of Education is required to provide technical assistance to boards of education in meeting this requirement, including advice on methods and strategies for assessing students at risk of failing to learn to read by the end of first grade, and the development of in-service training programs on the teaching of the reading and assessment of reading competency for teachers in grades kindergarten through three. Conn. Gen. Stat. § 10-221i.

These responsibilities were further specified in 1999. Under Conn. Gen. Stat. § 10-221j, the State Department of Education convened an Early

Reading Success Panel to review research on how reading is learned and the knowledge and skills necessary for teachers to deliver effective instruction in reading, and the State-Wide Early Reading Success Institute was created as a result. This Institute is to use a curriculum as specified in the statute. *Id.* There are special rules regarding plans for instruction in reading that apply to priority school districts. Conn. Gen. Stat. § 10-221m.

Since 1999, boards of education have been required to have a written policy concerning weighted grading for honors and advanced placement classes. Such policies must provide for advising parents and students whether grades in such courses are or are not given added weight for purposes of calculating grade point average and class rank. Conn. Gen. Stat. § 10-220g. Grading more generally is discussed in Chapter Four, Section B(2)(c).

Boards of education have been required since 2000 to review and revise policies for promotion from grade to grade in order to ensure that such policies foster student achievement and reduce the incidence of social promotion. Conn. Gen. Stat. § 1-223a. These requirements are reviewed in Section (4), below.

Since 2001, boards of education have been required to have policies prohibiting school personnel from recommending psychotropic medications, though school medical staff may recommend appropriate medical evaluation of students. Conn. Gen. Stat. § 10-212b. This same public act provides that the refusal of a parent to administer or to consent to the administration of a psychotropic drug is not, by itself, grounds for DCF to take the child into custody.

2002 brought new policy requirements from the General Assembly. Boards of education must have a policy in place to assure that time is available each school day for students who wish to do so to say the Pledge of Allegiance. Conn. Gen. Stat. § 10-230(c). The statute specifies, however, that it should not be construed to require anyone to say the Pledge. For those who do, it is a safe bet that the words "under God" will continue to be permissible. After the Ninth Circuit ruled that inclusion of these words violated the Establishment Clause, the United States Supreme Court vacated the ruling on the basis that the plaintiff father did not have standing to make the complaint on behalf his daughter. *Elk Grove Unified School District v. Newdow*, ___ U.S. __, 124 S. Ct. 2301 (2004).

More complicated is the requirement concerning bullying policies. Conn. Gen. Stat. § 10-222d. Boards of education must develop and implement policies to address the existence of bullying in the schools. This law defines "bullying" as "any overt act by a student or a group of students directed against another student with the intent to ridicule, humiliate or intimidate the other student while on school grounds or at a school-sponsored activity which acts are repeated against the same student over time." The law is quite prescriptive, and requires that such policies include a number of detailed provisions. While it is easy enough to write such a policy, the implementation of these requirements is a challenge. School officials must assure that such policies do not over-promise, and they must respect the confidentiality rights of all students as they investigate such matters.

We are now seeing litigation over bullying issues. In one case, the court ruled that claims of racial bullying did not raise constitutional issues because the student could not show "deliberate indifference" by school officials, the standard applicable to claims of student-student harassment per *Davis v. Monroe Country Board of Education*, 526 U.S. 629 (1999). *Crispim v. Athanson*, No. 3:01CV558 (GLG) (D. Conn. 2003). By contrast, the Third Circuit ruled in 2004 that a proposed program did not constitute an appropriate program because of continued bullying. *Shore Regional High School Board of Education v. P.S.*, No. 03-3438 (3d. Cir. 2004). Negligence claims under *Burns v. Board of Education*, 228 Conn. 640 (1994), are also likely. *See also Gasper v. Sniffen*, No. CV010343743S, 2003 Conn. Super. LEXIS 1363 (Conn. Super. Ct. 2003) (student permitted to sue another student for bullying). Given the potential for such claims, it is important that school officials carefully follow the terms of the district's bullying policy.

School districts must now also adopt policies to provide for the safe use of the Internet. As described in greater detail in Section (F)(15), below, such policies are required under the Children's Internet Protection Act, 47 U.S.C. § 254, if school districts wish to be eligible for the "e-rate" subsidy for telecommunications and/or Internet access.

Finally, there are new policy requirements concerning students and medication. Conn. Gen. Stat. § 10-212a provides that any district that permits nurses and other school personnel to administer medication must adopt a related policy. Moreover, any such policy must then be approved by the school medical adviser or other licensed physician. Previously, the state regulations simply required that school districts submit their procedures to the Department of Health.

district should be his or her responsibility. Also, volunteer board of education members would typically have neither the time nor expertise to decide operational issues. Finally, the day-to-day operation of a school district requires prompt responses to situations as they arise.

Boards of education should seek to draw the distinction between policy and administration in their actions and in their policies. One common approach is to have the board of education deal with broad issues of responsibility through policy statements, with the specific procedures that will implement the policy set out thereafter by the superintendent and his or her staff in administrative regulations. Such an approach distinguishes policy from operational issues. Also, it provides the district with needed flexibility. District procedures must be changed whenever either the law changes or a problem is discovered. It is typical that board bylaws require two readings before a policy can be adopted or amended, which can involve weeks or months of delay. By contrast, administrative regulations can typically be changed by the superintendent with notification to the board of education. By utilizing administrative regulations for operational issues, districts can avoid troublesome delays in responding to changed circumstances.

c. Recommended policies

A comprehensive set of policies is the guiding document for district operation. The circumstances of an individual school district will determine how important a particular policy will be for that district. In any event, it is important that boards of education regularly review their policies to assure that they meet current legal requirements and that they are serving the best interests of the school district. CABE has a policy service that can assist boards of education in reviewing and revising existing policies, as well as proposing other policies that are advisable. Contact information is available at http://www.cabe.org.

2. School buildings, grounds and equipment

The board of education is responsible for all property used for school purposes. Conn. Gen. Stat. § 10-220 provides that the board of education "shall have charge of the schools of its respective school district; shall make a continuing study of the need for school facilities and of a long-term school building program; . . . [and] shall have the care and maintenance and operation of buildings, lands, apparatus and other property used for school purposes . . . ." The board, therefore, has the authority over such buildings and lands. Indeed, a board of education may be aggrieved by a zoning decision made by local officials and even sue the municipality over such matters. *New Haven Board of Education v. Zoning Board of Appeals*, 26 Conn. L. Rptr. No. 16, 565 (May 15, 2000).

a. Statutory obligations

One specific duty regarding school facilities relates to fire drills. Conn. Gen. Stat. § 10-231 requires that local and regional boards of education provide for a fire drill to be held in the schools of the district at least once each month. School districts, however, may substitute a crisis response drill for one of the required monthly fire drills every three months. *See also* Conn. Gen. Stat. § 29-315(a)(2) (sprinklers required for school construction put to bid after July 1, 2004).

Another specific duty regarding school facilities relates to flags. Conn. Gen. Stat. § 10-230 requires that each classroom in Connecticut have a flag, and that each school building display a flag on the school grounds as well. Moreover, boards of education are required to develop policies to ensure that time is available each school day for students in the schools to recite the Pledge of Allegiance, provided that such policies may not require students to do so.

Another duty regarding school facilities relates to smoking. Conn. Gen. Stat. § 31-40q provides that employers must designate no-smoking areas, and further provides that employers may designate the entire facility as no-smoking. Conn. Gen. Stat. § 19a-342, however, is broader, and it prohibits smoking in school buildings as follows: "No person shall smoke . . . (5) notwithstanding the provisions of section 31-40q, within a public school building while school is in session or student activities are being conducted." Notably, the express prohibition is limited to school buildings at times when students are present. Most districts have gone beyond this statutory requirement and adopted policies that totally ban smoking on school grounds, as is their right to do. The adoption of such policies, however, can require impact negotiations with unions representing affected employees. *See* Chapter Six, Section A(4).

In regulating school property, school districts should consider adopting a policy that clearly specifies that weapons are not allowed on school property. Conn. Gen. Stat. § 53a-217b provides that a person is guilty of the crime of possession of a weapon on school grounds if s/he possesses a weapon on school grounds or at a school-sponsored activity even though s/he knows that s/he is not permitted to do so. Such a policy gives school personnel the authority to enforce the prohibition, even when the person has a permit, because Conn. Gen. Stat. § 29-28a(e) provides that a permit does not authorize a person to carry a weapon where the owner of the premises does not allow it.

Finally, since the physical plant may present health issues for students and staff, both the federal and state governments have imposed requirements on school districts. The EPA requires that boards of education create asbestos management plans and notify parent and employee organizations each year that these plans are available. 40 C.F.R. § 763.93(g)(4).

The General Assembly has addressed environmental issues as well. Under Conn. Gen. Stat. § 10-283, the maximization of natural light must be considered in any school construction project. Also, school districts must use only certified pesticide application companies in school buildings or on school grounds, except in emergencies. Conn. Gen. Stat. § 10-231a *et seq.* imposes various obligations concerning the use of pesticides in schools, including (1) notifying parents and staff of the district policy concerning pesticide applications at the beginning of each school year, and (2) permitting parents and staff who wish to do so to register to receive notification of pesticide applications. Notification to parents must be provided by mail (if the district does not have an integrated pest management plan consistent with the model plan provided by the Commissioner of Environmental Protection) or by any means practicable (if the district has such a plan). Notification to staff may be by any means practicable. Special rules apply to any pesticide application made on an emergency basis.

The General Assembly has also addressed indoor air quality. School districts are now authorized to create indoor air quality committees at their facilities to increase awareness of this issue, but there are also specific new obligations. Under Conn. Gen. Stat. § 10-220, "proper maintenance of facilities" is now a basic school board responsibility. Specifically, school boards are now obligated to "adopt and implement an indoor air quality program that provides for ongoing maintenance and facility reviews necessary for the maintenance and improvement of the indoor air quality of its facilities," and they must report annually to the Commissioner of Education on these efforts as part of the report on the district's long-term school building program. Whenever a heating, ventilation and air conditioning (HVAC) system is installed or renovated, the school district must now assure that it is maintained and operated in accordance with prevailing industry maintenance standards. HVAC systems must also be operated continuously during the hours in which students or school personnel are present except for scheduled maintenance and emergency repairs, unless the quantity of outdoor air supplied by the system meets specified requirements for air changes per hour. The retention period for such maintenance records is at least five years.

In addition, for school facilities that are constructed, extended, renovated or replaced after January 1, 2003, school districts must establish a comprehensive inspection and evaluation program of indoor air quality within the building, such as the EPA "Tools for Schools" program. Such programs must be implemented by January 1, 2008, and must be repeated every five years. Before constructing any new facilities, districts must conduct a Phase 1 environmental assessment to check for radon and other hazards. There are also new provisions for identifying a "certified air quality emergency," which will be treated as a safety code violation for purposes of expediting state school construction grants.

b. Equal educational opportunity

In addressing the issues raised in the *Sheff* case in Public Act 97-290, the General Assembly addressed the issue of school facilities as a component of an equal educational opportunity. Conn. Gen. Stat. § 10-220 now includes specific reference to the duty to provide appropriate facilities and to assure that all students in the district are treated equitably in this regard. Section 10-220 states that a board of education shall:

> provide an appropriate learning environment for its students which includes (1) adequate instructional books, supplies, materials, equipment, staffing, facilities and technology, (2) equitable allocation of resources among its schools, and (3) a safe school setting . . . .

In preparing the strategic school profiles each year, school boards are required to include a report on "school resources, including technological resources and utilization of such resources and infrastructure." Conn. Gen. Stat. § 10-220(c).

c. Ownership

Regional boards of education own property used for school purposes, holding it in trust for the participating towns. By contrast, local boards of education do not "own" such property; it is owned by the municipality and is dedicated to use for school purposes. By statute, however, the local board of education has control over such property while it is being used for school purposes. Conn. Gen. Stat. § 10-220; Conn. Gen. Stat. § 10-239; Conn. Gen. Stat. § 10-240. The term "school purposes" can be construed broadly. For example, a board of education could unilaterally decide to close an elementary school and convert it to administrative offices. However, the board could not close a school and convert it to a senior center. If property is no longer used for school purposes, the board of education no longer controls it, and such property reverts (or is "rededicated") to the control of the town. The board of education may not "sell" a building and/or land to the town. Rather, in such a circumstance it would formally vote to relinquish control of such property, causing control to pass back to the town.

d. School building projects

A board of education may not unilaterally apply for a school construction grant. In order to qualify for state reimbursement for a school building project, the town must authorize the board of education to submit the proposed project to the State Department of Education. Conn. Gen. Stat. § 10-283. Applications for such projects under this statute must now show how maximization of natural light and wireless connectivity technology were considered, and for school facilities put to bid after July 1, 2004 sprinklers are required. Conn. Gen. Stat. § 29-315(a)(2). Also, prior to any construction on a school building project, the plans must be approved by the State Department of Education, the board of education, and the building committee. Conn. Gen. Stat. § 10-291. Any related contracts must be awarded to the lowest responsible bidder. Conn. Gen. Stat. § 10-287(b).

The responsibility for overseeing a school construction project is typically delegated to a school building committee appointed by the municipality. Such committees act as the agent for the municipality and do not have separate standing to assert legal claims. *Elementary School Building Committee of the Town of Fairfield v. Placko*, No. CV020398162S, 2003 Conn. Super. LEXIS 474 (Conn. Super. Ct. 2003). Information on the school construction grant process is posted on the Internet at http://www.state.ct.us/sde/dgm/sfu/index.htm.

e. Use of school facilities

The jurisdiction of the board of education over property used for school purposes extends beyond the regular school day. The local or regional board of education may permit the use of any room, building or school facility for "nonprofit educational or community purposes whether or not school is in session." In addition, when school is not in session, the authority of the board of education is even greater. It may grant the temporary use of "rooms, halls, school buildings or grounds or any other school facilities" under its control for "public, educational or other purposes or for the purpose of holding political discussions . . . ." Conn. Gen. Stat. § 10-239.

This broad grant of authority is not unlimited, and decisions concerning the use school facilities can give rise to constitutional claims involving equal protection and free speech. There have been a number of federal court decisions holding that school districts may not pick and choose from among groups seeking to use school facilities on the basis of their political or religious affiliation or viewpoint. Just as the Nazis may march in Skokie, so too may they use a school auditorium, if such use is permitted to the public generally. The district may certainly insist on insurance and require all groups to go through an approval procedure. But school districts may not generally discriminate among applicants based on whether the members of the board support or do not support the activities of the organization. Fortunately it is not Nazis who generally request use of school facilities. The three most common legal issues that come up involve community groups, commercial enterprises, and church groups.

The No Child Left Behind Act imposes new obligations on school districts as regards school facilities. Any district that permits use of school facilities by community groups (thereby creating an open forum or a "limited public forum") must permit the Boy Scouts or any other group designated in the Act as a "patriotic organization" (set out in a list that includes Big Brothers/ Big Sisters; Boys' and Girls' Clubs of America; Future Farmers of America; Girl Scouts; and Little League Baseball) the same access to use the facilities irrespective of any membership or leadership criteria or oath of allegiance to God or country. No Child Left Behind Act, Section 9525. This requirement is consistent with recent case law affirming the First Amendment rights of the Boy Scouts. *See, e.g., Boy Scouts of America, South Florida Council v. Till*, 136 F. Supp.2d 1295 (S.D. Fla. 2001).

There is not much legal guidance with regard to commercial enterprises. However, the statute does draw a distinction between non-profit and for-profit organizations. Since commercial speech is often subject to greater regulation, a school district could decide that it will not permit commercial enterprises to use school facilities, or to decide that the charges to such enterprises will differ from those for non-profit groups. However, if the district decides to let some commercial enterprises use school facilities, other commercial enterprises must be given the same opportunity.

Finally, church groups have the right to use school facilities on the same basis as other groups. School officials have been concerned about appearing to support religion by permitting such use. However, absent special circumstances (*e.g.*, a request to conduct services when students are in school), permitting such use is not a violation of the Establishment Clause. Reversing the Second Circuit, the United States Supreme Court ruled in 2001 that a school district violated the rights of a religious organization when it denied use of school facilities to that group, even though it permitted non-sectarian groups to use school facilities. *Good News Club v. Milford Central School*, 533 U.S. 98 (2001). *See also* Chapter Two, Section A(4). Moreover, given the broad language of this decision, the Second Circuit has ruled that the right to use school facilities equally even extends to religious worship, at least during non-school hours. *Bronx Household of Faith v. Board of Education*, 331 F.3d 342 (2d Cir. 2003).

3. <u>School year and school day</u>

Schools must be maintained in each town for at least 180 days of "actual school sessions." Conn. Gen. Stat. § 10-15. These days must be scheduled before June 30 each year because the statutes define the school year as running from July 1 through June 30. Conn. Gen. Stat. § 10-259. In 1996, the General Assembly eliminated the concept of a minimum school day of four hours, given concerns that students could be held in school unnecessarily during inclement weather in order to have the day count toward the required 180 days of instruction. Now, districts are required to hold 180 school day sessions, but they may now count a shortened day, even if it is less than four hours of actual school work. Conn. Gen. Stat. § 10-16. Also, a day may still count as one of the 180 days of required instruction for kindergarten students even if a morning or afternoon kindergarten session is canceled due to weather conditions. *Id.*

Rather than specifying the number of hours required for a school day to count, the statutes now impose an overall time requirement to assure that students receive no less than a stated amount of education each year. There are, however, a few specific requirements for the school day. All students must be offered a lunch period of at least twenty minutes, and the regular school day for students in grades kindergarten through five must include "a period of physical exercise" (without further specification). P.A. 04-224. Students in full-day kindergarten and in grades one through twelve must receive at least 900 hours of "actual school work" each year. Students in half-day kindergarten must receive at least 450 hours of actual instruction. Conn. Gen. Stat. § 10-16. In monitoring compliance with the 900 or 450 hour requirement respectively, the State Department of Education will not count passing time, lunch time, recess and other non-instructional time.

Students may be permitted to graduate with fewer than 180 school sessions in their last year under certain circumstances due to school cancellations. Specifically, Conn. Gen. Stat. § 10-16l provides that a board of education may establish a firm graduation date at the beginning of the school year, as long as it is no earlier than the one hundred eighty-fifth day noted in the school calendar as originally adopted by the board of education. Moreover, after April 1, boards of education can establish a firm graduation date and stick to it, even if school days are canceled later. *Id.* As long as the school calendar provides for at least 180 days of school at the time the firm date is set, districts may hold to the graduation date, even if school is canceled due to weather or other emergencies thereafter. Notwithstanding these statutory provisions, however, the Commissioner's position is that graduated seniors should not be short-changed and thus must be invited back to make up the missed school sessions to complete 180 days of school. Series 2000-2001, Circular Letter C-21 (March 21, 2001).

School days may not be scheduled on any of the specified state holidays, except under limited circumstances. School may be held on a holiday provided that the schools hold "a suitable nonsectarian educational program in observance of such holiday." Conn. Gen. Stat. § 1-4. This provision does not apply to holidays that fall in December and January, and thus school may not be held on Christmas Day, New Year's Day or Martin Luther King Day. *Id.* In addition, when inclement weather causes schools to be canceled, the rescheduled sessions may not be held on Saturday or Sunday. Finally, the statute authorizes the Commissioner of Education to approve special school schedules to permit year-round use of school facilities, even though a student may not receive 180 days of instruction in a particular year, as long as the student will receive an average of 180 days over thirteen years of schooling. Conn. Gen. Stat. § 10-15.

4. <u>Enumeration and assignment of students</u>

School districts are obligated to provide educational services to children from age five to twenty-one or high school graduation, whichever comes first. Conn. Gen. Stat. § 10-186. In addition, Conn. Gen. Stat. § 10-220 provides that boards of education "shall cause each child five years of age and over and under eighteen years of age living in the school district to attend school in accordance with the provisions of section 10-184. . . ." As discussed in Chapter Four, Section A(2), Conn. Gen. Stat. § 10-184 permits parents to show that their children are elsewhere receiving instruction, and resident children of school age may attend school elsewhere. It is important for school districts, therefore, to establish policies or procedures for the enrollment and disenrollment of students. If a student is not attending school, that circumstance should be identified so that appropriate action may be taken. Moreover, enrollment data should be accurate, because some state funding depends on the number of enrolled students.

In order to meet this responsibility, school districts must first identify the resident school-age children. The statutes require that the board of education identify children of compulsory education age on an annual basis, either by enumerating each child individually or by any other reasonable means approved by the Commissioner of Education. Conn. Gen. Stat. § 10-249. This statute, which has been essentially unchanged for over fifty years, provides that, if a child of school age is not attending school, the superintendent must make a reasonable effort to ascertain the reason for nonattendance. Of course, issues of nonattendance now raise issues of potential neglect, discussed in Chapter Four, Section F.

Conn. Gen. Stat. § 10-220 also provides that boards of education "shall determine the number, age and qualifications of the pupils to be admitted into each school; [and] shall designate the school which shall be attended by the various children with the school district . . . ." School officials thus have the right to determine hours of operation, school assignments for students, grade placement decisions, and other operational issues. Where residence for school purposes is disputed, or there is a dispute over transportation, students and families can seek review under Conn. Gen. Stat. § 10-186, as described in Chapter Four, Section A. Any child who receives special education services has extensive rights to challenge district decisions through the special education review process, as described in Chapter Five. However, aside from these special situations, school officials retain the right to make these decisions, which are not generally subject to review by another agency or appeal to the courts.

This broad discretion is apparent in a case involving the Hamden Board of Education. In 1999, parents challenged its decision to eliminate sibling preference in admissions to an interdistrict magnet school. Parents of children already enrolled in the school challenged this action on the basis of promissory estoppel (*i.e.* a promise relied upon can be enforced). The

Superior Court rejected their argument, holding that the sibling preference was a policy that the school board had the right to change. *Whiting v. Hamden Board of Education*, 5 Conn. Ops. 493 (May 3, 1999).

5. Testing, promotion and retention of students

Connecticut law imposes upon boards of education the duty to test students in various ways. In 2003, however, the General Assembly imposed a troublesome restriction – now no test required under Chapter 163c (state mastery testing) or under the No Child Left Behind Act may begin before 9 a.m. P.A. 03-174, § 5.

The "mastery test" is required when students are in the fourth grade to measure whether a student has mastered essential grade level skills in reading, language arts and mathematics. Conn. Gen. Stat. § 10-14n. Mastery tests are also required of students in the sixth grade, the eighth grade, and the tenth grade. School districts may include tenth grade mastery test scores on the transcript of any student who takes the test. When students meet or exceed the mastery level on any component of the test, notation of that fact must be included in the permanent record and the transcript of the student, and a certificate of mastery of such component(s) must be issued to the student. If a student does not meet the standards on any component of the tenth grade mastery test, s/he may retake the examination until s/he reaches mastery, graduates or reaches age 21.

Effective with the 2005-2006 school year, additional testing will be required consistent with the provisions of the No Child Left Behind Act. Specifically, mastery testing will occur in April. In addition, there will be annual mastery testing in reading, writing and mathematics of all students in grades three through eight and grade ten, and beginning in the 2007-2008 school year, there will be annual mastery testing in science of students enrolled in grades five, eight and ten. Conn. Gen. Stat. § 10-14n.

Historically, the statute has provided for exceptions to mastery testing. Special education students were exempt whenever the planning and placement team found it appropriate, and students enrolled in a bilingual program or an English-as-a-second-language program for three years or less were automatically exempt. In 2001, however, the General Assembly tightened up the rules. Exemption of a special education student is considered the exception, not the rule, and is permitted only in "the rare case" that the planning and placement team determines that an alternative assessment would be appropriate. Similarly, the automatic exemption for students whose first language is not English was reduced to those enrolled for ten months or less. Effective July 1, 2003, limited English proficient students who have been enrolled from ten to twenty months and who score below standard on the English mastery test in the previous month will also be exempt. Conn. Gen. Stat. § 10-14q.

The No Child Left Behind Act has significantly affected both the scope of mastery testing and the stakes. In 2004, for example, some forty-two high schools in Connecticut were identified as having failed to demonstrate "adequate yearly progress" (AYP) under NCLB. State Department of Education News Release, September 8, 2004. Under NCLB, ninety-five percent of the students in a school (and in each subgroup) are expected to participate, and many schools did not show AYP because of insufficient participation rates. There is therefore significant (bordering on irrational) emphasis on student participation levels. *See, e.g.*, Letter from Sternberg dated January 20, 2004, "Elimination of Out-of-Level Testing."

School officials have the right and responsibility to determine grade placement for students, and to determine whether and when such students will be promoted. With the exception of special education students (who may seek due process hearing review of virtually anything), there is no statutory right for parents to challenge promotion/retention decisions. Clearly, parent input is important, and some districts have adopted policies providing that such decisions will be made only with parental concurrence. Legally, however, the final decision rests with school personnel.

The General Assembly has required that school districts establish policies concerning promotion from grade to grade (or retention). The stated purpose for requiring such policies is to ensure that such policies foster student achievement and reduce the incidence of social promotion. Such policies must (1) include objective criteria for the promotion and graduation of students, (2) provide for the measuring of the progress of students against such criteria and the reporting of such information to parents and students, (3) include alternatives to promotion, such as transition programs, and (4) provide for supplemental services. The law specifies that school districts may require students who have substantial academic deficiencies that jeopardize their eligibility for promotion or graduation to attend after-school programs, summer school programs or other similar programs. Conn. Gen. Stat. § 10-223a(a).

The General Assembly has imposed new obligations on boards of education related to standards for academic progress. By September 1, 2002, boards of education were required to specify the basic skills necessary to graduate, with such requirements applying first to the class of 2006. Conn. Gen. Stat. § 10-223a(b). There is no specific provision in the statute exempting, for example, bilingual students or special education students, but the statute appears to provide discretion in this regard. After all, the graduation credit requirements set out in Section 10-221a may be waived by the planning and placement team, as discussed in Section F(6)(c), below.

If a student in a priority school district fails to reach the state-wide standards for remedial assistance on the reading component of the fourth grade mastery examination or on such sixth grade mastery examination, s/he must attend summer school, and if summer school is offered but s/he did not attend, s/he may not be promoted. The superintendent may exempt a student from this requirement upon the recommendation of the principal. Conn. Gen. Stat. § 10-265l.

6. Library books, textbooks, and curriculum

Boards of education also have responsibilities concerning library books, textbooks and curriculum. Here, student rights under the First Amendment must be balanced with the need for school officials to be able to make appropriate decisions. Each responsibility warrants separate review.

a. Library books

Boards of education must "make rules for the control, within their respective jurisdictions, of school library media centers and approve the selection of books and other educational media therefor." Conn. Gen. Stat. § 10-221(a). This provision has long been in the education statutes, and it has simply been updated to include references to "media center" and "other educational media." School boards do not generally approve all books and other material purchased for the school library media centers in the schools. Rather, they generally delegate this responsibility to the administration and teachers. Such delegation has not been challenged legally.

Removing books once they have been placed in the library raises different issues. On occasion, school districts have taken such action in response to complaints from parents, and thereafter others have challenged such action as a violation of the constitutional right of free speech. The United States Supreme Court has reviewed this question of whether school library books achieve "tenure" on the shelf. *Board of Education, Island Trees Union Free School District No 26 v. Pico*, 457 U.S. 853 (1982). A plurality of the Court found that removal of certain books (including The Naked Ape and Soul on Ice) from the shelves of the school library violated the First Amendment: "local school boards may not remove books from school library shelves simply because they dislike the ideas contained in those books and seek by their removal to 'prescribe what shall be orthodox in politics, nationalism, religion, or other matters of opinion.'" Since there was no majority opinion, this case does not provide definitive guidance for school districts, but it illustrates the First Amendment issues that can arise regarding library books.

A more recent decision of the Court suggests a new test for determining whether books may be removed from the school library. In *Hazelwood School District v. Kuhlmeier*, 484 U.S. 260 (1988), the United States Supreme Court held that school officials may censor the content of a school newspaper "so long as their actions are reasonably related to legitimate pedagogical concerns." Central to the Court's analysis is the idea that the district can decide for itself what will carry the "imprimatur" of the district as the official school newspaper. Subsequently, the Eleventh Circuit Court of Appeals applied this reasoning in reviewing a challenge to a school district decision to remove "The Miller's Tale" and "Lysistrata" from a reading list for a high school humanities course. *Virgil v. School Board of Columbia County, Florida*, 862 F.2d 1517 (11th Cir. 1989). The court held that the district was within its rights to remove the books, given that it could reasonably have concerns over vulgarity contained in these works. It is reasonable to anticipate that the result would be the same with regard to books in a school library. *But see Counts v. Cedarville School District*, 295 F. Supp. 3d 996 (W.D. Ark. 2003) (citing *Pico*, court holds that requirement for parent consent to read "Harry Potter" books violates First Amendment).

A more recent challenge against required reading brought by a parent illustrates the balance that school districts must strike in presenting a curriculum and assuring that the school environment is free of discrimination or harassment. In *Monteiro v. Tempe Union High School District*, 158 F.3d 1022 (9th Cir. 1998), the parent sought to enjoin the school district from assigning The Adventures of Huckleberry Finn by Mark Twain and a short story by William Faulkner, because both works of literature included a racial epithet. Moreover, the parent sought to enjoin alleged harassment of her children and other children, which she alleged increased following the assignment of the works in question. The *Hazelwood* rule did not apply, because it was a parent, not the school district, seeking removal of the books. The Ninth Circuit relied on *Pico* (discussed above) and dismissed the claim that these works should not be in the curriculum, because such action would deny students the ability to receive material that school officials appropriately found to have literary value. As to the claim of racial harassment, however, the court permitted further evidentiary proceedings since a school district has an obligation to maintain a school environment free of racial harassment.

b. Textbooks

The education laws impose upon boards of education the duty to provide textbooks for the use of students in the schools. Conn. Gen. Stat. § 10-228 provides that school districts will purchase

> such books, either as regular texts, as supplementary books or as library books, and such supplies, material and equipment, as it deems necessary to meet the needs of instruction in its schools. In day and evening schools of elementary and secondary grades, all books and equipment shall be loaned and materials and supplies furnished to all pupils free of charge, subject to such rules and regulations as to their care and use as the board of education prescribes.

Occasionally, a parent will question whether school districts are obligated to provide *all* supplies necessary for instruction, ranging from pencils and paper to gym shoes for physical education. There are no cases interpreting Section 10-228 on this point. School districts typically (and appropriately) take the position that basic parent responsibilities include providing equipment (pencils, pens, calculator) and supplies (paper, notebooks) so that students may attend school and do their homework. It is also appropriate, however, to make arrangements to provide for scholarship assistance to students whose parents cannot afford to provide them with these basic supplies. This statute may be among those that have not caught up with the realities of the modern school. *See also* Conn. Gen. Stat. § 10-185 (daily fine on parents for not sending their children to school "shall not be incurred when it appears that the child is destitute of clothing suitable for attending school and the parent or person having control of such child is unable to provide such clothing").

Some districts offer supplementary activities on the condition that students pay the cost of additional materials, and similarly there are no court cases in Connecticut prohibiting such arrangements. However, for basic instructional activities, this statute makes clear that such textbooks and other necessary equipment must be provided at no cost to the students.

Another statute authorizes local and regional boards of education to loan textbooks which are currently in use in the public schools to students enrolled in the private schools located in the district. Such requests may be made either by the student or the parent or guardian. These loans are not required, but rather the decision is left to the individual board of education. Conn. Gen. Stat. § 10-228a. Such textbook loan programs have long been allowed even for students in religious schools. *Board of Education of Central School District No. 1 v. Allen*, 392 U.S. 236 (1968).

Boards of education have substantial discretion in deciding which textbooks are to be used in district schools. The statutes direct that boards of education select textbooks that "accurately present the achievements and accomplishments of individuals and groups from all ethnic and racial backgrounds and of both sexes," unless a legitimate educational purpose will otherwise be served. Conn. Gen. Stat. § 10-18a. There is, however, no express requirement that the board of education itself approve textbooks to be used in the schools, and it appears possible that a board of education could delegate such decisions to the superintendent and/or to a committee that it or the superintendent may create.

By contrast, the statutes specifically set out the requirements for board of education action to change textbooks. Conn. Gen. Stat. § 10-229 provides that boards of education may not change textbooks except by a two-thirds vote of all the members of the board after given at least one week's written notice. It also provides that the board may loan such unused textbooks to another school district. While the need for this provision is not clear on its face (particularly the part about loaning out the old book that was just added in 1995), the statute safeguards against a minority of the board of education taking action with regard to textbooks. The requirement that the change be made only if supported by a two-thirds vote of all the members of the board, however, is extreme, and this requirement could permit a minority on the board to prevent a change in textbooks. The Connecticut courts, however, have never interpreted Section 10-229, quoted above. In light of the *Hazelwood* case, we expect that the courts will defer to the reasonable judgments of school administrators and school board members.

In recent years, religious conservatives have challenged textbook selection in some cases. The prevailing view, however, is that religious objections to specified textbooks by certain parents cannot force the school district as a whole to change textbooks. In *Mozert v. Hawkins County Board of Education*, 827 F.2d 1058 (6th Cir. 1987), parents challenged the use of a particular reading series at the elementary level. They claimed that use of the series forced their children to read books that teach values contrary to their religious beliefs, in violation of their right of free exercise of religion. The parents' concerns about the textbooks ranged from evolution and secular humanism to "futuristic supernaturalism" and magic. The parents were actually successful in district court, but the Sixth Circuit rejected their claims. It held that the use of these books did not compel the students to act contrary to their religion, and it vacated the injunction against their use.

The Eleventh Circuit also considered a challenge against the use of textbooks. There, the parents claimed that the books were improper because they promoted a new religion, "secular humanism," in violation of the constitutional separation of church and state. The federal trial court agreed with the parents, but again the appellate court reversed and upheld the right of the school board to use the books. *Smith v. Board of School Commissioners of Mobile County*, 827 F.2d 684 (11th Cir. 1987).

c. Curriculum

The statutes provide that boards of education are to establish the program of studies for the public schools, and several statutes impose specific requirements. At the outset, however, it should be noted that this responsibility should be interpreted as the broad duty to create teaching positions and to establish courses. The development of the specific curriculum may be delegated to the superintendent, administrators and the teaching staff. Such delegation is, of course, reasonable because the professional educators employed by the district are best able to develop the specific curriculum.

The major statutory provision dealing with curriculum is set out in Conn. Gen. Stat. § 10-16b. This statute specifies the various subjects in which instruction must be provided by "legally qualified instructors." In *Nonnewaug Teachers' Association Petition for Declaratory Ruling*, (St. Bd. Ed. May 7, 2003), the State Board of Education considered the claim of the Nonnewaug Education Association that the assignment of teachers to grade student work done primarily through a program of computer-assisted instruction was a violation of the certification requirements. On its own, the State Board redefined the issue as one of whether the school district was complying with the requirements of Section 10-16b. While it found reason to be critical of the original implementation of the program, the State Board noted that the program had evolved so that there was greater direct teacher-student contact. The State Board held that the program was not a violation of the certification regulations and, as implemented, complied with Section 10-16b.

Boards of education are required to provide instruction in other areas as well. Districts must provide instruction regarding the "knowledge, skills and attitudes required to understand and avoid the effects of alcohol, of nicotine or tobacco and of drugs . . . on health, character, citizenship and personality development . . . in accordance with a planned, ongoing and systematic program of instruction." Conn. Gen. Stat. § 10-19. A similar requirement applies with regard to instruction on acquired immunity deficiency syndrome, except that the board of education is further required to adopt a policy concerning the exemption of pupils from such instruction upon the written request of the parent or guardian. *Id.* Finally, all public or private elementary or secondary schools must provide a program of instruction concerning United States history, including instruction on government at the national, state and local levels, and on the duties, responsibilities, and rights of United States citizenship. Conn. Gen. Stat. § 10-18. The statute provides that no student is to be graduated from any such school "who has not been found to be familiar with said subjects." There is no evidence that this provision has been applied in the memory of man to deny a student a diploma.

In addition to these required courses, the statute provides that school districts may, but are not required to, provide instruction on family life education (including but not limited to family planning, human sexuality, parenting, nutrition and the emotional, physical, psychological, hygienic, economic and social aspects of family life). Conn. Gen. Stat. § 10-16c. The State Department of Education is to provide curriculum guides on family life education, with the proviso that these curriculum guides may not include information pertaining to abortion as an alternative to family planning. The statutes also provide that a local or regional board of education may not require participation in such a course, and parents may simply provide written notification to the board to exempt their children from such courses. Conn. Gen. Stat. § 10-16c through Conn. Gen. Stat. § 10-16f.

The State Board of Education is also required to encourage and assist local boards of education to include in the program of instruction and in teacher in-service training the following subjects: Holocaust education and awareness, the historical events surrounding the Great Famine in Ireland, African-American History, Puerto Rican History, Native American History, and personal financial management. The State Board of Education is required to make curriculum materials available for these subjects. Conn.

Gen. Stat. § 10-16b(d). Districts may also offer instruction in firearm safety for students in grades kindergarten through eight. Conn. Gen. Stat. § 10-18c. As with family life education, parents can have their children excused from such instruction by written request.

The statutes also set forth the credits necessary for graduation. Interestingly, this requirement first arose in the context of the *Horton v. Meskill* case. Adoption of uniform graduation requirements was a way to help assure that all students in Connecticut receive a substantially equal educational opportunity. *See Horton v. Meskill (II)*, 195 Conn. 24 (1985). Students in Connecticut high schools must earn minimum credits in various subjects as specified in Conn. Gen. Stat. § 10-221a. Students graduating in 2004 and thereafter must have at least one-half credit course on civics and American government as part of the three social studies credits. Each of these credits is defined as the equivalent of one forty-minute class period for each day of a school year. Some of these credits may be earned at other institutions, and for special education students, the PPT can waive these requirements. *Id.* In addition, boards of education are now authorized to confer a diploma on a veteran of World War II who left high school prior to graduation in order to serve in the armed forces and did not receive a diploma as a consequence of such service. Conn. Gen. Stat. § 10-221a.

School districts have broad discretion in establishing courses to address these curriculum requirements, an authority that the courts have affirmed on the rare occasions that parents have challenged curriculum decisions in court. Years ago, for example, parents challenged the required health education courses provided by the Hamden Board of Education. However, since the requirements were applied equally and parents had other options available such as private or home instruction, their challenge was dismissed. *Hopkins v. Hamden Board of Education*, 29 Conn. Supp. 397 (1971). More recently, a parent in Fairfield asked that his son be excused from health education. The district responded by granting the requested excusal as provided by law, *i.e.* from the course segments on family life education and AIDS, but otherwise denied the broader request for excusal from the health curriculum as a whole. When the student then received a failing grade for not attending, his father sued in federal court, claiming a violation of his First Amendment right of free exercise and of his Fourteenth Amendment right to due process. The Second Circuit, however, rejected these claims, affirming a ruling that the board's mandatory health curriculum was reasonably related to legitimate educational objectives. *Leebaert v. Harrington*, 332 F.3d 134 (2d Cir. 2003).

Similarly, parents in West Haven were unsuccessful in an attempt to force a change in the curriculum through legal action. *Bell v. West Haven Board of Education*, 55 Conn. App. 400 (1999). There, parents alleged that the school district employed a teaching program called "Responsive Classroom" that emphasized social skills at the expense of discipline and academics. The plaintiffs further claimed that, as a result of this teaching program, their children were deprived of an education comparable to that received by children of other Connecticut elementary schools and that their children suffered extreme emotional distress. The appellate court followed the precedents in Connecticut and elsewhere that courts will not consider claims of educational malpractice. *See, e.g., Gupta v. New Britain General Hospital*, 239 Conn. 574 (1996). It also held, however, that the facts as alleged could support the plaintiff's claim that the district had intentionally inflicted emotional harm by adopting the program in question (notwithstanding the very high standard for misconduct required to establish this tort). Upon remand, the trial court held that factual issues precluded summary judgment, which permitted the parents to have a trial on the case. *Bell v. West Haven Board of Education*, 2001 Conn. Super. LEXIS 286 (January 31, 2001).

7. Student health issues

Connecticut law imposes a number of responsibilities upon local and regional boards of education regarding student health issues. Each local or regional board of education in a town that has a population of ten thousand or more is required to appoint a school medical advisor. In some towns where the department of health exercises these responsibilities, the board of health may appoint the school medical advisor, subject to the approval of the board of education. Towns can join together in the hiring of the school medical advisor. Conn. Gen. Stat. § 10-205. The duties of school medical advisors are set out in the statutes, and these duties include health inspections of the schools, medical examinations of employees and excluding or readmitting students with communicable diseases. Conn. Gen. Stat. § 10-207.

School districts are also required to appoint one or more school nurses or nurse practitioners. Conn. Gen. Stat. § 10-212. However, there is no requirement that the board of education appoint a nurse for each school. Such judgments are left to the determination of the board of education. Effective in 2004, however, any school nurse or nurse practitioner appointed by or under contract with a board of education (including nurses who provide services to private schools under Conn. Gen. Stat. § 10-217a) is subject to a criminal records check in accordance with Conn. Gen. Stat. § 29-17a.

School districts must require proof of immunization against specified diseases, including diphtheria, pertussis, tetanus, measles, mumps, rubella and other diseases. Conn. Gen. Stat. § 10-204a. Health care providers conducting such immunizations must provide reports to designated school personnel. Conn. Gen. Stat. § 10-209. However, parents may be excused from assuring that their children have such immunizations in certain circumstances, such as when a physician provides a certificate stating that such immunization is contraindicated because of the physical condition of the child, or, in the case of measles, mumps or rubella, a certificate that the child already had a confirmed case of the disease. In addition, such immunizations may not be required if the parents provide a statement that such immunization would be contrary to the religious beliefs of the child. Conn. Gen. Stat. § 10-204a. Finally, under the Title X, Section 1032 of the No Child Left Behind Act (the "McKinney-Vento Homeless Assistance Act"), lack of immunization records may not prevent a student from being enrolled in school.

Students are required to have health assessments prior to enrolling in school, prior to either grade six or grade seven, and prior to either grade ten or grade eleven. Conn. Gen. Stat. § 10-206. These assessments must include a "chronic disease assessment which may include but not be limited to, asthma." *Id.* When the parents or guardians of such students meet the eligibility requirements for free or reduced meals under the National School Lunch Program, the district is to provide these assessments at no cost to the parents. Conn. Gen. Stat. § 10-206a. Similarly, school districts are to provide vision screenings and hearing screenings to students in specified grades. Conn. Gen. Stat. § 10-214. Health care providers conducting such assessments are required to provide reports of such assessments to designated school personnel. Conn. Gen. Stat. § 10-209.

There are special rules concerning the administration of medication. Conn. Gen. Stat. § 10-212a now requires that each board of education that permits the school nurse or other personnel to administer medication in school or that permits students to self-administer medication (*i.e.*, all school districts) to adopt related policies and procedures. This requirement had previously be in the regulations implementing Section 10-212a, Conn. St. Reg. §§ 10-212a-1 through 10-212a-7, which were adopted by the Department of Public Health. Now, the authority to adopt such regulations is vested in the State Board of Education in consultation with the Department of Public Health, and the statute requires that such board policies and procedures (1) must conform to those regulations, and (2) must be approved by the school medical advisor or other licensed physician. Also, in February 2004, the State Board of Education promulgated Guidelines for Glucose Self-Monitoring in School, a new right described below.

Conn. Gen. Stat. § 10-212a permits the school nurse, or in the absence of the school nurse, the principal, any teacher, any coach of intramural or interscholastic athletics, or any licensed occupational or physical therapist to administer medication if authorized in writing by the parents and the student's physician, dentist, licensed advance practice registered nurse or licensed physician's assistant. In addition, a paraprofessional may be identified and trained to administer medication to a student. Any administration of medication in school, however, remains under the general supervision of the school nurse. School personnel administering medication in accordance with the statute are immune from liability for negligence in so doing unless such it is gross, wanton or willful. *Id.*

Administration of medication by injection is subject to additional rules. Paraprofessionals identified and trained as set forth above may administer medication by cartridge injector to students having a dangerous allergic reaction. Conn. Gen. Stat. § 10-212a(d). More generally, Conn. Gen. Stat. § 52-557b protects a teacher or other school employee from liability for any injury caused by administration of medication by injection in emergency circumstances on school property or at a school-sponsored function. To qualify for this protection, the school official must have completed a first aid course and training by the school medical advisor or licensed physician, and their actions must not have been "gross, willful or wanton negligence." *See* Section G(1)(d), below.

Boards of education are also required to adopt policies prohibiting board personnel from recommending that a student be administered psychotropic medication. Conn. Gen. Stat. § 10-212b. Medical evaluation, however, is a different story. As clarified in 2003, this statute provides that school health or mental health professionals (*e.g.*, school medical advisers, nurses, psychologists, social workers, counselors or other personnel designated to communicate with a parent about a need for medical evaluation) may communicate with other school personnel about a child who may require a medical evaluation and may recommend medical evaluation. Such policies are also required to set forth how school health or mental health personnel should communicate a recommendation for medical evaluation to a parent or guardian, as well as the process for obtaining proper parental consent for such personnel to communicate about such child with an outside medical practitioner. Finally, the statute specifies that the planning and placement team may recommend medical evaluation to determine eligibility for special education services or to determine the services a child needs.

Parents and students themselves have rights concerning student health needs in the school setting. Parents may administer medication to their own children on school grounds. Conn. Gen. Stat. § 10-212(b). Also, students must be permitted to self-test blood glucose when their physician or advanced practice registered nurse provides a written order specifying the need and the capability of the child to conduct such testing. P.A. 03-211. *See* Series 2003-2004, Circular Letter C-19 (February 6, 2004), "Guidelines for Blood Glucose Monitoring in School." School districts may not deny a student access to school transportation because of his/her need to carry a cartridge injector while traveling on a school vehicle used for student transportation. *Id.* Finally, school personnel must honor any written notice of limitations on student physical activity provided by a physician or advanced practice registered nurse. Conn. Gen. Stat. § 10-208a.

Connecticut law also requires that children in non-public schools receive health services. Each town or regional school district that provides health services to children enrolled in the public schools must provide the same health services to children enrolled in non-public schools in the town, as long as a majority of the children attending the non-public school reside in Connecticut. Conn. Gen. Stat. § 10-217a. Such services need not be provided to children who are not residents of Connecticut. A non-public school can enforce this requirement directly. *Bennett v. Town of Sprague*, 7 Conn. Ops. 275 (March 12, 2001).

The statute describes such services as "the services of a school physician, school nurse and dental hygienist." The statute excludes any services that would be special education services. That exclusion was more important before 1991, when the listed services under this statute included "school psychologist, speech remedial services, school social worker's services, special language teachers for non-English speaking students and such clerical, supervisory and administrative services necessary to the provision of the [listed] services . . . ." The General Assembly deleted these services in 1991, relieving towns and regional school districts from the duty to provide such services to children in non-public schools. The statute provides for some reimbursement of these expenses.

Finally, in recent years the General Assembly has enacted a number of new laws addressing student health more broadly, ranging from environmental concerns to requirements for recess and food served in the school cafeteria. Statutes addressing environmental concerns include the following. Any art and craft material used for instruction in the elementary or secondary schools must contain a warning label if that material contains a carcinogenic substance or a potential human carcinogen. Conn. Gen. Stat. § 10-217c *et seq*. School districts are also obligated under Conn. Gen. Stat. § 10-231a *et seq*. to take special measures with regard to pesticide applications, including notification of parents, as described in greater detail in Section F(2)(a) above. In addition, boards of education are required to file with the Department of Public Health and the local health department certain information concerning students diagnosed with asthma as recorded on school health assessment forms, and the Department of Public Health must review the asthma screening information and report back to the General Assembly on "asthma trends and distributions among pupils enrolled in the public schools." Conn. Gen. Stat. § 10-206(f).

In 2004, new obligations were imposed on school districts out of concern for student health and well-being. Now, school districts must assure that students are offered a daily lunch period of not less than twenty minutes. Also, the school day must include "a period of physical exercise" (without further specification) for grades kindergarten through five (subject to modification for special education students through the PPT process). In addition, school districts must now make "nutritious, low-fat foods and drinks" available to students as specified in Public Act 04-224. This is "feel-good" legislation on two levels.

8. Vocational education

In addition to the responsibilities of boards of education regarding students who are regularly enrolled, school districts must provide opportunities for vocational education. As authorized by the statutes, the state board of education has established vocational-technical schools (now the "Connecticut Technical High School System") that are operated separately from local and regional school districts. Conn. Gen. Stat. § 10-95. Students apply to and enroll in these schools separately from their local or regional school district. Conn. Gen. Stat. § 10-95j.

Local and regional boards of education remain responsible for providing such students transportation as is reasonable and necessary. In 1996, however, the General Assembly capped the responsibility of the local or regional board of education for providing such transportation at the "foundation" amount under Conn. Gen. Stat. § 10-262j. Where students attend vocational-technical schools outside their town of residence, the sending school district is entitled to reimbursement from the state at a special rate twenty percentage points higher than regular reimbursement for costs in excess of $800. Conn. Gen. Stat. § 10-97(a). If a student is denied such reasonable and necessary transportation, his or her parents may appeal through the school accommodations hearing process set out in Conn. Gen. Stat. § 10-186. Conn. Gen. Stat. § 10-97.

In addition to providing transportation to vocational-technical schools, local and regional school districts must provide opportunities for vocational agricultural education. If the school district does not provide such vocational agricultural training approved by the state board of education, it must designate another school district that its students may attend, and the sending district is responsible for the tuition and for reasonable and necessary transportation for such students, subject to the same reimbursement and cost-cap provisions that apply to students attending vocational-technical schools. Conn. Gen. Stat. § 10-64(d); Conn. Gen. Stat. § 10-97(b).

Boards of education are now obligated to permit regional vocational-technical schools and regional vocational-agricultural schools (as well as interdistrict magnet schools, charter schools and interdistrict student attendance programs) full access for the purpose of recruitment of students. The only limitation on this right is that the recruitment may not be for the purpose of interscholastic athletic competition. Conn. Gen. Stat. § 10-220d.

9. <u>Adult education</u>

In addition to vocational-technical and vocational-agricultural programs, school districts in Connecticut are responsible for providing adult education programs. Such educational programs must be made available for any person sixteen years of age or older who is not enrolled in school. All school districts are required to provide a program of adult education or to enter into a cooperative arrangement with another school district to assure that its adult residents may participate in such a program. Such programs must include instruction in Americanization and United States citizenship, English for adults with limited English proficiency, and elementary and secondary school completion programs or classes. In addition, districts may provide for instruction in any subject taught in the public schools, including vocational education, adult literacy, parenting skills, and in any other subject or activity. Conn. Gen. Stat. § 10-69. School districts may not charge tuition for the required subjects, but may charge tuition for other courses offered. Conn. Gen. Stat. § 10-73a.

School districts may award an adult education diploma only if the student meets specified requirements for credits across a required distribution, including English, mathematics, history and other subjects. Conn. Gen. Stat. § 10-69(b).

10. Bilingual education

As a matter of federal law, local and regional school districts must take special steps to assure that students with limited English language proficiency have an opportunity to participate equally in educational programs.

a. National issues

The United States Supreme Court addressed this issue in 1974. *Lau v. Nichols*, 414 U.S. 563 (1974). In that case, the Court considered the rights of non-English speaking Chinese students who sued the San Francisco school district under the Civil Rights Act of 1964, which prohibits discrimination based on "race, color, or national origin." The Department of Health, Education and Welfare, the then-responsible federal agency, had enacted regulations concerning non-English proficient students to implement this non-discrimination requirement. These regulations required school districts to take affirmative steps to rectify the language deficiencies of such students. In *Lau*, the Court agreed with the plaintiffs that these requirements were valid. In the Court's view, the fact that non-English speaking students could not participate in the educational programs constituted illegal discrimination against such students.

That same year, Congress passed the Equal Educational Opportunities Act, which provides in relevant part that:

> No state shall deny educational opportunity to an individual on account of his or her race, color, sex, or national origin, by . . . the failure by an educational agency to take appropriate action to overcome language barriers that impede equal participation by its students in its instructional programs.

20 U.S.C. § 1703(f). While this law clearly imposes responsibilities upon school districts with regard to non-English speaking students, it did not define with precision exactly what "appropriate action" school districts were to take.

Some advocates of bilingual education have claimed that the law requires bilingual education. However, the courts have disagreed. Typical is the response by the Ninth Circuit, which ruled in 1978 that approaches other than bilingual education may be sufficient to overcome language deficiencies of students. *Guadalupe Organization, Inc. v. Tempe Elementary School District*, 587 F.2d 1022 (9th Cir. 1978). In a leading case on the subject, the Fifth Circuit Court of Appeals ruled in 1981 that a school district may meet its obligations in this regard in various ways. *Castaneda v. Pickard*, 648 F.2d 989 (5th Cir. 1981). The court reviewed the obligations of school districts, and stated that compliance with these federal requirements is based on whether the chosen model effectively addresses the needs of students whose first language is not English. The court ruled that effectiveness can be measured by asking three questions:

- Is the district's program based upon recognized, sound educational principles?
- Is the district's program designed to implement the adopted theory?
- Has the program produced satisfactory results?

Id. at 1009-10. Whether a district has adopted the bilingual education model, the "English as a second language" model, or some other approach, it will meet its obligations under federal law if it can answer the listed questions affirmatively.

Districts are free to adopt models other than traditional bilingual education to assist children whose first language is not English, as long as they are effective. By voter initiative in 1998, the statutes were changed to replace bilingual education in California with an alternative approach known as "sheltered English immersion" or "structured English immersion." This law was challenged on the basis that it did not provide appropriate instruction for such children. Relying on the *Castaneda* decision, the federal district court in California ruled that there was little probability that the elimination of bilingual education in favor of these alternative approaches would violate either Title VI of the Civil Rights Act of 1964 or the equal protection clause of the Fourteen Amendment. School officials were thus free to adopt other models for educating children whose first language is not English. *Valeria G. v. Wilson*, 12 F. Supp.2d 1007 (N.D. Cal. 1998).

b. State requirements

Following the *Lau* case, the General Assembly addressed the needs of non-English speaking students in Connecticut. Prior to 1977, districts were authorized, but not required, to provide such programs. Now, bilingual education must be provided in Connecticut whenever there are twenty or more students in any school dominant in any one language other than English. Conn. Gen. Stat. § 10-17f. Special rules apply to such students as regards mastery testing. *See* Section F(5), above.

In 1999, the General Assembly enacted comprehensive revisions to the statutes on bilingual education. It revised the definition of bilingual education to emphasize that (1) instruction in English as well as the student's native language is appropriate, (2) the goal of bilingual education is to enable students to achieve English proficiency and academic mastery of subject matter content and higher order skills, and (3) the use of English should continuously increase and the use of the native language should continuously decrease, so that English is used for more than half of the time after the first year. Conn. Gen. Stat. § 10-17e(2). The General Assembly also added a definition of "English as a second language program." Conn. Gen. Stat. § 10-17e(3).

These changes were significant. Rather than permitting parents to seek to exempt their child from bilingual education, the statute now reverses the process, and students may be placed in bilingual education only if the parent consents following a meeting at which school officials explain options, including language immersion programs as well as bilingual education. Conn. Gen. Stat. § 10-17f(e). Students are now limited to thirty months in bilingual education (which need not be consecutive). Conn. Gen. Stat. § 10-17f(d). School districts must continue to provide support for students who are not English proficient after thirty months, and such support may include English as a second language programs, sheltered English programs, English immersion programs, tutoring and homework assistance. *Id.*

Teacher applicants for bilingual programs must also demonstrate competence in English and the other language of instruction, and there are new certification requirements for bilingual teachers. Conn. Gen. Stat. § 10-17f(e); Conn. Gen. Stat. § 10-145b(l)(1). The State Department of Education was obligated to develop a state English mastery standard in 2000, and districts must now assess student progress toward that standard. Conn. Gen. Stat. § 10-17f(c).

11. Racial integration and racial balance

Since the landmark decision in *Brown v. Board of Education*, 347 U.S. 483 (1954), racial integration of our schools has been a public policy of the highest importance. There have been a number of decisions in the federal courts following *Brown*, but these cases have been of limited relevance in Connecticut. The federal courts have declined to assert jurisdiction when segregation is based on living patterns and personal choices, which is known as *de facto* segregation. *See, e.g., Freeman v. Pitts*, 503 U.S. 467 (1992); *Bell v. School City of Gary*, 324 F.2d 209 (7th Cir. 1963), *cert. denied* 377 U.S. 924 (1964). Rather, the federal courts have issued remedies in school desegregation cases only when the governmental entity involved as engaged in *de jure* segregation, *i.e.*, past segregation that was legally-sanctioned by direct or indirect means. Moreover, even in cases of *de jure* segregation, the courts do not have the authority to issue multi-district remedies against districts that did not participate in the *de jure* segregation. *Milliken v. Bradley*, 418 U.S. 717 (1974).

By contrast, our Connecticut Supreme Court addressed issues of *de facto* segregation in *Sheff v. O'Neill,* 238 Conn. 1 (1996). The court's decision requires that the General Assembly address the issues of racial isolation and equal educational opportunity in and among school districts, and the General Assembly has taken many steps to address this obligation. *See* Section A(1)(c) above.

The current law on racial balance, however, addresses the issue of racial balance only within the individual school districts in Connecticut. Following *Sheff*, the statutes concerning racial balance were amended to require that each school district report on the racial composition of its teaching staff as well as of its student body. Conn. Gen. Stat. § 10-226a. Moreover, now each board of education is required to develop and implement a written policy for minority staff recruitment. Conn. Gen. Stat. § 10-220(a). The remedial provisions of the racial balance law, however, continue to be limited to students within individual school districts.

"Racial imbalance" is defined by statute as a condition where the proportion of racial minorities in all the grades of a school taken together:

> substantially exceeds or falls substantially short of the proportion of such public school pupils in all of the same grades of the school district in which said school is situated taken together.

Conn. Gen. Stat. § 10-226b(b). This definition does not establish any specific standards. The statute, however, also authorizes the State Board of Education to establish regulations to fix standards for determination of racial imbalance, which it has done. Conn. St. Reg. §§ 10-226e-1 through 10-226e-9.

The regulations define racial imbalance as a difference of twenty-five percent or more between the percentage of racial minorities in a particular school as compared to the percentage of racial minorities in the same grades in the district as a whole. Conn. St. Reg. § 10-226e-3. Also, the regulations provide that a difference of fifteen percent between a particular school and the district as a whole is considered impending racial imbalance. Conn. St. Reg. § 10-226e-4.

When a school is determined to have impending racial imbalance, the school board may but need not file a plan to correct the impending imbalance. However, once a determination of racial imbalance is made, the district must submit a plan to the State Board of Education for approval. Conn. St. Reg. § 10-226e-5. School districts can address imbalance at a particular school without necessarily implementing a district-wide plan. Conn. Gen. Stat. § 10-226c. Also, a board of education may request an extension of time within which to address issues of racial balance if the imbalance is fewer than five students at a school. The State Department of Education has revised its regulations for assuring racial balance within the individual school districts in Connecticut. *Id.*

12. <u>Non-discrimination</u>

While boards of education have significant discretion in the assignment and transfer of students, they must comply with state and federal legislation prohibiting discrimination against students on any prohibited basis. Federal law, for example, sets out prohibitions against discrimination on the basis of sex in Title IX, 20 U.S.C. § 1681, discussed in Chapter Four, Section G(6). Federal law also prohibits discrimination on the basis of race, discussed in Chapter Seven, Section B(1)(a), and discrimination on the basis of disability, discussed in Chapter Five, Section B.

State law expressly prohibits discrimination against students on the basis of race, color, sex, religion, national origin or sexual orientation. Conn. Gen. Stat. § 10-15c. These prohibitions are long-standing, except for that against discrimination on the basis of sexual orientation, which was added to the statute in 1997. Questions have arisen concerning the enforcement of these provisions. Clearly, Conn. Gen. Stat. § 10-15c may be enforced by the State Department of Education. It is a law related to education, and it may be the subject of a complaint to the State Board of Education under Conn. Gen. Stat. § 10-4b, discussed in Section A(1)(d), above.

On occasion, parents and students have filed complaints with the Connecticut Commission on Human Rights and Opportunities alleging illegal discrimination by school districts. In the past, hearing officers appointed by the Commission have ruled, however, that a school district is not a "public accommodation" subject to the jurisdiction of the Commission. *CHRO ex rel Dawn Alston v. East Haven Board of Education*, 6 Conn. Ops. 564 (May 22, 2000) (Commission on Human Rights and Opportunities, Docket No. 9830205, May 3, 2000); *Commission on Human Rights and Opportunities ex rel Chillon Ballard v. Cheshire Board of Education*, Commission on Human Rights and Opportunities, Docket No. 9830294, (May 31, 2000).

Under these rulings, a proceeding under Conn. Gen. Stat. § 10-4b, rather than a complaint with the Commission, would be the appropriate means for seeking review of an alleged violation of Conn. Gen. Stat. § 10-15c. The Connecticut Supreme Court, however, reversed the decision in *Ballard*, above. The court ruled that the jurisdiction of the State Board of Education under Conn. Gen. Stat. § 10-4b is not exclusive, and that the Connecticut Commission on Human Rights and Opportunities also may take jurisdiction of such claims under Conn. Gen. Stat. § 46a-58(a). *Commission on Human Rights and Opportunities v. Cheshire Board of Education*, 270 Conn. 665 (2004).

The courts have also entertained claims of discrimination brought against boards of education under federal law or other state laws. In a recent decision, the Superior Court held that a parent can maintain an action for injunctive and declaratory relief, and perhaps for money damages, for the alleged denial of an elementary and secondary education to which all students are entitled under the Connecticut Constitution. *McPhail v. City of Milford*, 5 Conn. Ops. 326 (March 22, 1999). *See also Gant v. Wallingford Board of Education*, 69 F.3d 669 (2d Cir. 1995) (parents permitted to bring Section 1983 claims against school district). The claims in the *Gant* case were eventually dismissed, but only after further litigation. *Gant v. Wallingford Board of Education*, 195 F.3d 134 (2d Cir. 1999).

13. Charter schools

Conn. Gen. Stat. § 10-66aa through Conn. Gen. Stat. § 10-66gg set out provisions authorizing "charter schools," special schools approved by either the local or regional board of education and by the State Board of Education, or by the State Board of Education alone. The thrust of the legislation is to encourage such schools to be innovative by relieving them of various statutory mandates. Applicants for charter schools may request a waiver from the various statutory provisions that apply to local and regional boards of education. Conn. Gen. Stat. § 10-66bb. Mandates regarding health, safety, certification, mastery testing and collective bargaining, however, may not be waived. Conn. Gen. Stat. § 10-66dd.

The legislation provides for an application process for approval either as a local charter school or a state charter school. Application for approval as a local charter school is to be made to the local or regional board of education in which the charter school is to be located. If the local or regional board of education approves the school, the application then goes to the State Board of Education for action. Application for approval as a state charter school is made directly to the State Board of Education.

Proposed charter schools in priority school districts, in districts that have a minority population of at least seventy-five percent, or that are located at a work-site or that are affiliated with institutions of higher education must now be given priority. The statute also requires that the State consider the impact of a proposed charter school on the racial, ethnic and economic isolation of the student population in both the charter school and in the district as a whole. Admission criteria are to "promote a diverse student body." Such criteria, however, must also be in compliance with Conn. Gen. Stat. § 10-15c, which prohibits discrimination on the basis of race, color or national origin. When an applicant is successful, a charter may be granted for up to five years. The legislation limits the overall number of charter schools to twenty-four. Conn. Gen. Stat. § 10-66bb(c).

The statutes now provide standards for renewal, probation and revocation of charters. A charter may be revoked if the school fails to demonstrate student progress, fails to comply with the terms of its charter, fails to make adequate progress in reducing racial, ethnic and economic isolation, or fails to ensure that public funds are expended prudently (among other obligations). Conn. Gen. Stat. § 10-66bb.

Once approved, a charter school is a separate statutory entity. The law provides that the charter school may hold property, make contracts, sue or be sued and borrow money, though the law specifically states that neither the State nor a local or regional board of education that has approved a charter school are liable for the debts or other actions of a charter school except as such obligations may be created by contract. Charter schools may now carry over up to ten percent of amounts received but unexpended and may now create a reserve fund for specified, approved purposes. Conn. Gen Stat. § 10-66ee. Members of a charter school governing council are prohibited from having a personal or financial interest in the assets of the school. Conn. Gen. Stat. § 10-66aa.

If a local charter school is approved, the local or regional board of education must pay the amount specified in the charter for each student enrolled in the school. If a state charter school is approved, currently the State will provide $7,250 per student. Charter schools may also receive federal, state or private funds. The local board of education of the school district in which the charter school is located is obligated to provide transportation to students enrolled in the charter school unless the school makes other arrangements. Conn. Gen Stat. § 10-66ee. Moreover, this law now provides that parents may challenge transportation decisions through the hearing and court processes set out in Conn. Gen. Stat. § 10-186 and Conn. Gen. Stat. § 10-187.

Under the No Child Left Behind Act, states are required to have procedures assuring the transfer of school records between school districts and charter school. No Child Left Behind Act, Section 5208. Conn. Gen. Stat. § 10-220h, which provides for the transfer of records between school districts, may meet this requirement, but clarification of the statute is advisable.

In addition, school districts are responsible for conducting planning and placement team meetings regarding resident children with disabilities who attend charter schools. Conn. Gen Stat. § 10-66ee. Under the IDEA, children enrolled in public charter schools retain all their rights to an appropriate educational program. 34 C.F.R. § 300.312. Under state law, the district is required to invite representatives from the charter school, and it must pay the difference between the amount received by the charter school and the reasonable cost of special education instruction on a quarterly basis.

Conn. Gen Stat. § 10-66ee. This requirement can be very expensive, given the greater difficulty in consolidating special education services than is the case for programs within the district schools. The charter school is responsible for assuring that the student receives the services set out in the IEP, either by the charter school or by the school district in which the student resides. Conn. Gen Stat. § 10-66ee.

Much of the charter schools legislation is devoted to protecting the rights of employees who choose to work for a charter school. Teachers at local charter schools are to be subject to the collective bargaining agreement that applies to teachers in the district in which the charter school is located, and the terms of the contract may be modified only upon a majority vote of the teachers employed at the charter school. The law also provides that teachers employed by a local or regional board of education shall be granted a two-year leave of absence to work in a charter school, which may be extended at the request of the teacher for an additional two-year period. The teacher may return to the same or a comparable position at any time during the leave, and such leave time may not operate as an interruption of service for purposes of seniority and teacher's retirement. The teacher, however, may not include such time for the purpose of achieving tenure. A teacher who is not on leave from a school district and who works at the charter school for forty school months, however, will achieve tenure after twenty school months if subsequently employed by a local or regional board of education. Conn. Gen. Stat. § 10-66dd.

14. Staff training

Boards of education are required to adopt and update comprehensive plans on teacher professional development based on the educational goals of the board of education. The plan must include systematic assessment and improvement of both teacher evaluation and professional development, including personnel management and evaluation training or experience for administrations. Conn. Gen. Stat. § 10-220a(b). The requirements of the district teacher evaluation plan(s) for teachers and administrators are described in greater detail in Chapter Three, Section D(2). Conn. Gen. Stat. § 10-220a(a) lists the various topics on which districts must provide in-service training to teachers, administrators and pupil personnel staff.

15. Technology issues

Boards of education rely increasingly on technology to implement the instructional program, and this use of technology gives rise to a number of related legal issues. In dealing with these issues, school officials must be aware of current requirements. Moreover, continuing vigilance is warranted because new technology will likely give rise to new legal issues.

a. Regulation of technology use

Boards of education are well-advised to develop policies to regulate the use of technology. Typically called "Acceptable Use" policies, such policies set out the most important rules for the use of technology and assure that technology users are on notice of these rules. Some districts have one policy of general application, and others have separate policies for student and employee use of technology. By promulgating such policies, school districts can protect themselves from claims by parents that their children were given unauthorized access to inappropriate materials and can deal more effectively with disciplinary issues.

These rules should be distributed at least annually. The school district must make a policy judgment on whether to require staff and/or students (and their parents) to sign-off each year. One appropriate decision is to publicize the rules to employees annually, but to require students and parents to sign off each year. The distinction may be justified by the view that parents may otherwise claim that they were not aware that their child was permitted access to the Internet.

b. Website filtering and related issues

The United States Congress has tried, with varying degrees of success, to regulate the use of the Internet. Its first attempts were aimed at senders of information, but these legislative efforts were struck down by the courts. *See Reno v. American Civil Liberties Union (I)*, 521 U.S. 844 (1997) (striking down the Communications Decency Act of 1996, 47 U.S.C. § 223(a)(1)(B)(ii) as overly broad). In the *Reno (I)* case, the Court found that the Internet was more like print media than broadcast media, because it is "non-invasive" and its use requires deliberate, affirmative steps to access the information. Accordingly, the Court held that regulation of the Internet is subject to strict scrutiny standard, *i.e.* whether there is a compelling governmental interest and whether the regulation is the least restrictive means of achieving that governmental interest.

Congress tried again in 1998, with the Child Online Protection Act, 47 U.S.C. § 231(a)(1), as amended by P.L. 105-277 ("COPA"). Again, this law was aimed at the senders of information, and again the courts struck it down.

ACLU v. Reno (II), 31 F. Supp.2d 473 (E.D. Pa. 1999), *affirmed* 217 F.3d 162 (3d Cir. 2000). In 2002, the United States Supreme Court remanded the case back to the Third Circuit, *Ashcroft v. ALCU (I)*, 535 U.S. 564 (2002), but after the Third Circuit again affirmed the injunction against enforcement of COPA, the United States Supreme Court affirmed. *Ashcroft v. ACLU (II)*, 542 U.S. __, 124 S.Ct. 2783 (2004). A 5-4 majority of the Court ruled that filtering is a less restrictive (and possibly more effective) means of protecting children from harmful material.

In 2001, Congress tried a different approach to regulating the Internet, the Children's Internet Protection Act, 47 U.S.C. § 254 ("CIPA"). Rather than seeking to regulate the senders of information, however, this law is focused on the recipients. It imposes certain obligations on school districts and libraries as a condition of continued eligibility under the Communications Act of 1934 for discounted Internet access, Internet services and internal connection services (the "e-rate" program).

School districts must adopt policies to comply with the law as follows. First, such policies must provide for the implementation of a technology protection measure (*i.e.* filtering software) to assure against Internet access by both adults and minors to visual depictions that are obscene, child pornography or (as to minors) harmful. Second, such policies must provide for safe use of the Internet by addressing access by minors to inappropriate matter on the Internet; safety and security of minors when using electronic mail, chat rooms, and other forms of direct electronic communications; and other unlawful activities by minors online; and other specified matters.

Under CIPA, school districts were required to certify by October 28, 2001, that the required policies and technology measures were in place, or that they were undertaking such actions, including any necessary procurement procedures, to put them in place for the following funding year. The Certification had to be provided on FCC Form 486 (or on FCC Form 479 if the district is an eligible member of a consortium, but not the billed entity). The Certification did not need to describe the policy or technology measures, but rather simply had to attest that the district was either in compliance or was in the process of procurement to assure compliance for the following funding year.

New challenges were promptly filed concerning the obligations of CIPA. This litigation has proceeded on behalf of libraries only, even though CIPA applies to both schools and libraries. *See, e.g., Mainstream Loudoun v. Board of Trustees of the Loudoun County Library*, 24 F. Supp. 552 (E.D. Va.

1998) (use of mandatory blocking software on Internet access in a public library violates the First Amendment). However, in 2003, the United States Supreme Court reversed a lower court decision enjoining enforcement of CIPA as against libraries. *United States v. American Library Association*, 539 U.S. 194 (2003). There, the Court held that the First Amendment does not prohibit Congress from conditioning the "e-rate" subsidy to libraries on compliance with requirement that filters be installed to limit Internet access to obscenity. Given the special responsibilities of school officials for student welfare, this ruling effectively precludes any viable challenge to such requirements in the school setting. Filtering of Website access for students will thus continue.

c. Copyright issues

With the increased use of technology in the schools, educators now frequently confront issues of copyright. Copyright is generally held by the person who created the work except if the work is a "work for hire," discussed below. No special filing is required, and a work may be copyrighted by operation of law, whether or not it has been registered and whether or not the symbol © identifies it as a copyrighted work. That being said, use of a copyright notice on a work is important because it informs the public that the work is protected by copyright, identifies the copyright owner and shows the year of first publication. The copyright notice should be placed on the work to give reasonable notice of the claim of copyright and should contain the following three elements: (1) the symbol © (the letter C in a circle) or the word "Copyright" or the abbreviation "Copr."; (2) the year of first publication of the work; and (3) the name of the owner of the copyright, or an abbreviation by which the name can be recognized or a generally known alternative designation of the owner.

Violation of copyright can occur in various ways. If material is used without permission, a violation occurs unless there is an applicable exception to the copyright protection, such as "fair use," discussed below. In addition, a violation of copyright may occur if a use is made of the material that falls outside of the applicable license. For example, we are permitted to watch a movie we bought on tape, and we may be permitted to make copies for our own personal use by our license. If we show the copy to others, whether or not for payment, we may violate our license, a copyright violation. This violation can even occur in the educational setting. The copyright law permits a teacher to show a video for instructional purposes, but not purely for entertainment, unless the teacher or school district has a license for such use. 17 U.S.C. § 110(1).

Sensitivity to copyright issues is important, especially now as technology facilitates both the creation and the expropriation of intellectual property. Teachers who create works outside the scope of their employment may establish an unexpected ownership interest. Even student work is protected by copyright law. Conversely, students and staff members who violate copyright law may be liable for the violation. In addition, while this area of the law is developing, it is possible that the school district could be liable for contributory and/or vicarious infringement if policies or procedures permit copyright law to be violated. *See, e.g., Fonovisa, Inc. v. Cherry Auction, Inc.*, 76 F.3d 259 (9th Cir. 1996); *Shapiro, Bernstein and Co. v. H. L. Green Co.*, 316 F.2d 304 (2d Cir. 1963). The following briefly addresses the two most common copyright issues that confront educators – the scope of "fair use" and the concept of "work for hire," which gives the employer a copyright interest in an employee's creation.

1. "Fair use" of copyrighted material

The United States Copyright Act, 17 U.S.C. § 107, (the "Act") specifically states:

> "[Notwithstanding copyright protections,] the fair use of a copyrighted work, including such use by reproduction in copies or phonorecords or by any other means specified by that section, for purposes such as criticism, comment, news reporting, teaching (including multiple copies for classroom use), scholarship, or research, is not infringement of copyright.

In determining whether "fair use" has occurred, the courts will apply four nonexclusive factors that are set out in the same statute:

- the purpose and character of the use, including whether such use is of a commercial nature or is for nonprofit educational purposes;
- the nature of the copyrighted work;
- the amount and substantiality of the portion used in relation to the copyrighted work as a whole;
- the effect of the use upon the potential market for or value of the copyrighted work.

Educators have no trouble meeting the first test, of course. Under the second test concerning the nature of the work, a distinction is drawn between published or unpublished works. The scope of fair use is narrower with respect to unpublished works. *Wright v. Warner Books, Inc.*, 953 F.2d 731 (2d Cir. 1991). Also, the courts distinguish between informational and creative works, with this factor weighing in favor of "fair use" of informational works.

The third factor concerns both the percentage of the original work that was copied, and whether that portion constitutes the essence of the copyrighted work. Finally, application of the fourth factor considers whether the actions at issue would result in a substantially adverse impact on the potential market for the original. Given that copyright protects property interests, this factor, which affects the value of the work, is central to the fair use analysis.

With these four, non-exclusive factors in play, it can be difficult to predict reliably whether a particular use is "fair use" permissible under the copyright laws. Incidental copying of magazine articles, or excerpts of small parts of works, would typically be a permissible "fair use." By contrast, wholesale copying of workbooks for use in the classroom would not. *See Princeton University Press v. Michigan Document Services, Inc.*, 40 U.S.P.Q.2d 1641 (1996) (production of course packs with excerpts of various works for college students held to be copyright violation, even though authors did not object because they were not copyright holders).

2. Copyright ownership and "works for hire"

The general rule is that the creator of an original work is the author and owner of the copyright to the work. "Works for hire," however, are an important exception to this rule. Since educators often create copyrightable works, ranging from lesson plans to workbooks to computer software programs, whether the educator or his or her employer is the owner of the copyrightable work often turns on whether the work is a "work for hire," as defined in the Act. Under the Act a "work for hire" is either (1) a work prepared by an employee within the scope of his employment or (2) a work specially commissioned, that fits into any one of nine specially enumerated categories. Under this exception, "the employer or other person for whom the work was prepared is considered the author for purposes of copyright." 17 U.S.C. § 201(b).

For teachers, the question of whether their employer owns the work that they have created is a tricky issue. The Seventh Circuit has articulated the test regarding when an employer owns a copyright in a work — an employer owns the copyright if: (1) the work meets the requirements for copyrightability; (2) an employee prepared the work; (3) the employee prepared the work within the scope of his/her employment; and (4) the parties have not expressly agreed that the employee will own the copyright to the work in a signed, written agreement. *See Foraste v. Brown University*, 248 F. Supp.2d. 71 (D. R.I. 2003) citing *Baltimore Orioles, Inc. v. Major League Baseball Players Assn.*, 805 F.2d 663 (7th Cir. 1986). Generally, preparation of a work will be considered "within the scope of employment" if: (1) it is the kind of work the employee is employed to do; (2) it occurs substantially within authorized work hours and space; and (3) it is created, at least in part, by a purpose to serve the employer. *See Foraste v. Brown University*, 248 F. Supp. 2d. 71 (D. R.I. 2003).

For an independent contractor who is hired to create a specially commissioned work, the work is a "work for hire" (and therefore the work is owned by the employer) if it falls into one of nine categories. The nine categories are: (1) a contribution to a collective work; (2) a part of a motion picture or audiovisual work; (3) a translation; (4) a supplementary work; (5) a compilation; (6) an instructional text; (7) a test; (8) answer material for a test; and (9) an atlas. In addition, for an independent contractor's work to be considered a "work for hire," there must be a written agreement, signed by both parties, that the work will be a "work for hire."

Thus, for teachers, the general rule is that the school, as their employer, will own the copyright for academic materials they create that fall within the scope of their employment. Examples of such materials include tests, lesson plans and/or a course syllabus for assigned classes. If a teacher creates academic materials outside the scope of his/her employment, however, then the teacher will own the copyright to those materials, unless the work meets the requirements of a "work for hire" for an independent contractor, described above. For example, if a teacher prepares a manual outside the scope of his or her employment to assist students in working with a particular computer program, it is likely that copyright ownership remains with the teacher. *See Hays v. Sony Corporation of America*, 847 F.2d 412 (7th Cir. 1988).

d. Freedom of Information Act issues

Technology affects the obligations of public agencies to retain information (*e.g.,* retention of recordings of board meetings), to disclose information (*e.g.*, e-mails), and even to create computer programs to retrieve information. With advances in technology the law has imposed new obligations, such as the duty to maintain existing electronic records once a claim is made. In Section D, above, there is a comprehensive review of these issues under the Freedom of Information Act (FOIA). Given the forward march of technological innovations and their use in our public schools, we can expect a steady stream of new legal issues. It is therefore critically important to keep up-to-date on related legal obligations.

G. Board Liability

Increasingly common today are claims that school officials have somehow been negligent or have violated the constitutional or statutory rights of students or teachers, in situations ranging from free speech to sexual abuse. In dealing with these claims, school districts will be able to establish immunity from liability in some cases and will be held liable in others. In any event, there is a strong public policy in Connecticut in favor of protecting school board members, school employees and even volunteers from personal liability, and the indemnity statute confers that protection. Conn. Gen. Stat. § 10-235.

1. Negligence

It may come as a surprise to some that school districts and their employees are not the insurers of the safety of all who come onto school property. If, for example, a student who is appropriately supervised hits a fellow student in the head with his lunch bucket, his/her parents may be liable for the assault under Conn. Gen. Stat. § 52-572 (parents liable for torts of minor children up to $5,000). The school district, however, will not be liable. In order to establish liability for negligence, a plaintiff must show that the school district employees or agents acted negligently.

a. Elements of negligence

A person will be liable for negligence only if each of four elements of negligence is met. First, there must be a duty of care. School officials generally have a duty of care for students at school. However it is equally clear that there are other situations where there is no such duty. For example, a student injured in a fight on the school playground on a Sunday would have no claim that school officials owed her a duty of care to intervene. Similarly, a student who leaves school grounds pursuant to an open-campus policy should have no expectation that the district would have a continuing duty of care to supervise him. *See Heigl v. Board of Education*, 218 Conn. 1 (1991).

The existence and scope of any duty of care will depend on the facts of the particular case. Teachers of students in the lower grades, for example, have a duty of care which includes physical supervision, and such students should certainly not be left to their own devices on the school playground. Conversely, school officials generally do not have any continuing duty of care to students who leave school grounds to walk home along a route that is not otherwise hazardous. The nature of the duty of care owed to students, teachers and others on school property thus will depend on their age and ability to take care of themselves.

Second, the plaintiff must show that the school district has breached that duty of care, *i.e.* a school official must act unreasonably under the specific facts of the case. For example, it would be unreasonable for a school custodian to leave soapy water on the stairway during passing period. Similarly, it would be unreasonable for a teacher to permit a student to maintain possession of fireworks on school property. Conversely, if the defendant has acted reasonably, there will be no breach of the duty of care. *See Carter v. Laidlaw Transit, Inc.*, No. CV020175182S, 2004 Conn. Super. LEXIS 1355 (Conn. Super. Ct. 2004) (no liability for injuries when student slipped on wet stairs entering school bus; driver had no duty to warn of the evident (and not inherently dangerous) circumstance).

Third, the plaintiff must establish that the unreasonable action or failure to act caused the injury. The student who is pushed down the stairway may not be able to show that the soapy water had anything to do with his injuries. It is not enough to show that someone made a mistake.

Finally, the plaintiff must show that that there is a direct connection between the unreasonable action or failure to act and the injury suffered. Of all the elements of a negligence claim, this is perhaps the easiest to establish. When an injured student sits in court and demonstrates that unreasonable action by a school employee caused an injury, a jury will likely be ready to consider the injury to be foreseeable. Hindsight is 20/20.

Applying these principles in the school setting, it is clear that there are many situations where students or others are injured on school grounds without the school district being liable. For example, if a teacher turns to write on the board and one student injures another by throwing a pencil, the teacher's actions were neither unreasonable nor caused the injury. Nonetheless, school districts are increasingly confronted with claims of negligence in a variety of situations, ranging from student injuries in extracurricular activities to student suicides. In each case, the courts will apply the principles outlined above. Liability will be established only if there was a duty of care, district personnel breached that duty by acting other than reasonably, the unreasonable action caused an injury, and the injury was the proximate cause of the injury.

A related point is whether one student can sue another student for negligence following an injury during a physical education class or athletic contest. The courts have ruled that claims for simple negligence cannot be brought against fellow students. *Baer v. Regional School District No. 16 et al.*, 25 Conn. L. Rptr. No. 11, 376 (November 15, 1999), *citing Jaworski v. Kiernan*, 241 Conn. 399 (1997) (voluntary participants in local co-ed soccer league subject to suit only for reckless or intentional conduct, not mere negligence). *But see Hendry v. Fratus*, No. 558176, 2002 Conn. Super. LEXIS 2824 (Conn. Super. Ct. 2002) (conduct of coach who injured student subject to review under normal rules, not the higher standard for liability of *Jaworski* applicable to participants); *Jagger v. Mohawk Mountain Ski Area, Inc.*, 262 Conn. 672 (2004) (*Jaworski* rule does not apply to skiing because physical contact between participants is not necessarily involved).

b. Board policies

In considering issues of negligence, board members and school administrators should be aware that adopting policies can raise liability concerns. Specifically, in adopting a policy, the board of education defines what is reasonable conduct. If, for example, the youth suicide prevention policy states that the parents will be notified whenever the student assistance team convenes to consider a report of suicidal ideation, the policy has defined what action is reasonable under the circumstances. A failure to follow the policy will thus be considered unreasonable, increasing the likelihood that liability will be found if a person is injured. It is therefore critically important to take care in drafting policies. It is far better to do more than is set out in policy than to do less. The drafting of policies is not the time to give voice to aspirations and hopes. Rather, boards of education should take care to promise only what they and school staff can deliver.

c. Educational malpractice

A discussion concerning negligence would be incomplete without a short mention of educational malpractice, *i.e.* a claim that school officials should somehow be liable for negligence in failing to provide a student with an appropriate education. The discussion of such claims is indeed short because Connecticut has followed the general rule that claims for educational malpractice are against public policy and will not be considered by the courts. *Gupta v. New Britain General Hospital*, 239 Conn. 574 (1996); *Bell v. West Haven Board of Education*, 55 Conn. App. 400 (1999); *Vogel v. Maimonides Academy*, 58 Conn. App. 624 (2000).

The result may be different, however, if the actions are not purely educational. For example, the concept of educational malpractice does not preclude a claim on the basis that negligent action caused a physical injury, even in the educational setting. *Doe v. Yale University*, 252 Conn. 641 (2000). Also, the *Gupta* court stated that a specific contractual promise above and beyond the general exception of an appropriate educational program may be actionable. Similarly, a guidance counselor was held liable for giving wrong information to a student, causing the student to lose a valuable scholarship. *Sain v. Cedar Rapids Community School District*, 626 N.W.2d 115 (Iowa 2001). Irrespective of how a complaint is framed, however, if the underlying claim is inadequacy of an educational program, the courts will likely dismiss the claim. *See Faigel v. Fairfield University*, 75 Conn. App. 37 (2002).

d. Immunity from liability

Even where negligence may be shown, the school districts and school officials may be immune from suit. First, there is statutory immunity – *i.e.* situations in which the legislature has determined that public policy is best served by conferring immunity upon a person who takes action under certain circumstances. Second, there is sovereign or governmental immunity. When immunity is found, the injured party cannot recover.

It is important to keep the concept of "immunity" separate from the concept of "indemnity." Immunity means that liability cannot be imposed. By contrast, where there is indemnity the injured party still recovers, but the party that would otherwise be liable is held harmless against financial loss. For example, liability may be imposed on a teacher whose negligent actions result in an injury to a student (if he or she is not immune from liability – more about that later). Pursuant to the indemnity provisions in Conn. Gen. Stat. § 10-235, however, the associated costs (including attorney's fees) will typically be borne by the school district, because usually it must indemnify the teacher for such claims.

1. Statutory immunity

Statutory immunity exists when a statute provides that a person acting in a particular situation is not liable for any injuries that may result.

This concept reflects a public policy judgment that we should encourage "good deeds" by protecting those who take the specified action, usually on behalf of another. Typically, however, any such protection is limited to actions that may constitute simple negligence; wanton or reckless conduct is typically excluded from a provision for statutory immunity.

A good example of statutory immunity is the "Good Samaritan" law, Conn. Gen. Stat. § 52-557b. This statute provides that a "teacher or other school personnel on the school grounds or in the school building or at a school function" will be immune from liability for providing "emergency first aid" if they meet the statutory requirements for immunity, *i.e.* (1) they must have completed a course in first aid offered by the American Red Cross, the Department of Health or a local health director (among others), and (2) any mistakes they make must be "ordinary negligence." The law specifies that immunity is not available for actions or omissions that constitute "gross, willful or wanton negligence." Other examples of statutory immunity include Conn. Gen. Stat. § 10-212a, described below, or Conn. Gen. Stat. § 17a-101e, which provides that a person who files a report of suspected child abuse in good faith is immune from liability, civil or criminal, that could otherwise be imposed.

The concept of statutory immunity protects school personnel who administer medication to students in two ways. First, Conn. Gen. Stat. § 10-212a provides that a school nurse or, in her/his absence, a principal or teacher will not be liable for administering medication to a student pursuant to the written order of a physician, dentist, licensed advanced practice registered nurse or physician assistant, and the written authorization of a parent. Second, Conn. Gen. Stat. § 52-557b(e) provides that a school employee who renders emergency care by administration of medication by injection will not be liable for acts that are found to be ordinary negligence. To be eligible for this immunity, however, the school employee must have completed both a course in first aid as described above *and* a course in the administration of medication by injection given by the school medical advisor or by a licensed physician. Moreover, neither provision for immunity applies to acts or omissions that are gross, willful or wanton negligence.

2. Governmental immunity

Historically, boards of education in Connecticut have been immune from liability for the discretionary acts of their agents. This immunity dates back to the middles ages when the king could do no wrong and was immune from legal claims. The concept of "sovereign immunity" still applies to claims against the State, and the State can be sued only as provided by statute or otherwise with the permission of the Claims Commissioner. For towns, boards of education and other governmental entities, a related concept of "governmental immunity" has evolved. These entities (and the officials and employees who act on their behalf) also enjoy limited immunity from suit. The term "limited" is used advisedly, because the exceptions to governmental immunity are significant and are growing.

There are three major exceptions to the doctrine of governmental immunity. Public officers and employees are not immune from suit (1) when their alleged acts involve malice, wantonness or intent to injure, rather than simple negligence, (2) when a statute permits lawsuits, and (3) when the failure to act will subject an identifiable person to imminent harm. Each of these exceptions can be briefly described as follows.

First, if a public officer or employee acts maliciously, wantonly or with the intent to injure, the law presumes that he or she is not acting on behalf of the government and therefore is not protected by governmental immunity. The Connecticut Supreme Court affirmed this principle in 2004, holding that a municipality is not responsible for the intentional torts of its employees. *Pane v. City of Danbury*, 267 Conn. 669 (2004).

The second exception to the doctrine of governmental immunity is statutory abrogation, *i.e.* a decision by the legislature to permit persons to sue the government under specific circumstances. Conn. Gen. Stat. § 52-557 is an example of statutory abrogation of governmental immunity. In relevant part, this statute provides that the defense of governmental immunity is not available in claims against school districts in legal actions alleging personal injuries received while being transported to or from school in a vehicle owned, leased or hired by a school district. The General Assembly clarified the law in 2000 to provide that special education students have the same right to sue for injuries, even though they receive their programs pursuant to an IEP mandated by federal law. Conn. Gen. Stat. § 52-557. *See Nisinzweig v. Kurien*, 30 Conn. L. Rptr. No. 9 342 (October 15, 2001). *But see Goode v. Town of Wilton*, 31 Conn. L. Rptr. 25 (October 9, 2001); *Goode v. Town of Wilton*, 2002 Conn. Super. LEXIS 1232 (April 16, 2002) (school district immune from liability for actions related to injuries suffered during transportation to school athletic contest provided by student).

Conn. Gen. Stat. § 52-557n is another example of statutory abrogation, and it authorizes an action against the political subdivision for negligence under specified circumstances. *Spears v. Garcia*, 263 Conn. 22

(2003). Codifying a common-law exception to governmental immunity, it provides that a political subdivision of the state (*e.g.*, municipality, board of education) can be liable for damages for negligence as long as the action claimed to be negligence was a "ministerial" act (an action not requiring the exercise of judgment) as opposed to a "governmental act." *See Gauvin* v. *New Haven*, 187 Conn. 180, 184, (1982) ("Governmental acts are performed wholly for the direct benefit of the public and are supervisory or discretionary in nature."). The rationale of this limitation is that government officials should be free to decide how to fulfill their duties without fear of being sued. *Elliott v. Waterbury*, 245 Conn. 385 (1998). However, if a duty is "ministerial," *i.e.* it is to be performed in a prescribed manner, school officials may be sued for their actions or their failure to act. *See Doe v. Voluntown Board of Education*, 25 Conn. L. Rptr. No. 18, 629 (January 10, 2000) (district can be sued for failing to conduct mandatory postural scoliosis screening required by Conn. Gen. Stat. § 10-214; such screening is considered to be a ministerial act).

The third exception, liability for conduct that subjects an identifiable person to imminent harm, has been the subject of much litigation. In *Burns v. Board of Education*, 228 Conn. 640 (1994), the Connecticut Supreme Court held that a superintendent could be held liable for injuries suffered when a student slipped on a sheet of ice. It held that students attending public schools during school hours are entitled to a special duty of care, and that during school hours the "superintendent bears the responsibility for failing to act to prevent the risk of imminent harm to school children as an identifiable class of beneficiaries of his statutory duty of care." The designation of the head custodian as the person responsible for such matters did not absolve the superintendent of responsibility in that case (subject of course to indemnity, as discussed in Section G(4) below).

After *Burns*, the lower courts have followed and extended its principles to find that school districts may be liable for various injuries to students. In *Cannato v. Stamford Board of Education*, 5 Conn. Ops. 556 (May 17, 1999), the Superior Court held that a student who slipped on condensation puddled on a staircase was "one of a class of foreseeable victims" of negligence who, therefore, could maintain an action against the responsible school officials. This concept was extended even further in *Matthews v. Sklarz*, 5 Conn. Ops. 303 (March 15, 1999) (Superior Court). There, a student was injured when he was struck by a car while walking to school. The defendant school district moved to dismiss the claim on the basis of governmental immunity. The court held, however, that the student was required to walk to school and therefore was "a foreseeable victim" who could sue the district for alleged negligence. By contrast, the Superior Court has held that the "imminent harm" exception to governmental immunity does not apply when students are permitted to transport themselves and other students to athletic contests. *See, e.g., Goode v. Town of Wilton*, 31 Conn. L. Rptr. 25 (October 9, 2001); *Goode v. Town of Wilton*, No. CV000180777, 2002 Conn. Super. LEXIS 1232 (Conn. Super. Ct. April 16, 2002).

In considering this exception to governmental immunity, school officials should be aware of "Megan's Law." Conn. Gen. Stat. §§ 54-250 *et seq.* requires that sexual offenders register pursuant to specified statutory requirements, and this information is maintained by the Department of Public Safety on its website. In 2003, the United States Supreme Court upheld this requirement, ruling that it did not deny registrants due process. *Department of Public Safety v. Doe*, 538 U.S. 1 (2003). It is advisable, therefore, to have a process in place to check this registry as part of the application process or approval of volunteers.

The rule in *Burns* has even been applied to student-to-student misconduct. *Purzycki v. Town of Fairfield*, 244 Conn. 101 (1998). In this case, the Connecticut Supreme Court considered whether the imminent harm exception to governmental immunity applied to a situation in which one elementary school student tripped another in the hallway, causing injury, while both were unsupervised during the lunch recess period. The Appellate Court had held that a jury could not reasonably conclude that the lack of supervision in the hallway, standing alone, would subject the student to imminent harm. The Supreme Court reversed, however, and held that the failure to provide supervision to students in the hallway during this period did subject students to imminent harm. The Court relied on the testimony of the principal at trial, who said that students are likely to engage in horseplay if left unsupervised, and on the fact that students were otherwise supervised throughout the lunch recess period.

The extension of the *Burns* case in the *Purzycki* decision is disturbing because the Court finds that school officials may be liable for student misconduct that injures another student. *See, e.g., Domejczyk v. New Britain Board of Education*, No. CV98491816, 2002 Conn. Super. LEXIS 741 (Conn. Super. Ct. March 6, 2002) (district may be liable for injuries after student was attacked by another student in school during school hours); *Kendall v. West Haven Department of Education*, 6 Conn. Ops. 1357 (December 4, 2000) (liability when district took no action to prevent student attack against another student, despite prior warning).

The courts are refining this exception so that it does not subsume the general rule that governmental actors are immune from liability for their discretionary acts. Parents are not considered members of the identifiable class subject to the protection of this exception. *Prescott v. City of Meriden*, No. CV000446162S, 2002 Conn. Super. LEXIS 3152 (Conn. Super. Ct. 2002). As to students, the courts have narrowed this exception to governmental immunity by requiring that a danger be specific as to time and place before a student will be considered an identifiable person subject to immediate harm. *See Doe v. Klingberg Family Centers*, No. CV 00 504520 (Conn. Super. Ct., August 9, 2001) (sexual assault alleged against teaching assistant was not limited to time and place, defeating claim of "imminent harm" exception); *Rodriquez v. City of Bridgeport*, No. CV950332509S, 2002 Conn. Super. LEXIS 3199 (Conn. Super. Ct. 2002) (no liability to student injured in fight at school).

In *Doe v. Board of Education*, 76 Conn. App. 296 (2003), for example, a student was sexually assaulted by other students. She claimed that the New Haven Public Schools had assigned insufficient security personnel and had implemented inadequate safety controls. The Appellate Court found, however, that these general allegations were not sufficiently specific to establish liability. *See also Eberle v. Town of Coventry*, No. X07CV020078407S, 2003 Conn. Super. LEXIS 2081 (Conn. Super. Ct. 2003) (student injured in locker room as sports participant cannot overcome governmental immunity under *Burns*); *Drago v. Town of Madison*, No. 478215, 2003 Conn. Super. LEXIS 3030 (Conn. Super. Ct. 2003) (injury on playground not sufficiently limited as to time to fall within *Burns* rule). These more recent cases may represent a narrowing of the circumstances under which school districts will lose the benefit of governmental immunity.

The lesson of these cases is that one cannot predict with certainty when a court will permit a student injured in school to sue because s/he was a member of an identifiable class of victims subject to imminent harm. It is therefore imperative that school personnel be vigilant in reviewing their actions to assure that they are reasonable and do not subject students to risk. Equally important, school officials should assure that appropriate insurance is in place and that, if and when a claim is made, the insurance carrier is promptly notified so that coverage under the policy is preserved.

e. Permission slips and waivers

Given the risks of liability for negligence, school officials might ask whether they may guard against liability by requiring that parents execute releases absolving the district of liability in certain situations, such as field trips or participation in athletics. As tempting as such a strategy might be, it may not work. Even as to adults, the courts view releases of future liability with suspicion, and often will not enforce them. The Connecticut Supreme Court has ruled that a party cannot be released from liability resulting from his or her future negligence in the absence of clear language so providing. *Hyson v. White Water Mountain Resorts*, 265 Conn. 636 (2003). Where the language is clear and the parties have equal bargaining power, however, such releases may be enforced. *Fischer v. Rivest*, 33 Conn. L. Rptr. 119, (Conn. Super. Ct. August 15, 2002) (waiver to play youth hockey enforced); *Brown v. Sol*, 2004 Conn. Super. LEXIS 1517 (Conn. Super. Ct. 2004) (waiver for racing school enforced).

The school setting is unique, in that students are required to attend school and schools have a special responsibility of care. It is therefore possible that a release would not be enforceable even if it specifically refers to negligence of school personnel. To be sure, the Supreme Judicial Court in Massachusetts recently enforced a waiver signed by parents. *See Sharon v. City of Newton*, 769 NE.2d 738 (Mass. 2002) (cheerleader who broke her arm falling from pyramid cannot sue because her parents signed waiver form as a condition of participation). While there are no Connecticut cases directly on point, however, almost fifty years ago the Attorney General opined that a release from liability would not be effective as to teachers and employees of the Mansfield Training School. 28 *Opinions of the Attorney General* 245 (1954). Moreover, the courts have ruled that waivers are against public policy when the defendant is engaged in a business involving the public interest and/or when the bargaining power between the parties is unequal. Many years ago, for example, the Connecticut courts ruled unenforceable a waiver signed on behalf of a minor attending a boy scout camp. *Fedor v. Mauwehu Council*, 21 Conn. Supp. 38 (1958). *See also Cooper v. Aspen Skiing Co.*, 2002 WL 1358723 (Colo. 2002) (release ineffective after skiing accident). Complicating the picture even further is the judicial doctrine of parent immunity, which prohibits a child from suing his/her parents for injury. *Squeglia v. Squeglia*, 234 Conn. 259 (1995). Any waiver that would seek to have the parent indemnify the school district for damages awarded the child due to injury may be unenforceable under this doctrine as well.

The question of permission slips stands on a different footing. Permission slips do not purport to serve as a waiver of future liability claims, but rather provide notification to parents of school activities that are out of the ordinary. These permission slips can serve an important function — they provide the parents notice of the special situation and give the parents the opportunity to bring any special concerns to the attention of school personnel.

The use of permission slips has its downside as well. If a parent puts school personnel on notice of special circumstances, through a permission slip or through emergency health information, it is far more likely that a failure to take precautions will result in a finding of liability. Since the district was aware of the special circumstance in such a case, its failure to follow through would likely be seen as unreasonable and thus would lead to a finding of liability for negligence.

f. Insurance

Risks relating to liability for negligence claims are not generally personal risks because in most cases school board members and other school officials are indemnified and held personally harmless by statute, as discussed below at Section G(4). However, indemnity does not reduce liability, but rather simply shifts the responsibility for payment. School boards are therefore well advised to audit their insurance policies to assure that they have protection against such claims, including claims for injuries suffered in an assault under Conn. Gen. Stat. § 10-236a.

If insurance is in place, it is critically important to notify the insurance company promptly of any claim. Coverage may be denied if the district delays unreasonably in notifying the carrier of the claim because such delay may prejudice the rights of the carrier and may violate the terms of the insurance policy.

2. Defamation

Another liability issue that occasionally arises in school districts is defamation, *i.e.* libelous (printed) or slanderous (verbal) comments that damage one's reputation. School board members, administrators and even teachers may be unfairly criticized by parents or others and wish to sue. Teachers may feel that they have been defamed through a negative evaluation. Sometimes a claim of defamation may be valid. In such cases, the provisions of Conn. Gen. Stat. § 52-237 may be of interest. This statute provides that damages in a defamation case may be limited to actual, economic damage if within a reasonable time the defendant retracts the defamatory statement in as public a manner as the original statement was made. Defamation claims in the public sector, however, will generally be unsuccessful for four reasons.

First, there are basic limitations on the scope of a defamation claim. No one can recover in defamation unless he or she can prove the communication of an untrue statement of fact concerning him or her. Truth is an absolute defense (at least to defamation claims). Moreover, if a statement expresses an opinion (rather than presents a claim of fact), there is no defamation. For example, a supervisor's statement that he had "serious concerns" regarding an employee's performance was not defamatory because it was his opinion, not an assertion of fact. *Iosa v. Gentiva Health Services, Inc.*, 299 F. Supp.2d 29 (D. Conn. 2004). *But see Milkovich v. Lorain Journal*, 497 U.S. 1 (1990) (a statement of opinion that can be interpreted as a factual allegation can support a defamation claim).

Second, when school officials testify in court or in administrative proceedings, there is an absolute privilege against liability for defamation. The courts have held that the interest in unfettered testimony in judicial and/or quasi-judicial proceedings outweighs the public interest in protecting people against defamation. This principle was extended in an appellate court decision to grievance proceedings in a case in which an employee sued his former girlfriend for defamation after she testified against him in an arbitration proceeding over his termination. *Preston v. O'Rourke*, 74 Conn. App. 301 (2002). There is also an absolute privilege when one fills out the UC-61 form (the "pink slip") reporting the reason for termination for purposes of a possible unemployment compensation claim because employers must be free to provide such information without fear of a lawsuit. *Petyan v. Ellis*, 200 Conn. 243 (1986).

Third, when school officials are otherwise fulfilling their responsibilities (to evaluate a teacher or to fill out an unemployment form, for example), they have a qualified privilege against liability and will not be liable for defamation claims as long as they are acting in good faith. When one must make a statement to perform a job, the law confers a qualified privilege against defamation claims, because such claims could otherwise interfere with the proper operation of the agency.

This privilege against liability for defamation, however, is "qualified" in two respects. It applies only if (1) the statement was necessary to perform a job responsibility, and (2) the statement was made in good faith. For example, school officials were immune in conveying information a parent considered defamatory, because in good faith they were fulfilling their duty to communicate with parents. *Lowe v. City of Shelton*, No. CV000069780S, 2003 Conn. Super. LEXIS 2206 (Conn. Super. Ct. 2003). *See also Muldoon v.*

Anderson, No. CV990336964S, 2003 Conn. Super. LEXIS 494 (Conn. Super. Ct. 2003) (qualified privilege extended to students who reported what appeared to them to be cheating on a quiz).

Finally, given their public responsibilities, school officials (including teachers) are "public figures" under the law of defamation. Public figures cannot recover damages against persons making defamatory remarks unless they can show malice or a reckless disregard for the truth. The rule that applies to public officials was announced by the United States Supreme Court in *New York Times v. Sullivan*, 376 U.S. 254 (1964). The Court established this higher standard for public figures because of the chilling effect defamation claims could have on persons who wish to comment on matters of public concern.

The public figure status of school board members and school administrators is clear, at least as to their public responsibilities. As we go further down the chain of command from policy-makers and executives to regular employees, however, it is not always clear who is and who is not a public figure. The case law in the various states is mixed on whether teachers are public figures subject to the *New York Times v. Sullivan* rule. Our Supreme Court, however, has resolved this issue in Connecticut. In *Kelley v. Bonney*, 221 Conn. 549 (1992), a retired teacher claimed that board members defamed him by raising questions concerning his conduct as a teacher. The court ruled, however, that teachers are public figures who must show malice or reckless disregard of the truth to recover damages for defamation. Since the teacher was unable to meet this standard, the court dismissed his claim for defamation. *See also Izzo v. Deafenbaugh*, 4 Conn. Ops. 1159 (October 12, 1998) (Superior Court).

3. Constitutional and statutory claims

School districts are bound by the same constitutional requirements as other agencies of government. In addition, school districts are subject to a variety of state and federal laws, the violation of which can give rise to a liability claim. For example, in 1992 the United States Supreme Court decided that a female student could sue her school district for money damages for violating her rights under Title IX, the federal statute prohibiting discrimination on the basis of gender. *Franklin v. Gwinnett County Public Schools*, 503 U.S. 60 (1992).

The primary source of liability for the violation of statutory and constitutional rights of third persons is 42 U.S.C. § 1983, a law first passed as part of the Civil Rights Act of 1871. That law provides people who claim that their constitutional or statutory rights were violated by an official of government have the right to sue that official for damages. Such claims are called "Section 1983" claims because they are authorized by the quoted statute, 42 U.S.C. § 1983.

In 1978, the United States Supreme Court held that local governments, including school districts, are "persons" under this statute and therefore may be sued for damages. *Monell v. Department of Social Services*, 436 U.S. 658 (1978). Moreover, the Court has held that members of a board of education may be sued individually for actions that violate a person's constitutional or statutory rights. *Wood v. Strickland*, 420 U.S. 308 (1975). Thus, if a student were expelled from school without the hearing provided for by statute, he could sue the school board under 42 U.S.C. § 1983. Similarly, a teacher who alleges that she was transferred because of her exercise of her free speech rights may sue the school board under Section 1983.

Section 1983 claims are very troublesome for boards of education. First, school officials may be liable for damages in such cases. The United States Supreme Court has ruled that damages in such cases must be designed to compensate the injured party for the wrong he or she suffered, and the courts are not to base damages on the abstract "value" of constitutional rights. *Memphis Community School District v. Stachura*, 477 U.S. 299 (1986). Nonetheless, "actual damages" can include a variety of claims in addition to out of pocket losses (as in an illegal dismissal), such as claims for impairment of reputation, personal humiliation, mental anguish and suffering, and mental and emotional distress. *Id.* In one case, a teacher alleged that his school district retaliated against him for speaking out concerning the grievance procedure, travel reimbursement and other issues. The federal district court awarded him damages of $514,333. While the Court of Appeals found that amount to be excessive, it remanded with a direction that damages should fall in the "reasonable" range of between $200,000 and $400,000. *Knapp v. Whitaker*, 757 F.2d. 827 (7th Cir. 1985).

Two recent decisions of the United States Supreme Court concerning sexual harassment show the expanding scope of civil rights litigation in the schools. In 1998, the United States Supreme Court decided that in limited circumstances school districts may be held liable in a Section 1983 action under Title IX for sexual harassment of students by teachers. *Gebser v. Lago Vista Independent School District*, 524 U.S. 274 (1998). Then, in 1999 the Court held that school districts can be liable for student-to-student sexual harassment. *Davis v. Monroe Country Board of Education*, 526 U.S. 629

(1999). These cases, both decided on a 5 to 4 vote, hold that school districts can be liable for sexual harassment of students if school officials with the authority to act are actually aware of sexual harassment but fail to respond or respond so inadequately that the response can be considered "deliberate indifference." This high standard makes it unlikely that a single incident would result in liability, but it opens the door to related litigation.

These decisions underscore the need for school officials to take immediate and appropriate action when sexual harassment or abuse is alleged. Moreover, school officials who fail to respond vigorously to any potential problem of sexual harassment or abuse by teachers may be found liable for damages under principles of negligence law, irrespective of Title IX. One Superior Court decision holds that a school district may be liable for a teacher's abuse of a student if the district was negligent in hiring a teacher with a criminal record involving sexual misconduct. *Doe v. Edwards*, 16 Conn. L. Rptr. No. 6, 202 (April 8, 1996). In 1999, another Superior Court decision held that a school district may be liable at common law for the negligent failure to adopt and enforce policies and procedures for the prevention of sexual abuse of students by teachers. *Doe v. Vibert*, 5 Conn. Ops. 874 (August 2, 1999) (Superior Court).

Constitutional claims have been permitted in Connecticut in situations other than sexual harassment or abuse. In *Davis v. City of Hartford*, 4 Conn. Ops. 1321 (November 16, 1998) (D. Conn.), the federal district court ruled that there is a private direct cause of action for an unlawful search and seizure in violation of the Fourth Amendment. Though this case arose in a criminal law context, its reasoning could be applied by a student who claimed that a search by school officials violated his/her Fourth Amendment rights.

In *McPhail v. City of Milford*, 5 Conn. Ops. 326 (March 22, 1999), the Superior Court held that a parent can even maintain an action for injunctive and declaratory relief, and perhaps for money damages, for the alleged denial of an elementary and secondary education to which all students are entitled under the Connecticut Constitution. The *Davis* and *McPhail* cases were not decided on the merits, but rather simply on the ability of parents to maintain such lawsuits. They show, however, that it will be difficult for school districts to avoid trials on such allegations, which can be very costly.

In addition to the risks of damages in such cases, school districts often have to be even more concerned about attorney's fees. 42 U.S.C. § 1988 provides that a person who prevails in a Section 1983 case is entitled to reimbursement of his or her attorney's fees. The United States Supreme Court has ruled that a person prevails if the litigation results in a change in the government's position on any point of significance. *Hensley v. Eckerhart*, 461 U.S. 424 (1983). Therefore, a school district may be liable for attorney's fees even when the plaintiff loses on many of his claims against the district as long as he prevails on one point.

Two additional issues regarding attorney's fees in Section 1983 litigation should be considered. First, the award of attorney's fees need not be related to the size of the damage award. *City of Riverside v. Rivera*, 477 U.S. 561 (1986). If a district defends against a Section 1983 claim and loses, it will be liable for the plaintiff's fees, even if the plaintiff only receives nominal damages. Since the district has no control over how aggressively opposing counsel pursues the case, and since litigation is very expensive to resolve problems under the best of circumstances, fee awards under Section 1983 can be very expensive.

Second, the United States Supreme Court recently eliminated the basis for many attorneys' fees awards. In *Buckhannon Board & Care Home, Inc. v. West Virginia Department of Health and Human Services*, 532 U.S. 598 (2001), the Court rejected the "catalyst" theory that the lower courts had used in many fee awards. Previously, if a government defendant changed its position in response to a lawsuit, the courts would find that the plaintiff was a "prevailing party" because the relationship between the parties had changed. In *Buckhannon*, however, the Court ruled that a plaintiff attains prevailing party status (and the attendant eligibility for attorneys' fees) only when there is a court decision or court-supervised consent decree. While the Court was addressing claims made under the ADA and the Fair Housing Amendments, the principle in *Buckhannon* has been applied to fee-shifting statutes across the board, including Section 1983 and the IDEA. *See J.C. v. Regional School District 10*, 278 F.3d 119 (2d Cir. 2002). Settlement agreements, therefore, do not create an entitlement to attorneys' fees under Section 1983, IDEA, Section 504 or other fee-shifting statutes.

As with negligence claims, in some situations school officials may be immune from suit, even when their actions result in the violation of constitutional or statutory rights. In *Wood v. Strickland*, 420 U.S. 308 (1975), the court held that school officials are entitled to a good faith qualified immunity for decisions they make in the course of their official responsibilities. School officials will not be liable if their action was taken "in the good faith fulfillment of their responsibilities and within the bounds of reason under all the circumstances . . . ." 420 U.S. at 321.

Such immunity, then, depends on two factors. First, the school official must have acted in good faith. "We'll get you!" or similar threats can result in the school official losing immunity. Second, the action must be reasonable. Whether action is "reasonable" as a matter of constitutional law often depends on whether the law was clear at the time, not whether the state actor was aware of the law. For example, it is clear that students have a right to a hearing before they can be expelled. A school board member who takes such an action without providing a hearing will not be immune from liability because he did not intend to act unconstitutionally. If a school official knew or reasonably should have known that the action violates constitutional rights, or if the school official acts with malice, he or she will be liable, despite the qualified immunity otherwise available in Section 1983 actions. *Harlow v. Fitzgerald*, 457 U.S. 800 (1982). *See Gruenke v. Seip*, 225 F.3d 290 (3rd Cir. 2000).

4. <u>Indemnification</u>

Despite the various risks of liability outlined above, school officials have extensive protection from personal liability under Connecticut law. Conn. Gen. Stat. § 10-235 provides that the school district must indemnify and hold school board members, school board employees, student teachers, and volunteers harmless from civil liability in most situations. For any such board member, teacher, other employee, student teacher or volunteer, the school district must pay any damages awarded to a plaintiff in an action brought alleging negligence or other act resulting in injury, including infringement of that person's civil rights.

Also, of equal or perhaps even greater interest, the school district is responsible for the reasonable attorney's fees incurred in defending the school district employee or school board member against such claims. Generally the school district will simply refer the matter to the insurance carrier, which will then appoint counsel, and the employee will not have to pay any money up front for legal fees. Given that the school district must hold the employee harmless against such fees, the employee or other school official could retain counsel and send the district the bill. However, employees generally do not take this approach, because there could be a dispute over whether such fees were "reasonable." Moreover, in interpreting the analogous indemnity statutes applicable to municipal employees (Conn. Gen. Stat. § 7-101a and Conn. Gen. Stat. § 7-465) the Superior Court held in one case that the municipality had the right to appoint legal counsel for a municipal defendant. *Cusick v. City of New Haven*, No. CV010453210S, 2002 Conn. Super. LEXIS

2906 (Conn. Super. Ct. 2002). Where there are no conflicts in interests among various school district defendants, it is more economical and more reasonable for one lawyer to represent the various defendants in the lawsuit.

There are two special rules that apply to volunteers. First, Conn. Gen. Stat. § 10-235 extends the protection of the indemnity statute to volunteers as long as the volunteer is (1) approved by the board of education to carry out a duty prescribed by the board, and (2) under the direction of a certified staff member. In addition, in 1997 the United States Congress passed the Volunteer Protection Act, 42 U.S.C. § 14501 *et seq.* This new law provides that volunteers are protected from liability for accidents that occur when volunteering for a non-profit organization or governmental entity. The Superior Court applied this law to find that a volunteer member of the Booster Club for Regional School District No. 9 was immune from liability for injuries suffered by a person selling tickets, who was injured when the ticket booth constructed by the Boosters' Club collapsed on her. *Gaudet v. Braca*, 31 Conn. L. Rptr. No. 2, 53 (January 21, 2002).

There are two conditions to the obligation to indemnify board members, board employees, student teachers and volunteers. First, the person must be acting "in the discharge of his or her duties or within the scope of employment or under the direction of such board of education." Conn. Gen. Stat. § 10-235. Normally, it is clear when a person is acting within the scope of his or her duties. Ambiguous situations can arise, however, such as when an English teacher takes two students to watch a play in New York, without following the established procedures for field trips. School districts, therefore, should adopt and implement clear procedures for special activities to be reviewed and approved. If a teacher does not identify an activity as a school-sponsored activity by following such procedures, he or she may act at his/her own risk. If approval procedures are in place, the district is better able to argue that it is not obligated to provide indemnification for the private actions of the teacher.

The second requirement is that the actions complained of not be "wanton, reckless or malicious." A problem can arise in defending school officials when such conduct is alleged because if the allegations are proven, there is no protection under the indemnity statute. In 1990, the General Assembly addressed this issue by adding Conn. Gen. Stat. § 10-235(b). That provision states that the school district must protect and save harmless any school board member or other school official against whom a claim is made that he or she has committed a "malicious, wanton or willful act or *ultra vires* act," *i.e.* an act outside his or her statutory authority. If the school official is found not to have engaged in such action, he or she is fully protected. However, if ultimately it is determined that the school official did commit such a malicious or *ultra vires* act, the employee must reimburse the district for the expense of providing a defense. Moreover, that school employee will not be indemnified against any verdict that results from such a finding.

The Connecticut Supreme Court interpreted this provision in the indemnity statute in 2002. The case involved a teacher who admitted to allegations of serious misconduct, including sexual assault and battery against a female student. Nonetheless, when the student sued for damages, he demanded that the school district provide a legal defense, and he brought suit against the school district when it refused. The trial court ruled in his favor, but the Supreme Court, reversed. *Vibert v. Board of Education of Regional School District No. 10*, 260 Conn. 167 (2002). The court held that boards of education need not provide a defense under Conn. Gen. Stat. § 10-235. It noted, however, that boards of education act at their peril in such cases, because they will be liable for indemnification of any liability *and* reasonable attorney's fees if it is found that the acts in question were within the scope of employment and were not malicious, wanton or willful. Under the circumstances of the *Vibert* case, however, the decision of the school district was understandable, given the serious misconduct to which the teacher admitted.

There is need for further clarification by the courts concerning one aspect of Conn. Gen. Stat. § 10-235. Some plaintiffs have tried to make the school district (the "deep pocket") a defendant by asserting that Section 10-235 creates a direct cause of action against the school district (since the district will likely indemnify the teacher eventually anyway). The Superior Court, however, has split on this issue, and neither the Appellate Court nor the Connecticut Supreme Court has ruled on the subject. The majority view is that Conn. Gen. Stat. § 10-235 does not establish a direct cause of action against a school district. *See, e.g., Duffs v. McClendon*, No. CV010182286S, 2001 Conn. Super. LEXIS 1024 (Conn. Super. Ct. April 12, 2001).

The broad protections conferred by the indemnity statute reflect a strong public policy in favor of protecting public employees. In construing the statute, the courts will generally apply this public policy to find for public employees in most cases. *King v. Watertown Board of Education*, 195 Conn. 90 (1985). The *Vibert* case, described above, is the exception, not the rule. Public employees doing the public's work in good faith will be protected.

CHAPTER TWO
RELIGION AND THE SCHOOLS

The matter of religion in the schools has received more attention from the United States Supreme Court than any other issue of school law. The relevant provision in the United States Constitution is short. The First Amendment provides:

> Congress shall make no law respecting an establishment of religion, or prohibiting the free exercise thereof; or abridging the freedom of speech, or of the press; or the right of the people peaceably to assemble, and to petition the Government for a redress of grievances.

There are only eleven words dealing with religion. However, almost every year the United States Supreme Court issues a new decision on religion in the schools. Can students have a Bible study club? Can there be prayer at graduation? Can legislators enact a voucher program that benefits sectarian schools? Can the state provide computers to religious schools? Can a separate school district be set up for persons of a particular religious group? May a school district refuse to permit a religious group to rent the school auditorium? Must it? The Court has addressed all of these questions and many others just since 1990.

There are two basic issues involving religion in the schools. First, and more common, the question is whether a particular action by government (and here the "government" can be the Congress, the state legislature, the mayor or the school board) should be considered an "establishment of religion" in violation of the First Amendment. Text book loans, tax breaks, vouchers, state funding for religious schools, prayer at graduation—all of these matters and more have been challenged as state support for religion in violation of the Establishment Clause.

Free exercise of religion is the other major issue for school districts. The government may not interfere with the rights of students, their parents, or employees to exercise their religion freely, and that prohibition has led to a number of challenges. Parents have sought to have their children excused from the mandatory attendance laws or from certain school activities. Other parents have sought to force school districts to change the curriculum to conform to their religious views. Teachers get into the act as well, with claims that they should be allowed extensive leave for religious activities or should be permitted to wear religious dress while teaching.

The two basic issues in the First Amendment religion cases may be stated separately, but they are interrelated. For example, the "free exercise" right of the teacher to wear religious dress in school can be the "establishment" problem for the parent who claims that his or her child is being proselytized at school. Accommodation to one parent's demands regarding the curriculum on Free Exercise grounds can result in an Establishment Clause claim by another. Often school officials try to reconcile these two obligations without knowing for certain whether they are violating one or the other.

Religion in the schools has been the subject of entire books, and a comprehensive analysis is beyond the scope of this Guide. However, the following review of the general principles and the major cases may be helpful in understanding district obligations in such matters.

A. "Congress shall make no law respecting an establishment of religion"

The issue of religion in the schools first assumed prominence in the 1960s. In 1962, the United States Supreme Court held that the reading of a daily prayer in the New York schools was unconstitutional, *Engel v. Vitale,* 370 U.S. 421 (1962). The very next year the Court held that laws in Pennsylvania and Maryland requiring the reading of Bible verses in the schools violated the First Amendment. *Abington v. Schempp*, 374 U.S. 203 (1963). These cases signaled a major shift in the law concerning religion in the schools.

Since 1971, the actions of school districts and other agents of government have been considered under a three-part test announced by the United States Supreme Court in *Lemon v. Kurtzman*, 403 U.S. 602 (1971). To determine whether government action regarding religion in the schools is consistent with constitutional obligations imposed by the Establishment Clause, the courts will ask the following questions:

- Is there a secular purpose for the action?
- Does the action have a primary effect that neither advances nor inhibits religion?
- Does the action avoid an excessive government entanglement with religion?

The Court has applied this "*Lemon* test" in most of the Establishment Clause cases since 1971, though the courts focus sometimes on the "coercion" inherent in governmental endorsement of prayer or other religious activities.

For example, in deciding *Lee v. Weisman* in 1992, the Court did not use the *Lemon* test when it held that prayer at graduation exercises is unconstitutional. Moreover, in a 1993 case, Justice Scalia issued a strong dissent which described the *Lemon* test as follows:

> As to the Court's invocation of the *Lemon* test: Like some ghoul in a late-night horror movie that repeatedly sits up in its grave and shuffles abroad, after being repeatedly killed and buried, *Lemon* stalks our Establishment Clause jurisprudence once again, frightening the little children and school attorneys . . . .

Lamb's Chapel v. Center Moriches Union Free School District, 508 U.S. 384 (1993) (Scalia, J. dissenting). Given these developments, the demise of the *Lemon* test appeared imminent. However, since *Lee v. Weisman*, the Court has applied the *Lemon* test in a number of different cases. Consequently, unless and until the Court takes a different approach to Establishment Clause issues, the *Lemon* test remains a good place to start the analysis.

1. Transportation, textbooks, materials and equipment

Parents of students in parochial schools already support the public schools through their taxes, and some legislators have attempted to enact laws requiring the state to provide these students with some of the same benefits that are provided to students in public school. When one can establish that the benefit of the law goes to the children, not to the religious school, such laws will be held constitutional. When the primary beneficiary of the legislation is the religious school, historically the law has been struck down. Recent case developments, however, are breaking down this distinction, and in the past several years the United States Supreme Court has shown itself to be willing to overturn past precedents and to permit aid in various forms to be provided on the site of sectarian schools, and in one case even to go to the religious schools themselves.

a. Transportation

The United States Supreme Court dealt with both transportation and textbooks in cases decided before the *Lemon* test was announced. In 1947, the Court held constitutional a program of reimbursement to parents for the expense of providing transportation to either public or non-public schools. The Court relied on the "child benefit" theory, *i.e.* government benefits may be extended to children enrolled in parochial schools if there is a secular purpose in the enactment (here, safe transportation to school) and the primary beneficiaries of such government action are the children. *Everson v. Board of Education*, 330 U.S. 1 (1947).

This decision left the issue of transportation for students enrolled in private schools up to the individual state legislatures. In Connecticut, municipalities or school districts are required to provide the same transportation services to students enrolled in non-public schools within the town as are provided to the public school students, as long as a majority of the children attending the non-public school are residents of Connecticut. Conn. Gen. Stat. § 10-281. If the cost of such transportation exceeds double the cost of transportation for students in the public schools, the municipality or school district may pay the proportionate share of such costs up to a maximum of twice the regular per pupil cost. Also, parents of students receiving such transportation have the same right to review the provision of transportation services as do parents of students in the public schools under Conn. Gen. Stat. § 10-186. *Id.* In providing such transportation services, school districts will be reimbursed by the state on the same basis as they are reimbursed for transportation costs for students enrolled in the public schools.

The scope of the obligation to provide transportation services to students in private schools was clarified by the Connecticut Supreme Court in 1998. The Court ruled that boards of education are obligated to provide transportation to such schools on all school days, whether or not the public schools are open on the day in question. *Board of Education of the Town of Stafford v. State Board of Education*, 243 Conn. 772 (1998). The Court rejected the Board's argument that such transportation was not "the same kind of transportation" since the public schools were not in session on those days. In addition, the Court rejected the argument that requiring school districts to provide such transportation to sectarian schools would violate the Establishment Clause.

School districts in Connecticut also have the option of providing transportation to students enrolled in non-public schools outside of the school district. Conn. Gen. Stat. § 10-280a. This law was first passed in 1978 and was promptly challenged in federal court. Plaintiffs claimed that such transportation was a special benefit to students enrolled in parochial schools, because students enrolled in the public schools could not receive transportation to a school of their choice out of district. The court ruled, however, that such transportation is constitutional and confers no special benefit on such students. *Cromwell Property Owners Association v. Toffolon*, 495 F. Supp. 915 (D. Conn. 1979). However, since this case was decided, the General Assembly has eliminated all provisions for state reimbursement for such transportation services, and few if any Connecticut school districts provide such transportation services to non-public schools outside of the town. Conn. Gen. Stat. § 10-280a.

b. Textbooks

The United States Supreme Court has also considered whether school districts may provide textbooks to children enrolled in non-public schools, including parochial schools. In 1968, the Court reviewed a New York statute which required local boards of education to loan textbooks to students enrolled in the non-public schools. Again the Court relied on the "child benefit" theory and held that such loans are permissible. *Board of Education of Central School District No. 1 v. Allen*, 392 U.S. 236 (1968). While Connecticut does not require that textbooks be loaned to students in non-public schools, the law permits local and regional boards of education to loan textbooks to such pupils, at the request of the student or his/her parent. Conn. Gen. Stat. § 10-228a.

c. Educational materials and equipment

The analysis of the Establishment Clause becomes murkier, if not incoherent, when we consider cases involving other attempts by government to provide services to children enrolled in non-public schools. Over the years, different states have attempted to enact various measures in addition to textbook programs to provide assistance to the non-public schools. For years, such attempts failed under the *Lemon* test, because most non-public schools are sectarian, and support for education in such schools was considered support for religious activity. *Meek v. Pittinger*, 421 U.S. 349 (1975); *Wolman v. Walter*, 433 U.S. 229 (1977). In addition, in several decisions the Court held that instructional services supported by public funds must be provided on a neutral site. More recently, however, the United States Supreme Court has been more tolerant of aid programs that benefit private sectarian schools, with the only limitation being that such schools cannot be singled out for special benefit.

The requirement that state-supported services be provided on a neutral site died some years ago in *Zobrest* and *Agostini*, discussed below at Section A(3). The broader prohibitions of *Meek* and *Wolman*, however, were eliminated in 2000. In *Mitchell v. Helms*, 530 U.S. 793 (2000), the Court considered a federal program that distributes aid to local and state governments, which those governments then use to lend educational materials to public and private schools. Plaintiffs claimed that lending educational materials to sectarian schools violated the Establishment Clause, because such aid benefited the sectarian schools directly. They distinguished programs that provided benefits to individual children (which can be defended under the "child benefit theory," discussed above), and asked the Court to rule the program unconstitutional.

Under *Meek* and *Wolman*, the program would have been deemed unconstitutional. However, in recent years, the Court has taken a different view of neutrality, and it has held that benefits that are generally available should not be denied to religious organizations solely because of their involvement with religion. *See, e.g., Lamb's Chapel v. Center Moriches Union Free School District*, 508 U.S. 384 (1993). It was no big surprise, therefore, that the Court explicitly reversed its prior rulings in *Meek* and *Wolman* to hold that a program that provides aid equally to all schools, whether or not they are sectarian, meets the strictures of the Establishment Clause.

Clearly, there is a trend of greater tolerance of providing funds to support religious activities, either indirectly or even directly. It remains difficult, however, to determine just where to draw the line. It has been permissible to provide transportation and textbooks to students enrolled in sectarian schools for many years. It has not been clear, however, when public funds can be used for programs that provide educational equipment to sectarian schools. Given the sharply divided Court, it does not appear that *Mitchell* has resolved this thorny issue.

2. Reimbursements, tax breaks and vouchers

Various efforts have also been made over the years to provide the parents of children in parochial schools with reimbursement of their tuition and other expenses. Shortly after the United States Supreme Court decided the *Lemon* case, Pennsylvania passed a new statute which provided for tuition reimbursement to parents. However, the Court ruled that this statute was unconstitutional, because its effect was to support religious schools. *Sloan v. Lemon*, 413 U.S. 825 (1973). In a companion case involving a similar New York law, the Court ruled that the fact that the parents were the recipients of the funds did not change the analysis—the program was unconstitutional because the money would go to the parochial institution. *Committee for Public Education v. Nyquist*, 413 U.S. 756 (1973).

At the same time, the Court also addressed challenges to other statutes which provided for reimbursement directly to parochial schools for maintenance and repair expenses. Sponsors of these laws had argued that such expenses did not relate to the "religious" activities of the schools and thus could be reimbursed. However, the Court found that such state programs had the purpose and/or effect of advancing religion and, as such, were unconstitutional. *Committee for Public Education v. Nyquist*, 413 U.S. 756 (1973); *Levitt v. Committee for Public Education and Religious Liberty*, 413 U.S. 472 (1973).

Another challenged provision in the New York statute in question in the *Nyquist* case concerned income tax benefits. Parents of children in private schools were permitted to reduce their gross income by a specified amount, which of course conferred a tax benefit on such families. The Court found this provision to be unconstitutional because it "rewarded" parents who sent their children to non-public schools, the vast majority of which were religious schools.

Ten years later, however, the Court reviewed and upheld a Minnesota law which provided deductions for parents of actual expenses (up to a stated maximum) for tuition, textbooks and transportation of any dependent attending school. The Court found the statute to be constitutional even though children in the public schools received these services without cost, and thus the beneficiaries of this law were overwhelmingly families with children in religious schools. The Court determined that support for parents' expenses in educating their children was a secular purpose, that any benefit to the parochial schools was incidental, and that the entanglement problems were no worse than those implicated in a textbook loan program. *Mueller v. Allen*, 463 U.S. 388 (1983).

The *Mueller* decision was a harbinger of the Court's ruling in 2002 on vouchers in *Zelman v. Simmons-Harris*, 536 U.S. 639 (2002). The voucher program at issue in *Zelman* involved two forms of assistance, tuition assistance and tutorial aid. In 1999-2000, no public school districts elected to participate in the program, but forty-six private schools elected to do so. Of these, 82% had a religious affiliation, accounting for 96% of the students participating in the program. As a consequence, the federal district court found that the program violated the Establishment Clause, and this decision was affirmed by the Court of Appeals. The United States Supreme Court, however, reversed.

Writing for the majority, Chief Justice Rehnquist stated that the voucher program in Cleveland does not violate the Establishment Clause because any public funds that benefit sectarian schools are directed by the private choice of the individual participants, not by direct government action. The Court cited *Mueller v. Allen*, 463 U.S. 388 (1983), as well as *Witters v. Washington Department of Services for the Blind*, 474 U.S. 481 (1986), (federal funds can be spent to support tuition at a religious institution), and *Zobrest v. Catalina Foothills School District*, 509 U.S. 1 (1993) (IDEA Part B funds may be used to pay for a sign language interpreter at a parochial school). Common to each of these situations was that the benefit, direct or indirect, to the sectarian institution was the result of the private choice of the parent (or student in *Witters*). Based on these precedents, the Court upheld the voucher program.

This decision was presaged by decisions of various state courts. For example, the Wisconsin Supreme Court ruled in 1998 that the amended Milwaukee Parental Choice Program does not violate the Establishment Clause. *Jackson v. Benson*, 578 N.W.2d 602 (Wisconsin, 1998). The court applied the *Lemon* test, and held that the provision of vouchers that may be used in private non-sectarian or private sectarian schools was neutral as regards religion. In so ruling, the court relied upon a number of decisions of the United States Supreme Court, including *Zobrest*, *Agostini*, and *Rosenberger*, discussed at Section A(6). *See also Kotterman v. Killian*, 972 P.2d 606 (Ariz. 1999), *cert. denied*, 528 U.S. 921 (1999) (tax credit for donations to organization that makes grants for tuition, mainly for sectarian schools, is permissible under the Establishment Clause).

In addition, state courts have considered challenges to school vouchers under state constitutional principles. Given that a voucher program has not been adopted in Connecticut, there are no court decisions considering state constitutional issues here. In *Jackson v. Benson*, discussed above, however, the Wisconsin Supreme Court also held that the voucher program did not violate the Wisconsin constitution. In a case involving the voucher program at issue in *Zelman,* the Ohio Supreme Court reached the same conclusion, holding that the intervening parent choice to send children to private schools (the vast majority of which are sectarian) eliminates concern that the state is supporting religion. *Simmons-Harris v. Goff*, 711 N.E.2d 203 (Ohio 1999). By contrast, an appellate court in Florida has ruled that a voucher program violates the Florida constitution. *Holmes v. Bush*, 2002 WL 1809079 (Fla. Cir. Ct. 2002).

The *Zelman* decision moves the voucher debate from issues of constitutional law to issues of public policy. It will likely encourage proponents of voucher programs, and it is important that arguments against such programs be marshaled. Many argue that vouchers would inappropriately divert scarce public dollars to schools that, unlike the public schools, do not subject their students to the rigors of state testing and that do not have to provide education to all children, irrespective of disability or discipline issues. Moreover, the case against vouchers is especially strong now, following the No Child Left Behind Act. Under that law, schools must demonstrate adequate yearly progress, and when schools do not do so for a specified period, students have the right to obtain third-party support services and/or to transfer to another school in the school district. Given this new statutory scheme, a separate program for vouchers would be ill-advised.

Finally, the fact that voucher programs may be legal does not prevent states from deciding to exclude religious schools from such programs. In *Locke v. Davey*, 124 S.Ct. 1307 (2004), the United States Supreme Court upheld a law in Washington state that excluded devotional theology from a scholarship program. The Court ruled that, though the Establishment Clause did not require exclusion of such studies from the scholarship program, the statute doing so did not violate the free exercise rights of the student. Similarly, since the program was not a forum for student speech, the Court dismissed the student's free speech claims as well. *See also Strout v. Albanese*, 178 F.3d 57 (1st Cir. 1999), *cert. denied*, 528 U.S. 931 (1999) (no violation of the Free Exercise or Establishment Clauses in excluding religious schools from tuition subsidy program for districts that do not operate their own schools).

3. <u>Teachers and educational services</u>

Direct subsidy of teacher salaries in sectarian schools was prohibited early on, in the *Lemon* case itself. After *Lemon*, therefore, there were several attempts to establish publicly-funded instructional programs at non-public schools. However, in large part, these programs were struck down as well. Two leading cases dealt with a program for supplementary instruction in Grand Rapids and a program for educationally disadvantaged children in New York. *School District of the City of Grand Rapids v. Ball*, 473 U.S. 373 (1985); *Aguilar v. Felton*, 473 U.S. 402 (1985). In both cases, the Court held the programs had the impermissible effect of advancing religion by funding teaching activities on the site of the sectarian school. The Supreme Court reversed these decisions in 1997 and teaching and other services may now be provided on the site of the sectarian school. *Agostini v. Felton*, 521 U.S. 203 (1997) (discussed below). *Aguilar and Grand Rapids*, however, are an important part of the history and analysis of the Establishment Clause.

Following *Aguilar* and *Grand Rapids*, many members of the Supreme Court expressed concern that the Establishment Clause may not prohibit provision of educational services on the site of a sectarian school. In 1993, for example, the Court ruled that public funds could be used to pay for the services of a sign language interpreter at a parochial school site. *Zobrest v. Catalina Foothills School District*, 509 U.S. 1 (1993). There, a student enrolled in a sectarian school claimed that the regulations under the federal special education law mandated that this service be provided. The United States Department of Education took the position that the regulations in force at the time did not require the provision of such services. When it decided *Zobrest*, however, the Court considered only the constitutional issue. The Court held that the provision of a sign language interpreter on the parochial school site was constitutional, because the service provided was a neutral benefit that the student could receive regardless of whether he was enrolled in a public or in a sectarian school.

A Supreme Court decision in 1994 further suggested that the Court would reconsider the issue of providing services on the site of a religious school. In *Board of Education of Kiryas Joel v. Grumet*, 512 U.S. 687 (1994), the Court considered the situation of the Village of Kiryas Joel, a community of Hasidic Jews. Most of the children in the village were educated in private yeshivas, but the children with disabilities were educated in annexes to the religious schools. Following the rulings in *Aguilar* and *Grand Rapids,* school officials determined that they could not continue to provide the services at the religious schools and offered services to children with disabilities at the public schools. However, the parents did not want to send their children to the public schools outside the Hasidic community, and the children with disabilities were left in the middle. To break the impasse, the legislature created a new school district with the same boundaries as the village. Public officials then established a new "public school" providing special education solely for these disabled Hasidic children residing in the new district (*i.e.* the village). This action was challenged as an establishment of religion.

The United States Supreme Court agreed, holding that the action violated the duty to remain neutral in matters of religion. The Court found that, by drawing the boundaries to create a district that includes only persons of the one religious sect (a "district" with only thirteen local, full-time students in special education and remedial programs), the legislature was acting to benefit members of one particular religion, in violation of the Establishment Clause. *See also Grumet v. Pataki*, 93 N.Y.2d 677 (1999), *cert. denied*, 528 U.S. 946 (1999) (subsequent legislative attempt to enable the Village of Kiryas Joel to reestablish its own publicly funded school district struck down). Significantly, however, in *Kiryas Joel* a majority of the Court noted in passing that the *Aguilar* and *Grand Rapids* decisions should be reconsidered and perhaps overruled.

In 1997, the Court followed formally overruled *Aguilar* and that portion of *Grand Rapids* that dealt with a similar provision. *Agostini v. Felton*, 521 U.S. 203 (1997). A group of parents in New York noted the evolution of the Court's pronouncements in this area and challenged the prohibition against Title I services on the site of a parochial school. The Court held that it would no longer presume that the presence of a publicly paid teacher on the site of a parochial school would have the impermissible effect of advancing religion by creating a symbolic union between government and religion. Relying on its decision in *Zobrest*, the Court held that the provision of Title I services was analogous to provision of services by a sign language interpreter, and that such services could be provided on the site of the religious school without violating the First Amendment.

In *Agostini*, the Court elaborated on the second prong of the *Lemon* test, and provided a framework for analyzing whether a program impermissibly advances religion: (1) whether the aid results in governmental indoctrination, (2) whether the paid program defines its recipients by religious affiliation, and (3) whether the aid creates an excessive entanglement between government and religion. As with the *Lemon* test, these considerations are not self-defining, and they can be applied to the same situation by different people and yield different results. These factors were cited in both the plurality and concurring opinions in *Mitchell v. Helms*, for example, but the two sides analyzed them very differently.

4. <u>School facilities</u>

Church groups also request opportunities to use school facilities, and here too we see an evolution in the law. Traditionally, school districts have been reluctant to permit church groups to use school facilities, because school officials have been concerned that such use would be seen as support for religion. However, under the First Amendment school districts generally may not treat church groups less favorably than other groups. Federal courts have held, for example, that churches should have the same right to rent school facilities outside of school hours as do other community groups. In 1993, the United States Supreme Court got into the act, ruling against a school district that had denied a church-related group the right to rent the school auditorium to show a movie series that dealt with family issues "from a Christian perspective." In *Lamb's Chapel v. Center Moriches Union Free School District*, 508 U.S. 384 (1993), the Court ruled that the district could not discriminate against the religious viewpoint of the church group.

In 2001, the United States Supreme Court addressed this issue again. *Good News Club v. Milford Central School*, 533 U.S. 98 (2001). There, the Court ruled that a school district could not discriminate against a group that sought to use school facilities after school for religious activities. The district had been concerned that permitting the group to use the facilities would violate the Establishment Clause because the activities (which included Bible lessons, memorizing scripture, and singing religious songs) involved elementary school students. The Court ruled, however, that it was illegal viewpoint discrimination to single out the religious group.

Consistent with the requirement of equal treatment, school districts must take care not to discriminate between religious groups. *See Full Gospel Tabernacle v. Community School District No. 27*, 164 F.3d 829 (2d Cir. 1999). Moreover, the school district must assure that a religious group is treated as are other groups (because a favorable rental rate only for religious groups would be support for religion), and must take care to assure that such use does not convey a message of governmental support for religion (by limiting such use to non-school hours). *See also Campbell v. St. Tammany's School Board*, 206 F.3d 482 (5th Cir. 2000).

Similar claims can arise concerning access by persons with a religious message. In *DiLoreto v. Board of Education of Downey United School District*, 196 F.3d 958 (9th Cir. 1999) *cert. den.* 529 U.S. 1067 (2000), the Ninth Circuit Court of Appeals reviewed a claim by a member of the public who wanted to post a copy of the Ten Commandments on the school's athletic field fence. Since the fence was available for commercial advertising, he claimed that it was a violation of his First Amendment rights not to be able to buy space for his message, albeit a religious one. The court disagreed, however, and ruled that the athletic fence was not a public forum. Given legitimate pedagogical concerns about having a religious message on the outfield fence, the court held that the school district was within its rights to deny permission.

Twenty-two years ago, the United States Supreme Court invalidated a Kentucky statute that required that the Ten Commandments be posted in all public school classrooms. *Stone v. Graham*, 440 U.S. 39 (1980). Nonetheless there have been several attempts recently to bring the Ten Commandments into our public schools and other buildings, either alone on in the context of some sort of historical display. These recent efforts, however, have been unsuccessful because the courts have held that such displays advance religion in violation of the Establishment Clause. *Doe v. Harlan County School District*, 96 F. Supp.2d 667 (E.D. Ky. 2000); *Glassroth v. Moore*, 335 F.3d 1282 (11th Cir. 2003) (Ten Commandments monolith in court lobby violates Establishment Clause). *But see Freethought Society v. Chester County*, 334 F.3d 247 (3d Cir. 2003) (County not required to remove courthouse façade with Ten Commandments 80 years after installation).

5. <u>Curriculum, school activities, release time and school calendar</u>

Various state legislatures have also passed laws dealing with the curriculum, school activities, release time and the school calendar. In the constitutional challenges that followed, legislative action clearly promoting the interests of a particular religion has been struck down. Other activities, however, have been judged on whether they have the purpose or effect of advancing religion.

a. Curriculum requirements

In *Epperson v. Arkansas*, 393 U.S. 97 (1968), the United States Supreme Court considered a statute adopted by the State of Arkansas that made it unlawful for a teacher in any state-supported school "to teach the theory or doctrine that mankind ascended or descended from a lower order of animals." The Court held that the State could not require that teaching and learning be tailored to the principles of any one religious dogma, and it ruled that this prohibition against teaching evolution was unconstitutional.

Almost twenty years later, the Court reviewed another variation on this theme. In Louisiana, the legislature passed the "Balanced Treatment for Creation-Science and Evolution-Science in Public School Instruction Act." That law required that if either the theory of evolution or creation science is taught, the other theory must be taught as well. The Court found that this law was unconstitutional as well. It rejected the claim made by its defenders that the statute was intended simply to assure fairness in the presentation of these alternative theories of the creation of humanity. Rather, the Court held, the law had as its purpose the advancement of one particular religious doctrine, which has as one of its tenets "the creation of humankind by a divine creator," and therefore the law violated the First Amendment. *Edwards v. Aguillard*, 482 U.S. 578 (1987).

Most recently, the Court declined to review a decision of the Fifth Circuit Court of Appeals that struck down a "disclaimer" requirement related to the teaching of evolution. Specifically, one board of education required that teachers read a disclaimer before teaching a lesson on evolution, which included the following:

> "The lesson to be presented, regarding the origin of life and matter, is know as the Scientific Theory of Evolution and should be presented to inform students of the scientific concept and not intended to influence or dissuade the Biblical version of Creation or any other concept."

The Fifth Circuit ruled that, while theoretically a disclaimer could be neutral, this disclaimer had the effect of advancing religion (here Creationism) and was thus impermissible. *Freiler v. Tangipahoa Parish Board of Education*, 201 F.3d 602 (5th Cir. 2000), *cert. denied*, 530 U.S. 1251 (2000). Unfortunately, the court gave no guidance on how a disclaimer could be written to be "neutral."

b. Holiday celebrations and other classroom activities

One common concern is the handling of holiday celebrations in the public schools. Activities that clearly promote a particular religious faith will not be permitted. However, it is also true that holiday traditions have become part of our culture. It is not always easy to draw the line. School events that involve music and other activities related to various religious faiths, without proselytizing on behalf of any, will be appropriate under the First Amendment.

In an early decision on the subject, the Eighth Circuit Court of Appeals held that the curriculum could include discussion of holidays having both religious and secular significance, and that the study of these holidays could include religious symbols and religious music "in a prudent and objective manner and as a traditional part of the cultural and religious heritage of the particular holiday." *Florey v. Sioux Falls School District*, 619 F.2d 1311 (8th Cir. 1980), *cert. denied,* 449 U.S. 987 (1980). While people can differ as to what is a prudent and objective approach to this sensitive subject, it is clear that it is not necessary to ban traditional holiday music from the schoolhouse. *See also Bauchman by Bauchman v. West High School*, 132 F.3d 542, (10th Cir. 1997), *cert. denied*, 524 U.S. 953 (1998) (performance of religious songs, even at Christian religious sites, did not violate Establishment Clause because there was a reasonable secular purpose and a reasonable observer would not conclude that the activity had the purpose or effect of endorsing religion). *But see Skarin v. Woodbine Community School District*, 204 F. Supp.2d 1195 (S.D. Iowa 2002) (singing of "The Lord's Prayer" at graduation had the principal effect of advancing Christianity and thus violated the Constitution).

When other school activities have been challenged as advancing religion, however, the results have been mixed. The courts have considered the specific activity and whether the activity, as a matter of fact, has the effect of advancing religion in the schools in violation of the Establishment Clause. Many years ago, for example, a class on transcendental meditation was disallowed. While there was no evidence that the course would in fact cause students to convert to Hinduism, the court found that the class was based on the tenets of Hinduism and thus would advance those religious beliefs. *Malnak v. Maharashi Mahesh Yogi*, 440 F. Supp. 1284 (D. N.J. 1977).

More recently, parents in Bedford, New York claimed with some success that school activities without overt religious significance violated their rights under the Establishment Clause. The court rejected the parents' basic claim that the district was responsible for advancing different religious beliefs, but it did find that certain lessons and practices by individual teachers were objectionable. *Altman v. Bedford Central School District,* 45 F. Supp.2d 368 (S.D.N.Y. 1999). Specifically, third graders learning about Hindu gods were to be asked to construct a paper image of the Hindu god Ganesha, a "graven image" that the court found objectionable. Similarly, fourth grade students made "worry dolls," brightly colored dolls and were told that they would chase away bad dreams if they were kept under the pillow. The court found that this activity endorsed superstition over religion and thus violated the Establishment Clause. The court even found that an Earth Day celebration crossed the line because the earth was "deified" in the celebration.

The Second Circuit reversed the trial court on the issue of Earth Day. It found that the celebration had a secular purpose, there was little mention of Gaia (the "Earth Goddess") during the celebration, and no one suggested that the Earth is a deity who should be worshipped. Moreover, the Free Exercise rights of the students were not burdened, because attendance was not compulsory. As to the other rulings, however, the court did not provide any further guidance; it found that these issues became moot when the students moved or graduated. *DiBari v. Bedford Central School District*, 245 F.3d 49 (2d Cir. 2001), *cert. denied* 534 U.S. 827 (2001).

Issues also arise when students bring religion into classroom discussions on their own. The courts generally side with school officials who restrict student actions related to religion, because of the legitimate concern that permitting such activities could convey a message of state support for religion. For example, a student in one district drew a picture of Jesus for a Thanksgiving assignment in kindergarten, and in first grade he brought in a book with Bible stories for an in-class oral reading activity. His mother sued after school district officials removed the picture from the display in the hallway, and after his teacher required that he select a different book (without a religious theme) for the reading activity. The school district prevailed in court, given its authority to control curriculum activities based on "legitimate pedagogical interests" as described in *Hazelwood* (discussed in Chapter Four, Section E(1)). *C.H. v. Oliva*, 990 F. Supp. 341, 352 (D.N.J. 1997), *aff'd in part, rev'd in part*, 226 F.3d 198 (3d Cir. 2000), *cert. denied*, 533 U.S. 915 (2001). *See also Gernetzke v. Kenosha United School District No. 1*, 274 F.3d 464 (7th Cir. 2001), *cert. denied* 535 U.S. 1017 (2002) (principal acted within his authority by banning the Bible Club from including a large cross in the group's hallway mural); *Walz v. Egg Harbor Township Board of Education*, 342 F.3d 271 (3d Cir. 2003), *cert. denied* 124 S. Ct. 1658 (2004) (district had right to restrict distribution of religious gifts during school-sponsored party).

These cases illustrate the difficulty for districts in avoiding illegal support for religion on the one hand, and violating the First Amendment rights of the students on the other. While school officials retain broad authority to control the curriculum and classroom activities, they must be careful neither to advance religion nor to be hostile to religious expression by individual students absent a legitimate pedagogical concern.

c. Release time and the school calendar

School districts and other governmental agencies have also attempted to make accommodations for religious activities conducted by others. The United States Supreme Court has reviewed the question of release time for religious activities on two separate occasions. In each case, the location of such activities was critical to the outcome. In *McCollum v. Board of Education*, 333 U.S. 203 (1948), the Court reviewed the practice of a school district in Illinois. There, the district permitted clergy to come into the schools during the regular school day and provide religious instruction in three separate classes (Protestant, Catholic and Jewish) to those children who chose to participate. Given the use of public school facilities and use of time during the school day for such religious instruction, the Court found that the program violated the First Amendment. However, release time programs are not unconstitutional *per se.* In a related case decided in 1952, the Court reviewed a release time program in the New York City schools. There, the students were released from school responsibilities and received religious instruction off school property. Since the public schools did not participate directly, but rather simply provided release time, the Court found that the program was constitutional. *Zorach v. Clauson*, 343 U.S. 306 (1952).

Consistent with the *McCollum* decision, the Fifth Circuit ruled in 1999 that a school district violated the First Amendment when it invited local clerics to counsel students during the school day on civic virtues and morality. After rehearing the case *en banc*, however, the court remanded the case to the district court to determine whether the program can be considered neutral in matters of religion. *Doe v. Beaumont Indep. School District*, 173 F.3d 274 (5th Cir. 1999), *rehearing en banc granted*, 1999 U.S. App. LEXIS 14810 (5th Cir. 1999), *decision on remand*, 240 F.3d 462 (5th Cir. 2001).

There are two lessons in these cases. First, direct involvement in religious activities by public school authorities is unconstitutional, though after *Agostini* and *Mitchell* it is more difficult to know what is prohibited direct involvement in religious activities. Second, accommodation to the religious activities of students is permissible as long as the actions of public officials do not promote religion. For example, the school calendar generally includes the major Christian holidays, and many districts also include holidays celebrated by students of the Jewish faith. Such accommodation to different faiths in setting the calendar is not required, but the First Amendment does not prevent school authorities from taking religious holidays into account in setting the school calendar or from otherwise making reasonable accommodation to the religious practices of students. *Zorach v. Clauson*, 343 U.S. 306 (1952); *Koenick v. Felton*, 190 F.3d 259 (4th Cir. 1999), *cert. denied* 528 U.S. 1118 (2000) (Maryland statute providing that Good Friday is a holiday does not violate the Establishment Clause).

6. Prayer

Prayer in the schools has been a concern of the courts since 1962, when the United States Supreme Court decided that a New York law requiring a daily prayer reading in the public schools was unconstitutional. *Engel v. Vitale*, 370 U.S. 421 (1962). The Court has ruled that prayer may be allowed at legislative sessions, *Marsh v. Chambers*, 463 U.S. 783 (1983), and it opens its own sessions with "May God bless this honorable Court." In the schools, however, the Court has strictly prohibited prayer. The concern has been that such prayer would advance religion by conveying an impression of state support for religion to impressionable children in school.

In 1985, the Court dealt with an Alabama law which required one minute of silence at the start of the school day for "meditation." The statute also authorized a period of silence for meditation or "voluntary prayer," and further authorized teachers to lead "willing students" in a prescribed prayer to "Almighty God, . . . the Creator and Supreme Judge of the World." The Supreme Court ruled that the references to prayer were unconstitutional, holding that the law did not even pass the first prong of the *Lemon* test, *i.e.* its defenders could not show a secular purpose for the enactment. *Wallace v. Jaffree*, 472 U.S. 38 (1985).

A related issue is whether a statute may require that schools provide a moment of silence for reflection without expressly stating that this opportunity is for prayer. The Alabama statute under review in *Wallace* included such a provision, but the United States Supreme Court did not specifically rule on it. However, it did comment on the fact that the appellants had not questioned the validity of that portion of the statute. In her concurring opinion, Justice O'Connor stated that she would find the moment of silence requirement constitutional.

In 1997, the United States Court of Appeals for the Eleventh Circuit ruled that a Georgia law mandating a moment of silence in public schools does not violate the Establishment clause. When a high school teacher defied the law and was fired, he challenged it on constitutional grounds. The court held that, even though the prior law had called for silent prayer, the provision for "quiet reflection" at the opening of each school day "with the participation of all the pupils therein assembled" did not have the purpose or effect of advancing religion. *Bown v. Gwinnett County School District*, 112 F.3d 1464 (11th Cir. 1997). Indeed, even a reference to "prayer" in such a statute may not, alone, cause it to be unconstitutional. In *Brown v. Gilmore*, 258 F.3d 265 (4th Cir. 2001), *cert. denied* 533 U.S. 1301 (2001) the court upheld a Virginia statue providing students with one minute of silence, during which students may "mediate, pray, or engage in any other silent activity." *But see Doe v. School Board of Ouachita Parish*, 274 F.3d 289 (5th

Cir. 2001) (statutory amendment deleting "silent" from statute authorizing "silent prayer or meditation" violates Establishment Clause).

Given these precedents, it is clear that the Connecticut law requiring a moment of silent meditation is permissible. Conn. Gen. Stat. § 10-16a provides in its entirety:

> Each local or regional board of education shall provide opportunity at the start of each school day to allow those students and teachers who wish to do so, the opportunity to observe such time in silent meditation.

As a practical matter, individual school districts (and individual teachers) in Connecticut approach this obligation differently. However, this provision has never been challenged on constitutional grounds. Conversely, apparently no student or teacher has found it necessary to bring suit to claim that this required opportunity has been denied to him or her.

The decisive factor in these cases is whether government sponsorship of actual prayer is involved; when it is, the activity will violate the Establishment Clause. Even prayer that occurs outside of school can create problems. In 1999, the Sixth Circuit ruled that opening a public school board meeting with a prayer violates the First Amendment because it creates the appearance of state support for religion. *Coles v. Cleveland Board of Education*, 171 F.3d 369 (6th Cir. 1999), *rehearing denied*, 183 F.3d 538 (6th Cir. 1999). The court held that, because both students and teachers attend school board meetings, the situation was more similar to *Lee v. Weisman* (prohibiting prayer at graduation ceremony) than to *Marsh v. Chambers* (permitting a prayer to open a legislative session), as discussed above. A federal court in California saw the matter differently, but the Ninth Circuit reversed on appeal. *Bacus v. Palo Verde Unified School District Board of Education*, 11 F. Supp.2d 1192 (C.D. Cal. 1998); 2002 WL 31724273 (9th Cir. Dec. 3, 2002 unpublished).

In any event, the *Marsh* rule has been applied to local agencies other than school boards, where an opening prayer has been allowed. *Snyder v. Murray City Corporation*, 159 F.3d 1227 (10th Cir. 1998), *cert. denied*, 526 U.S. 1039 (1999). *But see Wynne v. Town of Great Falls*, No. 03-2069 (4th Cir. 2004) (prayer at town council meeting advances religion). Similarly, the Sixth Circuit rejected a challenge to the Ohio state motto, "With God, All Things Are Possible," even when it was to be included on a ten foot by twelve foot bronze panel in the statehouse plaza. *ACLU of Ohio v. Capitol Square Review and Advisory Board*, 243 F.3d 289 (6th Cir. en banc 2001).

Invocatory prayer involving students has kept the courts busy in recent years, but the United States Supreme Court has continued to hold that such prayer violates the Establishment Clause. In 1992, the Court held that prayer by a member of the clergy at a public school graduation ceremony is unconstitutional. *Lee v. Weisman*, 505 U.S. 577 (1992). Not even a year later, however, the Fifth Circuit Court of Appeals upheld action by a school district permitting the members of the senior class to vote that they would include an invocation at the graduation ceremony. *Jones v. Clear Creek Independent School District*, 977 F.2d 963 (5th Cir. 1992), *cert. denied* 508 U.S. 967 (1993). The lower court distinguished the *Lee* decision by pointing out that school officials did not make the decision or have any guidelines for any prayer except that it be "nonsectarian and non-proselytizing." By contrast, the Ninth Circuit Court of Appeals ruled that a practice similar to that in *Jones* violated the Establishment Clause. *Harris v. Joint School District,* 41 F.3d 447 (9th Cir. 1994).

The Supreme Court later vacated the judgment of the Ninth Circuit as moot, 515 U.S. 1154 (1995) (mem.), but did not review the *Jones* case. Meanwhile, even the Fifth Circuit attempted to draw fine distinctions in the matter of school prayer. It ruled that prayer at football games is unconstitutional, notwithstanding the fact that the speaker was elected by the student body. *Doe v. Santa Fe Independent School District*, 168 F.3d 806 (5th Cir. 1999), *rehearing denied*, 171 F.3d 1013 (5th Cir. 1999). Confusion reigned in other judicial districts as well. The Eleventh Circuit, for example, ruled that permitting students to vote on whether to allow prayer at graduation violated the First Amendment, but then less than a month later vacated that ruling, reheard the case and decided that the practice was constitutional. *Adler v. Duval County School Board*, 174 F.3d 1236 (11th Cir. 1999), *vacated*, 1999 U.S. App. LEXIS 13190 (11th Cir. unpublished 1999), *reinstated* 250 F.3d 1330 (11th Cir. 2001), *cert. denied* 122 S.Ct. 664 (2001). Clearly, the time was ripe for the United States Supreme Court to address this issue again.

In 2000, the United Supreme Court ruled that the process of having students select a student speaker with the understanding that the student speaker would give an invocation is state endorsement and encouragement of religion, and, as such, is unconstitutional. *Santa Fe Independent School District v. Doe*, 530 U.S. 290 (2000). The Court stated:

> There is a crucial difference between government speech endorsing religion, which the Establishment Clause forbids, and private speech endorsing religion, which the Free Speech and Free Exercise Clauses protect.

The school district had claimed that the student selection process insulated it from involvement in any religious activity that students may choose to undertake. The Court found, however, that there was a history of prayer at football games and that the student selection process would simply perpetuate this practice, given the requirement that the student chosen must give an invocation. Moreover, under these circumstances, the Court rejected the claim that the speech at issue was private student speech. This ruling (which included a strong dissent) was based on the history and involvement of the district in the selection process.

From the ruling, it appears that a student may make the free and individual choice to profess his or her religious faith in a school-sponsored activity without violating the Constitution. For example, the Eleventh Circuit reviewed a policy permitting students to vote on whether to have an opening and/or closing message at graduation, and it ruled that the policy is constitutional, notwithstanding *Santa Fe. Adler v. Duval County School Board*, 174 F.3d 1236 (11th Cir. 1999), *vacated*, 1999 U.S. App. LEXIS 13190 (11th Cir. unpublished 1999); *reinstated* 250 F.3d 1330 (11th Cir. 2001), *cert. denied* 122 S.Ct. 664 (2001).

Whenever these issues arise, however, the difficulty for school officials is to steer between an Establishment Clause claim for permitting such speech and a First Amendment claim for restricting such speech. The Ninth Circuit, for example, recently rejected the claim of student graduation speakers who were not permitted to include religious content in their speeches. *Cole v. Oroville Union High School District*, 228 F.3d 1092 (9th Cir. 2000), *cert denied Niemeyer v. Oroville High School District*, 532 U.S. 905 (2001). There, one student proposed to give a proselytizing speech with repeated reference to God and Jesus, and "if anyone was offended, they could leave the graduation." The other student proposed an invocation that, *e.g.*, called upon the audience to "yield to God in our lives." Given the legitimate concern of school officials over these comments, the court rejected the students' claim that the directives not to make these statements violated their free speech rights. *See also Lassonde v. Pleasanton Unified School District*, 320 F.3d 979 (9th Cir. 2003). The result may be different, however, if a student's comments simply refer to his/her religious faith, without antagonizing others or seeking to proselytize. *See, e.g., Chandler v.*

Siegelman, 230 F.3d 1313 (11th Cir. 2000), *cert. denied* 533 U.S. 916 (2001) (permanent injunction against all student religious speech struck down as overbroad; student prayer, even at student assemblies, may be permitted if it is "genuinely student-initiated").

Finally, in the federal No Child Left Behind Act, the United States Congress could not resist getting involved in the school prayer imbroglio. Section 9524 of the Act provides that the Secretary of Education must provide guidance to school districts every other year on the "current state of the law concerning constitutionally protected prayer in public elementary schools and secondary schools." Moreover, school districts receiving Title I funds must certify each year that they do not prevent or deny students the right to participate in constitutionally-protected prayer as identified in the guidance from the Secretary. Neither the Secretary's guidance nor the related certification, however, will insulate a district from a challenge that it should have or should not have permitted student expression on a religious topic.

7. Bible study clubs and other student activities

In 1984, Congress passed the Equal Access Act, 20 U.S.C. §§ 4071-4074. Prior to that time, the federal courts had uniformly ruled that Bible study clubs at the secondary level were unconstitutional, because they would give the impression of state support for religion to the students. In 1980, the Second Circuit Court of Appeals so ruled, *Brandon v. Board of Education of Guilderland Central School District*, 635 F.2d 971 (2d Cir. 1980), *cert. denied*, 454 U.S. 1123 (1981), and other courts reached similar conclusions. However, Congress passed the Equal Access Act with such decisions in mind, and with the express purpose of requiring that school boards permit student Bible study clubs in the public secondary schools.

The law was written more broadly, of course. It provides that schools that create a "limited open forum" by permitting some non-curriculum student groups to meet at school during non-instructional time must give any other such groups the same right to meet (absent concern for disruption or illegal activities). The Equal Access Act provides:

> It shall be unlawful for any public secondary school which receives Federal financial assistance and which has a limited open forum to deny equal access or a fair opportunity to, or discriminate against, any students who wish to conduct a meeting within that limited open forum *on the basis of the*

> *religious, political, philosophical, or other content of the speech* at such meetings.

20 U.S.C. § 4071(a) (emphasis added). Under this law, a student Bible study group has the right to be recognized as a student group and to have access to school facilities if any other non-curriculum related groups, such as Chess Club or Key Club, are granted such access.

The Equal Access Act, albeit quite short, presents a number of difficulties in statutory interpretation. It leaves the definition of "secondary school" to state law, for example, but Connecticut law does not define "secondary school." It is simply not clear whether students in a middle school in Connecticut can claim rights under the Equal Access Act. Similarly, the law does not define "non-curriculum related" activities, and its "non-instructional time" leaves room for interpretation. *See Donovan v. Punxsutawney Area School Board*, 336 F.3d 211 (3rd Cir. 2003) ("non-instructional time" can include time during the school day when students are not in class). School districts and the courts have been sorting out these difficulties, and the law has been interpreted broadly to confer the rights Congress intended upon secondary students.

Given the lower court decisions in *Brandon* and other cases, it originally appeared that the Equal Access Act would be found unconstitutional. However, in 1990, the United States Supreme Court ruled that the Act is constitutional, and that school districts are obligated to permit student Bible study groups on the same basis as other student groups. *Board of Education of the Westside Community Schools v. Mergens*, 496 U.S. 226 (1990).

In *Mergens*, the Court relied heavily on its decision in *Widmar v. Vincent*, 454 U.S. 263 (1981), an earlier decision that involved college students. In *Widmar*, the Court invalidated a state university rule prohibiting use of school property for religious worship or religious teaching. The Court held that this prohibition was not required by the Establishment Clause, and therefore such discrimination against religious activity could not be justified. The Court applied this analysis to the Equal Access Act in *Mergens*. It held that Congress could extend this requirement of equal treatment to the secondary school level without violating the Establishment Clause. The Court distinguished between government speech supporting religion, which is prohibited, and student speech supporting religion, which is not. It held that Congress could fairly conclude that secondary school students are mature enough to recognize the difference.

After *Mergens*, it is clear that the Equal Access Act is enforceable. Moreover, the "trigger" for the Act's protection, the existence of "non-curriculum related groups," will be defined broadly. In *Mergens*, the Court reviewed the argument made by the school district that it had not created a limited forum. The district claimed that the various student organizations it permitted were all curriculum-related, because they furthered the goals of particular aspects of the school curriculum. Citing the clear purposes of the Equal Access Act, the Court disagreed, and held that social service clubs and other activities such as Chess Club do not directly relate to the curriculum. Therefore, the existence of even one such activity creates a limited open forum, to which Bible study clubs must be given access under the Equal Access Act.

The impact of the Equal Access Act goes far beyond religious clubs. With some frequency, gay-straight alliances have sought – and won – rights under the Equal Access Act. *East High Gay/Straight Alliance v. Board of Education*, 81 F. Supp.2d 1166 (D. Utah 1999); *Colin ex rel. Colin v. Orange Unified School District*, 83 F. Supp.2d 1135 (C.D. Cal. 2000). In some cases, however, school officials will be permitted to apply a general prohibition against discussion of sexual matters in school to deny recognition of such a club. *See Caudillo v. Lubbock Independent School District*, 311 F. Supp. 2d. 550 (N.D. Tex. 2004) (denial of access to gay-straight club upheld because district had general prohibition against discussion of sexual matters).

Finally, the case law is evolving beyond the provisions of the Equal Access Act, and the court are now also applying more general First Amendment principles to require that religious activity on school property be treated the same as other student activity as long as it is not sponsored by the school. This requirement of equal treatment is also seen in *Lamb's Chapel v. Center Moriches Union Free School District*, 508 U.S. 384 (1993) (equal access to rental of school facilities). School officials should be aware of this development in the law. For example, if a group wishes to pray at the flagpole on a given day, they should be afforded the same right to do so as a group that wishes to gather to "save the whales" or protest Republican efforts to abolish the estate tax.

The requirement that church and state be separated does not require or permit school districts to be hostile to religious activities. Any restriction on religious speech, however, must be based on a legitimate educational concern that the speech would be ascribed to the school. *See Gernetzke v. Kenosha United School District No. 1*, 274 F.3d 464 (7th Cir. 2001), *cert.*

denied 535 U.S. 1017 (2002) (principal's decision to deny permission to allow Bible Club to erect mural with large cross and Bible passage did not violate rights under Equal Access Act, given legitimate pedagogical concerns); *Fleming v. Jefferson County School District R-1*, 298 F.3d 918 (10th Cir. 2002), *cert. denied* 123 S. Ct. 893 (2003) (Principal permitted to prohibit religious messages in student-created tiles to commemorate Columbine shootings).

A 1995 decision of the United States Supreme Court in the higher education setting demonstrates how difficult it can be to navigate between prohibited establishment of religion, on the one hand, and prohibited hostility toward religion, on the other. In *Rosenberger v. Rector and Visitors of the University of Virginia,* 515 U.S. 819 (1995), the Court upheld a challenge by a student group that had applied for and had been denied university funding. The University of Virginia recognizes various student groups and extracurricular activities and provides funding for many. Its guidelines, however, provided that certain activities would not be funded, including religious activities, political activities or social entertainment. Here, plaintiffs were denied funding for their publication, which provides a Christian viewpoint on a number of subjects.

On a 5-4 vote, the Supreme Court reversed the lower court's finding that funding the group would violate the Establishment Clause, which in the Court's view does not "even justify, much less require, a refusal to extend free speech rights to religious speakers who participate in broad-reaching government programs neutral in design." *See also Board of Regents v. Southworth*, 529 U.S. 217 (2000) (viewpoint neutral mandatory student activity fee permissible despite objections by students that funds were used to support speech with which they disagreed).

The *Rosenberger* decision is consistent with the continuing trend of the Court to interpret the First Amendment to require that a religious activity be treated the same way as other activities, as long as the government agency is not actively sponsoring the activity. The close vote in *Rosenberger*, however, reflects how difficult these issues can be. Moreover, since this case involved students at the university level, it does not provide any definitive guidance on such matters for public school districts serving students at the elementary and secondary levels.

Even at the elementary and secondary level, however, we see greater tolerance of religious activities in the name of neutrality toward religion. In *Prince v. Jacoby*, 303 F.3d 1074 (9th Cir. 2002), *cert denied* 124 S. Ct. 62 (2003) for example, the Ninth Circuit ruled that a school district violated the rights of a student religious club under both the Equal Access Act and the First Amendment when it denied the group the same rights as other student groups, including access to the public address system and even funding. Similarly, in *Halls v. Scottsdale Unified School District*, 329 F.3d 1044 (9th Cir. 2003), *cert. denied* 124 S. Ct. 1146 (2004) the Ninth Circuit ruled that school officials violated the First Amendment rights of a summer camp operator by refusing to permit him to distribute flyers advertising "Bible Heroes" and "Bible Tales" because the school otherwise permitted non-profit groups to distribute literature of interest to children. One district court even ruled that a school district could permit private religious groups to place Bibles on tables in public secondary schools one day per year for students to take if they wished. *Peck v. Upshur County Board of Education*, 155 F.3d 274 (4th Cir. 1998). The court relied on *Lamb's Chapel* and held this activity was neutral toward religion, because various groups were permitted to leave information for students. When a principal started handing out the Bibles himself, however, the result was different. *Jahr v. Rapides Parish School Board*, 171 F. Supp.2d 653 (W.D. La. 2001).

B. "Congress shall make no law . . . prohibiting the free exercise thereof"

The other half of the First Amendment provision on religion provides protection for the free exercise of religion. However, the "Free Exercise" cases are far less numerous than those dealing with establishment of religion. School districts are obligated to make reasonable accommodation for the religious practices of both students and employees. Such accommodations generally involve excusal from certain activities or time off to meet religious obligations. Accommodations are not required, however, if they would interfere significantly with school operation, either because it would preclude the school from educating the student effectively, or because it would interfere unreasonably with the ability of the employee to perform his/her job responsibilities. In considering claims under the Free Exercise Clause, the key is whether there is coercion, *i.e.* does the school district rule or directive require the student or employee to do something that conflicts with his or her religious obligations? If so, such school district action is permissible only if there is a compelling state interest involved and there is no less intrusive way to accomplish that interest. If not, however, the test is simply whether the district's actions are reasonable and not discriminatory. School districts need not accommodate to the religious preferences of the student or employee. Rather, they are obligated only to accommodate their religious obligations

1. Accommodation of students

The courts have been sensitive to the need to make requested accommodations for religious reasons unless such accommodations significantly interfere with the educational process, either for the requesting student or for other students. The courts have been especially concerned that "accommodations" do not result in impermissible endorsement of religion by the school or its agents. Sometimes, the only workable accommodation is to permit the family to educate the child outside of the public schools, through sectarian education or home instruction. Moreover, as to changing the curriculum, the courts have not been willing to permit individual students' families to dictate what the curriculum for all students should be.

a. School attendance, enrollment and excusal

The United States Supreme Court considered the balance between mandatory school attendance and accommodation to religious beliefs in 1972, in a unique case involving the Amish faith. There, Amish students sought excusal from the mandatory attendance laws after eighth grade. While the elementary schools were located in the Amish communities, attendance at the secondary level would involve interaction with others and, in the parents' view, a risk to their religious practices. When the parents kept their children home after completion of eighth grade, however, the State of Wisconsin sought to enforce the mandatory attendance laws, which required school attendance to age sixteen. The Court reviewed the well-established practices of the Amish people and concluded that they had shown that requiring these children to attend secondary school would gravely endanger the Amish way of life. The Court balanced this risk against the benefit of the years of instruction between eighth grade and age sixteen and ruled that the First Amendment rights of the children and their families outweighed the state's interest in enforcing the mandatory attendance laws for those years. *Wisconsin v. Yoder*, 406 U.S. 205 (1972).

In subsequent years, other parents have attempted to obtain similar excusal from the mandatory attendance laws for their children, but these efforts have failed. *See Johnson v. Charles City Community Schools Board of Education*, 368 N.W.2d 74 (Iowa 1985). The unique circumstances of the *Yoder* case (a separate religious community for centuries) were not present in other cases. Moreover, such parents have the option of withdrawing their children from the public schools and providing them with instruction at religious schools or at home so that they could be educated without conflict with their religious practices.

Given that parents have alternatives to the public schools, school officials need not accede to parent demands to modify the curriculum or to excuse attendance. *Leebaert v. Harrington*, 332 F.3d 134 (2d Cir. 2003). There, the court denied a parent's claim that his rights and the rights of his son were violated when the school district denied his request for excusal from the mandatory health curriculum. The court noted that excusal was permitted from the "family life education" and AIDS education portion of the curriculum, in accordance with Conn. Gen. Stat. § 10-16e and Conn. Gen. Stat. § 10-19(b). More generally, however, the court held that school officials have the right and responsibility to determine the curriculum.

The court considered the parent's claim that other topics in the curriculum conflicted with his sincerely-held religious beliefs, but it rejected the parent's claim that his free exercise rights required accommodation under the "strict scrutiny" standard (explained in Chapter Four, Section E(3)(b)). Rather, the court ruled that free exercise rights are not violated by exposure to ideas that an individual parent finds offensive on religious grounds. Only if a student were forced to accept (or to espouse) principles inconsistent with his/her religious beliefs would free exercise rights come into play. Therefore, the court applied the "rational basis" test and upheld the school district's mandatory health curriculum on the basis that it is rationally related to a legitimate state interest.

1. Sectarian education and home instruction

Connecticut law permits parents to educate their children either in private schools or at home as an alternative to the public schools. Conn. Gen. Stat. § 10-184 requires that parents assure that their children ages five to eighteen attend school "unless the parent or person having control of such child is able to show that the child is elsewhere receiving equivalent instruction in the studies taught in the public schools." If a student is enrolled in a private school, the parent is deemed to have met this requirement, whether the school is sectarian or non-sectarian.

Parents also have the option of declaring that a child will receive home instruction instead of being enrolled in a private school. The State Department of Education does not supervise home instruction programs, nor does it expect local and regional boards of education to supervise such programs. See Series 1994-95, Circular Letter C-14, "Revised Procedures Concerning Requests from Parents to Educate Their Child at Home" (July 15, 1994). Rather, a parent simply must file a notification with the superintendent of the school district, and the superintendent must simply send an acknowledgment to the parent. The recommended form for that acknowledgment states that the superintendent takes no responsibility for the adequacy of the proposed program of home instruction.

It is difficult to square these procedures with the statutory duty of parents to show that the child is "elsewhere receiving equivalent instruction in the studies taught in the public schools." Conn. Gen. Stat. § 10-184. There is essentially no mechanism for assuring that a student is receiving an adequate education in the home setting. The reluctance of the State Department of Education to establish a review procedure is understandable, since it does not exercise any review authority over the parochial and other private schools in the state. A parent seeking to educate his or her child at home could well claim that special scrutiny of home instruction with no similar scrutiny of private school education is a violation of equal protection of the laws. Generally, however, the courts have sided with state authorities in their efforts to establish criteria for exemption from compulsory attendance laws. *See State v. Bowman*, 653 P.2d 374 (Or. App. 1982). For example, in *Murphy v. State of Arkansas*, 852 F.2d 1039 (8th Cir. 1988), the court held that the State of Arkansas had the right to require that students receiving home instruction be given achievement testing. The law also provides that the students must be placed in a public, private or parochial school if testing reveals that they are more than eight months below grade level. Similarly, the North Dakota Supreme Court has ruled that the State may require that home instruction be provided by certified instructors. *State v. Melin*, 428 N.W.2d 227 (N.D. 1988).

2. "Dual enrollment"

Questions arise concerning the right, if any, of parents who choose to provide for private school education or home instruction to enroll their children in the public schools for part of the day. School officials have a legitimate concern in assuring that students enrolled in the public schools participate in a common curriculum, and there is no statutory or constitutional right of dual enrollment. The State Department of Education has taken the position that school districts are not obligated to permit dual enrollment of students receiving home instruction. *See Letter to Olson from Flanagan*, (State Department of Education, Office of Legal and Governmental Affairs, September 27, 1997). Also, the courts have rejected "free exercise" claims made by parents seeking dual enrollment. *See Swanson v. Guthrie Independent School District*, 135 F.3d 694 (10th Cir. 1998) (a home-schooled eighth grader did not have the right to attend public school on a part-time basis, notwithstanding parent claim that denial of dual enrollment burdened his free exercise of religion). Consequently, school districts in Connecticut have the option to grant or deny requests for dual enrollment.

Most school districts in Connecticut do not permit dual enrollment. Under the Equal Protection Clause, districts are obligated to treat similarly-situated persons the same. The small burden of granting one request can become a significant burden if a number of parents make similar requests. Moreover, it can be difficult to coordinate the home instruction (or private school) curriculum with the public school curriculum. Dual enrollment can also raise issues concerning proper credit, other curriculum requirements, participation in extracurricular activities, liability and even special education. Given all of these concerns, school officials must carefully consider the potential consequences in reviewing requests for dual enrollment.

b. Curriculum

While courts have recognized a duty to accommodate religious practices of students by excusing them from particular activities, the courts have been less sympathetic to parent requests that the curriculum be modified because of concerns over perceived conflict between the family's religious beliefs and the content of the curriculum. Parents remain free to seek excusal or even to elect alternative instruction for their children (and thus avoid the influences of the public schools). However, parents have not been able to impose their viewpoint on the public school curriculum or other educational programs through free exercise claims. *See Brown v. Hot, Sexy & Safer Productions, Inc.*, 68 F.3d 525 (1st Cir. 1995) (parent challenge to school assembly based on privacy and free exercise claims dismissed). Two cases illustrate this principle.

In an infamous case, parents attacked the selection of a particular reading series by a Tennessee board of education, claiming that references to evolution, secular humanism, "futuristic supernaturalism," pacifism, magic and false views of death violated their free exercise rights. The lower court agreed and enjoined the district from using the reading series. The federal appeals court reversed. It rejected the parents' claims, since it found that no student was ever required to affirm or disavow any particular religious creed in using the reading series. *Mozert v. Hawkins County Board of Education*, 827 F.2d 1058 (6th Cir. 1987).

Parents in Alabama tried a somewhat different tack. They claimed that the curriculum materials used in their district denied theistic religious views and advanced self-reliance in lieu of divine guidance. They brought suit and argued that the curriculum thus had the effect of promoting a "religion" of "secular humanism." As luck would have it, the parents were able to make their argument to the same federal judge who had found prayer in the schools to be constitutional (a decision which the Supreme Court reversed in *Wallace v. Jaffree*, 472 U.S. 38 (1985). The district court agreed with these parents, but the federal appeals court promptly reversed. The absence of religious references in the books used did not constitute an advancement of religion or active hostility toward theistic religion. Consequently, the claims were dismissed, and the school district was free to establish the curriculum as it felt appropriate to the needs of the students. *Smith v. Board of Commissioners of Mobile County*, 827 F.2d 684 (11th Cir. 1987).

c. Religious practices

Since the free exercise of religion is a right guaranteed by the United States Constitution, government agencies, including local and regional boards of education, must assure that any direct interference with a student's ability to practice his or her religion is justified by a compelling state interest and is only as intrusive as necessary to protect that interest. This obligation under the United States Constitution is codified under Connecticut law in the State Religious Freedom Restoration Act, Conn. Gen. Stat. § 52-571b, discussed below. Consequently, where students' religious practices affect their lives at school, accommodations must be made wherever reasonable. For example, if a student must miss school because of religious obligations, accommodations must be made to (1) permit the absence, and (2) permit any work missed to be made up.

The scope of such required accommodation can, of course, be the subject of dispute and debate. For example, a Muslim student might ask for the opportunity to be absent from class in order to pray several times per day. The scope of the duty must be determined on a case-by-case basis, with consideration of the religious need and of the disruption, if any, of the educational process.

Unfortunately, there are few cases on the subject, and school districts do not have a great deal of judicial guidance in such matters. Interestingly, in ruling that student Bible clubs are unconstitutional (before the Supreme Court decision in *Mergens*), the Second Circuit addressed the situation of the

Muslim student in *dicta*, *i.e.* a comment that was not necessary to the court's decision:

> We do not have before us the case of a Moslem who must prostrate himself five times daily in the direction of Mecca, or children whose beliefs require prayer before lunch, sports or other school activities. If faced with these religious demands from students, a school board might have to make additional accommodations to permit the student to withdraw momentarily from the class.

Brandon v. Board of Education of Guilderland Central School District, 635 F.2d 971 (2d Cir. 1980), *cert. denied*, 454 U.S. 1123 (1981).

Many of the accommodation issues that have come to the courts have had to do with requests to be excused from particular courses. In cases involving the Free Exercise Clause, the issue is usually whether the student has been coerced into activities that are contrary to his or her religious beliefs. Consequently, if a student may be excused from a particular course such as sex education, courts will generally dismiss any free exercise complaints. Such excusal removes the issues of coercion, and the courts will not interfere with the judgments of the school officials. *See, e.g., Medieros v. Kiyosaki*, 478 P.2d 314 (Hawaii 1970); *Smith v. Ricci*, 446 A.2d 501 (N.J. 1982), *app. dism.*, 459 U.S. 962 (1982). However, some courts have upheld required courses in sex education even though there was no provision for excusal. *Cornwell v. State Board of Education*, 428 F.2d 471 (4th Cir. 1970), *cert. denied*, 400 U.S. 942 (1970). *See also Hopkins v. Hamden Board of Education*, 29 Conn. Supp. 397 (1971).

In Connecticut, specific statutes permit parents to have their children excused from certain subject matter in the curriculum. Parents may request in writing that their children be excused from required instruction on HIV, as provided in Conn. Gen. Stat. § 10-19(b). A similar exemption provision exists with regard to firearm safety programs. Conn. Gen. Stat. § 10-18c(b). Perhaps the most frequently utilized exemption provision, Conn. Gen. Stat. § 10-16e, provides that parents may provide written notification and thereby automatically exempt their children from any family life education program. The statute even provides that the exemption shall be from the family life education program "in its entirety or from any portion thereof so specified by the parent or legal guardian." *Id.* By providing these specific exemptions, the General Assembly has arguably established the public policy in this area, leaving any other requests for exemption from portions of the curriculum to the discretion of the school district. *See Leebaert v. Harrington*, discussed above (student can be required to attend other elements of the health curriculum, notwithstanding objection on religious grounds by parent).

Sometimes, excusal requests exceed any reasonable expectation of accommodation to religious beliefs. In such cases, courts have been unwilling to require that school boards make such major accommodations. For example, in *Davis v. Page*, 385 F. Supp. 395 (D. N.H. 1974), parents objected to the use of any audio-visual equipment in school, and asked that their children be excused from any such activities. The court dismissed the parents' claims and noted that granting the parents' request would effectively deny the child an education.

Another issue of accommodation concerns student dress. In one case, a student and her parents objected to her participating in physical education, claiming that the required uniform was immodest and therefore against their religious beliefs. The court held that the student should be excused from wearing the uniform but nonetheless would be required to participate in the activity, despite her protestation that she did not want to see others so dressed. *Mitchell v. McCall*, 143 So. 2d 629 (Ala. 1962). While the district was required to accommodate the personal beliefs of the student and her parents, it was not required to release her from this curriculum requirement altogether.

More recently, students in Texas successfully asserted the right under the Free Exercise Clause to wear rosaries and other religious symbols notwithstanding a prohibition against such objects based on concern that, for other students, they were gang symbols. *Chalifoux v. New Caney Independent School District,* 976 F. Supp. 659 (S.D. Tex. 1997). The court ruled that the students' interest in wearing the rosaries outweighed any legitimate school concern that rosaries (in other situations) were gang-related symbols.

One of the most interesting cases on accommodation arose in a small, rural community in Missouri. There, some of the local churches had as a tenet of their religion a proscription against social dancing, which was described as "sinful." As a result, the local school board adopted a rule which stated: "School dances are not authorized, and school premises shall not be used for purposes of conducting a dance." Opponents of the rule brought suit in federal court, claiming that the rule violated the Establishment Clause. The district court agreed with this claim, but the Eighth Circuit Court of

Appeals reversed. The court found that, since dancing is a wholly secular activity, a rule prohibiting dancing was secular as well. It also found that a no-dancing rule did not promote any one religion, and it certainly did not cause any entanglement with religion. *Clayton v. Place*, 884 F.2d 376 (8th Cir. 1989). While one might question the conclusion that a no-dancing rule has a secular purpose, this case illustrates the difference between support for religion and accommodation of religion, and the deference the courts give to school authorities in the latter case.

These cases require a balance between the rights of parents and children to practice their religion and the obligation of parents and the state to assure that children receive an education. When a direct conflict between curriculum requirements and religious obligations can be shown, some accommodation is generally required. If that accommodation makes it impossible for the school district to provide an appropriate education to the children in question, or if the accommodation interferes with the education of other children, however, the free exercise rights of the parents and children must yield.

2. Accommodation of employees

In addition to the free exercise claims by students and their parents, school districts must deal with such claims by employees. In this regard, school boards are not only subject to the constitutional requirements that apply to school boards as agents of the government, but they also must comply with the statutory duty of employers not to discriminate against employees on the basis of their religion.

Under the 1972 Amendments to Title VII of the Civil Rights Act of 1964, all employers are required to "reasonably accommodate an employee's . . . religious observance or practice without undue hardship on the conduct of the employer's business." 42 U.S.C. § 2000e(j). Often this duty to accommodate to the religious practices of employees relates to employee absences due to religious obligations. Generally, the courts have held that employers are required to permit absence for necessary religious activities. *See, e.g. Wangsness v. Watertown School District No. 14-4*, 541 F. Supp. 332 (D.S.D. 1982); *Pinsker v. Joint School District No. 28J*, 554 F. Supp. 1049 (D. Colo. 1983). The duty of the employer, however, is simply to provide a reasonable accommodation. *Trans World Airlines, Inc. v. Hardison*, 432 U.S. 63 (1977).

The scope of this obligation was in issue in a case involving a teacher employed by the Board of Education in Ansonia, Connecticut. The teacher, Ronald Philbrook, asked that he be permitted to use all three days provided in the contract for religious days and three additional personal days with pay to assure that he could take six days of religious observance off with pay. However, because the contract did not require the Board to permit Mr. Philbrook to use personal days for religious reasons, the Board denied Mr. Philbrook's request. Mr. Philbrook brought suit under Title VII, claiming that he had proposed a reasonable accommodation and that the Board of Education was therefore obligated to grant his request. The United States Supreme Court rejected Mr. Philbrook's claim. It held that an employer is not obligated to agree with a reasonable accommodation proposed by the employee, but rather may determine what accommodation to make. As long as it is reasonable, the employer's decision regarding accommodation will meet the employer's obligation under Title VII. *Ansonia Board of Education v. Philbrook*, 479 U.S. 60 (1986). *See also Bruff v. North Mississippi Health Services, Inc.*, 244 F.3d 495 (5th Cir. 2001) (a counselor had no right to be excused from specific job duties on the basis of religious objection).

Teachers have also made free exercise claims with regard to religious speech or particular religious garments that they wish to wear in the classroom. For example, in 1986, the Oregon Supreme Court considered the case of a teacher, who became a Sikh and began wearing white clothes and a turban in accordance with her religion. She refused directives to desist, and when she eventually lost her certification, she sued. The court, however, held that the right of school authorities to avoid creating the appearance of approval of a particular religion outweighed the teacher's free exercise rights. *Cooper v. Eugene School District No. 4J*, 723 P.2d 298 (Or. 1986). *See also United States v. Board of Education for School District of Philadelphia*, 911 F.2d 882 (3d Cir. 1990) (district permitted to prohibit teacher from wearing traditional religious dress in school).

Rulings on religious speech claims have been to similar effect. In 1999, a teacher in New York State claimed that his free exercise rights were violated by a directive to refrain from using "references to religion in the delivery of [his] instructional program unless it is a required element of a course of instruction . . . and has prior approval by [his] supervisor." This directive came after the teacher discussed his conversion with his students and discussed "forgiveness, reconciliation, and God" in his teaching. When he refused to conform to this directive, he was suspended for six months for insubordination. When he again got in trouble upon his return, he sued the district, claiming that the directive violated his free exercise rights. The

Second Circuit ruled, however, that the directive did not violate his rights because school districts (and the teachers they employ) have a duty to avoid conveying the impression that they are promoting religion. *Marchi v. Board of Cooperative Educational Services*, 173 F.3d 469 (2d Cir. 1999).

In *Downing v. West Haven Board of Education*, 162 F. Supp.2d 19 (D. Conn. 2001), a teacher wore a "Jesus 2000, J-2K" T-shirt to school. She sued when she was told to stop wearing the T-shirt during instructional time. The court held that the school district's action was reasonable because (1) it could otherwise be seen as endorsing religion, and (2) her inability to wear the T-shirt did not interfere with her ability to practice her religion. *See also Anderson v. USF Logistics*, 274 F.3d 470 (7th Cir. 2001) (employee unlikely to prevail on her religious discrimination claim that she has the right to end her correspondence and her telephone conversations with "Have a Blessed Day"). These rulings demonstrate the willingness of the courts to support school district action taken to assure a religiously neutral school environment.

Congress attempted to require greater accommodation to the religious activities of employees in 1993. That year, it enacted the Religious Freedom Restoration Act, 42 U.S.C. § 2000bb *et seq*. This law provided that an employer may impose a substantial burden upon a person's free exercise of religion only if (1) it establishes that it has a compelling interest and (2) it has adopted the least restrictive approach to accomplish this compelling interest. In 1997, the Connecticut General Assembly passed a very similar law. Conn. Gen. Stat. § 52-571b. The federal law, however, did not pass constitutional muster. The United States Supreme Court ruled in 1997 that the Religious Freedom Restoration Act is unconstitutional. *Boerne, Texas v. Flores*, 521 U.S. 507 (1997). The Court held that rather than enforcing rights under the Fourteenth Amendment Congress had attempted to change the rights of persons under the First Amendment. As such, the Court ruled that Congress had exceeded its authority, and it struck down the law.

Given the demise of the Religious Freedom Restoration Act, issues of employee free exercise are governed by the traditional standard of whether the employer's action is coercive, *i.e.* whether the employee remains free to practice his/her religion. Any direct interference with religious obligations must be narrowly tailored and be justified by a compelling state interest (the "strict scrutiny" test). If the issue is a matter of employee preference, however, employer actions will be upheld as long as they are reasonable. "Title VII requires only reasonable accommodation, not satisfaction of an employee's every desire." *Rodriguez v. City of Chicago*, 156 F.3d 771, 776 (7th Cir. 1998).

CHAPTER THREE
TEACHER EMPLOYMENT, EVALUATION AND DISMISSAL

The employment of teachers in Connecticut is governed by the Teacher Tenure Act, Conn. Gen. Stat. § 10-151. Teacher tenure in Connecticut is a relatively recent development. Tenure statutes were first passed as special acts amending the charters in the larger cities. *See Bauer v. Costello*, 7 Conn. Supp. 98 (1939). The General Assembly passed the first state-wide tenure law in 1941, and by 1955 the tenure law was quite similar to today's law. Originally justified by the perceived need to insulate teachers from political patronage decisions, teacher tenure continues today to provide teachers security by imposing procedural and substantive requirements before a teacher's contract can be terminated.

As a threshold matter, it is important to define a "teacher" under the tenure law. A "teacher" is a certified professional employee of a board of education below the rank of superintendent employed for at least ninety days in a position requiring a certificate issued by the State Board of Education. Conn. Gen. Stat. § 10-151(a)(2). Both certification conditions must be met, *i.e.* the person must possess a certificate and the person must be in a position requiring that certificate. Neither a paraprofessional who possesses a teaching certificate, nor a teacher whose certification has lapsed is a "teacher" under the tenure law. Similarly, a person who holds a DSAP is not a teacher, because a permit is distinct from a certificate. Conn. St. Reg. § 10-145d-421. Finally, for the first ninety calendar days, even a person who meets both requirements is still not a "teacher" who is entitled to the protections of the Teacher Tenure Act.

Administrators below the rank of superintendent fall within this definition and thus achieve tenure just as teachers do. Even assistant superintendents can achieve tenure status in Connecticut, because they do not hold the rank of superintendent. *Cimochowski v. Hartford Public Schools*, 261 Conn. 287 (2002). However, administrators do not achieve tenure in their administrative assignments. *Id.*; *Delagorges v. West Haven Board of Education*, 176 Conn. 630 (1976); *Candelori v. New Britain Board of Education*, 180 Conn. 66 (1980). While reassignment of an administrator to a teaching position can raise other questions, such action is not subject to review under the tenure law. Moreover, the *Cimochowski* case, cited above, suggests that administrators do not have a property interest in their administrative assignment. In ruling in that case that an assistant superintendent is covered by the Teacher Tenure Act, the Connecticut Supreme Court stated that such employees have a property interest in a job, but not in their assignment as assistant superintendent.

Part-time teachers are also covered by the tenure law. There is no minimum number of hours that a "teacher" must be employed in order to have protection of the tenure law. The critical issue is whether a certified employee is in a position requiring certification. After ninety days of employment, even a teacher assigned to teach only one class per day is covered by the tenure law (albeit as a non-tenured teacher) because his or her position requires certification. *See* Conn. Gen. Stat. § 10-151(a)(6)(A).

Substitute teachers are excluded from the scope of the tenure law if they are not in a position requiring teacher certification. Sometimes school districts characterize teachers as long-term substitutes or interim teachers because they are filling in for a teacher on leave. The regulations of the State Department of Education, however, require that a person employed in the same teaching assignment for more than forty days possess appropriate state certification. Conn. St. Reg. § 10-145d-420. A substitute or interim teacher who is employed in a position requiring certification for more than forty school days, therefore, will be considered a "teacher" for certain purposes, such as certification requirements and membership in the teachers' bargaining unit. After a total of ninety calendar days of employment (including the first forty), that teacher will also be entitled to the protections of the tenure law.

Finally, coaches do not attain tenure as coaches (even if they are otherwise certified), because their assignment requires a permit, not a certificate. *Dietter v. City of New Milford*, No. CV960070416, 1996 Conn. Super. LEXIS 1634 (Conn. Super. Ct. 1996); *Talmadge v. Bristol Board of Education*, No. 312200 (Conn. Super. Ct. 1986). However, coaches now have certain rights of job security and appeal, as set out in Public Act 04-243. *See* Chapter Seven(C)(5)(c).

A. Employment of Teachers

Under the tenure law, boards of education have the right to hire teachers. The board may delegate that responsibility to the superintendent of schools. Conn. Gen. Stat. § 10-151(b). The practice in Connecticut varies. Some boards of education employ all teachers, while others authorize the superintendent to do the hiring of teachers. Since the term "teachers" includes administrative employees, some boards of education authorize the superintendent to hire employees up to a certain rank, and reserve the final judgment on specified administrative positions to the board. That judgment is supported by the further provision in Section 10-151(b) that boards of education can require multiple nominations for administrative or supervisory positions. In such cases, the superintendent is authorized (but not required) to rank the candidates submitted to the board of education.

Even if it has retained the right to employ teachers, a board of education can only hire persons who are nominated by the superintendent. The tenure law provides that, when the superintendent is not authorized to employ teachers directly, he or she must nominate teacher candidates for the board's consideration. Conn. Gen. Stat. § 10-151. The board must accept or reject such nominations within thirty-five days of their submission by the superintendent, and if all the candidates are rejected, the superintendent must then submit other nominations. At that point, the board of education is required to act on the nominations within one month. *Id.*

B. Teacher Tenure

Once employed for at least ninety calendar days, a teacher is covered by the tenure law. However, there are situations in which a teacher either does not possess appropriate certification or fails to maintain certification. When an employee no longer possesses certification, he or she is no longer a "teacher," and the protections of the tenure law are no longer applicable. *Ames v. Regional School District No. 7 Board of Education*, 167 Conn. 444 (1974). In such cases, the employer should hold an informal hearing to give the employee an opportunity to explain his or her certification status before taking action. *See Cleveland Board of Education v. Loudermill*, 470 U.S. 532 (1985). But once it is determined that an employee does not hold certification, the superintendent may dismiss the employee without following the provisions of the tenure law.

The tenure law provides that a teacher's employment contract shall be in writing. Conn. Gen. Stat. § 10-151(b). Most districts confirm the appointment of teachers in writing and further provide annual salary agreements, setting forth the salary for the year.

Notwithstanding this requirement for a written contract, it is important to note that tenure is a statutory right, not a contractual right. Under the tenure statute, the contract of a teacher is renewed by operation of law from year to year, unless it is terminated in accordance with the statutory procedures. Thus, a teacher's contract of employment with the board of education continues in force unless it is actually non-renewed or terminated, whether or not the teacher receives a new document each year.

As a statutory right, tenure status will depend upon the application of the statute, not on agreements between the parties. The tenure statute is "remedial" legislation, *i.e.* legislation intended to protect individuals, and it may not be waived. A board of education could not ask an individual teacher to waive the tenure statute, for example, or to extend the nonrenewal period. Conversely, if a board of education mistakenly "confers" tenure prematurely, it will not be bound. *Cipu v. North Haven Board of Education*, 32 Conn. Supp. 264 (1974).

Teachers in Connecticut fall into two categories for purposes of the tenure law. A teacher has "non-tenure" status for the initial period of employment, generally the first four years. Subject to exceptions discussed below, the statute provides that a teacher must be employed for forty consecutive school months (which do not include July and August) before achieving tenure status. Until that time, he or she is considered to be a probationary employee, and the teacher is subject to nonrenewal or termination (discussed below). If a teacher is employed beyond this probationary period of employment, he or she achieves "tenure" status. Once tenure status is achieved, the teacher may be dismissed only upon a showing of cause in accordance with the tenure law.

1. <u>Achieving tenure status</u>

Obtaining tenure status is purely a function of length of service; if a teacher is employed for the requisite period, he or she attains tenure. Significantly, school boards in Connecticut do not grant tenure. In fact, one school district purported to grant tenure to a teacher and then changed its mind after it discovered that the first year of service had been under an emergency permit, rather than a certificate. When the teacher challenged that action, the court held that the teacher had not achieved tenure. The action of the school board was irrelevant, because tenure status is conferred by operation of statute, not by board action. *Cipu v. North Haven Board of Education*, 32 Conn. Supp. 264 (1974).

A teacher with no prior experience achieves tenure after forty school months of continuous service, provided that the superintendent offers the teacher a contract to return for the following year.

Meeting the first requirement is simply a function of time. By statute, neither July nor August can be counted as a school month. Thus, the typical pattern is employment in September of one school year and attainment of tenure status at the end of June of the fourth year of continuous employment, provided that the teacher's contract has not been non-renewed for the following year. Formerly, teachers had to be employed at the beginning of the fourth continuous year of employment to achieve tenure status. However, in 1983 that requirement was eliminated, and teachers attained tenure whenever they completed the required thirty months. The requirement for forty school months of continuous employment applied first to teachers employed on or after July 1, 1996.

The second requirement, that the superintendent must offer the teacher a contract to return, is not as clear. The requirement is met, of course, if there is a formal offer of reemployment, but such formal offers are not always made. Inaction, however, may be sufficient. A teacher's contract is renewed by operation of law unless it is non-renewed or terminated. If the superintendent fails to take action to terminate the contract, it is fair to presume that "the superintendent [has offered] the teacher a contract to return for the following school year."

The period of continuous employment commences with the first day of service, which can occur at any point in the year. The statute also provides that a teacher will be credited for a school month if he or she has worked one-half of the student school days for that month. Conn. Gen. Stat. § 10-151(a)(7). Given these provisions, teachers may now achieve tenure at different times during the school year, depending upon when in the year they were first hired, and whether their service toward tenure was interrupted for authorized leave or layoff.

2. <u>Part-time teachers</u>

Part-time teachers accrue service time toward tenure, with their service prorated according to a statutory formula. A teacher whose assignment is fifty percent or more (computed by the ratio of salary for the position) receives full credit for such time. A teacher whose assignment is between twenty-five and fifty percent receives one school month credit for each two months worked in that assignment. Even a teacher whose assignment is less than twenty-five percent accrues credit toward tenure, at the rate of one school month for each three months of service in such a part-time assignment. Conn. Gen. Stat. § 10-151(a)(6)(A).

3. <u>Continuous service</u>

It is essential that service toward tenure be continuous. A teacher who is on authorized leave maintains continuous employment status. If the leave is more than ninety days, it will not count toward tenure, but the teacher can resume accruing time toward tenure upon return. By contrast, if the leave is less than ninety days, the teacher receives full credit for such time. Conn. Gen. Stat. § 10-151(a)(6)(A). Continuous service will be broken, however, if a teacher resigns or is terminated before he or she accrues tenure. In such cases, when rehired the teacher must start over accruing continuous months of service for tenure purposes.

If a teacher is laid off and then rehired by the same board of education within the next five years, "continuous employment" for purposes of accrual of time for tenure will not be interrupted. Under those circumstances, the teacher may count prior service toward tenure (though the time spent on layoff may not be counted). Conn. Gen. Stat. § 10-151(a)(6)(B).

Questions can arise in applying this provision because the term "layoff" is not defined in the statute. Presumably, a teacher is "laid-off" if he or she had an expectation of continued employment, but was then identified for layoff through the contractual reduction-in-force procedure because of position elimination or loss of position. Conversely, one can argue that a teacher who is hired for a finite period to fill in for someone on an authorized leave is not "laid off" when that period comes to an end. In one case, the Superior Court ruled that termination of employment under such circumstances was not a "layoff." *Mazurek v. Wolcott Board of Education*, 1999 WL 512641 (Conn. Super. Ct. 1999) (unpublished).

4. <u>"Fast track" tenure status</u>

The rules are different for teachers who have previously achieved tenure status in Connecticut. Teachers whose employment terminates after they achieve tenure with one Connecticut school district reacquire that tenure status after only twenty consecutive school months of service for the same or another school district (even if their new assignment is different). The only restriction upon this "fast track" tenure is that the teacher must have been employed by some school district in Connecticut within the five years before the employment. Conn. Gen. Stat. § 10-151(a)(6)(C).

There are two wrinkles in the law regarding "fast track" tenure teachers. First, as discussed below, teachers who have not attained tenure status are subject to nonrenewal and the statute designates April 1 as the deadline for such action. However, the provision for "fast track" tenure is separate. Conn. Gen. Stat. § 10-151(a)(6)(C) provides that such teachers shall not achieve tenure if "prior to the completion of the twentieth school month following commencement of employment by such board, such teacher has been notified in writing that his or her contract will not be renewed for the following school year." Section 10-151(c) separately provides, however, that the contract of teachers who have not achieved tenure shall be renewed from year to year unless they have received notification of nonrenewal by April 1. The law does not directly address the status of a "fast track" teacher who receives notification of nonrenewal after April 1. It is clear that the teacher will not achieve tenure status after twenty months, but it is unclear whether that teacher, nonetheless, will have a contract for the following year.

Second, a teacher will not be entitled to "fast track" tenure status if "for a period of five or more calendar years immediately prior to such subsequent employment, such teacher has not been employed by any board of education." *Id.* This limitation seems clear enough; if the teacher did not have tenure with another district in the preceding five years, he or she will have to start over. For purposes of this provision, the Connecticut Appellate Court has interpreted "five or more calendar years" to mean five periods of twelve months, not at least five complete calendar years, as claimed by one non-tenure teacher contesting her termination. *Drahan v. Regional School District No. 18 Board of Education*, 42 Conn. App. 480, *cert. denied,* 239 Conn. 921 (1996).

The law does not specifically state that the teacher must have had tenure status in the preceding five years; it simply refers to the teacher's employment by any board of education during that period. Moreover, the statute does not even refer to employment as a teacher or to the previously employing board of education being in Connecticut. Consistent with the logic of the provision, however, it is fair to interpret the reference to "such teacher" as a person who within the prior five years had been in a tenure status under Conn. Gen. Stat. § 10-151, a status unique to Connecticut employment.

C. Teacher Dismissal

The status of a teacher as tenure or non-tenure determines his or her rights when termination of employment is proposed. Non-tenure teachers are subject either to nonrenewal or termination, but the employment of tenure teachers may be terminated only through termination proceedings, as discussed below. However, both tenure and non-tenure teachers alike have the right to request a hearing before the board of education prior to contract termination.

When boards of education conduct either nonrenewal or termination hearings, they act in a "quasi-judicial" capacity, *i.e.* as a judge would act. *Conley v. New Britain Board of Education*, 143 Conn. 488 (1956); *Miller v. Monroe Board of Education*, 166 Conn. 189 (1974). Therefore it is important that any such hearings be conducted fairly and impartially. Board of education members must make their decision on the basis of the evidence presented at the hearing, and they should not undertake independent investigation of the situation outside the hearing. Also, since the board must be impartial when it considers the superintendent's recommendation for termination, the same lawyer must not represent both the board of education and the superintendent.

The Connecticut Supreme Court has ruled that boards of education must comply with the procedural requirements of the Tenure Act. *Petrovich v. Board of Education,* 189 Conn. 585, 590 (1983); *LaCroix v. Board of Education*, 199 Conn. 70 (1986) (board of education was permitted to reinitiate proceedings and comply with procedural requirements). If a board of education fails to afford the teacher a full and fair hearing, action terminating a teacher's contract may be reversed. *See Zanavich v. Waterbury Board of Education*, 8 Conn. App. 508, *cert. denied*, 201 Conn. 809 (1986).

A threshold question concerning the tenure law is whether the teacher has been terminated, permitting review under the Act, or whether the teacher voluntarily resigned, relinquishing any rights under the statute. In *Geren v. Brookfield Board of Education*, 36 Conn. App. 282, *cert. denied,* 232 Conn. 907 (1994), the appellate court held that the teacher was not entitled to proceed under the tenure law to pursue claims concerning whether his resignation was voluntary. Similarly, in *Kolenberg v. Stamford Board of Education*, 206 Conn. 113, *cert. denied,* 487 U.S. 1236 (1985), the Connecticut Supreme Court ruled that a teacher was not entitled to proceed under the tenure law; rather, the teacher's employment had terminated independent of the statute because of the teacher's failure to provide timely notice of intent to return from leave in accordance with the collective bargaining agreement. *See also Mitchell v. New Haven Board of Education*, 7 Conn. Ops. 1159 (Superior Court, October 15, 2001) (reinstatement agreement that includes resignation on date certain binds teacher).

A related question is whether a teacher may seek judicial relief without going through the procedures of the Teacher Tenure Act by resigning and then claiming that he or she was constructively terminated. Generally, exhaustion of procedures under Section 10-151 is required before a teacher may seek judicial review of his or her termination of employment. *Murphy v.*

Young, 44 Conn. App. 677 (1997). *See also Shields v. City of Bridgeport*, 22 Conn. L. Rptr. No. 15, 520 (October 12, 1998) (terminated teacher not permitted to assert claim of discrimination on the basis of mental disability; Section 10-151 is exclusive remedy). Also, a teacher's failure to appeal action taken pursuant to the tenure law precludes an independent court action alleging wrongful conduct related to the termination. *Drahan v. Board of Education of Regional School District No. 18*, 42 Conn. App. 480, *cert. denied,* 239 Conn. 921 (1996).

In rare circumstances, teachers may proceed with litigation after resigning. The Connecticut Supreme Court has held that exhaustion of remedies under the Tenure Act is not necessary if the teacher's claim is constructive discharge and such administrative proceedings would be demonstrably futile or inadequate. In *Mendillo v. Board of Education*, 246 Conn. 456 (1998), a principal claimed she resigned because she was being harassed. In its decision, the court emphasized the general rule that teachers must request a hearing under Section 10-151 and go through the process before seeking judicial review. Without ruling on the truth of the plaintiff's claims in *Mendillo*, however, the Court held that the principal (a "teacher" under the Tenure Act) could seek judicial redress notwithstanding her prior resignation, because proceedings under the Teacher Tenure Act are not designed to resolve claims of harassment and infliction of emotional distress, which she alleged. *See also Stallworth v. Town of Waterford*, No. 555312, 2003 Conn. Super. LEXIS 769 (Conn. Super. Ct. 2003).

This decision is the exception, not the rule. The courts will not consider a teacher's Section 10-151 claim if a teacher has resigned voluntarily. *See Appleton v. Stonington Board of Education*, 254 Conn. 205 (2000) (given teacher's voluntary resignation, court affirmed dismissal of her various claims); *Dollard v. Orange Board of Education*, 63 Conn. App. 550 (2001) (alleged cabal by school administrators to get school psychologist to resign does not meet standard for claim of intentional infliction of emotional distress). Similarly, the courts have ruled that they lack subject matter jurisdiction to consider a teacher's Section 10-151 claims if the teacher had an administrative remedy through the grievance procedure. *Kolenberg v. Board of Education*, 206 Conn. 113 (1988); *Schwab v. City of Hartford*, No. X10CV010806154S, 2003 Conn. Super. LEXIS 3102 (Conn. Super. Ct. 2003).

1. Non-tenure teachers

The contract of employment of a teacher who has not yet achieved tenure status may be terminated in either of two ways, either through "nonrenewal" procedures or through "termination" procedures. The Teacher Tenure Act provides that the contract of a teacher will be renewed from year to year, unless (1) the teacher receives written notification prior to April 1 of one school year that his or her contract will not be renewed for the next school year or (2) the contract is terminated in accordance with statutory procedures.

a. Nonrenewal

Nonrenewal is effected by providing written notification to the teacher that his or her contract will not be renewed for the following year. Questions have arisen, however, as to the proper method for providing such notification. Prior to 1995, it was the general practice to have the board of education vote to consider termination of contract or to notify a teacher of nonrenewal of the contract. In 1995, however, the General Assembly clarified Section 10-151 to give the superintendent the express authority under the tenure law to initiate termination proceedings.

Unfortunately, the General Assembly did not similarly clarify the provision in the Teacher Tenure Act concerning notification of nonrenewal. The statute requires that the teacher receive "written notice" of nonrenewal prior to April 1, but it does not specify who should send such notice. It is therefore not clear whether a board of education vote is necessary to effect nonrenewal of a teacher contract. Unless and until this question is answered through legislative clarification or judicial decision, however, the prudent course is to have the board of education vote to direct the superintendent to give written notice to the individual non-tenure teacher(s) that his or her contract will not be renewed for the following year. One can argue, however, that the superintendent may provide notification of nonrenewal without a board of education vote, since he or she has the authority without a board vote to notify the teacher that contract termination is under consideration. Moreover, teachers whose contracts have not been renewed have the right to request a hearing before the board of education. Any prior board vote on nonrenewal perforce would be technical in nature, because the board should not review the merits of the decision until the requested hearing, if any. Where a teacher admits receiving notification of nonrenewal and then participates fully in the nonrenewal hearing, the court ruled that the teacher can not later claim that notification issued by the superintendent was defective. *Joanou v. East Lyme Board of Education*, 165 Conn. 671 (1974).

An affected teacher could wait until after April 1 and then claim that a notification issued by the superintendent was defective under the statute.

First, the teacher would argue that a nonrenewal operates to terminate employment as a teacher, while a notification that contract termination is under consideration does not. Second, the General Assembly did not change the provision regarding notification of nonrenewal in 1995 when it amended the law to authorize superintendents to initiate termination proceedings. Third, teachers who are not renewed for reasons other than reduction in force have the right to a hearing before the board of education, which is to "*rescind* a nonrenewal decision only if the board finds such decision to be arbitrary and capricious," which the teacher could argue refers to prior board action. Conn. Gen. Stat. § 10-151(c) (emphasis added). Consequently, pending further clarification, boards of education may wish to take the safe course and vote to direct the superintendent to provide written notification to the designated teachers that their contracts of employment will not be renewed.

The teacher must actually *receive* the written notification before April 1. When these steps are taken, the contract will terminate at the end of that school year. It is not enough, however, to have a board vote or to provide the affected teacher with verbal notification. It is advisable, therefore, for school districts not to wait until the last minute before providing such notification.

As stated above, there is some question concerning the notice requirement when a teacher has achieved tenure previously in another Connecticut school district within the preceding five years. The statute provides that such teacher achieve tenure unless they receive notification of nonrenewal "prior to the completion of the twentieth school month of employment." Conn. Gen. Stat. § 10-151(a)(6)(C). In accordance with the terms of the statute, notification of nonrenewal at any time during the twenty-month period should result in nonrenewal of the contract for the following year. No courts have ruled, however, on the impact, if any, of the April 1 date on that action. The most a "fast track" teacher notified after April 1 could claim, however, would be that he or she has a contract for the following year, albeit in a non-tenure capacity, and such a claim would be inconsistent with the purposes of the statute as clarified in 1995.

A teacher who receives notification of nonrenewal has the right to request a written statement of the reason or reasons for nonrenewal. When such a request is received, the district must provide that statement of reasons within seven days of receipt of the request. Conn. Gen. Stat. § 10-151(c). Such a statement is likely subject to disclosure under the Freedom of Information Act, however, and therefore a teacher should think twice before asking that such a record be created.

A teacher who receives notification of nonrenewal is also entitled to request a hearing before the board of education unless the reason for the nonrenewal is elimination of position or loss of position to another teacher. The law further provides, however, that the hearing is not to consider the matter *de novo*, *i.e.* independently of the prior decision. Rather, it provides that the board of education should rescind the nonrenewal decision only if it finds the decision to be arbitrary and capricious. *Id.* Given this responsibility to consider rescinding a nonrenewal decision, discussion of the merits of the nonrenewal decision should be limited to such a hearing, and the board should not consider the merits of the nonrenewal decision in its initial vote (if any) to give the affected teacher notification of nonrenewal of his or her contract.

The decision whether to non-renew the contract of a non-tenure teacher is within the discretion of the superintendent. In sharp contrast to termination, discussed below, a nonrenewal decision does not require a finding of incompetence or even poor performance. A decision not to renew the contract of a non-tenured teacher can be based on the judgment that the teacher's performance is simply not up to district standards. School districts in Connecticut may even establish "excellent performance or the potential for excellent performance" as the standard for nonrenewal, and teachers who do not meet that standard may be subject to nonrenewal. Of course, the superintendent should never base a decision to non-renew a contract on an improper reason, such as union activity or the filing of a workers' compensation claim. As long as the superintendent's reasons are not improper, however, he or she has broad discretion. Indeed, one decision describes nonrenewal as a "discretionary act concerning a probationary employee." *Shanbrom v. Orange Board of Education*, 2 Conn. L. Rptr. 396, 398 (1990); *see also Devlin v. Bennett*, 26 Conn. Supp. 102 (1965).

Once nonrenewal notification has been given, the teacher's employment terminates at the end of the then-current school year. If no hearing is requested, employment will terminate at the end of the school year without further action, in accordance with the notification of nonrenewal. If a hearing is requested and held, the board of education must affirmatively vote to rescind the nonrenewal decision, or it will stand. Moreover, the statute does not provide for an appeal to court in cases of nonrenewal. Absent some collateral attack (*e.g.* free speech, due process), the nonrenewal decision is final. Conn. Gen. Stat. § 10-151(c); *Neyland v. Redding Board of Education*, 195 Conn. 174 (1985).

b. Contract termination

In addition to nonrenewal, a board of education may terminate the contract of a non-tenure teacher at any time for one or more of the six reasons set out in the tenure law (*i.e.* inefficiency or incompetence, insubordination against the reasonable rules of the board, moral misconduct, disability as shown by competent medical evidence, reduction in force, or other due and sufficient cause). Conn. Gen. Stat. § 10-151(c) and (d). If the nonrenewal deadline is missed or if cause arises during the year, contract termination may be the appropriate course of action.

Once the superintendent has notified a teacher that termination of his or her contract is under consideration, the teacher may request reasons for the proposed termination. The superintendent must provide the statement of reasons within the succeeding seven days. Also, the teacher may request a hearing within twenty days after receipt of notice that contract termination is under consideration. *Id.* If the teacher does not exercise this right within the prescribed twenty day period, the board may then vote to terminate the contract without holding a hearing. *But see Norris v. Board of Education Town of Waterford*, No. 539528 (Conn. Super. Ct. 1998) (twenty-day time limit directory, *i.e.* not mandatory). It is advisable, however, that the superintendent present to the board the reason or reasons for contract termination, so that it is clear that the termination was properly based on one or more of the statutory reasons for contract termination.

For non-tenure teachers, the hearing will be held before the board of education unless *both* the teacher and the board request either (1) that the hearing be conducted by an impartial hearing panel, or (2) that the hearing be conducted by a single impartial hearing officer. The superintendent, therefore, may deny a request from a non-tenure teacher for an impartial hearing panel.

The standard for contract termination is significantly different from that for nonrenewal. A decision to terminate must be based on findings made on the evidence presented at the hearing. Those findings must establish cause under one or more of the six reasons for contract termination, discussed in detail below in Section C(2). Also, as a matter of due process the board of education must adopt a written decision, setting out the findings on which the termination decision is based. *Lee v. Bristol Board of Education*, 181 Conn. 69 (1980).

If the board votes to terminate the teacher's contract, the contract is terminated immediately (unlike nonrenewal, which is effective at the end of the school year). Also, following a board of education vote on contract termination, a non-tenure teacher has limited rights of appeal. Appeal is permitted under the statute only if the reason for termination was either "moral misconduct" or "disability as shown by competent medical evidence." Conn. Gen. Stat. § 10-151(c), (d)(3), (4). Notwithstanding this limitation, a non-tenured teacher who claims that his or her termination violated his or her constitutional rights (which includes the right to "due process") may file an independent lawsuit to seek review of that claim. *Simard v. Groton Board of Education*, 473 F.2d 988 (2d Cir. 1973).

2. Tenure teachers

Termination of the contract of a tenure teacher (other than by a voluntary resignation or retirement) must be effected by the procedures set out in the tenure law. Conn. Gen. Stat. § 10-151(d). To initiate the process, the superintendent provides written notification that contract termination is under consideration. However, it is still necessary for the board of education to vote to terminate.

Generally, that vote is taken after a hearing, as described below. If the teacher does not request a hearing within the specified twenty day period, however, the board of education may vote to terminate. A late request for hearing, however, may not constitute a waiver of the right to a hearing. In *Norris v. Board of Education Town of Waterford*, No. 539528 (Conn. Super. Ct. 1998), the Superior Court held that the twenty day time limit was directory (not mandatory), and it ruled that the board of education should have given the teacher a hearing since it received her request for a hearing before it took action on the contract. Where no request is received before board action, the superintendent should present to the board of education the basis for the termination, so that it is clear that the action to terminate the contract is based on one or more of the statutory reasons.

a. Statement of reasons

Within seven days after receipt of written notification from the superintendent that contract termination is under consideration, the teacher can request a statement of reasons, which the superintendent must provide within the succeeding seven days. The statement of reasons should identify the statutory grounds for the proposed termination, *i.e.* which of the reasons enumerated in Conn. Gen. Stat. § 10-151(d) are in issue. The statement of reasons should also include a narrative description of the facts that support the proposed termination, but the statement of reasons does not have to list exhaustively all relevant facts. *See Meehan v. East Lyme Board of Education*, 9 CSCR 366, 367 (1994); *Sperrow v. Region 7 Board of Education*, No. CV010085019S, 2002 Conn. Super. LEXIS 3766 (Conn. Super. Ct. 2002). Rather, the superintendent, acting with the assistance of legal counsel, should simply describe the circumstances on which the recommendation for termination is based with sufficient specificity to give the teacher in question fair notice of the charges against him or her.

b. Hearing

Within twenty days of receipt of notification that contract termination is under consideration, the teacher can request a hearing. The statute provides that the board of education may hear the case, and it further permits the board of education to designate a subcommittee of three or more members to hear the case and submit written findings and a recommendation to the entire board for action. When the teacher in question has tenure, either the teacher or the board of education can unilaterally request that the hearing be conducted by an impartial hearing panel. If an impartial hearing panel is requested, one representative is selected by the teacher, another by the superintendent, and a chair is selected by those two members. Alternatively, by mutual agreement the tenure teacher and the superintendent may agree on a single impartial hearing officer. Conn. Gen. Stat. § 10-151(d). Teachers typically elect to have such cases heard by an impartial panel, and less frequently the teacher and the superintendent agree upon a single impartial hearing officer. Board hearings in such cases, however, are rare.

The hearing, whether before the board of education, a subcommittee, a hearing panel or a single impartial hearing officer, is to commence within fifteen days of the board's receipt of the request for a hearing, unless the parties agree to an extension. Given widespread concern over delays in adjudicating teacher dismissal cases, in 1995 the General Assembly included in the tenure law the limitation that any such extension in the time for commencing the hearing may not exceed fifteen days. Conn. Gen. Stat. § 10-151(d).

If an impartial hearing panel is to hear the case, the panel members designed by the teacher and the superintendent respectively must then select a third panel member to serve as chair. In the past, a reason for delay in starting such hearings was the absence of a statutory mechanism for forcing agreement on a chairperson for the impartial panel. In 1995, the law was amended to addresses this situation. Now, if the two panel members selected by the parties are unable to agree upon the choice of the third panel member within five days after the decision to use a hearing panel, the third panel member is to be selected with the assistance of the American Arbitration Association, using its expedited selection process in accordance with its rules for the selection of a neutral arbitrator in grievance arbitration. The statute now includes a "fail-safe" provision; if the third panel member is not selected with the assistance of the American Arbitration Association within five days, the hearing is to be held before the board of education or a designated subcommittee of the board. Conn. Gen. Stat. § 10-151(d).

Either the teacher or the body hearing the case (the hearing panel, single hearing officer, board of education, or board subcommittee, as the case may be) may designate that the hearing be in public; otherwise the hearing will be conducted in private. If the board of education or a committee of the board hears the case, the hearing will be a "meeting" under the Freedom of Information Act, and the hearing therefore must be posted, though unless the teacher requests otherwise, the board or committee may convene into executive session for the purpose of "discussion concerning the . . . employment . . . of a public employee . . . ." Any vote on contract termination, however, must be taken in public session.

The teacher has the right to appear at the hearing with counsel. Also, the board of education is responsible for maintaining a verbatim record of the proceedings, and the board of education must provide the teacher with a copy of the transcript of the hearing within fifteen days of the board's decision. The statute further provides, however, that the teacher bears the cost of any such copy. Conn. Gen. Stat. § 10-151(d). Given these provisions, the teacher (through the collective bargaining agent or otherwise) and the school district often share the cost of the transcript. The transcript is usually used in the preparation of briefs, which, of course, occurs prior to the decision of the board of education.

The superintendent has the burden of proving that cause for termination exists, and therefore he or she present his or her case first. Then the teacher has an opportunity to present his or her evidence and argument that there is no cause for termination. The scope of the hearing should be limited to the reasons given for the recommendation of termination, and it need not be a forum for reviewing education policy decisions of the board of education. For example, in *Harhay v. Ellington Board of Education*, 44 Conn. App. 179 (1997), the teacher claimed that the hearing panel improperly excluded evidence concerning her claim that the elimination of her position violated the duty of the board of education to implement the educational interests of the state. The panel ruled (and the court affirmed), however, that the hearing was properly limited to the questions of whether the teacher's position was eliminated, and whether there was another position available for which the teacher was qualified. *See also Yaffe v. Meriden Board of Education*, 34 Conn. Supp. 115 (1977) (hearing concerning laid-off teacher was appropriately limited to the question of whether the position was eliminated and, if so, whether the teacher's contract was properly identified for termination).

If the hearing is held before the board, the board must deliberate on the evidence and vote. Also, as a matter of due process, if a board of education hears a termination case, it is obligated to provide the teacher with a written decision that summarizes the evidence relied upon and the basis for the decision. *Lee v. Bristol Board of Education*, 181 Conn. 69 (1980).

When the matter is heard by an impartial hearing panel, a single hearing officer or a subcommittee of the board, the hearing body must make findings of fact and a recommendation as to contract termination within seventy-five days after receipt of the request for a hearing, unless the parties mutually agree to an extension. Conn. Gen. Stat. § 10-151(d). The statute specifically provides, however, that the parties may only agree to extend the time for providing such findings of fact and recommendation by a maximum of fifteen days, for a total of ninety days from receipt of the request for a hearing. Any extensions agreed upon concerning the convening of the hearing do not extend the timelines for the panel's concluding the hearing and issuing its report. *Id.* These strict timelines were imposed by the General Assembly in 1995. There was widespread concern over long delays in concluding such hearings, and these changes were enacted after an infamous case in which the administrative hearings alone took over one year to complete. *Sekor v. Ridgefield Board of Education*, 240 Conn. 119 (1997).

Notwithstanding the interest in a prompt resolution, it can be very difficult to conclude a complicated case within these timelines. Hearings take time to schedule, and the presentation of evidence, particularly in a competence case, can be time-consuming. Before the panel can even consider the matter, moreover, the transcript must be produced, and the parties must prepare and submit briefs. Limiting the hearing due to time constraints, however, could result in the teacher's raising due process issues, particularly in a complicated case. There is no discovery in teacher termination hearings, and the teacher could claim a need for additional time to rebut evidence presented by the administration. Finally, calling an end to the hearing due to time constraints is more likely to affect the teacher's presentation of his or her case, because the administration presents its case first.

Given these problems, creative lawyers have devised a way to comply with the statutory timelines and still assure that the teacher involved receives due process. If it appears that the panel will not be able to complete its work, the parties occasionally agree on the following procedure for giving the process more time. The superintendent withdraws his letter initiating termination proceedings. The superintendent then reinitiates termination proceedings pursuant to an agreement that the same panel will be designated and that all testimony and evidence presented in the prior hearing will be accepted by the "new" panel in the "new" hearing. The process assures both due process and preserves the information that was presented at the prior hearing.

c. The decision

The board of education must make the ultimate judgment on contract termination. At the conclusion of the hearing, the board must vote on the proposed termination within fifteen days, measured from the close of the hearings if before the board, or from receipt of the written findings of fact and recommendation if before an impartial panel, impartial hearing officer, or a subcommittee of the board. Conn. Gen. Stat. § 10-151(d). Neither the superintendent nor the teacher has the right to present further argument before the Board of Education. In *Pagano v. Torrington*, 4 Conn. App. 1 (1985), the Appellate Court ruled that a teacher's right of due process is satisfied by the hearing process before the impartial hearing panel, and that the teacher may not insist as a matter of due process on addressing the board of education as it considers a panel's report.

The board of education is not bound by the recommendation, and where the findings of fact reasonably support a decision to terminate, the board of education may reject a contrary recommendation and vote to terminate. For example, in a case where the teacher was found guilty of shoplifting, the panel recommended against termination, but the board of education voted to terminate despite the recommendation. The Connecticut Supreme Court upheld the Board's decision and dismissed the teacher's appeal. *Petrino v. Shelton Board of Education*, 179 Conn. 428 (1980).

If the findings of fact do not reasonably support termination, however, a board of education will not be permitted to reject the panel's recommendation and terminate the contract. *Catino v. Hamden Board of Education*, 174 Conn. 414 (1978). Finally, while courts will generally defer to the judgment of the board of education, in one well-known case, the Connecticut Supreme Court reversed a termination based on one incident of insubordination. Given the teacher's otherwise good record, the court held that the board's decision was an abuse of discretion. *Tucker v. Norfolk Board of Education*, 177 Conn. 572 (1979). More recently, however, the court has held that one incident can establish cause to terminate, notwithstanding the panel's recommendation otherwise. *Rogers v. New Haven Board of Education*, 252 Conn. 753 (2000) (dismissal of tenured administrator upheld, notwithstanding panel recommendation to the contrary, for failing to intervene in a strip search of students and failure to familiarize herself with applicable Board policy).

It is thus clear that the board of education can terminate notwithstanding a recommendation to the contrary from the panel. It is not clear, however, whether a board of education can rely upon findings of a single member of the hearing panel. In *Barnett v. Board of Education*, 232 Conn. 198 (1995), the panel recommended against termination of a teacher. One of the panel members, however, dissented from the recommendation, and set forth additional findings. Because these findings were supported by evidence in the record, the Connecticut Supreme Court held that the board of education acted properly in relying on these additional findings, in rejecting the recommendation of the panel, and in voting to terminate the contract of the teacher. By contrast, in *Rogers v. New Haven Board of Education*, 252 Conn. 753 (2000), the Connecticut Supreme Court considered an appeal based in part on the fact that one of the panel members dissented from the findings. The court ruled, however, that the board of education had relied solely on the majority findings of the panel and dismissed the appeal.

d. Appeal

If the employing board of education terminates a tenured teacher's contract, he or she may appeal to superior court. Significantly, any such appeal does not stay the termination, and the teacher will be off the payroll during the appeal process. Moreover, the appeal is based on the record that was created during the Section 10-151 hearing process. In 1995, the General Assembly amended the law to delete the provision permitting the parties to present additional evidence to the court on appeal. *See Hanes v. Bridgeport Board of Education*, 23 Conn. L. Rptr. No. 5, 163 (December 21, 1998). The courts will not permit teachers to bring an action based on Section 10-151 claims if the teacher had an administrative remedy through the grievance procedure. *Kolenberg v. Board of Education*, 206 Conn. 113 (1988); *Schwab v. City of Hartford*, No. X10CV010806154S, 2003 Conn. Super. LEXIS 3102 (Conn. Super. Ct. 2003). Except in extreme situations similar to those described in the *Mendillo* case (described above), teachers must pursue their grievance remedies and Section 10-151 remedies. If they do not, the court will dismiss their claim for lack of subject matter jurisdiction. *Myers v. City of Hartford*, No. 3:03ev652 (PCD) (D. Conn. 2003).

3. <u>Reasons for contract termination</u>

The grounds for contract termination are the same for both tenure and non-tenure teachers. They are:

1) inefficiency or incompetence, provided, if a teacher is notified that termination is under consideration due to incompetence, the determination of incompetence is based on evaluation of the teacher using teacher evaluation guidelines established pursuant to Section 10-151b;
2) insubordination against the reasonable rules of the board of education;
3) moral misconduct;
4) disability, as shown by competent medical evidence;
5) elimination of the position to which the teacher was appointed or loss of position to another teacher, provided:
    a. there is no vacant position for which the teacher is qualified;
    b. (in the case of a tenure teacher) there is no position held by a non-tenure teacher for which the tenure teacher is qualified; and
    c. the teacher whose contract is to be terminated is identified in accordance with a negotiated reduction-in-force procedure or a written board policy; and/or
6) other due and sufficient cause.

Conn. Gen. Stat. § 10-151(d). While a comprehensive review of the case law is beyond our scope here, a few general comments on each of these reasons may be helpful.

a. "Inefficiency or incompetence"

The first reason for contract termination under the statute is inefficiency or incompetence. Conn. Gen. Stat. § 10-151(d)(1). Hearings involving such issues will generally be lengthy, because proving that a teacher is incompetent involves evidence spanning months and sometimes years of teaching, observation and evaluation. In reviewing whether such cause has been demonstrated, a hearing panel or a court will typically look to see whether the district has followed the principle of progressive discipline. Applied to competency determinations, this concept means that (1) the employee must be warned about unsatisfactory performance and the consequences (contract termination) of failing to show the necessary improvement, and (2) the employee must be given time and assistance in meeting job requirements. These expectations are typically fulfilled through the teacher evaluation process. Through that process, the teacher's deficiencies are brought to his or her attention, and a remediation plan is devised to help the teacher improve his or her performance. To establish cause for termination based on inefficiency or incompetence, the administration must show that it made escalating remediation efforts to assist the teacher, and that the teacher failed to demonstrate competence notwithstanding these efforts.

The statute includes both "inefficiency" and "incompetence" as alternative grounds for termination. Neither the statute nor the case law, however, provides guidance as to what, if any, difference there is between these two terms. One might argue that "inefficiency" is a failure to teach in effective manner even though one has the ability to do so, whereas "incompetence" is an inability to do so. These terms are typically both included when this ground for termination is cited. The distinction, if any exists, has not been significant in any reported cases.

We now have more guidance concerning "incompetence." Since 2000, the statute specifies that a determination of incompetence must be based on evaluation of the teacher using the teacher evaluation guidelines established pursuant to Section 10-151b. That statute obligates each local and regional board of education to develop and implement a teacher evaluation program consistent with the guidelines established by the State Board of Education, discussed in Section D, below. In accordance with these guidelines, local evaluation plans are required to incorporate the Connecticut Common Core of Teaching, which was published by the State Department of Education in May 1999, as the definition of effective teaching. A teacher's failure to demonstrate competent teaching as described in the Common Core of

Teaching (and/or in a "teacher" job description adopted by the board of education) can establish that the teacher is "incompetent."

Typically, administrators determine whether a teacher's performance is competent through the teacher evaluation plan. This process begins by observing the teacher's classroom performance, and comparing that performance with these indicators of competent performance set out in the local plan (incorporating the Common Core of Teaching described above). If the teacher's performance is not satisfactory, the teacher evaluation plan will typically provide for a process of intensive supervision and assistance to the teacher. Frequently, such assistance results in the remediation of the performance problems. If the teacher is not able to demonstrate competent performance, however, such plans (and the professional responsibilities of administration) require either that the teacher be counseled out of the profession or that termination proceedings be initiated.

b. "Insubordination against the reasonable rules of the board of education"

Insubordination can be a basis for the termination of any employee. The tenure statute specifies that this reason for termination of a teacher's employment must relate to the "reasonable rules of the board of education." Conn. Gen. Stat. § 10-151(d)(2). Given this wording, such a case against the teacher would involve a violation of specific board policy or other rules. *See Rogers v. New Haven Board of Education*, 252 Conn. 753 (2000). Arguably, in the absence of specific board rules prohibiting such conduct, a teacher who is repeatedly insubordinate to his or her principal, would not be subject to dismissal under this provision. However, a teacher who engages in such misconduct would be subject to contract termination under the standard of "other due and sufficient cause," discussed below. *Tucker v. Norfolk Board of Education*, 177 Conn. 572 (1979).

c. "Moral misconduct"

Termination of a teacher's contract for moral misconduct is obviously a most serious matter, and the superintendent has a heavy burden in such cases. However, such action is expressly authorized by the tenure statute. Conn. Gen. Stat. § 10-151(d)(3). The term "moral misconduct" may be interpreted broadly. The Connecticut Supreme Court declined to provide an exhaustive definition of "moral misconduct," but it held that "moral misconduct" includes criminal conduct, such as the commission of a felony. *Rado v. Naugatuck Board of Education*, 216 Conn. 541 (1990). On a related note, school officials are required to notify the Commissioner of Education if they learn that a teacher (or a holder of a permit or authorization) has been convicted of any crime, presumably so that the Commissioner can determine whether to initiate certification revocation proceedings. Conn. Gen. Stat. § 10-221d(a). *See* Chapter Seven, Section C(5)(a).

When the moral misconduct involves child abuse, there are other statutory responsibilities. *See* Chapter Four, Section F. Mandated reporters must report immediately to the Department of Children and Families (DCF) if they have reasonable cause to suspect or believe that abuse or neglect has occurred. Also, when a report relates to a school employee, there are special responsibilities. The mandated reporter must notify not only DCF, but also the person "in charge of such school," presumably the superintendent. Conn. Gen. Stat. § 17a-101i. The superintendent is then obligated to provide immediate notification to the parent or other person responsible for the child's care.

By statute, the investigation of these matters is the responsibility of DCF, not the superintendent. Given the need to take prompt action in the school setting, however, the superintendent will likely want to conduct a review independent of the DCF investigation, provided that he or she may do so without compromising the results of the investigation by DCF. The superintendent has the express authority to suspend a teacher with pay during the investigation of any such allegations, provided that he or she notifies the board and the Commissioner of Education within seventy-two hours of such action. *Id.* If the investigation leads to action terminating the teacher's contract under the tenure law, within seventy-two hours of such termination the superintendent must again notify the Commissioner of Education, who may then initiate certification revocation proceedings. Conn. Gen. Stat. § 17a-101i. If the teacher is convicted of a crime of child abuse, however, there is no need for separate revocation proceedings because upon such conviction the Commissioner of Education may now deem the certificate of that teacher revoked. Conn. Gen. Stat. § 10-145b(m).

d. "Disability, as shown by competent medical evidence"

If a teacher's disability, whether physical or mental, prevents him or her from successfully serving as a teacher, his or her contract of employment is subject to termination. Conn. Gen. Stat. § 10-151(d)(4). As the statute indicates, this basis for contract termination involves the presentation and evaluation of medical evidence, rather than the judgments of the teacher's supervisors as to his or her ability to perform the duties of a teacher. If performance is unsatisfactory and there is some question as to disability, termination should be based on inefficiency or incompetence and/or other due and sufficient cause, either apart from or in conjunction with "disability as shown by competent medical evidence."

The scope of this provision may be affected by state and federal obligations of boards of education. As recipients of federal funds, school districts have been subject to the requirements of Section 504 of the Rehabilitation Act of 1973, 29 U.S.C. § 794(a), for over thirty years. This law prohibits discrimination against staff members, as well as parents and students, on the basis of disability. In 1990, Congress passed the Americans with Disabilities Act, 42 U.S.C. § 12101 *et seq.*, which expands these prohibitions and extends them to private companies. Finally, state law prohibits discrimination on the basis of disability. Any consideration of contract termination due to disability must take into account the rights and protections of persons with disabilities under these laws. *See* Chapter Seven, Section B(1)(d).

Notwithstanding these protections, it still may be appropriate to terminate a teacher's contract if he or she cannot perform his or her responsibilities due to disability. However, before making the determination that the person cannot perform his or her job, the employer must make reasonable accommodations to the disability if such accommodations will allow the individual to perform the essential job duties of his/her position fully and satisfactorily. Whether an accommodation is reasonable and thus will be required, will depend upon whether and how any such accommodation affects the performance of job responsibilities and, possibly, upon the cost of the accommodation. If the teacher cannot perform the essential job functions with or without reasonable accommodation, the teacher is considered disabled and his or her contract may be terminated under the tenure law. *See* Chapter Seven, Section B(1)(d).

e. Reduction in force

Elimination of position is the most common cause for teacher contract termination. In such cases, three conditions set out in the statute must be satisfied. First, there must be no vacant position for which the teacher to be terminated is qualified. Second, termination is not permitted if there is a position held by a non-tenure teacher, for which the teacher to be terminated is qualified. Third, the teacher's contract must be identified in accordance with a written board policy or a negotiated reduction-in-force procedure. Conn. Gen. Stat. § 10-151(d)(5). These requirements raise two related questions.

First, how does one determine whether a teacher is qualified under the tenure law to claim a vacancy or to displace a non-tenure teacher? Minimum qualification is, of course, certification, because teachers must be properly certified. However, the certification statute expressly permits school districts to prescribe qualifications in addition to certification for particular positions. Conn. Gen. Stat. § 10-145. Should a board of education wish to adopt qualifications beyond certification, it must do so for bona fide reasons in advance of a layoff. For example, one board of education facing the need to reduce music teachers attempted to require that music teachers have experience at specific levels, elementary, intermediate or high school, in order to be "qualified" to displace a non-tenure teacher. The court held, however, that the board of education could not adopt classifications at the time of impending layoffs to limit the rights of a tenure teacher. *Fedele v. Branford Board of Education*, 35 Conn. Supp. 55 (1977).

In the first instance, adoption of such qualifications is a prerogative of the board of education. However, the board may have a duty to bargain over the impact of any such decision. In another case, for example, a qualification of dual certification for a particular position was held unenforceable, because the district could not show that such a qualification was required under the negotiated reduction-in-force procedure. *McKee v. Watertown Board of Education*, 32 Conn. App. 6 (1993). However, if a qualification is adopted as part of the process of establishing and filling a position, it is likely that using such additional qualifications in the reduction-in-force procedure will be permitted.

Second, how should we identify the teacher to be laid off? This statutory provision requires that the contract of the teacher to be terminated be identified through a written board of education policy or a negotiated reduction-in-force procedure. Such procedures may be very specific, such as those that use seniority, prior experience at a particular level or other factors to identify a teacher for contract termination. Others may provide that the superintendent or the board will apply listed factors to identify the teacher affected. In any event, it is essential that the procedure set out specifically how the teacher to be affected will be identified for layoff. In the absence of such a procedure, it is not possible to terminate a teacher's contract under this provision. *Theriault v. Bloomfield Board of Education*, 31 Conn. App. 690, *cert. denied*, 227 Conn. 922 (1993). Moreover, since layoff relates to a mandatory subject of negotiations, the board of education may not unilaterally adopt or modify reduction-in-force criteria, even if they are set out in a board of education policy.

Finally, there are special rules that apply to reductions in force from the administrators' bargaining unit. Under Conn. Gen. Stat. § 10-151(d)(5), the contract to be terminated due to reduction in force is to be identified through negotiated reduction in force procedure. Administrators are "teachers" under the Teacher Tenure Act, but they are members of the separate "administrators' unit" under the Teacher Negotiation Act. As such, they negotiate a separate reduction-in-force procedure. It was thus not clear which reduction-in-force procedure should apply. The Connecticut Appellate Court answered this question in *Connecticut Education Association v. State Board of Labor Relations*, 5 Conn. App. 253, *cert. denied*, 197 Conn. 814, 815 (1985). Administrators who lose their positions due to reduction in force take their place in the teachers' bargaining unit and may exercise bumping rights within that unit on the same basis as other teachers. Notably, however, teachers are not permitted to "bump up" into the administrators' bargaining unit. *Trotta v. Plymouth Board of Education*, 32 Conn. App. 395, *cert. denied*, 227 Conn. 922 (1993).

f. "Other due and sufficient cause"

Finally, it may be that serious misconduct does not neatly fit into one of the first five reasons, but termination of contract may still be appropriate and necessary. The sixth reason for termination, "other due and sufficient cause," will support termination in such cases. Given the recent limitation of "incompetence" to determinations under the teacher evaluation plan, this ground for termination may take on even greater importance than in the past.

"Other due and sufficient cause" was challenged as too vague, but that challenge was rejected. *diLeo v. Greenfield*, 541 F.2d 949 (2d Cir. 1976). The court in *diLeo* recognized that there may be cases in which conduct similar but not identical to the other stated reasons provides cause for contract termination. However, the court cautioned that the misconduct must be of a serious nature similar to that of the other reasons.

The Connecticut courts have given meaning to the term "other due and sufficient cause." In *Rogers v. New Haven Board of Education*, 252 Conn. 753, 769-70 (2000), the Court upheld the termination of an administrator for her actions in connection with the strip search of students, stating that the courts have "treated that phrase as equivalent to good cause . . . . Thus in deciding whether particular conduct constitutes due and sufficient cause for termination, the impact of that conduct upon the operation of the school is a significant consideration." *See also Hanes v. Bridgeport Board of Education*, 65 Conn. App. 224 (2001) (falsifying reading scores is cause for contract termination); *Sperrow v. Region 7 Board of Education*, No. CV010085019S, 2002 Conn. Super. LEXIS 3766 (Conn. Super. Ct. 2002) (continuing pattern of mistreating students is cause for termination).

One source of authority for conduct that may constitute "other due and sufficient cause" is the Certification Regulations. Conn. St. Reg. § 10-145d-400a set forth the Code of Professional Responsibility for Teachers. By its terms, it "shall serve as a basis for decisions on issues pertaining to licensure and employment." These standards of conduct reflect the fact that teachers have a position of trust, and expressly prohibit a number of things, such as engaging in misconduct that would put students at risk, or misrepresenting one's professional qualifications. Conduct that would constitute other due and sufficient cause for termination will often be found in this Code. *See also* Code of Professional Responsibility for School Administrators, Conn. St. Reg. § 10-145d-400b.

Given the specificity of some of the other reasons (*e.g.*, insubordination must be against the reasonable rules of the board of education; incompetence must be shown through the teacher evaluation plan), when a teacher's serious misconduct warrants termination of contract, it is often advisable to include a reference to "other due and sufficient cause" in the statement of reasons for contract termination.

4. <u>Suspension</u>

The tenure statute provides that teachers may be suspended:

> Nothing herein contained shall deprive a board of education or superintendent of the power to suspend a teacher from duty immediately when serious misconduct is charged without prejudice to the rights of the teacher as otherwise provided in this section.

Conn. Gen. Stat. § 10-151(d). Suspension of a teacher will typically be effected in one of three situations. First, when a recommendation for contract termination is made, the teacher will generally be suspended from duty during the hearing process. Since the quoted provision makes clear that any such suspension be "without prejudice," conventional wisdom is that the suspension will be with pay.

Second, a teacher may be suspended while allegations of misconduct are being investigated, whether or not termination proceedings are ever brought under the Teacher Tenure Act. Such a suspension is, of course, with pay and without prejudice, and it does not reflect a finding on the merits of the allegations. Rather, such a suspension simply removes the teacher from the school environment while the investigation is conducted.

Conn. Gen Stat. § 17a-101i(a) addresses one such situation of suspension during an investigation. It requires that the superintendent suspend a certified teacher whenever an investigation of child abuse by the Department of Children and Families establishes that there is evidence of abuse. The law requires that the superintendent notify the board of education and the Commissioner of Education within seventy-two hours of the reasons for and conditions of the suspension.

Third, a teacher may be suspended as a disciplinary measure without regard to the tenure law. Under the concept of progressive discipline, suspension without pay is a disciplinary intervention that is on the continuum of progressively severe disciplinary actions of oral warning, written warning, suspension and termination. Any such suspension is not subject to review under the tenure statute, because it does not involve termination of the teacher's contract. *Tucker v. Norfolk Board of Education*, 190 Conn. 748 (1983). Moreover, a suspension is not subject to judicial review. *Tucker v. Norfolk Board of Education*, 4 Conn. App. 87 (1985). However, since such a suspension involves loss of pay, due process obligations come into play. It is appropriate, therefore, to give the affected teacher an opportunity for a hearing, either before the superintendent or the board of education, before the suspension is imposed. Also, some boards impose such hearing requirements or otherwise limit the authority of the superintendent to suspend through board policy. Finally, in some collective bargaining agreements, there is provision for review through the grievance procedure of whether disciplinary action, including a suspension, is for "just cause."

D. Teacher Evaluation

Connecticut law vests in the superintendent of schools responsibility for the evaluation of all certified staff, *i.e.* teachers, principals and all other administrators. Conn. Gen. Stat. § 10-151b provides that the superintendent shall "continuously evaluate or cause to be evaluated each teacher." The statute further specifies minimum requirements for such evaluations:

> An evaluation pursuant to this subsection shall include, but need not be limited to, strengths, areas needing improvement and strategies for improvement.

Such evaluations may be conducted either by the superintendent or, as is generally the case, by administrators to whom the superintendent has delegated such authority. In recent years, the General Assembly has underscored the critical importance of evaluation pursuant to Section 10-151b in at least three ways.

First, superintendents and other administrators must receive at least fifteen hours of training on teacher evaluation pursuant to Conn. Gen. Stat. § 10-151b as part of the mandatory ninety hours of CEU activities during each five-year period. Conn. Gen. Stat. § 10-145a(l)(1).

Second, under the Teacher Tenure Act the superintendent must base any offer of reemployment to a non-tenure teacher on "records of such evaluation" conducted in accordance with Section 10-151b. Conn. Gen. Stat. § 10-151(b). Before this requirement was included in the statute, the Superior Court ruled that a failure to evaluate in strict compliance with the established teacher evaluation program does not prevent a board of education from exercising its discretion to non-renew a teacher's contract. *Shanbrom v. Orange Board of Education*, 2 Conn. L. Rptr. 396, 398 (1990). Similarly, the Court of Appeals has ruled that Section 10-151b does not create a cause of action for negligent evaluation. *Drahan v. Board of Education*, 42 Conn. App. 480, 499, *cert. denied,* 239 Conn. 921 (1996). Nonetheless, to avoid possible claims under this provision, administrators should take pains to comply with the local teacher evaluation program, especially since grievances over procedural violations in teacher evaluation are permitted for contracts negotiated after July 1, 2004, as discussed below.

Third, in 2000 the General Assembly amended the definition of "incompetence," tying it directly to the teacher evaluation plan. Now, any determination that a teacher is not competent must be based on teacher evaluation conducted in accordance with the guidelines of the State Board of Education. *See* Section C(3)(a) above.

By statute the superintendent must report on the status of evaluations each year before June 1, and the board does not have any direct responsibility for the evaluation of staff (except of course for that of the superintendent). *See* Conn. Gen. Stat. § 10-157, discussed in Chapter One, Section C. As discussed below, however, the board of education has the crucial responsibility for adopting a teacher evaluation plan for the school district. Conn. Gen. Stat. § 10-151b(b).

1. Access to evaluations

Conn. Gen. Stat. § 10-151a provides that teachers are entitled to knowledge of and access to supervisory records and reports that relate to an evaluation of their performance. In addition, teachers have the right under the Freedom of Information Act, Conn. Gen. Stat. § 1-210, to have access to documents relating to their service with their employing board of education. However, access by others may be limited.

Under Conn. Gen. Stat. § 10-151c, records of teacher performance and evaluation (excluding records of teacher misconduct) are not considered to be public records, and therefore they are not subject to public disclosure unless the teacher in question consents in writing to the release of such records. Given the special confidentiality protection of such documents, questions arise concerning the right, if any, of board members to review evaluations of certified staff members. An individual board member has no greater right than any other member of the public to review records of teacher performance and evaluation. However, when the board, acting as a board, authorizes itself or some of its members to review teacher evaluations, the situation is different, and it appears that the board members, acting in this capacity, can have access to teacher evaluations.

Two cautions should be noted. First, any such information would be privileged, and the board member would be obligated to maintain the confidentiality of any such information obtained in the course of fulfilling his or her official responsibilities. Second, it may be unwise for members of the board to review evaluations in particular cases. It is necessary to balance the board's interest in reviewing teacher evaluations, either specifically or in general, against its need to remain impartial, should the board be called upon to consider the termination of a particular teacher's contract.

In one case, a board was considering the termination of teacher contracts due to a reduction in force, and some members unilaterally reviewed the evaluations of the teachers who would potentially be affected. Since the board members considered evidence outside of the formal hearing process (thus calling into question its ability to be a neutral decision-maker), the board's decision was overturned in court. *DeTour v. Regional School District No. 13*, No. 7320, slip op. (Conn. C.P., July 25, 1977). However, if board of education members receive information in the normal course of performing their duties, there is no presumption that such information has impaired their ability to act impartially in termination cases. The United States Supreme Court held in one case that board of education members still had the ability to act "impartially" (for constitutional purposes) in terminating the contracts of teachers for illegally participating in a strike, even though those board members had been involved in the negotiations with the teachers that led to the strike. *Hortonville School District No. 1 v. Hortonville Education Association*, 426 U.S. 482 (1976).

The bottom line is that a board should rarely review the evaluations of specific teachers outside the administrative hearing process. If the question is how the evaluation process is working, the board can ask that the superintendent provide for the board's review a random sample of teacher evaluations, with or without names redacted, reflecting the different cycles of the evaluation process.

2. The evaluation plan

The format of the evaluation process is regulated by statute and guidelines of the State Board of Education. Conn. Gen. Stat. § 10-151b(b) provides that the board of education "shall develop and implement teacher evaluation programs consistent with guidelines established by State Board of Education . . . ." In addition, Conn. Gen. Stat. § 10-220a(b) requires that such plans be consistent with the plan the board of education must develop to provide for professional staff development, including teacher evaluation.

The law also provides that evaluations should be conducted in accordance with the guidelines of the State Board of Education and such other guidelines as are mutually agreed upon by the board and the "teachers' representative" under the Teacher Negotiation Act. Conn. Gen. Stat. § 10-151b(a). This reference slights administrators, who are subject to the evaluation plan but not represented by the "teachers' representative," because they are (almost always) in a separate bargaining unit. More important, the reference to "other guidelines as are mutually agreed" means what it says. Absent mutual agreement, boards of education are not obligated to negotiate over the terms of the teacher evaluation plan, as long as the plan conforms to the State Guidelines.

As discussed in Section D(2)(a)(2) below, in 2002, the State Board of Education adopted guidelines for administrator evaluation, and thus a separate plan for administrator evaluation is now required, with final implementation by the 2004-2005 school year. The statutory rights and responsibilities of boards of education in this regard, however, were not changed with the promulgation of these new guidelines for administrators.

The Connecticut Supreme Court reviewed Conn. Gen. Stat. § 10-151b(a) in light of a demand by a teachers' union to negotiate over teacher evaluation, and it ruled that teacher evaluation is a permissive subject of bargaining. *Wethersfield Board of Education v. State Board of Labor Relations*, 201 Conn. 685 (1986). A board of education, therefore, can, but need not, negotiate over teacher evaluation. Such negotiations could occur either at the bargaining table or in the development of the teacher evaluation plan, but most school districts do not engage in such negotiations. As long as the district teacher evaluation plan is consistent with the State Guidelines, the board retains the final decision on the content of the plan.

While the evaluation plan is not subject to negotiations, for contracts negotiated after July 1, 2004 "claims of failure to follow the established procedures of such evaluation programs" are now by statute subject to the grievance procedure. Conn. Gen. Stat. § 10-151b(a). It is advisable, therefore, that changes in the contractual grievance procedure be negotiated to limit the scope of review of such issues. Since the superintendent is ultimately responsible for the evaluation process by statute, one possible approach would be to limit such review to the superintendent level. In any event, the State Guidelines provide that there should be a process for resolving disputes between the evaluatee and the evaluator, and any disputes over the substance of a teacher evaluation should be left to that process, rather than to the contractual grievance procedure.

As stated above, in developing teacher evaluation plans, boards of education are required to comply with the State Guidelines as well as the requirements for local professional development plans, including teacher evaluation. Each requirement warrants separate review.

a. The State Guidelines

For many years, the statute on teacher evaluation has included a reference to guidelines established by the State Board of Education for the development of evaluation programs. From time to time, the State Board reviews and revised these guidelines. The most recent guidelines at this time are Guidelines for Teacher Evaluation and Professional Development published by the State Department of Education in May, 1999. For many years, there were no separate guidelines for administrator evaluation. The State Board of Education remedied this problem in 2002, when it adopted new guidelines for administrator evaluation. Each will be separately reviewed.

1. Teacher evaluation

The Connecticut Guidelines for Teacher Evaluation and Professional Development are divided into two main parts. The first part of the Guidelines set forth broad requirements, such as the need to use *Connecticut's Common Core of Teaching* for the definition of effective teaching. The Guidelines also set out "Key Elements for the Development of a Teacher Evaluation and Professional Development Plan."

These Guidelines, especially the Key Elements, are broad, practical principles that provide structure and assistance to boards of education in developing teacher evaluation plans, and to administrators and teachers who must implement such plans. The Guidelines, however, do not mandate the specific terms of the plan. Rather, they leave significant discretion to local and regional boards of education in the development and implementation of the staff development plan, which includes teacher evaluation.

2. Administrator evaluation

In June 2002, the State Board of Education adopted new School Leader Evaluation and Professional Development Guidelines. Many school districts started by drafting an evaluation plan consistent with these guidelines during the 2002-2003 school year and by piloting the program in 2003-2004. School districts were required to have fully implemented plans for evaluation of school administrators by the 2004-2005 school year. Series 2002-2003, Circular Letter C-1 (July 2, 2002).

These School Leader Guidelines supplement the 1999 Guidelines for Teacher Evaluation and Professional Development, and apply specifically to the responsibilities of school administrators. Like the teacher evaluation Guidelines, they are general in nature, and they leave significant discretion to the individual school districts. As with the teacher evaluation guidelines, the statutes require that there be input from the professional staff, but the final decision on the plan is left to the local or regional board of education, provided that the plan is consistent with the guidelines from the State Board of Education. Finally, the Guidelines incorporate the Standards for School Leaders developed by the State Board of Education. These standards are the administrator equivalent of the Common Core of Teaching, which sets forth the standards for effective teaching. The Standards for School Leaders set forth specific, concrete standards under three headings: "Knowledge and Skills," "Dispositions," and "Performances." These standards provide a comprehensive and helpful description of the qualities of the successful and effective school administrator.

b. The local staff development plan, including teacher evaluation

Teacher evaluation plans adopted by local and regional boards of education must also conform to the requirements of Conn. Gen. Stat. § 10-220a. That statute requires that boards of education develop a comprehensive staff development plan, including teacher evaluation. The plan must be directly related to the educational goals of the district, as are established by the board of education in accordance with Conn. Gen. Stat. § 10-220a(b). Also, it must provide for the systematic assessment and improvement of both teacher evaluation and professional development of the certified staff, including "personnel management and evaluation training or experience for administrators." It must also be related to regular and special student needs, and may include provisions concerning career incentives and parent involvement. *Id.*

Under this statute, the board must have the "advice and assistance" of the teachers and administrators, including representatives of the exclusive bargaining agents of both groups, in the development of the teacher evaluation plan. Such "advice and assistance" does not include negotiation. Rather, when such plans are first adopted and periodically revised, the board of education must assure that it has the input of these groups. Given the expertise of the professional staff, such input is not only legally required; it is essential.

The statute requires the systematic assessment and improvement of the teacher evaluation plan, which, given the definition of "teacher" as including certified staff below the rank of superintendent, includes the provisions for administrator evaluation. The implementation of the teacher evaluation plan is therefore an ongoing process. Boards of education should regularly review and revise these plans, and there should be a standing committee on teacher evaluation. Ideas for change may come from teachers and administrators working with the plan, the superintendent, and even from board members themselves. Whenever boards adopt teacher evaluation plans or consider changes to such plans, those proposed changes should be presented to the committee for its input. The professional expertise of certified staff members is invaluable, and this process ensures compliance with the statutory requirement for participation of teachers and administrators, including the bargaining representatives of both groups. The ultimate decision for adopting the teacher evaluation plan, including action on any revisions suggested by the teacher evaluation committee, however, remains with the board. *See Wethersfield Board of Education v. State Board of Labor Relations*, 201 Conn. 685 (1986), discussed above.

c. Implementation of the teacher evaluation plan

Such plans typically include provision for supervision at varying levels of intensity. Where no particular problems are noted, the teacher evaluation plan may permit a teacher to set goals with the assistance of his or her supervisor for the upcoming year. The plan may not require formal classroom observation of the experienced classroom teacher each year, but rather may provide other means for the evaluation of such teachers in such years. However, most plans require a more comprehensive evaluation at least once every three years and/or when problems arise.

When problems are noted, such plans provide for remediation and intensive assistance. Typically, the teacher and his or her evaluator collaborate on the elements of a remediation plan, which identifies areas in which improvement is needed, and which sets out the support that will be available to the teacher, such as specialized training, peer support, materials and intensive supervision. The State Guidelines, quoted above, provide helpful assistance as to the process of intensive supervision. The Guidelines provide, for example, that the intensive supervision phase should include sufficient opportunities for the teacher to obtain assistance from peers and administrators. They also provide that special training to help the teacher meet district standards is also an appropriate element of a remediation plan. The Guidelines specify that "sufficient time must be allocated to enable the teacher an opportunity to improve." Finally, consistent with the concept of "progressive discipline," discussed in Chapter Six, Section A(7), the Guidelines specify that "consequences of the teacher's performance must be clearly articulated" (*e.g.*, "improve or you will be fired"), and all steps in the process must be "well-documented."

It is not always possible to have agreement between the teacher and the evaluator in the development and implementation of a remediation plan.

The Guidelines, therefore, require that there be a process for resolving any disputes. Given that the superintendent is ultimately responsible for evaluating all teachers, it is appropriate to have the superintendent be the authority to resolve such disputes. Since evaluation is not a mandatory subject of bargaining in Connecticut, it is not required (or appropriate) to have disputes over the substance of an evaluation resolved through the contractual grievance procedure because board of education members and arbitrators involved in contractual grievance procedures would not typically have the expertise to rule on such matters. Claims of procedural violations are now subject to the grievance procedure in contracts negotiated after July 1, 2004. Conn. Gen. Stat. § 10-151b(a). Appropriate limitations on any such review, however, should be negotiated for the same reasons.

Teachers often may elect to have union representation in meetings to review their evaluation or to develop a remediation plan. The State Board of Labor Relations has ruled that employees have the right to union representation in any conference with the employer in which they may reasonably fear for their job security. *East Hartford Board of Education*, Dec. No. 2256 (St. Bd. Lab. Rel. 1983). The union representative may attend such meetings to assure that questions posed are clear. The union representative may also confer with the teacher and provide other reasonable assistance in such meetings. The representative, however, is neither the lawyer nor the surrogate for the employee, and the administrator involved may require that the employee answer questions and otherwise actively participate in the meeting.

In any event, it is important for district personnel to separate teacher evaluation from other supervision and discipline. The evaluation plan should not impose specific time requirements before a teacher's contract may be considered for termination; the variety of situations in which contract termination may be appropriate defies categorization in rigid time tables. In accordance with the tenure law, termination proceedings may be initiated at any time.

Finally, it is also important that administrators not limit the supervision of teachers to the evaluation process. If, for example, a teacher is late to class or fails properly to supervise his or her students, that conduct can and should be the subject of discipline, such as a warning to the teacher that his or her conduct is unacceptable. Depending on the circumstances, that warning may take the form of an oral warning, a written reprimand or even a suspension. While the same problem may be referenced in the evaluation process, administrators supervising teachers may, and often should, utilize disciplinary procedures in appropriate cases.

E. Teacher Certification

Certification is central to the very definition of a "teacher" in Connecticut. To be a "teacher," a person must hold certification from the State Board of Education, and the person must be employed in a position requiring certification. Certification is required when one has direct responsibility to provide instruction and to assess student achievement. Conn. St. Reg. § 10-145d-401(b). Conversely, if a person's assignment does not require certification, he or she does not have status as a teacher. Similarly, once a person no longer holds certification, he or she is no longer entitled to the protections of the Teacher Tenure Act. *Ames v. Regional School District No. 7 Board of Education*, 167 Conn. 444 (1974).

1. State responsibilities

The State Board of Education is responsible for establishing certification requirements for teachers, supervisors, administrators, special services staff members, and school superintendents. Conn. Gen. Stat. § 10-145d. The State Board of Education fulfills this responsibility by promulgating regulations that govern the various types of certificates and required subject matter endorsements. These regulations are amended from time to time. The current regulations are available online at http://www.state.ct.us/sde/dtl/cert/regtoc.htm and were first effective in 1998. Originally, there were plans to enact new regulations to be effective July 1, 2003, but implementation of new regulations is on indefinite hold, and thus the current regulations are still in effect. While a detailed review of the regulations is beyond the scope of this Guide, the following overview of the certification regulations illustrates how they generally work.

In exercising its responsibilities to certify persons to serve as teachers, the State Department of Education may not issue or reissue certificates in certain cases. Conn. Gen. Stat. § 10-145 provides that a person is not eligible to receive a teaching certificate, authorization or a permit if he or she has been convicted of various, serious crimes, including a crime involving an act of child abuse or neglect, second degree sexual assault, third degree sexual assault, and/or fourth degree sexual assault, and served the sentence for such conviction within the five years immediately preceding the date of the application. The crimes of second degree and fourth degree sexual assault include sexual contact and sexual intercourse respectively between a school employee or a coach or other responsible person (among other people) and any student of the school district. Conn. Gen. Stat. § 53a-71; Conn. Gen. Stat. § 53a-73a.

2. Teacher responsibilities

Under current law, prospective teachers must either pass competency tests or achieve certain performance levels on standardized tests such as the SAT. Also, in order to receive subject matter endorsement in specified areas, prospective teachers must pass subject examinations, if available.

Once the prospective teacher meets the applicable qualifications, he or she will be eligible for the appropriate certification. Beginning teachers now work under an initial educator certificate for the first three years of teaching. During this time they must complete the Beginning Educator Support and Training (BEST) Program in order to be eligible for the next level of certification, the provisional educator certification. For some certification areas, the BEST program provides support for one year, but for most certification areas, the BEST program is a two-year program. In the first year, the teacher works with a mentor teacher and receives additional support through the State Department of Education. Work with the mentor teacher and support from the State Department of Education continues in the second year, and in the spring the teacher must submit a teaching portfolio for assessment. Teachers who receive a satisfactory grade on the portfolio complete the program. Those who do not continue to receive support and must submit a new portfolio by January 1 of the third year.

Upon successful completion of the BEST process, teachers are eligible for the provisional educator certification. Such certification is valid for up to eight years. During that time, the teacher must fulfill the requirements for professional educator certification.

The highest level of certification under Connecticut law is now the professional educator certificate. To be eligible for this certificate, the teacher must have at least three years of successful teaching experience in Connecticut and must complete at least thirty semester hours of study beyond the bachelor's degree. That program, however, need not lead to a master's degree. Previously, the highest level of certification was the standard or permanent certificate. When the General Assembly changed the law, it provided that all teachers who possessed a standard or permanent certificate on July 1, 1989 were automatically eligible for a professional educator certificate.

The significance of the change to the professional educator certificate is that teaching certification in Connecticut is no longer permanent. Rather, in order to maintain valid professional educator certification, a teacher must participate in continuing education activities. Specifically, the teacher must participate in at least ninety hours of continuing education activities every five years to maintain his or her professional educator certification. If a teacher has completed a national board certification assessment in the appropriate endorsement area in the previous five years, s/he will automatically satisfy this requirement for continuing education activities. Conn. Gen. Stat. § 10-145b(l)(1).

The Connecticut Education Association challenged the change from permanent certification to the current system as unconstitutional after it was enacted by the General Assembly. The Association argued, among other things, that abolishing permanent certification interfered with the teachers' property rights, and that it unconstitutionally abrogated contract rights. However, the Connecticut Supreme Court dismissed the challenge, holding that these changes in the law did not deprive teachers of any constitutional rights. *CEA v. Tirozzi*, 210 Conn. 286 (1989).

The General Assembly has also imposed various requirements that teachers in certain certification areas receive training through continuing education activities. For example, teachers with an early childhood nursery through grade three or elementary endorsement in positions requiring such endorsement must complete at least fifteen hours of training in the teaching of reading and reading readiness and assessment of reading performance during each five year period. Conn. Gen. Stat. § 10-145b(l). Teachers at all levels must receive fifteen hours of training in the use of computers in the classroom every five years as well, unless they are able to demonstrate technology competence as determined by the board of education based on state-wide standards for teacher competency in the use of technology for instructional purposes. *Id.* During each five-year period, superintendents and other administrators must complete at least fifteen hours of training in the evaluation of teachers. *Id.*

3. <u>School district responsibilities</u>

School districts, acting through the superintendent of schools, are responsible for assuring that all teachers working in the schools have appropriate certification and subject matter endorsement for their assignments. This responsibility is significant, because the statutes provide that the State Board of Education may impose fines on districts that employ persons without proper certification. Conn. Gen. Stat. § 10-145. The statute provides that such fines shall be determined by the State Board of Education, and it specifies that such fines may range from $1,000 to $10,000. The statute further provided that the State Department of Education may impose these fines by withholding state grant funds.

School districts are also required to offer at least eighteen hours of continuing education activities at no cost to the certified staff. The statute provides that such activities may be provided by the board itself, or through cooperative arrangements with other boards of education, or through regional educational service centers. The activities offered are to be determined with the "advice and assistance" of the teachers employed, including representatives of the teachers' exclusive bargaining representative. Boards of education are required to give credit for any activities teachers are required to attend, and the time and location of such activities is to be determined through an agreement with the bargaining agents, or otherwise by the board of education. Conn. Gen. Stat. § 10-145b(l)(1).

It is noteworthy that local and regional school districts may impose hiring requirements that exceed the state certification standards, which ensure a minimum qualification level. Conn. Gen. Stat. § 10-145(a) specifically authorizes local school districts to impose qualifications for specific positions beyond those imposed by the certification regulations. In exercising this authority, however, boards of education must be careful to assure that the reduction-in-force policy or contract provision incorporates such qualifications into the process of identifying the contracts to be terminated under Section 10-151(d)(5). *See McKee v. Watertown Board of Education*, 32 Conn. App. 6 (1993).

Finally, the school district has responsibility not only to assure that the teacher is certified, but is also to assure that the teacher has the appropriate subject matter endorsement for the particular assignment. The regulations contain complicated rules concerning subject matter endorsement requirements and exceptions for minor or temporary assignments. In any event, if a school district assigns a teacher who otherwise holds proper certification outside his or her certification area, he or she remains entitled to the protections of the tenure law, notwithstanding the fact that he or she does not have appropriate certification for his or her assigned position. *Loftus v. Fairfield Board of Education*, 200 Conn. 21 (1986).

a. "Teacher" positions that require certification

It is not always clear whether a particular position requires certification. The determination of whether the person so employed requires certification is a function of (1) the duties of the position and (2) the period of time the person holds that position.

The Commissioner of Education first addressed the question of what duties cause a school employee to be a teacher in a decision in 1987 concerning tutors for the Milford Board of Education. These requirements have since been incorporated into the certification regulations. In brief, a person employed by a board of education must have appropriate certification if he or she

- is not directly supervised in the delivery of instructional services by a certified professional; or
- is responsible for planning of the instructional program for a student; or
- evaluates student progress; or
- does not receive specific directions from his/her supervising teacher or administrator that constitute a lesson plan for each lesson.

Conn. St. Reg. § 10-145d-401(b). When a person has such responsibilities, the school district must ensure that he or she has appropriate certification. Requiring such certification has other consequences as well; persons in positions requiring certification are "teachers" and as such are entitled to the protections of the Teacher Tenure Act after ninety days of employment.

b. Substitutes and temporary employment

Temporary substitutes may not work more than forty days in the same assignment without appropriate certification. After that limitation is exceeded, generally the substitute must be properly certified for the position. Conn. St. Reg. § 10-145d-420. If the person does not have appropriate certification, the board of education may request substitute authorization, and the State Department of Education may issue such an authorization, provided that an appropriately certified person is not available, and that the school district has made appropriate efforts to secure a certified person for the position. Given these requirements, it is much more common for districts simply to assure that any substitute in an assignment for more than forty school days possesses appropriate certification.

When a substitute teacher has certification and has been in the same position more than forty days in a school year, he or she is a "long-term substitute" under the certification regulations. Conn. St. Reg. § 10-145d-400(mm). Since that person must be appropriately certified, he or she is a member of the teachers' bargaining unit, notwithstanding his or her status as a substitute. Conn. Gen. Stat. § 10-153b(a). Given the temporary nature of the employment, however, most school districts provide long term substitutes salary and benefits different from teachers who are permanently employed by the district. In many school districts long term substitute teachers are entitled to placement on the teachers' salary schedule, usually at step one of the BA column, and rarely are such substitute teachers entitled to benefits. Given the temporary nature of the employment of such substitutes, to date most teacher bargaining representatives have not invested much energy in the salary and benefits for these temporary employees.

The State Department of Education may also issue durational shortage area permits ("DSAP") upon the application of a school district when it is not possible to hire a teacher with appropriate certification for the position. Conn. St. Reg. § 10-145d-421. To be eligible for a DSAP, an individual must have a bachelors' degree, must have passed Praxis I, must have completed at least twelve semester hours in the subject for which the permit will be issued, and must file an intent to be or actually be in a planned program leading to certification (if such a program is required). The regulations permit the Department to reissue a DSAP up to two times provided that specified conditions are met. Conn. St. Reg. § 10-145d-422.

Commencing in 2003, persons holding a DSAP are included by statute in the teachers' bargaining unit. Conn. Gen. Stat. § 10-153b(a). Boards of education are therefore required to negotiate with the teacher union over their terms and conditions of employment. Typically boards of education simply treat DSAP holders as "teachers" for purposes of the collective bargaining agreement. Significantly, however, DSAP holders are not subject to the Teacher Tenure Act, because "teachers" for that purpose must be certified, Conn. Gen. Stat. § 10-151(a)(2) , but DSAP holders have a permit "in lieu of a certificate." Conn. St. Reg. § 10-145d-421. It is advisable therefore to clarify that DSAP holders are at-will employees and are not subject to contract provisions concerning "just cause."

Finally, the statutes also permit school districts to retain the services of private sector specialists. Conn. Gen. Stat. § 10-21c provides that businesses may donate the services of private sector specialists to teach in critical shortage areas or in areas of projected workforce shortages, and such individuals may provide instruction even though they are not certified teachers. Such instruction is limited, however, so that no such specialist may (1) teach more than half the maximum classroom hours of a certified teacher, (2) ever have sole responsibility for a classroom, (3) ever displace a certified teacher.

c. Administrators

The certification regulations require that certain certified staff possess not only a teaching certificate, but also an appropriate administrative certificate. There are separate certificates for superintendents, other administrators (*e.g.* directors, principals, assistant principals), department chairpersons, and reading and language arts consultants.

The most common administrative certificate is the "intermediate administration or supervision certificate" (the "092"). This certificate (or another appropriate certificate) is required for the following responsibilities:

> deputy superintendent, assistant superintendent, principal, assistant principal, curriculum coordinator, supervisor of instruction or any person who has the primary responsibility for directing or coordinating or managing certified staff or resources, or any person responsible for summative evaluation of certified staff.

Conn. St. Reg. § 10-145d-572. This certificate authorizes service in the most common administrative positions. It is noteworthy that this certificate is required if one is responsible for "summative" evaluation, *i.e.* the overall, final evaluation of the teacher.

A relatively new certificate is that of "department chairperson." This certificate is required of any certified staff member who (1) is designated by the board of education as a department chairperson, and (2) has the responsibility for directing, coordinating or managing staff and resources. Conn. St. Reg. § 10-145d-577. The certification regulations expressly provide that this certificate does not authorize summative evaluation. If a department chairperson's job function includes summative evaluation, he or she must have the intermediate administration or supervision certificate.

d. School business officials

There are also special rules that relate to school business officials. The certification regulations address such positions, and require that school business officials hold appropriate certification if they are responsible for six or more of the following areas of school business administration:

- accounting and supervision;
- financial planning and budgeting;
- operation and maintenance of plant;
- administering personnel functions;
- purchasing and supply management;
- data processing;
- food service operations;
- grant applications and reporting;
- insurance;
- collective bargaining;
- transportation.

This certificate is unique, however, in that a person holding this certificate is not thereby subject to the protections of the Tenure Act. Conn. Gen. Stat. § 10-145d(c). Also, persons holding the school business administrator certificate are not thereby eligible for membership in the teacher retirement system. Conn. Gen. Stat. § 10-145d(d). In both cases, however, the statute provides that such a certificate does not make the holder ineligible. Rather, a staff member with responsibilities in the areas above may still participate in the teacher retirement system and be covered by the Tenure Act if his or her position requires teacher or administrator certification.

4. <u>Certification revocation</u>

When a teacher commits misconduct, his or her actions may demonstrate that he or she is not fit to continue to hold certification as a teacher. Indeed, since 2001, boards of education have been required to notify the Commissioner of Education whenever they receive notification that a teacher has been convicted of a crime (any crime, without limitation). Conn. Gen. Stat. § 10-221d(a). Whenever a teacher commits an act of serious misconduct, any interested person may initiate certification revocation proceedings, whether or not the teacher is convicted of a crime. In 2001, the General Assembly clarified that these procedures apply not only to certification, but also to any authorization or permit issued by the State

Board of Education. Conn. Gen. Stat. § 10-145b(m). In the following, the term "certification" shall refer to all three credentials.

Given the importance of certification in the employment of teachers, it is clear that certification is a property right for the teacher, creating a constitutional right to due process before a teacher's certification can be revoked. The certification regulations contain detailed procedures for a hearing and decision when revocation is recommended.

The statutes and regulations set forth reasons for which a teacher's certification, authorization or permit may be revoked. They include:

- The holder of the certification obtained it through fraud;
- The holder persistently has neglected to perform the duties for which certification was granted;
- The holder is "professionally unfit" to perform the duties for which certification was granted;
- The holder is convicted in a court of law of a crime involving moral turpitude or of another crime that, in the opinion of the State Board of Education, would impair the standing of certificates issued by the Board;
- The holder is found to have improperly disclosed questions or answers or otherwise breached the security of any state-wide examinations; or
- Other due and sufficient cause.

Conn. Gen. Stat. § 10-145b(m); Conn. St. Reg. § 10-145d-612.

The regulations provide that a request for certification revocation may be made by a board of education, a superintendent or "by any person with a legitimate interest." When a valid request for revocation is made, the Commissioner of Education (acting through his or her designee) will investigate. The Commissioner may also dismiss the request or ask for additional information before determining whether to investigate. If, based upon the results of the investigation, no probable cause to revoke is found, no further action is taken. However, if there is a finding of probable cause, the certificate holder may request a hearing. If he or she does, the hearing is held before the State Board of Education itself, before a committee of the Board or before an impartial hearing officer, at the option of the State Board of Education. If no hearing is requested, the State Board may rely on the Commissioner's report. The standard of proof in such proceedings is "by a preponderance of the evidence." Conn. Gen. Stat. § 10-145b(m).

In 1994, the General Assembly streamlined this process with regard to teachers who are convicted of the crime of child abuse. As was previously the case, school superintendents are required to notify the Commissioner of Education whenever a certified school employee is suspended after investigation of alleged child abuse, and they are further required to notify the Commissioner if the teacher's contract is terminated following such a suspension. Conn. Gen. Stat. § 17a-101i. While the statute does not so require, it would also be appropriate to notify the Commissioner if a teacher resigns his or her employment in the face of such allegations. In any event, the State's Attorney is also required to notify the Commissioner if a certificate holder is convicted of the crime of child abuse.

Crimes of child abuse include sexual contact between a student and any employee in the school district (among other persons), Conn. Gen. Stat. § 53a-73a (Class A misdemeanor) and sexual intercourse between a student and any employee in the school district (among other persons) (Class C felony). Conn. Gen. Stat. § 53a-71. If the Commissioner is notified that a certificate holder has been convicted of a crime involving an act of child abuse, the person's certificate is deemed to have been revoked. While the person may request reconsideration, there is no longer a duty to hold a hearing in the first instance. If reconsideration is requested, it is the burden of the former certificate holder to demonstrate why his or her certification should be reinstated. Conn. Gen. Stat. § 10-145b(m).

F. Other Teacher Rights

The education statutes in Connecticut contain a number of provisions that relate solely to teachers. While these statutes do not separately define a "teacher," it is reasonable to apply the same definition as is set out in the tenure law: a certified staff member below the rank of superintendent.

1. Sick leave

Teachers are entitled by law to an annual minimum of fifteen days paid sick leave. Since the law does not provide for accrual over the course of the year, it appears that teachers are entitled to all fifteen days at the beginning of the year. In addition, unused sick leave must be permitted to accumulate to no less than one hundred fifty days. Conn. Gen. Stat. § 10-156. Many teacher units have negotiated sick leave entitlements beyond these statutory minimums.

The statute does not address the issue of mid-year or part-time employment, and there are no court cases that provide guidance in this regard. However, school districts may likely make proportionate adjustments in sick leave accruals as teachers move from full- to part-time and vice versa. It is advisable to review how such adjustments will be made with the bargaining representative to assure common understanding.

2. Military leave

Teachers are entitled to be absent from work to fulfill military obligations. Conn. Gen. Stat. § 10-156c provides that professional employees of boards of education are entitled to up to thirty days leave each year to perform military duties, including service in the reserves of any branch of the military. Such leave must be without "loss or reduction of vacation or holiday privileges" (if applicable), and must be without prejudice with regard to promotion, continuation or employment or re-employment.

Also, if a professional employee of a board of education leaves employment to assume active duty status, he or she is entitled to be re-employed as long as he or she makes application within ninety days of separation from military service. For service of less than three years in addition to war service and the ninety day reapplication period, the returning employee is entitled to credit for all such time on the same basis as teachers serving in the district received for salary and other purposes. The statute expressly states, "[a]ny employee returning to the employ of the board of education as herein provided shall be credited with the period of such service in said armed forces to the same extent as though it had been a part of the term of employment by such board of education." It is not clear, however, whether "other purposes" includes accrual of time for tenure purposes. Conn. Gen. Stat. § 10-156d. *See also* Chapter Seven, Section C(5)(g).

3. Residency requirements

Teachers may not be required to live within the municipality or school district as a condition of appointment or continued employment. Conn. Gen. Stat. § 10-155f. Since the superintendent is not a "teacher" under the statute, this prohibition does not apply to him or her.

4. Lunch period

The statutes specifically require that teachers have a duty-free lunch period. Conn. Gen. Stat. § 10-156a provides that all certified professional employees of a board of education who work directly with children must have a guaranteed duty-free lunch period which is to be scheduled as a single period of consecutive minutes. However, the statute does not specify a minimum length of time for teacher lunch periods.

5. Discrimination on the basis of sex or marital status

While discrimination laws now protect persons generally from disparate treatment in employment on the basis of sex or marital status, teachers have been so protected for over fifty years. Conn. Gen. Stat. § 10-153.

6. Personnel records

The statutes have guaranteed teachers special rights of access to their personnel files since 1967, some years before the Freedom of Information Act provided such rights to public employees more generally. All professional employees certified by the State Board of Education are entitled to "knowledge of, access to, and upon request, a copy of supervisory records and reports of competence, personal character and efficiency maintained in such employee's personnel file with reference to evaluation of performance as a professional employee of such board of education." Conn. Gen. Stat. § 10-151a.

The Freedom of Information Act provides that most information in the personnel files of public employees must be disclosed, and that is true for teachers as well. While Conn. Gen. Stat. § 10-151c provides that "records of teacher performance and evaluation" are not considered to be public records under the Freedom of Information Act, this provision was amended in 2002. Now, it expressly states that "records of the personal misconduct of a teacher shall be deemed to be public records." *See* Chapter One(D)(4)(c)(2).

7. Professional communications

Given the special role that teachers can play in students' lives, teachers (as well as administrators and school nurses) have special rights concerning "professional communications" from students. If a student shares information confidentially with a teacher concerning alcohol or drug abuse or any alcohol or drug problem of the student, the teacher may not be required to disclose that information. Moreover, the teacher has immunity with regard to a decision to disclose or not to disclose such information, as long as that decision is made in good faith. Conn. Gen. Stat. § 10-154a.

This right belongs to the teacher. The teacher need not disclose this information to others, including school administrators. Significantly, however, the statute leaves the decision as to confidentiality with the teacher, and the student who shares such information with the teacher does not have the legal right to enforce confidentiality. Rather, that judgment is left to the teacher, and the teacher may disclose such information as he or she sees fit. In many cases the teacher may decide to disclose the information, out of concern for the student or for the other students. Some district policies concerning the use, possession or sale of drugs or alcohol, required under Conn. Gen. Stat. § 10-221(d), provide that such information shall be kept confidential. Such an assurance is not required, and could conflict with the rights of the professional employee under this section. The decision as to disclosure is left to that employee.

This privilege is limited to oral or written communication. If the professional employee receives physical evidence that a crime has been or is being committed by the student, such evidence must be turned over to school administrators or law enforcement officials within two days from when it was received. In turn, a school administrator who receives such evidence must turn it over to either the Commissioner of Consumer Protection or the appropriate law enforcement officials within three days of receipt. Conn. Gen. Stat. § 10-154a.

8. <u>Teacher retirement</u>

A significant advantage to being a "teacher" (*i.e.* teachers, administrators and superintendents) in Connecticut is eligibility to participate in the State Teacher Retirement System, and all such persons are "members" of this exclusive club. The rules regarding retirement benefits can be complicated, and they are beyond the scope of this <u>Guide</u>. Some general observations, however, may be helpful.

a. Required contributions

Teachers in Connecticut do not have a choice concerning contributions to the Teacher Retirement System. Members must contribute six percent of their "annual salary" for retirement benefits and one and one-quarter percent of their "annual salary" for medical retirement benefits. Conn. Gen. Stat. § 10-183b(7). The board of education is required to withhold these amounts and remit them each month (except July and August) to the State Teacher Retirement Board. Conn. Gen. Stat. § 10-183n. These contributions are withheld pre-tax, and taxable salary is reduced by the amount of the contributions. Conn. Gen. Stat. § 10-183kk.

b. "Annual salary"

The "annual salary" is the established rate that applies to the teacher's position. As long as the member receives salary on the first working day of the month, that salary is used to compute "annual salary" and the amount paid is subject to the mandatory contributions described above. Conversely, if a teacher is absent without pay (*e.g.*, after running out of paid sick leave or during an unpaid disciplinary suspension), such time would not be credited unless the time is paid for as a leave of absence.

The statutes describe in some detail what components of compensation are, and are not, included in "annual salary." The inclusion or exclusion of amounts from annual salary is highly significant, because it affects the contributions that teachers must make. Even more important, the definition of "annual salary" affects the benefits that the teacher will receive upon retirement.

"Annual salary" is defined as the annual salary rate for service as a Connecticut teacher during a school year. This amount includes compensation that a teacher receives as part of his/her basic assignment, such as a chairperson stipend, and it includes amounts paid to a member during a sabbatical leave during which mandatory contributions were made, provided that the member returns to full-time teaching for at least five full years following the completion of the leave. Conn. Gen. Stat. § 10-183b(3).

The statute excludes from annual salary any supplementary payments, such as payments for unused sick leave (if any), unused vacation, terminal pay, and coaching or extra duty assignments. Similarly, any amount the timing of which can be controlled by the member (such as a retirement incentive payment) is excluded from annual salary. Moreover, to prevent actions that would artificially inflate annual salary near retirement, the statute provides that any amount determined to have been included for the purpose of inflating the teacher's average annual salary will be excluded from the benefit calculation. Conn. Gen. Stat. § 10-183b(3).

There can be special problems in computing "annual salary" for school superintendents and other employees who have special contracts. Conn. Gen. Stat. § 10-183b(3) establishes a presumption that inclusion in salary of any amounts that were previously paid by the employer and not included in salary are for the purpose of inflating average annual salary. For example, if a superintendent received a car allowance for ten years and then three years before retirement that amount is added to salary in lieu of a car allowance, the Teachers Retirement Board will exclude this amount from final salary unless the member can establish that there was a reason for the change other than to inflate "annual salary" for retirement purposes.

The critical determinant of whether an amount can be included in annual salary for superintendents (and others with special contracts) is whether the amount is part of base salary. Conn. Gen. Stat. § 10-183b(3) expressly provides that annual salary does not include any payment to a superintendent that is not part of base salary. Accordingly, if a board of education and superintendent wish to include in annual salary payments made on behalf of the superintendent to an annuity company, those payments must be expressly described in the contract as part of base salary. Similarly, a performance incentive component to be determined over the course of the year can be included in base salary only if the contract specifically so states. By including such components in base salary, the parties assure that the superintendent makes contributions on all components of salary and concomitantly that retirement benefits will be computed on those components.

c. Benefit levels

The Teacher Retirement System is a defined benefit plan, *i.e.,* the amount of the retirement benefit is defined and the State bears all the investment risk. Indeed, when the teacher contribution was increased in 2003 to a total of 7.25%, the statute was amended to provide that this benefit is in the nature of a contract, which insulates the benefit from legislative change. Conn. Gen. Stat. § 10-183c.

The formula for computing a member's benefit upon normal retirement is two percent of "average annual salary" times years of service, computed to the nearest month. Conn. Gen. Stat. § 10-183g. Under certain circumstances specified in the statute, teachers can purchase credit for other past service, including out-of-state service, service for national teacher organizations, and substitute service in excess of forty school days (at the rate of eighteen days of such service for each school month to be purchased). Conn. Gen. Stat. § 10-183e.

Average annual salary is defined by statute as the salary received during the three years of highest salary, no matter when they occurred.

Conn. Gen. Stat. § 10-183b. If a member retires prior to normal retirement, his or her benefit is reduced actuarially.

d. Retirement

The statutes provide that members may retire normally, *i.e.* with no reduction in the benefit formula, under two circumstances: (1) with thirty-five years of service (of which at least twenty-five years are Connecticut service), regardless of age, or (2) at age sixty, with at least twenty years of credited service in Connecticut. In addition, there are other options for retirement that entail an actuarial reduction in the benefit, including proratable retirement, early retirement, and deferred vested retirement, all with different benefit levels. Conn. Gen. Stat. § 10-183f. Members are eligible for a proratable retirement upon attaining age sixty with at least ten years of credited service. Members are eligible for early retirement if they have twenty-five years of credited service, at least twenty of which were in Connecticut, or if they attain fifty-five years of age and have at least twenty years of credited service, at least fifteen of which were in Connecticut. Finally, a member is eligible for a vested deferred retirement at age sixty if the member has ten years of credited service in Connecticut and terminates service before becoming eligible for any other benefit. *Id.*

In addition to these retirement options, members who become disabled and are unable to perform their teaching or administrative duties are eligible for a disability allowance. Conn. Gen. Stat. § 10-183aa. Significantly, application for and receipt of a disability allowance does not operate to sever employment with the employing board of education. Obviously, the disabling condition that confers eligibility for the disability allowance will often cause the teacher to resign employment, or in rare circumstances will cause the board to terminate the teacher's contract in accordance with the Tenure Act. Notably, however, the issue of disability allowance and continued employment are separate.

e. Medical benefits

Teachers are required to contribute six percent of their salary plus one and one-quarter percent of their salary (for a total of seven and one-quarter percent) toward their retirement benefits. Conn. Gen. Stat. § 10-183b(7). The one and one-quarter percent contribution is earmarked to offset the cost of providing members health insurance benefits upon retirement, and the State Teachers' Retirement Board is required to maintain the one and one-quarter percent contributions in a separate fund for that purpose. Conn. Gen. Stat. § 10-183t.

Upon retirement, teachers are eligible to receive health insurance benefits. Their eligibility for benefits depends upon their eligibility to participate in Medicare Part A, which in turn depends upon their having paid into the social security system or being the spouse of a person who did. The number of such teachers eligible to participate in Medicare Part A will increase over time, because in 1987 the law was changed to require participation. Employees hired by boards of education that year and after are required to pay into Medicare, causing them to be eligible for Medicare upon retirement.

Conn. Gen. Stat. § 10-183t provides that teachers have two options regarding health insurance. The Teacher Retirement Board is obligated to offer members (and their spouse or their surviving spouse or a disabled dependent if there is no surviving spouse) a basic health insurance plan upon retirement, provided that the teacher or spouse is eligible for Medicare Part A Hospital insurance. Members (and spouses) participating in this plan must pay a twenty-five percent premium cost share. In addition, the Teacher Retirement Board is also obligated to offer members and/or their spouses one or more optional plans, with the participating member or spouse paying the cost difference.

Alternatively, a member (either retired or receiving a disability allowance) who is not participating in Medicare Part A hospital insurance "may fully participate in any or all group health insurance plans maintained for active teachers by such member's last employing board of education." This right may be exercised at any time and is not lost if the teacher does not enroll with the board of education plan at the time of retirement. The law also specifies that the term "group health insurance plans" is to be construed broadly as the "hospital, medical, major medical, dental, prescription drug or auditory benefit plans that are available to active teachers."

The statute also provides for payment of a portion of the expense of participation for retired teachers. First, it clarifies that its provisions do not affect other obligations boards of education may have assumed for such costs through collective bargaining. In the absence of such a contractual obligation of the board of education, the cost of participating in the plan is to be borne by the member. The statute provides, however, that the Teacher Retirement Board will pay a subsidy to the local or regional board of education in whose plan the member is participating. This subsidy is to be equal to the subsidy paid on June 30, 2000, which is $110 per month for the member and another $110 per month for any dependent. Moreover, this subsidy is doubled if a member is at least sixty-five years of age and has at least twenty-five or more years of full-time service, is not receiving a spousal subsidy, is not participating in Medicare Part A, and is receiving a monthly benefit of less than $1,500. The statute specifies that subsidy must be used to reduce the costs for the member and/or spouse absent any contractual provisions to the contrary. *Id.*

Finally, the law now provides that boards of education must notify the Teacher Retirement Board prior to canceling coverage of participating members in its health insurance plan due to non-payment of premiums. Such notification must be provided at least thirty days prior to the date of cancellation.

f. Re-employment

Members who retire and begin to receive benefits from the Teachers Retirement System may obtain any employment not subject to membership in the System (*i.e.* employment in a position requiring certification) without jeopardizing their eligibility for benefits. Moreover, members can even be re-employed in a certified position on a temporary basis. The law permits members to earn annually up to forty-five percent of the maximum-level salary for the assigned subject area (or responsibility) without losing their retirement benefits. Members who are re-employed in shortage areas (as specified by the Commissioner of Education) have an even better deal – they are entitled to be re-employed without any earnings limitation for one year and, with the approval of the Teacher Retirement Board, a second year. Conn. Gen. Stat. § 10-183v(a). *See* Series 2003-2004, Circular Letter C-2 (July 11, 2003). Such teachers must be offered health insurance benefits on the same basis as other active staff members, but they cannot accrue any further service credit for such additional teaching time.

Members may even suspend their retirement and again be employed. If a board of education certifies that such re-employment is in its best interests, the member can be re-employed on a continuing basis and be paid at the regular rate for teachers in that position. TRB benefits terminate on the first day of the month of such re-employment, and they resume on the first day of the month after such re-employment ends. In any event, such re-employment is not considered service as a teacher under the Tenure Act. Conn. Gen. Stat. § 10-183v(b), (c), (e).

CHAPTER FOUR
STUDENTS

School districts encounter many legal issues involving the students they serve. Historically, school districts were seen as acting *in loco parentis*, in the place of the parent, and as such were subject to few legal restrictions. However, more recently the courts have recognized that students are people too, with many of the same rights as adults have. Over the years, the courts have struggled to decide when students' rights must be recognized, and when school officials can exercise supervision and control over students.

A. Residency and School Attendance

The obligation to provide school accommodations raises two separate issues: what are the rights of students to attend school in a particular district, and what are the obligations of parents and guardians to assure that children attend school?

1. The right to attend school

The General Assembly has delegated the State's responsibility for education to local and regional school boards, which are obliged to "make such provisions as will enable each child of school age, residing in the district to attend some public day school for the period required by law and provide for the transportation of children wherever transportation is reasonable and desirable." Conn. Gen. Stat. § 10-220(a). Local and regional boards of education must permit any child residing in the district who is between the ages of five and twenty-one (and not yet a high school graduate) to attend public school. Conn. Gen. Stat. § 10-186. Moreover, this basic obligation includes the duty to provide transportation to students whenever such transportation is reasonable or desirable. Conn. Gen. Stat. § 10-220(a).

When a school district does not operate its own high school, it is obligated by statute to designate a school that resident children can attend. Conn. Gen. Stat. § 10-33. To do so the district must contract with a neighboring school district that operates a high school and is willing to accept such students on a tuition basis. If a receiving district does not wish to continue to provide such services, it must give prior notice of at least one year. Conn. Gen. Stat. § 10-35.

School districts may designate more than one high school for resident children to attend. The Attorney General has opined that the board of education must pay full tuition for and the reasonable cost of transportation to any designated school. *Opinion to Sergi, Opinions of the Attorney General* #1996-019 (December 13, 1996). This opinion also states, however, that a school district not maintaining a high school may agree with a parent to pay full tuition and share in the cost of transportation to a school other than the designated high school.

a. Eligibility for school privileges

Students are eligible for school accommodations if they reach the age of five prior to January 1 in that year. Conn. Gen. Stat. § 10-15c. Parents sometimes press to get their children into the public schools before that time. Early admission may be required because of the special education needs of the child, as discussed in Chapter Five. More generally, the statute provides that boards of education may admit students prior to that time by a formal vote. In considering such requests, however, boards of education must keep in mind the responsibility to provide "equal protection of the laws." Early admission for one student may result in other parent claims for equal treatment of their children.

The right to school accommodations ends with high school graduation or attainment of age twenty-one, whichever comes first. In addition, the General Assembly has limited the right to school accommodations in two respects. If a student sixteen years of age or older voluntarily terminates enrollment (*i.e.* drops out), he or she may be denied readmission to that school district for up to ninety school days from the date of termination. Conn. Gen. Stat. § 10-186(d). Second, a board of education may now place a student enrolling at age nineteen or older in "an alternative school program or other suitable educational program" if that student cannot acquire a sufficient number of credits for graduation by age twenty-one. Conn. Gen. Stat. § 10-220(a).

b. School assignment

Designating the schools children attend is a basic responsibility of boards of education. Conn. Gen. Stat. § 10-220(a). School boards typically accomplish this responsibility by establishing attendance zones that determine which of the district's schools a particular student will attend. Under state law, once attendance zones are set, that is it, and there is no right of a parent to appeal. Conn. Gen. Stat. § 10-221e provides that school districts may establish intradistrict assignment programs that give students the option to attend a different school within the district, and transportation need not be provided to students electing a different school. School districts, however, do not generally utilize this option.

A student's right to transfer in various situations under the No Child Left Behind Act can now trump a local school assignment decision. First, as discussed in Chapter One, Section (A)(2)(a), students who attend schools "in need of improvement" may be entitled to transfer to other schools within the district.

Second, also under the NCLB, a student who "becomes a victim of a violent criminal offense, as determined by State law, while in or on the grounds of a public elementary school or secondary school that the student attends" must be allowed to transfer to a different school if one is available within the school district. No Child Left Behind Act, Section 9532. The State Board of Education has defined a "violent criminal offense" as having three required components. First, the student must suffer bodily injury as a result of intentional, knowing, or reckless acts committed by another person. Second, the police must have been notified and a report taken (though significantly there is no requirement that such notification come from school officials). Third, the facts alleged in the police report must be sufficient to constitute a crime as described in the Penal Code, Title 53a. Series 2003-2004, Circular Letter C-12 (August 27, 2003).

Third, the No Child Left Behind Act, Section 9532 also requires that states receiving Title I funds identify "persistently dangerous public elementary school[s] or secondary school[s]," and provide students attending such schools the option to attend a "safe public elementary or secondary school within the [district], including a public charter school." A "persistently dangerous" school is defined as a school that meets two of the following three criteria for three years in a row:

- Two or more gun-free schools violations (possession of a firearm or explosive device that resulted in expulsion from school); or
- One "Other Weapon" incident resulting in expulsion per 200 students with a minimum of three such incidents; or
- One violent criminal offense resulting in expulsion per 200 students with a minimum of three such incidents.

Series 2003-2004, Circular Letter C-12 (August 27, 2003). In the first year that a school meets two of these criteria, the State Department of Education will notify the school and require that it develop a written plan to develop a positive school environment. In the second year, it will warn the school, which then must revise the plan. In the third year, the district must notify parents of the option to transfer to a school that is not "persistently dangerous. Many Connecticut school districts, however, only have one school at a particular level. Some students in Connecticut, therefore, may find themselves without any transfer rights even though they attend "a persistently dangerous school" or are the "victim of a violent criminal offense."

c. Residency determinations

At the outset, it is important to understand that there is a public policy in favor of education. Rulings on residency and the concomitant right to attend school are based on the premise that each child has the right to attend school somewhere. For example, over a hundred years ago, the Connecticut Supreme Court ruled that "residence" for school purposes is not to be interpreted technically, but rather in the "ordinary and popular meaning of the word." Given this rule and the public policy in favor of educating children, it is fair to say that, if the child is actually present within the district, he or she is to be educated. *Yale v. West Middle School*, 59 Conn. 489, 491 (1890). *See also New Haven v. Torrington*, 132 Conn. 194 (1945).

By law, the burden of proof in residency disputes is on the family; the "party denied schooling shall have the burden of providing residency by a preponderance of the evidence." Conn. Gen. Stat. § 10-186(b)(1). Given the strong public policy in favor of education, however, the child will be found eligible for school privileges in at least one, and sometimes more than one, school district. Practically speaking, to establish that a student is not entitled to school privileges in a particular district, district personnel generally must be able to point to another district in which the student would be able to attend school.

Despite these rules favoring claims that a student may attend the schools of a particular district, residency disputes can and do arise. School districts may exclude children who are actually residing in another district (subject to the right under Conn. Gen. Stat. § 10-186 to continue in attendance during any hearing process). The term "residence" is not self-defining, however, and disagreements over whether a child is actually a resident of a particular district are common.

Each of the typical family situations is addressed below. It is important that building administrators make a residency determination before permitting a parent or guardian to enroll a student. Once a student is enrolled in school, the district must permit the student to remain in attendance until hearings over eligibility for school privileges are complete. Conn. Gen. Stat. § 10-186(b)(2). By statute, school officials may recoup the cost of tuition if a state hearing officer finds that the student was not entitled to school privileges, but such after-the-fact relief does not directly benefit the school board, if in fact the parents ever pay up.

1. Student living with parents

If a student is living with parents or guardians, the school district must ascertain whether they are living in the district. The parents should be asked to give the address of their house or apartment, and to provide evidence of residence, such as a driver's license for that address, utility bills made out to that family at that address or other information to establish that they are actually living at the house or apartment in question. District officials can ask for a copy of the lease if the family is renting.

2. Student living with one parent (when parents are divorced)

Practically speaking, a student will be eligible to attend school in the school district if either parent resides there, regardless of whether the parent residing in the district has custody. Legal custody is not required for a student to be eligible for school accommodations. Rather, the question is simply whether the child is actually residing in the district. A student would not be eligible for school privileges in the district if he or she were actually living with the other parent in another school district (irrespective of which parent has custody). If a student claims to be living with a parent in a particular school district, however, it is difficult for the district to show otherwise. Spending some nights with the other parent will not change the residency of the student, and hearing officers and the courts will be sympathetic to the wishes of divorced parents to have their children spend substantial time with each parent. The facts of the case will govern, however, and the actual residence of the student, as opposed to the wishes of the parents, is the dispositive factor. *See West Hartford Board of Education v. State Board of Education*, 8 Conn. Ops. 807 (July 15, 2002).

3. Student living in homes on the town boundary

In rare cases, a student's residence rests on the boundary of two towns, and the question arises as to where the student is entitled to attend school. There have been both litigation and statutory changes concerning this matter. In *Baerst v. State Board of Education*, 34 Conn. App. 567, *cert. denied*, 230 Conn. 915 (1994), the Appellate Court applied a "constellation of interests" test to find that a student whose family's property was in both Norwalk and New Canaan (though the house was entirely within the town of Norwalk) was eligible to attend the New Canaan Public Schools because the focus of his life was New Canaan, not Norwalk. This ruling caused consternation because it made it difficult to predict with certainty where a student would be entitled to attend school.

The General Assembly has clarified the situation through legislation. It tried several different approaches (such as providing school privileges in the town to which the family paid the most real estate tax), but it established the current rule in 1997. The town of residence is where the dwelling is located, *i.e.* the house or apartment in which the family resides, not the plot on which the house or apartment stands. *See McGarry v. State Board of Education*, 7 Conn. Ops. 509 (May 7, 2001) (student residing on parcel in Waterford and Montville must attend Montville schools because the dwelling is solely in Montville). If a town line intersects the dwelling, however, the student is entitled to attend school in either school district. Conn. Gen. Stat. § 10-186(a).

4. Illegal foreign nationals

Sometimes questions arise concerning a student who is indisputably residing within the district, but who is not legally a resident of this country. These situations can put districts between a rock and a hard place, but some general comments may be helpful. The United States Supreme Court has ruled that a child's legal status should not affect his or her right to attend school. The Court struck down a Texas law that permitted school districts to deny educational services to children of illegal foreign nationals. *Plyler v. Doe*, 457 U.S. 202 (1982). The bottom line is that school districts will generally be responsible for children who are actually living in their district, regardless of their immigration status.

In 1996, the United States Congress passed a new law that limits the rights of a student to attend public school districts on an F-1 visa. The law provides that F-1 nonimmigrant student status is not available to a foreign national who seeks to attend a public elementary school. The law further provides that entry into this country to attend a public secondary school is prohibited unless the aggregate period of F-1 status does not exceed one year (cumulative total of twelve months) and the foreign national reimburses the school for the unsubsidized per capita costs of providing the education. 8 U.S.C. § 1184(m)(1). The J-1 visa remains available, however, for foreign nationals who attend school in the United States pursuant to approved foreign exchange programs.

These new provisions have caused some confusion. If the federal law now states that students whose legal residence is in another country may not obtain an F-1 visa to attend school, should such a child be permitted to attend school? Does such attendance violate federal law? The answers are yes and no. Given the *Plyler v. Doe* case cited above, and the strong public policy in favor of education, visa status and school attendance must be kept separate. If the student appears not to be a permanent resident, as when s/he is in this country on a tourist visa, the district may deny school accommodations. The district must notify the family, however, of their right to a hearing before the board of education over the denial. Conn. Gen. Stat. § 10-186(a). The burden will then be on the family and/or student to show that s/he is a permanent resident, notwithstanding his or her immigration status. If the family and/or student establishes that s/he is actually residing in the school district, however, the student will be entitled to school privileges. As the Connecticut Supreme Court stated in 1890, if the child is "actually present," *i.e.* is residing in the district, he or she is entitled to attend school. *Yale v. West Middle School*, 59 Conn. 489, 491 (1890). Providing education to such a child is not a violation of federal law. To be sure, the student may be residing in this country illegally, and he or she may be subject to deportation. As long as the child actually resides within the school district, however, the child is entitled to attend school.

5. Student living with other family members or friends

Under limited circumstances, students may establish residence in a district and attend school there even though neither parent lives in the district. Students often wish to move in with other family members or friends to attend school. The challenge is to determine when the student has actually established a residence apart from his or her parents, and when he or she has not.

The legislature has attempted in two ways to assure that only bona fide resident children may attend school in a district. First, the statutes provide that the family claiming eligibility for school privileges must establish residency by a preponderance of the evidence. Conn. Gen. Stat. § 10-186(b)(1). Second, the statutes set out specific requirements to establish "residency" when students do not live with their parents or guardians. Conn. Gen. Stat. § 10-253(d) provides that students may attend school in a district even though their parents or guardians do not live there under the following conditions. It must be the intention of the parents or the child and of the host family that the residence in the district be:

- permanent,
- provided without pay, and
- not for the sole purpose of obtaining school accommodations.

As a threshold matter, we note that a student may be eligible for school privileges in a district even over the specific protest of the parents. Since the public policy is strongly in favor of assuring access to education, the General Assembly has provided that it is sufficient that it is the intent of the child and of the host family that the child will reside in a school district. When students run away from home and live with friends, for example, they may in fact be "residing" with their friends in that district. If so, they are entitled to school privileges there.

Also, Conn. Gen. Stat. § 10-253(d) provides that school officials may request that a parent provide documentation of the child's residency. The statute further provides, however, that the district must first provide the family a written statement specifying the basis on which the district has reason to believe that the child is not entitled to school accommodations. This requirement appears not to apply, however, in the case of verifying residence upon initial enrollment. At that point, the district would not have made a determination concerning eligibility for school privileges, and could certainly not provide a written statement concerning grounds for ineligibility.

a. "Permanent"

"Permanent" residence is difficult to define. The State Department of Education has provided guidelines to assist school districts in making residency determinations. These Guidelines are set out in the School Accommodations Workshop Package, available at the State Department of Education website. These guidelines define a "permanent resident" as "one who resides in a district and who has a present intention to remain with the district." The notion of present intention to remain is of little help, of course; a student whose family is planning to move to another town, for example, remains entitled to school privileges until the day the family actually moves. All the facts and circumstances of the student's residence, therefore, must be considered in determining whether a claimed residence is permanent. If a student resides with friends during the school year and lives with parents during vacation and summer periods, for example, those facts would support a finding that the residence with friends within the school district is not permanent.

The State Guidelines set out factors that school districts may consider. The Guidelines recognize that residency determinations are complex, and the list of factors is not exhaustive: "There are a number of factors enumerated in court cases that boards may consider relevant to a determination of residency. These and other factors may be used as evidence of permanency and residency or the lack thereof. These may include, among others:

a) Where the majority of the student's clothing and personal possessions are located.
b) Address listed on the student's driver's license;
c) Town of issue of library card;
d) Where the student attends church;
e) Place of club affiliations, *e.g.* cub scouts, boy scouts;
f) Residence of child's immediate family;
g) Where the student spends substantial time when school is not in session;
h) Age and emancipation status of the child."

The Guidelines address the issue of custody as follows:

> As evidence of permanent residency, a district may request, but not require, as an indicator, that the person with whom the child resides has primary and direct responsibility over such child's daily and general affairs (e.g. ability to consent to school trips and medical treatment, attend parent-teacher conferences, receive report cards, etc.).

As stated above, legal custody in the host family is not required, because the determination is not who has custody, but rather simply where the child resides.

b. "Provided without pay"

The next factor listed in the statute is "provided without pay." This requirement has been in the statute for many years, and presumably it was originally intended to avoid the "rooming house" situation in which a person would set up shop to host children so that they could attend school in a particular district. The State Guidelines address this factor as follows:

> Pay shall include any monetary remuneration from a parent or legal guardian for the support of a child either to the relative or non-relative or to the child. It shall not include gifts to the child for purposes other than support.

In addition, the Guidelines state that "pay" does not include maintaining the child's health insurance, taking the child as a deduction for income tax purposes, or making support payments pursuant to a court order.

c. "Not for the sole purpose of obtaining school accommodations"

The last factor is "not for the sole purpose of obtaining school accommodations." Application of this factor will typically depend upon the specific facts of the case. If a student says that he is going to live with his friend so that he can complete his education in a school district, for example, he has just provided evidence that he is not entitled to attend school there. Sophisticated parents, however, can come up with some explanation other than completing school for the separate residence of their child (*e.g.*, "we are not getting along," "she was living with my parents to help them remember to take their medication").

In an effort to ensure that these statutory requirements are met, many districts require that parents and host families execute affidavits attesting to the fact that the residence is permanent, provided without pay and not for the sole purpose of education. These forms can also warn parents and others that they may be liable for tuition charges if it is later determined that the student attended school illegally.

6. State agency placements

Students who are placed in a district by state agencies are entitled to attend school in that district. The district in which the child would otherwise be attending school is financially responsible for the student's education. Generally, the receiving school district may charge tuition to the school district where the child would otherwise be attending school. However, it is not always possible to identify such a district, and the financial responsibility will then be imposed on the district where the student resides as a result of the placement. Conn. Gen. Stat. § 10-253(a). When students requiring special education services are placed in residence on state-owned property, special provisions apply to require the State to reimburse the local or regional district for one hundred percent of the cost. Conn. Gen. Stat. § 10-76d(e).

7. Homeless children

Questions can arise when a student has no permanent residence in a school district. In 1987, the General Assembly addressed this situation, and the No Child Left Behind Act sets forth new rules. Conn. Gen. Stat. § 10-253(e) provides that students who reside in temporary shelters are entitled to free school privileges from the school district in which the shelter is located or from the school district where they would otherwise reside if not for the need for temporary shelter. The statute provides that the district in which the temporary shelter is located shall notify the district where the student would otherwise be attending school. The district may either continue to provide educational services, including transportation between the temporary shelter and school in the "home" district, or it may pay tuition to the district in which the temporary shelter is located. Also, when the student is placed out of district in order to receive special education services, the district where the student would otherwise attend school remains responsible for the placement until a new residence is established. However, where it is not possible to identify the district where the student would otherwise be attending school, the district in which the temporary shelter is located must provide school accommodations to the student.

The statute also states that when the Department of Children and Families places a child requiring special education in a temporary shelter, the district in which the child resided immediately prior to the placement is responsible for the costs of special education instruction. This responsibility, however, is limited to a period of one year (or earlier if the child is returned to his or her parents or is committed to the state), after which time DCF is financially responsible.

Title X, Section 1032 of the No Child Left Behind Act (known as the McKinney-Vento Homeless Education Assistance Improvements Act of 2001, 42 U.S.C. § 11431 *et seq.*) amended the federal law concerning homeless children, and Conn. Gen. Stat. § 10-253(f) incorporates these federal requirements by reference. Unfortunately, at this point it is not clear whether and how the state and federal laws interrelate, because we do not know how the reference in the federal law to "emergency or transitional shelters" relates to the definition of "temporary shelters" in state law.

The McKinney-Vento Homeless Education Assistance Improvements Act defines "homelessness" broadly to mean "individuals who lack a fixed, regular, and adequate nighttime residence," including:

- children who are sharing the housing of other persons due to loss of housing, economic hardship, or a similar reason;
- children who are living in motels, hotels, trailer parks, or camping grounds due to the lack of alternative adequate accommodations;
- children who are living in emergency or transitional shelters, or who are abandoned in hospitals, or are awaiting foster care placement;
- children who have a primary nighttime residence that is a public or private place not designed for or ordinarily used as a regular sleeping accommodation for human beings;
- children and youths who are living in cars, parks, public spaces, abandoned buildings, substandard housing, bus or train stations, or similar settings; and
- migratory children who qualify as homeless because they are living in circumstances described above.

This law obligates school districts to assure that students enrolled in their schools who become homeless during a school year continue to receive educational services for that year. It further provides that students who become homeless between school years must continue to receive educational services for the following school year. In both cases, the school district responsible for assuring continued educational services is the district in which the student was last enrolled before becoming homeless (the district of origin). This obligation continues throughout the period of homelessness.

Moreover, such children may now continue in enrollment in the school of origin at least for the rest of the school year, even if they establish a new residence. The school district of origin and the new school district must confer on how best to share costs, but if they cannot, the law specifies that they must split the costs equally. Obviously, the obligation to assure that such children get to school each day can be a logistical nightmare. To meet these obligations, school districts are now required to designate an appropriate staff person, who may also be a coordinator for other federal programs, such as a local educational agency liaison for homeless children and youths.

Under McKinney-Vento, the district of origin (where the child was enrolled when s/he last had a permanent residence) is obligated to maintain the child in the school of origin "to the extent feasible," unless the parent or guardian objects. The district may continue to provide educational services in the school of origin, *i.e.* the school that the student attended when last permanently housed or the school of last enrollment. The responsible district may provide for the child to attend school in the school that is attended by other students living in the same attendance area where the homeless child lives, but if the parent or guardian insists, transportation must be provided to the school of origin if that school is within the school district.

The McKinney-Vento Act further requires that homeless children be provided with educational services that are comparable to those provided to the other students enrolled in the same school, including transportation services, compensatory educational programs and the like. The 2001 Amendments impose significant new obligations, including the right of students to attend their school of origin (the last school attended before they became homeless), and the right to attend school even though immunizations and other conditions are not met and even though school records are not available. A child who claims that he or she is homeless and has been denied school accommodations has the same right to seek a hearing as other children, as outlined below. Significantly, however, if a child is homeless, under the McKinney-Vento Act he or she is entitled to "stay-put" and may attend school in the district where enrollment is sought pending a decision through the hearing process.

d. Denial of school accommodations and hearing procedures

If district personnel conclude that a student seeking admission or a student already attending district schools is not eligible for school accommodations, they must notify the family of that determination, and the basis for it. Typically, such written notification also informs the family that the child should be withdrawn from school by a specified date. Also, if the determination is made on the basis that the student resides in another school district, that other school district must be notified of the denial of school accommodations to the student. Conn. Gen. Stat. § 10-186(a). If a parent claims that his or her child has been wrongfully denied school accommodations, he or she may request a hearing.

After a school district notifies a family of denial of school privileges, it may not simply exclude the student from school. The courts have held that such action without at least offering a prior hearing is a denial of due process. Rather, whenever a school district provides notification that a child is not eligible for school accommodations, it must inform the parents or guardians of their right to request a hearing under Conn. Gen. Stat. § 10-186(b) if they dispute the determination. The statute further provides that the parent, guardian or student may in writing request a hearing from the board of education on the denial of accommodations. Interestingly, the statute does not contain a time limitation for the filing of such a written request. It is advisable, therefore, for a school district to include in its original notification of ineligibility a date by which the parents should either remove the child from school or request a hearing.

Within ten days after receipt of the request, the local or regional board of education must hold a hearing. The statutes now provide that the board may (1) itself conduct the hearing, (2) designate a subcommittee of the board composed of three members to conduct the hearing, or (3) establish a local impartial hearing board of one or more members who are not members of the board of education to conduct the hearing. At such hearings, the burden is on the student to establish residency by a preponderance of evidence. However, if a school district claims that a student is ineligible for a reason other than residency, it has the burden of proving such ineligibility. The school board must maintain a record of the hearing and make its decision on the question of eligibility for school privileges within ten days after the close of the hearing. Conn. Gen. Stat. § 10-186(b)(2).

When a student is already enrolled in school, he or she has the right to remain in school during the hearing process and any subsequent appeals. However, the district has the right to seek payment of tuition for such period if the student is ultimately found ineligible for school privileges. Conn. Gen. Stat. § 10-186(b)(2) and (4). If the child has not yet been admitted to school, there is no obligation to enroll the child pending the results of the hearing process (except as may be required under the McKinney-Vento Act, discussed above).

A decision to deny school accommodations to the student may be appealed to the State Board of Education. Conn. Gen. Stat. § 10-186(b)(2). Such an appeal must be filed within twenty days of the mailing of the board of education decision, or the appeal will be dismissed. Hearing officers appointed by the State have strictly enforced this time limitation.

In addition, the parent may request and receive within thirty days a tape recording or a transcript of the hearing before the local or regional board of education. Conn. Gen. Stat. § 10-186(b)(2). However, since the party requesting the transcript must pay for it, it is more common for the parties simply to submit the tape recording of the board level hearing to the State Board of Education. *See* Conn. Gen. Stat. § 4-177(e).

The local or regional board must file the record of its hearing with the State Board of Education within ten days of receipt of an appeal. An impartial hearing officer of the State Board of Education will hold the hearing on the appeal in the local or regional school district, must maintain a record of the hearing, and has the right to join as a party to the hearing any school district that could be responsible for the student's education. In fact, the statute expressly states that the hearing officer may not make a determination concerning the obligations of another school district unless that district is also a party to the hearing. Conn. Gen. Stat. § 10-186(b)(2). Therefore, whenever a school district contests eligibility for school accommodations and claims that another district is responsible for the child, it should make sure that the other district is made a party to the hearing.

The hearing officer is required to make a decision within forty-five days of the request for a hearing, but the hearing officer may request extensions from the Commissioner of Education. Extensions are normally granted when good cause is shown. These time limits are not mandatory, but rather directory, *i.e.* they provide guidance to the hearing officer. *Blau v. State Board of Education*, 19 Conn. App. 428, *cert. denied*, 212 Conn. 816 (1989).

The hearing officer must consider the record of the hearing before the local or regional school board. In cases of residency disputes, the hearing officer makes an independent determination, and s/he is not required to give deference to the decision of the board of education below. In all other cases (including denial of school accommodations for other reasons or denial of transportation services), the decision of the local or regional board of education is to be sustained unless the hearing officer finds that the decision was arbitrary, capricious, or unreasonable. Conn. Gen. Stat. § 10-186(b)(4). It is especially important in such cases, therefore, that the local or regional board of education make written findings. Such findings make clear the basis for the decision of the local or regional board of education, and the hearing officer is better able to determine whether the decision should stand.

If parents or school officials are dissatisfied with the decision of the hearing officer, they may appeal to Superior Court. Such an appeal must be filed within forty-five days of the mailing of the decision. Conn. Gen. Stat. §

10-187, Conn. Gen. Stat. § 4-183. As with other court appeals, any dispute may then be appealed further, to a final ruling by the Connecticut Supreme Court. Once the process is concluded, however, the school district may disenroll the student. *Dunbar v. Hamden Board of Education*, 267 F. Supp.2d 178 (D. Conn. 2003).

e. Transportation

Under Connecticut law, "each local or regional board of education shall furnish, by transportation or otherwise, school accommodations" to resident children. Conn. Gen. Stat. § 10-186(a). Such transportation must also be provided to students enrolled in non-public, non-profit schools within the district. Conn. Gen. Stat. § 10-281. School boards must also provide transportation to students enrolled in vocational-technical schools, vocational agricultural schools and to charter schools located within the district. The key to the duty to provide transportation is that it must be a necessary part of school accommodations. If a student does not need transportation in order to have reasonable access to school accommodations, there is no duty to provide it.

In 2002, the General Assembly amended the statutes concerning the operation of school buses as they provide transportation to school children. Operators are now prohibited from running the engine of a stopped school bus for more than three consecutive minutes except when it is necessary in specified circumstances, including traffic conditions, keeping the bus warm for students, and discharging passengers. Conn. Gen. Stat. § 14-277.

School districts have the right to suspend students from transportation services for up to ten days if their conduct while awaiting or receiving transportation to or from school endangers persons or property or is violative of a publicized policy of the board. Conn. Gen. Stat. § 10-233c. This right to suspend transportation services applies to students enrolled in private schools as well. Conn. Gen. Stat. § 10-281. School officials should be cautious, however, in any suspension of transportation services. Transportation is typically provided because the district has determined that the walking route to school presents a hazard due to distance or other danger. If such transportation is to be suspended, the district should ascertain through discussion with the parents how the student will otherwise be getting to school. The district should not create a situation where the student is exposed to hazards because he or she is expected to get to school on his or her own without any safe way to do so. If the parents will not take responsibility for providing transportation, it may be more appropriate to suspend the student from school altogether.

1. Transportation to public schools

Whether transportation services are necessary to provide reasonable access to school depends, of course, on the particular facts. The statute does not prescribe the situations in which transportation must be provided to students. Most districts have specific policies as to when students will be entitled to transportation based on both the student's grade level and the distance from the student's designated school. For example, a district might set one-half mile as the requisite distance for grades kindergarten through 3, one mile for grades 4 through 8, and two miles for grades 9 through 12. However, where walking exposes the students to hazards or other dangers, such as high speed streets, unguarded intersections on busy streets, or unfenced waterways, transportation must be provided regardless of distance. The State Department of Education has developed guidelines concerning the provision of transportation that, although not binding, are a helpful starting point for boards of education in developing their own policies. These Guidelines are set out in the School Accommodations Workshop Package, available at the website of the State Department of Education.

2. Transportation to state technical high schools, vocational agricultural schools, charter schools, and interdistrict magnet schools

Students may elect to attend state technical high schools or vocational agricultural programs. *See* Chapter One, Section F(8). In such cases, their district of residence must provide transportation to the school (for vo-ag programs, the reasonable costs thereof). The statutes set forth special reimbursement percentages for the district providing such transportation, and limit the cost for vo-ag programs to the foundation as defined in Section 10-262f(9). Conn. Gen. Stat. § 10-97.

As described in Chapter One, Section F(13), students may also elect to attend charter schools. The school district in which the student resides must provide transportation to any charter school located within the school district. Conn. Gen. Stat. § 10-66ee(e). School districts may also elect to provide transportation to students attending charter schools outside of the district, and if they do so, they will be eligible for reimbursement for some of the costs of such transportation. *Id.*; Conn. Gen. Stat. § 10-266m.

Providing support for interdistrict magnet schools is one way in which the State is addressing its obligations under *Sheff v. O'Neill*. Students who elect to attend interdistrict magnet schools may also be entitled to transportation to such schools, which may be provided by the participating local or regional school district. If the school is located within the district, eligibility and reimbursement for such transportation is determined on the same basis as for other in-district transportation. If the interdistrict magnet school is located outside of the student's district of residence, the district is not obligated to provide transportation, but it may do so. If it does, the school district transporting the student will receive reimbursement for the cost of such transportation in accordance with Conn. Gen. Stat. § 10-264i. For interdistrict magnet schools to be successful long-term, however, a greater state commitment to paying the cost of such transportation may be essential.

3. Transportation to private schools

School districts are obligated to provide "the same kind of transportation services" to resident children enrolled in "nonpublic nonprofit schools" that are located within the district. Conn. Gen. Stat. § 10-281. Accordingly, school districts typically apply the same policies regarding distance to school and the existence of hazards on the way to determine whether children enrolled in such private schools are entitled to transportation services.

The statute sets out certain limitations on the duty of board of education to provide such transportation to students enrolled in private schools. First, a majority of the students must be residents of Connecticut. Second, the local or regional board of education may not be required to expend more than twice the local per pupil expenditure for public schools transportation for the last completed school year. If the transportation costs exceed this limitation, the local or regional board of education may, at its option, either allocate its share of the transportation costs on a per pupil, per school basis, or may pay the provider directly until the limitation is reached, even if that is for less than the entire school year.

The Connecticut Supreme Court clarified the obligation to transport private school children within the district in 1998. The Stafford Board of Education declined to provide transportation services to such students on days on which the public schools were not in session. The Court ruled, however, that the Board of Education was obligated to provide transportation on days when the private school was in session. *Board of Education of the*

Town of Stafford v. State Board of Education, 243 Conn. 772 (1998). The Court rejected the Board's argument that such transportation was not "the same kind of transportation" since the public schools were not in session on those days. The Court noted that "[r]easonable equality would limit the Town's transportation to no more than the 180 days mandated by law." In addition, the Court rejected the argument that requiring school districts to provide such transportation to sectarian schools would violate the Establishment Clause of the United States Constitution. *See Everson v. Board of Education*, 330 U.S. 1 (1947) and Chapter Two, Section A(1)(a).

In addition, school districts also have the discretion to provide transportation services to students who attend private schools outside the school district. Conn. Gen. Stat. § 10-280a. Because there is no state reimbursement for such transportation, however, school districts seldom provide transportation for students enrolled in schools outside the district.

4. Review of transportation decisions

If parents feel that their child is being denied school accommodations because necessary transportation is not being provided, they have the right to seek review before the board of education. This right of appeal exists concerning transportation to vocational-technical, vocational agricultural programs and to private schools, as well as public schools, including interdistrict magnet schools and charter schools, within the district. Conn. Gen. Stat. § 10-97(d); Conn. Gen. Stat. § 10-281. Also, transportation disputes can arise with regard to "riders." When a school district provides transportation, it must also establish a bus stop to which the student must walk. If parents believe that the walking route to the bus stop is too far or otherwise subjects a student to hazard, they also have the right to seek review under Conn. Gen. Stat. § 10-186.

The same procedures that apply to school accommodations hearings also apply to review of transportation decisions. The decision by the board of education may be appealed to the state, and if so, the hearing officer must uphold the decision of the board of education unless s/he finds that the board's decision was "arbitrary, capricious or unreasonable." Conn. Gen. Stat. § 10-186(b)(4).

2. <u>Parent responsibilities for the education of their children</u>

The parents or guardians of school-age students have responsibilities as well. The law, perhaps somewhat optimistically, requires that "parents and those who have the care of children shall bring them up in some lawful and honest employment and instruct them or cause them to be instructed in reading, writing, spelling, English grammar, geography, arithmetic and United States history and in citizenship, including a study of the town, state and federal governments." Conn. Gen. Stat. § 10-184. This long-standing duty to provide for the education of children continues to be the subject of legislative change and judicial action.

a. Mandatory school attendance

Parents or other persons having control of children between the ages of five and eighteen must assure that their children attend public school "regularly during the hours and terms the public school in the district wherein such student resides is in session." Conn. Gen. Stat. § 10-184. There are special provisions, however, permitting children not to attend school at ages five and six, and ages sixteen and seventeen.

In 1998, the mandatory age of school attendance was reduced from seven to five. Parents may opt out of mandatory school attendance for their children on an annual basis, however, when the children are either five or six. Specifically, Conn. Gen. Stat. § 10-184 now provides that parents and guardians are obligated to assure that children attend school starting at age five unless they personally appear at the school district office and sign an option form exercising their right not to have their child attend school. At that time, district officials must provide the parents or guardians with information on the educational opportunities available within the district. A parent or guardian who wishes to exercise this option for a child six years of age must follow the same procedure, even if he or she exercised this option in the prior year when the child was five years of age.

In 2000, the General Assembly took similar action with respect to students ages sixteen to eighteen. Students under eighteen are now subject to the mandatory attendance laws unless their parent (or other person having control of the child) consents to their withdrawal from school. Again, the parent or other person must personally appear at the school district office and sign a withdrawal form. At that time, the school district is required to provide the parent or other person with "information on the educational options available in the school system and in the community." Conn. Gen. Stat. § 10-184. As described in Section B(2)(b) below, this change has given towns a new authority to enact ordinances empowering the police to stop children up to age eighteen and, if truant, send them back to school.

In addition, parents sending their children to the public schools are obligated to comply with the related requirements necessary for school attendance, including obtaining the required immunizations (absent medical contraindications or religious objections), Conn. Gen. Stat.§ 10-204a, and the required health assessments, Conn. Gen. Stat. § 10-206. These obligations may be waived, however, for homeless students. *See* Section A(1)(c)(7), above.

Failure to comply with the requirement that children attend the public schools is a violation of law, unless the parent provides alternative instruction, as discussed below. Conn. Gen. Stat. § 10-185. Each day's failure to provide schooling is a separate violation, punishable by a fine of up to twenty-five dollars (increased from five dollars a week in 1990). *Id.* Curiously, the statute goes on to excuse a failure to have a child attend school if "the child is destitute of clothing suitable for attending school and the parent or person having control of such child is unable to provide such clothing." *Id.* This statute requires revision.

Where a parent fails to send a child to school, the responsible school officials should consider at least three different actions.

First, failure by parents or guardians to assure that a child attends school may constitute educational neglect, which should be reported to the Department of Children and Families. "Mandated reporters" (including teachers, principals, guidance counselors, paraprofessionals, licensed nurses, social workers, school coaches and licensed professional counselors) who are aware of abuse or neglect of children are required to file a report with the Department of Children and Families. Such reports must be made as soon as practicable, but in any case within twelve hours, and followed up with a written report within seventy-two hours. Conn. Gen. Stat. § 17a-101.

Second, school officials must follow the procedures set forth in Conn. Gen. Stat. § 10-198a. This statute defines a "truant" as an enrolled student age five through eighteen who has four unexcused absences in a month or ten unexcused absences in a year. Boards of education are required to adopt policies concerning truants. Such policies must include a provision for having a meeting with parents whose child is a truant. Such policies must also require that the superintendent file a "family with service needs" petition with the Superior Court whenever the parent or other person having control of a student who is a "truant" fails to attend the required meeting to discuss the truancy problem with school officials, or otherwise if such person fails to cooperate with the school in attempting to solve the truancy problem. *Id.* In addition, when a student is beyond the control of his/her parents or has more than four unexcused absences in a month or ten unexcused absences in a year, the statutes now permit the superintendent to file a petition with the court alleging that a student is a "youth in crisis." Conn. Gen. Stat. § 46b-150f.

When such petitions are filed, the court determines whether a family has special needs and, if so, it can take action appropriate under the circumstances. Such action can include an order that the local or regional board of education (or the private school, if the child is enrolled) conduct an educational evaluation of the child at its cost, if no such evaluation has been conducted within a year, or an order that the child receive services from the Department of Children and Families, or even that the child be committed to the custody of the Department of Children and Families. The court has jurisdiction to take further action if the child and/or parent does not comply with the orders of the court.

Third, a possible need for special education services should be considered. The state regulations implementing the special education laws provide that a child must be referred for special education evaluation if his or her behavior or attendance is unacceptable or at a marginal level of acceptability. Connecticut State Regulations, § 10-76d-7. Consequently, whenever students are excessively absent without excuse, the district should ensure that it has referred the child to the planning and placement team for evaluation for a possible disability.

b. Private schools and home instruction

Parents have an alternative to public school instruction. A parent meets his or her duty regarding the education of children if "the parent or person having control of such child is able to show that the child is elsewhere receiving equivalent instruction in the studies taught in the public schools." Conn. Gen. Stat. § 10-184. Absent special circumstances, enrollment in a private school meets that requirement, whether the school is secular or sectarian. Such schools, however, are required to file student attendance reports with the State Department of Education. Conn. Gen. Stat. § 10-188.

In addition, parents may choose to exercise their right to educate their children at home. When parents make this choice, school officials can be uncertain of their own rights and obligations. The statute clearly states that the parent must show that the child is elsewhere receiving education equivalent to that provided in the public schools. Do school districts have the right to judge the quality of the parents' home instruction? Can school districts require that instruction be provided through certified personnel? Do school officials have the right to visit the home, observe instruction, ask for work samples, conduct pre- and post-instruction testing, and the like? With home-schooling there are more questions than answers.

The Connecticut statute does not explicitly permit home schooling. However, since the statute provides that mandatory attendance will be excused if the parent can show that the child is elsewhere receiving equivalent instruction, the State Board of Education has held that home instruction is permitted. In the past, school boards were expected to review such programs and forward their approval to the State Department of Education. But there were disputes over the respective rights of parents and school districts in such cases, and neither state law nor the regulations provided any guidance on how far districts could or had to go in supervising home instruction programs.

After committee review and further discussion, the State Board of Education adopted a policy and procedure for local school districts to follow. Now the State Department of Education simply asks that local school districts obtain a notification from parents who wish to home-school that they are taking responsibility for the education of their children. The State Department of Education does not require (or apparently expect) that school districts will exercise any oversight responsibility over home instructional programs. *See Series 1994-95, Circular Letter C-14*, "Revised Procedures Concerning Requests from Parents to Educate Their Child at Home" (July 15, 1994).

The acknowledgment form recommended for use by local and regional school districts by the State Department of Education includes an express disclaimer to the effect that the superintendent does not express any opinion as to the adequacy of the program. Such a laissez-faire approach is questionable, given the continuing statutory responsibility on parents to show that their children are "elsewhere receiving equivalent instruction." Moreover, as "mandated reporters" school officials who are aware that a student is not receiving educational services have a duty to report such educational neglect to the Department of Children and Families. Conn. Gen. Stat. § 17a-101b. However, at present the only thing the State Department of Education asks of local or regional school districts is that they collect simple one page forms from parents before permitting them to educate their children at home in the manner that they see fit.

B. Supervision of Students

Historically, school districts have exercised great control over students. Generally the courts will defer to the judgments of school officials. However, since the 1960s, limitations on the right of school officials to regulate student conduct have evolved. Citing the provisions of the Fifth and Fourteenth Amendments to the United States Constitution, judicial decisions have recognized the following principles in reviewing action taken by school officials.

1. General principles

While courts generally defer to judgments by school officials, parents often do not. Over the years, various parent challenges to actions by school officials have led the courts to develop rules by which to decide whether a particular school rule under challenge will be sustained.

First, for a school rule to be valid, it must be clear and understandable. Courts have held that it is a denial of due process of law to impose a penalty on the basis of a rule that is overly vague. *Crossen v. Fatsi*, 309 F. Supp. 114 (D. Conn. 1970); *Coy v. Board of Education of North Canton*, 205 F. Supp.2d 791 (N.D. Ohio 2002). Before a student can face discipline for violating a rule, the rule must be sufficiently clear so that the student can reasonably understand what conduct is permitted and what is prohibited.

Second, the student must have fair notice of the rule. The statutes provide that school districts must assure that all pupils are informed at least annually of board policies governing student conduct. Typically, school districts set out the school rules in a student handbook. Some districts even require that parents and/or students acknowledge receipt of the handbook. Such special acknowledgment may be particularly helpful where districts impose strict rules that apply to participants in interscholastic sports. *See* Section G, Extracurricular Activities, below.

It is important that any enumeration of school rules include broad language to counter parent or student arguments that particular conduct is not prohibited. For example, is a weapon facsimile considered to be a "weapon" under the language of the school rules? To avoid such arguments between parents and school personnel, the school handbook should clearly and broadly define terms like "weapon." More generally, board policy and the student handbook should specify that prohibited conduct is not limited to the listed types of misconduct, and that misconduct in any of these three categories may result in suspension or expulsion:

- conduct that endangers persons or property;
- conduct that is seriously disruptive of the educational process; or
- conduct that violates a publicized policy of the board of education.

This list comes from Conn. Gen. Stat. § 10-233d, which authorizes boards of education to expel students for such conduct. Admittedly, these standards are vague. However, they are good enough for the General Assembly, and thus this list can be a good "catch-all" to avoid student or parent arguments that the misconduct in issue is not prohibited by the code of conduct.

Given changes to the student discipline statutes in 1996, it is particularly important that board of education rules governing student conduct be broadly written. Under Conn. Gen. Stat. § 10-233c and 10-233d, school districts are authorized under certain circumstances to discipline students for conduct that occurs off campus. Significantly, however, discipline for off campus conduct is permitted only if the conduct is both seriously disruptive of the educational process *and* is violative of a publicized policy of the board of education. *See* Section C(1)(d) below. Discipline policies, therefore, should be broadly worded to encompass seriously disruptive conduct that occurs off-campus.

Third, there must be a rational relationship between the rule enacted and its purpose. This requirement is not hard to meet. A school district need not show that its rule is the best approach. Rather, the district must be able to establish that its rule is one reasonable way to accomplish a legitimate educational goal. As long as a school district can show that connection between the rule it has adopted and a legitimate educational purpose, the rule will generally be upheld. Avoiding disruption, promoting a positive learning environment, safeguarding student and staff safety, and protecting the physical plant are all examples of valid educational purposes.

When a school rule implicates constitutional rights, the standard will be different. As discussed in Section E, below, rules that impinge upon constitutional protections will be permissible only if they pass the "strict scrutiny" test, *i.e.* they must relate to a compelling state interest and they must be narrowly tailored to achieving that compelling interest. In *Saxe v. State College Area School District*, 240 F.3d 200 (3d Cir. 2001), for example, the Third Circuit struck down an anti-harassment policy adopted by a local school district because, in the court's view, it limited student speech without a showing of a reasonable forecast that such speech would substantially interfere with or materially disrupt the educational process.

Lawmakers generally defer to the judgments of local school officials concerning school rules. Recently, however, there have been a number of legislative efforts to prescribe certain school rules. Now, there are several offenses that automatically result in expulsion. *See* Section C(1)(b). Also, the General Assembly has specifically prohibited possession or use of a "beeper" in a public school unless the student obtains the written permission of the school principal for such possession and use. The principal is to grant such permission only if the student or his or her parent or guardian establishes to the satisfaction of the principal that a reasonable basis exists for the possession and use of the device. Conn. Gen. Stat. § 10-233j. Similarly, in 1996 the General Assembly specified that boards of education may restrict student possession or use of cellular mobile telephones, though in doing so, districts are required to consider the special needs of parents and students. *Id.* That year, the legislature also passed Conn. Gen. Stat. § 10-221f, which authorizes boards of education to specify a school uniform for students under its jurisdiction. While districts are not obligated to specify uniforms, the legislative history makes clear that, once specified, such uniforms may be mandated. *See Byars v. City of Waterbury*, 5 Conn. Ops. 707 (June 21, 1999) (Superior Court).

In sum, the courts will generally defer to the decisions of school officials in enacting rules of conduct. However, school officials must be ready to show how a rule relates to legitimate school concerns, such as avoiding disruption, maintaining a safe school environment, or promoting learning by students. Moreover, where a school rule affects the constitutional rights of students, it will be held enforceable only if it relates to a compelling school interest and if there is no other less intrusive way to accomplish the goal that the rule is designed to achieve.

2. <u>Specific school rules</u>

In addition to the foregoing review of these guiding principles, it may be helpful to consider three issues that school districts commonly confront.

a. Dress codes

First, some districts have enacted dress codes, and within limits such codes are enforceable. In assessing a particular dress code, courts will generally focus on two issues. First, the courts must find that the provisions of the code promote legitimate educational interests. Such educational interests include the need to avoid disruption of the educational process, student safety, or maintenance of the physical plant. Rules that reasonably relate to such educational interests include prohibitions against sexually provocative clothing, dangerous jewelry (such as multi-finger rings), or the infamous black-soled shoes.

More recently, given concerns over gang violence, courts have ruled that school districts may prohibit gang colors and other insignia, even in the face of free speech and free association claims. *Jeglin v. San Jacinto Unified School District*, 827 F. Supp. 1459 (C.D. Cal. 1993); *Olesin v. Board of Education*, 676 F. Supp. 820 (N.D. Ill. 1987). In any such policy, however, it is necessary that the prohibitions relate to real concerns and that they be clearly stated. In the *Jeglin* case, for example, the court permitted the prohibitions at the high school level, but not at the middle school level, because the district was not able to show any gang-related problems at the middle school level. Also, in a decision by the Eighth Circuit, such a dress code prohibition was struck down as unconstitutionally vague; the court found that the term "gang-related" dress is not self-defining, and thus that students had no fair notice of what was prohibited. *Stephenson v. Davenport Community School District*, 110 F.3d 1303 (8th Cir. 1997). *See also Chalifoux v. New Caney Independent School District*, 976 F. Supp. 659 (S.D. Tex. 1997), discussed in Chapter Two, Section B(1)(a)(3).

In addition to assuring that there is a valid reason for dress code provisions, the courts will ask whether the code is understandable and may be fairly applied. For example, in *Crossen v. Fatsi*, 309 F. Supp. 114 (D. Conn. 1970), the federal district court in Connecticut held that any grooming and/or dress code must define with reasonable specificity the type of dress that is prohibited. In that case, the court considered the following dress and grooming code:

> Students are to be neatly dressed and groomed, maintaining standards of modesty, and good taste conducive to an educational atmosphere. It is expected that clothing and grooming not be of an extreme style and fashion.

Since different people could have very different ideas of what grooming and/or dress is "neat," the court ruled that the code was unconstitutionally vague and unenforceable as written. *See also Stephenson v. Davenport Community School District*, 110 F.3d 1303 (8th Cir. 1997). However, in

Crossen the court noted that its ruling was based on the code before it, and it stressed that a school district has the authority to adopt a code regulating student dress as long as the code is sufficiently specific and is reasonably related to legitimate educational concerns.

By contrast, in 1969 a Connecticut court reached a different result with regard to grooming codes (*e.g.*, rules governing hair length or facial hair for boys). The Superior Court ruled that a school district may not maintain a regulation prohibiting long hair unless it causes disruption of school activities or poses a sanitary or health hazard. *Yoo v. Moynihan*, 28 Conn. Supp. 375 (1969).

Until recently, judicial activity in this area had subsided (perhaps as a result of an increased tolerance of student appearance). The federal courts are about evenly split on whether school officials may adopt rules governing student grooming, and neither the Second Circuit (which includes Connecticut) nor the United States Supreme Court has ever addressed codes concerning student grooming or dress. Increasingly, however, the pendulum appears to be swinging back to support for the ability of school officials to regulate student appearance. In Connecticut, we even have Conn. Gen. Stat. § 10-221f, which states *in toto* that "[a] local or regional board of education may specify a school uniform for students in schools under its jurisdiction." The legislative history makes clear that, while school districts are not required to specify a uniform for students to wear, once they do, students can be required to wear the uniform.

The Waterbury Board of Education adopted a uniform policy/dress code for students (which included a prohibition against the wearing of blue jeans), and parents challenged this action as a violation of their rights of parental autonomy and their children's right to free public education. The Superior Court denied their request that the Board's uniform policy/dress code be temporarily enjoined, based on Section 10-221f and the rational relationship between appropriate student dress and legitimate educational concerns. *Byars v. City of Waterbury*, 5 Conn. Ops. 707 (June 21, 1999).

After hearing evidence, the Superior Court subsequently ruled on the merits of the case. *Byars v. City of Waterbury*, 2001 Conn. Super. LEXIS 3313 (Conn. Super. Ct. November 19, 2001). It affirmed its earlier ruling that school districts in Connecticut may enact mandatory dress codes, and that the provision in the dress code prohibiting baggy blue jeans that impede climbing stairs is authorized because it has a rational basis, safety. The court found that prior to the dress code, student dress issues had caused distractions, confrontations between students, and even thefts. Given the procedural posture of the case, however, the court limited its ruling to the prohibition against wearing blue jeans to school. It found that there is no fundamental right to wear blue jeans to school, and that the dress code was rationally related to reducing actual disruptions and loss of instructional time caused by students' preoccupations with fashionable clothing, including blue jeans. The dress code therefore did not violate the student's right to due process or the parent's right to autonomy in raising children.

This decision is consistent with rulings in other jurisdictions. In *Littlefield v. Forney Independent School District*, 268 F.3d 275 (5th Cir. 2001), the Fifth Circuit upheld a school uniform policy. The parents had complained that the policy interfered with their free speech, religious rights, and parental rights. The court however, sustained the policy, holding that it was subject only to rational basis review because that was the proper level of review for each component of the parents' claims. *See also Canady v. Bossier Parish School Board*, 240 F.3d 437 (5th Cir. 2001) (mandatory school uniform policy upheld).

These rulings are consistent with societal trends. Indeed, in 1996 the United States Department of Education issued a Manual on School Uniforms, which presents the view that school uniforms are effective in promoting an orderly school environment.

b. Student truancy

A second common area of concern is student truancy. Since 1991, school districts in Connecticut have been required to adopt procedures governing "truants." The definition of "truant" is now "a child age five to eighteen, inclusive, who is enrolled in a public or private school and has four or more unexcused absences from school in any one month or ten unexcused absences from school in any school year." Conn. Gen. Stat. § 10-198a. Such required procedures include the following: (1) holding a meeting with the parents of any truant child within ten school days after the fourth unexcused absence; (2) coordinating services and referring such children to community agencies; (3) providing notification annually to parents of their obligations under the mandatory attendance laws; (4) obtaining a telephone number where parents can be contacted; and (5) providing notification to parents when their child does not arrive at school. Finally, the law now requires that the superintendent file a "family with service needs" petition with the Superior Court if the parent or other person responsible for the education of a child fails to attend the meeting described in subparagraph (1) above or otherwise fails to cooperate with the school in attempting to solve the truancy problem.

In 1995, the General Assembly eliminated the requirement that such policies address the issue of "habitual truants" (students enrolled in public or private school who have twenty or more unexcused absences within a school year). Conn. Gen. Stat. § 10-200, however, provides that municipalities may adopt ordinances concerning such habitual truants, and such ordinances may include provision for stopping such students during school hours and sending them back to school. This authority was enhanced in 2000, when the mandatory attendance age was raised to eighteen (subject to parental waiver), effective July 1, 2001. Conn. Gen. Stat. § 10-186. Now, any such ordinance would permit the police to send such students to school as well.

c. Grading

For as important it is to students and their families, there is little guidance in Connecticut concerning the grading process. As discussed in Chapter One, Section F(1)(a)(1), school districts must have a written policy concerning weighted grading for honors and advanced placement classes. Such policies must provide for advising parents and students whether grades in such courses are or are not given added weight for purposes of calculating grade point average and class rank. Conn. Gen. Stat. § 10-220g.

Other than this one statute, there are no Connecticut laws on the subject. By contrast, in other states the legislature has regulated the grading process by statute. In California, for example, a statute provides that the grade a teacher assigns is final and can only be changed for limited reasons, such as clerical error or teacher bad faith. *See Las Virgenes Educators Association v. Las Virgenes United School District*, 2001 WL 20512 (Ca. Ct. App., 2d Dist. 2000). In Connecticut, therefore, the assignment of grades is a teacher responsibility, and there is no statutory process for review and/or appeal. One student sought to challenge a grade through the process under the Family Educational Rights and Privacy Act (FERPA) for seeking change to records that are "inaccurate, misleading or in violation of the student's rights of privacy." 34 C.F.R. § 99.20. The court ruled, however, that this process is not available to challenge the substance of a grade. *Tarka v. Cunningham*, 917 F.2d 890 (5th Cir. 1990).

Questions sometimes arise as to the right of a school administrator to change a grade issued by a teacher. Clearly, the grading process is part of a teacher's professional responsibilities, and the teacher may be held accountable (*i.e.* may be subject to discipline) for inappropriate or unfair grading practices. There is no case law for the premise, however, that the courts would ever intercede on behalf of a student, even when there is a problem with a grade. *See, e.g., Board of Curators v. Horowitz,* 435 U.S. 78, 84-85 (1978); *Board of Regents of the University of Michigan v. Ewing,* 474 U.S. 214, 223 (1985). Moreover, it appears that the teacher would not have a claim against an administrator for supervising the assessment of students and the assignment of grades. The Third Circuit recently ruled that the assignment of grades is a school responsibility, even at the university level, and that a university did not violate a professor's rights of free speech and academic freedom by ordering him to change a grade. *Brown v. Armenti,* 247 F.3d 69 (3d Cir. 2001). *But see Parate v. Isibor*, 868 F.2d 821 (6th Cir. 1989).

The dilemma thus arises when upon investigating a student (or parent) complaint about a grade, an administrator determines that a grade was determined unfairly. The administrator should first determine whether there is a board policy on the subject. If there is not (as will likely be the case), the matter is for the sound business judgment of the school administrator. In the first instance, the administrator should meet with the teacher to seek a remedy to the inappropriate grading practice. If such a remedy is not established by mutual agreement, however, the administrator should take care not to make a bad situation worse. Specifically, if the administrator does not have any basis for grading the student, the administrator should not change the grade, *i.e.* assign a new grade. Rather, in an extreme situation, unless a grade can be reconstructed reliably, it would seem appropriate simply to vacate the unfairly derived grade, so that it neither helps nor harms the student.

Another related issue that can arise involves the rights of children receiving special education services. The Office for Civil Rights has provided some guidance on this issue, but questions remain. In *Letter to Runkel,* 25 IDELR ¶ 387 (1996), *quoted in Ann Arbor (MI) Public School District*, 30 IDELR 405 (1998), OCR stated that school districts may not designate a class on the transcript as "special education," but that the transcript can generally describe course content and also note curriculum modifications if such notations are used uniformly in all cases. In *Ann Arbor (MI),* OCR conceded that "there is yet no definitive standard enunciated in any court or OCR decision to indicate exactly what terms are permissible to use and what are not." There, OCR clarified the situation somewhat, and stated that in limited circumstances, a designation for a special education course that is based on content, rather than the manner in which the course is taught, does not violate the student's rights under Section 504 and the ADA. *Id.* Any such modifications, of course, should be reviewed and approved through the IEP process.

Finally, it is important to separate grading from school discipline. Clearly, it is appropriate to punish students for academic offenses, such as plagiarism or stealing tests. *Zellman v. Independent School District No. 2758,* 594 N.W.2d 216 (Minn. Ct. App. 1999); *Reed v. Vermilion Local School District*, 614 N.E.2d 1101 (Ohio App.6th Dist. 1992). A grade reduction for misconduct unrelated to academic achievement, however, may violate equal protection. *Smith v. School City of Hobart*, 811 F. Supp. 391 (N.D. Ind. 1993).

Some school districts have enacted grade reduction policies, which may provide, for example, that a student's grade will be reduced by five points for each unexcused absence, and/or that a student will lose course credit if he or she misses more than fourteen classes. Within broad limits governed by basic fairness, the Connecticut Supreme Court held that school districts have the authority to enact such policies. *Campbell v. New Milford Board of Education*, 193 Conn. 93 (1984). The student in *Campbell* claimed that the policy was, in effect, a disciplinary policy that was not authorized by statute. However, ruling that school districts have broad discretion in making academic decisions, the court found that the grade reduction policy was one permissible measure of student effort, and it dismissed the student's claim. The key in adopting any such policy is to ensure that the purpose and effect of the policy are academic, not disciplinary.

C. Student Discipline

In 1975, the United States Supreme Court decided that students are entitled to due process before being deprived of educational opportunities as a result of disciplinary action by school officials. *Goss v. Lopez*, 419 U.S. 565 (1975). In *Goss*, the Court sharply distinguished between short exclusions (of up to ten days), for which only rudimentary due process is necessary, and longer exclusions (in excess of ten days), for which more formal procedures are required.

Following the *Goss* case, the General Assembly rewrote the statutes governing student discipline to make them consistent with constitutional requirements. Now, the statutes describe various levels of disciplinary action, and each carries with it specific requirements and limitations. Conn. Gen. Stat. § 10-233a *et seq*. Districts must inform all students and their parents or guardians or surrogate parents annually of any board policies governing student conduct and discipline. Boards of education must also provide for an effective means of notifying parents within twenty-four hours of any disciplinary action taken against their children, and this obligation extends to surrogate parents appointed under Conn. Gen. Stat. § 10-94g. Conn. Gen. Stat. § 10-233e.

1. Student expulsion

Expulsion is authorized if a student's conduct on campus or at a school-sponsored activity violates a publicized rule of the board of education, seriously disrupts the educational process or endangers persons or property. Conn. Gen. Stat. § 10-233d. Expulsion is defined as any exclusion from school privileges for more than ten days up to one calendar year. *See Rosa R. v. Connelly*, 889 F.2d 435 (2d Cir. 1989) (three month postponement of hearing by mutual agreement does not reduce the length of permissible expulsion, then 180 days). An expulsion is also defined as exclusion from the school to which a student was assigned at the time of the disciplinary action. Conn. Gen. Stat. § 10-233a(e). The law, however, now provides that the reassignment of a student to a regular classroom program in another school in the district does not constitute either a suspension or an expulsion. Conn. Gen. Stat. § 10-233f(b).

The decision of a board of education concerning a proposed expulsion is final. The expulsion statute incorporates certain provisions of the Uniform Administrative Procedures Act, but it does not incorporate the provisions governing appeal of administrative decisions. *Roach v. North Haven Board of Education*, No. 440118, 2002 Conn. Super. LEXIS 4028 (Conn. Super. Ct. 2002), *citing Lee v. Board of Education*, 181 Conn. 69 (1980); *Lebron v. Bridge Academy*, No. CV023981426, 2002 Conn. Super LEXIS 3927 (Conn. Super. Ct. 2002). To be sure, if there is an allegation that disciplinary action taken by a board of education has violated the constitutional rights of the student, courts will hear such a claim when it is brought through an independent lawsuit. However, since there is no general right of appeal, the courts will not usually entertain parent or student challenges to an expulsion decision or to a proposed alternative educational opportunity.

a. Procedures

As to children who are not identified as in need of special education, the authority to expel is clear. Only the board of education has the legal authority to expel students. The statute provides that any recommendation for expulsion must be heard by the board of education in a formal hearing consistent with the certain requirements of the Uniform Administrative

Procedures Act. Conn. Gen. Stat. § 10-233d, *citing* 4-176e to 4-180a, inclusive, and 4-181a. Such requirements include providing written notice including a "short and plain statement of the matters asserted," maintaining a record (either stenographic or tape recording), permitting the student to appear with counsel and offer evidence and argument, permitting cross-examination of witnesses, assuring an impartial decision-maker, and providing a final decision.

In addition, Section 10-233d requires that at least three board of education members sit on an expulsion hearing. From this provision it is fair to infer that a board of education can delegate the responsibility to conduct an expulsion hearing to less than a quorum of the board, as long as at least three members are present. Even if fewer members than a quorum meet, however, an expulsion hearing is a "hearing or other proceeding" under the Freedom of Information Act. Conn. Gen. Stat. § 1-200(2). Such hearings, therefore, must be posted, and while the hearing can be conducted in executive session, the vote must be taken in open session, as discussed below.

Section 10-233d also requires that there be at least three affirmative votes in order for an expulsion to be effective. Consequently, depending upon the number of board members present, the vote required for an expulsion would be a unanimous vote if only three members are present.

School boards have another option with regard to conducting expulsion hearings. The statute authorizes school boards to appoint an impartial hearing officer to hear expulsions. The only restriction is that such hearing officers may not be members of the board of education that appoints them. If appointed, such hearing officers have full authority to decide expulsion cases, including whether provision will be made for an alternative educational program. There is no provision for such decisions to come back to the board of education for approval. Conn. Gen. Stat. § 10-233d(b).

Expulsion hearings must be held within ten school days of any suspension unless there is an emergency; any ongoing exclusion from school for longer than ten school days would itself be an "expulsion." Such hearings generally begin with the presentation by the administration of the underlying facts. The student and his or her representative have the right to cross examine any witnesses. After the administration has presented its evidence and testimony, the student and his or her representatives have the right to present evidence and testimony, and the administration similarly has the right to conduct cross examination. The members of the board of education are also free to ask questions, though it often makes sense to let the parties present their cases first, because the parties may answer any such potential questions in their presentations. At the conclusion of the evidence, both parties typically present argument to the board of education, which must then decide whether the facts established at the hearing warrant expulsion.

Some boards deliberate and make this determination before proceeding to hear the recommendation of the superintendent concerning expulsion. Other boards of education continue with the hearing and hear the recommendation before making a decision on the facts of the case. Either approach is appropriate, though a bifurcated hearing on (1) the facts and (2) the recommendation may be preferable. The board is authorized to receive and consider evidence "of past disciplinary problems which have led to removal from a classroom, suspension or expulsion of such pupil" expressly for the purpose of considering the length of an expulsion and any alternative educational opportunity to be offered. Conn. Gen. Stat. § 10-233d(c). It is therefore not appropriate to consider past conduct in determining whether the student committed the offense alleged. A bifurcated hearing keeps the two issues separate.

In conducting such hearings, school boards (or impartial hearing officers) have some discretion. The formal rules of evidence do not apply, and it is not necessary to adopt rigid procedures for hearing such cases. However, it is essential that the student in question have a fair hearing. School board members should not discuss the case outside the hearing with the superintendent or others, and they must make their decision on the evidence presented at the hearing. In addition, the same lawyer may not represent the board and the administration. There is no requirement that either the administration or the board be represented by counsel, but if they are, it cannot be the same lawyer, because the courts have held that such joint representation impairs the board's ability to decide the case impartially.

In 1997, the General Assembly clarified that police records may be used in expulsion hearings. Previously, police officials were sometimes reluctant to cooperate in the presentation of evidence of misconduct, because juvenile records are by law subject to special confidentiality provisions. Conn. Gen. Stat. § 10-233h now makes clear, however, that police may provide such information at expulsion hearings:

> If an expulsion hearing is held . . . a representative of the municipal police department or the division of state police, as appropriate, may testify and provide reports and information on the arrest at such hearing, provided such police

> participation is requested by any of the following: the local or regional board of education, the impartial hearing board, the principal of the school or the student or his parent or guardian. Such information with respect to a child under sixteen years of age shall be confidential in accordance with section 46b-124, and shall only be disclosed as provided in this section and shall not be further disclosed.

On rare occasions police representatives and prosecutors resist providing such information, based on the position that the statute permits but does not mandate the release of such information. That reading ignores the fact that this provision is found in statutory provisions that impose affirmative duties upon the superintendent to expel students for off-campus conduct. Fortunately, such officials generally cooperate with school requests for such information, which can be critically important in determining the facts at a student expulsion hearing.

The critical procedural question is whether the student facing expulsion has a fair opportunity to be heard and defend him- or herself. To ensure that an expulsion hearing is fair, it is important to avoid reliance on hearsay testimony if possible. Hearsay evidence is evidence concerning statements made by persons not present at the hearing that is offered to establish the truth of such statements. For example, it would be hearsay if a school administrator testified at an expulsion hearing that Student A told him that he saw Student B (the subject of the hearing) with a weapon in school, if that testimony were offered to prove that Student B did have the weapon. If that were the only "evidence" before the board of education, it may not be proper to expel the student, because the student facing expulsion could not effectively cross-examine the administrator in the example above, because he did not himself see the weapon.

In the interest of fairness (and thus of due process), absent exceptional circumstances a board of education should not rely on hearsay testimony alone in deciding whether the student in question violated school rules. A federal court in Connecticut found that a board of education violated the due process rights of a student by relying on hearsay in imposing a thirty-day expulsion. *DeJesus v. Penberthy*, 344 F. Supp. 70 (D. Conn. 1972). *See also In the Matter of the Expulsion of E.J.W.*, 632 N.W.2d 775 (Minn. Ct. App. 2001). The case law is mixed, however, and specific circumstances may warrant proceeding with an expulsion based on hearsay information. *See Schneider v. Board of School Trustees, Fort Wayne Community Schools*, 255 F. Supp.2d 891 (N.D. Indiana 2003) (expulsion for inappropriate sexual conduct upheld despite hearsay testimony and even though student not entitled to cross-examine witnesses).

Once the board of education has heard all of the evidence, it must make a decision on the recommendation for expulsion and on the recommendation, if any, for an alternative educational program. While the deliberations can be conducted in executive session, the vote on the expulsion itself must be held in open session, typically in a format that sets forth the necessary information while protecting the confidentiality of the student's name and any other personally identifiable information, such as

> Moved: that the Board finds that Student ID # ____ engaged in [describe misconduct] and therefore is hereby expelled from [Name] School and all school activities and all property of the [Name] Public Schools for __ days.

The motion may also describe provisions for an alternative educational opportunity. The board of education must describe the misconduct so that its findings are clear. It must make a judgment, however, concerning the level of detail in its decision. A description of conduct that resulted in an expulsion may serve as a warning to other students. It may also be on the evening news ("Student attempts to poison teacher!!").

b. Mandatory expulsion

The United States Congress and the Connecticut General Assembly have both enacted legislation mandating expulsion of students for certain misconduct that is considered to be especially dangerous. The federal legislation, the Gun-Free Schools Act, imposes obligations on the states to require that local school districts expel students from school for bringing guns and certain other weapons to school. The General Assembly amended the student discipline statutes to address the need to comply with this federal law. It also further expanded the state law that requires expulsion in a number of situations that go beyond the provisions of federal law.

The Gun-Free Schools Act, which was recodified as part of the No Child Left Behind Act, Section 4141, obligates state educational agencies that receive federal funds to require that local educational agencies expel students who bring a "weapon" to school for not less than one calendar year, subject to exceptions on a case-by-case basis. The law defines "weapon" as a firearm as defined in 18 U.S.C. § 921(a), summarized as follows:

- any weapon that will or is designed to or may readily be converted to expel a projectile by the action of an explosive;
- the frame or receiver of such a weapon;
- any firearm muffler or firearm silencer;
- any explosive, incendiary, or poison gas, including

  (1) a bomb,
  (2) a grenade,
  (3) a rocket having a propellant charge of more than four ounces,
  (4) a missile having an explosive or incendiary charge of more than one-quarter ounce,
  (5) a mine, or
  (6) a similar device.

The statutory definition also includes any combination of parts designed or intended for use in readily constructing a "weapon" as defined above. The definition of a "weapon" under the Gun-Free Schools Act, however, does not include rifles intended for sporting, recreational, or cultural purposes (*e.g.*, a musket brought during the unit on the Revolutionary War) or knives.

The Act requires that students who bring such weapons to school be expelled for one calendar year. It permits the chief executive officer of the school district to make case by case exceptions in writing. The Department of Education, however, has issued guidelines to make clear that such exceptions should be rare, and would typically result from the operation of other laws, such as the federal special education laws, which prohibit the expulsion of a student whose disability caused him or her to bring a weapon to school. *OSEP Memorandum 95-16* (April 26, 1995), 22 IDELR 531 (1995). *See* Chapter Five, Section C, for a more detailed explanation of the application of these requirements to special education students.

Mandatory expulsion in Connecticut was first introduced in 1994, and the provisions concerning mandatory expulsion were amended in 1995 and again in 1996. The law now provides that students must be expelled in the following three situations.

1. On-campus conduct

First, if the superintendent has reason to believe that a student was in possession of a firearm (described with reference to the Gun-Free Schools Act, above), deadly weapon, dangerous instrument, or martial arts weapon on school property or at a school sponsored activity, he or she must recommend expulsion. Each of these terms are defined in Conn. Gen. Stat. § 53a-3:

Deadly weapon	any weapon, whether loaded or unloaded, from which a shot may be discharged, or a switchblade knife, gravity knife, billy, blackjack, bludgeon, or metal knuckles.
Dangerous instrument	any instrument, article or substance which, under the circumstances in which it is used or attempted or threatened to be used, is capable of causing death or serious injury, and includes a 'vehicle' as that term is defined in this section and includes a dog that has been commanded to attack (except police dogs on duty).
Martial arts weapon	a nunchaku, kama, kasari-fundo, octagon sai, tonfa, or Chinese star.

The last definition is not terribly helpful, and you may need pictures from the local police department to know what a marital arts weapon is. If the board of education finds that the student possessed any of these objects on school property or at a school sponsored activity, it must expel the student. The statute further provides that a mandatory expulsion for such conduct must be for one calendar year, subject to modification by the board of education or hearing board on a case-by-case basis. Conn. Gen. Stat. § 10-233d(a).

2. Off-campus conduct

If conduct occurs "off campus" (neither on school property nor at a school sponsored activity), the rules are different. Expulsion is required if the student possessed a "firearm" under federal law (described with reference to the Gun-Free Schools Act, above) in violation of Conn. Gen. Stat. § 29-35 (which sets out the permit requirement for carrying a firearm). *See State v. Hopes*, 26 Conn. App. 367 (1992) (possessing a weapon without a permit violates Section 29-35; transportation of the weapon is not required). Expulsion is also mandatory if a student possessed and used such a "firearm" or a deadly weapon, dangerous instrument, or martial arts weapon (as defined above) off-campus in the commission of a crime listed as an offense in the Penal Code, Connecticut General Statutes, § 53a-24 *et seq*. As above, if the board of education finds that the student engaged in such conduct, the statute directs that the board expel the student for one calendar year, with the right to modify the period of expulsion on a case-by-case basis.

3. Conduct on- or off-campus

Expulsion is also mandatory whenever a student is found to have engaged in the sale or distribution of drugs, whether that conduct occurred on school property, at a school sponsored activity, or off of school property. As with other mandatory expulsion situations, the statute directs the board to expel the student for one calendar year, with the right to modify the period of expulsion on a case-by-case basis. The drug in question must be a "controlled substance" as defined in Conn. Gen. Stat. § 21a-240, the sale, distribution, etc. of which is subject to criminal penalties under Conn. Gen. Stat. § 21a-277 or Conn. Gen. Stat. § 21a-278. These statutes include the various substances that we think of as "drugs," including marijuana, cocaine, heroin, and hallucinogenic substances. While these statutes also set out minimal quantities that trigger the mandatory minimum sentences in these statutes (*e.g.* five years for selling a kilo of marijuana), it is fair to read these statutes as establishing the categories of substances that will trigger mandatory expulsion without regard to the amount possessed.

The rules concerning mandatory expulsion for off-campus conduct are not affected by the *Thomaston* decision, discussed below in Section C(1)(d). The issue there was whether a student is fairly on notice that his or her conduct could result in expulsion even though it occurs off-campus. These specific statutory provisions concerning mandatory expulsion for off-campus conduct provide such notice. It may be helpful, however, to include reference to these rules in student handbooks to avoid any debate over whether the student had appropriate notice.

The scope of the state law requirement for mandatory expulsion for one calendar year is significantly broader than the federal statute. For example, under state law a pellet gun or a BB gun may be considered a "deadly weapon," since these weapons discharge a shot. Conn. Gen. Stat. § 53a-3. Such weapons are not covered by the federal statute, because they do not discharge a shot by means of an explosive, as is included in the federal definition of a "weapon." Similarly, there is no provision in federal law for a mandatory expulsion for the sale or distribution of drugs or for possession of a gravity knife, a switchblade knife, a billy, a bludgeon or metal knuckles, a dangerous instrument, or a martial arts weapon.

In imposing a period of expulsion on a student in a mandatory expulsion situation, boards of education may wish to differentiate between expulsions required under state law and those required under the federal Gun-Free Schools Act. The state law incorporates the provision from the federal Gun-Free Schools Act permitting exceptions on a case-by-case basis. Such exceptions, however, should not be applied in a way that eviscerates the requirement for a calendar year expulsion, at least when the federal law applies. The Office of Special Education Programs of the United States Department of Education has advised school districts that such exceptions are to be limited to compelling circumstances, such as when an expulsion is not permitted because the misconduct is caused by the student's disability. *OSEP Memorandum 95-16* (April 26, 1995), 22 IDELR 531 (1995). The State Department of Education has not provided any similar guidance regarding how boards of education should exercise their discretion in modifying the period of expulsion under the state law.

c. Alternative educational programs

School districts must provide an alternative educational opportunity to many of the students who are expelled, as described below. With one exception, the statutes do not define the "alternative education opportunity" that school districts must provide. The one definition that exists was added to the law in 1995. Conn. Gen. Stat. § 10-233d(d) provides that "such alternative may include, but shall not be limited to, the placement of a pupil who is at least sixteen years of age in an adult education program . . . ." More generally, districts are guided by the provisions in the state education regulations concerning homebound tutoring, which provide that homebound students at the secondary level are entitled to ten hours of tutoring per week. Conn. St. Reg. § 10-76d-15. In any event, school districts have significant discretion in deciding what sort of alternative educational opportunity to provide. Indeed, in 1995 the General Assembly clarified that school districts have the authority to provide alternative educational opportunities even when they are not obligated to do so. Conn. Gen. Stat. § 10-233d(d). The statutes are much more prescriptive in describing which students have a right to an alternative educational opportunity, as follows.

1. Students under sixteen years of age

For students who are under sixteen years of age, the duty to provide an alternative educational opportunity is unconditional. Moreover, school districts may not impose the costs of such an alternative program on the student or his or her family, because such an alternative program is the "school accommodations" to which the student is entitled.

2. Students ages sixteen to eighteen

For students ages sixteen to eighteen, the duty to provide an alternative educational opportunity depends upon the nature of the misconduct, and the recent increase in the mandatory school age to eighteen did not change these provisions. Generally, a student between sixteen and eighteen is entitled to an alternative educational program, as long as "he or she complies with conditions established by his or her local or regional board of education." Conn. Gen. Stat. § 10-233d(d). However, school districts have the option not to provide an alternative educational opportunity to such students in various situations.

First, school districts are not obligated to provide an alternative educational opportunity to students ages sixteen to eighteen who have been expelled previously. This provision applies even if the previous expulsion occurred before the student was sixteen years of age. Conn. Gen. Stat. § 10-233d(d).

Second, school districts are not obligated to provide an alternative educational opportunity to students ages sixteen to eighteen if they are expelled for possessing a firearm (as defined under federal law), deadly weapon, dangerous instrument, or martial arts weapon on school property or at a school-sponsored activity. Each of these terms is defined in Conn. Gen. Stat. § 53a-3, quoted above. It is important to note that this limitation on the duty to provide an alternative educational program applies only if the conduct occurs on campus or at a school-sponsored activity. For example, a student who used a gun in an armed robbery would be subject to mandatory expulsion. He or she would still be entitled to an alternative educational program if under eighteen, however, if this conduct did not occur at school or at a school sponsored activity.

Third, a student between sixteen and eighteen is not entitled to an alternative educational program when he or she is expelled for offering a controlled substance for sale or distribution on school property or at a school-sponsored activity. Where expulsion is for sale or distribution of drugs, the district is also required to refer the pupil to an appropriate state or local agency for rehabilitation, intervention, or job training. Again, however, the student remains entitled to an alternative educational program if the proscribed conduct occurs off-campus.

Conn. Gen. Stat. § 10-233d provides that the notice of hearing shall include a statement that the district is not obligated to provide an alternative educational opportunity to such students who have engaged in the conduct described above. This notice requirement applies in all cases, and a failure to provide such notice may prevent the board of education from deciding not to provide an alternative educational opportunity in an appropriate case.

3. Students eighteen years of age and older

For students who are over eighteen, there is no duty at all to provide an alternative program (except for special education students). Boards of education often choose, however, to provide an alternative educational opportunity (which may include adult education). Such action often is good public policy, given the alternative of having the student return at the end of the expulsion period no closer to high school graduation.

4. Special education students

Special education students are not subject to these rules. Students eligible for special education under the IDEA remain entitled to an appropriate program regardless of their age or their misconduct up to age twenty-one or high school graduation. Prior to the expulsion of a special education student, school districts must convene a planning and placement team meeting to determine whether the student's misconduct was a manifestation of the student's disability. The conditions for making this determination under the IDEA are described in detail in Chapter Five, Section C(1)(b)(2). If the misconduct is determined to be causally related to the disability, the PPT must review and modify the IEP to address the misconduct and to ensure the safety of the other children and staff in the school. Even when the misconduct was not caused by the disability, school districts are required in all cases to provide special education students with "an alternative educational opportunity consistent with such child's educational needs." Conn. Gen. Stat. § 10-233d(i).

d. Off-campus conduct

Student misconduct off-campus can be a legitimate concern. In 1925, the Connecticut Supreme Court held that school officials could discipline a student who was hassling other children on their way home, even though he was at his own home at the time. *O'Rourke v. Walker*, 102 Conn. 130 (1925). More recently, many school boards have included in their disciplinary codes provision for discipline of students for conduct off-campus. Such provisions can be valid where there is a direct connection between the conduct and legitimate school concerns. A student who disrupts students engaged in a school activity off campus can expect to face the music in school the next day.

More recent and dramatic concerns over violence and drugs in and out of school have renewed interest in off-campus conduct. School administrators and board members have questioned whether they can discipline students who engage in serious misconduct outside of school, as for example a student who is arrested in the community for armed robbery. In 1989, the Connecticut Attorney General advised the Commissioner of Education that school districts may take disciplinary action against students for off-campus conduct in certain situations. *Opinions of the Attorney General* 89-23 (August 22, 1989). *See also Howard v. Colonial School District*, 621 A.2d 362 (Del. Super. 1992) (sale of drugs off-campus); *see also Durso v. Taylor*, 624 A. 2d 449 (D.C. App. 1993) (sale of drugs off-campus).

In 1996, the General Assembly amended the suspension and expulsion statutes so that they expressly permit discipline for off-campus misconduct. Conn. Gen. Stat. § 10-233c (suspension) and Section 10-233d (expulsion) provide that students may be disciplined for off-campus conduct if both of two conditions are met. First, the conduct must violate a publicized policy of the board of education. Second, the conduct must be seriously disruptive of the educational process.

1. "Violative of a publicized policy of the board"

To meet the first requirement, the school administration must prove that the misconduct in question actually occurred and violated school rules. A report of an arrest is certainly not proof of misconduct, and off-campus conduct can be difficult to prove. Police reports, including confidential juvenile arrest records, may be used at expulsion hearings. Conn. Gen. Stat. § 10-233h. However, it is still necessary to have direct evidence of the alleged misconduct, and in some situations proving that prohibited off-campus conduct occurred can be difficult or impossible.

2. "Seriously disruptive of the educational process"

To meet the second requirement, the school administration must prove to the board of education that the misconduct in question is "seriously disruptive of the educational process." Questions over the meaning of this phrase resulted in a trial court decision, further legislative change, and finally a decision of the Connecticut Supreme Court.

These events began when the Thomaston Board of Education expelled a high school student for possession of marijuana off-campus. The student sued the school district, claiming that his constitutional rights had been violated. The Superior Court agreed, and even ruled more generally that the statutory provisions authorizing discipline for off-campus conduct were unconstitutionally vague and therefore unenforceable. This decision resulted in both a decision by the Connecticut Supreme Court and a statutory amendment.

Even before the appeal was decided, the General Assembly amended Conn. Gen. Stat. § 10-233d(a)(1) to address the concern expressed by the trial court that the phrase "seriously disruptive of the educational process" was unconstitutionally vague. Now, the statute provides that boards of education may consider, but their consideration is not limited to, certain factors in determining whether conduct is "seriously disruptive of the educational process." These factors are (a) whether the incident occurred within close proximity of a school, (b) whether other students from the school were involved or whether there was any gang involvement, (c) whether the conduct involved violence, threats of violence or the unlawful use of a weapon as defined in Conn. Gen. Stat. § 29-38, and whether any injuries occurred, and (d) whether the conduct involved the use of alcohol.

While the motivation was clear, some of the details of this amendment are odd. The amendment uses a new definition of "weapon" that appears nowhere else in the statutes concerning student discipline. Moreover, in the (non-exhaustive) list it provided of permissible considerations, the General Assembly included reference to conduct that involved the use of alcohol, but not drugs. Sale or distribution of drugs, whether on- or off-campus, however, is a mandatory expulsion.

In any event, the Connecticut Supreme Court issued its decision later in 1998. It agreed with the trial court that the student should not have been expelled, given the specific facts of the case. In the Court's view, the Thomaston Board of Education had violated the student's rights in the expulsion because it had not shown a direct connection between legitimate school concerns and the specific misconduct of the student, *i.e.* possession of a small quantity of drugs off-campus. *Packer v. Thomaston Board of Education*, 246 Conn. 89 (1998).

Of greater significance, the Court reversed the trial court on the broader question of discipline for off-campus conduct. The court ruled that the statute is constitutional on its face and that discipline may be imposed for off-campus misconduct. Moreover, in its ruling the Court provided guidance to school districts on the circumstances that may justify a student expulsion for conduct that occurs off-campus. The Court stated that the phrase "seriously disruptive of the educational process" has a core meaning of sufficient clarity because the legislature intended the phrase "to mean conduct that markedly interrupts or severely impedes the day-to-day operation of a school." 246 Conn. at 119. School officials must now ask whether the off-campus conduct in issue has such a direct impact on the operation of the school before they bring expulsion proceedings related to conduct that occurs off-campus. Note, however, that this issue arises when the expulsion is discretionary. In cases of mandatory expulsion for conduct off-campus, discussed in Section C(1)(b), the offenses requiring expulsion are specified in the statute, obviating the need for further consideration of whether the conduct disrupted the educational process.

A case involving the Trumbull Public Schools provided further clarification of the meaning "seriously disruptive of the educational process." *The Administration of the Trumbull Public Schools and Christopher Weiner*, Hearing Officer Decision dated November 6, 1998 (Eagan, Hearing Officer). Christopher Weiner, a senior at Trumbull High School, was convicted of sexual assault of a younger girl who was also a student at the same school. Following his conviction, school officials brought expulsion proceedings against the student, and the Board of Education hired a retired magistrate to serve as hearing officer. Judge Eagan considered testimony of school officials about the conviction and about the disruption and distraction caused by Mr. Weiner's attendance at school. He decided that the conduct for which the student was convicted violated the policies of the Trumbull Board of Education, and that, given the evidence of disruption and distraction, there was a sufficient nexus between this conduct and the operation of the school. Therefore, he ordered the student expelled.

e. Criminal conduct and reporting obligations

When a student between the ages of seven and twenty-one is arrested for a felony or a Class A misdemeanor, the municipal police department or division of the state police that made the arrest must orally notify the superintendent of schools of the district where the student attends school not later than the end of the weekday following the arrest, with written notification to follow within seventy-two hours of the arrest. Conn.

Gen. Stat. § 10-233h. The superintendent is to keep such information confidential, but may disclose the information to the principal of the school that the student attends. The principal may in turn disclose it to special services staff members for the purposes of assessing the risk of danger posed by the student to himself of herself, to other students, or to staff. School district personnel must conclude any such assessment not later than the next school day following notification. This new law also provides procedures for coordination between the school superintendent and the courts in matters of probation and school attendance. *Id.* This same statute also provides that police officials may testify and disclose juvenile arrest records in student expulsion proceedings, as quoted in Section C(1)(a), above.

In 1999, the General Assembly dealt with serious juvenile offenders in two new ways. First, it established an alternative to criminal adjudication for such juvenile offenders. If a child is charged with an offense involving the use or threatened use of physical violence in or on the real property comprising a public or private elementary or secondary school or at a school sponsored activity, upon motion, the court may order the suspension of further delinquency proceedings for up to one year and order the child to participate in a school violence prevention program. Conn. Gen. Stat. § 46b-133e. If the child completes the program successfully, he or she will not be subject to further delinquency proceedings. Conditions for participation in the program include (1) no previous participation in the program, (2) participation in no less than eight group counseling sessions (at parent cost), (3) compliance with any other orders of the court, and (4) certification by the child and his or her parents (or guardian) that to the best of their knowledge neither they nor the child possess any firearms, dangerous weapons, controlled substances, or other property or materials the possession of which is prohibited by law.

Second, the General Assembly imposed a reporting obligation upon the Department of Children and Families similar to that imposed on police officials. Conn. Gen. Stat. § 10-233k requires that DCF notify the superintendent of schools if DCF officials believe that there is risk of imminent personal injury from a child who has been adjudicated a serious juvenile offender. As with Conn. Gen. Stat. § 10-233h, the superintendent must then notify the principal, who can make further disclosure of such information only to special services staff as is necessary to assess the risk of danger posed by the student. In 2001, the law was clarified to provide that DCF and the Judicial Department must also provide to the superintendent "any educational records" in their custody, and the superintendent is authorized to release these records to the principal, who may disclose the records to "appropriate staff" members who are responsible for the education or care of the student. In addition, DCF and the Judicial Department must require that any contracting agency that holds such records provide them to the superintendent. Conn. Gen. Stat. § 10-233k.

Reporting obligations go both ways. When a student is expelled for possession of a firearm or deadly weapon, the board of education must report the violation to the local police department. Conn. Gen. Stat. § 10-233d(e). Also, if a teacher or other school employee files with the school principal a written report concerning an assault on him or her in the performance of his or her duties, the principal must report that assault to the local police authority. Moreover, the statute further provides that no school administrator may interfere with the right of a teacher or other school employee to file a report with the local police concerning threats of assault or actual assault by a student. Conn. Gen. Stat. § 10-233g.

f. Special education students

The "stay-put" and other rights of students who have disabilities can complicate or even prohibit an expulsion. Chapter Five, Section C sets forth the special rules that apply when considering the expulsion of a child identified as having a disability under either the IDEA or Section 504.

g. General matters

Expulsion decisions are final. There is no provision in Connecticut law for the appeal of expulsion decisions. For the procedure at the hearing, the statute incorporates selected provisions of the Uniform Administrative Procedures Act, but not the provision for appeal of administrative rulings. Conn. Gen. Stat. § 10-233d. The only way to have court review of such decisions, therefore, is by making a constitutional claim in an independent legal action. *See, e.g., Packer v. Thomaston Board of Education*, 246 Conn. 89 (1998); *Harris v. Robinson*, 273 F.3d 927 (10th Cir. 2001) (no substantive due process violation when principal made student clean out toilet under mistaken belief that he had clogged it).

Conn. Gen. Stat. § 10-233d(j) now provides, however, that a student may apply for early readmission following an expulsion. Any such readmission is at the discretion of the board of education, which can delegate the authority to consider such requests to the superintendent, and there is no duty to convene a hearing on the request. Either the board or the superintendent may impose conditions on any readmission, and the law specifies that readmission decisions are not subject to appeal to Superior Court.

Also, when a district expels a student, the expulsion and the conduct for which the student was expelled must now be noted on the student's cumulative educational record. The statutes do not define the "cumulative educational record," and there is no requirement that such a notation be included on the student's transcript. This notation must be expunged from the cumulative record upon graduation from high school. Notation of expulsion, however, should not be expunged in cases of a mandatory expulsion based on possession of a firearm or deadly weapon. Conn. Gen. Stat. § 10-233d(f).

Finally, the General Assembly has addressed the problem of students moving from one district to another in two ways. First, if a student is expelled by one school district and then presents him- or herself for admission to a second school district, the "receiving" district may adopt the decision of the first school district and expel the student without conducting a full hearing on the facts of the matter. The scope of the second hearing, rather, is limited to a determination of whether the misconduct established in the hearing in the first district would warrant expulsion under the board policies in the second. This hearing is therefore not an opportunity to retry the case. In any event, the second district must provide an alternative educational opportunity during the period of expulsion to the same extent as in other cases. Conn. Gen. Stat. § 10-233d(g).

Second, if a student withdraws from school when an expulsion hearing is "pending," the school district that scheduled the hearing must (1) note the pending expulsion hearing on the student's cumulative educational record, and (2) conclude the hearing and render a decision. The term "pending" is not defined in the statute, but it is reasonable to conclude that an expulsion is "pending" if notification of the proposed expulsion hearing has been provided to the student and/or parent. If the student enrolls in another district after receiving such notification, this statutory provision applies. The receiving district may suspend the student and either wait for the first district to conclude the ongoing hearing, or it may conduct its own expulsion hearing. If the second district decides to wait, it can then adopt the decision made by the prior district in accordance with Section 10-233d(g), described above. Unless an emergency exists, however, any such suspension must not exceed ten days. Conn. Gen. Stat. § 10-233d(h), and it thus may be necessary for the receiving school district to take action.

2. Student suspension

The requirements for a suspension from school are significantly different from the detailed procedures that apply in cases of expulsion. A suspension is any exclusion from school privileges for no more than ten school days for conduct that endangers persons or property, is seriously disruptive of the educational process, or violates a publicized policy of the board of education. The statutes provide that the board of education may authorize its administration to suspend, and such authorization should be contained in board policy. Conn. Gen. Stat. § 10-233c.

In 1996, the General Assembly amended Conn. Gen. Stat. § 10-233c to address suspension for off-campus conduct. Similar to the change made regarding expulsion, the statute now provides that students may be suspended for conduct off-campus if their conduct both violates a publicized policy of the board of education and is seriously disruptive of the educational process. In exercising this authority, however, school officials should keep in mind the definition of "seriously disruptive of the educational process" that the Connecticut Supreme Court provided in the *Thomaston* case, discussed above. Suspension for off-campus conduct is permitted only when the conduct "markedly interrupts or severely impedes the day-to-day operation of the school." *Packer v. Thomaston Board of Education*, 246 Conn. 89, 119 (1998). Conduct meeting this standard would likely warrant an expulsion, rather than only a suspension.

A suspension is limited to no more than ten school days at a time, and it may not extend beyond the end of the school year in which it is imposed. Conn. Gen. Stat. § 10-233a(d). In addition, school administrators may not suspend students more than ten times in a school year or for a total of more than fifty days without following the more formal procedures required for an expulsion. Conn. Gen. Stat. § 10-233c. As with expulsions, special rules may apply for children with disabilities, especially where there is more than one suspension. While there is no prohibition against suspending children with disabilities, districts must take care not to impose suspensions that, when taken together, in effect constitute a change in placement. Also, depending upon the nature of the student's disability and the length and number of suspensions, such actions with regard to children with disabilities can result in a claim of discrimination on the basis of disability. *See* Chapter Five, Section C.

The procedural rights of students facing suspension are modest in comparison to those that apply in cases of expulsion. *Goss v. Lopez*, 419 U.S.

565 (1975). Prior to imposing a suspension, school administrators simply must inform the student of the reasons for the disciplinary action and give him or her an opportunity to explain the situation. If this modest due process is provided, the courts will not review the underlying factual issues. *McDonald v. Sweetman*, 2004 U.S. Dist. LEXIS 5558 (D. Conn. 2004). Unless an emergency exists, this informal hearing must be held before the suspension is imposed. In determining the length of any suspension, the administration may consider evidence of past disciplinary problems that have led to previous disciplinary actions of removal, suspension, or expulsion. Conn. Gen. Stat. § 10-233c(b).

The statutes impose a few other requirements on school administrators in cases of suspension. As with all disciplinary action, the parents of the student should be notified within twenty-four hours of the suspension. Moreover, the student has the right to make up any work he or she missed during the period of suspension, including any examinations. Conn. Gen. Stat. § 10-233c(c) and (d).

School boards in Connecticut may also authorize the administration to suspend transportation services only to students whose conduct while receiving or awaiting transportation endangers persons or property or violates a publicized policy of the board. As with other suspensions, such action is limited to a maximum of ten consecutive school days. Conn. Gen. Stat. § 10-233c. In considering this option, it is advisable for school administrators to assure that alternative arrangements are made with the parents for the safe transportation of the student to school and, if no such arrangements can be made, to consider other alternatives to such disciplinary action. There is risk in simply suspending such services without making such arrangements. If a student were then injured on the way to school, he or she could claim that the board had acted unreasonably in expecting the child to get to school on his or her own.

Finally, as with expulsions, notice of any suspension and the conduct for which the pupil was suspended must also be included in the student's cumulative educational record. Notice of suspension is to be expunged upon high school graduation. Conn. Gen. Stat. § 10-233c(e).

3. Other disciplinary action

The statutes specify two other types of disciplinary actions. Boards of education can authorize their teachers to remove a student from class when the student deliberately causes a serious disruption within the classroom, *i.e.* to send the student to the office. There are limitations on such action. The teacher is required to inform the building principal or designee of the action immediately, along with the reasons for the action. Also, such "removals" should not occur more than twice in a week or six times during a school year without an informal hearing before the administration, as would occur in cases of suspension. Conn. Gen. Stat. § 10-233b.

Boards of education can also authorize the administration to impose in-school suspension on students whose conduct would otherwise justify an "out-of-school" suspension. Such in-school suspensions are defined as an exclusion from regular classroom activity for no more than five consecutive school days. Conn. Gen. Stat. § 10-233a(c). Before imposing an in-school suspension, administrators are required to provide the student with the same type of informal hearing that is required for suspensions generally. Also, no student may be placed on in-school suspension more than fifteen times during a school year, or for a total of more than fifty days, whichever is less. Conn. Gen. Stat. § 10-233f. In considering this limitation one may ask whether in-school and out-of-school suspensions should be considered together. There are no court decisions interpreting these statutes in this regard. Since the limits are set forth separately in separate statutes, however, it is reasonable to conclude that the limits on in-school and out-of-school suspension may be kept separate.

Notably, there is no provision in Connecticut law for corporal punishment of students as a disciplinary tool. The United States Supreme Court has ruled that corporal punishment of students may be imposed without violating the Eighth Amendment, which prohibits cruel and unusual punishment. *Ingraham v. Wright*, 430 U.S. 651 (1977). In Connecticut, however, such action would be taken at the teacher's peril because the teacher could be committing an assault. A teacher or other person entrusted with the care and supervision of a minor for school purposes who uses reasonable physical force is not guilty of assault only if that person reasonably believes that such force is necessary to (1) protect himself or others from immediate physical injury, (2) to obtain possession of a dangerous instrument or controlled substance, (3) to protect property from physical damage, or (4) to restrain a minor student or to remove a minor student to another area to maintain order. Conn. Gen. Stat. § 53a-18. If the teacher or other person who uses force on a student cannot point to one of these provisions, or if the force used exceeds what is reasonable, the teacher may be guilty of assault under this statute. Moreover, the teacher would also be subject to the additional claims described below, and would be subject to discipline or even termination.

A mandated reporter who has reasonable cause to suspect or believe that a school employee has engaged in child abuse by using excessive force must report that suspicion or belief to the Department of Children and Families. *See* Section F, below. In addition, a teacher who uses excessive force on a student may also face civil liability for any injuries caused by such conduct. *See Sansone v. Bechtel*, 180 Conn. 96 (1980). While the indemnity statute, Conn. Gen. Stat. § 10-235, will generally protect teachers from liability for injuries they cause in the scope of their employment, this protection does not apply to conduct that is "wanton, reckless or malicious." An extreme use of excessive force may fall within this exception and be outside the scope of the indemnity statute.

D. Student Records

Under federal law, parents and students have extensive rights with regard to student records. These rights may be exercised by the parents while the students are children, and these rights transfer to the students themselves when they reach the age of eighteen (which makes them "eligible students" under the law). Parents remain entitled to access to school records without the consent of the student even after a student has reached age eighteen, as long as the student is a dependent of the parent for federal tax purposes. The law gives parents and eligible students the right to inspect all school records relating to the student. Also, the law requires that any personally identifiable information contained in these records be kept confidential, unless either consent for disclosure is given or one of the legal exceptions to these confidentiality requirements applies. This law, the Family Educational Rights and Privacy Act, 20 U.S.C. § 1232g, or "FERPA" is also sometimes known as the "Buckley Amendment" after its primary sponsor in 1974, Senator James Buckley.

At the heart of the law is the definition of "education records." If information is personally identifiable and is an education record, the provisions of FERPA apply, both as to parent and student access, and as to confidentiality. FERPA defines "education record" broadly to be material that directly relates to a student and that is maintained by the educational institution. In 2002, the Sixth Circuit Court of Appeals applied the plain language of this provision, for example, to hold that student disciplinary records, even at the college level, are "education records." *United States v. Miami University*, 294 F.3d 797 (6th Cir. 2002).

In 2002 the United States Supreme Court provided guidance on the scope of "educational records." *Owasso Independent School District I-011 v. Falvo*, 534 U.S. 426 (2002). There, a parent claimed that a teacher's practice of having the students in class grade each other's papers and call out the grades humiliated her son and violated FERPA by causing the disclosure of information contained in educational records. Reversing the appellate court, the Court ruled that student work is not covered by FERPA until the papers are graded and those grades recorded by school personnel. The Court also noted that the practice used by the teacher was common, and that an overly broad definition of "educational records" would be burdensome, given the requirement, for example, of maintaining a log of access to such records by non-school personnel.

1. <u>Access rights</u>

Under FERPA, parents and eligible students (those who have reached age eighteen -- for simplicity hereinafter just "parents") have the right to review school records. However, in Connecticut it is important to remember that parents may also exercise rights under the Freedom of Information Act, Conn. Gen. Stat. § 1-200 *et seq.*, as discussed in Chapter One, Section D, and those rights are often more extensive than the rights under FERPA.

While the law itself is fairly short, the implementing regulations set out the rights of parents and the duties of school districts in some detail. 34 C.F.R. § 99.1 *et seq.* Parents have the right to inspect all "education records" pertaining to their children. School districts must afford parents this right of access and inspection within forty-five days of the request, though of course records are generally shared much more quickly. Also, under the Freedom of Information Act, a parent making a request would be entitled to "prompt" access to such records. Conn. Gen. Stat. § 1-210.

Under FERPA school officials must respond to reasonable requests for an explanation and interpretation of the records. 34 C.F.R. § 99.10. In addition, school districts must provide a copy of such records or make other arrangements for the parents to inspect them if circumstances effectively prevent the parents from exercising the right to inspect such records (though the regulations do not provide an example of such circumstances). If a copy of an education record is made for the parents, school districts can generally charge a fee for such copies. 34 C.F.R. § 99.11. Under the special education regulations, however, parents are entitled to access to all educational records,

34 C.F.R. § 300.501, and to one copy of the IEP at no cost. 34 C.F.R. § 300.345(f).

Parent and eligible student rights to see educational records are subject to certain limitations set out in FERPA. 34 C.F.R. § 99.3. Perhaps most frequently cited is the "sole possession record" provision. FERPA provides that a record that a teacher or other school employee maintains in his or her sole possession (except as to share with a temporary substitute for the maker of the record) is not an education record that must be disclosed. *Id.* However, this provision does not affect the rights of parents (or appropriate others) to obtain such information pursuant to a subpoena when there is an ongoing legal proceeding, or possibly under the state Freedom of Information Act, Conn. Gen. Stat §§ 1-200 *et seq.*

In addition to the "sole possession record" exception, other exclusions from the definition of education records include certain records of law enforcement units of educational institutions, employment records of students who are also employed (not usually relevant at the elementary and secondary level), certain treatment records created by a psychiatrist or psychologist, or records that contain information about an individual after he or she is no longer a student at that institution. 34 C.F.R. § 99.3.

Finally, with regard to access rights, it is important to recognize that non-custodial parents have rights of access to student records under both state and federal law. Under FERPA, either parent of a child has the full rights of access unless the school district has received evidence that there is a court order, state statute, or other legally binding document relating to separation, divorce, or custody that specifically revokes such rights. 34 C.F.R. § 99.4. *See also* Conn. Gen. Stat. § 46b-56(e), reviewed in Section D(4) below. The Second Circuit Court of Appeals has also ruled that non-custodial parents have rights under FERPA. *Fay v. South Colonie Central School District*, 802 F.2d 21 (2d Cir. 1986).

That case also held that non-custodial parents may recover damages for violations of FERPA. This holding, however, was superseded by the decision of the United States Supreme Court in *Gonzaga University v. Doe*, 536 U.S. 273 (2002). There, University employees disclosed information contained in a student's file about an alleged sexual assault by him, and he was therefore unable to get certified as a teacher. The former student sued under FERPA and was awarded $1,155,000 in damages, including $450,000 in damages under FERPA from Gonzaga University for the release of that information. The United States Supreme Court reversed, holding that

FERPA does not authorize private lawsuits against educational institutions for FERPA violations. The Court explained that Congress must speak unambiguously when it creates a private right of action under the Spending Clause. The sole remedy for a FERPA violation thus is through the Department of Education. Unauthorized release of information that is confidential by law, however, may result in an invasion of privacy or other tort claim.

2. Confidentiality rights

The other key provision in FERPA relates to confidentiality of education records. Except as noted below, school districts are obligated to maintain the confidentiality of personally identifiable student information. 34 C.F.R. § 99.7(a)(2)(iii). In 1997, the Freedom of Information Act was amended so that it now expressly provides that matters privileged from disclosure under FERPA are also exempt from disclosure under Conn. Gen. Stat. § 1-210(b)(17).

The duty to maintain the confidentiality of student records can sometimes collide with the realities of a public school setting. In *Owasso Independent School District I-011 v. Falvo*, 534 U.S. 426 (2002), discussed above, a parent claimed that a classroom practice of having students grade papers of other students and call out their own grades violated FERPA. The Court held that student grades on quizzes, etc. are not "student records" under FERPA until they are recorded by school officials. This ruling is consistent with the interpretation of FERPA provided by the enforcing agency, the United States Department of Education. The Department's Family Policy Compliance Division has stated that "a thoughtful, common sense, and flexible approach is necessary in judging the impact of some classroom activities on a student's right to privacy . . . ," and that FERPA does not prohibit teachers from allowing students to grade the work of other students. *Letter from LeRoy S. Rooker, Director, to Wallace N. Raupp* (July 15, 1993).

a. Disclosure with written consent

Except as is provided in FERPA, written consent of the parent (or of the eligible student) is required before confidential student information is disclosed. Such consent must specify the records to be disclosed and the purpose of the disclosure, and must identify the party to whom the records are to be disclosed. Electronic consent is now permitted as long as it "(1) identifies and authenticates a particular person as the source of the electronic consent, and (2) indicates such person's approval of the information contained in the electronic consent." 66 Fed. Reg. 21,670 *et seq.* (Apr. 21, 2004) (to be codified at 34 C.F.R. § 99.30)

b. Disclosure without written consent

FERPA sets out several situations where prior written consent is not required before personally identifiable information may be disclosed. Directory information is addressed in subsection c, below, and the following review identifies the other most common provisions.

First, and most common, consent is not required when disclosure is to a "school official" of the district, if that person has a legitimate educational interest in the information. 34 C.F.R. § 99.31(a)(1). Persons who may have a legitimate educational interest include teachers and other school employees working directly with a student, as well as school administrators, school district lawyers and, where appropriate, even outside consultants who are employed to assist with the particular student's educational program.

Also, when a student transfers from one school district to another, written consent is not required before records may be sent to the receiving district unless board policy requires otherwise. 34 C.F.R. § 99.31(a)(2), 34 C.F.R. § 99.34. A local requirement that prior parent consent be obtained is not advisable, moreover, given the administrative burden involved. Under state law, however, school districts are now required to send written notification to the "sending" school district when a student enrolls, and that "sending" school district must send the educational records within ten calendar days of receipt of the notification. Conn. Gen. Stat. § 10-220h. Also, if the notification from the "receiving" school district does not establish that the parents provided written consent for the transfer, the "sending" school district is required to send notification of the transfer to the parents at the same time it transfers the records. *Id.*

Consent is not required when disclosure of educational records is made to state and local educational authorities, when such disclosure is made in an audit, evaluation, or compliance review of educational programs. 34 C.F.R. § 99.31(a)(3), 34 C.F.R. § 99.35.

School officials may also disclose educational records without prior written consent pursuant to a court order or subpoena. 34 C.F.R. § 99.31(a)(9). However, before complying with such an order or subpoena, the district must make a reasonable effort to notify the parent or eligible student of the court order or subpoena in advance of the disclosure. The theory is that the parents would then have the right to seek to have the subpoena quashed or the court order stayed. In 2001, FERPA was amended to provide that pursuant to an *ex parte* order schools must disclose information to the Attorney General related to investigation of terrorism. If a school makes a disclosure in such a case (which presumably will be rare), the school district is not to keep a record of the disclosure. 20 U.S.C. § 1232g(j).

Confidential student information may also be disclosed in health and safety emergencies. Knowledge of the information, however, must be necessary to protect the health or safety of the student or other individuals, and the regulations provide that this requirement will be strictly construed. 34 C.F.R. § 99.31(a)(10), 34 C.F.R. § 99.36.

Finally, questions can arise as to releasing information to victims of student misconduct. FERPA permits student disciplinary information to be disclosed to a victim of a crime of violence or a non-forcible sex offense. 34 C.F.R. §§ 99.31(13), (14). This new provision applies only to institutions of postsecondary education, however, and it does not affect school districts. Typically, therefore, school officials should not disclose to other parties the disciplinary consequences imposed upon a student. The Tenth Circuit has ruled that even at the elementary and secondary level, a contemporaneous release of information to parents of children who were victims of misbehavior by another student is not a release of an "education record" under FERPA and thus did not violate that student's confidentiality rights under that statute. *Jensen v. Reeves*, 456 F.3d 681 (10th Cir. 2001). It is not clear that that United States Department of Education would agree with this approach generally, and a better alternative would be to maintain as confidential the specific discipline imposed, but to release to both the perpetrator and the victim a summary of the disposition of the complaint. Such a record of such disposition would be an education record that directly relates to both students and thus could be disclosed to both.

c. Directory information

School districts do not have to obtain written consent before disclosing personally identifiable information that is designated as "directory information." The regulations provide that school districts may, but need not, designate certain categories of information as directory information. Such information is that which would not generally be considered harmful or an invasion of privacy if disclosed. The regulations provide examples of such information, such as name, address, telephone listing, electronic mail address, photograph, date and place of birth, major field of study, dates of attendance, grade level, enrollment status, participation in officially recognized activities and sports, weight and height of members of athletic teams, degrees and awards received, and the most recent school previously attended. 34 C.F.R. § 99.3, 34 C.F.R. § 99.31(11). As described below, FERPA requires that school districts give annual notice to parents of their rights. The district may describe what information it has designated as directory information, and if it does, it must notify parents of their right to refuse to permit disclosure of any or all such information. 34 C.F.R. § 99.37. If a parent or eligible student does not object within the time specified in the notification, the school district can release such information without the consent of the parents or eligible student. It is important, however, to follow this procedure, because if directory information has not been designated or if parents have not been notified, it would be a FERPA violation to release any personally identifiable student information, even a list of students on an honor roll.

Since FERPA does not require disclosure of directory information, some school districts have declined to release directory information when it is requested by third parties, while reserving the district's right to release directory information when district officials believe it appropriate. The federal No Child Left Behind Act, P.L. 107-100, however, requires the disclosure of certain directory information upon request to military recruiters and to institutions of higher education, *i.e.* name, address and telephone number of secondary students. No Child Left Behind Act, Section 9528. This obligation is similar to the general provision for the release of directory information, described above. School districts therefore must either (1) designate such information as directory information in the annual notification of FERPA rights sent to parents, or (2) provide a separate notification to parents of the obligation to release such information to military recruiters and institutions of higher education unless the parent objects.

3. District obligations

In 1996, there was a significant change in the obligations the regulations impose on school districts. Previously each school district was required (1) to adopt a policy setting forth how it would meet the requirements of the law and (2) to publish an annual notification of rights for parents. Pursuant to the 1996 amendments to FERPA, school districts are no longer required to adopt such policies. The amended regulations expand the previous requirement of an annual notification of rights under FERPA to parents, however, and a more elaborate and extensive notification is now required.

Pursuant to 34 C.F.R. § 99.7, the annual notification must now inform parents that they have the right to:

- inspect and review the student's education records;
- seek amendment of the student's education records if they believe such records to be inaccurate, misleading, or otherwise in violation of the student's privacy rights;
- consent to disclosures of personally identifiable information contained in such records, except to the extent disclosure is authorized without consent;
- refuse to permit disclosure of directory information (the notice should describe what information the district has designated as "directory information");
- file a complaint with the federal Department of Education concerning alleged failures by the district to comply with its obligations under FERPA or the regulations.

In addition, the annual notification must include the following items:

- procedures for exercising the right to inspect and review education records;
- procedures for requesting amendment of records under 34 C.F.R. § 99.20;
- the district's criteria for determining who constitutes a "school official" and what constitutes a "legitimate educational interest" if the district has a policy of disclosing education records to its own employees within the district under 34 C.F.R. § 99.31(a)(1).

The regulations do not specify how such notification is to be provided, but rather simply specify that the notification must be provided by any means that is reasonably likely to inform parents of their rights. Also, the district must provide effective notification for parents who are disabled or whose primary language is not English. 34 C.F.R. § 99.7. Model notification language has been developed by the United States Department of Education, and it is available online or from the Office of Legal Affairs of the State Department of Education.

The most commonly asserted right is that of access. While the Freedom of Information Act requires "prompt" access to records, FERPA requires that educational records be provided within forty-five (calendar) days of the request. 34 C.F.R. § 99.10.

In addition, the district must have a procedure for permitting parents to request amendment of the records when they believe that the record is "inaccurate, misleading or in violation of the student's rights of privacy." 34 C.F.R. § 99.20. This process may not be used to challenge a particular grade, however, except as to mathematical correctness or the intent of the grader. *Tarka v. Cunningham*, 917 F.2d 890 (5th Cir. 1990).

The required review procedures include the opportunity to request a change and an opportunity for a hearing if the district declines to make the requested change. The matter must be heard "within a reasonable time" after the request is made, and the decision must be made by an official who does not have a "direct interest" in the matter, though the hearing officer may be an employee of the district. If, after hearing, the district does not make the requested change, it must inform the parent of his or her right to place a statement in the record commenting on the information or stating why he or she disagrees with the record. When that record is then disclosed by the school district to third parties, any such statement by the parent must also be disclosed. 34 C.F.R. § 99.21.

These duties must be taken seriously. Failure to maintain confidentiality of personally identifiable student information, or violation of any of the other requirements of the law may result in a finding by the Department of Education against the district and an order of remedial action. The United States Supreme Court recently ruled that FERPA does not establish a private right of action by students for alleged violations of their rights under the statute. *Gonzaga University v. Doe*, 536 U.S. 273 (2002). Given the requirements of the law, however, a parent could still bring an action for negligence or invasion of privacy if information contained in student records is disclosed without consent.

4. State law

FERPA is the most detailed statutory provision concerning student records. However, there are also six state laws of note related to student records.

a. General access rights

Conn. Gen. Stat. § 10-15b expressly provides that parents or legal guardians of students are entitled to knowledge of and access to "all educational, medical, or similar records maintained in such student's cumulative record," except as such records may be privileged under Conn. Gen. Stat. § 10-154a, discussed in Section D(4)(e), below. This statute also sets forth the procedure for complying with subpoenas relating to student records. It provides that student records that are subpoenaed to court may be delivered to the court in a sealed envelope marked as required by the statute (case name, etc.). If the records are accompanied by an affidavit attesting to the fact that the records are maintained in the normal course of business, it is not necessary for a school official to attend the court proceedings to authenticate the records.

b. Non-custodial parents

As with the federal law, the matter of custody does not necessarily affect a parent's right to access to school and other records. Under Connecticut law, a non-custodial parent may not be denied access to "academic, medical, hospital or other health records of such minor child unless otherwise ordered by the court for good cause shown." Conn. Gen. Stat. § 46b-56(e).

c. HIV information

HIV information is strictly confidential, and the statutes impose significant responsibilities on school districts. Conn. Gen. Stat. §§ 19a-581 *et seq.* provide that confidential information concerning HIV status may not be released to anyone except a health care provider without a written release from the parents. When school officials become aware of a student's HIV status, they may not share that information with other school personnel as they do with other educational records. Rather, further release of information is subject to the special requirement for a written release. Where such information may be relevant in educating a student, the school medical advisor may be helpful in obtaining consent from the parents.

d. FOIA and FERPA

Since 1997, the Freedom of Information Act has included express recognition of the confidentiality obligations of FERPA. Any document that is confidential under FERPA is exempt from disclosure under Conn. Gen. Stat. § 1-210(b)(17).

e. Professional communications

Under state law, communications concerning drug or alcohol abuse or a drug or alcohol problem made in confidence by a student to a teacher (or other professional including the school nurse) need not be disclosed by the professional employee. Conn. Gen. Stat. § 10-154a. *See* Chapter Three, Section F(7). Significantly, the professional employee may decide to disclose the information; the choice is up to the employee, and he or she is immune from liability for good faith decisions to disclose or not to disclose such information. *Id.* By contrast, records of medical treatment from substance abuse treatment facilities are confidential under federal law. 42 U.S.C. § 290dd-2. While certain exceptions apply, as when the disclosure is ordered by a court to protect against an existing threat to life or of serious bodily injury, school personnel should be cautious and determine their legal obligations before further disclosure of any such information they receive concerning students.

f. Record transfer requirements

When a student enrolls in a new school district, the new school district must provide written notification of such enrollment to the school district in which the student previously attended school. The "sending" school district must transfer the student's educational records within ten days after receipt of such notification, and, if the student's parent or guardian did not given written authorization for the transfer of such records, the "sending" district must send the parent or guardian notification of the transfer to the parent or guardian at the same time it transfers the records. Conn. Gen. Stat. § 10-220h. In addition, Section 4155 of the federal No Child Left Behind Act requires states to assure that they have in place a process to facilitate the transfer of records concerning student suspension and expulsion to any public or private school in which the student is enrolling. This requirement may require amendment of Conn. Gen. Stat. § 10-220h.

5. <u>Student surveys, analyses, and evaluations</u>

In addition to their right to obtain access to the student records directly related to their children, parents also have a right under federal law to review certain instructional materials. The Protection of Pupil Rights Amendment, or PPRA (also known as the "Hatch Amendment"), requires schools to make available to parents for inspection instructional materials used as part of any survey, analysis, or evaluation, funded in whole or in part by the U.S. Department of Education. *See* 20 U.S.C. § 1232h(a); 34 C.F.R. § 98.1 *et seq.* 20 U.S.C. § 1232h(b) provides that school districts must obtain written parental consent before requiring minor students to participate in any survey, analysis, or evaluation funded by the U.S. Department of Education that reveals information concerning:

- political affiliations;
- mental and psychological problems potentially embarrassing to the student or his or her family;
- sexual behavior and attitudes;
- illegal, anti-social, self-incriminating, and demeaning behavior;
- critical appraisals of other individuals with whom respondents have close family relationships;
- legally recognized privileged or analogous relationships, such as those of lawyers, physicians, and ministers; or
- income (other than that required by law to determine eligibility for participation in program or for receiving financial assistance under such program);
- religious practices, affiliations, or beliefs of the student or student's parents.

The PPRA was amended by the No Child Left Behind Act, P.L. 107-110, which requires that boards of education develop student privacy policies in consultation with parents, including provisions on (1) the parents' right to inspect third-party surveys before they are administered; (2) the parents' right to inspect any instructional material used in the curriculum; (3) the administration of any physical examination or screenings; and (4) the collection and use of personal information collected from students for the purpose of marketing that information. No Child Left Behind Act, Section 1061.

The PPRA now also requires schools to provide parents annual notification of these policies. This notification must explain that parents have the right to "opt the student out of participation" in the following activities (and identify when during the school year they are scheduled to occur): 1) the collection and use of personal information gathered from students for the purpose of marketing that information; 2) the administration of any survey that delves into the restricted sensitive subject areas identified;

3) the administration of any non-emergency, invasive physical examination or screening that is not otherwise permitted or required by state law.

Prior to these changes, it was clear that the PPRA applied in only very limited circumstances. Because the scope of the law is specifically limited to a survey, analysis, or evaluation funded by the Department of Education, the requirements of PPRA will apply to a particular survey, analysis, or evaluation only if:

- the development and/or administration of the survey, analysis or evaluation is funded, in whole or in part, with federal education funds;
- the students are required to participate in the survey, analysis or evaluation; and,
- the survey, analysis, or evaluation is designed to reveal information about one or more of the seven categories of information listed above and noted in the law.

The facts and circumstances of a particular case will determine whether student participation is required. Obviously, if students are told that they must participate in a survey, analysis, or evaluation, their participation would be characterized as "required." Even if students are told they need not complete all or a portion of a survey, but the option is presented to them in circumstances that prohibit a free and informed choice, administration of that survey may also be deemed "required."

Given the fact that the requirement for written parent consent applies only to surveys, analyses, and evaluations funded by the Department of Education, the impact of the PPRA on school districts may continue to be limited. It remains to be seen, however, whether the recent changes (required privacy policies, annual notification, etc.) will cause this law to be a more significant concern for school districts. In any event, it appears unlikely that parents would be able to assert a private right of action for violation of the terms of this statute. *See Gonzaga University v. Doe*, 536 U.S. 273 (2002).

E. Student Rights

The United States Supreme Court first recognized that students may have constitutional rights in the school setting in 1943, when it decided that a state law requiring students to pledge allegiance to the flag could not be enforced. In that case, the student, a Jehovah's Witness, refused to participate in the Pledge, claiming that his religion prohibited him from doing so. Though the decision was reached in the dark days of World War II, the Court agreed with the student and held that enforcement of the statute violated the First Amendment. *West Virginia v. Barnette*, 319 U.S. 624 (1943).

Though dramatic, the *Barnette* case was an isolated case, and there was no general recognition of students rights for another quarter-century. In 1969, the legal landscape changed when the United States Supreme Court decided *Tinker v. Des Moines Independent Community School District*, 393 U.S. 503 (1969), the seminal case recognizing the rights of students in the public schools. There, Justice Fortas wrote the famous words that students do not "shed their constitutional rights to freedom of speech and/or expression at the schoolhouse gate."

In the years since *Tinker* was decided, school districts, parents, and the courts have struggled to define the scope of student rights. While the courts still recognize that school districts must respect constitutional rights of students, times have changed since 1969 when *Tinker* was decided. Recently, the courts appear to be more willing to defer to judgments made by school administrators and school board members concerning student rights.

1. Free speech

Mary Beth Tinker participated in a planned protest against the Vietnam war, in which the students were to wear black armbands. When school officials heard about these plans, they quickly passed a new school rule prohibiting students from wearing black armbands in school. Mary Beth wore her armband anyway and was suspended from school. She then challenged the rule as a violation of her constitutional rights. The lower courts dismissed her claims on the ground that the rule was reasonable in order to prevent disruption of school discipline. The United States Supreme Court reversed, holding that students have constitutional rights that school officials must consider in regulating student conduct. The Court announced the *Tinker* standard for when school officials can regulate student speech, and this test has guided school officials ever since.

a. The *Tinker* standard

The Court held in *Tinker* that students have a right of free speech, even while they are in school. The Court recognized that this right must be balanced against the legitimate concerns and responsibilities of school officials in maintaining an orderly school environment. To strike this balance, the Court held that school officials may regulate the First Amendment rights of students only when they reasonably forecast that permitting such speech will result in:

- substantial disruption of the educational process;
- material interference with school activities; or
- invasion of the rights of others.

Where school officials reasonably make such a forecast, they may prohibit the particular student speech in question. However, it is important to recognize that the courts have not simply accepted forecasts of disruption by school administrators; rather, there must be specific facts reasonably supporting such a forecast. Where such a potential for disruption cannot be established, the First Amendment rights of students will prevail.

When *Tinker* was first decided, it was controversial. Justice Black dissented, lamenting that this new rule would subject the public schools "to the whims and caprices of their loudest-mouthed, but maybe not their brightest students." It was indeed revolutionary to think that students have rights in school. However, now the rule in *Tinker* seems self-evident, and it is well-known to school officials and students alike.

Following *Tinker*, there have been a number of cases that illustrate its principles. In one case, students chose not to stand for the Pledge of Allegiance, and school officials expelled them because of their actions. The federal court in New York enjoined such disciplinary action; as long as the actions by the students were not disruptive and did not interfere with the rights of the other students to participate in the activity, school officials had to respect their right of symbolic free speech. *Frain v. Baron*, 307 F. Supp. 27 (E.D.N.Y. 1969). *See also Goetz v. Ansell*, 477 F.2d 636 (2d Cir. 1973).

By contrast, when there was a history of disruption and confrontation in a racially charged school atmosphere, school officials were permitted to prohibit students from wearing any kind of button, including buttons protesting the Vietnam war. *Guzick v. Drebus*, 431 F.2d 594 (6th Cir. 1970). The unique facts confronting school administrators in that district made it reasonable to forecast substantial disruption or material interference if they permitted students to wear buttons in school. Similarly, in 2002 a student in West Virginia lost her challenge against discipline imposed for wearing a T-shirt shortly after 9/11 that said, "When I saw the dead and dying Afghani children on TV, I felt a newly recovered sense of national security. God Bless America." The jury awarded her $1.00 in damages, however, for the violation of her right to form an Anarchy Club. While the broad principles are clear, the facts of a specific case will determine whether school officials will be permitted to regulate student speech.

More recently, the courts have differentiated between the free speech rights of young students and those of older students. In *Walker-Serrano v. Leonard*, 325 F.3d 412 (3d Cir. 2003), the Third Circuit rejected a claim that a third-grader had the right to circulate a petition protesting the class trip to the circus, and it questioned more generally whether *Tinker* confers any free speech rights at all upon children of such tender years. *See also S.G. v. Sayreville Board of Education*, 333 F.3d 417 (3d Cir. 2003).

1. The Internet

The Internet poses special challenges for school officials. Clearly, if a student misuses school equipment or engages in computer misconduct on school property, he or she is subject to disciplinary action. With increasing frequency, however, the problem is that students are posting insulting or offensive material on their web pages or elsewhere off-campus. School officials are often inclined to judge such conduct harshly, as they would judge such conduct in the school setting. Applying the *Tinker* standard to such student speech, however, the courts have frequently ruled against school officials in such cases because it is very difficult for them to show that they reasonably forecast that the students' speech off-campus will substantially disrupt or materially interfere with the educational process. *See, e.g., Beussink v. Woodland R-IV School District*, 30 F. Supp.2d 1175 (E.D. Mo. 1998). Discipline for such conduct is especially difficult in Connecticut because discipline for off-campus conduct is permitted if the conduct severely interrupts or impedes the day-to-day operation of the school. *Packer v. Thomaston Board of Education*, 246 Conn. 89 (1998).

Vulgarity is frequently the concern, but off-campus vulgarity is typically not disruptive. In one case, a student created a satirical website that parodied one of the school's assistant principals harshly, including suggestions that he supported book burning, was a spokesman for Viagra, and even engaged in sex with livestock. The court granted summary judgment for the student because, in its opinion that school district failed to prove that the student's website caused a serious disruption to the educational process. *Beidler v. North Thurston School District No. 3*, (No. 99-00236, Washington Superior Court, July 18, 2000). The student was later awarded $10,000 in damages, plus attorneys' fees. Education Week, February 28, 2001, at 4. *See also Killion v. Franklin Regional School District*,

136 F. Supp.2d 446 (W.D. Pa. 2001) (student e-mailed Top Ten list to friends regarding size of athletic director's stomach and genitals; free speech under *Tinker* because student's off-campus actions were not disruptive).

Notwithstanding this high standard, discipline for off-campus student speech (including that on the Internet) is permitted in appropriate cases. For example, when students threaten school staff or other students, prediction of disruption may be reasonable, justifying discipline, as discussed below. Similarly, when off-campus conduct actually threatens disruption of the school's operation, discipline may be imposed. In *Boucher v. School Board of Greenfield*, 134 F.3d 821 (7th Cir. 1998), for example, the Seventh Circuit held that a student was properly disciplined after he wrote an article advocating hacking into the school's computer, complete with instructions. The school's interest in preventing such misconduct outweighed any free speech rights he had to share that information.

2. Threats

Given the concern for student safety following a number of shootings across the country, courts have been willing to grant school districts some latitude in addressing student threats, notwithstanding the protections of *Tinker*. Some threats are direct, and as such have no First Amendment protection. One student, for example, wrote a female student a note that included a rap song with words such as "you better run bitch, cuz I can't control what I do." The Arkansas Supreme Court held that this note did not have First Amendment protection because it was a "true threat." *Jones v. State*, 347 Ark. 455, 65 S.W.3d 402 (2002). *See also In the Interest of A.S.*, 243 Wis. 173, 626 N.W.2d 712 (Wis. 2001) (detailed threats against authority figures found to be criminal acts). A divided Eighth Circuit struggled with the discipline of a student for writing a threatening letter in his home that another student brought to the attention of school authorities, and ultimately it upheld the student's expulsion. *Doe v. Pulaski County Special School District*, 306 F.3d 616 (8th Cir. 2002).

Even when the student does not make a true threat, the courts may find that school discipline is warranted for inappropriate threatening speech. In *Lovell v. Poway United School District*, 90 F.3d 367 (9th Cir. 1996), for example, the court permitted discipline of an exasperated student who said that she would shoot her guidance counselor if she did not her change schedule. *See also In re Douglas D.*, 243 Wis. 204, 626 N.W.2d 725 (Wis. 2001) (creative writing assignment that refers to beheading a teacher not a "true threat;" criminal adjudication vacated but school discipline for crude and repugnant writing not affected); *S.G. v. Sayreville Board of Education*, 333 F.3d 417 (3d Cir. 2003). (three day suspension of kindergarten student for saying "I'll shoot you" upheld).

Threats can occur on the Internet as well, and subject to the *Packer* standard, discussed above, discipline can be imposed for such threats. One student created a Website called "Teacher Sux," in which he set out a picture showing violence against his algebra teacher and asked the question, "why should she die?" The student was permanently expelled (which apparently is permissible in Pennsylvania), and the court rejected his claims on appeal. The Pennsylvania Supreme Court found that, while the comments did not constitute a "true threat," the impact on the teacher (who missed the rest of the year) and school community was a serious educational concern that justified the expulsion. *J.S. v. Bethlehem School District*, 807 A.2d 803 (Pa. 2002). *But see Mahaffey v. Aldrich*, 236 F. Supp.2d 779 (E.D. Mich. 2002) (improper to suspend student who created "Satan's Website," including list of "people I wish would die").

Other threats are indirect, but even here the courts often rule in favor of school officials. In one case, a student distributed an anonymous pamphlet that included an essay in which the author "wondered what would happen" if he shot the principal, teachers or other students. The district searched the student and had him arrested. His subsequent claim that his constitutional rights were violated was dismissed by the court. *Cuesta v. School Board of Miami Dade County*, 285 F.3d 962 (11th Cir. 2002).

In another case, an eleventh grade student presented a poem, "Last Words" to his English teacher, which poem included the words, "I drew my gun and,/threw open the door,/Bang Bang, Bang-Bang/When it was all over, 28 were,/dead." The student was promptly referred to the police and to mental health professionals, but they found no cause for involuntary commitment. The next day, however, the principal invoked state procedures for emergency expulsion. The student later sued, claiming a violation of his First Amendment rights. The trial court agreed with the student, but the Ninth Circuit reversed in part. It held that school officials had reasonable cause for their actions. Given that it was later established that the student was not a threat, however, the appellate court agreed with the trial court that the record of the expulsion should be expunged. *Lavine v. Blaine School District*, 257 F.3d 981 (9th Cir. 2001), *rehearing denied*, 279 F.3d 712 (9th Cir. 2001), *cert. denied* 122 S.Ct. 2663 (2002).

When student writing raises issues of potential threat, expulsion is a possibility, and may be advisable, given the responsibility for the safety of all students. The threat of disciplinary action, however, need not always be carried out. It can be appropriate to inform the parents of the district's concerns and discuss psychiatric evaluation as an alternative to expulsion. The important thing is that school officials cannot ignore facts that would cause a reasonable person concern. Appropriate action to assure student safety, however, is not necessarily disciplinary action, and it is often possible to work with parents either to rule out a concern or to get the troubled student the help s/he needs.

b. "Legitimate pedagogical concerns"

Originally, the courts applied the *Tinker* standard across the board, to all situations involving student speech, whether in class, out of class, in the school newspaper, or elsewhere. This broad application of the *Tinker* standard, however, led to some serious problems. Specifically, school officials have a legitimate interest in maintaining standards of decorum in the school setting, in fairness to the other students and as part of teaching students socially acceptable behavior. However, the *Tinker* standard places a heavy burden on school officials when students assert a right of free speech. While school officials wished to regulate vulgarity, for example, it was difficult or impossible for them to establish that vulgar speech caused substantial interference or material disruption. To be sure, school officials were always able to prohibit obscenity, as a violation of the rights of the other students. However, in a classic Catch-22, vulgarity was difficult or impossible to regulate — the more vulgarity that students used, say, in the student newspaper, the more difficult it would be for school officials to forecast disruption, given the ever-higher "shock" thresholds that could develop.

In 1986, the United States Supreme Court addressed the question of student vulgarity in *Bethel School District No. 403 v. Fraser*, 478 U.S. 675 (1986), and gave school officials more authority to regulate student free speech when it is vulgar. In *Bethel*, the plaintiff student, Matthew Fraser, gave a nominating speech at a student assembly. The speech was essentially an elaborate sexual metaphor ("Jeff Kuhlman is a man who takes his point and pounds it in. . . . Jeff is a man who will go to the very end - even the climax, for each and every one of you," etc.). Two teachers had advised Matthew not to present the speech. After he did, school officials suspended him for three days and removed him from the list of candidates for graduation speaker.

Matthew brought suit against the district, alleging that his First Amendment rights had been violated. Relying on the *Tinker* standard, the federal district court agreed, awarding him damages and attorneys' fees. The Court of Appeals affirmed, holding that the school district had not carried its burden under *Tinker* to show that the sexual innuendo substantially disrupted or materially interfered with the educational process.

The United States Supreme Court reversed, and in so doing significantly modified the *Tinker* standard. After reviewing established expectations of decorum in various institutions, including the United States Congress, the Court ruled that school officials had the right to discipline Matthew Fraser for his offensively lewd and indecent speech:

> Surely it is a highly appropriate function of public school education to prohibit the use of vulgar and offensive terms in public discourse. Indeed, the "fundamental values necessary to the maintenance of a democratic political system" disfavor the use of terms of debate highly offensive or highly threatening to others. Nothing in the Constitution prohibits the states from insisting that certain modes of expression are inappropriate and subject to sanctions. The inculcation of these values is truly the "work of the schools." The determination of what manner of speech in the classroom or in school assembly is inappropriate properly rests with the school board.

478 U.S. at 683 (citation omitted). Significantly, the action of the school officials was not based on their political viewpoint, but rather on the manner of the speech. It is well-established that reasonable restrictions on the time, place and manner of one's exercising First Amendment rights are permissible.

Two years after deciding *Bethel*, the Court again ruled on the issue of student First Amendment rights, and again sided with school authorities. In *Hazelwood School District v. Kuhlmeier*, 484 U.S. 260 (1988), the Court considered a claim by student editors of a high school newspaper that the principal had violated their rights. There, the principal reviewed the final edition of the school newspaper for the year. He decided that an article on teen pregnancy was inappropriate, given the ages of some students, and he also objected to an article on children of divorce. Therefore he removed both articles from the newspaper.

The student editors brought suit, and the Court of Appeals found in their favor because the school district did not show disruption as required under *Tinker*. The Supreme Court, however, reversed, announcing another exception to the *Tinker* standard. The Court rejected the claim that the school newspaper should be considered a traditional public forum, subject to established First Amendment protections (and thus subject to regulation only under the *Tinker* standard). Instead, the Court found that the school newspaper was an extension of the educational process. In the Court's view, therefore, the *Tinker* standard did not apply, and regulation of the content of the school newspaper did not implicate student free speech concerns. The Court held that school officials have the right to exercise control over the type and content of student speech in school-sponsored activities such as the school newspaper if such action is reasonably related to legitimate pedagogical concerns.

The *Hazelwood* case has had a significant impact with regard to school activities other than the school newspaper. When an activity is school-sponsored, school officials have broad discretion as to what speech to allow in "their" activity. For example, in one case there were parent complaints about the sexual content of books used in a high school elective course on literature. When the school district removed these books (Aristophanes' "Lysistrata" and Chaucer's "The Miller's Tale") from the course, despite their clear literary merit, some other parents brought suit, claiming that the action violated the First Amendment. Given *Hazelwood*, the Eleventh Circuit Court of Appeals rejected the claim. Despite misgivings over the decision of school officials, the court ruled that it must defer to the legitimate pedagogical reasons the district offered to justify its action. *Virgil v. School Board of Columbia County, Florida*, 862 F.2d 1517 (11th Cir. 1989).

Similarly, the Eighth Circuit ruled that a school district did not violate the free speech rights of a student in disqualifying him from participating in a student election. As part of his campaign, he had distributed condoms in violation of the school rule requiring prior approval before distributing materials in school. The court held that the election was not an open forum, and that the school had a legitimate pedagogical interest under *Hazelwood* in its requirement that materials to be distributed have prior approval. *Henerey v. City of St. Charles School District*, 200 F.3d 1128 (8th Cir. 1999).

In summary, students continue to have the significant free speech rights announced in *Tinker* when they act independently, and school authorities can regulate that speech only when they can reasonably forecast substantial disruption or material interference with the educational process or the rights of others. *See, e.g., Thomas v. Board of Education, Granville Central School District*, 607 F.2d 1043 (2d Cir. 1979) (underground newspaper). However, where an activity can be considered an extension of the educational process or where an activity is school-sponsored or otherwise carries the "imprimatur" of the school, school officials have broad authority to regulate student speech. *See, e.g., Poling v. Murphy*, 872 F.2d 757, 761 (6th Cir. 1989) (student disqualified from a school election because he had made rude remarks about the school principal in a school assembly).

c. Evolution of free speech rules

Over time, the line between private speech (the *Tinker* standard) and school-sponsored speech (the *Bethel/Hazelwood* standard) has blurred, at least as to offensive or vulgar speech. For example, in *Gano v. School District No. 411 of Twin Falls County, Idaho*, 674 F. Supp. 796 (D. Idaho 1987), the court upheld a student suspension for wearing a T-shirt with a caricature of school administrators holding beer cans and appearing drunk, with the caption, "It Doesn't Get Any Better Than This." While the case arguably could have been decided on *Tinker*, the court looked to *Bethel* for guidance. It ruled that the message on the shirt falsely accused the administrators of being drunk and damaged the decorum of the school. *See also Broussard v. School Board of the City of Norfolk*, 801 F. Supp. 1526 (E.D. Va. 1992) (T-shirt with "Drugs Suck!" message may be prohibited). *But see Chambers v. Babbitt*, 145 F. Supp.2d 1068 (D. Minn. 2001) ("Straight Pride" T-shirt must be allowed under *Tinker*). Relying on *Bethel* and *Hazelwood*, one federal court even upheld the discipline of a student for using profanity in a non-instructional setting after missing her ride home. *Anderson v. Milbank School District 25-4*, 197 F.R.D. 682 (D. S.D. 2000).

Various courts have considered and affirmed disciplinary action based on violating prohibitions against the display of the Confederate flag. Significantly, the courts have not only considered *Tinker*, but they have also cited *Bethel* in affirming the right of school officials to prohibit such speech. *Scott v. School Board of Alachua County*, 2003 U.S. Appl. LEXIS 5392 (11th Cir. 2003). *See also West v. Derby Unified School District No. 260*, 206 F.3d 1358 (10th Cir. 2000), *cert. denied* 531 U.S. 825 (2000) (no free speech violation when student suspended for drawing a Confederate flag in violation of dress code prohibiting clothing which depicts a "racial implication"); *Denno v. School Board of Volusia County, Fla.*, 218 F.3d 1262 (11th Cir. 2000) (qualified immunity granted as to claim that student's free speech rights were violated by directive not to display Confederate flag). *But see Castorina v. Madison County School Board*, 246 F.3d 536 (6th Cir. 2001) (Hank Williams T-shirt with Confederate flag cannot be banned without a showing that it caused an actual disruption); *Sypniewski v. Warren Hills Regional Board of Education*, 307 F.3d 243 (3d Cir. 2002) (Jeff Foxworthy "redneck" T-shirt not disruptive).

Similarly, the courts are increasingly tolerant of school actions prohibiting vulgar speech. For example, even though it could not show any disruption, one public high school in Ohio was successful recently in asserting its right to prohibit student speech it found offensive, specifically a Marilyn Manson T-shirt depicting a three-faced Jesus. The court rejected the claim that *Tinker* applied, ruling that *Tinker* protects political speech. In considering this suppression of "vulgar or plainly offensive speech," the court looked rather to *Bethel*, and it ruled that the district did not violate the student's rights in prohibiting the T-shirt. *Boroff v. Ver Wert City Board of Education*, 220 F.3d 465 (6th Cir. 2000). *See also Pyle v. South Hadley School Committee*, 861 F. Supp. 157 (D. Mass. 1994) (certain "Co-Ed Naked . . . ." T-shirts may be banned).

The difficulties in deciding between legitimate student free speech concerns and legitimate school concerns is evident in a recent case involving symbolic free speech unrelated to vulgar or offensive speech. A student was not permitted to wear a headwrap in celebration of her African American heritage, and she sued the school district, claiming a violation of her First Amendment rights. Even though school officials did not forecast a material disruption or substantial interference in the educational process, the court rejected the student's challenge. The court held that school officials were enforcing a "no hats" rule to further an important government interest in providing a safe, respectful school environment, and that the rule was unrelated to the suppression of free expression. *Isaacs v. Board of Education of Howard County*, 40 F. Supp.2d 335 (D. Md. 1999).

From these cases, we may say that three different rules have evolved with regard to student free speech. First, where speech is student-initiated and unrelated to school activities, school officials can regulate the speech only if it meets the *Tinker* standard of disruption or interference. Examples of such speech include the expression of personal viewpoints through buttons or unofficial or "underground" newspapers. Second, where the speech occurs in the context of a school activity, such as the school newspaper, the school play, or student assemblies, school officials can control the content of that speech (for example by deciding what articles will appear or what play will be produced). In so doing, school officials need only demonstrate a legitimate pedagogical basis for the action. Third, and finally, after *Bethel,* it appears that school officials have increased authority to regulate the manner of student speech and take appropriate disciplinary action against lewd, vulgar, or offensive speech because it affects the school environment.

Finally, school rules themselves must also comply with First Amendment requirements. A Pennsylvania school district adopted an anti-harassment policy that defined punishable harassment in very broad terms. While the district court held that harassment is not protected by the First Amendment, the Third Circuit ruled that there is no "harassment exception" to the First Amendment, and that prohibitions that affect student speech must be drawn carefully to avoid overbreadth (which would unnecessarily interfere with student free speech rights). *Saxe v. State College Area School District*, 240 F.3d 200 (3rd Cir. 2001). Similarly, the Third Circuit struck down a portion of a code of conduct that prohibited written material that "creates ill will" as overly vague. *Sypniewski v. Warren Hills Regional Board of Education*, 307 F.3d 243 (3d Cir. 2002).

2. Search and seizure

The Fourth Amendment protects persons from unreasonable searches and seizures by agents of the government. As with the right of free expression, the Fourth Amendment rights of students were recognized only fairly recently. Lower court decisions acknowledging that students have the right to be secure from unreasonable searches and seizures first appeared in the 1960's, but it was not until 1985 that the United States Supreme Court affirmed the principle that students are protected by the Fourth Amendment. Now it is clear that school officials may search students and their effects only when they have reasonable suspicion that the search will lead to evidence that school rules or the law were violated.

The United States Supreme Court first addressed the issue of student Fourth Amendment rights in *New Jersey v. T.L.O.*, 469 U.S. 325 (1985). In this case, a student (T.L.O.) was accused of smoking and was brought down to the office. When she denied smoking on school grounds and even denied that she smoked at all, the administrator conducting the interview opened her purse and found cigarettes. However, he did not stop at that point. Rather, he searched further and found a small amount of marijuana, a pipe, a substantial amount of money in one dollar bills, and a list of students who owed her money. Eventually this evidence was used to convict the student of being a juvenile delinquent despite her motion to suppress the evidence. The New Jersey Supreme Court reversed her conviction, however, and held that the search by the administrator had violated her rights because it had been unreasonable. At the request of the State of New Jersey, the United States Supreme Court decided to review the case. Ultimately it reversed, finding that the search was reasonable and therefore permissible.

In *New Jersey v. T.L.O.*, the Court announced the rules that apply to searches by school officials in the school setting. First, it held that school officials are subject to the provisions of the Fourth Amendment, which provides:

> [N]o warrants shall issue except upon probable cause, and the right of the people to be free of unreasonable searches and seizures shall be secure.

Since school officials act on behalf of the government, they are subject to the requirements of the Fourth Amendment.

Although school officials must comply with the Fourth Amendment's prohibition against unreasonable searches, the Court further found that school officials do not have to obtain a warrant before conducting a search of students. The Court explained that it would not be reasonable to prohibit school officials from searching students without having a warrant because of the practical difficulties in so doing, the need for prompt action to avoid losing an opportunity to obtain evidence, and the need to assure a safe school environment. For the same reasons, the Court held that only reasonable cause, rather than probable cause, is required before school officials can conduct a student search.

Under *New Jersey v. T.L.O.*, the following standards apply in assessing whether a search of a student's person or effects is reasonable and, therefore, permissible. First, a search must be reasonable at its inception. Second, the scope of the search must be reasonably related to the purpose of the search and not excessively intrusive in light of the age and sex of the students involved.

a. Reasonable at inception

A school administrator conducting a search must have reasonable grounds at the inception of the search to believe that it will produce evidence that school rules or the law have been violated. What is "reasonable" will depend upon the facts of each case.

As stated above, the Court ruled that "probable cause" is not required for a search to be reasonable at its inception. The difference between probable cause and reasonable cause is that, in the former, the facts known must make it probable that the search will turn up evidence of a violation of the law. By contrast, reasonable cause means that the facts make the search a reasonable exercise of school authority, whether or not it is probable that the search will result in finding evidence of wrongdoing.

Generally, and perhaps most importantly, there must be cause to believe that the search of the particular student will result in finding evidence. While the United States Supreme Court expressly reserved judgment on whether individualized suspicion is a prerequisite to a reasonable search in all cases, lower court decisions both before and after *New Jersey v. T.L.O.* have generally held that it is unreasonable to conduct general searches of a number of students without reasonable suspicion as to the particular student or students searched.

In addition, there must be a connection between the suspicion and the purpose for the search. For example, one student was found hiding from a security guard in the student parking lot, and when she refused to identify herself, she was taken to the office and searched. The court held that her behavior, though suspicious, did not establish a reasonable basis for a search; indeed, school officials could not explain what they were searching for. *Cales v. Howell Public Schools*, 635 F. Supp. 454 (E.D. Mich. 1985).

Grounds for reasonable cause to search can be based on a number of things. For example, if a particular student is observed acting in a manner consistent with smoking marijuana or if the student smells of marijuana, there may be reasonable cause to search him or her for marijuana. By contrast, furtive actions trying to hide something may, but do not always, establish reasonable cause to initiate a search, because the administrator must still be able to describe what he or she is looking for in any search.

Tips from students often are adequate grounds for a search; whether the tip is reasonable will depend on whether the statement is based on personal knowledge or is otherwise reliable ("I saw Joe selling drugs" vs. "I heard that Joe was selling drugs"). By contrast, anonymous tips are often not reliable and thus may not be adequate to establish reasonable grounds for a search. In sum, the school administrator must be able to state a logical reason for believing that a search of a specific student will yield evidence of particular misconduct. If he or she is able to do so, the search will likely be held reasonable at its inception.

b. Reasonable in scope

The second test under *New Jersey v. T.L.O.* is whether the scope of the search is reasonable and not excessively intrusive in light of the age and sex of the students involved. This requirement raises two separate concerns. First, the school administrator must be able to show that the search is reasonably related to the object of the search. If the administrator is looking for a bottle of gin or a gun, it is not necessary that the administrator open the student's coin purse or ask him or her to remove clothing. Such searches would not be necessary to accomplish the purpose for which the search is justified, *i.e.* to find the bottle or the gun. For example, one administrator was searching a student's purse for a knife and, after unzipping a small compartment in the purse (which could not possibly hold the knife), he found drugs. The search failed the second requirement of *T.L.O.* and was thus invalid. *T.J. v. State*, 538 So.2d 1320 (Fla. Dist. Ct. App. 1989).

The other issue raised by this second requirement of *New Jersey v. T.L.O.* is that the search must not be excessively intrusive. This requirement necessarily involves some subjectivity, but the bottom line is that the courts will consider the extent to which the search invades the legitimate privacy expectations of students against the need for the search. In weighing this balance, school officials must understand that they will have a heavy burden to justify any strip search or other intrusive search of students. In one infamous case, an adolescent girl was awarded damages after she was strip-searched when a "sniffer dog" alerted on her. *Doe v. Renfrow*, 631 F.2d 91 (7th Cir. 1980). The search turned up nothing, and as it turned out the "alert" was a reaction to the fact that her dog at home was in heat. *See also Bellnier v. Lund*, 438 F. Supp. 47 (N.D.N.Y. 1977) (strip search of an elementary class to find missing $3.00 was excessively intrusive).

Where there is a compelling need to search (as with suspicion of drug possession) and significant reliability in the information leading to the search, even an intrusive strip search may be permitted. For example, in *Phaneuf v. Cipriano*, No. 3:03CV00372 (AVC) (D. Conn. 2004), the court dismissed the claims of a student whose underwear was searched for drugs by the school nurse (in the presence of her mother) after the principal received reliable information from students that the student possessed marijuana. In any event, school officials must exercise the right to search students with due regard for the significant and legitimate privacy rights of students. Failure to do so can result in discipline of the teacher or administrator, even termination. *See Rogers v. New Haven Board of Education,* 252 Conn. 753 (2000).

c. Applying *New Jersey v. T.L.O.*

In applying these rules to the question of students searches, school officials must consider a number of related issues:

1. Consent

One common notion is that school administrators do not have to worry about meeting Fourth Amendment standards when the student "consents" to a search of his or her person or effects. There is not much law on the subject, but school administrators must be sensitive to the difficulty of establishing that a student gave consent in an inherently coercive situation. This concern is especially true of younger children, who may not be capable of consent at all. For example, a student is hustled down to the office and is confronted by the assistant principal who barks "Empty your pockets." When the student complies, has he consented to the search? Clearly not. How different is the situation when the administrator prefaces the demand with "Would you please . . . "? While each situation will be judged on its own facts, administrators are well advised to meet the *T.L.O.* standards before undertaking a search.

Sometimes, school districts argue that "consent" will be inferred because the search relates to a voluntary activity, such as a field trip. However, *T.L.O.* did not make that distinction, and some courts have held that Fourth Amendment protections apply to all school activities. For example, school administrators in one district searched all luggage when students went on trips with the school band, and they left behind one student whose parents would not consent to the search. The Washington Supreme Court found that the general search was unreasonable and as such violated the Fourth Amendment because there was no individualized suspicion regarding the student. *Kuehn v. Reston School District No. 403*, 694 P.2d 1078 (1985). *But see Rhodes v. Guarricino*, 54 F. Supp.2d 186 (S.D.N.Y. 1999) (search of student rooms for marijuana during trip to Disney World held reasonable; students had no expectation of complete privacy in their rooms).

Notably, more recent case law suggests that a distinction may be drawn for voluntary activities, and that school officials may be able to conduct searches in those circumstances without meeting the *T.L.O.*

standards. In *Vernonia School District 47J v. Acton,* 515 U.S. 646 (1995), the United States Supreme Court ruled that a school district could require that students submit to suspicionless drug testing as a condition for participation on the football team. In 2002, this rule was extended to permit random drug testing of students who participate in extracurricular activities, even those activities that do not involve athletics. *Board of Education of Independent School District No. 92 of Pottawatomie County v. Earls*, 536 U.S. 822 (2002). *See* Section E(2)(c)(5).

2. "Fruits" of the search

Another frequent question is what happens when a search based on the reasonable suspicion that the student possesses one item, say a weapon, results in finding another item, say drugs. When that happens, the administrator has simply had a good day at the office. The administrator can punish the student for an offense related to the unexpected find, and he or she may even refer the student to the police for prosecution. In addition, the item seized may create cause for a further search (*e.g.* rolling papers may justify a search for marijuana).

In fact, even if a search violates the student's Fourth Amendment rights, the student may be disciplined. The common understanding that an item seized in an illegal search cannot be used is based on the "exclusionary rule" under the criminal law, and indeed such evidence is inadmissible at a criminal trial. This rule, however, does not affect the right of school officials to take disciplinary action when there has been a violation of the school rules or the law. Nonetheless, this fact should not weaken the commitment of school officials to meet the requirements of the Fourth Amendment. Violations can lead to liability under 42 U.S.C. § 1983 for infringing the student's civil rights.

3. Student's person and effects

Another common question is whether the rules differ with regard to a student's person versus a student's effects, such as the student's book bag, purse, or automobile (parked on school property). In a word — no. The Fourth Amendment applies when students have a legitimate expectation of privacy, and thus school officials must meet the *T.L.O.* standards before they may conduct a search of a student's person or effects.

A caution is in order. The second part of the *T.L.O.* test is that the scope of the search should not be excessively intrusive in light of the age and sex of the students involved. In searching either the student's person or his or her effects, school officials must be sensitive to this requirement. Thus, while a search of a student may be reasonable in general, a highly intrusive search (one that involves the removal of clothing, for example) may well be unreasonable and a violation of the Fourth Amendment. *See T.J. v. State*, 538 So.2d 1320 (Fla. Dist. Ct. App. 1989) (search of compartment in purse for knife intrusive).

4. Lockers and desks

In *T.L.O.*, the United States Supreme Court expressly left unanswered the question of the status of school lockers. In 1994, the General Assembly addressed the issue of locker and desk searches. Conn. Gen. Stat. § 54-33n expressly permits school boards to authorize school officials and law enforcement officials to search lockers and other school property available for use by students for the presence of contraband, weapons, or the fruits of a crime. Moreover, the law provides that such searches may occur only when the *T.L.O.* standards are met, *i.e.* the search must be justified at its inception, and the scope of the search must be reasonably related to the purpose for the search.

The question of whether access by school officials to a locker or desk is a search will depend upon whether the student had a reasonable expectation of privacy with regard to that locker or desk. The new law concerning such searches may have created an expectation of privacy by imposing the *T.L.O.* standard on locker and desk searches. Nonetheless, it is advisable for school officials to take measures to put students on notice that they should not have a privacy expectation in their lockers or desks. Such steps include (1) publishing a statement in the student handbook that lockers and desks are school property, are loaned to the students and may be searched, (2) exercising control over lockers and desks with reasonable frequency, such as periodic inspection for library books, etc., and (3) assuring that the administration either provides any locks on the lockers, or maintains the lock combination on file. If the student does not have a legitimate privacy expectation, access and control of student lockers and desks by school officials will not be considered a search. Given the provisions of Conn. Gen. Stat. § 54-33n, however, school officials are better advised to conduct locker or desk searches concerning specific students when the *T.L.O.* standards are met.

A final word of caution is in order. Even where it is appropriate for a school official to open and search a locker or desk, the same may not be true of the student effects in the desk or locker. The purpose of the search must be reasonably related to the objectives of the search, and the search must not be excessively intrusive in light of the age and sex of the student and the nature of the infraction. However, where reasonable suspicion exists, a search of student effects will be legal. *See, e.g. State of Washington v. Slattery*, 787 P.2d 932 (Wa. App. 1990).

5. Drug testing

The courts have held that drug testing is a search of the person. Generally, any requirement that a student submit to drug testing must be justified by the reasonable suspicion required under the *T.L.O.* case. Consequently, in one case, the court held that a school district's requirement that students submit to drug testing as part of the physical examination process was held to be unconstitutional. *Odenheim v. Carlstadt-East Rutherford Regional School District*, 510 A.2d 709 (N.J. 1985). The absence of any individualized suspicion made such blanket "searches" unreasonable. More recently, a program of testing all middle school and high school students in a Texas school district was held to violate the Fourth Amendment rights of the students. *Tannahill v. Lockney Independent School District*, 133 F. Supp.2d 919 (N.D. Tex. 2001). The court held that the general school population had a greater expectation of privacy than student athletes, discussed below.

The rules regarding the drug testing of students involved in extracurricular activities are different. In 1995, the Supreme Court reversed a lower court ruling, and held that individualized suspicion for required drug testing of student athletes was not required under the Fourth Amendment. *Vernonia School District 47J v. Acton,* 515 U.S. 646 (1995). The Court cited four factors in support of its conclusion: (1) the district had a serious problem with student drug use; (2) the program was limited to student athletes, who already give up some privacy to participate (as Justice Scalia wrote for the majority, "school sports are not for the bashful"); (3) the testing was carefully monitored to provide reliable results; and (4) the program was not purely punitive, and with a first positive result, students had the option of entering a drug assistance program in lieu of being suspended from sports for the season.

Following *Vernonia*, some school districts extended the *Vernonia* rule and initiated random drug test requirements for all extracurricular activities. Some courts upheld such programs, and others struck them down. The United States Supreme Court resolved this issue in *Board of Education of Independent School District No. 92 of Pottawatomie County v. Earls*, 536 U.S.

822 (2002). There, the Court ruled that school officials have a broad right to require random drug testing of students who participate in extracurricular activities, even those activities that do not involve athletics. Justice Thomas, writing for the majority, stated that the responsibility of school officials for the safety of students and concern over student use of drugs outweighed the privacy interests of students.

This decision is a surprising expansion of the right to adopt random drug testing programs for extracurricular activities. While the Court expressly stated that it was not offering its opinion on the wisdom of such programs, this decision dramatically reduces the ability of students to challenge such programs under the federal constitution. Theoretically, a student could now make a claim under the Connecticut Constitution, which includes in Article First, Section 7, a provision very similar to the Fourth Amendment. Unless and until the Connecticut courts signal a willingness to adopt a stricter state standard, however, the decision on such programs will depend more on business and policy judgments, rather than on the constitutional rights of the affected students.

Sometimes questions arise whether a district can impose drug testing on students who have been disciplined for selling or even possessing drugs. While under *Earls*, school officials may require random drug testing of students who participate in extracurricular activities, returning to school after expulsion is different, because the right to basic education is implicated. Until we have further guidance from the courts, school administrators are well-advised to impose drug testing requirements on students in the general school population, even such students returning from expulsion, only when there is reasonable suspicion.

Finally, there is one situation where school officials could impose such a requirement if appropriate. If a student were expelled for no more than the period permitted by law (up to one calendar year), in an appropriate case (as with prior drug involvement), a district could offer the student an opportunity to return to school early on the condition that he or she submit to random drug testing. Since the student has no right to attend school during the expulsion period, school officials can require testing as a condition of attendance during that period.

6. Sniffer dogs or metal detectors

Connecticut school districts have made limited use of trained "sniffer dogs" to find drugs on students or metal detectors to find weapons. However, litigation in some other states gives some guidance. The courts have held generally that the use of a sniffer dog to find drugs in lockers is not a search, because there is no personal intrusion. However, courts have held that the use of a dog to sniff a student's person is intrusive and must be justified by the reasonable suspicion standard of the *T.L.O.* case. *See, e.g., Horton v. Goose Creek Independent School District*, 690 F.2d 470 (5th Cir. 1982).

The use of metal detectors has been successfully justified in some school districts that have a significant problem with weapons. The initial screening is a search, albeit a minimally intrusive search. However, when the detector goes off, a personal search may ensue. The critical point in the use of metal detectors is that the circumstances of the particular school (high incidence of weapons, student violence, etc.) must justify the intrusion.

In either case, the method used must be reliable. If a dog alerts or a metal detector goes off, and school officials wish to conduct a further search, they must be prepared to show that it was reasonable to believe that a search of the student at that time would yield evidence of a violation of school rules or the law. If the dogs are not properly trained, or if a paper clip causes the detectors to sound, a further search would not be justified.

7. Breathalyzers

Given the problems (and attendant dangers) of students drinking before or during school functions, such as dances, some school districts have adopted requirements that students submit to breathalyzer testing as a condition of attending the dance. Given the broad ruling in *Earls* as it applies to extracurricular activities, it is a safe bet that such rules will pass constitutional muster, particularly if students are warned about such testing in advance, through the student handbook, printing a warning on the tickets, or other means. Such testing is much less intrusive than is drug testing. Moreover, such activities are purely voluntary. If a school district wished to be cautious with regard to student Fourth Amendment rights, however, it could employ breathalyzer testing only after personal observation that establishes reasonable cause to believe that a student has been drinking. Under those circumstances, the minimal "search" effected through the breathalyzer test will be squarely within the well-established *T.L.O.* rule.

8. Police involvement

Finally, it is important to distinguish the rules that apply to school officials from those that apply to the police. The *T.L.O.* case is based on the special rights and responsibilities that school officials have to supervise students during the school day. The rules that apply to the police were not changed. To be sure, students can be criminally prosecuted on the basis of any evidence legally seized by school officials acting as such, even when the evidence was obtained through a search justified only by reasonable suspicion. However, when police ask for assistance in investigating students, school officials should understand that they may be seen as police "surrogates." If they are so viewed, they will lose their special rights to search students under the *T.L.O.* standard, and the greater protections of the criminal law will apply. Indeed, in one case a teacher reported suspicions to the liaison police officer, who reported those suspicions to the administration. When administrators found contraband, it was suppressed by the court on the theory that the school administrators were operating as the agents of the police officer. *State v. Heirtzler*, 789 A.2d 634 (N.H. 2002). *But see Russell v. State*, 74 S.W.3d 887 (Tex. App. 2002) (school liaison officer may act on reasonable suspicion to conduct a search).

While it is important to keep in mind the distinction between school officials and police, the provisions of Conn. Gen. Stat. § 54-33n warrant special mention. This law expressly enables boards of education to authorize "school or law enforcement officials" to search lockers or other property available for student use. As discussed in Section E(2)(c)(4) above, such searches are permitted as long as the requirements set out in *T.L.O.* are met. The *T.L.O.* standard, however, would be easier for law enforcement officials to meet than the regular standards for search under the criminal law.

3. Other constitutional rights

In *Tinker v. Des Moines Independent Community School District*, 393 U.S. 503 (1969), the United States Supreme Court announced that students do not shed their constitutional rights at the school house gate, and over the years since the courts have determined that students have constitutional rights in addition to those under the First and Fourth Amendments. Given the breadth of the school experience, there are school law cases on virtually every constitutional right.

a. Due process

School officials are required under the Fifth and the Fourteenth Amendments to the United States Constitution to provide due process before depriving anyone of liberty or property. In interpreting this obligation, the courts have distinguished between procedural and substantive due process.

Early on, the United States Supreme Court decided that students have the right to procedural due process before they are excluded from school. *Goss v. Lopez*, 419 U.S. 565 (1975). While education is not a right conferred by the United States Constitution, education is a property right conferred by state law. Accordingly, students may be deprived of this property right only if they receive due process. The scope of the due process required, however, will depend on the nature of the proposed deprivation: "Due process is flexible and calls for such procedural protections as the particular situation demands," *Morrissey v. Brewer*, 408 U.S. 471 (1972). *See also Matthews v. Eldridge*, 424 U.S. 319 (1976). As discussed in Section C, above, for example, a suspension, as a less serious deprivation, requires significantly less process than does an expulsion. *See McDonald v. Sweetman*, 2004 U.S. Dist. LEXIS 5558 (D. Conn. 2004).

Procedural due process concerns arise in other areas as well. The "due process" rights set out in the Fifth and Fourteen Amendments involve liberty as well as property. Students and their parents sometimes claim that a particular rule interferes with their liberty interests, for example in personal freedom or in raising a family free of governmental interference. Unless the interference is significant and direct, however, the courts will defer to the judgments of school officials. *See, e.g., Campbell v. New Milford Board of Education*, 193 Conn. 93 (1984) (student attendance policy providing for grade reduction and/or loss of credit not a violation of substantive and procedural due process).

The courts have also held that school officials must not deny anyone substantive due process. This obligation relates not to procedures, but rather to actions. Violations of substantive due process, however, occur only rarely. "The protections of substantive due process are available only against egregious conduct which goes beyond merely offending some fastidious squeamishness or private sentimentalism and can fairly be viewed as so brutal and offensive to human dignity as to shock the conscience." *Smith v. Half Hollow Hills Cent. School District*, 298 F.3d 168, 173 (2d Cir. 2002). Nonetheless, on rare occasions the courts have found such violations in the school setting. *See Garcia by Garcia v. Miera*, 817 F.2d 650, 655 (10th Cir. 1987) (excessive corporal punishment excessive violates substantive due process); *Gerks v. Deathe*, 832 F. Supp. 1450 (W.D. Okla. 1993); *Kirkland v. Greene County Board of Education*, 347 F.3d 903 (11th Cir. 2003). *But see Harris v. Robinson*, 273 F.3d 927 (10th Cir. 2001) (no substantive due process violation when principal made student clean out toilet under mistaken belief that he had clogged it); *McDonald v. Sweetman*, 2004 U.S. Dist. LEXIS 5558

(D. Conn. 2004) (student claim of substantive due process violation dismissed; even if principal's decision to suspend student was erroneous, it was reasonable).

b. Equal protection

The Fourteenth Amendment also provides that the government (which includes school boards and school administrators) may not deny any person in the United States "equal protection of the laws." On its face, this constitutional provision simply means that people in the same situation should be treated the same. Through the years, however, this provision has evolved to establish three different standards of review, depending on the nature of the interest in question.

Normally, the actions of government are measured by a "rational relationship" test. This means that a governmental action (here, school rule) must bear a rational relationship to the goal it is attempting to achieve. For example, some school districts have adopted policies providing that students may participate in school sports only if they maintain a C average. Similarly, under the rules of the Connecticut Interscholastic Athletic Conference, under some circumstances students may not play sports immediately after transferring from one school to another. There are arguments for and against such rules. Since students have no statutory or constitutional right to participate in sports, however, the courts will consider simply whether such rules have a rational connection to the purpose for the rule. *See, e.g., Wajnowski v. The Connecticut Association of Schools*, 6 Conn. Ops. 35 (Superior Court, January 24, 2000).

The "rational relationship" test is fairly easy to meet. The Connecticut Supreme Court, for example, as described it as follows: "In general, the Equal Protection Clause is satisfied so long as there is a plausible policy reason for the classification." *Donahue v. Southington*, 259 Conn. 783, 795 (2002). On occasion, however, school rules have not even met this tolerant standard. For example, school districts have variously attempted to exclude married students, married pregnant students, unmarried pregnant students or students with children (whether married or not) from participating in school activities. Justifications offered for such rules, *e.g.*, to permit the student to attend to family responsibilities or to protect the other students from the influence of such students, have been uniformly rejected as not rationally connected to legitimate educational goals. *See, e.g., Perry v. Grenada Municipal Separate School District*, 300 F. Supp.

748 (N.D. Miss. 1969); *Ordway v. Hargraves*, 323 F. Supp. 1155 (D. Mass. 1971).

When a governmental action (here, school rule) is based on gender, the courts will apply a higher standard of review. It will not be enough for school officials to show a rational relationship between their rule and purpose. Rather, any rule that distinguishes between persons on the basis of gender will be subject to an intermediate level of scrutiny, *i.e.* whether the rule promotes important governmental objectives and whether the discriminatory means employed are substantially related to achieving those objectives. Under this higher standard, the United States Supreme Court struck down the rule excluding females from the Virginia Military Academy as a violation of the equal protection rights of females who may wish to attend. *United States v. Virginia*, 518 U.S. 515 (1996).

Finally, where school rules infringe upon constitutional rights, such as free expression or free exercise of religion, or when they are based on a suspect classification, such as race or national origin, school officials have a heavy burden to justify the rule. Such a rule will be upheld only if it passes the "strict scrutiny standard," *i.e.* (1) it is necessary to achieve a compelling state interest, and (2) the scope of the rule is drawn as narrowly as possible to achieve that objective.

For example, a school rule that penalizes students for absences would be unenforceable if it were applied to students who were absent because of religious obligations. The legitimate school objective of requiring regular attendance could be achieved less intrusively by penalizing students for unexcused absences. Conversely, a rule against secret societies at the high school level could likely be sustained against challenge, even though it infringes upon the free association rights of students, because such a rule can ultimately be construed as serving the important interest of student safety. *See Passel v. Fort Worth Independent School District*, 453 S.W.2d 888 (Tex. Civ. App. 1970).

c. Assignment of students

Rules that assign students on the basis of race raise serious legal issues. *Sheff v. O'Neill* requires that racial, ethnic, economic isolation of students in Connecticut be reduced, and local school officials may be obligated to reduce racial imbalance within a school district. The imperative to reduce racial, ethnic and economic isolation, however, comes at a time at which race-based remedies are being scrutinized under federal constitutional law.

In 1978, the United States Supreme Court ruled that race can be a factor in university admissions, but that strict racial quotas are not permissible. *Regents of the University of California v. Bakke*, 438 U.S. 265 (1978). The decision did not provide clear guidance, however, in that there were six different opinions written. Then, in 1989, in a different context the court ruled that race-based remedies are subject to review under a "strict scrutiny" standard. *City of Richmond v. J.A. Croson Co.*, 488 U.S. 469 (1989).

Given these rulings, the lower courts struggled with whether and how race may be considered in making school admissions decisions. *Compare Wessman v. Gittens*, 160 F.3d 790 (1st Cir. 1998) (racial and ethnic admissions criteria used in the Boston Public Schools struck down) and *Hopwood v. Texas*, 78 F.3d 932 (5th Cir. 1996), *cert. denied* 518 U.S. 1033 (1996) *with Hunter v. Regents of the University of California*, 190 F.3d 1061 (9th Cir. 1999), *cert. denied*, 531 U.S. 877 (2000) (racial screens for admission to a research-oriented public elementary school upheld); *Smith v. University of Washington*, 223 F.3d 1188 (9th Cir. 2000).

In 2003 the United States Supreme Court issued two rulings on this subject, and the answer to whether race may be used in school admissions decisions is a clear "maybe." In *Grutter v. Bollinger*, 539 U.S. 306 (2003), by a 5-4 vote the Court upheld the admissions procedure at the University of Michigan Law School, which gave special weight to race as one of the factors considered. The Court found first that assuring a diverse student body is a compelling state interest, a requirement of the "strict scrutiny" test. Then, it found that the School was not required to achieve that interest through less restrictive means, because racially-neutral criteria (such as a lottery) would not assure diversity. Key to the Court's ruling was the fact that race was not a defining characteristic in the admissions process, but rather only one of several "diversity factors," such as socio-economic status that were considered.

By contrast, in *Gratz v. Bollinger*, 539 U.S. 244 (2003), the Court found that the way in which the University of Michigan used race in making undergraduate admissions criteria violated constitutional principles. The University considered African-Americans, Hispanics and Native Americans to be underrepresented, and under its guidelines for admission it automatically awarded members of these groups twenty of the one hundred points needed to guarantee admission, with the result that virtually all such qualified applicants were admitted. By a 6-3 vote, the Court ruled that, while there can be a compelling state interest in assuring a diverse student body, the use of race there was not sufficiently narrow. The Court held that crediting such students with a specific number of points made it a decisive factor in the admissions process, akin to a quota system (which is unconstitutional because it precludes individual consideration of applicants).

Unfortunately, these two cases do not provide clear guidance as to how race may be used as a plus factor in school admissions decisions; we now simply know that race can be considered but not "too much." Moreover, these issues are also subject to review under state constitutional standards. *See Parents Involved in Community Schools v. Seattle School District No. 1*, No. 72712-1 (Wash. 2003). Race-based admissions decisions have not been a major issue in Connecticut to date, however, because student admission to schools is typically based on geography. It remains to be seen, however, whether race can be considered in making interdistrict magnet school decisions, especially since for programs commencing after July 1, 2005 no more than seventy-five percent of the students may be members of racial minorities. *Compare* Conn. Gen. Stat. § 10-264l *with* Conn. Gen. Stat. § 10-266aa(e); Conn. Gen. Stat. § 10-15c.

d. Other constitutional claims

The Eighth Amendment to the United States Constitution prohibits "cruel and unusual punishment," and the Thirteenth Amendment prohibits "involuntary servitude." At first blush, one could question how these constitutional provisions would even come up in the school setting. In challenging school policies, however, imaginative lawyers have raised both issues.

In Florida, school officials have been permitted to paddle students as a disciplinary intervention, subject to procedural protections set out in statute (*e.g.*, limits on the number of strikes, requirement for an observer). Some students who were paddled challenged this action as a violation of the prohibition against "cruel and unusual punishment." The United States Supreme Court, however, rejected this claim, stating that the Eighth Amendment was intended to regulate government action under the criminal laws, and that it does not apply in the school setting. *Ingraham v. Wright*, 430 U.S. 651 (1977). Punishment that is so disproportionate that it shocks the conscience, however, may be a violation of the substantive due process rights of the student punished, as discussed in Section E(3) above.

Similarly, the courts have been unwilling to apply the constitutional prohibition against involuntary servitude in the school setting. In 1990, for example, the Rye Neck, New York school district adopted a graduation requirement that students perform at least forty hours of community service during their four high school years. A student and his parents claimed that this requirement violated the Thirteenth Amendment prohibition against involuntary servitude, as well as the parents' right to raise their children, and the student's right to privacy and to personal liberty, both under the Fourteenth Amendment.

The Second Circuit Court of Appeals rejected each of these arguments, stating that "we have no trouble concluding that the mandatory community service program does not amount to involuntary servitude in the constitutional sense. The work required is not severe; students must perform only forty hours of service in four years." *Immediato v. Rye Neck School District*, 73 F.3d 454, 462 (2d Cir. 1996), *cert. denied* 519 U.S. 813 (1996). Furthermore, the court ruled that the requirement is rationally related to a legitimate governmental interest, and it upheld the community service requirement as a legitimate exercise of government authority. *See also Steier v. Bethlehem Area School District*, 987 F.2d 989 (3d Cir. 1993).

F. Child Abuse and Neglect

There is a strong public policy in Connecticut in favor of protecting children, which is evident in the laws concerning child abuse and neglect. Those laws require that mandated reporters must report to the Department of Children and Families (DCF) when they have reasonable cause to suspect or believe that a child is being neglected, abused, or placed in imminent risk of serious harm. The list of mandated reporters relevant to school operation includes teachers, principals, social workers, school guidance counselors, school paraprofessionals, licensed and registered nurses, school coaches, psychologists, certified substance abuse counselors, and licensed professional counselors. Each school district is required to adopt a policy concerning reporting of suspected abuse or neglect by school employees. Conn. Gen. Stat. § 17a-101i(e). If a mandated reporter violates his or her statutory obligations to report suspected child abuse or neglect, as described below, s/he may be required to go through training and is subject to criminal prosecution and can be fined no less than $500 and up to $2,500. Conn. Gen. Stat. § 17a-101a. Moreover, the prosecutor must notify the Commissioner of Education if a mandated reporter who holds a certificate, authorization or permit issued by the State Board of Education is convicted of or fined for violating this statute. Conn. Gen. Stat. § 10-149a.

A mandated reporter who has "reasonable cause to suspect or believe" that a child is being abused, neglected or placed in imminent risk of serious harm must make both an oral and a written report. Conn. Gen. Stat. § 17a-101a. Previously, this obligation was limited to situations in which such abuse, neglect or risk was caused by a person responsible for the child's care or a person given access to the child by such person. This limitation was deleted in 2002, which raised questions whether reporting is mandated, for example, if a student reports that she was assaulted by a peer on a date. DCF has taken the position, however, that the statute should be interpreted to require reporting concerning potentially abusive actions by peers or similar persons only if (1) one individual is being exploited because the relationship is non-consensual, hostile, or includes use of force or threats, (2) the child has emotional or intellectual disabilities that may preclude the child from consenting or of understanding the consequences of understanding (regardless of age), or (3) the child is under 16 years of age and the partner is 21 years of age or older. *Letter from Commissioner Kristine Ragaglia to Dr. David Larson* (January 29, 2003).

The oral report must be made to DCF or to local law enforcement authorities "as soon as practicable" but not later than twelve hours after the mandated reporter has reason to suspect or believe that abuse or neglect has occurred. This report must be made either by telephone or in person. Conn. Gen. Stat. § 17a-101b. The law now specifies that the DCF hotline must accept all reports of abuse or neglect. Conn. Gen. Stat. § 17a-103a.

The obligation to report suspected abuse or neglect does not permit the reporter to defer a report until he or she is certain that abuse or neglect has occurred. Moreover, the mandated reporter is not required to conduct an independent investigation before filing a report. *Morales v. Kagel*, 4 Conn. Ops. 1382 (Superior Court, November 30, 1998). A person who complies with this requirement in good faith is immune from liability whether or not the abuse is substantiated. Conn. Gen. Stat. § 17a-101e.

Within forty-eight hours of making an oral report, the mandated reporter is required to follow up with a written report. Conn. Gen. Stat. § 17a-101d. Employees in public or private schools must submit a copy of that report to the "person in charge of the institution." The following information is required when making an oral or written report: names and address(es) of the child and his or her parents or other responsible person, the age and gender of the child, the nature, extent and approximate date and time of the injury or injuries, maltreatment, or neglect, information concerning previous injury, injuries, maltreatment, or neglect of the child or his or her siblings, the circumstances in which the suspected abuse or neglect came to the reporter's attention, the name of the person believed to be responsible for the abuse or neglect, and action taken, if any, to treat the child. Conn. Gen. Stat. § 17a-101d.

Once it receives a report, DCF is then responsible for investigating and taking steps necessary to protect the child. Actions that DCF may take include immediate notification of the police authorities or removal of the child from the home situation, either with parental permission or upon the order of the Superior Court. Conn. Gen. Stat. § 17a-101g. Under certain circumstances, the Commissioner of DCF even has the right to remove the child immediately for up to ninety-six hours, without parental permission or authorization from the court. *Id.* A principal and school nurse were immune from liability, therefore, for not preventing the DCF worker from physically checking a child for bruises following a report, even though the parents claimed that the inspection of the child by the DCF worker was an illegal search. *Smart v. Morgillo*, 7 Conn. Ops. 898 (D. Conn., August 6, 2001).

Failure by a mandated reporter to comply with this reporting requirement can be a serious matter. The statute provides that failure to report in accordance with the law may lead to the imposition of fines. Conn. Gen. Stat. § 17a-101a. Conversely, the law provides that persons filing such reports in good faith will be immune from liability, criminal or civil, that might otherwise be incurred or imposed, provided that the person reporting did not perpetrate or cause the abuse or neglect. Conn. Gen. Stat. § 17a-101e. The law also provides that individuals making false reports will be subject to fines. When DCF has reasonable cause to believe that a person has knowingly filed a false report, it may disclose the names of individuals making such false reports to law enforcement authorities and to the alleged perpetrator. Conn. Gen. Stat. § 17a-103(b).

Special rules apply to allegations of abuse against a school employee. Mandated reporters who suspect abuse by a school employee are expressly obligated to report to both DCF and the "person in charge of such . . . school," presumably the superintendent. The superintendent must immediately notify the parent or other person responsible for the child's care. Conn. Gen. Stat. § 17a-101b. If an employee holds a certificate, authorization or permit issued by the State Department of Education, the superintendent is also required to send a copy of the report to the Commissioner of Education. Conn. Gen. Stat. § 17a-101c. The DCF reports and the information contained in such reports are confidential documents not subject to disclosure under the Freedom of Information Act. Conn. Gen. Stat. § 17a-101k.

DCF is the agency responsible for investigating reports that a school employee has abused a child. If DCF finds that a school employee who holds a certification, permit, or authorization issued by the State Board of Education has abused a child, the Commissioner of DCF must inform the superintendent of the finding and to provide all related records to the superintendent. This notification must be provided whether or not the victim is a student in that district. *Opinion to Dunbar*, *Opinions of the Attorney General*, #2004-014 (August 30, 2004). In such cases, the superintendent is required to suspend the employee with pay, and to notify the board of education and the Commissioner of Education within seventy-two hours of the suspension and the reasons for it. Conn. Gen. Stat. § 17a-101i(b). DCF is also obligated to inform the issuing agency if the person found guilty of abuse holds a license, certificate, permit or authorization. *Id.*

When the superintendent receives records concerning abuse by a school employee, he or she must disclose these records to the Commissioner of Education and to the local or regional board of education so that they may be reviewed by these authorities prior to acting on the subject employee's employment status or certification. If the alleged perpetrator is a certified employee, the statute provides that his or her suspension remains in force "until the board of education acts pursuant to the provisions of Section 10-151" (the Teacher Tenure Act). Conn. Gen. Stat. § 17a-101i(a). The problem with this provision is that there can be findings of abuse that do not rise to the level of a termination offense. In the interest of protecting children, DCF may find that a teacher's ill-conceived punishment of a child was "emotional abuse" or that a teacher's pushing a student to get into line was physical abuse. Without condoning such behavior, school officials could well decide that such conduct, while justifying disciplinary action, falls short of a "termination offense" under the Teacher Tenure Act. In such cases, it is appropriate simply to report the disposition of the matter to the board of education, and to the Commissioner of Education, and then reinstate the employee following the disciplinary suspension, if any.

If the contract of a certified employee is terminated as a result of a finding of child abuse, the Commissioner of Education must be notified within seventy-two hours of termination, and he or she may then initiate certification revocation proceedings. While the law does not specifically so provide, it is also advisable to notify the Commissioner if a staff member resigns in the face of likely termination proceedings for such misconduct. If a staff member holding a certificate, permit, or authorization is convicted of a crime involving an act of child abuse or neglect, the state's attorney for the district is required to notify both the superintendent and the Commissioner of Education. Conn. Gen. Stat. § 17a-101i(c). The certificate of such person is thereupon deemed revoked. Conn. Gen. Stat. § 10-145b(m).

These laws require that doubts be resolved in favor of protecting children. The duty to report falls on every mandated reporter, and any such school employee must assure that reports are filed whenever appropriate. Therefore, it is inappropriate for a school district to impose conditions, such as an internal review process, on the filing of such reports. Rather, reports must be filed whenever a mandated reporter has reasonable cause to suspect or believe that abuse has occurred. Many allegations will not be substantiated. However, these determinations are the responsibility of DCF, and once such reasonable cause exists, individual reporters should not delay filing a report based on their personal wish to be certain of the validity of the allegation.

These laws can put school officials in the middle between DCF, on the one hand, and parents or other persons, on the other. The law provides that persons authorized to investigate allegations of abuse shall coordinate investigatory activities to minimize the number of interviews with the child and to share information with other persons authorized to investigate the matter. DCF is also required to obtain the consent of the child's parents before any such interview, unless the alleged perpetrator is the parent or other person from whom such consent would be sought. Conn. Gen. Stat. § 17a-101h. In such cases, any interview with the child is generally to be conducted in the presence of a disinterested adult.

The bottom line is that school officials may have to make judgments concerning investigation of such matters. The law also provides that "All law enforcement officials, courts of competent jurisdiction, school personnel, and all appropriate state agencies providing human services in relation to preventing, identifying and treating child abuse and neglect shall cooperate toward the prevention, identification and treatment of child abuse and neglect." Conn. Gen. Stat. § 17a-106. This broad mandate and the public policy in favor of protecting children establishes that school officials have the right and obligation to cooperate with DCF during the course of these investigations, and that DCF has a similar obligation to cooperate with all other agencies who have an interest in the outcome of the investigation.

Finally, it should be noted that there is a separate reporting obligation when a mandated reporter as defined in Conn. Gen. Stat. § 46a-11b has reasonable cause to suspect or believe that a person with mental retardation who is at least eighteen years of age has been abused or neglected. Mandated reporters under this statute include social workers, school teachers, school principals, school guidance counselors, and school paraprofessionals. Required reports under this statute are to be made to the Office of Protection and Advocacy as soon as practical, but in no event more than seventy-two hours after the suspicion or belief arises, followed up with a written report no more than five days from the initial report.

G. Extracurricular Activities

Each board of education has the authority under Connecticut law to "provide such other educational activities as in its judgment will best serve the interests of the school district." Conn. Gen. Stat. § 10-220(a). In exercising this authority, boards of education typically offer a variety of activities that supplement the basic curriculum, such as intra- and interscholastic athletic teams, drama activities, the school newspaper, clubs, and other activities. The basic principle concerning such extracurricular activities is that, since they are not part of the basic right to education, school officials have discretion in determining whether to offer an activity, and in setting conditions for participation. Such activities are viewed as a privilege, not a right. The courts, therefore, have been reluctant to entertain challenges against school officials over extracurricular activities. Nonetheless, legal issues arise, and the most common are addressed below.

1. Constitutional issues

Many of the constitutional principles that apply to educational issues generally do not apply to participation in extracurricular activities. A basic constitutional right, for example, is the right to due process before being deprived of a property right. The courts have generally held, however, that students do not have a right of due process before being excluded from an extracurricular activity. *See, e.g., Poling v. Murphy*, 872 F.2d 757, 764 (6th Cir. 1989) (no protected right to participate in student council elections); *Farver v. Board of Education of Carroll County*, 40 F. Supp.2d 323 (D. Md. 1999) (injunction to prevent suspension from extracurricular activities, such as sports, clubs and the National Honor Society, denied to group of high school students who allegedly violated the school alcohol policy). This commonsense result avoids the need for hearings and appeals, for example, in determining whether a student will be excluded for violating a "no-alcohol" rule or who will be cut from the football team.

Another constitutional right is to be free of unreasonable searches and seizures. In its 1995 decision in *Vernonia School District 47J v. Acton,* 515 U.S. 646 (1995), however, the United States Supreme Court ruled that an Oregon school district could adopt a requirement for suspicionless drug testing of student athletes. The Court based its decision on the fact that students participate voluntarily in extracurricular activities. Since such participation is a privilege, the Court ruled that a requirement that football players submit to random drug testing did not violate their Fourth Amendment rights. In 2002, the Court extended this rule to any student who participates in extracurricular activities, including the Future Farmers of America. *Board of Education of Independent School District No. 92 of Pottawatomie County v. Earls*, 536 U.S. 822 (2002).

Despite the distinction courts have drawn regarding extracurricular activities, students do not lose their basic constitutional rights when participating in extracurricular activities. Under the Equal Protection clause of the Fourteenth Amendment, for example, people have a constitutional right to be treated fairly, *i.e.* the laws must be rational and applied in the same way to persons similarly situated. Under the Equal Protection Clause, a student can challenge a rule regarding participation in extracurricular activities that is not rational. *See, e.g., Perry v. Grenada Municipal Separate School District*, 300 F. Supp. 748 (N.D. Miss. 1969); *Ordway v. Hargraves*, 323 F. Supp. 1155 (D. Mass. 1971) (prohibitions against married or pregnant students participating in sports struck down). The standard in such cases is high, however, and the courts will defer to the judgments of school officials as long as they can show a rational relationship between the rule in question and a legitimate school interest.

Also, while school officials have broad discretion in these matters, they must exercise that discretion in a way that does not violate other constitutional or statutory rights of a student. The Eighth Circuit ruled, for example, that a school district did not violate the free speech rights of a student in disqualifying him from participating in a student election. As part of his campaign, he had distributed condoms in violation of the school rule requiring prior approval before distributing materials in school. *Henerey v. City of St. Charles School District*, 200 F.3d 1128 (8th Cir. 1999). This case is significant not because the district prevailed, but rather because the court heard the claim. Participating in a student election is a privilege, not a right. However, in supervising an extracurricular activity school officials are still constrained by constitutional principles, and students remain free to raise such issues through litigation. Here, although the student's claim was dismissed, he had the chance to argue that his First Amendment rights had been violated. Extracurricular activities may be optional, but they can still embroil school districts in constitutional litigation.

Finally, some parents have claimed that they have the right to home-school their children, on the one hand, and have their children participate in extracurricular activities on the other. The State Department of Education has taken the position that school districts are not obligated to permit dual enrollment of students receiving home instruction. *See Letter to Olson from Flanagan*, (State Department of Education, Office of Legal and Governmental Affairs, September 27, 1997).

Courts throughout the country similarly have rejected free exercise claims made by parents of home-schoolers, seeking either dual enrollment or to have their children in extra-curricular activities. In *Swanson v. Guthrie Independent School District*, 135 F.3d 694 (10th Cir. 1998), the court ruled that a home-schooled eighth grader did not have the right to attend public school on a part-time basis, notwithstanding his parents' claim that denial of this request burdened his free exercise of religion. In *Goulert v. Meadows*, 345 F.3d 239 (4th Cir. 2003), the court held that denial to home-schoolers of community center to conduct lessons did not violate their free speech and equal protection rights. *See also Angstadt v. Midd-West School District*, No. 03-3912 (3d Cir. 2004) (cyber-student did not have constitutional right to participate in extracurricular activities); *Reid v. Kenowa Hills Public Schools*, No. 239473 (Mich. Ct. App. March 2, 2004) (no Equal Protection or First Amendment violation to deny opportunity to home-schooled children to participate in extracurricular activities). Consequently, school districts in Connecticut have the option to grant or deny requests by home-school families to participate in extracurricular activities. In responding to such requests, however, school district must keep in mind their obligations under the Equal Protection Clause, discussed in Section E(3)(b) above. If the school district grants one request, it must generally grant all similar requests.

2. Discipline issues

A related point concerns discipline of student athletes or other students involved in extracurricular activities. As discussed above in Section C, Student Discipline, above, there are statutory rules concerning removal, suspension, and expulsion, and required procedures that apply when such discipline is imposed Consistent with the premise that participation in extracurricular activities is a privilege, however, the normal rules regarding discipline do not apply when students are excluded from such activities. Rather, exclusion from such activities is a matter for the discretion of the school officials supervising the activity. Any exclusion must not violate other statutory or constitutional rights of the student, of course, but absent such a claim, there is no legal requirement that school officials provide due process or otherwise hold hearings concerning such matters. Clearly, there may be good educational and/or policy reasons for having a hearing and/or appeal process, but the law leaves those judgments to the school officials.

School officials have broad discretion in adopting rules concerning participation in extracurricular activities. Many school districts require, for example, that students sign a written acknowledgment that they must refrain from using alcohol, drugs, or tobacco products during the season. Such written acknowledgments can be helpful, both in promoting good conduct and in giving fair notice of consequences for violating these expectations. Since these rules extend the reach of the school beyond the campus to the student's every waking hour, however, one may question whether these rules are enforceable. In a word – absolutely. Such activities are a privilege, and school officials may impose any reasonable requirement for participation. Such rules relate not only to the training regimen for student athletes, but also to the role of the student athlete as a model for the other students. Based on that reasoning, some school districts have announced rules requiring student athletes to refrain from even attending parties where illegal drinking or use of drugs occurs. While there are no court cases in Connecticut, such a rule would almost certainly be upheld. The rule is rational in that it would be very difficult to prove use of alcohol (as compared to establishing that the student attended the party). Moreover, given that student athletes may serve as role models for the other students, their attendance at such parties may actually promote such harmful conduct.

3. "Pay for play"

In determining whether to offer certain activities, boards of education are often confronted with difficult choices, given the limited funds available. One way to offer a greater range of activities for students, therefore, has been to establish participation fees for students. When school districts around the country first started imposing such required fees, there were court challenges. Given that such activities are supplementary to the basic curriculum, these challenges uniformly failed.

There are no reported cases in Connecticut challenging school district decisions to implement participation fees for extracurricular activities, and the practice is common. It is also common, and appropriate, for boards of education to make provision for scholarship assistance to students whose families cannot afford such participation fees.

In establishing cost-sharing arrangements related to school activities, school officials should take care to avoid imposing charges for activities that are part of the basic educational opportunity offered to students. Conn. Gen. Stat. § 10-228 provides:

> Each local and regional board of education shall purchase such books, either as regular texts, as supplementary books or as library books, and such supplies, material and equipment, as it deems *necessary* to meet the needs of instruction in its schools. In day and evening schools of elementary and secondary grades, *all books and equipment shall be loaned and materials and supplies furnished to all pupils free of charge*, subject to such rules and regulations as to their care and use as the board of education prescribes.

(Emphasis added). Given this requirement, costs may be imposed only for supplementary activities.

If an activity would enrich a student's experience but is not a required activity, the board of education has the right to impose costs. The only limitation is set forth in the statutory provisions concerning priority school districts, Conn. Gen. Stat. § 10-266t(h), which provides that priority school districts may charge fees for after-school academic enrichment, support or recreational programs as long as the charges are no more than seventy-five percent of the cost of the program and no student is excluded from the program because of financial inability to pay the fee. Problems can arise, however, in distinguishing between required activities and enrichment activities in at least two different situations.

First, as to activities within the curriculum (*i.e.* activities for which secondary school students earn credit), the question is whether the supplies, material and/or equipment are "necessary to meet the needs of instruction" as provided in Conn. Gen. Stat. § 10-228. A student may have the right, for example, to participate in the school orchestra, but the district would meet its obligation by making *some* arrangements for participation. The student does not have the right to decide to play the violin and require the district to purchase such an instrument. Happily, these cost issues rarely come up, and there are no reported cases in Connecticut regarding such matters.

Second, school officials must distinguish between extracurricular enrichment activities and curricular activities. For example, if German students who can afford it go to Germany on a school trip during the school year and those who cannot sit in study hall, one could persuasively argue that costs are impermissibly interfering with a student's ability to participate in the basic curriculum. Caution is therefore warranted with respect to activities that occur during the school day and/or school year.

4. Interscholastic competition

Interscholastic competition in Connecticut is regulated by the Connecticut Interscholastic Athletic Conference, an organization run by the Connecticut Association of Schools. The CIAC organizes conferences in the various girls' and boys' sports throughout the state. Among its described purposes are "to develop intelligent recognition for the proper place of interscholastic athletics in education, to encourage good sportsmanship, to nurture more cordial relationships among member schools, and to foster equitable competition among schools." *Wajnowski v. The Connecticut Association of Schools*, 6 Conn. Ops. 35 (January 24, 2000).

The CIAC establishes eligibility rules to assure that students participating in interscholastic athletics are successfully participating in their academic studies. In addition, there are strict prohibitions against recruiting. Students are not permitted to participate in interscholastic competition for one year if they have changed schools without their parents having moved; this prohibition, the "transfer rule," is intended to prevent students from changing their living arrangements in order to change the teams on which they would compete.

These eligibility rules serve an important public good, to assure that athletics remain an enrichment activity, rather than an end in itself. Some school districts have adopted eligibility rules regarding academic standards that are even more rigorous than those adopted by the CIAC, and reasonable people can debate over the efficacy of such rules. Given that athletics is a privilege rather than a right under law, however, deference is generally given to the rules for participation established by school districts and the CIAC.

This deference is evident in a recent case in which a student challenged a determination by the CIAC that he was not eligible to participate in interscholastic athletics. *Wajnowski v. The Connecticut Association of Schools*, 6 Conn. Ops. 35 (January 24, 2000). There, a student transferring from Notre Dame High School in West Haven to the West Haven Public Schools challenged the decision not to grant a "hardship" exception to the transfer rule (which generally prohibits a student from competing in the same sport for another school for one year if his residence has not changed). After the CIAC Eligibility Committee denied his request for an exception and the Board of Control declined to hold further hearing, the student challenged this decision in court.

In ruling against the student, the Connecticut court found it unnecessary to determine whether the CIAC was subject to the court's jurisdiction as a "state actor." The court ruled, rather, that application of the "transfer" rule in this case did not violate any constitutional rights of the student. The court simply inquired whether the "transfer" rule bears a rational relationship to a legitimate state interest. The court found that the rule more than met that standard, given the determination by CIAC that unrestricted eligibility upon transfers among member schools can cause the problems that the rule avoids. Such problems could include recruitment or even coercion of an athlete or family to the detriment of the student. The CIAC rule, therefore, was upheld and the request for injunction was denied. By contrast, the United States Supreme Court held in 2001 (on a five-four vote) that the Tennessee Secondary School Athletic Association is a "state actor," *i.e.* a governmental body subject to constitutional strictures. *Brentwood Academy v. Tennessee Secondary School Athletic Association*, 531 U.S. 288 (2001). This ruling permitted a member school to sue under the First and Fourteenth Amendments over sanctions that had been imposed.

5. Students with disabilities

Assuring that the rights of students with disabilities can participate in extracurricular activities can pose special challenges. Under the Individuals with Disabilities Education Act (IDEA), 20 U.S.C. § 1400 *et seq.*, school districts are required to assure that children with disabilities have appropriate opportunities to participate in extracurricular activities. Under Section 504 of the Rehabilitation Act of 1973, 29 U.S.C. § 794(a), students (and others) with disabilities who are otherwise qualified may not be excluded from, or denied the benefits of participation in, activities that receive federal funds. These issues are discussed generally in Chapter Five.

As to extracurricular activities, these statutes impose two separate responsibilities. First, school officials have an affirmative duty to make provision through the PPT process for students with disabilities to participate in extracurricular activities. Second, school officials must assure that students with disabilities are not excluded from participation on the basis of their disabilities. In order to meet these responsibilities, school districts can be required to provide disabled students significant accommodations.

Under the IDEA, each individualized education program (IEP) must include a statement describing the supplementary aids and services to be provided to the child, as well as a statement of the program modifications or supports for school personnel that will be provided in order for the child, *inter alia*, to participate in extracurricular and other non-academic activities, and to be educated and participate in such activities with other children with disabilities and children without disabilities. 34 C.F.R. § 300.347, *discussed* in Chapter Five, Section A(3)(e).

In working to meet these obligations, school officials must keep (at least) three things in mind. First, a basic principle of special education law is that students must be considered individually. Rather than relying on rules that were developed to apply to students without disabilities, school officials should consider the individual circumstances of the student in question. Does the rule make sense as to that student? Would an exception to the rule undermine the purpose of the rule? These decisions must be based on the unique facts of the specific case.

The principle of individual consideration is reflected in two separate cases. In one case the federal district court in Connecticut ruled that an exception should be made for a young man with Down Syndrome to the CIAC rule prohibiting students nineteen years of age from competing in interscholastic activities. While the rule is reasonable in general (because it protects student competitors from older students), the court found that it worked to discriminate against the disabled student, who was an enthusiastic, albeit not-gifted, member of the swim team. *Dennin v. CIAC*, 913 F. Supp. 663 (D. Conn. 1996), *dismissed as moot,* 94 F.3d 96 (2d Cir. 1996).

By contrast, in *Stearns v. Board of Education for Warren Township High School District No. 121*, No. 99C5813, 1999 WL 1044832 (N.D. Ill, November 10, 1999), a student was dismissed from varsity basketball team for violating a "no-alcohol" rule. He claimed that his exclusion was discriminatory because his alcoholism (a disability) caused him to use alcohol. The court, however, rejected that claim. Neither he nor the school officials were aware of the disability at the time of exclusion. Moreover, the court ruled, an accommodation that would permit him to violate the "no-alcohol" rule was not reasonable, because it undermined the very purpose of the rule, which was intended to establish ideals of good sportsmanship and respect for rules and authority.

It can be difficult to know just how far to go in making accommodations so that disabled students can participate in extracurricular activities. In fairness to the other competitors and to the underlying purpose of the activity, there are limits to the duty to make accommodations. Modifications to the rules or activity need not be made if they fundamentally alter the nature of the activity. *Compare PGA Tour, Inc. v. Martin*, 532 U.S. 661 (2001) (professional golfer with disability has the right to use a golf cart in competition; walking between the holes held not a fundamental aspect of the competition). The key point, however, is that school officials must consider the matter on an individual basis.

Second, cost is not likely to be a valid defense. If a student would be able to participate in an activity but for special transportation, for example, the district must make provision for such transportation. The IDEA contemplates that program modifications and supplementary services and supports will be provided to permit students with disabilities to participate in extracurricular activities.

Third, total exclusion of students from extracurricular activities simply will not be permitted. If there is individual consideration, school districts need not make provision for a student to participate in all activities identified by the student and/or the parents. Exclusion from all activities (or even an especially important activity, such as the class trip to Washington, D.C.), however, can be an emotional flashpoint for parents. Given the clear right of children with disabilities to participate with their non-disabled peers in such activities, school officials have a heavy burden to make provision for such participation. Actions to meet this responsibility can include hiring special support people for the activity, or even modifying the activity itself.

6. <u>Title IX</u>

Title IX of the Educational Amendments of 1972 prohibits discrimination on the basis of gender. With exceptions that are not relevant, the prohibition is stated as follows:

> No person in the United States shall, on the basis of sex, be excluded from participation in, be denied the benefits of, or be subjected to discrimination under any education program or activity receiving Federal financial assistance.

20 U.S.C. § 1681. This law caused significant changes in the operation of the public schools, and issues of compliance and liability continue today.

a. Basic obligations

Title IX applies to all educational institutions that receive federal funds. Much of the litigation involving Title IX involves institutions of post-secondary learning. Since public schools in Connecticut (and throughout the country) receive federal funds, however, school officials must assure that they comply with the proscription in Title IX against sex discrimination as well. This prohibition applies to all facets of school operation, including admission, recruitment, course offerings, textbooks and curricular materials, and even employment. Indeed, the United States Supreme Court addressed the scope of Title IX in a case from Connecticut, *North Haven Board of Education v. Bell*, 456 U.S. 521 (1982). There, the court held that the Department of Health, Education, and Welfare had the authority under Title IX to adopt regulations concerning prohibited sex discrimination in employment practices. *See* 34 C.F.R. § 106.51.

Disputes over the scope of Title IX continue even though it has been over thirty years since Title IX was adopted and over twenty years since *North Haven Board of Education v. Bell.* In 2002, the Eleventh Circuit ruled that private individuals who are not covered by the protections of Title IX cannot sue to enforce its prohibitions (no private right of action for girls' basketball coach who claimed he was fired for complaining about Title IX violations). *Jackson v. Birmingham Board of Education*, 309 F.3d 1333 (11th Cir 2002). The Solicitor General, however, expressed support for his claim, and the United States Supreme Court has accepted the case for review. Closer to home, the federal district court in Connecticut ruled in 2003 that a student intern has a private right of action under Title IX. *Hiler v. Hyde School*, No. 3:02CV416 (DJS) (D. Conn. 2003). In so doing, the court noted that the appellate courts are split on the question of whether employees have a private right of action under Title IX.

The No Child Left Behind Act includes a provision that could cause a change in how Title IX is interpreted. At present, single sex programs are permitted in physical education and in sex education. 34 C.F.R. § 106.34. A provision in the No Child Left Behind Act, however, directs the Secretary of Education to issue guidelines on single sex programs, which he did in 2002. Guidelines on Current Title IX Requirements related to Single-Sex Classes and Schools (May 3, 2002). At the same time, the Secretary issued a notification of proposed rule-making in this regard. Federal Register: May 8, 2002 (Volume 67, Number 89), at 31097-31099. In March 2004 the Secretary proposed regulations on single-sex schools that would increase flexibility and would specify when single-sex schools will be permitted. The final regulations, however, have not yet been adopted.

b. Athletics

Perhaps the most common compliance issue for elementary and secondary schools is whether girls have opportunities to participate in athletics equal to those provided to boys. The Title IX regulations set forth a list of non-exclusive factors that local and regional boards of education must consider in determining whether they are providing equal opportunity to students of both sexes:

- Whether the selection of sports and levels of competition effectively accommodate the interests and abilities of members of both sexes;
- The provision of equipment and supplies;
- Scheduling of games and practice time;
- Travel and per diem allowance;
- Opportunity to receive coaching and academic tutoring;
- Assignment and compensation of coaches and tutors;
- Provision of locker rooms, practice and competitive facilities;
- Provision of medical and training facilities and services;
- Provision of housing and dining facilities and services;
- Publicity.

The regulation also states that unequal expenditures for boys and girls teams do not, alone, constitute noncompliance with the requirement that equal opportunities be provided to students of both sexes. 34 C.F.R. § 106.41(c). However, when there are significant disparities in spending, school officials have explaining to do.

The listed factors address the issue of equal opportunity in a number of different ways. The Office for Civil Rights will not determine compliance by relying on a single factor, but rather will consider the whole picture in determining whether the school district has provided an equal opportunity to boys and girls. Since 1979, there has been a three-part test to determine compliance with Title IX (at least as regards intercollegiate athletics), and the Office for Civil Rights of the Department of Education will likely find compliance if a school district can meet any of the following three tests:

- Are the opportunities for boys and girls substantially proportionate to their respective enrollments?
- Where one sex has been historically underrepresented, is there a continuing practice of program expansion to develop the interests and abilities of that sex?
- Where one sex has been historically underrepresented and the school cannot show a continuing practice of program expansion, are the interests and abilities of the underrepresented sex fully and effectively accommodated by the present program?

Policy Interpretation of the Department of HEW, 44 Fed. Reg. 71,418 (1979).

The first test, "substantial proportionality," is typically the test used. It can be difficult or impossible for a school district to show that there is a continuing practice of program expansion. It may be even more difficult to establish that the interests and abilities of girls are "fully and effectively accommodated" even if they are underrepresented. Rather, it is often easiest for school districts to assure that the opportunities for boys and girls are substantially proportionate, and school districts often find themselves in a numbers game, seeking to have a similar number of girls sports and boys sports. *See Price v. Wilton Public School District et al.*, No. 3:97CV2218 (D. Conn. September 27, 2001), digested at 7 Conn. Ops. 1200 (October 22, 2001) (average difference of 2.9% over ten years between girls and boys participating in sports is "substantially proportionate").

If necessary, it is permissible to reduce opportunities for one sex to assure substantial proportionality of participation. *See, e.g., Boulahanis v. Board of Regents*, 198 F.3d 633 (7th Cir. 1999) (university's elimination of men's intercollegiate wrestling and soccer programs to reduce disparity in participation in athletics did not violate Title IX); *Neal v. Board of Trustees*, 198 F.3d 763 (9th Cir. 1999) (remedial action may include reducing opportunities for men's sports). In *Miami University Wrestling Club v. University of Miami*, 302 F.3d 608 (6th Cir. 2002), the Sixth Circuit held that the disbanding of the male wrestling team to eliminate part of the disparity of between men and women in athletics did not violate the equal protection rights of the men. *See also Chalenor v. University of North Dakota* , 291 F.3d 1042 (8th Cir. 2002) (termination of men's wrestling program to reduce disparity upheld, despite availability of private funds).

Equal opportunity is not simply a matter of equality in funding or proportionality in participation. In 2004, the Second Circuit ruled that a decision to offer girls' soccer in the spring rather than in the fall (as is the case with boys' soccer) can operate to deny female students their rights under Title IX. *McCormick v. School District of Mamaroneck*, 370 F.3d 275 (2d Cir. 2004). Critical to the court's decision was the fact that the state championships in soccer come at the end of the fall season. The court ruled that the school district could submit an alternative compliance plan, such as alternating the scheduling of soccer in the spring between the boys and the girls teams. The original decision to schedule girls' soccer in the spring, however, denied girls an important opportunity to compete for the state championship and was discriminatory under Title IX.

School districts do not have to run teams in the same sport for both sexes. If they do not operate a team for that sex, then students must be permitted to participate on the same team if "athletic opportunities for members of that sex have previously been limited." 34 C.F.R. § 106.41(b). The regulations go on to provide that this obligation does not extend to contact sports ("boxing, wrestling, rugby, ice hockey, football, basketball and other sports the purpose or major activity of which involves bodily contact"). However, the federal courts have ruled on equal protection grounds that this exclusion may not be enforced, and girls have successfully asserted the right to wrestle or play football on the boys' team as a matter of equal protection. *See, e.g. Darrin v. Gould*, 540 P.2d 882 (Wash. 1975) (voiding rule forbidding female participation on football team).

By contrast, boys who on occasion have sought to participate on girls' teams have not fared as well. To be sure, in one case, the federal district court in Rhode Island issued a preliminary injunction in favor of a boy who sought to participate on the girls' volleyball team. *Gomes v. Rhode Island Interscholastic League*, 469 F. Supp. 659 (D. R.I. 1979), *vacated as moot*, 604 F.2d 733 (1st Cir. 1979). The courts have generally ruled, however, that boys do not have the right to participate on girls' teams, either under 34 C.F.R. § 106.41(b) or under the Equal Protection clause of the United States Constitution. *See, e.g., Williams v. School District of Bethlehem, Pennsylvania*, 998 F.2d 168 (3d Cir. 1993), *cert. denied*, 519 U.S. 1043 (1994) (boy properly excluded from participating on girls' field hockey team).

c. Policy and grievance procedure

The Title IX regulations require that all educational institutions publicize their policy of non-discrimination on the basis of sex in all of its programs. 34 C.F.R. § 106.9. In addition, all educational institutions are required to name a person responsible for assuring compliance with Title IX, typically called the Title IX Officer or Coordinator. Moreover, educational institutions are required to establish and maintain "grievance procedures providing for prompt and equitable resolution of student and employee complaints alleging" violation of Title IX. 34 C.F.R. § 106.8.

d. Liability issues

In addition to compliance issues, school districts may face liability under Title IX. The appellate courts are split on whether employees can sue under Title IX. *See Hiler v. Hyde School*, No. 3:02CV416 (DJS) (D. Conn. 2003). The United States Supreme Court has, however, ruled that school districts may be liable in damages to students whose rights under Title IX were violated. *Franklin v. Gwinnett County Public Schools*, 503 U.S. 60 (1992). Since that time, the United States Supreme Court has elaborated twice on the circumstances when school districts will be liable for such violations, as described below.

The Second Circuit has ruled that Title IX is a comprehensive remedial scheme, and that plaintiffs may not also bring claims against school districts under 42 U.S.C. § 1983. *Bruneau v. South Kortright Central School District*, 163 F.3d 749 (2d Cir. 1998). This ruling, however, does not preclude Section 1983 claims against individuals. *Price v. Wilton Public School District*, No. 3:97CV2218 (D. Conn. September 27, 2001), *digested at* 7 Conn. Ops. 1200 (October 22, 2001). In addition, with increasing frequency, school districts find themselves in class action litigation over alleged violations of Title IX. *See Price v. Wilton Public Schools*, 4 Conn. Ops. 1163 (D. Conn. 1998) (Title IX claim brought by coach and parent certified as a class action in federal court involving "female students currently participating, or who are deterred from participating, in female athletic programs"); *Communities for Equity v. Michigan High School Athletic Association*, 192 F.R.D. 568 (W.D. Mich. 1999). One court has ruled, however, that school districts are not liable for punitive damages in Title IX cases. *Schultzen v. Woodbury Central Community School District*, 187 F. Supp.2d 1099 (N.D. Iowa 2002).

The potential for liability under Title IX is not limited to issues involving program offerings or other official actions of the school district.

Two recent decisions of the United States Supreme Court concerning sexual harassment hold that in limited circumstances school districts may even be held liable under Title IX for sexual harassment of students by teachers or by other students.

In *Gebser v. Lago Vista Independent School District*, 524 U.S. 274 (1998), a teacher initiated sexual relations with a student when she was a freshman in high school. The student did not report the situation to school officials, but after approximately one year, the teacher and the student were discovered having sexual relations. The district fired the teacher, and his license was also revoked. Despite the actions by the school district, the student and her parents then sued the school district under Title IX. On a 5-4 vote, the Court held that a school district can be liable to a student in cases of teacher/student sexual harassment, but only under narrow circumstances, *i.e.* liability will be found only if (1) an official who has authority to address the alleged discrimination and to take corrective measures has actual knowledge of the conduct, and (2) the response of that official is so inadequate that it constitutes "deliberate indifference" to discrimination.

This standard is difficult to meet. In *Norris v. Norwalk Public Schools*, 124 F. Supp.2d 791 (D. Conn. 2000), for example, the federal district court in Connecticut ruled that a Title IX plaintiff could not prevail in her claim under 42 U.S.C. § 1983 that actions by a coach that were annoying (slapping, pinching, and sexually suggestive comments) violated her right to substantive due process, and based on the *Gebser* standard set forth below, the court ultimately dismissed all claims.

In 1999, the United States Supreme held that school districts can be liable for student-to-student sexual harassment as well. *Davis v. Monroe County Board of Education*, 526 U.S. 629 (1999). In another 5-4 vote, the Court established a standard for district liability that is similar to that announced in the *Gebser* decision. Specifically, a school district may be liable for student-to-student sexual harassment if school officials with the authority to take corrective action exhibit deliberate indifference to known sexual harassment that is "so severe, pervasive, and objectively offensive that it effectively bars the victim's access to educational opportunity or benefit." This high standard makes it unlikely that a single incident would result in liability. If action is taken, school officials may not even be liable for a continuing course of harassment. *Gabrielle M. v. Park Forest-Chicago Heights, Ill. School District 163*, 315 F.3d. 817 (7th Cir. 2003). The *Davis* decision, however, permits plaintiffs who allege such conduct by school officials to have their day in court. *See, e.g., Warren ex rel. Good v. Reading*

School District, 278 F.3d 163 (3d Cir. 2002) (remanded for trial on whether principal, a person with authority to take action, had actual notice of the alleged abuse).

These cases underscore the need for school districts to comply with Title IX requirements and to be proactive in addressing complaints. It is critically important to have in place appropriate policies and procedures concerning Title IX and sexual harassment. These policies and procedures must provide an effective mechanism for receiving and investigating complaints of Title IX violation. The threshold of liability for teacher-student and student-student sexual harassment is high, as described above. The problem is that the expenses of the related litigation can be crushing. These problems are thus best avoided by assuring that any complaints are thoroughly investigated and promptly resolved.

CHAPTER FIVE
SPECIAL EDUCATION

Connecticut has long been a leader in providing appropriate programs to children with disabilities. The first known school for children with disabilities was established in Hartford by Thomas Gallaudet in 1817, and the American School for the Deaf continues to meet the needs of deaf children today. More recently, the General Assembly enacted its first comprehensive special education legislation in 1967, before the following seminal developments at the national level.

Children with disabilities were first afforded legal protection by the federal courts in 1971. That year the federal district court in Pennsylvania built on the abolition of the "separate but equal" doctrine in *Brown v. Board of Education*, 347 U.S. 483 (1954), and ruled that children with disabilities had the same right to be educated as do other children. *Pennsylvania Association of Retarded Children v. Commonwealth*, 334 F. Supp. 1257 (E.D. Pa. 1971). The PARC case was soon followed by *Mills v. Board of Education of District of Columbia*, 348 F. Supp. 866 (D. D.C. 1972), which reached a similar conclusion. The consent decree issued in that case included many elements that are now standard procedure in special education, including parent notice and participation in the placement planning process, evaluation, consideration of the individual needs of the child, a preference for education in the same setting with children without disabilities, and a process for reviewing whether educational services are appropriate.

Following *PARC* and *Mills*, the United States Congress first addressed the needs of children with disabilities with P.L. 94-142, the Education for All Handicapped Children Act of 1975. Since then, the framework for special education programs nationwide has been in place, with some minor changes in the intervening years, including renaming the law in 1990 to the Individuals with Disabilities Education Act, or IDEA, 20 U.S.C. § 1400 *et seq.* In 1997, Congress undertook a comprehensive revision of the IDEA, and that version of the law sets out the current procedures under the IDEA as described below. Acronyms abound in special education, with IEP's, PPT's, FAPE and the like. However, the basic provisions are readily understandable. The hard part comes in determining what specific services are needed to meet the unique needs of an individual child.

Children who are identified as having a disability are entitled to a "free appropriate public education" or "FAPE." The elements of such a program, including goals and objectives, the services to be provided and the placement for such services, are determined by a multi-disciplinary team, called the "IEP team" in the federal regulations and the planning and placement team (the "PPT") in the state regulations. This team includes representatives of the teaching, administrative and pupil personnel staffs and well as the parents. The PPT is responsible for the evaluation of students, and the planning for services for eligible students. Parent participation in educational decision-making concerning their child is a key element of the procedures under the IDEA. *See* Section A(3)(c), below.

One of the major responsibilities of the PPT is to develop and periodically revise the individualized education plan, (the "IEP"), on at least an annual basis. The IEP sets forth the specific services required for the student, the "free appropriate public education" to which all children with disabilities are entitled. Parents have the right to attend and actively participate in any PPT meeting to develop, review and/or revise the IEP. Also, if parents disagree over whether the planned program appropriately meets the needs of the student, they have a right to request mediation of the dispute or a more formal review before an impartial hearing officer appointed by the State Department of Education in a "due process hearing." Either party may then appeal the hearing officer's decision to either state or (more commonly) federal court.

State law has specific provisions concerning special education, including provision for the identification of gifted students (with no concomitant duty to provide programs) and due process hearing procedures. While the state law is necessarily written to comply with all federal requirements, some of its unique features bear review. In the following pages, we will review each of these laws affecting the rights of children with disabilities.

In addition to the IDEA, another federal law affects the rights of students with disabilities. Section 504 of the Rehabilitation Act of 1973 prohibits discrimination against persons with disabilities. As reviewed in Section B, the concept of "discrimination" is broadly drawn under Section 504, and the requirement to avoid discrimination carries with it the duty to provide services to disabled children so that they have an opportunity to participate in education as do their non-disabled peers.

Finally, discipline of children with disabilities has been a contentious issue. Issues regarding discipline of children with disabilities directly implicate the rights of other students to be educated without distraction and disruption. In 1997, significant changes were made to IDEA in this regard, and efforts for further change continue. Nonetheless, discipline of special education children can be difficult, and it is certainly complicated, as reviewed in Section C.

A. The Individuals with Disabilities Education Act

The IDEA is the principal source for the legal responsibilities of boards of education with respect to special education. Since first enacted as the Education for All Handicapped Children Act in 1975, it has guided school districts in their responsibility to provide individualized instruction to meet the needs of children with disabilities. In 1997 a comprehensive revision of IDEA clarified some of the more vexing problems, such as the obligations to students placed by their parents in private schools. Unfortunately, many problems and uncertainties remain.

1. "Free appropriate public education"

Basic to special education is the concept of the "free appropriate public education" or FAPE. The law does not purport to establish a substantive standard for what is appropriate for a particular student. That would be impossible, because the needs of children with disabilities vary greatly. Rather, the law establishes a procedure for determining the elements of a program to meet the unique needs of each child with disabilities. This focus is on the *process* of developing the IEP and providing FAPE, and it is thus crucially important that districts comply with the various procedural requirements of the IDEA. *Board of Education of Hendrick Hudson Central School District v. Rowley*, 458 U.S. 176 (1982).

The statute defines FAPE as follows:

> The term "free appropriate public education" means special education and related services that—
>
> (A) have been provided at public expense, under public supervision and direction, and without charge,
> (B) meet the standards of the State educational agency,
> (C) include an appropriate preschool, elementary, or secondary school education in the State involved, and
> (D) are provided in conformity with the individualized education program required under [this law].

20 U.S.C. § 1401(a)(18). Perhaps most notable about this definition is that it tells us almost nothing about what FAPE is. The statute makes clear that the program must be at no cost to the parents. Otherwise the definition is somewhat circular—a free appropriate public education must be free and appropriate.

In 1982, the United States Supreme Court decided its first case on special education, and it squarely addressed the definition of FAPE. In *Board of Education of Hendrick Hudson Central School District v. Rowley*, 458 U.S. 176 (1982), the Court was confronted with a request by the parents of Amy Rowley, a first grader with impaired hearing, that she be provided a full-time sign language interpreter. The district court found that Amy was entitled to the services as part of an appropriate education, reasoning that the law required the school district to provide services that would permit Amy to reach her maximum potential to the same degree that children without disabilities could reach theirs. The Second Circuit Court of Appeals agreed, albeit with the caveat that its decision should not be cited as precedent in any other case. The United States Supreme Court reversed, finding that the services of a full-time sign language interpreter were not a necessary part of an appropriate program for Amy Rowley.

The Court reviewed the statutory definitions of the terms "special education" and "related services" and concluded that the law contains no substantive standard, no definition of what "appropriate" means in a particular case. Rather the Court found that the law establishes a "basic floor of opportunity" which the Court described as follows:

> When the language of the Act and its legislative history are considered together, the requirements imposed by Congress become tolerably clear. Insofar as a State is required to provide a handicapped child with a "free appropriate public education," we hold that it satisfies this requirement by providing personalized instruction with sufficient support services to permit the child to benefit educationally from the instruction. Such instruction and services must be provided at public expense, must meet the State's educational standards, must approximate the grade levels used in the State's regular education, and must comport with the child's IEP. In addition, the IEP, and therefore the personalized instruction, should be formulated in accordance with the requirements of the Act and, if the child is being educated in the regular classrooms of the public education system, should

> be reasonably calculated to enable the child to achieve passing marks and advance from grade to grade.

Id. at 203-04. The Court cautioned that the courts generally lack the specialized expertise and experience to resolve questions as to whether a program is appropriate in a particular case, and stated, "Therefore, once a court determines that the requirements of the Act have been met, questions of methodology are for resolution by the States." *Id.* at 208.

The last part of the Court's definition, that the IEP must be formulated in accordance with the Act, is the critical part of the decision. The Court emphasized that the required procedures are at the heart of the law; the presumption is that if an individual educational program is developed with the proper procedures, including appropriate evaluation, input from a multi-disciplinary team and the active involvement of the parents, the resulting program will be appropriate to meet the needs of the child with disabilities:

> Congress placed every bit as much emphasis upon compliance with procedures giving parents and guardians a large measure of participation at every stage of the administrative process . . . as it did upon the measurement of the resulting IEP against a substantive standard . . . [such that] adequate compliance with the procedures prescribed would in most cases assure much if not all of what Congress wished in the way of substantive content in an IEP.

458 U.S. at 205-206. The Court reinforced that view in another case some three years after *Rowley*. *School Committee of Burlington v. Massachusetts Department of Education*, 471 U.S. 359, 368 (1985).

Given this emphasis on procedural matters, when the question has been whether proper procedures have been met, the courts have not been shy in reviewing the actions of school officials. When a school district has committed a significant violation of proper procedures, courts have held in some cases that such a violation may itself constitute a denial of an appropriate education. *See, e.g. Hall v. Vance County Board of Education*, 774 F.2d 629, 635 (4th Cir. 1985); *Board of Education of Cabell v. Dienelt*, 843 F.2d 813 (4th Cir. 1988).

The *Rowley* case also guides hearing officers and the lower courts by establishing that the obligation of school districts under state and federal law is clearly not to maximize educational opportunities. Rather, under IDEA school districts must provide individually designed instruction intended to confer a reasonable educational benefit. Indeed, even if all members of the PPT express support for recommended changes to a child's program, these changes are not required if the program is otherwise appropriate. *W.A. v. Pascarella*, 153 F. Supp.2d 144 (D. Conn. 2001). One federal judge described the duty to provide an appropriate education as follows:

> The Act requires that the Tullahoma schools provide the educational equivalent of a serviceable Chevrolet to every handicapped student. Appellant, however, demands that the Tullahoma school system provide a Cadillac solely for appellant's use. . . . [W]e hold that the board is not required to provide a Cadillac, and that the proposed IEP is reasonably calculated to provide educational benefits to appellant, and is therefore in compliance with the requirements of the IDEA.

Doe v. Board of Education of Tullahoma City Schools, 9 F.3d 455, 459-60 (6th Cir. 1993). This is as concrete and as practical a definition of "appropriate" as one will find.

Given the legal definition of an "appropriate education," it can be difficult to predict where a hearing officer will draw the line between an "appropriate" program and one that must be changed in order to become appropriate. Unfortunately, that question is typically at the heart of a special education dispute, and generally both parents and districts will present expert testimony from professionals from in and outside the district, holding opinions that are often widely divergent. Consequently, it is between difficult and impossible to reliably predict how a hearing officer will resolve a special education dispute. This uncertainty, the natural sympathy for parents of children with disabilities, and the high cost of hearings cause school districts to consider any reasonable alternative to resolving disputes through the hearing process.

a. "Special education"

The definition of a "free appropriate public education" includes two basic components, special education and related services. The first element, special education, is the individually designed instruction to which the Court in *Rowley* referred. Indeed, in developing its definition of FAPE, the Court relied on the statutory definition of special education:

> "Special education" means "specially designed instruction, at no cost to parents or guardians, to meet the unique needs of a handicapped child, including classroom instruction, instruction in physical education, home instruction, and instruction in hospitals and institutions."

Rowley, 458 U.S. at 188, citing 20 U.S.C. § 1401(16). Under IDEA, the IEP team is responsible for determining the elements of the required "specially designed instruction . . . to meet the unique needs of a handicapped child."

In most cases the law leaves questions of educational methodology to the states and thus to the local educators. At least in theory, as long as the chosen methodology can be defended as effective for the particular child, it will be considered appropriate, notwithstanding preferences for other approaches a parent may express.

1. "Specially designed instruction . . . to meet the unique needs of a child with a disability"

Fundamental to the definition of "special education" is that it is individually designed instruction. As we will see when we review the PPT process, the law requires that a team of knowledgeable professionals and the parents work together and develop a specific plan to address the needs of the particular child. This process requires that the participants keep foremost in mind that their task is to identify the individual needs and develop a program to meet the needs of that individual student. Decisions based on administrative convenience or district practice, rather than the student's individual needs, are inconsistent with the procedural requirements of the IDEA.

Given these requirements, school districts must assure that the development of an "appropriate" special education program follows the proper sequence. For children in regular education, school districts define the educational opportunities available in the normal course by deciding whether to offer French or Spanish, statistics or trigonometry. Once those opportunities are defined, students can select their programs of study.

By contrast, under the IDEA it is not adequate or appropriate for school districts, first, to establish programs for children with disabilities, such as programs for the emotionally disturbed, and then limit the planning process to a discussion of the programs available. Rather, the PPT must consider what specialized instruction is necessary to meet the unique needs of that child and only then determine the appropriate placement for that child. Indeed, one federal court found that a school district violated the procedural rights under the IDEA of a child with disabilities by first deciding to change a student's placement and then developing an IEP. *Spielberg v. Henrico County Public Schools*, 853 F.2d 256 (4th Cir. 1988).

One good way to keep the IDEA requirements for "specially designed instruction" in mind is consistently to address needs of children with disabilities in the following sequence:

(1) evaluation of the child's needs,
(2) development of an appropriate plan of services to meet those needs,
(3) placement in a program to provide such services.

This sequence is similar to the Connecticut law defining the jurisdiction of hearing officers. Conn. Gen. Stat. § 10-76h. By following this sequence in considering the needs of the child, the PPT can best meet its duty to prepare an educational plan on an individualized basis. First, the PPT must identify the child's needs through evaluation. After those needs are known, the PPT can identify the services needed to meet those unique needs. Only after both these steps are taken is it appropriate to decide where the program to meet those needs can be provided, *i.e.* the placement for the child.

This focus on the consideration of the unique needs of students may require that school districts suspend administrative rules that normally apply. A sure way to create a problem under the IDEA is to respond to a proposed element of an IEP with "we don't provide summer programs" or "we don't provide one-to-one instruction." To be sure, such interventions are not required for all students. But those decisions must be made after considering the individual needs of the child, not on the basis of administrative rules. Similarly, a team should not respond to a parent's request by stating that such decisions must be made by the director of special education or the superintendent. Decisions as to a student's program should be made by the IEP team members. If a request is problematic, a more appropriate response is to reconvene the team after district personnel gather information concerning an unusual request.

The courts have addressed the question of extended year programming on several occasions, and the decisions in these cases underscore the need for individualized consideration of what programs will be provided. In *Battle v. Commonwealth of Pennsylvania*, 629 F.2d 269 (3d Cir. 1980), the court of appeals considered a challenge to a Pennsylvania law which provided that all students, disabled or not, were entitled to 180 days of instruction, and no more. Rejecting this limitation, the court stated:

> Rather than ascertaining the reasonable educational needs of each child in light of reasonable education goals, and establishing a reasonable program to attain those goals, the 180 day rule imposes with rigid certainty a program restriction that may be wholly inappropriate to the child's educational objectives.

Id. at 280. Since this case, several other courts have followed suit. *See, e.g., Georgia Association of Retarded Citizens v. McDaniel*, 511 F. Supp. 1263 (N.D. Ga. 1981), *affirmed*, 716 F.2d 1565 (11th Cir. 1983). It is now clear that extended year programming may be required as a necessary part of an appropriate special education program. It is not as clear, however, when such services will be required.

In Connecticut, the State Department of Education has offered guidance on this point. *Update # 28*, Memorandum from George P. Dowaliby (January 10, 2002). *See also Reusch v. Fountain*, 872 F. Supp. 1421 (D. Md. 1994). To determine whether a student should receive extended school year (ESY) services, the PPT should consider factors that relate to both regression and non-regression, as follows: (1) the nature of the student's disability or the severity of the disabling condition; (2) regression and recoupment (*i.e.* is the student likely to lose critical skills or fail to recover these skills within a reasonable time (4-8 weeks), as compared to typical students?); (3) the student's progress in the areas of learning crucial to attaining self-sufficiency and independence from caregivers; (4) stereotypic, ritualistic, aggressive or self-injurious behaviors that interfere and prevent the student from receiving same educational benefit during the school year; (5) rate of progression (*i.e.* is the student moving through grades at an expected rate or is it slower?); (6) alternative resources available to the student, such as parks and recreation, DMR; (7) peer relationships (*i.e.* the ability of the student to interact with other disabled and non-disabled students); (8) whether there are areas of the student's curriculum that need continuous attention; (9) vocational needs for summer as indicated on the IEP; and (10) whether ESY services would be considered extraordinary considering the disability of the student. Considering these factors, ESY services are required only if they are an essential element of an appropriate program. As we know from *Rowley*, ESY services need not be provided in order to assure an optimal program. These factors, however, underscore the need to consider each child as an individual.

2. "At no cost"

The definition of "special education" expressly includes the requirement that special education be "at no cost to parents or guardians." The duty to provide FAPE to children with disabilities is unconditional, and a school district cannot excuse its failure to provide an appropriate program on the basis of expense. If a particular service is necessary to appropriately meet the special education needs of a student, whether it is one-to-one instruction, speech therapy or a residential placement, that service must be provided without regard to cost.

Cost may not be a factor in determining whether to provide an appropriate program, but it may certainly be a factor in choosing among alternative ways to deliver an appropriate program. For example, Conn. Gen. Stat. § 10-76d(d) was amended in 1997 to provide that the presumption in favor of public facilities may be overridden and school districts may place students in private facilities when placement in the private facility is less costly. In addition, districts may (and sometimes must) seek to have other agencies assume costs as long as the child continues to receive an appropriate educational program. For example, Conn. Gen. Stat. § 10-76d(a)(2) provides that certain school districts may work with the State on a voluntary basis in identifying students eligible for Medicare services and in obtaining reimbursement for Medicare-eligible expenses.

3. "In the least restrictive environment"

A core concept in determining an appropriate educational program is the requirement that children with disabilities be educated to the maximum extent appropriate with their non-disabled peers. When IDEA was adopted in 1975, the United States Congress noted that over one million students were excluded from education or were educated in segregated settings. 20 U.S.C. § 1400. Significantly, the requirement that all placements be made in the "least restrictive environment" can cut both ways. It can cause problems for parents who may want their children to be educated in a private school setting. It may also present difficulty for school district personnel who may believe that a special education setting is most appropriate to meet the needs of a particular child. All placement decisions, however, must conform with this requirement.

b. "Related services"

In addition to special education, a free appropriate public education must include such related services as are required for that individual child. The IDEA defines "related services" as follows:

> The term related services means transportation, and such developmental, corrective, and other supportive services . . . as may be required to assist a child with a disability to benefit from special education and includes the early identification and assessment of disabling conditions in children.

20 U.S.C. § 1401(20). The essential quality of a related service is that it must be necessary in order for the child to benefit from special education. Transportation is easily understood in this regard; if the child cannot get to school, he or she cannot benefit from special education. Special transportation, even with support people attending, may be required. However, it is often unclear whether a particular service is or is not necessary for the child to benefit from special education.

The difficulty starts with the list of related services set out in the Act. It includes:

- speech pathology
- audiology
- psychological services
- physical therapy
- occupational therapy
- recreation, including therapeutic recreation
- social work services
- medical services for diagnostic and evaluation purposes
- counseling services, including rehabilitation counseling
- early identification and assessment of disabling conditions in children

20 U.S.C. § 1401(20). The list of developmental, corrective and other supportive services potentially required for a child to benefit from special education is not all-inclusive, and the regulations mention other potential related services, including parent counseling and training. 34 C.F.R. § 300.24. Moreover, some parents understandably will seek additional services for their children, even if such services are not necessary to an appropriate

educational program. As a result, there have been disputes over requests for various services, such as residential placement, psychiatric services or even vision therapy. Moreover, even when there is agreement that a particular related service should be provided as part of FAPE, there is often disagreement over how often and by whom such services are to be provided under the IEP.

1. Medical services

The United States Supreme Court has squarely confronted the issue of related services twice. In *Irving Independent School District v. Tatro*, 468 U.S. 883 (1984), the Court considered the refusal of a local school district to provide clean intermittent catheterization to Amber Tatro, a young student with spina bifida, who could not attend school unless she received this service, at least until she was old enough to do such catheterization herself. The Court unanimously rejected the school district claim that the service was medical in nature, because it could be provided by a lay person with minimal training. The Court announced a four-part test to determine whether a related service is required:

- The child must be identified as a child with disabilities;
- The related service must be necessary for the child to benefit from special education;
- The service requested cannot be medical in nature, *i.e.* services that only a physician can perform; and
- Only services, rather than equipment, are included.

Id. at 894-95. As to the last test, the law has changed; since the 1990 amendments to IDEA, school districts can be required to provide assistive technology devices and services when required for FAPE.

Following the *Tatro* decision, the Court considered the case of Garret F., who was wheelchair-bound and ventilator dependent and required a responsible individual nearby to attend to certain physical needs during the school day. The school district claimed that it was not responsible for one-to-one nursing care for Garret and that the student's needs were so complex and expensive that they should be considered "medical" needs for which the school district would not be responsible. In support of its claim, the school district cited the decision of the Second Circuit in *Detsel v. Board of Education*, 820 F.2d 587 (2d Cir. 1987), *cert. denied,* 484 U.S. 981 (1987). There, the court ruled that the term "school health services" should be determined through a "multi-factor test," and that a school district was not required to provide the extensive services one child required, including constant monitoring of her respiratory status and other assistance that required the expertise of at least a licensed practical nurse throughout the day. Relying on *Detsel* and the "multi-factor test," school officials asked the Court to rule that these complex services were not its responsibility.

In *Cedar Rapids Community School District v. Garret F.*, 526 U.S. 66 (1999), the Court rejected this argument and reaffirmed the *Tatro* decision. It re-applied the bright line test it announced in *Tatro*: where services need not be provided by a licensed physician, they will be required related services if they are necessary to assist a child with disabilities to benefit from his or her special education program. The Court acknowledged that its interpretation of school district obligations under IDEA may cause legitimate concerns over costs. It held, however, that any adoption of the "multi-factor" test is a legislative function, and that the wording of the IDEA requires the school district to provide the services.

Following *Tatro* and *Garret F.*, school districts are often asked to assume responsibilities that the man on the street would hardly consider to be educational. For example, districts have been held responsible for suctioning tracheotomy tubes, care of gastric tubes or even a special diet during the school day. In one extreme case (decided before *Garret F.*) a district was held responsible for providing special transportation to one student to permit monitoring and suctioning of his tracheotomy tube during the trip to and from school. *Macomb County Intermediate School District v. Joshua S.*, 715 F. Supp. 824 (E.D. Mich. 1989).

The medical problems of some students are so severe that they may even come to school with a "Do Not Resuscitate" order. Such orders relate to medical, not educational issues. The Department of Health has adopted regulations governing DNR orders. Conn. St. Reg.§ 19a-580d-1 *et seq.* The regulations specify that a DNR bracelet is the only valid indicator of a DNR order that will be recognized. Emergency medical personnel must then provide medical care in consultation with medical direction, recognizing the limitations of the DNR order. Conn. St. Reg. § 19a-580d-4, 5. No law in Connecticut, however, addresses the obligations of school personnel in such situations. It is advisable, therefore, to convene a Section 504 team meeting to develop a written health care plan for any such student. The team should establish emergency procedures in advance, which may include provision for calling EMS personnel in an emergency. When such personnel respond, they will be notified of the DNR order by the bracelet.

2. Residential placement

It is well established that residential services may be required at school district expense where such services are necessary to provide an appropriate educational program. The regulations under IDEA expressly contemplate this obligation, 34 C.F.R. § 300.302, and courts have found in favor of claims for residential placement in various situations. Such need for residential placement arises most frequently in two situations. First, the disabilities of some students are so pervasive that they require educational programming twenty-four hours per day. *Kruelle v. New Castle County School District*, 642 F.2d 687 (3d Cir. 1981). Second, some adolescents with emotional disturbance require programming integrated with psychological and counseling services in a "therapeutic milieu." *Papacoda v. Connecticut*, 528 F. Supp. 68 (D. Conn. 1981).

The circumstances when school districts will be required to fund residential placements were construed broadly by the Second Circuit in 1997. *Mrs. B. v. Milford Board of Education*, 103 F.3d 1114 (2d Cir. 1997). In that case, a student with serious emotional and educational problems had been placed residentially by DCF. The parent then sought full payment of the placement by the Board of Education through a due process hearing. The hearing officer ruled, however, that "where predominately and significantly the child's problems grow out of the home situation rather than the school environment, the school cannot be taken to task." *Id.* at 1119. The district court reversed this decision. It held that the student's educational and non-educational needs were so intertwined that they could not be separated, and it ordered the Board to pay the full cost. *See North v. District of Columbia Board of Education*, 471 F. Supp. 136 (D. D.C. 1979). Upon review the Second Circuit affirmed and interpreted the duties of boards of education in such cases broadly: "If institutionalization is required due to a child's emotional problems, and the child's emotional problems prevent the child from making meaningful educational progress, the Act requires the state to pay for the costs of the placement." *Mrs. B. v. Milford Board of Education, supra*, at 1122. *But see Walczak v. Florida Union Free School District*, 142 F.3d 119 (2d Cir. 1998) (residential placement not necessary for FAPE). Also, where the placement is necessary for other than educational reasons, the school district is not financially responsible for the placement. *Dale M. v. Board of Education of Bradley-Bourbonnais High School District No. 307*, 237 F.3d 813 (7th Cir. 2001).

Given the unconverted needs of some children, the question is often not whether residential placement is required, but rather whether the school district is responsible for the residential placement because of educational needs. Under IDEA, boards of education are the "lead agency," which must assure that students receive an appropriate education, though it can coordinate services with other agencies. If a service is a necessary educational service, it must be provided by the school district without condition. If it is not, however, parent and student access to the service from the Department of Children and Families, the Department of Mental Health or other state agencies may be subject to budgetary restrictions, parent contribution or other restrictions. The lead agency status of school districts, therefore, has led to unseemly disputes among parents, school districts, and state agencies over whether a need is educational. To address this concern, interagency agreements have been proposed, but much work remains to be done. In any event, one court ruled in 2002 that the Department of Children and Families is not subject to constitutional and statutory claims that it has denied needed educational services. *Fetto v. Sergi et al.*, 181 F. Supp.2d 53 (D. Conn. 2002).

If the issue of residential placement is raised in a hearing, issues of reimbursement may arise. First, if the school district has offered an appropriate program, there is no need to determine whether the placement made by the parent was appropriate. Conn. St. Reg. § 10-76h-14(b). If the school district has not offered an appropriate program, however, the parent must establish that the placement made was appropriate in order to be reimbursed. *Id.* Second, if the unilateral placement made by the parents is appropriate, the fact that the appropriate program is not approved by the state educational agency is not a bar to reimbursement. *Florence County School District Four v. Carter*, 510 U.S. 7 (1993). *See also* Section A(4)(c) below, for discussion concerning limitations on reimbursement of parent costs for unilateral placement.

Given that residential placement is the most restrictive educational placement available, there is a heavy burden on the party claiming that such an extreme intervention is necessary for educational reasons. However, it is important that the members of the PPT remember that the PPT is only responsible for educational issues, not the various other legitimate needs that the student may have. When a PPT recommends a residential placement, it may be conclusively presumed that this recommendation is made for educational reasons, obligating the school district to pay for the residential placement. Consequently, the PPT should maintain its focus solely on educational issues. For example, it may be clear in a particular case that the home situation is untenable. However, the PPT should not initiate a residential placement simply because the child cannot or should not remain at home (unless, of course, there is an educational need for such a placement). When the PPT has concluded that a residential placement is not required for educational reasons, it should draft an IEP that can provide FAPE and be implemented in other than a residential setting. Then, if the parents or another agency places the child residentially, it will be clear that such placement was made for other than educational reasons and, as such, is not the responsibility of the school district.

Conversely, the PPT cannot refuse to consider a residential placement for educational reasons simply because of concerns over the home situation or because the school district is waiting for intervention from another agency, such as DCF. The PPT must determine whether a child's educational needs require a residential setting independent of other factors.

Finally, the law recognizes that there are situations in which such placements in residential settings will be made for other than educational reasons, such as a need for "medical, psychiatric or institutional care or services." Conn. Gen. Stat. § 10-76d(d). In such cases, the obligation of the local school district is to provide or pay for the reasonable costs of special education instruction. While the district is not obligated to pay for the residential placement in such a situation, it still must meet its responsibility to provide an appropriate educational program to students in such placements. Conn. Gen. Stat. § 10-76d(d).

3. Other related services

The list of possible related services set out in the regulations is long. Moreover, it is not exhaustive, and services not included on the list may be found to be required related services. Some general comments may be helpful in considering these issues.

First, the related service must be necessary to assist the child to benefit from special education instruction. If the service is not necessary, but rather would simply be of benefit, it will not be required.

Second, hearing officers and courts will often defer to the reasonable discretion of school officials in their determination of how best to provide an appropriate educational program. The issue will be whether needed services are being provided, not by whom. For example, if the planning and placement team determines that school personnel can appropriately provide needed counseling, there would be no justification for requiring the district to hire the student's private psychotherapist. Indeed, school personnel can provide a more integrated program.

Third, the student's progress will be a crucial factor in determining the nature and scope of related services. If a student is making appropriate progress toward the goals of the IEP, a request for additional related services will be less compelling than if the student is not making such progress under the current IEP.

4. Assistive technology

Finally, since 1990 school districts have been required under the IDEA to provide supportive services to children with disabilities. The statute now includes definitions of "assistive technology device" and "assistive technology service." 20 U.S.C. § 1412(a)(12)(B)(i). The implementing regulations make clear that school districts must make such devices and services available to children with disabilities when required as part of the child's special education, related services or supplementary aids and services. 34 C.F.R. § 300.308.

Several interpretive letters from the federal Office of Special Education Programs make clear that such decisions must be made on an individual basis, and access to such devices may be required both at school and at home. Indeed, in 2000 the Connecticut General Assembly amended the statutes specifically to authorize school districts "to loan, lease or transfer an assistive device for the use and benefit of a student with a disability to such student or the parent or guardian of such student . . . or to an agency providing educational, health or rehabilitative services." Conn. Gen. Stat. § 10-76y.

As with related services, the tough question is when is a requested device required? Certainly, for example, school districts can neither afford nor are they obligated to provide laptop computers to all students with disabilities. Rather, the determination must be made on an individual student basis. The PPT must ask whether the device is necessary for the student to receive FAPE. In making that determination, the PPT should be guided by the *Rowley* standard: school districts are responsible for devising an educational plan that will confer a reasonable educational benefit; they are not responsible for maximizing educational opportunities for children with disabilities.

If the device is essential for FAPE, it will be required unless some other way to address the need is available. If it is not, the PPT should not recommend the device, whether or not the PPT considers the assistive technology device to be beneficial. As with residential placement, a recommendation by the PPT will likely be described as a determination that the service is necessary, whether or not the PPT made that determination. It is important, therefore, for school personnel to include provision for assistive technology devices in the IEP only when the device is in fact an essential element of an appropriate educational program.

2. <u>Eligibility for special education services</u>

The rights of children eligible for special education services are dramatically different from the rights of other children, as discussed throughout this Chapter Five. Eligibility determinations, therefore, have great significance. The determination of eligibility is described below.

a. Child find

The IDEA covers all students with disabilities, and there is an affirmative duty to identify all such children who reside within the school district, the "local education agency," or LEA as the term is used in the IDEA. This obligation is called "child find," and school districts are required to identify children in need of special education services from birth on. The note to the implementing regulations explains that the age range for the identification process, or "child find," is greater than that for mandated services so that school districts will be aware of and plan for younger children who will require special education and related services. 34 C.F.R. § 300.300, note 3. In order to fulfill this "child find" obligation, once children with a suspected disability have been identified, the school district must evaluate these children, whether they attend public or private school. 34 C.F.R. § 300.125 (a). In Connecticut, local and regional school districts refer children younger than three to the "birth to three system." In turn, the birth-to-three system must notify school districts annually of the students in the program who will turn age three in the next year, subject to confidentiality requirements. Conn. Gen. Stat. § 17a-248d(e).

b. Specific disabilities

To be eligible for special education services, a student has to have one or more of the disabilities listed in the IDEA, and that disability must adversely affect the child's educational performance, resulting in the need for special education and related services. In contrast to Section 504, which contains a broad definition of disability, the IDEA is very specific and lists and defines the disabilities that will establish eligibility for services under IDEA:

- autism
- deaf-blindness
- deafness
- hearing impairment
- mental retardation (intellectual disability)
- multiple disabilities
- orthopedic impairment
- other health impairment
- serious emotional disturbance
- specific learning disability
- speech or language impairment
- traumatic brain injury
- visual impairment

20 U.S.C. § 1401(3)(A) and (B); 34 C.F.R. § 300.7. In 2003, the General Assembly amended the state definitions of "children requiring special education" simply to track the federal definitions of disability as set forth above, eliminating the separate disability definitions under state law. Conn. Gen. Stat. § 10-76a(5).

c. Age requirements

A free appropriate public education must be provided to all children between the ages of three and twenty-one who is not yet a graduate of high school. 34 C.F.R. § 300.300(a). A preschool child, defined as a child three to five years of age, requiring special education and related services is entitled to receive a free, appropriate public education on and after his or her third birthday, notwithstanding the fact that the third birthday occurs outside the regular school year. Conn. St. Reg., §§ 10-76d-1; 10-76a-1(q). Otherwise, local and regional school districts in Connecticut are obligated to provide special education and related services to each child five years of age and older until the child graduates high school with a regular diploma or through the end of the school year in which the child turns age twenty-one. *See* 34 C.F.R. § 300.122(a)(3)(ii). The State Department of Education has interpreted this to mean that a student who reaches age twenty-one after July 1 in a given year is entitled to receive special education services for the following school year. *Update # 32* (March 26, 2003). *See also* Conn. Gen. Stat. § 10-259.

Conn. Gen. Stat. § 10-76a(5) extends eligibility for services to children ages three to five under specified circumstances. The statute now includes children ages "three to five who are experiencing developmental delay that causes the child to require special education" in the definition of "children requiring special education." "Developmental delay" is defined as significant delay in one or more of the following areas: "(A) physical development; (B) communication development; (C) cognitive development; (D) social or emotional development; or (E) adaptive development . . . ." Conn. Gen. Stat. § 10-76a(6). *See* Series 2002-2003, Circular Letter C-28 (April 2, 2003).

d. Nature of the disability

There has been debate over whether there must be a threshold of benefit that the child must show to be eligible for special education and related services. The federal law simply states that "children with disabilities are those "who, by reason [of those disabilities] need special education and related services." 20 U.S.C. § 1401(a)(1)(B). This definition has been interpreted to provide that all students with disabilities have the right to an appropriate educational program.

This issue was raised and then laid to rest in a case in New Hampshire. In *Timothy W. v. Rochester, New Hampshire School District*, 874 F.2d 954 (1st Cir. 1989), *cert. denied* 493 U.S. 983 (1989). the court considered the case of a severely retarded child. The school district took the position that the child's many disabilities made it impossible for him to benefit from special education. In a decision that caused quite a stir, the district court agreed with the school district and dismissed the case filed on behalf of the student. However, the First Circuit Court of Appeals disagreed. Relying on both the legislative history and the specific wording of the law, the court affirmed a basic principle of special education, which is sometimes referred to as "zero reject." It held that all children, regardless of the nature and severity of their disabilities, are entitled to an appropriate educational program.

e. Children placed in private schools by their parents

The IDEA regulations provide that local school districts must make services available to students placed in private schools by their parents. The scope of this obligation, however, was unclear, especially for students in sectarian schools. It was not clear whether these students were entitled to an appropriate special education program. Moreover, it was not clear whether providing services to students at sectarian schools would violate the First Amendment prohibition against state subsidy of religious activity. Recent court decisions and the provisions of IDEA as revised in 1997 (and implementing regulations), however, have clarified this issue. School districts can provide services on the site of a sectarian school, but the obligation to provide services is limited to (1) consultation with the private schools to assure that private school students with disabilities have a meaningful opportunity to participate in the proportionate share of the federal Part B funds, and (2) establishment of an individual services plan for those students who will receive services funded by the Part B funds. *See* discussion at Section A(4)(c)(1) below.

f. Children in charter schools and magnet schools

Under the IDEA, children enrolled in public charter schools retain all their rights to an appropriate educational program. 34 C.F.R. § 300.312; *Response to Gloeckler*, 22 IDELR ¶ 222 (2000). Under state law, a student attending a local charter school is considered to be enrolled in the school district where the student resides, and is entitled to special education services as any other enrolled student. A student attending a state charter school is not considered to be enrolled in the school district where he resides, but the statutes impose similar obligations on the responsible school district. That district must hold a PPT meeting, must invite representatives from the charter school, and must pay the difference between the amount received by the charter school and the reasonable cost of special education instruction on a quarterly basis. The charter school must assure that the student receives the services set out in the IEP planned by the responsible school district, either by the charter school or by the school district in which the student resides. Conn. Gen. Stat. § 10-66ee.

Similarly, children with special needs who are enrolled in interdistrict magnet schools retain their right to a free, appropriate public education. Conn. Gen. Stat. § 10-264l(h) provides that the district in which the student resides must hold the PPT meeting to plan the program for the child, and that district must also pay the interdistrict magnet school the difference between the reasonable costs of educating the student and the amounts otherwise received by the magnet school for educating the student. The interdistrict magnet school, however, has the responsibility for ensuring that the students receives the services set out in the student's IEP. *Id.*

These requirements can be very expensive, since there is no provision for consolidating special education services, as is the case for programs within the district schools. Conversely, some of the unique features of the charter school or magnet school (*e.g.*, small class sizes) may make it unnecessary to provide the same level of support to the student that would be required in the public schools. The key issue is that the child must receive an appropriate educational program, which by definition requires individual consideration of the child's needs for special education and related services.

g. Gifted and talented students

In Connecticut, the definition of "children requiring special education" includes not only children with disabilities, but also students who are gifted or talented, *i.e.* children who have "extraordinary learning ability or outstanding talent in the creative arts, the development of which requires programs or services beyond the level of those ordinarily provided in regular school programs but which may be provided through special education as part of the public school program." Conn. Gen. Stat. § 10-76a(5). Since children requiring special education must be identified, procedures must be in place for the identification of gifted and talented children. Parents can even challenge a decision not to identify a student as gifted or talented through a due process hearing. However, school districts may, but are not required to, provide special education to the gifted and talented students. Conn. Gen. Stat. § 10-76d(b). When parents challenged this distinction on equal protection grounds, the Connecticut Supreme Court upheld this law. *Broadley v. Meriden Board of Education*, 229 Conn. 1 (1994).

h. Children coming from other districts and states

It should be noted that children who have previously been identified by other school districts as in need of special education have rights as well. If the child comes to the district from another Connecticut school district, his/her IEP is binding and is thus a "stay-put" placement. If a child comes from out of state, however, the receiving district must consider the child as an initial referral and is thus permitted to conduct its own evaluation and make its own determination as to eligibility, program and placement. *Letter of Clarification* from Thomas Hehir dated December 6, 1995 (OSEP 96-5).

3. <u>The PPT/IEP team process</u>

The procedures contained in the IDEA are designed to assure that the process of planning an IEP includes involvement of appropriate professionals, active participation of the parents, and access to necessary evaluation information. The IDEA and the implementing regulations include the following requirements.

a. Parent participation

Since its inception in 1975 IDEA has provided for parent participation in the planning process, and the 1997 amendments provide for even greater participation by parents in the special education of their children with disabilities. The regulations define a parent as including the natural or adoptive parents, guardians, persons acting as parents (such as grandparents) and surrogate parents. 34 C.F.R. § 300.20. The right of parents to participate in planning the educational program for their children is not affected by divorce or the determination of the primary custodial parent, unless the divorce decree specifically limits a parent's rights in this respect. If a divorce decree limits a parent's right to participate in decisions concerning the education of his/her child, however, he/she has no standing to initiate a due process hearing. *Taylor v. Vermont Department of Education*, 313 F.3d 768 (2d Cir. 2004).

1. Right of consent

A basic right of parents is to consent to evaluation and placement of their child in special education. The regulations detail the conditions under which parent consent may be obtained. The parent must be fully informed "of all information relevant to the activity for which consent is sought, in his or her native language, or other mode of communication," and the parent must understand that the granting of consent is voluntary and may be withdrawn at any time. The consent granted by the parent must describe the activity proposed and identify the records to be released, if any, and to whom. 34 C.F.R. § 300.500(b).

IDEA requires parent consent in various circumstances. Parents must provide written consent to the initial evaluation of their child. Parents must provide written consent to the initial provision of special education and related services to their child. Parent consent is now also required for reevaluation, subject to the conditions set out in the regulations (discussed at Section A(3)(d)). 34 C.F.R. § 300.505. Finally, under state law, written parent consent is required to place a child requiring special education in a private facility. Conn. St. Reg., § 10-76d-8.

Given human nature and the potential for disagreement over whether special education services are necessary, parents do on occasion refuse to consent to evaluation or placement in special education programs. The federal regulations authorize school districts to initiate due process proceedings to override parent refusal to give consent for evaluation or reevaluation, 34 C.F.R. § 300.505(b). OSEP has taken the position that school districts may not initiate due process hearings to override parent consent to special education services, notwithstanding the broad language in 34 C.F.R. § 300.507(a). *Letter to Cox*, 36 IDELR 66 (OSEP 2001); *Letter to Manasevit*, 41 IDELR 36 (OSEP 2003). This position appears to fly in the face of the child's substantive right to an appropriate program. Nonetheless, Conn. Gen. Stat. § 10-76h(a) was amended in 2003 to provide that a hearing officer may override a parent's refusal to give consent only in situations in which the parent has refused consent for initial evaluation or has already given consent to special education services and now refuses consent for reevaluation or private placement. In any event, the statute also provides that, if the parent appeals any such decision, the student shall not be evaluated or placed until that appeal is concluded. Conn. Gen. Stat. § 10-76h(d)(3).

On occasion, a parent will revoke consent for special education services and demand that such services terminate. Such revocation of consent, however, does not require that result. The regulations permit parents to revoke consent at any time, but they specify that such revocation is not retroactive, and it does not negate an action that was taken after consent was granted and before it was revoked. 34 C.F.R. § 300.500(b)(iii)(B). If the child has already been placed in special education when consent is revoked, a PPT should be convened to review relevant information and determine the child's status. If school personnel agree with the parent to terminate services, the PPT should make that decision and the child will no longer be subject to the provisions of IDEA. If school personnel believe that the child should continue to receive special education, however, the child remains in his or her special education program, and the revocation of consent operates as a request for due process. *J.J. Garcia v. Ridgefield Board of Education*, 1986-1987 E.H.L.R. Dec. 558:152 (D. Conn. 1986).

2. Attendance at PPT meetings

A key role for parents, of course, is participation in the PPT/IEP team process, and parents are expressly included in the list of members of the IEP team. 34 C.F.R. § 300.344(a); 20 U.S.C. § 1414(d)(1). The law imposes upon school districts an affirmative duty to attempt to convince parents to participate. The law is clear that a district may proceed with writing the IEP for a child with disabilities even if the parent chooses not to attend. A school district may go forward with the PPT without the parent in attendance, however, only if it "is unable to convince the parents that they should attend." In such situations, the regulations further provide that the school district must have records of efforts to arrange a mutually agreed-on time and place for the PPT. Examples of such efforts listed are detailed records of telephone calls made or attempted, and the results of those calls, copies of correspondence sent to parents and responses, if any. The regulation even mentions "detailed records of visits made to the parent's home or place of employment and the results of those visits." 34 C.F.R. § 300.345(d). The law, however, permits parents to participate in placement decisions without actually attending the PPT meeting, including through individual or conference telephone calls or even video conferencing. 34 C.F.R. § 300.501(c)(3).

3. Other parent rights

Since IDEA was first written, it has provided parents with a number of rights to assist them to participate effectively at the PPT. They have had the right to examine all relevant records concerning identification, evaluation and educational placement of the child. 34 C.F.R. § 300.501(a). Parents have also had the right to obtain an independent educational evaluation, along with information, if requested, about where to obtain such an independent evaluation, as discussed below. 34 C.F.R. § 300.502.

The law has also provided that parents have the right to notice, effectively informing them (in their native language, if necessary) of (1) all of the procedural safeguards available under IDEA, (2) any proposal or refusal to initiate or change a child's identification, evaluation, or educational placement, (3) the evaluation procedures and instruments used by the district as a basis for its proposal or refusal to initiate or change a child's identification, evaluation, or educational placement, and (4) any other factors relevant to the district's proposal or refusal to initiate or change a child's identification, evaluation or placement. 34 C.F.R. § 300.503(b).

Parents of children with disabilities are to be informed of their child's progress at least as often as the parents of children who are not disabled. 20 U.S.C. § 1414(d)(1). Also, as discussed in Section A(3)(d), parents must give consent to reevaluation.

IDEA imposes a number of detailed procedural obligations on school districts. The State and local and regional school districts are to adopt procedures to guarantee procedural safeguards for children with disabilities and their parents. 34 C.F.R. § 300.500(a). Among the required procedures are the following:

- An opportunity to review all records, not just "relevant" records.
- Procedures to protect the rights of children when their parents are unknown or unavailable.
- Prior written notice when the district proposes to initiate or change, or refuses to initiate or change, the child's identification, evaluation or educational placement, or the provision of a free appropriate public education.
- Procedures to assure that such notice is in the native language of the parents unless it is clearly not feasible to do so.
- An opportunity for mediation.
- An opportunity to "present complaints," *i.e.* to request a due process hearing over the identification, evaluation, educational placement or provision of FAPE to the child.
- Procedures to require the parents requesting a due process hearing (or the child's attorney) to provide a (confidential) notice to the school district that includes: the name, address and school attended by the child with a disability; a description of the nature of the problem of the child relating to a proposed initiation or change in identification, evaluation, educational placement or FAPE provided to the child; and a proposed resolution of the problem to the extent known and available to parents at the time.
- Procedures to require the State to develop a model form to assist parents in "filing a complaint," *i.e.* requesting a due process hearing.

In addition, IDEA imposes specific requirements for the prior written notice to parents that is required when the district proposes to initiate or change, or refuses to initiate or change, the child's identification, evaluation or educational placement, or the provision of a free appropriate public education. This notice must include the following provisions:

- a description of the action proposed or refused by the district;
- an explanation of why the district proposes or refuses to take the action;
- a description of any other options that the district considered and the reasons why the district rejected those options;
- a description of each evaluation procedure, test, record or report the district used in its decision;
- a description of any other factors that are relevant to the district's decision;
- a statement that parents have procedural protections and the means by which parents can obtain a description of such protections;
- sources for parents to contact to obtain assistance in understanding their rights.

34 C.F.R. § 300.503.

Under IDEA, parents must receive written notification of their rights with the notification of each meeting of the PPT. *See also* Conn. Gen. Stat. § 10-76d(a)(8). Parents must also receive a copy of this notification whenever a student is referred for evaluation or reevaluation, or if parents request a due process hearing. 34 C.F.R. § 300.504. IDEA is highly prescriptive as to the content of such a notification of rights. It provides that the notice of procedural safeguards must set forth the parents' rights regarding the following:

- independent educational evaluations;
- prior written notice;
- parental consent;
- access to educational records;
- opportunity to present complaints;
- the child's placement during the pendency of due process hearings;
- procedures for students who are subject to placement in an interim alternative educational setting;
- requirements for unilateral placement by parents of children in private schools at public expense;
- mediation;
- due process hearings, including the requirement for disclosure of evaluation results and recommendations.

34 C.F.R. § 300.504. To comply with these detailed requirements, school districts are required to use the notification of rights forms that the State Department of Education has prepared.

b. Surrogate parents

IDEA makes special provision for assuring that children with disabilities have representation by a "parent" figure, even if the actual parents are not available. States must make provision for the appointment of a surrogate parent if no parent can be identified and the state or the school district cannot discover the whereabouts of the parents. 34 C.F.R. § 300.515. The law provides that the surrogate parent may not be an employee of the state or school district, and clarifies that payment for fulfilling this responsibility does not create employee status. *Id.* State statute provides for the appointment of surrogate parents by the Commissioner of Education. Conn. Gen. Stat. § 10-94f *et seq.* In 2000, the statutory responsibilities of surrogate parents were expanded; now surrogate parents are empowered to participate in the planning process under Section 504 if the child they are representing is exited from special education but is provided services pursuant to Section 504. Conn. Gen. Stat. § 10-94f, Conn. Gen. Stat. § 10-94g. Also, school districts are now obligated to notify surrogate parents of any disciplinary action taken with respect to the children they represent. Conn. Gen. Stat. § 10-233e.

c. PPT/IEP team requirements

Under IDEA, the IEP team is responsible for determining the program and placement of children with disabilities. Under Connecticut law, the PPT is defined somewhat differently, and it has somewhat broader responsibilities, as described below. In *Rowley*, the United States Supreme Court declared that the procedural requirements of IDEA are the very heart of the law. The IEP team and the PPT, respectively, therefore, have important responsibilities for complying with the procedural requirements of IDEA.

1. PPT/IEP team membership

Under state law, the planning and placement team (or PPT) is responsible for making decisions concerning the educational programs for children with disabilities. The specific requirements for the PPT under state law are somewhat different than those for the IEP team. Under Connecticut law, the PPT must include representatives of the teaching, administrative and pupil personnel staffs. Conn. St. Reg. § 10-76a-1(p). The PPT has all of the responsibilities of the IEP team under the IDEA. In addition, the PPT is responsible for making eligibility determinations and placement decisions. Under IDEA, by contrast, decisions as to eligibility are to be made by a qualified team of professionals and the parent(s), and decisions as to placement are to be made by a group of persons, including the parent(s), and other persons who are knowledgeable of the child, the evaluation data and placement options.

Given the distinction between the PPT under state law and the IEP team under federal law, school districts must first ensure that they convene a proper PPT to make decisions concerning children with disabilities. Then, when the action under consideration requires the convening of the IEP team under the IDEA, the additional personnel required to constitute the IEP team must also participate in the meeting. Under federal law, the IEP team is responsible for evaluations (along with other qualified individuals), the development, revision and review of the IEP, the determination of the any interim alternative educational setting, behavioral assessment, and manifestation determinations.

IDEA specifies who should attend IEP team meetings. In addition to including the parents of the child with a disability in the membership of the IEP team, the law requires that the IEP team include at least one regular education teacher of the child (if the child is, or may be, participating in the regular education environment). The law also requires that the regular education teacher, to the extent appropriate, participate in the development of the IEP, including the determination of appropriate positive behavioral interventions and strategies and the determination of supplementary aids and services, program modifications and support for school personnel. 34 C.F.R. § 300.346(d). The regular education teacher, however, need not participate in the entire IEP team meeting.

The Act further specifies that the IEP team should also include the following personnel:

- at least one special education teacher (or where appropriate at least one special education provider of such child);
- an educator who is qualified to provide or supervise the provision of a special education program who is knowledgeable about the general curriculum and is

knowledgeable about the availability of resources of the district;

- an individual (who may be one of the individuals above) who can interpret the educational implications of evaluation results;
- at the discretion of the district or the parent, other individuals who have knowledge or special expertise regarding the child, including related services personnel as appropriate; and
- whenever appropriate, the child with a disability.

34 C.F.R. § 300.344.

As to the last requirement, it is noteworthy that IDEA includes provisions concerning the participation of the child with disabilities in educational planning. When a student reaches majority age (eighteen in Connecticut), a state may provide that the rights accorded parents under IDEA transfer to the student, provided that in such cases any required notification must be sent to the parents as well as to the student. 34 C.F.R. § 300.517. *See* Conn. State Regulations, § 10-76a-1.

2. State requirements for the PPT

As outlined above, Connecticut school districts convening the IEP team as defined by IDEA must also meet the PPT membership requirements. In Connecticut, the PPT is also responsible for making eligibility determinations and for making placement decisions.

As amended in 1995, Conn. Gen. Stat. § 10-76h used to provide that any issue to be presented in a special education due process hearing must first be raised at a PPT meeting. This requirement, however, was eliminated in 2003 at the insistence of the United States Department of Education, notwithstanding a court ruling that the requirement supplemented the requirements of IDEA and thus was not preempted by federal law. *Lillbask v. Sergi*, 117 F. Supp.2d 182 (D. Conn. 2000). Accordingly, a parent (or school district) can now bring a matter to hearing without first discussing it at a PPT meeting.

A related question is whether and when a school district can refuse a parent request for a PPT meeting. The United States Department of Education has advised that a board of education "should grant any reasonable request for such a meeting." 34 C.F.R. § 300, Appendix C,

Question 11 (1996). Conversely, a school district need not grant requests for PPT meetings that are not reasonable. *Lillbask v. Sergi*, 117 F. Supp.2d 182 (D. Conn. 2000) (no need to conduct further PPT meetings when there had been a large number of meetings in previous six months and all issues had been discussed and investigated).

State law also sets out requirements as to notice of PPT meetings. Conn. Gen. Stat. § 10-76d(8) requires that parents must receive notification in writing of a PPT meeting at least five days in advance. In 1995, this notification requirement was expanded; now, in addition to parents or guardians, such notice is to be provided to students themselves, if emancipated or eighteen years of age or older, and to surrogate parents. Second, school districts must provide the same group five days advance notice in writing of any proposed change of the student's identification, evaluation or educational placement, or any proposed change in the provision of a free appropriate public education to the student. Third, since 1995 state law has required that school districts must inform parents, guardians, students (if emancipated or over eighteen years old), or surrogate parents of the laws relating to special education and their rights under those laws at every PPT meeting, similar to the requirement in IDEA. State law further requires, however, that the school district is obligated to mail such information to the parents (or person acting as the parent), if they do not attend the PPT meeting.

Compliance with this notification requirement is especially important for two reasons. Procedural violations can lead to the award of attorney's fees against the district, as discussed below. In addition, in Connecticut proper notification permits school districts to assert a statute of limitations against a special education claim. In 1995, Conn. Gen. Stat. § 10-76h(a)(3) was amended to establish for the first time a clear statute of limitations (the period within which a legal claim can be brought) of two years. This limitation applies, however, only from the time the parents have been given notice of procedural safeguards, including notice of the statute of limitations. Conn. Stat. Reg. § 10-76h-4. The federal courts have applied this statute to rule that certain special education claims are time-barred. *Mr. and Mrs. D. v. Southington Board of Education*, 119 F. Supp.2d 105 (D. Conn. 2000).

As described in Chapter One, Section F(7), school personnel are prohibited from recommending psychotropic medication for students whenever they are fulfilling their professional responsibilities. The PPT process, however, is where such a recommendation is most likely to be made.

Conn. Gen. Stat. § 10-212b now clarifies that the planning and placement team may recommend a medical evaluation as part of an initial evaluation or reevaluation, as needed to determine a child's eligibility for special education and related services, or to determine the child's educational needs. *Id. See* Chapter One, Section F(7).

d. Development of the IEP

IDEA specifies that the IEP team must consider specific information in developing the IEP.

1. Evaluations

After a child is referred, the PPT is obligated to conduct a full and individual evaluation for each child being considered for eligibility under the IDEA. The purpose of the evaluation is to determine whether the child qualifies under the IDEA, and what are the needs of the child.

Several provisions of the federal regulations deal with the duty of the PPT to consider such information. First, prior to initial placement in a special education program, the district is obligated to assure that "a full and individual evaluation of the student's educational needs [is] conducted." 34 C.F.R. § 300.531.

The regulations also provide that evaluation procedures must be selected and administered so as best to ensure that the test results accurately reflect the child's abilities, rather than his or her disabilities. Moreover, evaluation is to be done by a multi-disciplinary team, including at least one teacher or other specialist with knowledge in the area of the suspected disability. Also, to assure that reliable information is utilized, no single procedure is to be used as the sole criterion for determining an appropriate educational program for the child. 34 C.F.R. § 300.532.

In conducting evaluations, the PPT must consider information provided by the parent; information that will allow the child to participate in the general curriculum, and current classroom-based assessments and observations. Based on this information, the PPT may make the following determinations, or it may decide that additional information is required to make these decisions:

- whether the child has a disability (or in the case of reevaluation continues to have a disability),

- what are the current levels of performance and educational needs of the child,
- whether the child needs special education and related services (or in the case of an reevaluation whether the child continues to need such services), or
- whether any addition or modifications to the special education and related services are necessary to enable the child to meet the measurable annual goals set out in the IEP, and to participate, as appropriate, in the general curriculum.

34 C.F.R. § 300.533.

Under IDEA, the PPT must make a determination on continuing eligibility for special education services at least once every three years. In making that determination, the PPT must affirmatively consider whether and what additional assessments may be appropriate. Since 1997, the PPT has had the right to forego reevaluation if its members do not believe that additional evaluation information is necessary to plan for a child's program. Reevaluation is required, however, if requested by the parent or the teacher. 34 C.F.R. § 300.536.

School districts are obligated to seek written parent consent prior to any reevaluation conducted of a child with disabilities. If parents refuse to provide consent for reevaluation, the district may seek an order from a hearing officer authorizing the reevaluation. If the district takes reasonable steps to obtain such consent and the parents do not respond, however, the district can proceed with the reevaluation. 34 C.F.R. § 300.505.

There are special rules for evaluating students suspected of specific learning disabilities. The multi-disciplinary evaluation team must include the child's regular teacher or another regular teacher qualified to teach a student of his or her age, as well as a person qualified to conduct individual diagnostic examinations. At least one member of the team other than the child's regular teacher must observe the child's academic performance in the regular classroom setting, and the team is to prepare a written report of the results of the evaluation. 34 C.F.R. §§ 300.540-543.

2. Independent educational evaluations

In addition to the requirements that the school district conduct appropriate evaluations of children with disabilities, the regulations provide that parents have the right to obtain an independent educational evaluation at the expense of the school district under certain circumstances. 34 C.F.R. § 300.502. The school district is even required to provide parents, upon request, with information concerning where an independent evaluation can be obtained, and what criteria, if any, the district has for such evaluations (*e.g.* qualifications of the examiner). Most parents recognize that a truly independent evaluator trusted by both district and parents may provide information that both parties can best use in the planning process. However, under the regulations, any qualified examiner other than an employee of the school district is considered "independent." *Id.* Technically, the child's private therapist over the last ten years fits within this definition.

The right to obtain an independent evaluation arises if the parent disagrees with an evaluation conducted by the school district. Implicit in this provision is the fact that the local school district must have an opportunity to conduct its own evaluation first, since the parent cannot "disagree" until the district conducts the necessary evaluations. In any event, the PPT is obligated to consider the results of any such "independent" evaluation the parents obtain.

The preferred approach, of course, is for the parents and the school district to work together, identify situations where independent evaluation is necessary, and mutually select the evaluator. In such cases, districts will bear the expense of such evaluations. However, there can be disputes over whether an independent evaluation is necessary. When a parent requests an independent evaluation, the school district must "without unnecessary delay" either initiate a due process hearing to show that its evaluation is appropriate or ensure that an independent evaluation is provided. If the hearing officer decides that the district's evaluation is appropriate, the cost of the independent evaluation will be at parent expense. However, if the hearing officer decides that the school district evaluation is not appropriate, the school district will be responsible for the cost of the independent evaluation. 34 C.F.R. § 300.502.

3. Other factors that must be considered

IDEA requires that the IEP team consider specific factors in developing the IEP. 34 C.F.R. § 300.346. The IEP team must consider the strengths of the child and the concerns of the parents for enhancing the education of their child, as well as the results of the evaluation information. In addition, the IEP team must consider the following special factors:

Behavior problems. If a child's behavior impedes his or her learning or that of others, the PPT must consider, where appropriate, strategies, including positive behavioral interventions, strategies and supports to address that behavior.

Limited English language proficiency. The PPT must consider the language needs of such children.

Blind or visually impaired children. The PPT must provide for instruction in Braille and use of Braille unless the PPT determines after an evaluation of the child's writing and reading skills that instruction in and use of Braille is not appropriate for the child.

Communication needs. The PPT must consider the communication needs of the child, and for deaf or hard of hearing children, it must consider opportunities for direct communication with peers and professional personnel in the child's preferred language and communication mode, including direct instruction in that language and communication mode.

Assistive technology. The PPT must consider whether the child needs assistive technology devices and services.

34 C.F.R. § 300.346(a)(2). If the IEP team determines that a child needs a particular device or service (including an intervention, accommodation, or other program modification) in order to receive FAPE after considering the special factors above, it must include a statement to that effect in the IEP.

IDEA also emphasizes participation in athletics and extracurricular activities. The regulations specifically provide that children with disabilities must participate in the regular physical education program with their non-disabled peers unless they are placed in a separate school or the child needs specifically prescribed physical education, as set out in the IEP. 34 C.F.R. § 300.307. Also, as discussed below, each IEP must include a statement of the program modifications or supports for school personnel that will be provided for the child to participate in extracurricular and other non-academic activities. More generally, the regulations specifically require that school districts must assure that children with disabilities participate to the maximum extent appropriate with their non-disabled peers in nonacademic and extracurricular services and activities including meals, recess periods, and other activities such as athletics, recreational activities, and special interest groups or clubs. 34 C.F.R. § 300.553; 34 C.F.R. § 300.306. These provisions require that the PPT consider ways to assure participation in such activities. The district need not, however, fundamentally alter the nature of an activity, such as competitive team sports.

e. Required elements of the IEP

IDEA sets out very specific requirements concerning the content of the IEP. Each child with a disability must have an IEP in place at the beginning of each school year. The IEP is the document that sets out the specific services and modifications that will be made for a child with disabilities. From the inception of IDEA in 1975, it has required that the IEP include information concerning present level of functioning, long term goals reviewed at least annually, short-term objectives, and the services and service providers (by category, not name) who will implement the IEP. New required elements have been added over the years.

The detailed requirements for IEP are set out in 34 C.F.R. § 300.347 and include the following components:

1. a statement of the child's present level of functioning. This statement must address how the child's disability affects the child's involvement and progress in the general curriculum. For preschool children, this means how the disability affects the child's participation in appropriate activities.

2. a statement of measurable annual goals, including benchmarks or short-term objectives to meet the child's educational needs to enable the child to be involved in and progress in the general curriculum, or for preschoolers, to participate in appropriate activities.

3. a statement of special education and related services to be provided to the child. This statement must include the supplementary aids and services to be provided to the child, as well as a statement of the program modifications or supports for school personnel that will be provided for the child

- to advance appropriately toward his/her annual goals,
- to be involved and progress in the general curriculum,
- to participate in extracurricular and other non-academic activities,

- to be educated and participate in such activities with other children with disabilities and nondisabled children.

4. an explanation of the extent, if any, to which the child will not participate with nondisabled children in the regular class and other school activities.

5. a statement of the individual modifications in the administration of state or district-wide assessments of student achievement, or, if the PPT determines that such participation is not appropriate, the reason why and the way in which the student will be assessed.

6. a statement of the projected date when special education services will commence, and the anticipated frequency, location and duration of special education services.

7. beginning at age 14, and updated annually, a statement of transition service needs of the child under the applicable components of the IEP that focus on the child's courses of study, such as participation in advanced placement courses or a vocational education program; beginning at age 16 (or younger if determined appropriate by the IEP team), a statement of needed transition services for the child, including, when appropriate, a statement of the interagency responsibilities or any needed linkages; beginning at least one year before the child reaches the age of 18, a statement that the child has been informed of his or her rights under the IDEA, if any, that will transfer to the child upon reaching age 18.

8. a statement of how the child's progress toward annual goals will be measured, and how the child's parents will be regularly informed (by means such as periodic report cards) at least as frequently as parents of nondisabled children are informed of their child's progress toward the annual goals of the IEP, and the extent to which that progress is sufficient to enable the child to achieve the goals by the end of the year.

f. Review of the IEP

IDEA also sets out rules concerning review and revision of the IEP. 34 C.F.R. § 300.346(b). The IEP team (again specifically including the regular education teacher) is to review the IEP periodically, but not less than annually, to determine whether the annual goals for the child are being achieved. Under the new IDEA, the IEP is to be revised as appropriate to address:

- any lack of expected progress toward the annual goals;
- any lack of expected progress in the general curriculum;
- the results of any reevaluation;
- information about the child provided to or by the parents;
- transition objectives.

Also, if another agency does not provide the transition services identified in the IEP, the IEP team must reconvene and identify alternative strategies to meet the transition objectives.

4. Placement issues

At the end of the IEP process, the PPT, with the participation of the parent, will recommend the specific placement for the child to receive his or her special education program. 34 C.F.R. § 300.501(c). This recommendation involves a number of considerations, including compliance with the requirement that the placement be in the least restrictive environment. Also, parents will not always agree with the PPT recommendation, and on occasion will engage in self-help by making a unilateral placement. IDEA includes specific provisions to address (and reduce the incidence of) unilateral private placements by parents.

a. General principles

The placement decision comes at the end of the planning process. It is imperative that the placement decision be made only after the team has identified the child's educational needs and has identified the services necessary to address those needs. At that point, the PPT with the parent must determine whether the appropriate program of services can be provided in the regular classroom setting, with modifications and supports if necessary. If not, the PPT and parent must determine to what extent education can be provided with non-disabled peers. By following this procedure, the PPT and parent will help assure that it meets its obligation to provide a free appropriate public education to each child with disabilities in the least restrictive environment, as discussed below.

In making placement decisions, the PPT and the parent must also keep in mind the fact that its jurisdiction is limited to educational matters.

Children are presented to the PPT with a variety of educational and personal needs. The PPT members may believe that a child is receiving an appropriate educational program, but that difficulties with family or otherwise in his or her personal life would warrant residential placement. It is important that any recommendations or related discussion to that effect take place outside the PPT meeting. The role of the PPT is to plan an appropriate educational program. Given that the PPT is responsible for educational planning, when PPT members raise issues of residential placement at the PPT, it will be presumed that the recommendation is made for educational reasons. If such a placement is made for educational reasons, the board of education is obligated to fund the placement. 34 C.F.R. § 300.302. *See* discussion at Section A(1)(b)(2) above.

b. Least restrictive environment

A core concept in determining an appropriate educational program is the requirement that children with disabilities be educated to the maximum extent appropriate with their non-disabled peers. The IDEA enforces this obligation by requiring that states receiving federal funds for special education establish:

> procedures to assure that, to the maximum extent appropriate, children with disabilities, including children in public or private institutions or other care facilities, are educated with children who are not disabled, and that special classes, separate schooling, or other removal of children with disabilities from the regular education environment occurs only when the nature or severity of the disability is such that education in regular classes with the use of supplementary aids and services cannot be achieved satisfactorily.

20 U.S.C. § 1412; 34 C.F.R. § 300.550. This requirement is often referred to as the "mainstreaming" or "least restrictive environment" requirement of the IDEA, though neither term appears in the law. This requirement reflects a concern that Congress had in adopting the original law in 1975. In the preface to the Education for All Handicapped Children Act, Congress announced its finding that some one million of the children with disabilities were excluded entirely from the public school system and would not go through the educational process with their peers. 20 U.S.C. § 1400. Consequently, a major thrust of the federal special education law has been

and remains to assure that children with disabilities are educated in the least restrictive environment.

The issue of educating children with disabilities in the regular education setting is often a source of controversy and litigation. Some advocates demand that all children, regardless of the nature or severity of their disability, be educated in the regular classroom. Their demand of "inclusion" raises questions of educational methodology. However, in contrast to other such questions where there will be deference to the expertise of the educators, here the law creates a clear presumption in favor of education in the regular education environment.

Under the implementing regulations, it is clear that the burden for removing a child from the regular education environment rests with the school district. The regulations repeat the statutory presumption that education be provided to children with disabilities in the regular classroom setting, and that separate education may be provided "only when the nature or severity of the disability is such that education in regular classes with the use of supplementary aids and services cannot be achieved satisfactorily." 34 C.F.R. § 300.550. This provision requires that the PPT and the parent consider whether and how a child with disabilities can be educated in the regular education setting. It must consider whether the assistance of an aide, modified instruction, a behavior plan or any of a number of educational strategies could be employed to provide a satisfactory education in the regular education setting.

Two leading cases concerning "least restrictive environment" provide a conceptual framework for meeting this obligation. *Daniel R.R. v. State Board of Education*, 874 F.2d 1036 (5th Cir. 1989) and *Oberti v. Clementon School District*, 995 F.2d 1204 (3d Cir. 1993). The courts reached opposite conclusions in these cases—in *Daniel R.R.*, the court held that the district had appropriately decided to educate the student in a separate setting, and in *Oberti*, the court held that the district had not. *See also A.S. v. Norwalk Board of Education*, 183 F. Supp.2d 534 (D. Conn. 2002) (court affirms hearing officer decision requiring regular classroom placement). In any event, in determining the setting in which to provide an educational program, the PPT and the parent should consider the following four factors.

- Balancing of benefits

First, in considering a regular education versus special education placement, the PPT and parent must balance the benefits to the student in each setting. The PPT and parent may well take into account the nature and scope of the educational benefit that the child will receive in each setting. If, for example, a child would not receive educational benefit in a regular education setting, that fact would weigh heavily in favor of a special education placement. However, it is clear that the PPT and parent may not focus purely on academic benefit. For some children with disabilities, benefits may include communication, modeling of behaviors, socialization, issues of self-esteem and the like, all benefits that would be important factors for the child's progress toward his or her IEP goals.

- Disruption

The PPT must also consider whether the placement would be disruptive of the educational activities of the class. There are two types of disruption for the PPT and parent to consider.

First, a student may be disruptive because his or her social skills are deficient and he or she acts out in a way that disrupts the class. That is, of course, an important consideration. However, the potential for such disruption may not automatically result in exclusion from the regular education classroom, because supplementary aids or services may eliminate the disruptive behaviors. Such services may include, for example, the intervention of a behavioral specialist. In *Oberti*, for example, the court found that the district's efforts to maintain Rafael Oberti in the regular education classroom had been inadequate, and school officials, therefore, were unable to justify Rafael's exclusion from the regular education classroom on the basis of disruption. *See also Warton v. New Fairfield Board of Education*, 37 IDELR 281 (D. Conn. 2002) (evidence of disruption of classroom as found by the hearing officer not persuasive because student had not received appropriate supportive services).

Second, a student may be disruptive simply by virtue of the amount of attention the student requires of the teacher. In *Daniel R.R.*, the court noted that the extensive modifications necessary for the student monopolized the teacher's and/or the aide's time, depriving the other students of the benefits of their services, making it inappropriate to maintain the child full-time in that classroom.

- Efforts to try less restrictive options

Another consideration for the PPT and parent are the results of any efforts to attempt less restrictive options. The law specifies that a separate class setting may be appropriate only when a regular classroom placement cannot be achieved "satisfactorily" with the use of supplementary aids and services. It may not be practical in some cases to "experiment" with a regular education placement against great odds of success. However, in the absence of actual experience with the student, the PPT and parent should be prepared to explain the basis on which it concluded that a regular education placement could not be achieved satisfactorily, even with supplementary aids and services. Failure to work hard to support the child in the regular education classroom, and to document those efforts, can result in a finding that a separate educational setting is not warranted. *See Oberti v. Clementon School District*, 995 F.2d 1204 (3d Cir. 1993).

- Cost

Within very broad parameters the PPT and parent may consider the cost of any supplementary aids or services required to support a child in the regular education setting. Certainly, if there are alternatives means of providing an appropriate educational program, the PPT and parent can choose the less expensive approach. The issue of cost, however, cannot excuse a failure to provide an appropriate program in the least restrictive environment.

Finally, unrelated to these four factors, the Second Circuit recently issued two decisions that deal with the least restrictive environment requirements. First, the court also ruled that the extent of mainstreaming available was an appropriate consideration for a hearing officer considering a private placement made by a parent. *M.S. ex rel. S.S. v. Board of Education of the City School District of the City of Yonkers*, 231 F.3d 96 (2d Cir. 2000), *cert. denied* 532 U.S. 942 (2001). Second, it ruled that the least restrictive environment requirement of IDEA does not apply to private schools. A public school district that lacked a high school contracted with a private academy to provide an education to a student with a disability, but the academy refused to implement the "mainstreaming" provision in the student's IEP. The court held that the academy was not subject to the IDEA, including the least restrictive environment provision. Moreover, its decision not to mainstream did not violate Section 504, because the student was not "otherwise qualified" for the regular classroom placement. *St. Johnsbury Academy v. D.H.*, 240 F.3d 163 (2d Cir. 2001).

In summary, school districts must confront the issue of "inclusion" of most or all children with disabilities in regular education settings, and there has been an evolution in both the willingness and the ability of local school districts to provide an appropriate educational program to a wide range of students either mainly or completely in the regular education setting. The State of Connecticut settled a class action lawsuit in 2002 concerning inclusion, agreeing to provide training and technical support to parents and school districts concerning the "least restrictive environment" requirements in IDEA. *P.J. v. State of Connecticut Board of Education*, No. 291CV000180 (D. Conn. 2002). However, all parties to such disputes must keep in mind what may be the only ultimate truth in special education—each child must be considered individually. It is equally inappropriate for a district to say either (1) it does not provide instruction in regular education for such students, or (2) it provides instruction in regular education for all such students.

c. Private school placements

Given the cost, private school placements have historically been a source of conflict between school districts and some parents. The law contemplates that it will sometimes be necessary to place children in private schools in order to provide FAPE. The regulations specify that school districts are required to provide a continuum of alternative placements, including "instruction in regular classes, special classes, special schools, home instruction, and instruction in hospitals and institutions." 34 C.F.R. § 300.551. Districts must make provision for supplementary services, such as resource rooms or itinerant instruction provided along with instruction in the regular classroom. *Id.* If placement in a private school or residential setting is required, however, the school district must provide that service. 34 C.F.R. § 300.302, 34 C.F.R. § 300.401. When parents and the school district agree that such placement is necessary, there is no cause for disagreement. When parents exercise their right to educate their children privately, or when parents claim that their child requires private placement, however, disputes will occur.

When private school placement is required for an appropriate program, the school district, of course, must pay. In addition, the school district remains bound to assure that the placement complies with all provisions of the IDEA. Significantly, the private school itself is not bound by stay-put or the other provisions of the IDEA. The school district, however, remains obligated to meet the IDEA requirements, through contract with the private provider or otherwise. *St. Johnsbury Academy v. D.H.*, 240 F.3d 163 (2d Cir. 2001).

A threshold question concerning this obligation relates to the very definition of "private school" as it relates to home instruction. *See* Chapter

Two, Section A(1)(a)(1). Under IDEA, the provisions for sharing proportionately in the Part B funds (discussed below) applies to children who are enrolled in school, and states may decide that students on home instruction are not "in school" and, accordingly, are not entitled to such services. *Hooks v. Clark County School District*, 228 F.3d 1036 (9th Cir. 2000). Connecticut follows this rule and holds that students on home instruction are not entitled to share in Part B funds.

Students placed in private schools by their parents are not entitled to such a placement at public expense, unless, of course, the parent establishes that such placement is necessary to provide an appropriate education. 34 C.F.R. § 300.403(c). Rather, the obligations of the school district are limited. School districts must assure that such children have an opportunity to participate in Part B federal funds so that the amount expended by school districts on children placed in private schools is equal to the proportionate amount of the Part B federal funds. Also, school districts must assure that children with disabilities have been offered a free, appropriate public education in the public schools. If the child has been offered FAPE, parents are responsible for the costs of any private school placement they make.

The requirement that the school district offer an appropriate program makes it imperative that the district identify children with disabilities, even if they have been placed by their parents, and conduct any necessary evaluations. 34 C.F.R. § 300.451. As stated previously, the child find requirements apply to all children residing in the district, regardless of where they attend school. *See* Section A(2)(a) above. Furthermore, the district must then convene an IEP team meeting to plan an appropriate educational program for the child. The parents may choose to decline the proffered program, as is their right, but the district must write the IEP, at least initially, to assure that it can show that it has offered FAPE to the child. *See* 34 C.F.R. § 300.403(a).

A difficult question concerns the responsibility of the school district in future years for children in parent-funded private placements. Arguably, the district could write "ghost" IEP's for such children each year, to show that it has offered the child an appropriate program, which the parents have declined. The problem, of course, is that this time-consuming process will often be unnecessary, because the parents will wish to continue to provide for their child's education in a private placement, irrespective of the program offered by the public schools. Moreover, without up-to-date evaluations and information concerning the student's progress, it may not be reasonably possible to write an appropriate IEP. Accordingly, it is advisable to notify parents of children placed in private schools each year of their rights, and expressly to state that the district stands ready to convene a PPT to identify any needed evaluation or other information and to plan and provide an appropriate program. Parents who receive that notice and do not request that the district convene a PPT to review and revise the IEP originally offered will be hard-pressed to claim that the district has denied their child an appropriate program.

1. Placement by parents when FAPE is not in issue

IDEA provides that, while not responsible for the costs of placements made privately by parents, local school districts must make services available to such students. IDEA now clarifies that school districts may provide services on the site of a private school, including sectarian schools. The obligation to provide services to children placed in such schools by their parents, however, is limited to (1) consultation with the private schools to assure that private school students with disabilities have a meaningful opportunity to participate in the proportionate share of the federal Part B funds, and (2) establishment of an individual services plan for those students who will receive services funded by the Part B funds.

The implementing regulations set out the procedure for school districts to meet their obligation to children with disabilities who attend private school. 34 C.F.R. § 300.451 *et seq.* These private school children, in both sectarian and non-sectarian schools, must have a meaningful opportunity as a group to participate in the federal Part B funds. The regulations specify that, in order to meet this obligation, school districts must consult with appropriate representatives of the private school children with disabilities (which can include parents). Through such consultation, the school district must decide how to allocate its Part B funds. 34 C.F.R. § 300.454.

No individual student enrolled by parents in a private school has a right to services. Moreover, those who do receive services do not have the right to an appropriate education, or FAPE. When children are identified to receive services after consultation with appropriate representatives of private school children with disabilities over how the Part B funds will be spent, the district must develop a services plan for such children. *Id.* The procedures for developing a services plan are similar to those that apply to developing the IEP. 34 C.F.R. § 300.455. As stated above, however, the district is not required to provide FAPE to the student. Moreover, any disputes over the substance of the services plan are subject to review only through the state complaint procedures, not through a due process hearing. 34 C.F.R. § 300.457.

The Second Circuit Court of Appeals addressed the question of whether services can be provided on the site of a sectarian school in a case with a long and complicated history. *Russman v. Board of Education*, 85 F.3d 1050 (2d Cir. 1996) (*Russman (I)*), *vacated and remanded* 521 U.S. 1106 (1997), *remanded sub. nom. Russman v. Mills,* 150 F.3d 219 (2d Cir. 1998) (*Russman (II)*), *vacated and dismissed as moot* 260 F.2d. 114 (2001).

Citing *Zobrest v. Catalina Foothills School District*, 509 U.S. 1 (1993), in *Russman (I)* the court rejected the argument of the school district that the provision of these services on the site of the religious school was impermissible under the First Amendment. The court instead followed the trend in recent case law to require equal treatment of religious activity. *See* Chapter Two, Section A(3). This case was an extension of *Zobrest*, because it involved the provision of instructional services, in contrast to the sign language interpreter at issue in *Zobrest*, whose services the Supreme Court described as a technical aid. In *Agostini v. Felton*, 521 U.S. 203 (1997), however, the United States Supreme Court put the matter to rest and ruled that services that are available to students in private schools may be provided at religious schools without violating the First Amendment.

In the interim, *Russman (I)* was appealed to the United States Supreme Court. The Court vacated the decision, and remanded the case back to the Second Circuit in light of the 1997 IDEA Amendments. The Second Circuit maintained its position that services can be provided at the sectarian school. It further held, however, that parents who unilaterally place their children in private school (sectarian or otherwise) are not entitled to an appropriate program at the private school, if an appropriate program is offered in the public school. Rather, the school district must simply assure in accordance with IDEA that it expends a proportionate amount of the federal Part B funds for educational services to all of its children enrolled in the private schools. *Russman (II)*. That proportionate amount typically averages only several hundred dollars for each student attending the private schools, and the funds can be expended in the discretion of the local board of education as long as it has consulted with appropriate representatives of private school children with disabilities as required by the statute and regulations. 34 C.F.R. § 300.451 through 34 C.F.R. § 300.454. The parents then claimed in district court that their child had a right to receive appropriate services on the site of the religious school under New York law and under the Free Exercise Clause of the United States Constitution. The district court dismissed these claims. The *Russman* case finally ended, however, when the Second Circuit vacated this decision, holding that the dispute was moot, because the student had graduated from high school by this time.

2. Placement by parents when FAPE is in issue

A persistent problem under IDEA arises when parents believe that their children require private placement but school personnel conclude that the district can provide an appropriate program in the public schools. The right of parents to make unilateral placements in order to secure FAPE has long been recognized. Hearing officers and the courts may order a school district to reimburse parents for the cost of a unilateral placement if (1) the school district did not offer the child an appropriate placement and (2) the private placement made by the parents is appropriate. *School Committee of Burlington v. Massachusetts Department of Education*, 471 U.S. 359, 368 (1985); 34 C.F.R. § 300.403(c). In reviewing these matters, hearing officers may separate the two issues.

If the program offered by the school district is appropriate, the hearing officer need not consider further whether the placement made by the parents was also appropriate; the school district fulfilled any duty it had under IDEA by offering the appropriate program. *M.C. v. Voluntown Board of Education*, 226 F.2d 60 (2d Cir. 2000). *See also* Conn. St. Reg. § 10-76h-14. If the program offered by the school district was not appropriate, the parents must still establish that the unilateral placement they made was appropriate before they will be eligible for reimbursement. *Id.* In considering this issue, a hearing officer may consider the extent of mainstreaming available in the private school setting. *M.S. ex rel. S.S. v. Board of Education of the City School District of the City of Yonkers*, 231 F.3d 96 (2d Cir. 2000). If the unilateral placement is not an approved special education placement, however, parents will still be eligible for reimbursement, as long as the hearing officer finds that the placement was otherwise appropriate. *Florence County School District Four v. Carter*, 510 U.S. 7 (1993).

Under IDEA, reimbursement to parents for the cost of a private placement may be reduced or denied unless the parents comply with new requirements. Parents must now inform the district at the most recent PPT meeting that they are rejecting the placement proposed by the district. They must also provide a statement of their concerns and notice of their intention to place the child in a private school at public expense. Alternatively, they must provide written notice of such concerns and their intention to place a student in a private school at public expense at least ten (10) business days (including any holidays that fall on a business day) prior to the removal of the child from the public school placement. 34 C.F.R. § 300.403(d). *See Greenland School District v. Amy N.*, 358 F.3d 150 (1st Cir. 2004) The theory of these requirements is that the school district should be aware of the concern and should have an opportunity to modify the program to address that concern.

Parents must also make their child available for evaluation by the school district if the district notifies the parents of its intent to evaluate the child (including a statement of the purpose of the evaluation that is "appropriate and reasonable") prior to the parents' removal of the child. In addition, a court may deny reimbursement to parents for a unilateral placement if it finds that the parents' actions were unreasonable. *Id.* These limitations on the parents' right to reimbursement will not apply, however, if the parent(s) are illiterate and cannot write in English; if compliance with these requirements would likely result in physical or serious emotional harm to the student; if the school district prevented the parents from providing notice; or if the parents had not received notice of these requirements. *Id.* These limitations make it essential that school districts comply with the obligation to provide written notification to parents of their procedural rights, as discussed above.

5. "Due process" hearing procedures

A central procedural protection in the IDEA is the right of parents of children with disabilities and of school districts to have an impartial binding review of any disagreement over the program provided by the local or regional school district. Moreover, the law provides that any such administrative hearing decision may then be appealed to federal or state court. 20 U.S.C. § 1415(i)(2)(A); 34 C.F.R. § 300.507 through 34 C.F.R. § 300.514. Significantly, exhaustion of the hearing process is a prerequisite for any court appeal; parents cannot simply march into federal court with their concerns. *Garro v. State of Connecticut*, 23 F.3d 734 (2d Cir. 1994); *W. G. v. Senatore*, 18 F.3d 60 (2d Cir. 1992). *But see Weixel v. Board of Education of City of New York*, 287 F.3d 138 (2d Cir. 2002) (exhaustion requirement not inflexible; excused when parents not notified of procedural rights).

The federal law leaves to the states the determination of the specifics of the hearing process. The one requirement is that the review officer may not be an employee of the agency responsible for the education of the student.

In Connecticut, the General Assembly has established a one-step administrative hearing process that confers extensive authority on hearing officers. The statutes provide that the hearing officer shall hear testimony from both parties and may hear additional evidence the hearing officer deems relevant. The hearing officer may require a complete independent educational evaluation or prescription of educational programs by qualified persons, and the school district is required to pay for any such evaluation or prescription. Conn. Gen. Stat. § 10-76h(c)(3). The law provides further that the hearing officer has the authority to confirm, modify, or reject the identification, evaluation or educational placement of or the provision of a free appropriate public education to the child or pupil, to determine the appropriateness of a placement made by the parents, and to order evaluation or placement (except for the initial provision of special education services) where appropriate without parent consent. Conn. Gen. Stat. § 10-76h(d)(1).

a. Prehearing procedures

A hearing may be requested by either the parent or the school district. Under Connecticut law, the request for a hearing "shall contain a statement of the specific issues in dispute." Conn. Gen. Stat. § 10-76h(a)(2). At the insistence of the United States Department of Education, Connecticut was forced to drop its requirement that issues must first be raised at a PPT meeting, and now a hearing officer may no longer dismiss a due process hearing for lack of subject matter jurisdiction on that basis. Parents are obligated however, to raise hearing issues promptly. The statute of limitations for such claims has been enforced, and no issue can be presented to hearing more than two years after the action complained of, or more than two years from the time notice of procedural safeguards (including the two-year requirement) were provided, whichever is later. Conn. St. Reg. § 10-76h-4. *See M.D. v. Southington Board of Education*, 334 F.3d 217 (2d Cir. 2003) (two year statute of limitations applies to IDEA claims; three year statute of limitations applies to Section 504 claims).

A request for hearing may be filed by the parents, the Commissioner of Children and Families, or by a public agency, including a board of education. The regulations specify the information that must be included in the request, such as the name of the child, the school the child attends, a description of the nature of the dispute relating to the proposed or refused initiation or change, including facts relating to the dispute, and a proposed resolution of the dispute to the extent known and available to the parent at the time. Conn. St. Reg. § 10-76h-3.

Under Connecticut law, the parties are required to participate in a prehearing conference. The prehearing conference is intended to resolve the issues in dispute, if possible, and narrow the scope of the issues. Conn. Gen. Stat. § 10-76h(c)(2). At that conference, the parties typically identify the days on which the hearing will be held. The hearing officer may organize the submission of exhibits, identify witnesses and otherwise address administrative matters deemed necessary to complete the hearing in a timely manner. The hearing officer, however, should not engage in substantive settlement discussions. Conn. St. Reg. § 10-76h-7(b).

State regulations governing due process hearings clarify the procedures regarding the filing of motions prior to the commencement of the hearing. Motions are to be filed with the hearing officer, and they should state the reasons for the desired ruling or action, and shall also state whether a hearing on the motion is requested. Conn. St. Reg. § 10-76h-8. Typical motions are identified (motion to recuse, motion to dismiss, motion to consolidate, motion to clarify findings or decision), and procedures for motion practice are set out. The regulations specifically provide, however, that the hearing officer may waive any requirement in the interest of a fair and expedient resolution of the issues. *Id.*

Typically, the school district provides copies of all relevant educational records, parents supplement those records with their exhibits, and the parties both present testimony, including that of the parents, the teachers and administrators involved in the case, evaluators and independent expert witnesses. At least five business days before the hearing convenes, each party must disclose documentary evidence it intends to present at the hearing, as well as a list of the witnesses the party intends to call, as well as all completed evaluations and recommendations based on the offering party's evaluations that the party intends to use at the hearing. The hearing officer has the authority to bar the introduction of any material not disclosed in accordance with this rule, including any undisclosed evaluation or recommendation. Conn. Gen. Stat. § 10-76h(c)(2).

The IDEA regulations provide that there should be a final decision reached not later than forty-five calendar days after the receipt of a request for a hearing. These timelines are totally unreasonable, given the complexity of special education disputes and the difficulties in scheduling hearing dates. Under the IDEA regulations, therefore, hearing officers may grant specific extensions of time at the request of either party and typically do.

The state regulations now set out detailed procedures concerning postponements. Requests for extensions of time must be made in writing no later than 5:00 p.m. five business days prior to the scheduled hearing or deadline date unless a compelling reason is shown for a later request. The request is to include the reasons for the request, as well as to describe the efforts made to contact the opposing party and, if known, the position of the other party. If the other party objects, that party is required to object in writing (with reason) no later than 5 p.m. two business days prior to the scheduled date. Any extensions granted are to be for a specific period, not to exceed thirty calendar days. Conn. St. Reg. § 10-76h-9.

Section 10-76h-9 also sets out the considerations applicable to any request for postponement. The hearing officer may grant a postponement only after considering the cumulative impact of the following:

- The extent of danger to the child's educational interest or well being that might be occasioned by the delay;
- The need for a party for additional time to prepare and present the party's position at the hearing in accordance with the requirements of due process;
- Any financial or other detrimental consequences likely to be suffered by a party in the event of delay; and
- whether there has already been a delay in the proceedings through the actions of one of the parties.

The regulations limit the right of parties to engage in settlement discussions. Only one thirty calendar day postponement will be granted for continued settlement discussions, as long as the parties verify such discussions in writing. When that period expires, however, there are only three alternatives. The parties can report a settlement, or the parties can go forward with the hearing. The hearing officer cannot grant an additional postponement for settlement discussions, and the third alternative is that the hearing officer will dismiss the hearing without prejudice. The party may file again for a due process hearing at a later date. Conn. St. Reg. § 10-76h-9(e).

b. Mediation

If both parents and the school district agree, the dispute may be submitted to mediation through the State Department of Education. Conn. St. Reg. § 10-76h-5. The regulation provides, however, that the mediation process should not be used to deny or delay a parent's right to a due process hearing. *Id.* Any communications that occur during the mediation process are confidential and cannot be used in a hearing.

Mediation can be an effective way to resolve disagreements. Any formal mediation agreement reached is part of the student's educational record and can be introduced at a subsequent hearing. *Id.* Significantly, however, the process is otherwise confidential, and neither party may present at the hearing discussions that occur in mediation. Therefore, the parties may freely explore alternative resolutions to the dispute without fear that their willingness to discuss such alternatives will haunt them at a hearing. Moreover, the assistance of the experienced mediators appointed by the State Department of Education can often bring a new and helpful perspective to the parties.

The importance of the mediation process is apparent in IDEA. States are now required to offer mediation procedures. States may now adopt procedures to require parents who elect not to use mediation to meet with a disinterested party who will explain the benefits of the mediation process and who will encourage the parents to use the process. The regulations specify, however, that any such procedures may not delay a parent's right to a hearing. 34 C.F.R. § 300.506(d).

c. Advisory opinions

Parties to a due process hearing have a new opportunity to explore settlement of their dispute without going through a full hearing. Conn. St. Reg. § 10-76h-6 provides that a school district and a parent can submit their dispute to a hearing officer for an advisory ruling. This option is available only if both parties agree, and it is subject to special rules as set out in the regulation. The hearing officer providing an advisory opinion may not be the hearing officer who will conduct the full hearing, if one is needed. The parties must exchange documents at least five calendar days before the hearing, along with the names of no more than two witnesses. The party who requested the hearing must also provide a statement of the issues in dispute and a proposed resolution.

The hearing process itself is limited. The hearing officer is to accept only "essential and reliable" exhibits. The proceeding is not transcribed, and attendance is limited. Postponements will not generally be granted, and witnesses are not under oath. The party requesting the hearing is given forty-five minutes to present the case, which may include no more than two witnesses, who are not subject to cross examination at this time. A similar opportunity is then given to the responding party. Each party is then given fifteen minutes to ask questions of the other parties' witnesses and otherwise to elaborate on that party's case. The hearing officer may ask questions, but such questions do not extend these timelines. Within thirty minutes after the hearing is concluded, the hearing officer orally provides the parties his or her opinion on the case, and there is no written opinion. The hearing officer may then facilitate settlement discussions, but he or she may not be called as a witness in any subsequent hearing.

d. Settlement agreements

Often the parties reach a settlement before the hearing officer makes a final decision. The regulations provide that a settlement agreement is not a final decision, prescription or order of the hearing officer. However, it may be read into the record of the hearing as an agreement between the parties. Such agreements are binding and may be enforced in subsequent proceedings. *Mr. J. v. Board of Education*, 98 F. Supp.2d 226 (D. Conn. 2000).

Though such settlement agreements may be enforced by the courts, they do not cause parents to be considered "prevailing parties" and thus entitled to attorneys' fees under IDEA. As discussed in Section A(5)(f) below, prevailing party status is conferred only upon a decision on the merits of the case or a consent decree enforceable by the courts. *Buckhannon Board & Care Home, Inc. v. West Virginia Department of Health and Human Services*, 532 U.S. 598 (2001); *J.C. v. Regional School District 10*, 278 F.3d 119 (2d Cir. 2002).

e. "Stay-put"

A key provision in the due process procedures under state and federal law is the "stay-put" provision. The IDEA provides:

> . . . during the pendency of any proceedings conducted pursuant to this section, unless the State or local educational agency and the parents or guardian otherwise agree, the child shall remain in the then current educational placement of such child, or, if applying for initial admission to a public school, shall, with the consent of the parents or guardian, be placed in the public school program until all such proceedings have been completed.

20 U.S.C. § 1415(j). In plain English, this provision requires that a student generally has the right to stay in his or her placement during any due process proceedings. Such proceedings begin with the filing by parents or the school district for mediation, advisory opinion or hearing, and proceedings continue during any related court appeals. Parents and the educational agency can agree otherwise, and it is certainly possible for the parties to agree that a student's placement should be changed, even if there is some issue of disagreement that goes to a hearing. However, if the parties cannot agree, the child "stays put."

Given the State role in overseeing the provision of special education services to children with disabilities, there is a wrinkle in the "stay put" rules following a hearing officer decision. If the hearing officer agrees with the parent's position and orders a change in placement, stay-put does not apply, and the hearing decision is considered to be an agreement between the State educational agency and the parents to change the placement, even if the local or regional school district appeals the hearing officer decision to the courts. 34 C.F.R. § 300.514(c). *See Greenwich Board of Education v. Torok*, No. 3:03-CV-1407 (JCH) (D. Conn. 2003).

The courts have held that stay-put does not prohibit a change in physical location or the closing of a program, and the district must simply provide for the delivery of the services set forth in the IEP in another location. *Concerned Parents v. New York City Board of Education*, 629 F.2d 751 (2d. Cir. 1980), *cert. denied,* 449 U.S. 1078 (1981). *See also Wilson v. Fairfax County School Board*, 2004 WL 1405290 (4th Cir. 2004) (disciplinary transfer to equivalent program at another school not change in placement). Given this and other decisions, it is clear that the stay-put provision does not operate to prevent implementation of general administrative decisions, such as closing or relocating a program. Moreover, the Second Circuit has ruled that private schools are not bound by the requirements of the IDEA (which of course include stay-put), even as to students placed there by public school districts. *St. Johnsbury Academy v. D.H.*, 240 F.3d 163 (2d Cir. 2001). The IDEA thus does not compel a private school to maintain a student in a particular placement, and if the private school acts unilaterally, the public school district may be sent scrambling to duplicate the placement elsewhere. It is advisable, therefore, to address these issues in placement contracts.

Other issues are not as clear. For example, if the school district and parents disagree over the elements of a program, does the student move to the next grade if the dispute is pending at the beginning of the next school year? Is the elimination of a paraprofessional in the classroom a change in placement? What happens if a program closes, or if a private provider terminates a placement? Fortunately, parents and school districts generally remain committed to the best interests of the particular student, dispute or no dispute. Consequently, these problems rarely come up as the parties work together to identify an appropriate interim placement.

Where the parties are not able to agree, hearing officers have issued interim orders concerning placement, though the authority for such orders is not clear (unless the parent agrees). In one case, a hearing officer issued an interim order before deciding the case on the merits, and the federal district court later held that the interim placement became the stay-put placement. *Warton v. New Fairfield Board of Education*, 125 F. Supp.2d 22 (D. Conn. 2000). When the parent appealed the hearing officer's later decision on the merits (agreeing with the school district), however, implementation of the decision was subject to stay-put.

Finally, the "stay-put" provision is central to the special rules relating to discipline of students with disabilities. As discussed more fully in Section C below, the United States Supreme Court has interpreted this provision to mean that a school district may not unilaterally implement a decision to expel a student over parent objection. *Honig v. Doe*, 484 U.S. 305 (1988). In that case, the Court ruled that school officials may not unilaterally change a placement, even when there are safety concerns. It ruled further, however, that the courts have the authority to override stay-put through their equitable power to issue injunctions. Given that injunctions are an extraordinary power, the courts will issue injunctions only rarely. *See, e.g.*, *R.M. v. Vernon Board of Education*, 8 Conn. Ops. 722 (D. Conn. 2002) (injunction to place student in residential placement denied). Under Connecticut law, the plaintiff must establish each of the four standards for an injunction:(1) no adequate remedy at law, (2) irreparable injury if the injunction is denied; (3) likelihood of success on the merits; and (4) the balance of equities favors granting the injunction. *Waterbury Teachers Assn. v. Freedom of Information Commission*, 230 Conn. 441 (1994).

In addition to the possibility of an injunction, IDEA now provides for certain other exceptions to the stay-put rules. When a student brings a weapon to school or engages in possession, sale or distribution of drugs, school officials can place the child in an alternative educational placement for up to forty-five calendar days. In addition, hearing officers have new powers to override the stay-put requirement in specific situations where safety is in issue. These rather complicated rules are described in detail in Section C(1)(b)(2)(b), below.

f. The hearing process

When Public Law 94-142 (the predecessor of IDEA) was enacted in 1975 these due process procedures were seen as a way to resolve special education disputes promptly. Unfortunately, due process hearings have become quite formal, and frequently they can involve five or even ten days of hearing, and decisions can run for dozens of pages. Lawyers for both parties have an obligation to work together to resolve such matters promptly and with courtesy to all participants. No one ever "wins" a special education hearing.

Both parties have specific procedural rights in due process hearings. The following commentary describes the procedures that apply to most hearings. Under certain circumstances, parties may request an "expedited hearing." Conn. St. Reg. § 10-76h-10. These special rules apply in cases of discipline and/or removal of a child from an educational setting, as discussed in Section C, below.

Rights in due process hearings generally include the right to be represented by counsel, and to be accompanied by persons with special knowledge or training with respect to the problems of children with disabilities. Also, both parties have a reasonable opportunity to present evidence and to confront, compel the attendance of witnesses, and to cross-examine all witnesses. In addition, parties may prohibit the introduction of evidence that was not disclosed at least five business days before the hearing unless the hearing officer waives this requirement for good cause shown. Conn. St. Reg. § 10-76h-11.

Parents have special rights in the hearing process. In addition to the rights set out above, they may have the child who is the subject of the hearing present for the hearing. Parents may also open the hearing to the public, and obtain a written or electronic verbatim record of the hearing, including findings of facts and decision. The record of the hearing and the findings of fact must be provided to the parent at no cost. Conn. St. Reg. § 10-76h-11.

The hearing officer is responsible for running an orderly, efficient hearing. The hearing officer may exclude parties, counsel, or any other participant to ensure that they comport themselves civilly and that the hearing is conducted in a fair and orderly manner. Conn. St. Reg. § 10-76h-13. The formal rules of evidence do not apply, but the hearing officer is required to give effect to the rules of privilege recognized by law (*e.g.*, attorney-client privilege). The hearing officer may receive any oral, documentary or tangible evidence, and the hearing officer may exclude irrelevant, immaterial or unduly repetitious evidence. The hearing officer may even require additional evidence on any relevant matter, even when neither party has presented that evidence. Conn. St. Reg. § 10-76h-15.

The regulations governing hearings also address the issue of who goes first. The party who filed for due process has the burden of going forward with the evidence. This means that the requesting party must present its case first. Significantly, however, the burden of proving that the child is receiving or will receive an appropriate educational program remains with the school district. Except when the district is asking a hearing officer to override stay-put because a student is dangerous, the district may meet its burden to establish that its program is appropriate by a preponderance of the evidence. Conn. State. Reg. § 10-76h-14.

At the conclusion of the hearing, the hearing officer must issue a written decision. The written decision must set forth findings of fact, conclusions of law and the decision on the issues identified for hearing. Conn. St. Reg. § 10-76h-16. Hearing officers have broad powers to "confirm, modify or reject the identification, evaluation or educational placement of or the provision of a free appropriate public education to the student . . . ." Conn. Gen. Stat. § 10-76h(d)(1). In addition, hearing officers may order compensatory education (extended or expanded educational services) to remedy a past denial of an appropriate program. Such awards are rare, however, and are typically available only in cases of gross violations of the law. *Garro v. State of Connecticut*, 23 F.3d 734 (2d Cir. 1994); *Mrs. C. v. Wheaton*, 916 F.2d 69 (2d Cir. 1990). Such compensatory education awards, however, may even extend beyond age twenty-one or even graduation. *St. Johnsbury Academy v. D.H.*, 240 F.3d 163 (2d Cir. 2001); *Letter to Riffel*, 34 IDELR ¶ 292 (2001). The Second Circuit has ruled that students are not entitled to money damages under IDEA, but money damages may be available in Section 1983 actions based on violations of IDEA. *Polera v. Board of Education of the Newburgh Enlarged School District*, 288 F.3d 478 (2d Cir. 2002); *B.H. v. Southington Board of Education*, No. 3:02 CV 252 (SRU) (D. Conn. 2003).

Hearing officers may also include in their decisions "a comment on the conduct of the proceedings." Conn. Gen. Stat. § 10-76h(d)(1). Presumably, this provision was added so that commentary concerning the conduct of the parties will be available to courts upon review of any attorney's fees request. As discussed below, attorney's fee awards can be reduced or can be justified if one party or the other unduly protracted the proceedings.

The decision of the hearing officer is final and binding on both parties, unless either party appeals the decision to either state court, Conn. Gen. Stat. § 10-76h(d)(4), or to federal district court, 20 U.S.C. § 1415(i)(2)(A). The courts, however, are admonished to give "due weight" to the decision of the state hearing officer. *Grim v. Rhinebeck Central School District*, 346 F.3d 377 (2d Cir. 2003). It is therefore a challenge to have a hearing decision overturned on appeal. *See Banks v. Danbury Board of Education*, No. 3:01 CV 2040 (GLG) (D. Conn. 2002).

g. Attorney's fees

When P. L. 94-142 was first passed in 1975, there was no provision for payment of attorney's fees to parents who prevailed in hearings. However, in 1986 the United States Congress passed the "Handicapped Children Protection Act," which amended the IDEA. Now the federal courts may award reasonable attorney's fees to parents who prevail in "any action or proceeding brought" under the IDEA. 20 U.S.C. § 1415(i)(3). When the law was first passed, there was some question as to whether parents were entitled to attorney's fees for hearings that were concluded at the administrative level. However, in a series of decisions, the federal courts construed this provision liberally, and they have ruled that parents may in fact collect attorney's fees for actions that terminate at the administrative level. IDEA was amended to clarify this matter, and it permits the award of attorney's fees for time spent in administrative hearings. *Id.* There is, however, no entitlement to reimbursement of attorney's fees incurred in pursuing the State Department of Education complaint procedures. *Vultaggio v. Board of Education, Smithtown Central School District*, 343 F.3d 598 (2d Cir. 2003).

This provision in IDEA for reimbursement of attorney's fees causes difficulties for school districts in several respects. First, there is no requirement that parents first attempt to resolve any dispute amicably. Under the law parents have the right to request a hearing at any time, simply by writing a letter. The only change in this regard in the 1997 amendments to IDEA is that now the request for due process must include a description of the nature of the problem being brought to due process, as well as a proposed resolution to the problem, "to the extent known and available to the parents at the time." 34 C.F.R. § 300.507(c)(2). If a parent files such a request for a due process hearing, the parents and the school district are immediately "in due process." From that point on, any change in the program or the district's position can lead to a claim that the parent "prevailed," entitling the parent to attorney's fees. Connecticut attempted to address this problem through a requirement that parties must raise issues at a PPT before bringing such issues to hearing, but the United States Department of Education insisted that Connecticut drop this requirement. Conn. Gen. Stat. § 10-76h(a)(1), (2).

Second, the definition of a "prevailing party" is very broad. Whenever a parent achieves some measure of success on a point of significance in the dispute, that parent has prevailed. For example, if a parent asks that his child be placed in a private school at district expense and also asks for an additional 30 minutes per week of counseling services, the parent may be a prevailing party (at least in part) even if his success is limited to the relatively minor issue of counseling.

Third, a parent can prevail if he or she establishes a significant procedural violation of the law, even if the program as provided by the district would otherwise be appropriate to meet the needs of the child. The procedural requirements of IDEA are complex and numerous, and districts will make procedural mistakes. The problem is not only that districts are at risk for parents' attorney's fees because of procedural issues that may be so serious as to constitute a denial of FAPE. More fundamentally, the law encourages some parent attorneys to doggedly pursue procedural issues (at great expense to school districts) just so that they may then claim that the parents are prevailing parties.

The attorney's fees provisions under IDEA apply even where the parents do not incur any fees whatsoever. Reimbursement is to be based on "rates prevailing in the community in which the action or proceeding arose for the kind and quality of services furnished." 20 U.S.C. § 1415(i)(3)(C). Non-profit legal firms and others may make arrangements with parents that litigation will be brought against school districts at no cost to them. If the lawyers then "prevail" in the subsequent proceedings, however, the school district will be liable for attorney's fees. School districts are thus exposed to the risk of litigation without any countervailing economic pressures on the parents and their lawyers, promoting excessive litigation in special education disputes.

IDEA sets forth various limitations on attorney's fees. No award of attorney's fees will be made if (1) at least ten days before the hearing starts, the school district makes a settlement offer, (2) the parents decline to accept the offer, and (3) the relief finally obtained by the parents is not more favorable than the offer of settlement. 20 U.S.C. § 1415(i)(3)(D). However, the court can award fees even in such a case if the court finds that the parents were substantially justified in rejecting the offer (because for example it was not sufficiently specific). 20 U.S.C. § 1415(i)(3)(D), (E).

The court may also reduce fees if the parent unreasonably protracted the final resolution of the matter (a rare finding indeed). Attorney's fees may also be reduced if the amount of fees otherwise authorized "unreasonably exceeds the hourly rate prevailing in the community for similar services of similarly comparable skill, reputation and expertise," or if the time spent and the nature of the legal services provided were excessive concerning the nature of the action or proceeding. 20 U.S.C. § 1415(i)(3)(F)(ii), (iii). In addition, fees will not be awarded for any meeting of the IEP team unless the IEP team meeting is convened as a result of the hearing or a related court proceeding. 20 U.S.C. § 1415(i)(3)(D)(ii). Fees may also be reduced if the attorney representing the parent did not provide appropriate information in the due process complaint, as required by IDEA (*e.g.*, nature of the problem and proposed solution). 20 U.S.C. § 1415(i)(3)(F)(iv).

Finally, the courts have recently clarified that parents are not considered prevailing parties eligible for attorneys' fees if they enter into a settlement agreement with the school district. In *Buckhannon Board & Care Home, Inc. v. West Virginia Department of Health and Human Services*, 532 U.S. 598 (2001), the United States Supreme Court ruled that fee-shifting statutes require an actual decision on the merits or an enforceable consent decree before the plaintiff will be considered a "prevailing party" entitled to attorneys' fees.

There, the Court rejected the "catalyst theory" adopted by some lower courts, whereby a plaintiff was considered to be a prevailing party if his/her claim resulted in a settlement that materially changed the relationship between the parties. The Court ruled in *Buckhannon*, however, that settlement agreements do not create prevailing parties, because such agreements do not carry the judicial stamp of approval. While the decision in *Buckhannon* dealt with fee-shifting provisions under the Fair Housing Act and the ADA, the Second Circuit has applied this decision to the IDEA. It ruled that parents are not entitled to attorneys' fees as a prevailing party when they enter into settlement agreements rather than proceeding through a full hearing to a decision. *J.C. v. Regional School District 10*, 278 F.3d 119 (2d Cir. 2002); *C.D. v. Norwalk Board of Education*, No. 3: 01CV940 (WWE) (D. Conn. 2002).

6. <u>Student Records</u>

Student records issues typically involve the two questions of access and of confidentiality. The access rights conferred by FERPA apply to special education records. In addition, Conn. St. Reg. § 10-76d-18 provides that parents have the right to one free copy of all student records. Parents exercise this right by making a written request, and the school district has five days to respond.

FERPA confidentiality obligations also apply, of course, to special education records. 34 C.F.R. § 300.560 through 34 C.F.R. § 300.577 incorporate and cross-reference the confidentiality protections set out in FERPA, discussed in Chapter Four, Section D. In addition, however, there are a few provisions in IDEA that are supplementary to FERPA. Under IDEA, school officials must notify parents when information is no longer required for educational planning, and at the request of the parent, such information usually must be destroyed. 34 C.F.R. § 300.573. While FERPA rights transfer to the student at age eighteen, districts must continue to provide parents (as well as the student) any notice required under the IDEA due process procedures. 34 C.F.R. § 300.574. Under IDEA, school districts must have one person who is responsible for ensuring the confidentiality of any personally identifiable information, and that person must train others who are using such information, and must maintain a log of access to such information of persons *within the school district*. 34 C.F.R. § 300.572. By contrast, FERPA only requires that such a log be maintained regarding access by persons other than the parent, a person with written consent of the parent, or a school official with a legitimate educational interest. 34 C.F.R. § 99.32(d). *See generally Response to Schaffer* (OSERS, 2000), 34 IDELR ¶ 151 (5/12/01).

Given that the FERPA rules generally apply, school officials do not need special permission to send special education records to a new school district if a student transfers. Under Connecticut law, the sending district must forward the records within ten days of receiving the request from the receiving school district. Conn. Gen. Stat. § 10-220h. There is no exception in this statute for special education records. It does provide, however, that notification should be sent to the parent if the parent does not given written authorization for the transfer. If a parent refuses to consent to the transfer of special education records, therefore, the records may still be sent, but school officials must notify the parent of that action.

B. Section 504 of the Rehabilitation Act of 1973

Two years before the Congress passed IDEA, it passed the Rehabilitation Act of 1973. Section 504 of that law is quite short. In relevant part it states:

> No otherwise qualified individual with handicaps . . . shall, solely by reason of his or her handicap, be excluded from the participation in, be denied the benefits of, or be subjected to discrimination under any program or activity receiving Federal financial assistance . . . .

29 U.S.C. § 794(a). The law also provides that each federal agency shall promulgate regulations as are necessary to carry out this law. In 1980, the United States Department of Education adopted the regulations currently in force. These regulations apply to students, teachers, other employees and even parents, and prohibit discrimination against persons with disabilities. The anti-discrimination provisions that apply to employees will be reviewed in Chapter Seven. Here we look at the specific provisions that deal with students. Though these requirements have been around for thirty years, the nature and scope of the duties imposed on school districts by Section 504 are still evolving. In any event, the provisions concerning students are in some ways similar to IDEA and in other ways different. It is important for school districts to recognize that children with disabilities have separate rights under both statutes and their implementing regulations.

Section 504 is enforced by the Office of Civil Rights of the United States Department of Education (OCR). A person who feels that his or her rights under Section 504 have been violated may file a complaint with OCR, which will investigate. After investigation, OCR will make a finding that a violation did or did not occur. If it concludes that there was a violation of the requirements of Section 504, it may issue a remedial order that the violation be corrected.

When considering the role of OCR in such matters, it is important to understand its view of that role. By statute, OCR is responsible for enforcing the requirements of Section 504. If it receives a complaint and investigates, it will consider any information about potential violations of Section 504 fair game. It is not limited to the particular complaint before it, and it may then request more information about Section 504 issues that are beyond the scope of the complaint. Therefore, once OCR undertakes an investigation under

Section 504, it is impossible for school districts to know where or when that investigation will end.

In addition to the remedies that may be imposed through enforcement action by OCR, Section 504, and the related Americans with Disabilities Act (which was adopted in 1990), create statutory rights for persons covered. As compared with IDEA, which has a comprehensive procedure for resolving disputes, Section 504/ADA simply creates rights and requires only a simple review procedure. Since there are no administrative remedies, the courts have held that persons claiming violation of their rights under Section 504 or the ADA can seek review in federal court. Moreover, when violations of rights of Section 504 or the ADA can be proven, the courts may award damages against the school district. *Rodgers v. Magnet Cove Public Schools*, 34 F.3d 642 (8th Cir. 1994); *W.B. v. Matula*, 67 F.3d 484 (3d Cir. 1995). The United States Supreme Court ruled in 2002, however, that punitive damages are not available for violations of Section 504 or the ADA. *Barnes v. Gorman*, 536 U.S. 181 (2002). In any event, it is important to understand the provisions of Section 504/ADA and district obligations under the law.

1. <u>Disability</u>

Under Section 504, the definition of a handicap (or disability) is significantly broader than that under IDEA. Under the regulations, a "handicapped person" means any person who:

- has a physical or mental impairment that substantially limits one or more major life activities, such as walking, seeing, hearing, speaking, breathing, learning and working; or
- has a record of such impairment; or
- is regarded as having such an impairment.

34 C.F.R. § 104.3. In contrast to IDEA, Section 504 does not set out a list of specific disabilities. While the definition of disability refers broadly to an impairment, however, mere impairment is not sufficient for identification under Section 504. Rather, an impairment must substantially limit the student in a major life activity, before he or she will have rights under Section 504. Asthma, attention deficit disorder, or any number of impairments may create rights under Section 504 if they substantially limit a major life activity in a way that affects the student's ability to learn. Conversely, since 1990 current drug users have been excluded from the

protections of the ADA and Section 504. 42 U.S.C. § 12114(a). *See Fedorov v. Board of Regents for the University of Georgia*, 194 F. Supp.2d 1378 (S.D. Ga. 2002).

Students are protected from discrimination in various ways. Section 504 requires, for example, that facilities be accessible to persons with disabilities. 34 C.F.R. § 104.22. Moreover, the duties under Section 504 do not simply require that school districts refrain from discrimination. Rather, Section 504 imposes affirmative obligations on school districts to assure that persons with disabilities have the opportunity to participate in their programs.

2. <u>"Free appropriate public education"</u>

As is the case with the IDEA, the regulations under Section 504 require that students with disabilities be provided a "free appropriate public education" or FAPE. 34 C.F.R. § 104.33(a). The definition of a "free appropriate public education" under Section 504 is different from that set out in IDEA. The regulations provide:

> [T]he provision of an appropriate education is the provision of regular or special education and related aids and services that (i) are designed to meet individual educational needs of handicapped persons as adequately as the needs of non-handicapped persons are met and (ii) are based upon adherence to procedures that satisfy the requirements of [the Section 504 regulations].

34 C.F.R. § 104.33(b). From this definition, we see that FAPE under Section 504 includes two separate elements, (1) special education and related services, and (2) adherence to all procedural requirements.

a. Special education and related services

First, the program must provide special education and related services to meet the needs of the child with disabilities as adequately as the needs of children without disabilities are met. This standard is of course not self-defining. Moreover, the regulations under Section 504 do not define what is meant by "related services." Consequently, it may be difficult in a particular case to know what services a school district is obligated to provide in order to meet the needs of a child with disabilities as adequately as the needs of children without disabilities are met.

Some things are clear. First, any student who has a disability under IDEA is necessarily a child with a disability under Section 504, because the broader Section 504 definition automatically includes all IDEA students. Also, the Section 504 regulations provide that implementation of an IEP under IDEA is a "safe harbor," that is, it will automatically meet Section 504 requirements. Therefore, in many if not most potential Section 504 cases, the IDEA will guide the school district.

For students who do not receive services under IDEA, the picture is not as clear. As with IDEA, procedures are an important part of the Section 504 regulations. However, under Section 504 there is no requirement that a IEP team develop an IEP. Rather it is appropriate for district personnel to convene as a "Section 504 team" to review the child's needs and develop a written "Section 504 plan" to address those needs.

The standard for an appropriate plan is not the "reasonable accommodation" standard that pertains to employment situations under Section 504. The "reasonable accommodation" standard is that modifications and adjustments have to be made to accommodate the special needs of persons with disabilities, as long as those modifications are not unduly burdensome. In defining an appropriate program under Section 504, however, the regulations do not incorporate this limitation of "reasonable accommodation." School districts, therefore, could theoretically be required to provide services that could be characterized as very burdensome in order to meet the needs of a child with disabilities. For example, if a field trip to Washington D.C. is part of the school program and the only way a student with disabilities can attend is with separate transportation and a one-to-one aide, the district cannot deny that student the right to participate. In extreme cases, such costs could even result in a decision that the trip will be canceled altogether. The duty to provide an education that meets the needs of disabled children as adequately as the needs of non-disabled children is absolute. A district is not excused from its obligations by claiming that it took reasonable steps to accommodate the student.

b. Procedural requirements

The procedural requirements are the heart of the Section 504 regulations, and school districts must assure that the required procedures are in place and staff are aware of their obligations. *See* Series 2000-2001, Circular Letter C-9, "Section 504 of the Rehabilitation Act of 1973: Procedural Safeguards" (October 13, 2000). Some advocates who represent children with disabilities focus on these procedural aspects of Section 504, and school districts must be prepared. Three different sections of the regulations impose procedural requirements on school districts.

1. Educational setting

As with the IDEA, the concern is that children with disabilities be educated to the maximum extent appropriate with children who do not have disabilities. 34 C.F.R. § 104.34. The presumption is for the regular educational setting, as is the case under the IDEA, and the standard for alternative placements is the same as well, *i.e.* that education in the regular setting cannot be satisfactorily achieved with the use of supplementary aids and services. Also, districts that place students in alternative settings must take into account the proximity of the student's home.

Second, this provision applies to non-academic settings as well, and again the duty is to assure that students with disabilities remain with students without disabilities to the maximum extent appropriate. This requirement can arise in various situations, such as field trips or athletic activities. For example, one student in Connecticut challenged how the district provided him transportation on the separate "special education van," under both IDEA and Section 504. The hearing officer held that such separate transportation was not necessary and, as such, was not proper. *East Windsor Board of Education*, 20 IDELR 1478 (SEA 1994).

Finally, this regulation requires that students with disabilities be educated in facilities comparable to those provided to regular education students. Such issues can arise, for example, when the special education class is housed in the former broom closet. While such decisions may be made in good faith based upon the smaller number of students in these classes, they may have the effect of depriving students with disabilities of their right to be educated in comparable facilities. The Office of Civil Rights of the United States Department of Education has stated that this requirement is a particular concern and will be a focus of enforcement efforts.

2. Evaluation and placement

The second section of the regulations imposing procedural requirements on school districts deals with evaluation and placement procedures. Under Section 504, a school district must conduct an evaluation before it may take any action with respect to the initial placement of a child, who because of his or her disabilities, may require special education or related services. That evaluation must be based on tests and other materials that have been validated and will measure the abilities, rather than the disabilities of the child. 34 C.F.R. § 104.35.

This evaluation requirement also applies any time a district takes action with regard to a "significant change in placement." In contrast to IDEA, there is no stay-put requirement with regard to changes in placement. Under Section 504, however, district personnel must evaluate the child before implementing any significant change in placement. There is no similar requirement under IDEA, but of course all children who are eligible under IDEA are subject to the provisions of Section 504. The appropriate course, therefore, is to convene the PPT or the Section 504 team before a change in placement to consider the proposed change and whether any additional information is needed. That exercise, in and of itself, appears to comply with the Section 504 requirements for evaluation before a significant change in placement. The regulations do not define "evaluation," and the district thus has discretion in determining how to meet this obligation to conduct an "evaluation."

The regulations also impose requirements with regard to placement of students. Interpretation of evaluative information and placement decisions are to be based on information from a variety of sources, including aptitude and achievement tests, teacher recommendations, physical condition, social or cultural background, and adaptive behavior. Also, districts are required to adopt procedures to ensure that information obtained from all sources is documented and carefully considered and that placement decisions are made by persons who are knowledgeable about the child and about the evaluative data. 34 C.F.R. § 104.35(c).

Finally, under Section 504, students with disabilities are to be reevaluated periodically. The regulations do not further define what is meant by periodically, except to state that compliance with IDEA in this regard is one way to meet this requirement. 34 C.F.R. § 104.35(d).

3. Procedural safeguards

The regulations require that school districts adopt procedures with respect to the identification, evaluation or educational placement of students with disabilities who need or are believed to need special instruction or related services. 34 C.F.R. § 104.36. The regulation provides that such required procedures must include

- notice to parents, presumably of meetings to consider evaluation or placement of a student;
- an opportunity for the parents to examine relevant records;
- an impartial hearing with opportunity for the parents to participate and be represented by counsel; and
- a review procedure.

An example of a notification of rights approved by the Office of Civil Rights of the United States Department of Education is attached to Series 2000-2001, Circular Letter C-9, "Section 504 of the Rehabilitation Act of 1973: Procedural Safeguards" (October 13, 2000).

The existing hearing officer procedures established by the State Department of Education under IDEA would be an appropriate means of assuring that students raising issues under Section 504 have access to an impartial hearing process. At present, however, the State Department of Education takes the position that the hearing procedures it has created under Conn. Gen. Stat. § 10-76h and IDEA are not available for claims that arise solely under Section 504, even for claims related to a child's education. It is necessary, therefore, that individual districts adopt procedures to address these obligations unless and until the State Department of Education changes its position on this matter.

The Section 504 regulations impose a number of other procedural requirements. School districts are required to take appropriate steps to identify children with disabilities enrolled in the public schools and to notify such children and their parents of their rights under Section 504. 34 C.F.R. § 104.32. Districts are also required to designate a Section 504 coordinator to coordinate efforts to comply with the regulations. 34 C.F.R. § 104.7. In addition, districts must adopt a grievance procedure to review and resolve complaints alleging violations of the requirements of the regulations. 34 C.F.R. § 104.7(b). Finally, districts are required to provide for continuing notification to employees, students and the public of its policy of not discriminating on the basis of disabilities in its programs and activities. This notification should include the name of the Section 504 coordinator. 34 C.F.R. § 104.8. It is important that school districts develop procedures to comply with these various requirements. Equally important, district personnel must assure that these procedures are implemented. If such procedures are not in place, school officials start out on the defensive when a challenge is made.

3. Implications for school personnel

School districts must take care to comply with their obligations under Section 504. As outlined above, the Section 504 requirements are in large part procedural, and it is important to assure that procedures are in place, referrals are made, and parents are notified of their rights under Section 504. Also, if a child is identified and a Section 504 plan is developed, it is imperative that all personnel expected to participate in the plan are apprised of the plan and follow its provisions. Common, albeit unfortunate, mistakes are for a plan not to follow a student to the next grade or the next school, or for the district not to ensure that all the student's teachers are aware of the plan so that modifications or accommodations can be made consistently. If a school district has determined that a student is eligible for a Section 504 services plan, it must ensure that the plan is followed. Not to do so is a violation of the child's rights.

It is equally important, however, not to expand Section 504 beyond the requirements of federal law. A common mistake is to end the discussion when the existence of a disability is confirmed, either by accepting a report provided by the parent or after evaluation by district personnel. Section 504, however, requires more than proof of a disability. A medical or other condition is not a "disability" under Section 504 unless it substantially limits one or more major life activities, such as learning. The key word here is "substantially." Only if a disability substantially limits a major life activity should the child be identified as a Section 504 student.

Such disabilities are often health-related, and accommodations are necessary to assure that the child can receive an educational opportunity in the least restrictive environment commensurate with that provided their non-disabled peers. Severe asthma may require accommodations in physical education. A serious allergy problem may require transfer to a different setting or the administration of medication by school personnel. An attention deficit disorder may make accommodations necessary, such as preferential seating or a homework notebook.

School districts should take special care in considering a claim of disability under Section 504 related to a learning problem that does not rise to the level of an identified disability under IDEA. For example, if a student is a slow learner but does not qualify as a child with a learning disability or as a child with mental retardation, it is unlikely that the child would be considered a Section 504 child. Similarly, a student with psychological problems may have a DSM IV diagnosis, but may not meet the standards for "serious emotional disturbance" under IDEA. In enacting IDEA, the Congress identified the conditions that substantially inhibit students from learning. Section 504 identification should not be a consolation prize.

C. Student Discipline

The discipline of special education students presents special problems for school districts. An expulsion is a change in placement, because by definition an expulsion is a denial of school privileges for more than ten days. The "stay put" provision of the IDEA can require that students stay in their current educational placement when there is disagreement over a proposed change in placement. Since a due process administrative hearing can take months, and an appeal to federal court of any such decision can take years, adamant parent refusal to permit a student's placement to be changed for disciplinary reasons can make a prompt expulsion of a student receiving special education services difficult or impossible.

1. <u>IDEA issues</u>

In the IDEA Reauthorization of 1997, Congress tackled the thorny issue of student discipline. In some quarters, it was claimed that the provisions of IDEA did not provide school officials enough authority and discretion to deal with student misconduct. Others asserted, however, that the restrictions in IDEA on disciplinary action were necessary to protect the rights of children with disabilities to receive an appropriate educational program. Congress started its review of these problems even before the IDEA Reauthorization in 1997. In 1994, Congress amended the stay-put provision of IDEA in the Gun-Free Schools Act, otherwise known as the "Jeffords Amendment." This law amended the stay-put provision to permit school officials unilaterally to place a student who brought a gun to school in an interim alternative educational setting for not more than forty-five calendar days. This concept was later incorporated into IDEA, as discussed below.

a. IEP requirements

The 1997 amendments to IDEA reflects concern over student discipline in the provisions that relate to the IEP. The first approach is to be proactive, *i.e.* to take measures to reduce the need for disciplinary action. Accordingly, the PPT is required to consider "strategies, including positive behavioral interventions, strategies, and supports to address that behavior" for children whose behavior impedes his or her learning. This requirement also applies if the child's behavior impedes the learning of other children. 34

C.F.R. § 300.346(a)(2)(i). In addition, the role of the regular education teacher, who must now participate in the development of the IEP if the student will be receiving services in regular education, includes consideration of behavior issues. The regular education teacher must assist in the development of "appropriate positive behavioral interventions and strategies for the child." 34 C.F.R. § 300.346(d)(1).

From these requirements, we see that the IEP should address student behavior if that behavior is identified as a potential problem in planning an appropriate education. In order to determine whether behavior is a concern, the PPT may determine to conduct a functional behavioral assessment. From that assessment, the team will develop "interventions, strategies, and supports" to address the behavior as appropriate. Any such plan is part of the IEP, "the behavioral intervention plan." Significantly, the requirement for a behavior intervention plan depends on the needs of the child, regardless of disability category, and this requirement is certainly not limited to students who are identified as emotionally disturbed.

Under IDEA, the PPT is obligated to conduct a functional behavior assessment (sometimes called "FBA") and implement a behavior intervention plan (sometimes called "BIP") if a child is "removed" (which presumably includes in-school and/or out of school suspensions) for more than ten days in a school year (computed cumulatively over the course of the year) or placed in an alternative educational setting, discussed under Section C(1)(d) below. The team must meet within ten business days of the eleventh day of removal. 34 C.F.R. § 300.520(b). If the PPT already conducted a functional behavior assessment and has implemented a behavioral intervention plan and the student is excluded cumulatively for more than ten days, the PPT must convene to review the plan and its implementation and to make any necessary modifications to address the behavior. *Id.* If the child is subsequently suspended from regular class activities, the members of the IEP team are required to review the plan. If one or more believe that modifications to the plan are necessary, the IEP team must convene to modify the plan to the extent that the team members deem such action to be necessary. 34 C.F.R. § 300.520(c).

Neither IDEA nor the implementing regulations specify how a functional behavior assessment should be conducted or what a behavior intervention plan should contain. The PPT may therefore determine how best to meet these responsibilities based on the unique circumstances of the particular case. Whether the district will require consent to conduct a functional behavior assessment will depend on the circumstances. Such an assessment does not require parent consent as an evaluation if it is a review of existing data or administering of tests given to all children. 34 C.F.R. § 300.505(a)(3).

b. Disciplinary action

The 1997 Reauthorization of IDEA made significant changes in the area of student discipline. It specifies that in some cases children with disabilities may be disciplined in the same manner as their non-disabled peers. For discipline that is a removal that is in excess of ten consecutive schools days or that otherwise constitutes a change in placement, however, the district must assure that the misconduct was not a manifestation of the child's disability. Moreover, the district must assure that, irrespective of any removal, children with disabilities continue to receive an appropriate educational program. Finally, there are significant changes regarding change of placement and stay-put requirements. Now, school officials and hearing officers may override stay-put claims of parents under specified circumstances and place a child who engages in misconduct in an interim alternative educational placement. A summary of these options is set out by the Office of Special Education and Rehabilitative Services in *Response to Shows,* 22 IDELR ¶ 223 (2001). These rules are complicated, and are sorted out below.

1. Short term suspensions

School officials have always been free to suspend children with disabilities. The question that bedeviled school officials is how to compute when such suspensions would accumulate to constitute a change of placement, which triggers procedural requirements and the duty to conduct a manifestation determination, as discussed below. The language of the 1997 IDEA amendments appeared to require convening of the PPT after any disciplinary suspension, but the implementing regulations have clarified these requirements. Students with disabilities are subject to suspension for up to ten days in the school year without review by the PPT. As reviewed above, the PPT must convene either to develop or review the behavior intervention plan after ten cumulative days of suspension over the course of a school year. In addition, the PPT must convene and make a manifestation determination if a child is to be expelled (excluded from school for more than ten consecutive school days) or if multiple, short-term suspensions constitute a pattern of exclusions that triggers the procedural safeguards. This determination must be made on a case-by-case basis, applying the criteria set forth in 34 C.F.R. § 300.519. *See Joshua S. v. School Board of Indian River*

County, 37 IDELR 218 (S.D. Fla. 2002) (26 days of suspension not a change in placement given periodic review of program).

The regulations impose new requirements concerning services to children who are suspended for more than ten days cumulatively over the course of a school year. As stated above, in such cases a functional behavior assessment must be conducted and a behavior intervention plan must be implemented if not already in place or the existing plan must be reviewed. In addition, for days of exclusion in excess of ten in a school year, the child must be provided services so that he or she continues to receive an appropriate educational program. Significantly, however, the IEP team need not convene to make this determination. Rather, "school personnel, in consultation with the child's special education teacher" have the right to determine the extent to which services are necessary to enable the child appropriately to progress in the general curriculum and appropriately advance toward achieving the goals set in the IEP. 34 C.F.R. § 300.121(d)(3)(i). School personnel, rather than the IEP team, may determine services for this new version of FAPE only if the exclusions do not constitute a change in placement.

2. Long term suspensions or expulsions

Under Connecticut law, any exclusion from school privileges for more than ten consecutive school days is an expulsion, which may only be imposed by the board of education after a formal hearing, as discussed above in Chapter Four. Moreover, since 1995 Connecticut law has provided that, before any expulsion of a child with disabilities, the PPT must convene to determine whether the student's misconduct was a manifestation of his or her disability. If it is not, the child may be expelled. If it is, the student may not be expelled, and the PPT is required to reevaluate the child for the purpose of modifying the IEP to address the misconduct and to ensure the safety of other children and staff in the school. Conn. Gen. Stat. § 10-233d(i).

The 1997 amendments to IDEA contain similar provisions, but include new requirements that make it much more likely that a child's misconduct will be deemed a manifestation of his or her disability. Moreover, even if the removals never exceed ten consecutive days, a series of removals may constitute a pattern of exclusion that triggers the procedural safeguards of the law. 34 C.F.R. § 300.519(b). Also, the law specifies that children with disabilities who are expelled (or whose placement is considered changed because of a pattern of suspensions) continue to be entitled to a "free, appropriate public education," as that term is specially defined for this situation. In such cases, the FAPE to which the child is entitled is comprised of the services that are necessary to enable the child to appropriately progress in the general curriculum and appropriately advance toward the goals set in the IEP, as determined by the IEP team. 34 C.F.R. § 300.121(d)(3)(ii).

a. Manifestation determination

IDEA and the implementing regulations set forth specific requirements concerning the standards for making a manifestation determination, and they make it more difficult than ever to take disciplinary action against students with disabilities. These provisions establish a presumption that misconduct by children with disabilities is caused by their disability. The PPT can determine that a child's misconduct is not a manifestation of their disability only if the following conditions are met.

i. Definition

First, the IEP team must consider all relevant information, including evaluation and diagnostic results, including information provided by the parents, observations of the child and the child's IEP and placement. Based on the consideration of all that information, the IEP team must determine that "in relationship to the behavior subject to the disciplinary action," the IEP and placement were appropriate and that "special education services, supplementary aids and services, and behavior intervention strategies" were provided in accordance with the IEP.

Second, if the IEP team finds that the IEP was appropriate and being implemented, as described above, it must then find that the child's disability did not impair his ability to understand the impact and consequences of the behavior causing the review.

Third, the IEP team must further find that the child's disability did not impair his ability to control the behavior that caused the review. If the PPT makes all of these findings, the PPT can determine that the misconduct is not a manifestation of the disability. If not, the PPT must find that the misconduct was a manifestation of the disability. 34 C.F.R. § 300.523.

ii. When required

School personnel must conduct a manifestation determination only when a change in placement is proposed. 34 C.F.R. § 300.519. The regulations also require that a manifestation determination be made if (1) the

PPT proposes to exercise its right to move the child to an appropriate interim alternative educational setting, or (2) if the district asks a hearing officer to exercise his or her right to do so. 34 C.F.R. § 300.523. This determination must be made no later than ten school days after the decision to take the action that triggered the duty to conduct the manifestation determination. Also, parents must be notified no later than the date on which the decision to take such action is made, and the district must provide them with a copy of the procedural safeguards at that time. *Id.*

Under the regulations, a change in placement is a removal for more than ten consecutive school days, including moving a child into an interim alternative educational setting. In addition, however, the regulations provide that a series of exclusions that constitute a pattern and exceed ten school days may also be a change in placement, even when the days are not consecutive. The regulations specify that, in making that determination, the PPT must consider "factors such as the length of each removal, the total amount of time the child is removed, and the proximity of the removals to one another." 34 C.F.R. § 300.519. Significantly, the reference to "factors such as" those listed makes it clear that this list is not exhaustive, and another important factor to consider is whether the grounds for discipline are similar or different from incident to incident.

iii. Impact of determination

If the IEP team finds that the misconduct is a manifestation of the disability, school personnel may not discipline the student for the misconduct. Rather, the PPT is responsible for reviewing the child's IEP to determine whether and how to modify the program to address the problem behavior, and to provide for the safety of the student, other students and staff.

If the IEP team finds that the misconduct is not a manifestation of the disability, school personnel may discipline the student in the same manner as non-disabled students are disciplined, including an expulsion for up to one calendar year. 34 C.F.R. § 300.524. There is, however, a significant difference. The rights of the non-disabled students during any expulsion are a function of state law. As outlined in Chapter Four, when students sixteen to eighteen years of age are expelled, the school district may not have any responsibility for providing an alternative educational program, depending on the offense committed. Furthermore, there is no requirement at all for students eighteen and older. By contrast, when a child with disabilities is expelled, the school district must meet two additional requirements.

First, before a child with disabilities may be expelled, "the special education and disciplinary records" of the child must be provided to the person or body that will hear the recommendation for expulsion. The IDEA regulations do not further define these records. Until there is further definition of this requirement, it seems logical to comply with this requirement by sharing with the decision-maker (*e.g.* the board of education) the disciplinary record, the latest IEP and the minutes of the manifestation determination IEP team meeting. 34 C.F.R. § 300.524(b). The student and his/her advocate, of course, would be free to provide additional records.

Second, the school district must assure that the student continues to receive a free appropriate public education. The regulations define FAPE for this purpose to be the services that are necessary to enable the child to appropriately progress in the general curriculum and appropriately advance toward the goals set in the IEP, as determined by the PPT. 34 C.F.R. § 300.121(d)(3)(ii).

b. Stay-put

When students engage in misconduct that puts themselves or others at risk, there is often concern that the child's placement should be changed, typically to a more restrictive setting. Whether or not misconduct is a manifestation of disability, the stay-put provisions of the law apply whenever parents object to a proposed change in placement and file a request for due process.

i. The general rule

In 1988, the United States Supreme Court addressed the question of expulsion of students receiving special education services under the IDEA. *Honig v. Doe*, 484 U.S. 305 (1988). In this case, the Court dealt with two students who had assaulted other students in school. John Doe, an emotionally disturbed student, choked another student. Jack Smith, also emotionally disturbed, had a history of physical and verbal assaults on other students, and after stealing, extorting money and making sexual comments to female students, he too was expelled. Both sued their respective districts, claiming that the "stay-put" provision entitled them to stay in school.

The United States Supreme Court agreed, and it held that the expulsions did in fact violate the rights of the students. Writing for the majority, Justice Brennan stated that an exclusion in excess of ten consecutive school days is a change of placement. The number ten as the threshold for a change in placement comes from *Goss v. Lopez*, 419 U.S. 565 (1975). In *Goss*, the Court held that an exclusion of more than ten days implicates significant due process concerns. In *Honig v. Doe*, the Court held that any such exclusion (an expulsion under Connecticut law) over parent objection violates the IDEA, even when the district has acted out of concern for the safety of other students:

> The language of Section 1415(e)(3) [the stay-put provision] is unequivocal. It states plainly that during the pendency of any proceedings initiated under the Act, unless the state or local educational agency and the parents or guardian of a disabled child otherwise agree, "the child *shall* remain in the then current educational placement."

(Emphasis in original). In reaching this decision, the Court rejected the argument made by the California Commissioner of Education that school officials must have the right to act unilaterally when students pose a danger.

In *Honig v. Doe*, the Court recognized that there will be situations in which school officials must act to protect the safety of the other students, even over parent objection. In such situations, the Court held, school officials still may not act unilaterally. Rather, it is necessary in such cases to seek judicial intervention, specifically an injunction. When maintaining the student in the current placement during due process review would involve inappropriate risk to the student or others, the court will provide injunctive relief and change the placement:

> The burden in such cases, of course, rests with the school to demonstrate the futility or inadequacy of administrative review. [The law] effectively creates a presumption in favor of the child's current educational placement which school officials can overcome only by showing that maintaining the child in his or her current placement is substantially likely to result in injury either to himself or herself, or to others.

Honig, 484 U.S. at 327-28. Given this high standard, typically such relief will be available only when there are compelling issues of safety or disruption.

ii. The new exceptions

The stay-put provision was first changed in 1994 as part of the Gun-Free Schools Act (also known as the "Jeffords Amendment"). In 1997 the exceptions to stay-put were expanded, and theses changes have given both school officials and hearing officers the right to override stay-put in certain, limited situations.

First, school personnel can unilaterally place a child in an interim alternative educational setting if the child carries a "weapon" to school or to a school function. IDEA defines "weapon" for this purpose as "a weapon, device, instrument, material, or substance, animate or inanimate, that is used for, or is readily capable of, causing death or serious bodily injury, except that such term does not include a pocket knife with a blade of less than two ½ inches long." 18 U.S.C. § 930(g)(2). Second, school personnel can unilaterally override stay-put if the child knowingly possesses or uses illegal drugs or sells or solicits the sale of drugs while at school or at a school function.

In either case, the IEP team may unilaterally move the child to an appropriate interim alternative educational setting for the same amount of time a child without a disability would be subject to discipline, but not for more than forty-five calendar days. 34 C.F.R. § 300.520(a). Any interim alternative education setting must be determined by the IEP team, and it must be selected to enable the child to progress in the general curriculum (although in another setting), and to continue to receive the services set out in the IEP to enable the child to meet the IEP goals. 34 C.F.R. § 300.522. At the end of the period, the child must be returned to the prior, "stay-put" setting unless school personnel and parents agree to continue the alternative educational setting, a hearing officer exercises his or her right to override stay-put (as described below), or the courts issue an injunction. In short, this provision is not a permanent solution, but it gives school personnel a little breathing room to work with parents and/or exercise other legal rights.

In 1998, the federal district court in Connecticut decided a case concerning stay-put obligations following disciplinary action by school officials. *Mr. and Mrs. S. v. Ashford Board of Education*, 4 Conn. Ops. 1036 (D. Conn. 1998). A student identified under the IDEA had been suspended for theft and possession of alcohol on school property, and the PPT was divided as to whether this misconduct was causally related to the student's disability. The hearing officer ruled that "stay-put" was the suspension, but the court disagreed. It cited the statutory reference to the "then current educational placement," and observed that the suspension was not an educational placement at all. The court ruled that the stay-put placement, therefore, was the placement prior to the expulsion, and found that both the local school district and the state were responsible for this violation of the student's stay-put rights.

In addition, a hearing officer may order a change in a child's placement to an appropriate interim alternative educational placement, notwithstanding the provisions of "stay put," again for not more than 45 calendar days under specific circumstances. Under the IDEA regulations, the hearing officer must determine that the district has demonstrated by substantial evidence (*i.e.* by more than a preponderance of the evidence) that maintaining the child in the current educational placement is substantially likely to result in injury to the child or to others. This finding alone, however, is not enough. To override stay-put, the hearing officer must also (1) consider the appropriateness of the child's current placement and (2) consider whether the district has made reasonable efforts to minimize the risk of harm in the child's current placement, including the use of supplementary aids and services. Finally, after considering these issues, the hearing officer must determine that the interim alternative educational setting is selected to enable the child to participate in the general curriculum and to continue to receive services and modifications as set out in the IEP, and that the IEP includes services and modifications designed to address the behavior leading to the change so that it does not recur. 34 C.F.R. § 300.521.

The regulations provide that, following unilateral changes as permitted above, the stay-put placement is generally the "current placement." 34 C.F.R. § 300.526. If immediate action is necessary, therefore, school personnel must still seek a *Honig* injunction. If a school district determines to go forward with an expedited hearing alleging dangerousness, however, it may be possible to obtain relief for more than the forty-five day limit. The regulation provides that "if school personnel maintain that it is dangerous for the child to be in the current placement (the child's placement prior to the interim alternative educational setting)," they may request an expedited hearing. Any placement overriding stay-put ordered by the hearing officer is limited to forty-five days. However, the regulation provides that this procedure "may be repeated as necessary." *Id.* While the procedure thereby contemplated is not completely clear, apparently the hearing officer can retain jurisdiction, hold hearings and order extensions of the placement for additional forty-five day periods.

iii. Expedited hearings

Any request for such relief from the hearing officer is available only through an "expedited hearing." In addition, IDEA requires that an expedited hearing process be available to parents who wish to challenge a manifestation determination or unilateral action by school officials. 34 C.F.R. § 300.525. To enable school districts to comply with these provisions, the State Department of Education adopted a new regulation setting out the conditions for an expedited hearing consistent with the provisions of IDEA. Special rules apply to such hearings. No prehearing conference is required. The hearing officer is charged with the responsibility for limiting the introduction of documents and testimony as may be necessary to rule on the issue presented no later than forty-five days after receipt by the Due Process Unit of the State Department of Education, without exceptions or extensions. In addition, documents, evaluations and recommendations must be shared with the other party and the hearing officer at least two business days before the hearing starts, and either party has the right to prohibit the introduction of such evidence if it is not disclosed by that time. Conn. St. Reg. § 10-76h-10.

c. Children not yet identified

When expulsion of a regular education student is proposed, parents sometimes object on the basis that the child should have been identified under IDEA and thus should have the protections that apply to children with disabilities. These claims, sometimes called "hidden disabilities," previously caused confusion under IDEA, and the 1997 amendments addressed this issue. IDEA provides that children do have such protections if the school district "had knowledge" that the child should have been identified under the IDEA. The law and the implementing regulations provide that such "knowledge" will be presumed if:

- the parent of the child had expressed concern in writing that the child is in need of special education and related services, unless the parent is illiterate or has a disability preventing such written expression;
- the behavior or performance of the child indicates the need for such services;
- the parents had previously requested an evaluation of the child; or
- the teacher of the child or other district personnel had previously made a referral for special education evaluation in accordance with established procedures that apply in such cases.

34 C.F.R. § 300.527. If none of these bases for "knowledge" exists, the child may be disciplined in the same manner as other children. Also, the child may be disciplined in the same manner as other children if one of these circumstances did apply and the district (1) either conducted an evaluation and determined that the child is not eligible for special education services or determined that an evaluation was not necessary and (2) notified the parents of that determination. 34 C.F.R. § 300.527.

If the parents contest the finding of school personnel that none of these grounds for "knowledge" apply, they may challenge that finding in an expedited hearing. 34 C.F.R. § 300.525. Moreover, if the parents request an evaluation during any period of exclusion, such evaluation must be conducted on an expedited basis. The child will remain where placed by the district pending the results of the evaluation. If the child is then determined to require special education and related services, however, he or she shall receive such services and will be afforded all the applicable procedural protections. 34 C.F.R. § 300.527.

3. Reporting crimes by students with disabilities

School districts and other agencies may report crimes committed by children with disabilities, and such children may be prosecuted. If a school district or other agency reports a crime committed by a child with disabilities, it must ensure that copies of the special education and disciplinary records of the child are transmitted for consideration by the appropriate authorities to whom it reports the crime. As noted above with disciplinary actions concerning children following a "no-manifestation" finding, the regulations do not define the records to be sent. It would be reasonable, therefore, to send the disciplinary records, and the most recent IEP and related meeting notes. The regulation further provides, however, that any such transmission of student records must be authorized under the FERPA. 34 C.F.R. § 300.529. Accordingly, the district must have written parent permission to transmit the records or otherwise be able to establish authority for the release of the records, such as a subpoena related to the criminal proceedings.

2. <u>Section 504 issues</u>

As reviewed above, Section 504 of the Rehabilitation Act of 1973 prohibits discrimination against students on the basis of their disabilities. This prohibition can be relevant in matters of student discipline, because misconduct can be caused by a disability. For example, a student with

Tourette's Syndrome may exhibit involuntary tic behavior, which can include muttering swear words and other bizarre behavior. It is clear that it would not be appropriate to impose discipline in such cases. Moreover, any such discipline would violate that student's rights under Section 504 because the conduct is a manifestation of the disability.

The situation is less clear in cases where a student with disabilities engages in misconduct that would typically lead to serious disciplinary consequences. If a regular education student comes to school with a firearm or dangerous weapon, he or she must be expelled. Conn. Gen. Stat. § 10-233d. What about the emotionally disturbed child? Was the misconduct, bringing the weapon to school, a manifestation of the disability? If so, can the student be expelled? What about the student with learning disabilities?

For children who are identified under IDEA, the new and complicated rules above give us answers (if not solutions). When a student is identified as having a disability as solely under Section 504, however, such as attention deficit disorder, these new rules do not apply. School districts must avoid taking disciplinary action that discriminates against a student on the basis of his or her disability, even if the disability is recognized under the IDEA. To meet this obligation, school districts presumably must determine whether the misconduct is a manifestation of the disability. The Section 504 regulations, however, do not provide guidance on when and how such a determination must be made. Moreover, while the standards for a manifestation determination under IDEA provide an analogy for such determinations, it is not clear that the high standards adopted for a manifestation determination under IDEA are required or even warranted. Significantly, neither Congress nor the United States Department of Education has seen fit to adopt requirements under Section 504 similar to those under IDEA. It is reasonable, therefore, for the Section 504 team to employ more common sense than may be permissible under IDEA. Rather than employing a default assumption that the misconduct is a manifestation, it is appropriate for the Section 504 team to consider these issues from a factual, rather than procedural perspective.

These questions are of course impossible to answer in the abstract and are very difficult in the concrete. However, the key is that they must be addressed. When a Section 504 student has engaged in misconduct that could lead to expulsion, a Section 504 team must be convened to consider the relationship, if any, between the disability and the misconduct. Under the Section 504 regulations, evaluation is required before any significant change in placement, and a manifestation determination would be an appropriate review prior to the significant change in placement of expulsion. If the team finds no manifestation, the student may be expelled, even if the parent disagrees with that finding, because there is no stay-put under Section 504.

Even when misconduct will not lead to an expulsion, the Section 504 team should convene whenever serious disciplinary action (either in severity or frequency) is contemplated. If it appears that there is a causal connection between the conduct and the disability, the Section 504 team must assure that discrimination against the student does not occur on the basis of his or her disability. The PPT or Section 504 team should review the situation whenever there is a pattern of misconduct and suspension, because in such situations it may be that (1) the misconduct is related to the disability and/or (2) the program is not appropriate to meet the student's needs. *See Memorandum to OCR Senior Staff from LeGree Daniels dated October 28, 1988*, EHLR Special Report, Supplement 233 (January 27, 1989).

3. Disciplining students with disabilities

After considering the impact of both the IDEA and Section 504, some generalizations are possible.

First, it is possible to discipline students who have disabilities, but recent changes in the law have made it more difficult. Discipline short of a ten day exclusion does not operate as a change in placement and, where appropriate, it may be imposed. The decision in *Honig v. Doe* recognized this fact:

> Such [disciplinary] procedures may include the use of study carrels, time-outs, detention or the restriction of privileges. More drastically, where a student poses an immediate threat to the safety of others, officials may suspend him or her for up to ten school days.

Honig, 484 U.S. at 325. As revised in 1997, IDEA builds on this concept. Even where the district may find it appropriate to convene a PPT, a temporary suspension while awaiting the PPT will generally be appropriate.

Second, it is important to exercise the right to suspend students prudently and to maintain accurate related records. After a student has been suspended for a total of ten days in any school year, the district must conduct a functional behavior assessment within ten business days of the removal and then promptly implement a behavior intervention plan if it has not been done prior to the removal from school. School personnel, in consultation with the student's special education teacher, must determine whether and what services are necessary during any subsequent suspension to enable the student to progress in the general curriculum and to appropriately advance toward his or her IEP goals. Moreover, if a series of short term suspensions (each less than ten days) comprises a "pattern," even short term suspensions will be a change in placement, requiring that the PPT conduct a manifestation determination and consider the services that are necessary under the standard above.

Third, students with disabilities under IDEA may even be expelled under certain circumstances. If expulsion of a student requiring special education services is proposed, however, the district must first convene an IEP team meeting to determine whether the misconduct is a manifestation of the student's disability. If so, the student is not to be expelled. Under IDEA, a manifestation determination is required if the IEP is not appropriate or being fully implemented (at least in the area implicated by the misconduct). This stark consequence of failing to implement the IEP underscores the need to be vigilant in implementing the IEP, especially any provisions concerning behavioral interventions or supports.

Fourth, it is important to keep the provisions of Section 504 in mind. The state law requiring that the PPT convene to consider whether there is a causal relationship between the misconduct and the disability relates solely to students receiving special education services. However, it would not be appropriate to expel a student with a disability under Section 504 without first convening a Section 504 team to make a causal relationship determination. Such an evaluation of the situation is necessary to satisfy the requirement of Section 504 that there be an evaluation prior to any significant change in placement. 34 C.F.R. § 104.35(a). If there is no causal relationship, expulsion will not discriminate against the student in violation of Section 504. If there is a causal relationship, however, the district must find an alternative means for dealing appropriately with the misconduct, including provision for the safety of other students and staff.

Fifth, where a student with disabilities engages in conduct that is disruptive or puts other students at risk, it may be necessary to modify or even change his or her placement. Certain misconduct is so serious that expulsion for a full calendar year is mandatory in such cases. Under state law, such conduct includes bringing a "firearm" or "dangerous weapon" to school (which are defined in Chapter Four, Section C(1)(b)). Students receiving special education must be expelled in such cases if the PPT determines that the student's disability did not cause the misconduct. Even when the PPT determines that there is a causal relationship between the misconduct and the disability, the law specifies that the PPT must evaluate the child for the purpose of modifying the child's IEP to address the misconduct and to ensure the safety of other children and staff in the school. Such modifications may include a change to a more restrictive setting, and the law contemplates that such changes may be made.

Sixth, parents are not always cooperative when the expulsion of their child is proposed, notwithstanding the mandatory expulsion provisions in the law. In *Honig*, the Court recognized that there will be situations in which school officials must act to protect the safety of the other students, even over parent objection. If maintaining the student in the current placement during due process review would pose an significant risk to the student or others, it may be possible to convince the federal court to provide injunctive relief and change the placement, though it is difficult to obtain such relief.

As described above, after the 1997 amendments school officials may unilaterally change a student's placement to an interim alternative educational placement for a maximum of forty-five calendar days under narrow circumstances involving weapons or drugs. Also, hearing officers may now override "stay-put" for a maximum of forty-five calendar days if school personnel show by substantial evidence that the student is substantially likely to injure himself or others. These provisions are limited, however, and school districts may still have major problems with stay-put in particular cases.

Finally, whether or not a child receiving special education services is expelled, it is clear under state and federal law that he or she will continue to be entitled to educational services. Conn. Gen. Stat. § 10-233d(i) provides that a special education student who has been expelled shall be provided "an alternative educational opportunity consistent with the child's educational needs" during the period of expulsion. Similarly, under IDEA as revised in 1997, students continue to be entitled to receive appropriate educational services. IDEA and the implementing regulations have clarified that students excluded for more than ten school days for conduct that is not a manifestation of their disability are not entitled to the full "free, appropriate public education" that must generally be provided to children with disabilities. They are entitled, however, to services that will permit them to progress in the general curriculum and to advance toward achieving the goals in the IEP.

In some cases it may be difficult to reach agreement on the expulsion of children with disabilities, or on the elements of an appropriate program for a student who has been expelled. However, it would be inappropriate to conclude that children who have disabilities may not be held accountable for their misconduct. Given that responsibility for one's actions is a major lesson in life, expulsion in particular cases may be the best response for the education of that student and for the safety of the school community.

CHAPTER SIX
COLLECTIVE BARGAINING

Collective bargaining is a major concern for Connecticut school districts, because education is a labor intensive industry. There is no inherent right of public employees to bargain collectively. However, in most states there is some form of bargaining between public employees and their employers. Connecticut was an early leader in this regard. In 1951, the Connecticut Supreme Court held that teachers in Connecticut have the right to organize and to meet with their employing board of education to bargain collectively as long as the board of education does not "negotiate a contract which involves the surrender of the board's legal discretion, [which] is contrary to law or is otherwise *ultra vires*," *i.e.* beyond the board's legal authority. *Norwalk Teachers' Ass'n v. Board of Education*, 138 Conn. 269 (1951). Connecticut has continued to provide its public employees collective bargaining rights that are among the most extensive in the nation.

A. General Issues

School districts are subject to separate collective bargaining laws for certified staff and non-certified staff, the Teacher Negotiation Act (TNA), Conn. Gen. Stat. § 10-153a *et seq.*, and the Municipal Employees Relations Act (MERA), Conn. Gen. Stat. § 7-467 *et seq.* These laws are both modeled on the federal law, the National Labor Relations Act, 29 U.S.C. § 151 *et seq.* Both the TNA and MERA impose upon boards of education the duty to bargain in good faith. They both prohibit strikes by public employees, and instead both provide for impasse resolution through binding arbitration of disputes in negotiations. Consequently, there are many common labor relations issues with both certified and non-certified employee groups.

1. <u>The duty to bargain in good faith</u>

At the core of the collective bargaining obligation is the duty to bargain in good faith. Boards of education are required to meet with designated employee representatives at reasonable times and to participate actively so as to indicate a present intent to reach agreement. That means, for example, that neither party can insist to the point of impasse that it will only meet at night or only meet on working time. However, the obligation to bargain in good faith does not require the making of a concession. *See, e.g.*, Conn. Gen. Stat. § 10-153e(d). Rather, public employers and employee organizations are required to come to the table, to listen to the other side, and to make proposals and counterproposals. Conduct at the bargaining table will be reviewed in its totality, and either party is generally free to maintain a position at the table without concession for as long as it wishes.

The duty to bargain in good faith also includes obligations both before and after negotiations for a collective bargaining agreement. Employers must provide information that is relevant to the collective bargaining process. *See, e.g., Connecticut State Board of Labor Relations v. Board of Education of the Town of West Hartford*, 190 Conn. 235 (1983). This duty to provide information is broadly construed, and the burden will be on the employer to show that requested information is not relevant to collective bargaining or related matters (*e.g*, processing a grievance). *City of Bridgeport*, Dec. No. 3127 (St. Bd. Lab. Rel. 1993). In addition, health care providers and third party health care administrators must provide relevant information at the request of the exclusive collective bargaining representative. Conn. Gen. Stat. § 38a-981. Similarly, when an agreement is reached, it is an unfair labor practice to refuse to sign a written contract setting forth that agreement. Conn. Gen. Stat. § 7-470(c); Conn. Gen. Stat. § 10-153e(d).

Finally, whether an agreement is reached through negotiations or arbitration, the State Labor Board has ruled repeatedly that a deal is a deal, even if the public employer confronts significant economic problems. From time to time, employers have claimed financial impossibility of performance or impracticality, and have sought to make unilateral changes in collective bargaining agreements. The State Labor Board has refrained from ruling that such action could never be justified, but it has never found that the particular circumstances warrant such action. *See City of Waterbury*, Dec. No. 3945 (St. Bd. Lab. Rel. 2004).

2. Scope of bargaining

The duty to bargain in good faith is limited by the scope of bargaining. An employer or an employee organization has no duty to negotiate over issues unless they are mandatory subjects of bargaining. Both the TNA and the MERA require that the parties negotiate over "salaries, hours and conditions of employment," and there is no requirement that either party negotiate over any issue that does not relate to these subjects.

a. Mandatory subjects of bargaining

A mandatory subject of bargaining relates directly to "wages, hours and conditions of employment." Examples of mandatory subjects are salaries, benefits, leave provisions, work load and the like. An employer and a union must negotiate regarding mandatory subjects of bargaining if requested by either party. Similarly, as discussed in Section 3 below, it is an unfair labor practice to make unilateral changes in working conditions that relate to mandatory subjects of bargaining. Rather, the employer must negotiate with the employee representative before making such changes.

Not all changes trigger a duty to bargain. Some changes are considered *de minimis, i.e.* having such a minor impact on working conditions that it does not have to be negotiated. Conversely, some changes are so fundamental to the operation of the employer that it may make the change without negotiations over the decision. Decisions concerning the curriculum or closing schools, for example, need not be negotiated. As discussed in Section 4, however, it may be necessary to negotiate over the impact of such decisions. Finally, employers may adopt "prophylactic rules" to assure that employees work as directed or receive benefits only when they are eligible. As long as such rules do not significantly burden the employees, they may be adopted without negotiations. *See Town of East Haddam* Dec. No. 1730 (St. Bd. Lab. Rel. 1979) (time clocks can be installed without prior negotiation).

As school districts have struggled to operate more efficiently, they have on occasion explored the possibility of contracting out work done by members of one bargaining unit to another bargaining unit or to a private entity. The State Board of Labor Relations has ruled that contracting out work done by members of a bargaining unit relates to a mandatory subject of bargaining. If the school district has negotiated the right to contract work out, typically as a provision of the management rights clause, the district may exercise that right without further bargaining. If the contract is silent, however, the district must negotiate with the union over the proposal to contract out work. Such negotiations can be difficult, and often involve issues of job security and/or severance. Moreover, the rule is that the decision itself is to be negotiated; the school district cannot announce its decision and offer to negotiate over the impact of that decision. If the matter is not resolved through negotiations, the mid-term mediation and binding arbitration procedures of either the Teacher Negotiation Act or MERA will be imposed, as described in Section B(7) and Section C(7) below.

An important exception to the contracting out rule has been the "shared work" doctrine. Under that doctrine, shared work, *i.e.* work performed by other bargaining units or other persons, was not considered "bargaining unit work." As a consequence, the employer had the right to contract such work out of the unit, because it was never exclusively bargaining unit work. The State Board of Labor Relations, however, has limited the "shared work" doctrine dramatically. *City of New Britain*, Dec. No. 3290 (St. Bd. Lab. Rel. 1995). If a public employer proposes subcontracting or transfer of work from a bargaining unit, it must negotiate over the change with a unit that is adversely affected if three tests are met: (1) the work in question is bargaining unit work, (2) the subcontracting or transfer of the work at issue varies significantly in kind or degree from what had been customary under past established practice, and (3) the subcontracting or transfer work in question has a demonstrable adverse impact on the bargaining unit.

When contracting-out does not differ significantly from the past practice, there is no violation of the *New Britain* rule. *Torrington Board of Education and Education Connection*, Dec. No. 3726 (St. Bd. Lab. Rel. 1999) (contract with regional educational service center for program for behaviorally-disturbed students similar to other arrangements for outside services; no violation found); *New Haven Board of Education*, Dec. No. 3791 (St. Bd. Lab. Rel. 2000) (transfer of summer work to part-time employees did not differ significantly from past practice). In one interesting case, the Labor Board dismissed a complaint alleging violation of the *New Britain* rule by the Stamford Housing Authority. Technological innovation permitted it to eliminate the position of an inventory clerk, and the Labor Board ruled that the second test was not met because the tasks previously performed were no longer necessary. Since these tasks were not performed by other employees, there was contracting out of the work. *Stamford Housing Authority*, Dec. No. 3897 (2003), *aff'd AFSCME, Local 1303-260, Council 4, AFL-CIO v. Connecticut State Board of Labor Relations*, 2003 Conn. Super. LEXIS 3201 (Conn. Super. Ct. 2003).

b. Permissive subjects of bargaining

Other subjects may be categorized as permissive subjects of bargaining. That means that the parties may but need not bargain over the subject. Such subjects include teacher evaluation in certified staff negotiations and bargaining unit determination in non-certified staff negotiations. *See, e.g., Wethersfield Board of Education v. State Board of Labor Relations*, 201 Conn. 685 (1986). Either party may simply decline to negotiate over a permissive subject. If it does, the other party cannot require bargaining or submit the issue to impasse resolution. If the parties do negotiate and reach an agreement on a permissive subject, it will be binding for the term of the contract. However, when the contract comes up for renegotiation, either party can inform the other that it declines to bargain over the permissive subject(s). Since these provisions would not then have been renegotiated, they will simply not reappear in the successor agreement.

c. Illegal subjects of bargaining

Illegal subjects of bargaining are those over which parties cannot bargain. Illegal subjects of bargaining usually conflict with other statutory duties. It would be illegal, for example, for a school board to negotiate over procedures for teacher dismissal, because the responsibilities of school boards in such matters are set out in the Teacher Tenure Act, Conn. Gen. Stat. § 10-151. *West Hartford Education Association v. DeCourcy*, 162 Conn. 566 (1972). If parties reach agreement on an illegal subject of bargaining, no one goes to jail, but the illegal provision would not be enforceable.

3. Past practice

The duty to bargain in good faith also imposes obligations during the term of a contract. Employers may not make unilateral changes in conditions of employment when they relate to mandatory subjects of bargaining, even if there is no contract language addressing the matter. This rule results from the practical realities of the collective bargaining relationship. The parties are obliged to negotiate over wages, hours and conditions of employment. However, if the employer could take unilateral action with regard to any matter not nailed down in the contract, negotiations would be an interminable process. As a consequence, the concept of "past practice" evolved. If a change relates to a significant condition of employment not covered by the collective bargaining agreement, the employer cannot make that change without prior negotiation.

This duty can even arise with respect to matters where the employer originally acted unilaterally without negotiation. The paradigm is the "holiday turkey" example. If an employer gratuitously gives each employee a turkey at Christmas time for, say, three years, it will have (perhaps inadvertently) created a past practice. The employer may not then be able to decide unilaterally that it will end this generous practice. At that point the employer's unilateral act of largesse may bind the employer until it negotiates a change in the practice.

Significantly, the "past practice" rule cuts both ways. Sometimes unions will challenge action by an employer on a mandatory subject of negotiations that is not covered by the contract. When the employer regularly has exercised that prerogative in the past, the exercise of that prerogative in a particular case will not be a change, and therefore the employer will not be required to negotiate on that issue when it exercises that right in the future. For example, where there is no language in the contract concerning experience credit, if the school board always has given newly hired teachers full credit for their past teaching experience, it could not unilaterally change that practice and place all new hires on the first step of the salary schedule. However, if the superintendent has historically exercised his or her discretion to determine how much credit to give on the schedule to new hires, the superintendent may continue to act in accordance with the past practice whether the union likes it or not.

Not all management decisions are subject to the "past practice" rule. First, a given action may be a management prerogative. The employer has the fundamental right to manage the affairs of the enterprise. For boards of education, that means that the board may determine what educational activities will be provided and how many people will be employed to staff such activities. Related prerogatives include determining the qualifications for particular positions, and, perhaps the most basic management right, decisions over the creation and elimination of positions. When an issue involves such a fundamental management prerogative, there is no duty to bargain over the decision, regardless of the past practice. There may be an obligation to bargain over the impact of the decision, however, as discussed in Section A(4), below.

Second, the "past practice" rule does not apply if there is contract language controlling the situation. Past practice relates to matters that are not in the contract. It can also be helpful in construing ambiguous contract language, and arbitrators often resort to past practice to determine what specific contract language has meant to the parties. If the contract language is clear, however, a past practice will not bind the employer. For example, a contract may state that teachers may receive up to two years credit on the salary schedule for time spent in the military. Even if in the past the district has given more than two years credit, it will be free to enforce the contract language in the future, regardless of the past practice.

Third, a past practice must be consistent to be binding. One decision does not make a past practice. Rather a past practice will arise only through consistent treatment of a group of similarly situated employees over time. How much consistency and how much time will be a factual determination in each individual case. A past practice will not arise, however, in a particular school or with a particular teacher. As with other conditions of employment, a past practice will typically relate to all employees or a specific class of employees.

Finally, to be a binding past practice the employer's action must be known to the union. Since the duty to bargain is between the employer and the union, the employer may not establish a past practice with individual employees. When an employer takes action that it may later wish to describe as an established prerogative, it will generally be in a specific case, with a specific employee. However, if the union does not have notice of a particular action or practice because the employer has dealt directly with that employee, the employer may not be able to prevail with the claim that the prerogative being exercised conforms to a binding past practice.

4. Impact bargaining

Even if a decision is a legitimate exercise of a management prerogative, the employer may be obligated to bargain over the impact of such a decision. For example, the board of education could decide to eliminate recess or otherwise lengthen the school day without bargaining. But the union would have the right (which it would certainly exercise) to demand to bargain over the impact of such decisions on the conditions of employment of its members. *See, e.g., Bloomfield Board of Education*, Dec. No. 2821 (St. Bd. Lab. Rel. 1990) (board of education must bargain over the impact of changes in the early release schedule for teachers).

The Connecticut Supreme Court considered the issue of impact bargaining in *Local 1186 v. State Board of Labor Relations*, 224 Conn. 666 (1994). There, the New Britain Board of Education exercised its right to impose a smoke-free policy unilaterally without negotiations. All agreed (eventually) that the Board of Education did not have to bargain over this decision, which is a management right to set educational policy for the school district. *See, e.g., Portland Board of Education*, Dec. No. 1490 (St. Bd. Lab. Rel. 1981). The union claimed that the Board of Education had to bargain over the impact of its decision on the employees. The Board of Education and the State Labor Board, however, took the position that any obligation to undertake impact negotiations was preempted by the statutes obligating school districts to have smoke-free buildings (at least during school hours) and permitting employers to declare their facilities smoke-free. Conn. Gen. Stat. § 19a-342; Conn. Gen. Stat. § 31-40q.

The Court rejected those claims and ruled that employers must negotiate over the impact of a management decision if it has a substantial impact on working conditions. First, it noted that the State Board of Labor Relations had previously ruled that a no-smoking rule does have a significant impact on working conditions. Second, it noted that the statutes in question did not absolutely ban smoking in school buildings. Since the employer was exercising some discretion in its total ban, it was obligated to negotiate over the impact of this decision. *Local 1186 v. State Board of Labor Relations*, 224 Conn. 666 (1994).

5. Unfair labor practice charges

The State Board of Labor Relations is the administrative agency within the State Department of Labor that is responsible for enforcing the duty of certain employers (including school districts) and employee representatives to bargain in good faith. Conn. Gen. Stat. § 7-471; Conn. Gen Stat. § 10-153e. It is an unfair labor practice for a board of education to:

- interfere with the rights of employees to engage in concerted activity;
- dominate or interfere with the creation or activities of an exclusive representative of the employees (the union);
- discharge or otherwise discriminate against an employee for exercising rights under the labor statutes;
- refuse to negotiate in good faith;
- refuse to participate in good faith in mediation or arbitration; or to
- refuse to hear employee grievances or refuse to comply with a grievance settlement.

Conn. Gen. Stat. § 7-470; Conn. Gen. Stat. § 10-153e. Similar rules apply to the unions, and it is possible for a board of education to file charges against the union on any of the grounds set forth in the statute. In addition, with regard to certified employee unions, the law expressly provides that it is an unfair labor practice for the union to engage in "soliciting or advocating support from public school students for activities of certified professional employees or organizations of such employees." Conn. Gen Stat. § 10-153e(c)(5).

If either the board of education or the union files a complaint that a prohibited practice has been committed, the State Board of Labor Relations will investigate the complaint. The investigation involves an informal conference between the parties, conducted by an assistant agent of the State Board of Labor Relations. At the informal conference, the agent discusses the matter with both parties and seeks an informal resolution. This process usually involves mediation efforts by the agent, and unfair labor practice charges are frequently resolved at this stage.

When resolution is not possible at the informal stage, the matter is presented to the State Board of Labor Relations in a formal administrative hearing. That process can take months (or years), and there is provision for the State Board of Labor Relations to grant interim relief in extraordinary cases. However, the standard for granting such relief is quite high, and it is rarely granted. *Town of Killingly*, Dec. No. 3205 (St. Bd. Lab. Rel. 1994). After hearing the case, the State Board will issue a written decision, either dismissing the complaint or finding a violation. These published decisions establish rules and provide guidance to Connecticut employers and unions in the same way that court decisions do.

When a violation is found, the State Board has the authority to order remedial measures, which typically include restoration of the *status quo ante*, *i.e.* the prior condition, a bargaining order, and a requirement that the decision be posted. In exceptional cases, the State Board of Labor Relations can and will order that the party committing the violation must pay the attorney's fees and costs of the other party. *Killingly Board of Education*, Dec. No. 2118 (St. Bd. Lab. Rel. 1982). A party who is aggrieved by a decision of the State Labor Board may appeal to the Superior Court but, as with other administrative agencies, the courts will often defer to the expertise of the State Board of Labor Relations.

6. <u>Grievance procedures and arbitration</u>

Virtually all collective bargaining agreements include a grievance procedure for resolving disagreements over the meaning of the contract. When a dispute is subject to a grievance procedure, employees are typically required to go through this procedure (exhaust their remedies) before they will be allowed to litigate the dispute in court. *Labbe v. Pension Commission*, 229 Conn. 801 (1994).

The heart of the grievance procedure is the grievance definition. Most such procedures define a grievance as a claimed violation, misinterpretation or misapplication of any of the specific provisions of the agreement. For contracts negotiated after July 1, 2004, however, Conn. Gen. Stat. § 10-151b(a) now provides that "claims of failure to follow the established procedures of such evaluation programs" are also subject to the grievance procedure. This amendment to Section 10-151b makes it advisable to negotiate appropriate limitations on such grievances and related remedies.

Where a complaint falls outside the scope of the grievance definition, it is not properly subject to the grievance procedure. If such a complaint is appealed to the arbitration step, the employer may claim that the complaint is not "arbitrable," *i.e.* not subject to the arbitration procedure ("substantive arbitrability"). Similarly, if the grievant did not appeal a grievance decision in a timely manner, the grievance may not be arbitrable ("procedural arbitrability"). If the employer does not raise the issue of arbitrability, the question of arbitrability will be waived, and the matter will be heard on the merits.

Grievance procedures usually provide that complaints are first subject to informal discussion and then to formal review at successive steps of the grievance procedure. Typically, the grievance is heard first by the immediate supervisor, then the superintendent of schools, the board of education, and an impartial arbitrator or arbitration panel in the successive steps of the procedure. Sometimes, parties negotiate bifurcated grievance procedures, in which grievances based on contract claims go to binding arbitration, while all other claims go to advisory arbitration or even terminate at the board of education level of the procedure.

Since the two parties to a collective bargaining agreement are the employer and the designated employee representative, the union may participate in the grievance procedure at every step, even if the contract permits a grievant to pursue his or her grievance independently of the union. In addition, the union can appeal a grievance decision, regardless of the position of the individual grievant, because it too may be bound by grievance resolutions. In any event, it is advisable for both the board of education and the union to provide in the contract that only the union, and not an individual employee, may appeal to arbitration.

The grievance procedure is a mechanism for resolving disputes over collectively bargained agreements, and the grievance procedure is thus an extension of the bargaining process. *Board of Education v. State Board of Labor Relations*, 217 Conn. 110 (1991); *State of Conn. (Judicial Dept.)*, Dec. No. 2428 (St. Bd. Lab. Rel. 1985). As such, it can be an unfair practice for either party to refuse to participate in good faith in the grievance procedure. Also, statements made by employees in the grievance procedure are privileged and may not result in discipline of the employee unless the employer can prove that the employee committed perjury. *Meriden Police*

Union, Local 1016 v. Connecticut State Board of Labor Relations, 2004 Conn. Super. LEXIS 769 (Conn. Super. Ct. 2004).

Similarly, once a grievance settlement is reached at any stage of the grievance procedure (including a decision that is not appealed further), it is an unfair labor practice to refuse to comply with the grievance settlement. *Hartford v. Hartford Municipal Employees Association*, 259 Conn. 251 (2002). It is therefore important for decision-makers at lower levels of the grievance procedure to get guidance from the Superintendent or his/her designee before binding the board of education with a grievance response.

Grievance hearings conducted by public agencies (including school boards) are subject to the Freedom of Information Act, at least in part. *Waterbury Teachers Association v. Freedom of Information Commission*, 240 Conn. 835 (1997). In that case, the Connecticut Supreme Court held that a grievance hearing is a "meeting" under the FOIA, at least when evidence is presented, because the presentations of the parties on the grievance in question is not "strategy or negotiations." Unless some other exemption under the Freedom of Information Act applies (such as that permitting executive session for personnel matters), therefore, that portion of the hearing devoted to "receiving testimony and evidence from witnesses" must be held in open session. Discussion thereafter concerning appropriate remedies and settlements, however, may be closed to the public, because discussion of "strategy and negotiations with respect to collective bargaining" is not a meeting under the FOIA.

Executive session for many grievance hearings can be justified under the "personnel" reason for executive session, *i.e.* "discussion concerning the appointment, employment, performance, evaluation, health or dismissal of a public officer or employee, provided that such individual may require that discussion be held at an open meeting." However, this provision may be used to justify the executive session only when the grievance relates to a particular employee and when that employee does not exercise his or her right to require that the discussion be held in open session. Conn. Gen. Stat. § 1-200(6).

A similar analysis applies to grievance records. The Appellate Court has held that the grievance document is not exempt from disclosure as a document relating to collective bargaining, because it does not include statements of collective bargaining strategy. *Bloomfield Board of Education v. Frahm*, 35 Conn. App. 384 (1994). However, this decision does not address the question of whether any responses would be exempt. Presumably, a grievance response is part of the collective bargaining process, because it is an offer from one party to the contract to the other in an attempt to reach agreement on how the contract is to be interpreted.

Since the grievance procedure is related to the collective bargaining process, it is important to distinguish the role of the board of education in the grievance procedure from other board responsibilities. There are situations where by law the board of education must be an impartial decision-maker independent from the administration, such as in teacher dismissal cases, residency hearings and student discipline matters. By contrast, in collective bargaining and, by extension, in the grievance process, the board of education has no duty to be "neutral," and the superintendent often acts as the agent of the board. The board of education, including the superintendent as its agent, is one party, and the union is the other party to the collective bargaining agreement.

Some districts follow a quasi-judicial model in grievance hearings, that is, the process is modeled on court procedures, with the union in the role of plaintiff, the superintendent in the role of defendant, and the board as the "judge." Such an approach ignores the realities of the bargaining and grievance process. While unilateral (*ex parte*) communication with the board would be improper when the board acts as judge in, for example, a tenure case, the same rules do not apply in the grievance setting. Boards of education, therefore, should feel free to discuss grievances privately with the administration both before and after related hearings. Such communication is particularly important because a grievance decision in one case can set a precedent in other cases. The board should exercise its right to communicate freely with the superintendent and its other agents to assure that it makes the best decision with regard to the interpretation of the contract.

Most contracts provide for binding resolution of such disputes through impartial arbitration. As discussed above, there may be situations in which a grievance is not arbitrable because the subject matter is not covered by the grievance definition or because it was appealed late. In addition, there may be situations in which the grievant did not comply with deadlines or other procedural requirements for processing the grievance. In such situations, the grievance may not be arbitrable, and the board of education may object to arbitration on that basis.

When arbitrability is raised, the arbitrator(s) typically determine whether the grievance is arbitrable. However, under Connecticut law, arbitrability determinations are ultimately reserved to the courts. The

Connecticut Supreme Court has held that "a person can be compelled to arbitrate a dispute only if, to the extent that, and in the manner in which, he has agreed so to do." *Marsala v. Valve Corp. of America*, 157 Conn. 362, 365 (1969), *cited in White v. Kampner*, 229 Conn. 465, 471-72 (1994). Moreover, if a party raises arbitrability before the arbitrator, that party may then seek judicial review of any adverse ruling by the arbitrator. *White v. Kampner*, 229 Conn. 465, 478 (1994). Given that arbitration is a favored means to resolve disputes, however, the courts will typically rule that a matter is arbitrable unless it can be stated with "positive assurance" that it is not. *Carlin Pozzi Architects, P.C. v. Town of Bethel*, 62 Conn. App. 483 (2001). This standard derives from a 1960 decision of the United States Supreme Court, which holds that the courts should order arbitration unless it can be stated with "positive assurance that the arbitration clause is not susceptible of an interpretation that covers the asserted dispute." *United Steelworkers v. Warrior & Gulf Co.*, 363 U.S. 574 (1960).

The State Board of Mediation and Arbitration, another administrative agency of the Department of Labor, is often named as the arbitration panel in contracts between boards of education and non-certified employees. When the State Board of Mediation and Arbitration conducts an arbitration hearing, state law requires that any claim of arbitrability generally must be made in writing to the chair of the arbitration panel and to the other party at least ten days before the arbitration hearing. Conn. Gen. Stat. § 31-97. Even when arbitration is through another agency such as the American Arbitration Association, it is helpful to raise the arbitrability issue in the earlier steps of the grievance procedure to assure that the question of arbitrability has not been waived.

Aside from the willingness to review questions of arbitrability, the courts are loathe to disrupt arbitration awards. The favored status of arbitration as a means for resolving disputes is based in part on its finality, and the courts will not entertain appeals from arbitration awards except under very limited circumstances. As long as the award conforms to the submission, *i.e.* the arbitrator answers the question he or she was asked, the courts will typically let the award stand. *See, e.g., Local 1042, Council 4, AFSCME, AFL-CIO v. Norwalk Board of Education*, 66 Con. App. 457 (2001). Even the most convincing argument by a party that the arbitrator's decision is wrong will generally be rejected, given the strong presumption in favor of arbitration as a means for dispute resolution.

This strong presumption in favor of the finality of grievance arbitration awards is reflected in another statute that affects certified staff members. Conn. Gen. Stat. § 10-153m provides that if a party moves to vacate an arbitration award or if a party refuses to stipulate to the confirmation of that award, and the award later is not vacated or is confirmed, that party may be required to pay the other its reasonable attorney's fees. Whether an award of attorney's fees will be imposed is within the discretion of the court. *Bethel Board of Education v. Bethel Education Association*, 2003 Conn. Super. LEXIS 2048 (Conn. Super. Ct. 2003). In plain English, if a party loses in arbitration and brings the matter to court, it risks having to pay not only its own attorney's fees, but also those of the other party.

Appeal from arbitration awards is limited by statute. Conn Gen. Stat. § 52-418 provides that courts will vacate an arbitration awards only when (1) the award has been procured by corruption, fraud or undue means, (2) there has been evident partiality or corruption on the part of the arbitrator, (3) the arbitrator has been guilty of misconduct in refusing to postpone the hearing upon cause shown or in refusing to hear evidence pertinent and material to the dispute or in otherwise prejudicing the rights of a party, or (4) if the arbitrator has exceeded his/her authority or exercised his/her powers so imperfectly that a definite award was not made. Claims of corruption or evident partiality are rare, but arbitration awards are often appealed on two grounds: (1) that the arbitrator exceeded his/her authority, or (2) that the arbitrator's decision contravenes public policy.

Arbitrators have only the authority granted them by the parties, and when they exceed that authority, the award will be vacated. In one case, for example, the court vacated an arbitration award in which the issue was framed, "Was the Grievant suspended for just cause under the collective bargaining agreement? If not, what shall be the remedy be?" The arbitrator found just cause for suspension, but reduced its length. The Appellate Court, however, vacated the award, ruling that once the arbitrator had found just cause, the issue of remedy was not before him. *Hartford v. Local 760*, 6 Conn. App. 11 (1986).

In *Board of Education v. East Haven Education Association*, 66 Conn. App. 202 (2001), the Appellate Court vacated an award because the arbitrator had exceeded her authority and had issued an award without a specific remedy. The arbitrator had ruled in favor of the Association in a grievance arbitration hearing over the interpretation of contract language on block scheduling. The arbitrator failed, however, to restrict her award to the year in question and failed to issue a concrete remedy, instead simply ordering the parties to negotiate a resolution. Rejecting the claim of the plaintiff board of education to the contrary, the court ruled that it was appropriate to remand the matter back to the original arbitrator, rather than vacating the award and remanding it for a *de novo* hearing. *See also State v. ASCSME, Council 4, Local 1565*, 249 Conn. 474 (1999); *Rocky Hill Teachers' Association v. Board of Education of the Town of Rocky Hill*, 72 Conn. App. 274 (2002) (award that sends matter of dental premiums back to the parties vacated for being indefinite). *But see International Brotherhood of Police Officers v. New Milford*, 81 Conn. App. 726 (2003) (award that upholds indefinite suspension subject to submission to fitness for duty examination not indefinite).

In addition, if an arbitration award violates an important issue of public policy, the courts will vacate the award. *Schoonmaker v. Cummings & Lockwood of Connecticut, P.C.*, 252 Conn. 416 (2000). This doctrine is especially important in the public sector, where issues of public policy arise with great frequency. In *Groton v. United Steelworkers of America*, 254 Conn. 35 (2000), for example, the Connecticut Supreme Court considered whether it was against public policy to reinstate an employee who was convicted of charges of embezzlement from his employer, the Town of Groton. The arbitrator had found that the conduct at issue, pocketing municipal funds, would be just cause for termination, but held that the employee's *nolo contendere* plea did not establish proof of the misconduct. The court, however, stated that the employee had been convicted of embezzlement as a result of the plea bargain, and that it is against the public policy of this State to require an employer to reinstate an employee after such a conviction.

Since the *Groton* case was decided, there have been a number of decisions on whether to vacate an arbitration award on public policy grounds. In *State v. AFSCME, Council 4, Local 387, AFL-CIO*, 252 Conn. 467 (2000), the Connecticut Supreme Court affirmed a decision vacating an award that reinstated a corrections officer who was terminated for placing obscene, racist calls from work to a legislator. *See also City of Hartford v. Casati*, 2001 Conn. Super. LEXIS 3146 (Conn. Super. Ct. 2001) (vacated award ordering reinstatement of demoted deputy police chief to his position who had made racist remarks); *City of Hartford v. Local # 760, International Association of Firefighters*, 2003 Conn. Super. LEXIS 687 (Conn. Super. Ct. 2003) (vacating arbitration award requiring salary credit for "study" at diploma mill). Before a court will vacate an arbitration award on public policy grounds, however, it must find a clear violation of a broad public policy. *State of Connecticut v. New England Health Care Employees Union, District 1199, AFL-CIO*, 265 Conn. 771 (2003). *See also South Windsor v. South Windsor Police Union Local 1480, Council 15, AFSCME, AFL-CIO*, 255 Conn. 800 (2001) (confirmed arbitration award reinstating police officer who had been found psychologically unfit for duty, despite employer's public policy claim).

Since arbitration awards will be final and binding in the vast majority of cases, parties to grievance procedures should take care in three ways. First, in negotiations they should carefully define the scope of the grievance procedure. Second, they should specifically define the authority of the arbitrator. Most grievance procedures expressly state that the authority of the arbitrator is to interpret the contract, and that the arbitrator may not add to, subtract from, or modify any of the provisions of the contract in any way. Third, the submission to the arbitrator (the "issue") must be carefully worded. Such limitations are important, given the deference the courts usually give to arbitration awards.

7. Just cause

In addition to issues of contract interpretation, questions of disciplinary action are frequently reviewed under grievance and arbitration procedures. Contracts with both non-certified and certified employees often contain a provision that any disciplinary action taken against an employee must be for "just cause." "Just cause" is a term of art that is generally understood, but is not easily defined. The best description is that "just cause" is another way of asking whether the employee has been treated fairly.

In determining whether there is just cause for discipline, supervisors should consider the following:

- Did the employee have fair notice of the rule or requirement?
- Did the employee violate the rule or fail to satisfy the requirement (such as satisfactory job performance)?
- Was there any justifiable excuse for any such failure?
- Was the disciplinary action taken appropriate under the circumstances, *i.e.* did the punishment fit the crime?

The burden of proof in disciplinary cases is on the employer. However, when the employer can show that the employee was on notice of a problem and his or her performance did not improve, there will be "just cause" for discipline.

In determining the discipline to be imposed (which can range from a verbal reprimand to termination of employment), the employer must generally follow the principle of "progressive discipline." To do so, the employer must first consider the seriousness of the offense. For some offenses, termination is the only reasonable course. For most matters of employee discipline, however, the challenge is to determine discipline that is appropriate to the employee's misconduct. To do so, the employer must consider both seriousness of the offense and the employee's past record. Relatively minor misconduct in the face of prior warnings, for example, may warrant suspension or termination. Conversely, if an employee's record is otherwise unblemished, discipline short of termination may be the appropriate response to even a serious lapse in judgment (*e.g.*, getting caught calling in sick to go shopping).

The standard progression of disciplinary action (hence "progressive discipline") is oral warning, written warning, suspension and termination. This progression of discipline, however, is only a guide, and each case must be considered individually, based on the principles set out above. It is important, therefore, to avoid contract language that requires such a progression in every case, because the employer must remain free to take appropriate action in cases of serious misconduct, even if it is a first offense.

Arbitrators at the State Board of Mediation and Arbitration typically apply a traditional seven-part test to determine if just cause exists for discipline:

- Was the employee forewarned of the consequences of his misconduct?
- Was the employer's rule or order reasonably related to safe and efficient operations?
- Did the employer, before administering the discipline, investigate to discover whether the employee did in fact violate or disobey a rule or order?
- Was the employer's investigation conducted fairly and objectively?
- Did the investigation produce substantial evidence or proof that the employee was guilty as charged?
- Has the employer applied its rules, orders and penalties evenhandedly and without discrimination?
- Was the degree of discipline reasonably related to the seriousness of the employee's proven offense and the employee's past record?

See, e.g., New Britain Board of Education and AFSCME, Council 4, Local #1186, (St. Bd. Med. Arb., Halperin, Neutral Arbitrator, June 9, 2000), *citing Enterprise Wire Co.*, 46 LA 359, 362-365 (Daugherty, Arb. 1966).

These elements of the seven-part test will be considered in the context of the specific facts of the case. For example, many actions of serious misconduct are presumed to be understood by all, such as theft or striking a supervisor. The seven-part test, however, is a helpful framework to use when considering disciplinary action against an employee.

Discipline of certified staff members must be considered separately. First, dismissal is not subject to review through the grievance procedure; it is the exclusive province of the Teacher Tenure Act, Conn. Gen. Stat. § 10-151. *West Hartford Education Association v. DeCourcy*, 162 Conn. 566 (1972). However, discipline short of dismissal relates to working conditions, a mandatory subject of negotiations. Moreover, it is clear that the Teacher Tenure Act does not cover disciplinary action short of termination of contract. *Tucker v. Norfolk Board of Education*, 4 Conn. App. 87 (1985). As a result, many contracts with certified staff have provisions requiring just cause for discipline short of termination. By contrast, issues of unsatisfactory performance of teaching responsibilities are typically addressed through the teacher evaluation plan, which is not subject to collective bargaining except by agreement of the parties. *Wethersfield Board of Education v. State Board of Labor Relations*, 201 Conn. 685 (1986). However, the concepts of just cause and progressive discipline apply to the supervision and discipline of certified staff members as well. Should contract termination ever be proposed, the impartial panel will consider elements of just cause and progressive discipline in deciding the case.

Finally, increasingly there have been claims of "constructive discharge." This claim can arise when an employee resigns and then later claims that he or she was forced to do so, and thus effectively (or constructively) was fired. Typically, a resignation will be enforceable, and a subsequent grievance alleging that there was not just cause for termination will not be arbitrable. *See, e.g., City of Hartford*, Case No. 2003-A-0788 (St. Bd. Med. Arb. 2003) (employee resigned at *Loudermill* hearing (with union representation); subsequent grievance claiming that he was harassed into resignation dismissed as not arbitrable).

Under rare circumstances, the courts have been willing to consider claims of constructive discharge, even if the employee did not exhaust other remedies before resigning. *See Mendillo v. Board of Education*, 246 Conn. 456 (1998), discussed in Chapter Three, Section C. More generally, however, an employee who claims constructive discharge will be required to exhaust his/her contractual or statutory remedies and will not be permitted to bring a court action instead. *Appleton v. Board of Education*, 53 Conn. App. 252

(1999), *reversed in part on other grounds* 254 Conn. 205 (2000); *Lathrop v. Town of East Hampton*, 2001 Conn. Super. LEXIS 1469 (2000). The courts will consider the actual nature of the claim, not how the plaintiff attempts the frame it. *Saccardi v. Board of Education*, 45 Conn. App. 712 (1997). *See also Pennsylvania State Police v. Suders*, 542 U.S. __ (2004) (constructive discharge in sexual harassment case will only be recognized if adverse employment action was so severe that there was no reasonable alternative).

8. <u>Union representation</u>

Employees covered by collective bargaining agreements have the right to request union representation at any conference with the employer where they reasonably fear for their job security, *i.e.* that the employer may be considering adverse employment action. *East Hartford Board of Education*, Dec. No. 2256 (St. Bd. Lab. Rel. 1983). Union representation in such meetings is often referred to as *Weingarten* rights, named after a decision of the National Labor Relations Board, affirmed by the United States Supreme Court, that the right to such representation is inherent in the definition of concerted activity. *NLRB v. J. Weingarten, Inc.*, 420 U.S. 251 (1975). However, this requirement does not apply to a meeting in which predetermined discipline is communicated. If the employer does not ask the employee questions, union representation is not required, even upon request. *See, e.g., Pilgrims' Pride Corp.*, 116 LA 1441 (2001).

This right typically arises when misconduct is alleged, and the employer must investigate the allegations. Part of any appropriate investigation, of course, is an interview of the employee to give him or her the opportunity to respond to the charges. Such an "investigatory interview" is typically conducted after the employer has gathered all other relevant information so that this information can be reviewed with the employee. The NLRB and the courts have extended this right to have a representative in an investigatory interview even to non-union employees, because they too have the right to engage in protected activity under the law. *Epilepsy Foundation of Northeast Ohio v. NLRB*, 268 F.3d 1095 (D.C. Cir. 2001). The NLRB recently reversed itself on this point, however, and it not clear what the courts will do. *IBM Corporation and Schult, Bannon and Parsley*, Cases 11-CA-19324, 11-CA-19329, 11-CA-19334 (NLRB, June 9, 2004).

The employer does not have to notify the employee of his or her right to union representation prior to an investigatory interview or negative evaluation conference, but such notification is appropriate, and it underscores the seriousness of the situation. Once representation is requested, the employer must either grant the request or terminate the interview. This right, however, is limited to being represented by a co-worker or by the union at such an interview. It is appropriate to defer to the employee's choice in selecting a representative, unless the requested representative is not available. *See Anheuser-Busch, Inc. v. NLRB*, 338 F.3d 267 (4th Cir. 2003). The employee, however, does not have the right to bring private legal counsel to such a meeting unless the employer does so.

Weingarten rights do not apply to discussions where there is no reasonable fear for job security or when the employer simply informs the employee of disciplinary action. Discussion concerning performance evaluation issues, however, can trigger the duty to permit union representation as long as there is any reasonable concern for job security. Indeed, denying union representation in such a case could undermine a claim later that the employee should have known that his or her performance was deficient.

When union representation is granted, the employer must strike the appropriate balance between the legitimate interests of the employee in fair treatment against the employer's need to conduct an effective investigation. The employee must be permitted to confer with the representative, and the union representative may also ask that questions be clarified and/or that the employee have an opportunity fully to explain his position. The representative need not be permitted to dominate the meeting, however, and the employer can insist that the employee, rather than the union representative, answer the questions posed. An employee's refusal to respond can be considered insubordination, except for situations in which the employee asserts his or her right against self-incrimination.

Where alleged misconduct may also involve potential criminal prosecution, the public employer may be better off not threatening discipline for refusing to answer on Fifth Amendment grounds. The employer may simply terminate the interview when the employee asserts his right against self-incrimination. Such a response, of course, provides no exculpatory information. If the employer has gathered evidence of misconduct and the employee declines to provide a satisfactory explanation, the employer may act on the information obtained through the investigation and take appropriate disciplinary action.

Alternatively, in cases in which it is more important to determine the facts than to prosecute the employee under the criminal law, it may be possible to give the employee written assurance that his/her statements will not be used against him in a criminal prosecution. Such an assurance is known as a "*Garrity* warning," named after a 1967 United States Supreme Court decision, *Garrity v. New Jersey*, 385 US 493 (1967). If the employer is sure of the enforceability of the assurance (by working with the prosecutor), the employer may provide a *Garrity* warning and then direct the employee to answer the questions and find the employee insubordinate if the employee refuses to do so. Sometimes, the better approach, however, is simply to give the employee an opportunity to respond and move on.

Finally, the right to be the exclusive representative of employees carries with it the obligation to represent all employees, whether they are members of the union or not. It is important to note, however, that the union is not required to support the employee's position no matter what. Rather, the union is bound by the duty of "fair representation," which means that its decisions must be reasonable and not made for an improper reason, such as a decision not to support a grievance because the grievant is a union dissident. The State Board of Labor Relations has adopted the standard announced by the United States Supreme Court in 1967 in *Vaca v. Sipes*, 386 U.S. 411 (1967), *i.e.* "a Union breaches its duty of representation only when its conduct toward a member of the bargaining unit is arbitrary, discriminatory, or in bad faith. Only when the Union's conduct is motivated by hostility, bad faith or dishonesty does a prohibited practice exist." *Local 1565, Council 4, AFSCME, AFL-CIO (David Bishop)*, Dec. No. 3510 (St. Bd. Lab. Rel. 1997). A union representative may claim privately that he/she is representing the employee only because he/she must, but that is not always true. Unions may prefer to fight with management rather than with their own members.

B. Certified Staff

Negotiations between boards of education and certified staff are covered by the Teacher Negotiation Act. Conn. Gen. Stat. § 10-153a *et seq.* This law covers certified personnel who are employed in positions requiring certification, whether full-time or part-time, and it now includes in the teachers' bargaining unit persons who hold a durational shortage area permit. Conn. Gen. Stat. § 10-153b(a). However, in contrast to the Teacher Tenure Act, which includes as "teachers" all certified employees of a board of education below the rank of superintendent, the Teacher Negotiation Act expressly excludes the following employees from the scope of bargaining:

> The superintendent of schools, assistant superintendents, certified professional employees who act for the board of education in negotiations with certified professional

> personnel or are directly responsible to the board for personnel relations or budget preparation, temporary substitutes and all noncertified employees of the board of education . . . .

Conn. Gen. Stat. § 10-153b(b). All other certified employees and persons holding a durational shortage area permit are included by operation of law in either the "teachers' unit" or the "administrators' unit."

1. Unit determination

In collective bargaining, a basic question is the scope of the bargaining unit, *i.e.* the group of employees that the union represents with respect to wages, hours and conditions of employment. Generally, various groups of employees can form bargaining units, and typically the unit is comprised of one or more employee classifications (*e.g.* custodians, teachers). An essential requirement, however, is that unit members must all be employed. Employers have no duty to negotiate over issues involving persons who have retired from the bargaining unit. *Allied Chem. & Alkali Workers of America, Local Union No. 1 v. Pittsburgh Plate Glass Co.*, 404 U.S. 157 (1971).

The labor boards will often defer to the employees' wishes in petitioning to be recognized as a bargaining unit. However, for certified staff in Connecticut, there are no choices to make. The law itself specifies the two bargaining units that exist for certified employees — the "teachers' unit" or the "administrators' unit." If there is disagreement over the proper placement of specific positions, or whether the positions are exempt (as described above), the Commissioner of Education will hear the relevant facts through a designated hearing officer and make a unit determination. Interestingly, as opposed to the general rule that "collective" bargaining requires at least two employees, in Connecticut it is possible to have an administrators' unit with just one employee.

The "administrators' unit" includes all certified employees of a board of education employed in positions requiring administrative or supervisory certification (except those who are excluded, as listed above), and whose administrative or supervisory duties comprise fifty percent or more of the assigned time of the administrator. The "teachers' unit" is comprised of certified employees (or those who hold a durational shortage area permit) who are employed in positions requiring a teacher's or other certificate who are not included in the "administrators' unit." Given these definitions of the bargaining units, it is clear that many positions that require administrative certification will nonetheless be in the teachers' unit because teaching responsibilities will comprise more than fifty percent or more of the time the employee is assigned.

Unions representing each of these groups may petition for recognition as the exclusive bargaining representative of such employees, and that has occurred with teacher and administrator groups in most school districts in Connecticut. Generally, the administrators' unit and the teachers' unit are separate. However, the law provides that combined groups in existence on July 1, 1969, may continue to represent both teachers and administrators in the same unit. Over time, most of the combined units have been separated, and there are very few combined units left.

The Teacher Tenure Act applies to employees in both bargaining units, as well as all other persons employed in positions below the rank of superintendent. By contrast, the Teacher Negotiation Act separates these groups into the administrators' unit, the teachers' unit and the exempt employees. The intersection of these two laws has created difficulty in two situations.

First, what are an administrator's rights when he or she is reassigned to a teaching position? Is that a termination of employment under the Tenure Act? The Connecticut Supreme Court reviewed this issue in 1980 and held that it is not. *Candelori v. New Britain Board of Education*, 180 Conn. 66 (1980). Rather, the court ruled that a reassignment of an administrator to a teaching position does not trigger any rights under the Tenure Act. Such reassignments, however, may trigger rights under the collective bargaining agreement that covers administrators, such as severance benefits. In addition, such a reassignment places an administrator in the teachers' bargaining unit, and the applicable collective bargaining agreement may contain relevant provisions, such as reduction in force provisions, as outlined below.

Second, can an administrator facing layoff "bump" (displace) a teacher? Under the tenure law, the contract of a certified staff member can be terminated due to elimination of position or loss of position only if his or her contract is identified in accordance with a negotiated reduction in force (RIF) procedure. However, administrators and teachers typically negotiate different RIF procedures, and it was unclear how the negotiation law and the tenure law were to be harmonized. In 1985, the Connecticut Appellate Court reconciled these two laws in a review of a decision of the State Board of Labor

Relations. It agreed with the State Labor Board, which held that a certified staff member who is displaced from an administrative position may bump into the teachers' unit, subject to criteria negotiated between the board of education and the teachers' unit. The administrator does not automatically bump into a position, but can do so if his or her seniority or experience or other standing under the negotiated criteria would permit him or her to bump a teacher. *Connecticut Education Association v. State Board of Labor Relations*, 5 Conn. App. 253, *cert. denied*, 197 Conn. 814 (1985). The teachers' unit may not negotiate criteria that are uniquely adverse to administrators (*e.g.*, years of service as a teacher), but may negotiate criteria that can be applied to either group equally.

The *Connecticut Education Association* case left (at least) two questions unanswered. First, it did not address the respective rights of administrators who are exempt from collective bargaining, such as assistant superintendents or persons responsible to the board of education for budget preparation or personnel relations. *Compare Cimochowski v. Hartford Public Schools*, 261 Conn. 287 (2002) (assistant superintendents are "teachers" under the Tenure Act). A fair reading of this case suggests that these employees would first take their place in the administrators' unit and be subject to the negotiated criteria there. If identified for displacement from the administrators' unit under those criteria, they would then take their place in the teachers' unit. However, since the court did not address this situation, it is simply not clear. Unfortunately, the number of such exempt employees is relatively small and they lack political clout. Therefore, it is not clear whether the General Assembly will ever take action to clarify the rights of such employees under these statutes.

Second, the decision did not address the issue of whether a teacher who is displaced may "bump" up into the administrators' unit, provided of course that he or she holds the necessary administrative certification. While that scenario appears to violate the laws of nature, one teacher in Plymouth made precisely such a claim. Both the trial court and the Appellate Court rejected his claim, holding that there is no authority under the tenure law for a teacher to achieve a promotion to an administrative position by virtue of a reduction in force. *Trotta v. Plymouth Board of Education*, 32 Conn. App. 395 (1993).

2. <u>The duty to negotiate</u>

The Teacher Negotiation Act defines the duty to negotiate, and provides that certified staff may not engage in any strike or concerted refusal to render services. Conn. Gen Stat. § 10-153e. The statute provides for specific timelines for conducting such negotiations, and assures that negotiations will result in a new contract before the existing contract expires. These timelines and procedures apply with equal force to board of education negotiations with the teachers' unit and with the administrators' unit. The process is driven by the budget submission date, which is defined in Conn. Gen. Stat. § 10-153b(a)(5) as the

> date on which a school district is to submit its itemized estimate of the cost of the maintenance of the public schools for the next following year to the board of finance in each town having a board of finance, to the board of selectmen in each town having no board of finance and, in any city having a board of finance, to said board, and otherwise to the authority making appropriations therein.

Between the 240th and 210th day prior to the budget submission date, the board of education is to "meet and confer" with the municipal fiscal authority. The statute does not specify further the nature of this meeting. Presumably, it is to provide boards of education and municipal governments the opportunity to share information about the upcoming negotiations.

Negotiations must start by the 210th day prior to the budget submission date. Unfortunately, in some districts with early budget submission dates, this date falls early in the summer, making negotiations difficult to schedule. This problem is especially acute, given the short time that the parties have to negotiate for a successor agreement, as discussed below. In any event, the statute does not specify how negotiations are to "commence," and sometimes the parties simply exchange ground rule proposals by mail to comply with this statutory deadline.

The statute provides that a member of the board of finance, board of selectmen or other authority making appropriations "shall be permitted to be present during negotiations pursuant to this section and shall provide such fiscal information as may be requested by the board of education." Conn. Gen. Stat. § 10-153d(a). This provision does not give the representative of the fiscal authority any responsibility for decisions as to negotiations, but it does permit that representative to be present. Given that the duty here is to provide information to the board of education, it is also noteworthy that this representative does not have a statutory duty to keep the board of finance or other town agencies informed on the status of negotiations. If there are ground rules in place that provide that the negotiations process is confidential, the parties may wish to clarify that the representative of the fiscal authority attending negotiations is also bound by the ground rules and may not report to the town during the negotiations process.

The Teacher Negotiation Act gives the parties only fifty days to negotiate a successor agreement before they must designate a mediator, so it is important that the limited time for negotiations be used efficiently and effectively. At the outset of negotiations, the parties typically establish ground rules for the negotiations. Such ground rules are a mandatory subject of negotiations, and can themselves be the subject of impasse resolution. However, neither party can condition its willingness to negotiate over other mandatory subjects on agreement over the ground rules. If the parties are unable to reach agreement on the ground rules, they are well-advised to move into the negotiations over the substantive issues in the negotiations, especially since there is little time to negotiate before the process will impose mediation.

The substance of the ground rules will vary with the situation and the relationship between the parties. However, basic ground rules to consider are:

- will negotiations be conducted in private or in public?
- who may attend negotiations?
- when will negotiations take place?
- what is the last date by which all proposals must be made?
- what is the effect of a "tentative agreement," *i.e.* an agreement between the negotiations committees on an issue in dispute?
- is an overall agreement between the negotiations committees subject to ratification by the parties, *i.e.* approval by the full board and the full membership?

As a practical matter, it is often also a good idea to have a ground rule for setting the agenda for the next meeting at the end of each meeting so that the parties come prepared to the subsequent negotiations sessions.

The Teacher Negotiation Act defines the duty to negotiate in good faith as follows:

> "[T]o negotiate in good faith" is the performance of the mutual obligation of the board of education or its

> representatives or agents and the [union] to meet at reasonable times, including meetings appropriately related to the budget-making process, and to participate actively so as to indicate a present intention to reach agreement with respect to salaries, hours and other conditions of employment, or the negotiation of an agreement, or any question arising thereunder and the execution of a written contract incorporating any agreement reached if requested by either party, but such obligation shall not compel either party to agree to a proposal or require the making of a concession.

Conn. Gen Stat. § 10-153e(d).

From this statutory provision, two important principles are evident. First, neither party may put conditions on their willingness to negotiate. Given the duty to conduct negotiations so as to indicate a present intention to reach an agreement, a party cannot refuse to negotiate over a mandatory subject, whether or not agreement is reached on other mandatory subjects. For example, a board of education may not refuse to bargain over salary until the union drops its class size proposals. Second, the duty to bargain in good faith expressly does not include the obligation to make any concessions. Rather, both parties remain free to hold to their positions as long as desired provided that they participate in good faith in the process of discussion and negotiation. In our example, the board would not have any duty to offer concessions on salary, regardless of the union's position on class size. In a word, good faith bargaining includes saying "no."

3. <u>The scope of bargaining</u>

Boards of education are obligated to negotiate only over mandatory subjects of bargaining. Permissive or even illegal subjects of bargaining may be presented by either side in negotiations, but it is completely appropriate and most often advisable to refuse to negotiate on such subjects. The Teacher Negotiation Act defines the scope of negotiations as follows:

> The local or regional board of education and the [union] shall have the duty to negotiate with respect to salaries, hours and other conditions of employment about which either party wishes to negotiate. For purposes of [the Teacher Negotiation Act], (1) "hours" shall not include the length of the student school year; the scheduling of the student school

> year; the length of the student school day; the length and number of parent-teacher conferences; and the scheduling of the student school day, except for the length and scheduling of teacher lunch periods and teacher preparation periods and (2) "other conditions of employment" shall not include the establishment or provisions of any retirement plan authorized by section 10-183jj.

Conn. Gen. Stat. § 10-153d(b). In 1987, "hours" was added to this provision as a mandatory subject of bargaining. Boards of education, however, still retain the right to set the student school day and student school year unilaterally. In addition, boards of education still retain the right to establish the length and number of parent-teacher conferences. However, now unions representing certified staff may negotiate over work time that is not during the student school day and school year, such as professional development activities outside of the school year. The statute has been clarified further, however, to provide that negotiations are not required over proposed retirement plans that include purchase of credit from the Teacher Retirement Board, known as an "Ohio" plan.

Even when boards of education have the right to act unilaterally in setting the student school year or student school day, negotiations may be required. Unions retain the right to demand negotiations over the impact of any changes in the school day or school year that affect their hours of employment. The State Board of Labor Relations decided in one case, for example, that the elimination of some fifteen early release days and the reinstatement of full school days on those days triggered a duty to bargain over the impact such changes had on the teachers' work load. *Bloomfield Board of Education*, Decision No. 2821 (St. Bd. Lab. Rel. 1990).

Evaluation of certified staff is also a permissive subject of bargaining. Here there is express authority for discussion with the bargaining agent, but negotiations are not required. Conn. Gen. Stat. § 10-151b(a) provides:

> The superintendent of each local or regional board of education shall, in accordance with guidelines established by the state board of education for the development of evaluation programs and such other guidelines as may be established by mutual agreement between the local or regional board and the teachers' representative chosen pursuant to section 10-153b, continuously evaluate or cause to be evaluated each teacher.

This statute establishes that boards of education have the responsibility for adopting teacher evaluation plans, so long as such plans are developed in accordance with guidelines established by the State Board of Education. The Connecticut Supreme Court has ruled that boards of education may, but are not required to, agree to guidelines proposed by the teachers' bargaining representative. The statute states that such plans may include "such other guidelines as may be established by mutual agreement." The court held that the reference to mutual agreement as opposed to negotiations evinced a legislative intent that guidelines for evaluation plans additional to those established by the State Board of Education need not be negotiated. *Wethersfield Board of Education v. State Board of Labor Relations*, 201 Conn. 685 (1986). *See* Chapter Three, Section D. Significantly, however, for contracts negotiated after July 1, 2004, the statute now provides that "claims of failure to follow the established procedures of such evaluation programs" are subject to the contractual grievance procedure. It is advisable, therefore, to negotiate appropriate limitations on such grievances and related remedies. Conn. Gen. Stat. § 10-151b(a).

In addition to school day, school year and evaluation, there are other issues that might come up in negotiations over which boards of education need not negotiate. The State Board of Labor Relations and the Connecticut courts have recognized that there are certain issues that relate to the basic responsibilities of the board of education and, as such, are not subject to negotiations. Perhaps the most commonly exercised prerogative is that of creating and eliminating positions. The board of education has the sole discretion as to what courses to offer and, concomitantly, what positions will exist to provide those educational services. Any contract language purporting to restrict the board of education in exercising this prerogative would, at the least, be permissive and might even be illegal.

Even though boards of education have the right to create and eliminate positions unilaterally, the impact of those decisions must be negotiated. Indeed, the Teacher Tenure Act expressly contemplates that boards of education will negotiate reduction in force procedures with the designated bargaining representatives. Conn. Gen. Stat. § 10-151(b)(5) provides that the contract of a teacher or an administrator may be terminated due to reduction in force only if his or her contract is identified in accordance with a negotiated reduction in force procedure or a written board policy.

Other basic prerogatives over which boards need not negotiate include establishing the curriculum, selecting textbooks, establishing policies for the district, such as policies on student discipline, or exercising any other statutory responsibility as a board of education. However, where such actions significantly affect working conditions, the board of education may be required to negotiate with the bargaining representative over the impact of such decisions on members of the bargaining unit.

When a board of education confronts a permissive or illegal subject during negotiations, it may identify it as such and decline to bargain over it. While discussing a permissive subject does not appear to constitute a waiver of the right to decline to bargain over such subjects, prompt notification to the union as to the position of the board of education will avoid wasting time in bargaining or muddying the waters, should the question of whether the subject is indeed permissive be submitted to the arbitration panel or the State Board of Labor Relations.

4. Agreement

The Teacher Negotiation Act sets out the procedure that applies when a board of education and a certified employee group reach agreement on a successor agreement. Typically, the contract agreement must be ratified by the parties. The statute does not address the issue of ratification, but virtually all negotiated settlements lead to a tentative agreement, which is then submitted to the full board of education and the unit membership for approval, *i.e.* ratification. If a contract is not ratified, the matter is submitted to mediation (if it has not yet been conducted) and then to arbitration. In such cases, the arbitration panel will generally consider the tentative agreement very seriously, will give significant weight to the history of negotiations, and will often issue an award which is the same as the tentative agreement reached earlier.

If the tentative agreement is ratified, the final agreement must be signed and then filed with the town clerk and the Commissioner of Education. In regional school districts, the signed agreement must be filed with the town clerk of each member town. The town clerk(s) are required to give public notice of the filing. The terms of the agreement are binding upon the legislative body of the local or regional school district unless the body rejects the contract at a regular or special meeting called within thirty days of the filing. A regional board of education is required to call a district meeting to consider the contract within the thirty day period if a chief executive officer of any member town so requests in writing within fifteen days of receiving the signed copy of the contract from the town clerk. Conn. Gen. Stat. § 10-153d.

The law favors approval of such contracts. First, no vote to approve is necessary — if no vote to reject is taken, the contract is approved. Second, the time limits are strictly construed. The actual vote must occur within the thirty day period; it is not enough to start the process within that period. *Madison Education Association v. Town of Madison*, 174 Conn. 189 (1978). Finally, if the matter of the contract is petitioned to referendum, at least fifteen percent of the registered voters must participate in the vote and a majority of those must vote to reject for any rejection to be valid. However, if the contract is rejected, the matter of the contract is submitted to arbitration. The fifth day following rejection is treated as the "arbitration date," on which the parties either designate their party arbitrators or inform the Commissioner that they have chosen a single arbitrator. The law also provides that the parties must also have mediation at this point if either party so requests.

If a contract agreement is rejected by the town (or by district meeting for regional boards of education), it is important to determine what issues will be submitted to the arbitration panel. When no agreement is reached, it is usually clear that the unresolved issues will be submitted to arbitration, but where all issues have been resolved, the answer is not so clear. Often, however, the parties "negotiate" over the issues that will be submitted to arbitration. The board of education will attempt to address the concerns that led to rejection, and the union will seek to balance those issues with issues of its own. Those provisions that neither party disputes are incorporated into the agreed language, which in turn the arbitration panel must incorporate into its award.

Alternatively, the parties may stipulate to all issues in arbitration. Since the board of education has the exclusive right to determine its last best offers in arbitration, it may simply make last best offers on the issues identical to the provisions of the agreement that was rejected. To date, the result of such a stipulation has been considered a binding arbitration award. Under analogous provisions under MERA, however, the Connecticut Supreme Court has ruled that such a stipulation is actually an agreement subject to approval by the municipal authority. *IBPO v. Jewett City,* 234 Conn. 123 (1995). Application of this rule to the Teacher Negotiation Act is questionable, given that the entire statute is built on the assurance that the contract will be finalized (one way or another) *before* the budget submission date. Moreover, at least when arbitration is the result of a prior rejection, treating a stipulation as an "agreement" could lead to absurd result of having the "agreement" rejected again and circling back to arbitration.

5. Mediation

If the parties have not reached agreement in negotiations, they are obligated by the Teacher Negotiation Act to submit to mediation. The statute requires that the parties designate a mediator no later than the 160th day prior to budget submission. The parties can continue to negotiate during this period, but the mediation session must occur during the twenty-five day mediation period, that is, before the "arbitration date," the 135th day prior to the budget submission date. Conn. Gen. Stat. § 10-153f(b).

Mediators are typically chosen by mutual agreement of the parties from a list of mediators approved by the State Board of Education, but the statute permits the parties to designate a mediator who is not on the panel. If the parties fail to reach agreement on the designation of the mediator, the Commissioner of Education will name the mediator.

The parties generally identify issues in dispute and agreed language prior to the mediation session so that the scope of the dispute is clear. The mediator has no power to compel either party to make a concession or to reach an agreement. Also, the mediator does not file a report or make written recommendations. Indeed, the mediator cannot be compelled to disclose any confidential communication made to him or her during the course of mediation, unless that privilege is waived. Nonetheless, mediation is a very important part of the teacher and administrator contract negotiation process. A large number, typically the majority of agreements reached in a particular year, are reached in mediation. When agreement is reached in mediation, the board of education must follow the procedures for submitting the contract to the town(s) for approval described in Section (B)(4) above.

6. Arbitration

If the parties do not reach agreement in negotiations or mediation, or if that agreement is rejected either during the ratification process or by the town(s), the dispute is submitted to arbitration in accordance with the statutory timeline. The arbitration process in Connecticut is "last best offer, issue-by-issue." That means that the arbitration panel may not split the difference between the parties' positions, but rather can only accept the last best offer of either party on each issue in dispute.

Arbitrators are appointed by the Governor and represent the interests of the employee group, the interests of the board of education, or the interests of the public, respectively. The statute provides for the appointment of a panel of seven arbitrators representing the employers and seven arbitrators representing the employee groups. In addition, between ten and fifteen members of the panel are appointed as neutral arbitrators. The neutral arbitrators, who must be residents of Connecticut, chair the panel when three arbitrators are appointed in a particular case. Arbitrators are appointed with the advice and consent of the General Assembly for two year terms, during which they are not subject to removal except for just cause. Names submitted to the Governor to serve on the arbitration panel must include a report certifying that the process for soliciting applicants made adequate outreach to minority communities and documenting that the number and makeup of minority applicants considered reflect the State's racial and ethnic diversity. Conn. Gen. Stat. § 10-153f(a).

When there is no settlement, the arbitration process must commence by the 135th day prior to the budget submission date. By that date (the "arbitration date"), the parties must each notify the Commissioner of Education of their designated representative on the arbitration panel. In addition, within five days thereafter, they must jointly agree on a neutral arbitrator. If they do not, the Commissioner must randomly select a neutral arbitrator from the panel of arbitrators. In either event, the neutral arbitrator serves as the chair of the panel. Alternatively, the parties may jointly inform the Commissioner on the arbitration date of their decision to submit the dispute to a single, neutral arbitrator.

The arbitration panel is required to convene the hearing between the fifth and twelfth day following the selection of the neutral arbitrator. This initial session is informally called the "bump and run" session, and the main order of business is typically to schedule the actual hearing dates, and often to identify the issues that will be submitted to the arbitration panel. Written notice of the initial meeting is to be sent to the parties five days in advance. Such notice is also to be sent to the fiscal authority for the town or towns involved in the arbitration, by registered mail, return receipt requested. Conn. Gen. Stat. § 10-153f(c)(2).

The arbitration hearing must be conducted in the school district, and the hearing must be concluded within twenty-five days after the initial session. At the hearing, both parties present evidence and testimony. These presentations provide the panel information related to the statutory criteria described below. The law also provides that "a representative designated by [the fiscal authority having budgetary responsibility or charged with making appropriations for the school district] may be heard at the hearing as part of the presentation and participation of the board of education." Conn. Gen. Stat. § 10-153f(c)(2). The statute also provides that the fiscal authority "shall be heard regarding the financial capability of the school district, unless such opportunity to be heard is waived." *Id.* The board of education generally coordinates its presentation with the representative of the fiscal authority, but the latter, while not a party to the proceedings, has the right to make an independent presentation if it wishes. In any event, the board of education remains solely responsible for submitting its last best offers on each issue. The arbitration panel can only consider the last best offers made by the two parties, regardless of the position taken by the fiscal authority.

After hearing the evidence, the arbitrator(s) must issue a decision or "award" within the next twenty days. The decision must be in writing, and is comprised of two parts. First, the decision must incorporate all agreed language. In this regard, it is important to note that the parties can submit agreed language on all issues in dispute at any time prior to the issuance of the decision of the arbitrator(s), and the arbitrator(s) are required to incorporate such language in the award. If the parties negotiate further prior to the issuance of the decision and stipulate to all issues in dispute, the arbitration decision must incorporate these agreements. However, since these agreements are formalized in the form of an arbitration award, the board of education need not (and may not) submit the agreement to the town; it is binding as written. By contrast, the Connecticut Supreme Court has ruled that under MERA a complete stipulation in arbitration is not a binding award, but rather an agreement that must be submitted to the legislative body of the town. *IBPO v. Jewett City*, 234 Conn. 123 (1995). No similar challenges, however, have been made under the Teacher Negotiation Act.

The second part of the arbitration decision includes the last best offers of the parties on all issues still in dispute, the last best offer accepted by the panel on each issue, and the analysis of the panel on these issues. In making its decision on each issue, the arbitration panel is required to give priority consideration to the public interest and the financial capability of the town or towns in the school district, including consideration of other financial demands on that district. The arbitrators must further consider the following criteria in light of such financial capability:

> (A) The negotiations between the parties prior to arbitration, including the offers and the range of discussion of the issues;

> (B) the interests and welfare of the employee group; (C) changes in the cost of living averaged over the preceding three years; (D) the existing conditions of employment of the employee group and those of similar groups; and (E) the salaries, fringe benefits, and other conditions of employment prevailing in the state labor market, including the terms of recent contract settlements or awards in collective bargaining for other municipal employee organizations and developments in private sector wages and benefits.

Conn. Gen. Stat. § 10-153f(c)(4).

The statute requires that the arbitrator(s) explain their decision. It requires that the written decision must include a narrative explaining the evaluation by the arbitrators of the evidence presented for each issue on which a decision was reached, stating "with particularity the basis for the decision as to each disputed issue and the manner in which the factors enumerated . . . were considered in arriving at such decision, including, where applicable, the specific similar groups and conditions of employment presented for comparison and accepted by the arbitrators or the single arbitrator and the reason for such acceptance." *Id.* Finally, the arbitrator(s) are required to include in the decision an explanation of how the total cost of all offers accepted was considered.

The arbitration decision must be filed with the Commissioner, each town clerk in the school district, the board of education and the employee organization. The decision is binding on both parties. However, since 1993, the legislative body of the town or towns of the school district may reject the award by a two-thirds vote within twenty-five days after receiving it. In the case of a regional school district, the rejection must be by each of the towns in the district. When the legislative body for the town is the town meeting, the board of selectmen has the authority to reject the award. The substance of the action, rather than the form of the vote, will control. *City of Stamford v. Ferrandino,* 1 Conn. Ops. 808 (July 24, 1995) ("approval" of contract defeated by two-thirds vote properly considered a rejection). If the appropriate body does not act within the prescribed twenty-five days, the award is binding, subject to judicial review, as described below.

If the award is rejected, within ten days of the rejection the legislative body is required to notify the Commissioner and the representative of the certified group in writing of the vote to reject and the reasons for the rejection. The employees' representative shall and the board of education may prepare a written response to such rejection and must submit it to the legislative body or bodies that rejected the contract and to the Commissioner of Education. Within ten days of receipt from the town or towns of notification of rejection by the legislative body, the Commissioner must appoint a second panel of three neutral arbitrators (unless the parties mutually agree to one arbitrator). Conn. Gen. Stat. § 10-153f(c)(7).

The "second look" panel does not hold hearings, but rather reviews the case on the basis of (1) the record (the transcript and exhibits) of the first hearing, (2) the briefs of the first arbitration hearing, (3) the written reasons submitted by the town(s) for the rejection, and (4) the responses by both parties. Significantly, the parties cannot change their offers. The "second look" panel either confirms or reverses the award on each disputed issue by accepting the last best offer of one party or the other. It is even possible for the panel to reverse issues which had been awarded to the board of education in the first arbitration. Given this limitation of the authority of the "second look" panel, towns have limited options in rejecting arbitration awards. A rejection will only provide review of issues that were disputed in the first hearing. Where the award includes agreed language, even on issues of salary or insurance, for example, the review panel does not have any right to review those issues.

The review of the "second look" panel must be completed within twenty days, and the decision must be issued five days later. The statute provides that the decision must include the specific reasons and standards used by each arbitrator in making a decision in the case. The costs of the panel and the costs of the transcript must be paid by the legislative body of the town(s). Conn. Gen. Stat. § 10-153f(C)(7). This award is binding and may not be rejected by the parties or the town(s).

In 2001, the Connecticut Supreme Court described the authority of the "second look" panel. *Education Association of Clinton v. Clinton Board of Education*, 259 Conn. 5 (2002). The first arbitration panel accepted the following last best offer of the teachers' union: "At no time shall any teacher be compelled to provide physical restraint procedures." The Town rejected the award, and a review panel was convened in accordance with statute. The review panel reversed, stating that award was not supported by evidence in the record and was not in the public interest. The Association appealed to court, claiming that the review panel should have afforded deference to the first panel. The Connecticut Supreme Court held, however, that the "second look" arbitration panel appropriately conducted *de novo* review, and it affirmed the award.

Finally, either party to an arbitration proceeding under the Teacher Negotiation Act can appeal to the courts for judicial review. Any such appeal must be filed within thirty days of receipt of the final decision, either the original award, if not rejected, or the "second look" award. However, the grounds for any such appeal are quite limited:

> The Superior Court, after hearing, may vacate or modify the decision if substantial rights of a party have been prejudiced because such decision is: (A) in violation of constitutional or statutory provisions; (B) in excess of the statutory authority of the panel; (C) made upon unlawful procedure; (D) affected by other error of law; (E) clearly erroneous in view of the reliable, probative and substantial evidence on the whole record; or (F) arbitrary or capricious or characterized by abuse of discretion or clearly unwarranted exercise of discretion.

Conn. Gen. Stat. § 10-153f(c)(8). Given this high standard of review, it is generally not worth the effort to seek judicial review of arbitration awards. *See, e.g., Watertown Education Association v. Watertown Board of Education*, 6 Conn. Ops. 894 (August 14, 2000) (Superior Court, July 25, 2000). Moreover, such action can be expensive; the statute provides that a party that is unsuccessful in its action for review is responsible for the reasonable attorney's fees of the other side as well as its own.

7. <u>Mid-term negotiations and arbitration</u>

Since 1987, the Teacher Negotiation Act has contained a provision for mid-term bargaining and impasse resolution. If parties to a certified staff contract either agree or are required to negotiate (by the State Board of Labor Relations, for example) during the term of a contract, they are to notify the Commissioner of Education within five days of commencing such negotiations. If no agreement is reached after twenty-five days of negotiations, mediation is imposed upon the parties. If no agreement is reached in mediation, which may be conducted for the next twenty-five days, binding arbitration is imposed on the parties, and the procedures described above all apply. Conn. Gen. Stat. § 10-153f(e).

This provision applies without regard to the budget submission date. If agreement is reached in a mid-term negotiation, that agreement is subject to ratification if the parties so provide in the ground rules for the negotiations. There is no express requirement in Conn. Gen. Stat. § 10-153f(e) that any such agreement be submitted to the town(s) for approval. The position of the State Department of Education, however, is that agreements reached under this provision must be filed with the town. The Department's position is based on Conn. Gen. Stat. § 10-153d(b), which provides that the local or regional board of education shall file a copy of a contract negotiated under that section with the town and the Commissioner of Education. The courts have not ruled on whether the contract filing requirement of Conn. Gen. Stat. § 10-153d applies to agreements reached under Conn. Gen. Stat. § 10-153f(e).

C. Non-Certified Staff

Negotiations between boards of education and their non-certified staff are governed by the Municipal Employees' Relations Act (MERA), Conn. Gen. Stat. § 7-467 *et seq.* This same statute applies to negotiations between towns and cities and their employees, as well as other agencies of local government, such as housing authorities, water pollution control authorities and the like. While the MERA applies to town and board of education negotiations with non-certified staff, the two are usually separate employers, and the board of education negotiates independently with its employees.

Sometimes charter provisions apply to non-certified employees of the board of education. For example, in some towns, non-certified board employees are subject to civil service rules. *Wallingford v. Wallingford Board of Education*, 152 Conn. 568 (1965). Such charter provisions can be binding on the local board of education, even though boards of education are independent of the town in many other ways. *Local #1186, AFSCME v. New Britain*, 182 Conn. 93 (1980). However, when employees are paid by the board of education and are under the sole control and supervision of the board, the board of education is the employer under MERA, whether or not such employees are also subject to municipal civil service rules.

1. Unit determination

In contrast to the Teacher Negotiation Act, MERA does not dictate placement of employees in particular bargaining units. Rather, the State Board of Labor Relations has followed the lead of the National Labor Relations Board, and will generally permit the petitioning employee organization to establish any "appropriate" bargaining unit. A "community of interest" is required, but that standard is not hard to meet, and generally the State Labor Board will allow any "appropriate" unit, without requiring the "most appropriate" unit. Some board of education units under MERA can include a wide range of employees, including for example, custodians, school secretaries, health aides and cafeteria workers. Theoretically, the State Labor Board will not certify a new bargaining unit if the result would be fragmentation (*i.e.* a proliferation of bargaining units). However, in practice, the State Labor Board gives deference to employee petitions, with the result that a large number of separate units have been certified. Custodians, nurses, secretaries, aides, school security workers, and even printers can all be in separate units.

Current employment is a basic prerequisite for unit membership, and employers have no duty to negotiate over issues involving persons who have retired from the bargaining unit. *Allied Chem. & Alkali Workers of America, Local Union No. 1 v. Pittsburgh Plate Glass Co.*, 404 U.S. 157 (1971). If a post-retirement benefit is negotiated, however, it will be binding on the employer during the applicable period (which can be the lifetime of the employee). Since the retiree is not a member of the bargaining unit, any dispute over such benefits would not be typically subject to the grievance procedure. Such benefits, however, are enforceable through the courts, which will review such claims under ordinary principles of contract law. *Poole et al v. City of Waterbury*, 266 Conn. 68 (2003).

MERA also provides that supervisory employees cannot be in the same unit with the employees who they supervise. The Act defines supervisory employees as those in positions the principal functions of which are characterized by two or more of the following:

(A) Performing such management control duties as scheduling, assigning, overseeing and reviewing the work of subordinate employees;

(B) Performing such duties as are distinct and dissimilar from those performed by the employees supervised;

(C) Exercising judgment in adjusting grievances, applying other established personnel policies and procedures and in enforcing the provisions of a collective bargaining agreement; and

(D) Establishing or participating in the establishment of performance standards for subordinate employees and taking corrective measures to implement those standards.

Conn. Gen. Stat. § 7-471(2). When employees' duties meet two or more of these requirements, they are considered supervisory and may not be in the same unit as the employees they supervise. However, any group of more than two supervisory employees can themselves form a collective bargaining unit unless they are either department heads or administrative officials.

MERA also makes special provision for "professional employees," as in Section 7-472(3). Such employees may not be included in a unit with non-professional employees unless a majority of such professional employees vote to be included in the unit.

The State Board of Labor Relations has developed the "confidential employee" exclusion based on precedents of the National Labor Relations Board, though there is no direct provision in the statute for excluding such employees. Municipal employers are entitled to exclude employees who have access to confidential information with regard to collective bargaining. For boards of education, such positions would usually be the secretary to the superintendent, the secretary to the business administrator, the secretary to the personnel director, administrative assistants and the like. The State Labor Board will generally recognize between two and four such positions as confidential. However, if a board of education seeks to exclude more than four such employees, it will have a heavy burden to show that the responsibility for confidential information related to collective bargaining cannot be consolidated in fewer positions. *East Hartford Board of Education*, Dec. No. 1980 (St. Bd. Lab. Rel. 1981).

Finally, questions can arise over unit determination during the term of the contract. Generally, a bargaining unit cannot petition for new employees during the term of a contract. Rather, any such petition must be filed during the "window" period at the end of the contract term, the same time when a rival union must file to challenge an incumbent union. However, if a position is newly created or if the employee in question is not represented by a union, the petition for unit clarification or modification can be filed at any time. Conn. Gen. Stat. § 7-471(4).

2. <u>The duty to negotiate</u>

MERA requires that negotiations between a municipal employer, including a board of education, and the union representing a bargaining unit commence at least one hundred twenty days prior to the expiration date of the contract. Conn. Gen. Stat. § 7-473b. Even if the negotiations extend beyond the term of the agreement, strikes are prohibited. Rather, the statute automatically extends the contract until the successor is reached through negotiations, mediation and/or binding arbitration, if necessary. Conn. Gen. Stat. § 7-475. The extension of the contract may require that the employer grant step movement if there is a past practice of doing so even before agreement on the new contract is reached. *Hartford Board of Education*, Dec. No. 3989 (St. Bd. Lab. Rel. 2004).

In contrast to the Teacher Negotiation Act, there is no requirement for consultation prior to starting negotiations, and there is no provision for the fiscal authority of the town to be involved in the negotiation process. MERA provides that "the chief executive officer, whether elected or appointed, or his designated representative or representatives, shall represent the municipal employer in collective bargaining" with the union. Conn. Gen. Stat. § 7-474(a). Under Connecticut law, the superintendent of schools is the chief executive of the board of education. Conn. Gen. Stat. § 10-157.

3. The scope of negotiations

MERA defines the duty to bargain as follows:

> [T]o bargain collectively is the performance of the mutual obligation of the municipal employer or his designated representatives and the representative of the employees to meet at reasonable times, including meetings appropriately related to the budget-making process, and to confer in good faith with respect to wages, hours and other conditions of employment, or the negotiation of an agreement, or any question arising thereunder, and the execution of a written contract incorporating any agreement reached if requested by either party, but such obligation shall not compel either party to agree to a proposal or require the making of a concession.

Conn. Gen. Stat. § 7-470(c). As with certified staff the duty to negotiate expressly does not include the requirement that either party make concessions.

The parties to negotiations will wish to negotiate ground rules to establish procedures for the negotiations. The same considerations that are reviewed in Section B(2) above apply to negotiations with non-certified staff. For example, it is important to determine a cut-off date for new proposals, the status of tentative agreements, whether negotiations will be confidential and the like. Also, it is especially important to specify the process for making proposals under MERA. The statute provides that "no party may submit for binding arbitration . . . any issue or proposal that was not presented during the negotiation process, unless the submittal of such additional issue or proposal is agreed by the parties." Conn. Gen. Stat. § 7-473c(g).

The scope of negotiations with non-certified staff is somewhat broader than applies to negotiations with certified employees. MERA adopts the standard from the National Labor Relations Act and provides that the parties are required to negotiate over "wages, hours and other conditions of employment." Conn. Gen. Stat. § 7-470(c). Consequently, issues concerning mandatory and permissive subjects do not arise with the same frequency as in certified staff negotiations. This broader duty could, of course, lead to problems, as for example with a proposal that custodians not work on Lincoln's Birthday, even though school is in session. Happily, such concerns to date have been theoretical rather than real.

The same rules do apply with regard to fundamental prerogatives of the board of education, as it fulfills its statutory responsibilities. Non-certified units cannot bargain over program issues, or the related creation or elimination of positions. However, the impact of such decisions may be subject to negotiations in the same way that boards of education may have to conduct impact negotiations with certified units.

There is one area where the scope of bargaining may be affected by the fact that school boards are for some purposes an arm of municipal government. Pension plans are a mandatory subject of bargaining. However, in some cases non-certified employees of the board of education participate in a municipal pension plan created by charter or ordinance. Typically, the board of education cannot change the terms of the plan through negotiations. Where such is the case, the union must negotiate the terms of any proposed changes in the pension plan directly with the municipality. *City of Hartford and its Board of Education*, Dec. No. 2812 (St. Bd. Lab. Rel. 1990); *Town of Ridgefield*, Dec. No. 3921 (St. Bd. Lab. Rel. 2003) (no separate unit recognition by municipality required).

4. Agreement

If parties to negotiations under MERA reach an agreement, they must reduce it to writing. As with certified staff negotiations, the parties will typically require ratification of any agreement reached. Once the agreement is ratified by the board of education and the unit membership, it is binding on both.

Under MERA, agreements reached must generally be submitted to the legislative body of the town for approval (which constitutes the ratification). Conn. Gen. Stat. § 7-474(b). As discussed in Section C(6), below, a total agreement reached in the arbitration process must be considered an "agreement" subject to these procedures, rather than an arbitration award. However, these rules relate only to negotiations under MERA with municipal employees. The statute makes separate provision for negotiations by other municipal employers, including boards of education. It provides:

> If the municipal employer is a . . . school board, . . . such . . . school board shall represent such municipal employer in collective bargaining and shall have the authority to enter into collective bargaining agreements with the [union], and such agreements shall be binding . . . and no such agreement or any part thereof shall require approval of the legislative body of the municipality.

Conn. Gen. Stat. § 7-474(d). Once a school board approves an agreement, it is binding, and there is no provision for the town to review or to reject the contract. *New London Housing Authority v. State Board of Labor Relations*, 76 Conn. App. 194 (2003).

5. <u>Mediation</u>

As with the Teacher Negotiation Act, MERA provides that contract disputes be mediated before the matter goes to binding arbitration. Conn. Gen. Stat. § 7-473b provides that the State Board of Mediation and Arbitration shall appoint a mediator to assist the parties if there has been no agreement after fifty days of bargaining. The statute also provides that the parties can request mediation earlier by mutual agreement.

In contrast to mediation under the Teacher Negotiation Act, under MERA the parties do not select the mediator, but rather he or she is assigned to the dispute by the State Board of Mediation and Arbitration. The mediators assigned to such disputes are employees of the State Board of Mediation and Arbitration, and thus there is no cost for the mediation process.

As with the Teacher Negotiation Act, the mediator does not have the power to compel agreement, and the mediator does not make recommendations or write a report. Under prior law, there was a fact finding stage, during which such reports were written and could be binding on the parties if not rejected. However, fact finding was eliminated from MERA in 1992.

If mediation leads to an agreement, the same procedures for finalizing the agreement as described in Section C(4) above apply. If no agreement is reached, then the procedures for arbitration apply, as outlined below.

6. Arbitration

Thirty days after the contract expires, MERA requires that binding arbitration be imposed. These procedures (including the imposition of binding arbitration thirty days after the contract expires) also apply to contract reopeners, which typically provide for negotiations over limited issues, such as salary and/or insurance. In either case, the State Board of Mediation and Arbitration notifies both the board of education and the union that binding arbitration is imposed upon them. Conn. Gen. Stat. § 7-473c.

Within ten days of receipt of that notification, the board of education, through its superintendent (generally through counsel), and the union must each select their representative on the arbitration panel. Then, within five days of their notification, the two panel members representing the parties must select the neutral arbitrator, who serves as chair of the panel, from the panel of neutral arbitrators. If the two party arbitrators fail to select the chair, the State Board of Mediation and Arbitration will make the selection at random from the same panel of neutral arbitrators. Conn. Gen. Stat. § 7-473c(b). The panel of neutral arbitrators is appointed by a neutral arbitrator selection committee. The selection committee is a group of ten persons, five representing labor and five representing management, all appointed by the Commissioner of Labor. Conn. Gen. Stat. § 7-473c(a).

Within ten days of his or her appointment, the chair of a MERA arbitration panel is required to convene the arbitration hearing in the municipality involved. The statute provides that the hearing is to be completed within twenty days. The statute also provides that the parties are required to prepare proposed collective bargaining agreements that they would be willing to sign, and file such proposed agreements with the panel chairman and the other party at least two days before the hearing commences. Such proposed agreements are to be in numbered paragraphs and should also have cost data for all provisions of the proposed agreement. At the beginning of the hearing the parties are required to file with the panel a reply setting forth (A) the paragraphs of the agreement that they would be willing to accept, and (B) those paragraphs that the party is unwilling to accept.

The procedures further require that the arbitration panel issue an arbitration statement within five days after the conclusion of the hearings, wherein it identifies the issues in dispute and the provisions on which the parties agree. Then the parties are to present (1) last best offers on each of the unresolved issues within ten days after the hearing concludes, (2) briefs seven days after the distribution of the last best offers of the parties by the State Board of Mediation and Arbitration, and then (3) reply briefs within five days of the distribution of the briefs by the State Board of Mediation and Arbitration. Within the next twenty days, the panel is required to issue its decision. Conn. Gen. Stat. § 7-473c(d)(1).

These procedures are most notable for the fact that they are never followed. Conn. Gen. Stat. § 7-473c(f) provides that the parties may file a stipulation with the panel modifying, deferring or waiving any or all of the provisions of the arbitration procedures. Consequently, the first order of business at the first arbitration hearing is generally to execute a stipulation waiving all of the procedures set out above. The parties almost always waive the timelines, and often they also modify the order of events so that the parties file briefs before filing their last best offers. However, it is important to note that, since the municipal employer has the right to reject the award, as discussed below, the employer must maintain a verbatim record of the arbitration hearings so that the review panel, if any, will have the required transcript to review.

The arbitration panel will decide each issue in dispute separately, selecting the last best offer of one party or the other. Each member of the panel is required to state the specific reasons and standards used in deciding each issue in dispute. In making its decision, the panel is bound to give priority consideration to the public interest and the financial capability of the municipal employer, including consideration of the other demands on the financial capability of the municipal employer, and the panel is to further consider the following factors in light of such financial capability:

> (A) The negotiations between the parties prior to arbitration; (B) the interests and welfare of the employee group; (C)

> changes in the cost of living; (D) the existing conditions of employment of the employee group and those of similar groups; and (E) the wages, salaries, fringe benefits, and other conditions of employment prevailing in the state labor market, including developments in private sector wages and benefits.

Conn. Gen. Stat. § 7-473c(d)(2). These criteria are very similar but not identical to those that apply under the Teacher Negotiation Act. The decision of the arbitration panel is final and binding on both parties, unless it is rejected as set forth below.

Given the struggles of many Connecticut towns and cities, the General Assembly has modified the statutory arbitration procedures in certain cases in which a municipality confronts a dire economic situation. Since the arbitration procedures are based on statutes passed by the General Assembly, the courts have held that the General Assembly can modify these procedures without violating the rights of unions and employees. In *AFSCME, Council 4, Local 681, AFL-CIO v. City of West Haven,* 234 Conn. 217 (1995), the Court reviewed binding arbitration procedures under Special Act 92-5, which granted the City of West Haven the right to issue state-guaranteed municipal bonds, on the condition that it submit to oversight by a financial control board. In accordance with the terms of the legislation, the financial control board served as a binding interest arbitration panel to resolve pending contract disputes between the City and its municipal unions. AFSCME challenged the legislation on constitutional and statutory grounds. The trial court rejected all of the union's arguments, *AFSCME, Council 4, Local 681, AFL-CIO v. West Haven*, 43 Conn. Supp. 470 (1995), and the Connecticut Supreme Court affirmed. *See also Waterbury Firefighters Association, Local 1339 v. City of Waterbury et al.*, No. CV01-166380S (Superior Court, September 26, 2001).

In 1992, the General Assembly made significant changes in MERA. Most prominent are the elimination of fact finding and the provision that arbitration awards may now be rejected by the municipal employer. The statute now provides that the legislative body of the municipal employer may reject the arbitration decision within twenty-five days of receiving it. Such a rejection requires a two-thirds vote. Within ten days of the vote to reject, the legislative body or its authorized representative is required to provide a written statement of its reasons for rejecting the award, and submit such statement to the State Board of Mediation and Arbitration and the employee organization. Then, the employee organization must respond to such reasons in writing, and it must provide such response to the State Board of Mediation and Arbitration and to the legislative body of the municipal employer within ten days of receiving the statement of reasons.

The statute does not define the "legislative body of the municipal employer," the entity with the authority to reject an arbitration award under MERA. The term "legislative body" usually refers to the municipality, but the statute provides that the board of education is a separate municipal employer. The Connecticut Supreme Court resolved this question in 1996. It affirmed a Superior Court decision that held that the "legislative body of the municipal employer" under MERA refers to the municipality. *Town of Stratford v. Connecticut State Board of Mediation and Arbitration,* 239 Conn. 32 (1996) (town has authority to reject arbitration award involving board of education employees).

Within ten days of receiving the notification of rejection, the State Board of Mediation and Arbitration must select a review panel of three members (or one, if both parties agree) to review the decision. The "second look" panel review is limited to (1) the briefs, (2) the transcript of the first arbitration hearing, (3) the statement of reasons for rejection, and (4) the union response. Also, the panel is limited to the same criteria for decision as was the first panel, as set forth above. As with the "second look" panel under the Teacher Negotiation Act, the panel is limited to the final last best offers made in the first arbitration proceeding, and it can only affirm or reverse the decision of the first panel on each issue in dispute.

The "second look" panel is required to complete its review within twenty days of its appointment, and must issue a decision in writing within five days thereafter. The decision is to include the "specific reasons and standards used by each arbitrator in making his decision on each issue." Except for court review under Conn. Gen. Stat. §§ 52-418 or 52-419, discussed in Section A(5) above, the decision of the "second look" panel is binding on both parties. Conn. Gen. Stat. § 7-473c(d)(5).

Finally, the Connecticut Supreme Court has addressed the effect under MERA of a stipulation (*i.e.* agreement on all issues in dispute) during the arbitration process. *IBPO v. Jewett City,* 234 Conn. 123 (1995). There, the municipality and the union reached an impasse in negotiations, and the State Board of Mediation and Arbitration imposed binding arbitration. After the arbitration commenced, however, the parties waived all statutory requirements for arbitration and eventually reached agreement on all outstanding issues. The parties then submitted their agreement to the arbitration panel as a "stipulation," and the panel issued the stipulation as its award in the matter.

The Connecticut Supreme Court found, however, that no bona fide arbitration award was ever issued. It noted that the arbitrators never heard an actual case, never deliberated, never selected between "last best offers," and never rendered an award. As such, it ruled, the agreement was not subject to confirmation under Conn. Gen. Stat. § 52-417, but rather it was subject to the procedures in Conn. Gen. Stat. § 7-474 for rejecting a negotiated agreement. By contrast, despite the widespread use of stipulations as "arbitration awards" under the Teacher Negotiation Act, the courts have not yet addressed this issue under that law.

7. Mid-term negotiations

In 1987, the General Assembly amended MERA so that it now provides that mid-term negotiations are subject to the same binding arbitration procedures as are contract reopeners and full contract negotiations. Binding arbitration is imposed on the parties thirty days after "the date the parties to an existing collective bargaining agreement commence negotiations to revise said agreement on any matter affecting wages, hours, and other conditions of employment. . . ." Conn. Gen. Stat. § 7-473c(b).

It is hard to see the logic in providing only thirty days for such negotiations before binding arbitration is imposed. Also, there is no clear procedure for notifying the State Board of Mediation and Arbitration so that the State Board would know when to impose binding arbitration. However, it is now clear that mid-term negotiations are subject to the same impasse resolution procedures, including binding arbitration and "second look" review," as are other contract negotiations.

CHAPTER SEVEN
Obligations of School Boards as Employer

The greatest expenditure in any board of education budget is invariably salaries and benefits, given that education is a personnel-intensive industry. Consequently, it is no great surprise that the obligations of a school district as an employer are of major concern. Since this is not an employment law treatise, it is not possible to deal comprehensively with the various laws that regulate school districts in their role as employer. Rather, the following overview summarizes some of the major responsibilities of school districts as employers.

A. Constitutional Rights

Since boards of education are an arm of government, they are subject to the constitutional limitations that apply to government generally. In dealing with their employees, boards of education must be aware of the various constitutional requirements outlined below.

1. Due process

A fundamental constitutional principle is that the government may not deprive any person of "life, liberty or property" without due process. The two issues that typically arise in the context of public employment involve "property" and "liberty." If an employee is fired and thus loses the income from his or her job, has he or she been deprived of "property" without due process? If an employee is fired, has he or she been deprived of the "liberty" to pursue his or her chosen occupation? In either case, the employee may have a valid constitutional claim against the public employer.

First, the employee may have a property interest. Not every job confers a property right upon the employee. Rather, the United States Supreme Court has ruled that an employee has a property interest in his or her job only if there is a reasonable expectation that the employee will remain employed. *Board of Regents of State Colleges v. Roth*, 408 U.S. 564 (1972). A substitute teacher who is hired for a specific period would not have a reasonable expectation of continued employment and, as such, would not have a property interest at the end of that employment. Similarly, a probationary employee would not have a legitimate expectation of continued employment at the end of the probationary period, and the district is generally free to dismiss that employee without worrying about due process concerns.

One recent case illustrates the limits of property interests. In *Holloway v. Reeves*, 277 F.3d 1035 (8th Cir. 2002), a federal appeals court ruled that a superintendent's due process rights were not violated when his employing board of education voted to "buy out" the superintendent by paying him the remaining two years on his contract. The superintendent sued, claiming that the board had taken this action without notice or a hearing. The court ruled, however, that the superintendent was not deprived of any property interest (because he received the full value of the contract) and thus he was not entitled to due process. Moreover, noting that superintendents frequently change jobs with political changes, the court held the board's action did not implicate any liberty interest in vocation and/or reputation, as discussed below.

There are situations in which public employees have a reasonable expectation of continued employment. Most frequently, such expectations arise from statutory provisions, such as the Teacher Tenure Act (which gives even probationary, non-tenure teachers certain due process rights). Other facts may also lead to a similar conclusion, even in the absence of statutory provisions. In one public junior college, for example, there was a *de facto* tenure system, created by a handbook statement that teachers with satisfactory performance would be reemployed from year to year. *Perry v. Sinderman*, 408 U.S. 593 (1972). In another case, civil service provisions created the same expectation. *Cleveland Board of Education v. Loudermill*, 470 U.S. 532 (1985). If a reasonable expectation of continued employment exists, a school board cannot terminate an employee without providing him or her due process.

Second, the employee may have a "liberty" interest in his or her job, of which s/he may not be deprived without due process. The courts have defined a "liberty" interest in the employment context in relation to the employee's reputation. The underlying rationale is that one's reputation affects one's "liberty" to find another job. For example, in *Memphis Community School District v. Stachura*, 477 U.S. 299 (1986), after some parents complained about his showing films on human growth and sexuality, a teacher was suspended without a hearing (even though the films were approved for use in class). He sued, claiming that the action affected his reputation and as such violated his liberty interest in serving as a teacher. The jury awarded him $275,000, even though his suspension had been with pay. The United States Supreme Court reversed on the issue of how the damages were calculated, but this case nevertheless underscores the need to be aware of the due process rights of employees.

Liberty interest claims arise infrequently, but it is important for school board members and administrators to be aware of the potential for such claims under the due process clause when public comments damaging to an employee's reputation are made. If an employee is to be terminated, it is often advisable to make no public comment on the reason, to minimize the chance that the employee will claim a right to a "name-clearing" hearing under the Due Process Clause.

Not every claim that employees raise constitutes a liberty or property interest. In *Gordon v. Nicoletti*, 84 F. Supp.2d 304 (D. Conn. 2000), a teacher was reinstated after the panel in a 10-151 tenure hearing rejected the claim of the administration that she was incompetent. Following the tenure proceedings, however, the administration reassigned the teacher from the middle school to the high school. She objected and brought suit in federal court, claiming that the transfer violated her property and liberty interests. The federal court disagreed, however, holding that the transfer did not violate her constitutional rights.

If either a "property" interest or a "liberty" interest exists, the employee is entitled to due process. However, what process is "due" will vary from situation to situation. *Morrissey v. Brewer*, 408 U.S. 471 (1972). In the employment setting, the "process due" is often prescribed by statute, as in the Teacher Tenure Act. For example, even though a non-tenure teacher cannot appeal a nonrenewal decision directly, if the board were to terminate that teacher's employment without following the statutory procedures for conducting a nonrenewal hearing, the teacher could file suit alleging a due process violation. Indeed, even board policy can create a due process right in a particular situation. For example, if a board has a policy providing for employee hearings prior to termination, a failure to follow that procedure could lead to a finding that a dismissal violated due process.

Even when there is no procedure spelled out in a statute or policy, and/or when it is not clear that the employee has a reasonable expectation of employment, some minimal due process is advisable. In *Cleveland Board of Education v. Loudermill*, 470 U.S. 532 (1985), the United States Supreme Court held that the defendant board of education should have held an informal hearing before terminating the employment of a school custodian. The purpose of such a hearing would be simply to inform the employee of the reason for the proposed termination and to give him or her a chance to present his or her side of the story. This procedure, now known as a *Loudermill* hearing, is advisable whenever employees are terminated. While the right to due process will not always be clear (and may not exist), such hearings by the superintendent or his or her designee are a minimal burden and can avoid the costly process of litigating over whether the employee should have been given due process.

2. Equal protection

An important constitutional right that employees have is the "equal protection of the laws" under the Fifth and Fourteenth Amendments to the United States Constitution. As with students, this constitutional provision simply means that people in the same situation should be treated the same. Through the years, however, this provision has evolved to establish three different standards of review, depending on the nature of the interest in question.

Normally, the actions of government are measured by a "rational relationship" test. This means that a governmental action (here, school rule) must bear a rational relationship to the goal it is attempting to achieve. A decision, for example, not to hire convicted felons is a rational measure to avoid problems in the work place. Though such a rule creates a disfavored group (felons), differentiated treatment of such persons is permissible because it has a rational basis, as described above. *See Donahue v. Southington*, 259 Conn. 783, 795 (2002) (differential treatment permitted as long as there is a plausible policy reason); *Irizarry v. Chicago Board of Education*, 251 F.3d 604 (7th Cir. 2001) (decision to extend health benefits to domestic partners of the same sex does not deny equal protection to heterosexual domestic partners).

When a governmental action is based on gender, the courts will apply a higher standard of review. It will not be enough for school officials to show a rational relationship between their rule and purpose. Rather, any rule that distinguishes between persons on the basis of gender will be subject to an intermediate level of scrutiny, *i.e.* whether the rule promotes important governmental objectives and whether the discriminatory means employed are substantially related to achieving those objectives. Given that employers are prohibited by statute from discriminating on the basis of gender, equal protection claims based on gender rarely arise.

Finally, where school rules infringe upon constitutional rights, such as free expression or free exercise of religion, or when they are based on a suspect classification, such as race or national origin, school officials have a heavy burden to justify the rule. Such a rule will be upheld only if it passes the "strict scrutiny standard," *i.e.* (1) it is necessary to achieve a compelling state interest, and (2) the scope of the rule is drawn as narrowly as possible to achieve that objective. Employee rules that interfere with constitutionally protected rights, including the right to privacy, will be subject to (and will often not survive) review under this standard. In the 1970's, there were a number of court decisions that struck down rules that intruded into teachers' lives, such as prohibition against cohabitation without the benefit of marriage. At this point, however, the principle that employers must not intrude into the private lives of employees is well-understood.

3. Free speech

The First Amendment to the United States Constitution provides another common basis for litigation by public employees. When disciplinary action follows public comments by a public employee, he or she may file suit against the public employer and allege that the disciplinary action is improper retaliation for the exercise of the right of free speech. Since 1968, the United States Supreme Court has recognized that public employees have a right to free speech. *Pickering v. Board of Education*, 391 U.S. 563 (1968). It is difficult, however, to predict in specific cases whether speech will or will not be protected. Sometimes we find out the answer only after an expensive trial. *See, e.g., Johnson v. Ganim, Rapice and City of Bridgeport*, 342 F.3d 105 (2d Cir. 2003) (case remanded for trial on question of whether employee discipline was retaliation for exercise of First Amendment rights).

In *Pickering*, a teacher wrote to the newspaper and was critical of how the superintendent and the board of education had handled past proposals to raise revenue for the schools. He was fired for his trouble, and the Illinois Supreme Court upheld the action. The United States Supreme Court reversed, however, ruling that public employees generally have the right under the First Amendment to speak out on matters of public concern. This right applies not only to termination, but also to any adverse employment decision. *Knapp v. Whitaker*, 757 F.2d. 827 (7th Cir. 1985); *Burgess v. Independent School District No. I-4 of Noble County, Oklahoma*, No. 01-1216 (10th Cir. 2003).

The right of free speech for public employees is not and has never been unlimited. First, the speech must relate to a matter of public concern; statements on purely private concerns are not protected by the First Amendment. *Connick v. Myers*, 461 U.S. 138 (1983). In *Connick*, an assistant district attorney, who was about to be transferred over her objection, circulated a questionnaire about office operations, created a "mini-insurrection," and was fired. The Court held that the employee was not speaking on a matter of public concern and, therefore, the speech was not protected. *See also Rankin v. McPherson*, 483 U.S. 378 (1987). In that case, a clerk in a police department was fired after saying "The next time they go for him, I hope they get him" after President Reagan was shot. On a 5-4 vote, the Supreme Court ruled that her comment related to a matter of public concern, President Reagan's policies toward minorities, and was thus protected speech. Since the speech was not disruptive, her dismissal was overturned.

Second, as the Court noted in *Pickering*, there is an important interest in public debate, and it is not permissible to discipline an employee simply because a statement made is false. Rather, the Court drew on the broadly tolerant standard that applies to actions with regard to defamation claims made by public figures, and it ruled that inaccurate statements will be cause for discipline only when they are made with the knowledge that they are false or are made with reckless disregard for the truth (or when they are otherwise not protected speech).

Third, if a teacher speaks on a matter of public concern in a private setting, s/he will still have protection under the First Amendment. This is a logical conclusion that avoids forcing employees to go public. *Givhan v. Western Line Consolidated School District*, 439 U.S. 410 (1979).

Fourth, even if a statement would otherwise be protected, some speech is too damaging to the operation of the public enterprise to be protected from regulation. In *Connick*, the Court held that the free speech interests of public employees must be balanced against the legitimate interest of public agencies to operate efficiently. If the speech is a serious disruption, the employer can prohibit it and/or take related disciplinary action against the employee. Following *Connick*, courts have identified the following factors that must be considered in determining whether speech by a public employee is protected:

- the need for harmony in the public work place;
- whether there is a need for a close working relationship between the speaker and the persons who could be affected by the speech;
- the time, manner, and place of the speech;
- the context in which the dispute arose;
- the degree of public interest in the speech; and
- whether the speech impeded the ability of the other employees to perform their duties.

Roberts v. Van Buren Public Schools, 773 F.2d 948 (8th Cir. 1985). *See also Lewis v. Cowen,* 165 F.3d 154 (2d Cir. 1999) (speech by Director impaired operation of Connecticut Lottery Unit and was not protected); *Sierra v. State of Connecticut*, No. CV00-083588, *digested at* 9 Conn. Ops. 1300 (Conn. Super. Ct. 2003) (comments on cable show alleging joking about ethnic characteristics irreparably damaged relationship of assistant with state comptroller).

An early Connecticut case illustrates the principle that not all speech is protected. In *Burns v. Rovaldi*, 477 F. Supp. 270 (D. Conn. 1979), a teacher challenged his dismissal for insubordination and incompetence, claiming that the board's actions violated his First Amendment rights. An avowed Communist, he claimed that he had a right of academic freedom to include in the instructional program for his fifth grade students statements from his fiancée, such as, "We are both working hard for the day when you kids and the rest of us working people kick out all the rich rotten bosses and then we can all run everything ourselves." In rejecting his claims, the federal court held that the board's prohibition of sectarian or partisan instruction was an appropriate exercise of the board's responsibility to assure that instructional time is used efficiently.

More recently, in *Boring v. Buncombe*, 136 F.3d 364 (4th Cir. 1998), *cert. denied*, 525 U.S. 813 (1998), a teacher was transferred after parents complained about a play that she had her class present. She claimed that her free speech rights were violated, but the court dismissed her claim, holding that her actions in implementing the school curriculum (including her activities as a teacher selecting and directing the play) did not implicate her First Amendment rights. Similarly, the Appellate Court recently held that a teacher's interactions with parents (for which she was criticized, though not formally disciplined) were not protected speech. *Sivek v. Baljevic*, 46 Conn. Supp. 518 (1999), *affirmed* 60 Conn. App. 19 (2000). *Compare Alba v. Board of Education*, 999 F. Supp. 687 (D. Conn. 1998) (personal grievance) *with Mazurek v. Wolcott Board of Education*, 849 F. Supp. 154 (D. Conn. 1994) (protected speech).

Sometimes the speech in question is wholly unrelated to the job responsibilities of the school employee, but again the courts will balance the importance of the speech against the impact, if any, on the efficient operation of the school district. Where such speech causes significant disruption, discipline may be imposed. For example, one teacher was fired for his work in editing the newsletter for an organization that advocated sexual relations between men and boys, despite the fact that there was no evidence of actual misconduct. *Melzer v. Board of Education of the City of New York*, 336 F.3d 185 (2d Cir. 2003), *cert. denied,* ___ U.S. ___. 124 S. Ct. 1424 (2004). The court rejected his claim that his First Amendment rights were violated because such statements were likely to impair the teacher's effectiveness and to cause disruption.

Different facts and different judges make it very difficult to predict in a particular case whether the balance will be struck in favor of the employer or the employee. For example, in *Fales v. Garst*, 235 F.3d 1122 (8th Cir. 2001), the court found that a directive to teachers not to discuss incidents involving special education students at the middle school did not violate their free speech rights. By contrast, a teacher won her claim that her First Amendment rights were violated when she was disciplined after inviting Woody Harrelson (along with CNN) to speak to her fifth grade class on the benefits of industrial hemp. *Cockrel v. Shelby School District*, 270 F.3d 1036 (6th Cir. 2001) *cert. denied*, 123 S. Ct. 73 (2002). *See also Settlegood v. Portland Public Schools*, 362 F.3d 1118 (9th Cir. 2004) (affirming jury verdict for $1,000,000 for alleged retaliation for outspoken criticism to supervisor of services provided to special education students).

This difficulty in distinguishing legitimate employment decisions from prohibited retaliation for comment on matters of public concern is evident in a legal odyssey the Waterford Board of Education recently endured. A former employee brought suit alleging a violation of her right of free speech under the First Amendment. The school district asserted that it terminated her employment for just cause related to her conduct at work. The jury disagreed, and awarded the plaintiff $561,000 in damages for the alleged violation of her constitutional rights. The trial judge, however, vacated the award as unsupported by the evidence. There was a second trial, and ultimately the Board of Education prevailed. *Farrior v. Waterford Board of Education*, 277 F.3d 633 (2d Cir. 2002).

The rules are a little different with respect to speech by school administrators. Such employees have policy-making responsibilities, and they have close working relationships with the superintendent and the board of education. Accordingly, when they speak out against the superintendent or the board, even on a matter of public concern, their speech may not be protected. For example, the Sixth Circuit dismissed the free speech claim of a principal who was demoted after criticizing the superintendent, ruling that he had the right to expect cooperation and support from a close subordinate. *Sharp v. Lindsey*, 285 F.3d 479 (6th Cir. 2002). *See also Vargas-Harrison v.*

Racine Unified School District, 272 F.3d 964 (7th Cir. 2001) (demotion of principal for opposition to district efforts to participate in aid program allowed; as policy-maker she owed superiors a duty of loyalty).

The situation can also be complicated when grounds for discipline exist independent of any statements the employee has made. In one case, a teacher who swore at students and was antagonistic with other staff members went on a radio talk show and criticized the superintendent's new dress code for staff. When his contract was not renewed, he claimed that his First Amendment rights had been violated. However, the United States Supreme Court determined otherwise, holding that when an employee would have been disciplined without regard to his or her speech, there is no First Amendment violation, even if it is impossible completely to exclude motivation related to the speech. The Court reasoned that the employee should not be better off as a result of the speech, and the employer may act when there are independent grounds for termination. *Mt. Healthy School District Board of Education v. Doyle*, 429 U.S. 274 (1977).

Teachers and other school employees also have rights of symbolic free speech under the First Amendment. In *James v. Board of Education*, 461 F.2d 566 (2d Cir. 1972), the Second Circuit considered the rights of a teacher who was fired after he wore a black armband in protest of the war in Vietnam. Mr. James' actions were similar to those of Mary Beth Tinker, who wore the black armband in the seminal case on student rights, *Tinker v. Des Moines Independent Community School District*, 393 U.S. 503 (1969). The results were similar as well. In *James*, the court held that the teacher's rights under the First Amendment could not be restricted any more than those of students, at least in the absence of interference with the requirement of appropriate discipline in the operation of the school.

This right of symbolic free speech is not, however, unlimited, as Mr. Brimley, a teacher in East Hartford, found out. When he was reprimanded for failing to wear a tie in accordance with the district's dress code, Mr. Brimley sued the board, claiming violation of his First Amendment rights. Finding that Mr. Brimley's claims of free speech were "vague and unfocused" and that his claims of a liberty right to go without a tie were not sustainable, the Second Circuit Court of Appeals dismissed his complaint. *East Hartford Education Association v. Board of Education*, 562 F.2d 838 (2d Cir. 1977).

Finally, it is noteworthy that Connecticut employees have an additional claim in matters of free speech. Conn. Gen. Stat. § 31-51q prohibits all Connecticut employers, public and private, from taking adverse employment action against employees who exercise their free speech rights under the First Amendment and under Article First, Sections 3, 4 and 14 of the Connecticut Constitution. The Connecticut Supreme Court has applied a standard First Amendment analysis to such claims. *See, e.g., DiMartino v. Richens*, 263 Conn. 639 (2003). *See also Bracey v. Bridgeport Board of Education*, 368 F.3d 108 (2d Cir. 2004) (Section 31-51q properly reviewed under federal constitutional standards; case remanded for new trial on damages after $250,000 jury verdict). The Appellate Court has held that punitive damages are available under Section 31-51q if the employer acts with reckless indifference of the employee's rights or wantonly or intentionally violates those rights. *Arnone v. Town of Enfield*, 79 Conn. App. 501 (2003).

4. Search and seizure

It is clear that teachers and other board employees are protected by the Fourth Amendment to the United States Constitution, which prohibits unreasonable searches and seizures. However, it is also clear that the typical rules concerning warrants and probable cause that govern the conduct of law enforcement officials do not apply to school officials who conduct searches of their employees and/or their effects.

The United States Supreme Court has held that a public employer may search the person and effects of a public employee as long as two conditions are met. First, the employer must have reasonable (as opposed to probable) cause to suspect that the search will turn up evidence that the law or work rules have been violated. Second, the scope of the search must be reasonably related to the purpose of the search and must not be excessively intrusive. *O'Connor v. Ortega*, 480 U.S. 709 (1987). These standards may sound familiar, and they should. They are adopted virtually without change from the United States Supreme Court decision concerning student searches. *New Jersey v. T.L.O.*, 469 U.S. 325 (1985).

First, to establish a reasonable basis for the search at its inception, the employer need not establish probable cause (*i.e.*, that it is more probable than not that the search will yield particular evidence). Rather, there must be a reasonable suspicion, based on more than conjecture or a hunch. For example, an anonymous tip would likely provide reasonable cause for a search only in a rare and compelling situation. More typically, a search will be justified by pointing to particular conduct, appearance or another objective basis to believe that the search will yield evidence of a violation of work rules or the law.

Second, the scope of the search must be reasonable in light of the purpose of the search and may not be excessively intrusive. For example, if the issue is whether a teacher has done lesson plans, it is hard to imagine how the district could justify a search of the teacher's person or personal effects. By contrast, a strong suspicion that the teacher is in possession of drugs could provide a reasonable basis for the search of the employee. Given that the employee, as an adult, may have a greater privacy expectation than a student in school, however, searches of employees or their effects would be warranted only for very serious matters.

The Second Circuit reviewed a claim by an employee whose employer searched his work computer without his permission or even knowledge. It held that he had a legitimate expectation of privacy. Given that the employer had reasonable cause to conduct the search, however, the employer did not violate the employee's rights. *Leventhal v. Knapek*, 266 F.3d 64 (2d Cir. 2001). While the employer prevailed here, this case underscores the importance of clear notification to employees that computers provided by the employer are subject to search, to reduce the likelihood that the employee will be able to establish a privacy interest.

There are two related issues to note. First, whether the Fourth Amendment applies will depend upon whether the particular administrative action is in fact a search. For example, if a desk or a file cabinet is used by more than one teacher, it is hard for any one teacher to argue that he or she has an expectation of privacy in that desk or cabinet. If the teacher has no legitimate expectation of privacy, a principal's "search" of that area may not be a search for purposes of the Fourth Amendment. While personal effects such as purses, briefcases, and book bags will certainly generate that expectation, school property may not, especially if it is shared with others.

Second, the rules may be different if the police are involved. It may be that the police will ask school officials to cooperate in the investigation of a crime. If a search is undertaken at the behest of the police, it is unlikely that the more lenient rules with regard to reasonable cause will apply; when an employer acts as a police surrogate, the acts of the employer will likely be tested against the rules that apply to the police generally, *i.e.* the courts will require that there be probable cause and a warrant for any search of the employee's person or effects. However, it is important to note that a public employer is free to turn over to the police evidence (*e.g.,* drugs) that had been seized in an independent search made by the employer, based upon the reasonable cause standard.

The other main issue regarding the Fourth Amendment and school employees concerns drug testing. Private sector employers may require drug testing of their employees, subject to statutory limitations set out in Conn. Gen. Stat. § 10-31t *et seq.* The situation for public employees, however, is different. There is no controlling statute, and the courts have held that a drug test is a "search" that is subject to the Fourth Amendment.

In certain narrow circumstances, random or suspicionless drug testing of public employees will be permitted. In two cases, the United States Supreme Court ruled that such testing was allowed. In one case a federal statute required that certain employees responsible for operating a train be tested (regardless of suspicion) following a train accident. *Skinner v. Railway Labor Executives' Association*, 489 U.S. 602 (1989). In another case, the Court ruled that the United States Treasury Department could require random drug testing of agents who carried a firearm and were involved in the war on drugs. *National Treasury Employees Union v. Von Raab*, 489 U.S. 656 (1989). In both cases the Court held that there was compelling justification for the testing, which outweighed any personal privacy interest of the employees.

Applying these cases to the public schools, there are a few situations in which a school district could justify random testing of employees. The courts have recognized that the risks inherent in the operation of motor vehicles to transport children justify drug testing for school bus drivers on a random basis. *Jones v. Jenkins*, 833 F.2d 335 (D.C. Cir. 1987). Since 1990, persons employed as school bus drivers have had to submit to drug testing as part of the employment process. Conn. Gen. Stat. § 14-276a.

Other than situations directly related to student safety, the issue of teacher drug testing is unresolved. The board of education in New Orleans attempted to institute a broad program of drug testing of teachers, aides and clerical workers any time they are injured on the job, without any particularized suspicion concerning drug use. The Fifth Circuit Court of Appeals ruled in 1998, however, that such testing violates the Fourth Amendment. *United Teachers of New Orleans v. Orleans Parish School Board*, 142 F.3d 853 (5th Cir. 1998). In the absence of particularized suspicion or any showing that the program was responsive to a particular problem of drug use among such employees, the court ruled that such testing was unreasonable.

The Sixth Circuit Court of Appeals, however, reached the opposite result, also in 1998. *Knox County Education Association v. Knox County School Board*, 158 F.3d 361 (6th Cir. 1998), *cert. denied*, 120 S.Ct. 46 (1999). There, the court affirmed the district court decision permitting "reasonable suspicion" testing of all employees, but reversed its decision prohibiting suspicionless drug testing of all "safety-sensitive" employees, including teachers. The court held that teachers and administrators have a unique responsibility in the drug interdiction effort (similar to Treasury employees in *Von Raab*) that justifies suspicionless testing.

Given this split in the courts of appeals over the scope of employee privacy, caution by school districts is still warranted. Betting persons, however, would predict that the United States Supreme Court (as currently constituted) would affirm the right of public school employers to impose drug testing requirements on teachers. Drug testing is increasingly common in the private sector, especially upon application for initial employment. For example, Conn. Gen. Stat. § 31-51t, which applies only to private sector employment, expressly permits random or suspicionless drug testing for prospective employees. Moreover, a majority on the Court demonstrated its comfort with drug testing in the recent decision on student drug testing. *Board of Education of Independent School District No. 92 of Pottawatomie County v. Earls*, 536 US 822 (2002) (allowing random drug testing of all students involved in extracurricular activities).

Finally, a disgruntled applicant or teacher in Connecticut could bring a challenge to drug testing of school employees pursuant to the Connecticut Constitution, which has a provision similar to the Fourth Amendment in Article First, Section 7. We have no cases in Connecticut asserting state constitutional rights in this regard. The Alaska Supreme Court ruled in 2001, however, that a program of suspicionless drug testing of police and firefighters in certain situations (application, transfer, promotion, after a traffic accident) violated a similar provision in the Alaska Constitution. *Anchorage Police Department Employees Association v. Municipality of Anchorage*, 24 P.3d 547 (Alaska 2001).

B. Discrimination

Boards of education are of course subject to the state and federal discrimination statutes that apply to all employers. Connecticut law prohibits discrimination in employment on the basis of:

> race, color, religious creed, age, sex, marital status, national origin, ancestry, present or past history of mental disability, mental retardation, learning disability or physical disability, including but not limited to blindness.

Conn. Gen. Stat. § 46a-60(a)(1). In 2001, this statute was amended to substitute "mental disability" for "mental disorder," and to specify that a person has a mental disability if they have any one of the approximately 400 disorders in the most recent edition of the DSM IV or its successor.

Employers, including boards of education, are also prohibited from discriminating against employees or applicants on the basis of sexual orientation. Conn. Gen. Stat. § 46a-81c. In addition, the state anti-discrimination laws have included a prohibition against employer collection or use of genetic information since 1998. Conn. Gen. Stat. § 46a-60(a)(11). Employers may not request or require employees or applicants for employment to provide such information, and may not discharge or otherwise discriminate against any person on the basis of genetic information.

In addition to these state laws, federal laws, notably Title VII of the Civil Rights Act of 1964, Section 504, the Age Discrimination in Employment Act (the ADEA), and the Americans with Disabilities Act (the ADA), contain similar protections against discrimination in employment. Often, both state and federal remedies will be available to the employee.

1. Employment practices

School boards in Connecticut may not refuse to hire, or discharge from employment, or otherwise discriminate against any person on the basis of any of the characteristics listed above. In exceptional cases, the characteristic may be necessary to successful job performance, and as such it would constitute a "bona fide occupational qualification" (BFOQ). Conn. Gen. Stat. § 46a-60(a)(1). For example, the need for a male to supervise the boy's locker room may make gender a BFOQ in that case. However, such situations are rare, and the burden of proving a BFOQ is a heavy one for employers. *See, e.g., Connecticut Institute for the Blind v. CHRO*, 176 Conn. 88 (1978) (sight was not a BFOQ, even where students in the class to be supervised were themselves blind and retarded and required close supervision). Except for situations in which privacy issues require that gender be a BFOQ, courts are likely to strike down requirements that are discriminatory.

The prohibitions against discrimination affect all aspects of the employment relationship. In hiring, school boards may not advertise job opportunities limited by race, sex, age, or any of the other protected classes unless they can show that membership in a particular class is a BFOQ. Conn. Gen. Stat. § 46a-60(a)(6). During the application, interview and hiring process, agents of the board of education should not ask job applicants for information about membership in protected groups. For example, it is not appropriate to ask an applicant whether he or she is disabled. Even innocent questions, such as questions about an applicant's age, marital status or child care arrangements, can lead to a claim later by an unsuccessful applicant that an adverse decision was based on illegal discrimination. Also, while it is permissible (and for school employees required under Conn. Gen. Stat. § 10-221d) to ask whether the applicant has any criminal convictions, as of 2002, employers who ask applicants to disclose conviction information must now warn them that they do not have to provide information concerning convictions that have been erased. Moreover, it is illegal to discriminate against any applicant or employee on the basis of such erased conviction information. Conn. Gen. Stat. § 31-51i. Finally, the General Assembly even saw fit in 2003 to prohibit discrimination against a person because he or she is late or misses work because of service as a volunteer firefighter or ambulance driver. P.A. 03-259, § 53.

Questions that seem neutral on their face may be illegal if they have a special or "disparate" impact on a protected group. For example, it is inadvisable to solicit information about an applicant's arrest record since such information does not relate to a business necessity (because an arrest is not proof of anything), and since members of racial minorities are more likely than other groups to have been arrested. A rejected candidate may claim that the hiring decision was based on his or her answers to such questions.

Once an individual is hired, a school board may not make decisions about promotion, transfer, salary, layoff, or discharge based on any of the protected characteristics. Furthermore, a school board may not discriminate against persons who have opposed any discriminatory employment practice, or who have filed a complaint, testified or assisted in a complaint proceeding. Conn. Gen. Stat. § 46a-60(4). Finally, a school board may not assist in the commission of any discriminatory act toward an employee. Conn. Gen. Stat. § 46a-60(5).

While school districts are prohibited from discriminating against employees on any of the listed bases, some issues naturally come up more frequently than others. The following brief review identifies these situations.

a. Racial discrimination

Discrimination against employees on the basis of race is, of course, prohibited under both state and federal law. Conn. Gen. Stat. § 46a-60; Title VII of the Civil Rights Act of 1964, 42 U.S.C. § 2000e(j). In addition, Title VI of the Civil Rights Act specifically prohibits discrimination on the basis of "race, color or national origin" in programs receiving federal financial assistance. 42 U.S.C. § 2000d. Happily, the issue of racial discrimination in employment does not frequently arise with respect to Connecticut school districts. However, some basic concepts should be reviewed.

Claims of racial discrimination fall into two basic categories -- (1) claims of disparate treatment, and (2) claims of disparate impact. While these approaches may be applied to any claim of discrimination, they were first developed as a way to approach claims of racial discrimination.

The first category, disparate treatment, is conceptually simple. A member of a protected racial minority may claim that an adverse employment decision, such as a failure to hire or promote, or termination or other disciplinary action, was based on an illegal consideration of the person's race. To establish such a claim, the person must first present a prima facie case, *i.e.* facts from which one could infer that discrimination occurred. The claimant must show the following:

- that s/he belongs to a racial minority;
- that s/he applied and was qualified for a job for which the employer was seeking applicants;
- that, despite her/his qualifications, s/he was rejected; and
- that, after her/his rejection, the position remained open, and the employer continued to seek applicants from persons of complainant's qualifications.

McDonnell Douglas Corp. v. Green, 411 U.S. 792 (1973); *Reeves v. Sanderson Plumbing Products, Inc.*, 530 U.S. 133 (2000). Once the complainant has made this showing, to rebut the claim, the employer must identify legitimate, nondiscriminatory reasons for its decision. If it does, the complainant must then show that the employer's claimed reason for its action was merely a pretext for a discriminatory action. Such a finding, however, can be based on a determination that the proffered reason was false. *Board of Education of the City of Norwalk v. CHRO*, 266 Conn. 492 (2003). In any event the complainant maintains the ultimate burden of establishing that discrimination occurred. *St. Mary's Honor Center v. Hicks*, 509 U.S. 502 (1993).

In addition to such claims of disparate treatment, an applicant or employee may also bring a claim of disparate impact discrimination. Simply put, the claim is that the employer has adopted a requirement or policy that has an adverse impact on a protected person without a business necessity. *Griggs v. Duke Power Co.*, 401 U.S. 424 (1971). In the *Griggs* case, the United State Supreme Court struck down a requirement that custodial employees have a high school diploma. There, the requirement was imposed after a court had ordered desegregation of the work force, and it had the effect of excluding racial minorities from the work force without any legitimate business justification. The theory of disparate impact liability is now expressly incorporated in Title VII as a result of the Civil Rights Act of 1991. To prevail with such a claim, the plaintiff must identify the particular employment practice in question and demonstrate that it caused the disparate impact. 42 U.S.C. § 2000e-2(k).

Employers can and often do take affirmative action to remedy past discrimination and/or make the work force more representative of the community at large. Efforts, such as special recruiting trips and advertising in the minority community, can be helpful in achieving such goals. Indeed, all boards of education in Connecticut are required to adopt and implement a policy on minority staff recruitment. Conn. Gen. Stat. § 10-220(a). However, the prohibitions against discrimination on the basis of race apply to all racial groups, and school districts have found themselves in court when such efforts have resulted in the establishment of absolute preferences for members of minority groups.

Such cases can be complicated, and in one case the nine justices of the United States Supreme Court issued six different opinions. *Wygant v. Jackson Board of Education*, 476 U.S. 267 (1986). In that case, the Court invalidated a layoff procedure that had the effect of discriminating against non-minority teachers, since minority teachers were given special protection. The Second Circuit Court of Appeals cited *Wygant* in a case involving the Bridgeport Board of Education. There the court held that a layoff procedure that provided an absolute preference for minority teachers was unconstitutional because it deprived the non-minority teachers of equal protection of the laws. *Crompton v. Bridgeport Education Association*, 993 F.2d 1023 (2d Cir. 1993). *See also Britton v. South Bend Community School Corporation*, 819 F.2d 766 (7th Cir. 1987), *cert. denied*, 484 U.S. 925 (1987).

Generally, remedial plans that operate to discriminate against members of the racial majority will be illegal unless (1) there is a statistical disparity between the races in the employee group, (2) there is evidence of past discrimination, and (3) the remedial plan is narrowly drawn and temporary in nature. Any such efforts must be undertaken cautiously and with a full review of the latest court decisions. *See, e.g., Piscataway Township Board of Education v. Taxman*, 91 F.3d 1547 (3d Cir. 1996) (preference for African-American teacher in the interest of diversity (rather than to remedy past discrimination or to correct racial imbalance) violated rights of white teacher).

In 1995, the United States Supreme Court considered the standard of review appropriate for courts to use when considering challenges to affirmative action plans. The Court ruled that affirmative action plans that use race as a determining factor are subject to "strict scrutiny," that is, they will be permitted only in rare cases where there is a compelling need and no less restrictive means of addressing that need. *Adarand Constructors, Inc. v. Pena,* 515 U.S. 200 (1995). *See also City of Richmond v. J.A. Croson Co.,* 488 U.S. 469 (1989). Although the *Adarand* case involved a public construction contract, its holding is not confined to that situation. Rather, at least to date it appears that the courts will apply the strict scrutiny standard in reviewing actions by government officials applying race-based criteria in such areas as education, health, and hiring. *See also Gratz v. Bollinger*, 539 U.S. 244 (2003); *Grutter v. Bollinger*, 539 U.S. 306 (2003).

b. Age discrimination

Employment decisions may not be made on the basis of age, unless the employer can show that age is a BFOQ for that particular position, a proposition that is between very difficult and impossible for school districts (because they do not operate jet planes). The federal Age Discrimination in Employment Act (ADEA), 29 U.S.C.§ 621 *et seq.*, protects employees age 40 and older, and Connecticut's age discrimination law protects individuals of any age against illegal discrimination. Conn. Gen. Stat. § 46a-60(a). The United States Supreme Court has ruled, however, that the ADEA does not prohibit discrimination in favor of older workers in the offering of health insurance benefits. *General Dynamics Land Systems Inc. v. Cline,* ___ U.S. __, 124 S. Ct. 1236 (2004)

In 2000, the United States Supreme Court decided a case that may have a serious impact on age discrimination litigation in federal courts, at least as regards public agencies. In *Kimel v. Florida Board of Regents*, 528

U.S. 62 (2000), the Court held that states are immune from suit under the ADEA. In implementing the educational interests of the state, local and regional boards of education are state agencies, but they are also municipal agencies for other purposes. The impact of this decision on local and regional boards of education in Connecticut, however, is still not fully understood.

There are two areas where concern over age discrimination issues is more acute for boards of education - hiring and early retirement incentive programs. As stated above, if a requirement has a disparate impact on members of a protected group, it will not be allowed unless the employer can show a business necessity for the requirement. In hiring teachers, school districts are often understandably concerned about cost, and some districts have adopted policies stating that they will not hire teachers with more than some specified minimal level of experience, say five years. However, if such a requirement would disparately affect employment opportunities for the older teacher, it may be found to constitute illegal age discrimination. *Geller v. Markham*, 635 F.2d 1027 (2d Cir. 1980), *cert. denied*, 451 U.S. 945 (1981).

Also, as school districts have sought to provide retirement incentives to teachers, they have attempted on occasion to tailor the incentive to the target group, teachers in their fifties who may not otherwise be considering retirement. A sliding scale benefit, based on age, would be particularly effective in providing an incentive to this group. Since 1990, however, employers have been prohibited from providing lesser benefits to employees on the basis of age, except for circumstances narrowly defined in the statute. Benefits that are differentiated on the basis of age will likely violate the ADEA, as amended by the Older Workers' Benefits Protection Act of 1990. *Solon v. Gary Community School Corporation*, 180 F.3d 844 (7th Cir. 1999); *O'Brien v. Deer Park Union Free School District*, 127 F. Supp.2d 342 (E.D. N.Y. 2001). A narrowly tailored window of benefits, however, may withstand judicial scrutiny. *Auerbach v. Board of Education*, 136 F.3d 104 (2d Cir. 1998).

c. Sex discrimination

The statutory prohibition against sex discrimination may arise in different situations. Clearly, it is not proper to base an employment decision on the gender of the employee or applicant unless gender is a BFOQ, and it is never appropriate to consider sexual orientation in employment decisions. Sex discrimination also includes discrimination on the basis of pregnancy, child-bearing capacity, sterilization, fertility or related medical conditions.

Conn. Gen. Stat. § 46a-51(17). *See Green v. Waterford Board of Education*, 473 F.2d 629 (2d Cir. 1973).

Pay differences based on gender are specifically prohibited in the Equal Pay Act, 29 U.S.C. § 206(d) as well as Conn. Gen. Stat. § 31-75. Moreover, teachers in Connecticut have long had special protection against discrimination in employment or compensation on the basis of sex or marital status. Conn. Gen. Stat. § 10-153.

Sexual harassment is a type of illegal sex discrimination. Prohibited practices include any unwelcome advances and/or requests for sexual favors for which submission is an explicit or implicit condition of employment, or behavior that substantially interferes with work performance, or creates an intimidating, hostile or offensive work environment. Conn. Gen. Stat. § 46a-60(a)(8). The Connecticut Commission on Human Rights and Opportunities (CHRO), the state agency responsible for enforcing the prohibitions against discrimination, can require employers, including school boards, to post in permanent and accessible locations information concerning the illegality of sexual harassment and the remedies available to its victims. Additionally, school boards employing fifty or more persons are required to provide training and education concerning sexual harassment to all supervisory employees, and to all new supervisory employees within six months of their appointment to a supervisory position. Conn. Gen. Stat. § 46a-54(15).

d. Disability discrimination

Connecticut law prohibits discrimination on the basis of "physical disability, including but not limited to blindness." In addition, there are two federal laws prohibiting discrimination on the basis of disability. Since 1973, public schools receiving federal funds have been subject to Section 504 of the Rehabilitation Act of 1973, 29 U.S.C. § 794. The Americans with Disabilities Act (ADA), enacted by Congress in 1990, confers protection against discrimination on the basis of disability in both private and public employment. Given the similarities in these two federal laws with regard to employment, school districts already complying with Section 504 were not required to make significant changes to comply with the ADA. Both the ADA and Section 504 require equal access for disabled persons to the services, programs, or activities offered by a public entity.

In 2001, the United States Supreme Court held that states are immune from suit under the ADA. *Board of Trustees of the University of Alabama v. Garrett*, 531 U.S. 356 (2001). State immunity does not automatically extend, however, to creatures of state statute, such as municipalities and boards of education. Since school districts receive federal funds, however, they remain subject to Section 504, and this decision has had little practical impact on local and regional school districts.

In many respects, the ADA and Section 504 are similar. Both statutes protect any person who is otherwise qualified for a position and who:

1) has a physical or mental impairment that substantially limits one or more major life activities;
2) has a record of such impairment; or
3) is regarded as having such an impairment.

42 U.S.C. § 12102(2); 29 U.S.C. § 794.

In 2002, the United States Supreme Court interpreted this provision narrowly. It ruled that an assembly line worker with carpal tunnel syndrome was not disabled under the ADA. It interpreted "substantially limits" and "major life activity" to mean that a disability under the ADA must be one that "prevents or severely restricts the individual from doing activities that are of central importance to most people's daily lives." *Toyota Motor Manufacturing v. Williams*, 534 U.S. 184 (2002); *Cutler v. Hamden Board of Education*, 150 F. Supp. 2d 356 (D. Conn. 2001). *See also Sutton v. United Airlines, Inc.*, 527 U.S. 471 (1999) (corrective steps, *e.g.*, eyeglasses, to mitigate the effects of a disability must be considered to determine whether the disability is a substantial limitation in the major life activity of working).

The Second Circuit applied the Court's analysis in *Toyota* and ruled that an alcoholic teacher did not establish that she was disabled under the ADA. While alcoholism can be a disability, this teacher did not establish that her alcoholism substantially limited her in the major activities of life. Also, her poor performance gave ample, non-discriminatory grounds for her termination. Finally, in the court's view, her subsequent employment as a substitute teacher established that she was not substantially limited in the major life activity of working. *Nucifora v. Bridgeport Board of Education*, 3:99-CV-00079 (EBB), *aff'd* 36 Fed. Appx. 472 (2d Cir. 2002). By contrast, a teacher who alleged that he was perceived as unable to work in any teaching position in the education field was permitted to proceed with his ADA claim because "teaching" was deemed sufficiently broad a class of jobs to trigger the protections of the ADA. *Howell v. New Haven Board of Education*, 2004 U.S. Dist. LEXIS 4340 (D. Conn. 2004).

When an individual is "otherwise qualified" to serve as a teacher or other school employee, it is illegal to discriminate against that employee on the basis of disability. If the employer is not aware of the disability, it cannot discriminate. *See, e.g., Nobitz v. Town of Hamden*, 2004 Conn. Super. LEXIS 1373 (Conn. Super. Ct. 2004) (custodian who revealed disability after being terminated had no claim of disability discrimination). Awareness of a disability, however, may be imputed to the employer by facts that would put it on notice that the employee is disabled. For example, a teacher's comments about possible suicide were reported to the employers, who suspended her pending medical review. When her employment was subsequently not renewed, she filed a claim under Section 504. The Second Circuit held that the employer was on notice of a potential disability, and it thus permitted her to take her claim of disability discrimination to trial. *Peters v. Baldwin Union Free School District*, 320 F.3d 164 (2d Cir. 2002).

It is also noteworthy that both Section 504 and the ADA expressly exclude current drug users from the definition of disability, 42 U.S.C. § 12210, and both the Office of Civil Rights of the United States Department of Labor and the courts have held that a person cannot claim to have quit using drugs after getting caught and avoid the exclusion. *See, e.g., Burns v. Stafford Board of Education*, 1995 Conn. Super. LEXIS 1650 (Conn. Super. Ct. 1995). In addition, the ADA excludes a number of other conditions that may otherwise be claimed as a disability, including kleptomania, pyromania, voyeurism, sexual identity issues, and sexual aberrations. 42 U.S.C. § 12211.

When there is agreement on the existence of a disability, there can still be disagreement over whether an employee with a disability is "otherwise qualified" to perform the essential job functions. In 2002 the United States Supreme Court affirmed the EEOC's regulation that permits an employer to decline employment when a person's disability poses a direct threat to the safety of others and even him- or herself. *Chevron U.S.A. Inc. v. Echazabal* 536 U.S. 73 (2002). Many years earlier, the Court addressed the question of when a person with a disability will be considered "otherwise qualified," and thus subject to the protections of Section 504 (which analysis now also applies to the ADA):

> An otherwise qualified person is one who is able to meet all of a program's requirements in spite of his handicap. In the employment context, an otherwise qualified person is one who can perform "the essential functions" of the job in question. When a handicapped person is not able to perform the essential functions of the job, the court must also

> consider whether any "reasonable accommodation" by the employer would enable the handicapped person to perform those functions. Accommodation is not reasonable if it either imposes "undue financial and administrative burdens" on a grantee, or requires a "fundamental alteration in the nature of [the] program."

School Board of Nassau County v. Arline, 480 U.S. 273 (1987), *citing Southeastern Community College v. Davis*, 442 U.S. 397 (1979); *see also* 42 U.S.C. § 12111(8).

In the *Arline* case, quoted above, the United States Supreme Court ruled that a teacher with a record of tuberculosis is a person with a disability potentially subject to the protections of Section 504, and that it would be illegal to fire such a teacher if the teacher were "otherwise qualified" to perform her duties, *i.e.* if it were possible to make reasonable accommodations to enable the teacher to work without undue risk to the students. It remanded the case back to the lower court to determine whether such accommodations could be made. *See also Chalk v. United States District Court Central District of California*, 840 F.2d 701 (9th Cir. 1988) (teacher who has AIDS may not be excluded from the classroom absent medical evidence of risk of contagion). *But see Calef v. The Gillette Company*, 322 F.3d 75 (1st Cir. 2003) (employee with uncontrolled anger not "otherwise qualified").

It is important to separate claims of disability from proof of misconduct. Where action is taken against an employee because of misconduct, rather than because of a disability, no discrimination on the basis of disability will be found. For example, a tenured fourth grade teacher was terminated for criminal conduct involving drugs. He claimed, however, that he was addicted to cocaine, and that his dismissal for his related conduct was discrimination against him as a person with a disability in violation of Section 504 and the ADA. The Appellate Court rejected those claims, however, and held that the teacher had properly been dismissed for "moral misconduct" and "other due and sufficient cause." *Gedney v. Board of Education*, 47 Conn. App. 297, *cert. denied*, 243 Conn. 968 (1997); *see also Burns v. Stafford Board of Education*, No. CV 93-53581S, 1995 Conn. Super. LEXIS 1650 (Conn. Super. Ct. 1995).

While the prohibition against discrimination on the basis of disability is stated simply and broadly in Section 504, the ADA elaborates many of the issues that arise in considering claims of such discrimination. The ADA details seven specific types of actions constituting prohibited employment discrimination:

1) Limiting, segregating, or classifying a job applicant or employee in a way that adversely affects employment opportunities or status because of the disability;
2) Participating in a contractual or other arrangement that has the effect of subjecting a disabled individual to discrimination;
3) Using standards, criteria or methods of administration that have a discriminatory effect or perpetuate discrimination;
4) Excluding or denying equal jobs or benefits to a qualified individual because of the known disability of an individual with whom the qualified individual is known to have a relationship or association;
5) Refusing to make reasonable accommodations for a disabled applicant or employee or denying employment opportunities to a disabled applicant or employee based on his need for reasonable accommodation;
6) Using qualification standards, employment tests or other selection criteria that screen out disabled individuals unless the standards, tests, or selection criteria are job-related or consistent with business necessity; and
7) Failing to select and administer employment tests in the most effective manner to ensure that the test results reflect relevant skills, aptitude or other factors to be measured by the test, rather than reflect impaired sensory, manual, or speaking skills, except where the impaired skills are the ones the test purports to measure.

42 U.S.C. § 12112(b). Given these restrictions, school boards must cautiously ensure that employment inquiries and requirements are job-related and consistent with business necessity.

Unless and until an employee raises an issue of disability, it is generally advisable for the employer to refrain from asking the employee about a suspected disability. A premise of the ADA is that a disability is none of the employer's business unless the employee informs the employer that he or she has a disability that affects the employee's ability to perform his/her job duties. Once an employer is on notice of the disability, the law contemplates that the employer and the employee will engage in an interactive process to explore whether the employee can perform the "essential job duties," as described below, with or without accommodation, and if so, what reasonable accommodation is necessary.

This duty is affirmative, *i.e.* it is triggered when the employee identifies a disability that is interfering with job performance, and the employer is not off the hook if the employee does not specifically ask for accommodation. *See Humphrey v. Memorial Hospitals Association*, 239 F.3d 1128 (9th Cir. 2001) (employer failed in duty to seek to accommodate employee with obsessive-compulsive disorder).

Reasonable accommodations under Section 504 and the ADA include modifying equipment and training materials, making existing facilities readily acceptable, and restructuring job assignments and schedules. The United States Supreme Court has ruled, however, that absent special circumstances the duty to make reasonable accommodation does not include overriding established seniority systems to give preference to an employee with a disability. *US Airways, Inc. v. Barnett*, 535 U.S. 391 (2002). Also, the Seventh Circuit has held that a request for unlimited sick leave without being penalized is not a reasonable accommodation. *EEOC v. Yellow Freight Systems, Inc.*, 253 F.3d 943 (7th Cir. 2001). Moreover, reasonable accommodations do not include accommodations that would require elimination of an "essential function" of the job or place an undue hardship on the employer. Again, the ADA provides guidance in this regard.

An "essential function" is a fundamental job task. If the applicant cannot perform that task, the person is not a "qualified individual" and thus the school board does not have a duty under the ADA to accommodate. 42 U.S.C. § 12111(8) provides that job descriptions will be considered evidence as to what tasks are essential. Given this provision, it is advisable for employers to assure that job descriptions are "ADA-compliant," *i.e.* they set out the essential job functions to make it possible to determine the scope of required accommodation.

Under both Section 504 and the ADA, "undue hardship" on the employer will release or modify the school board's responsibility to make reasonable accommodations. Unfortunately, the law does not provide a general definition of the term "undue hardship." Employers must make a good faith judgment as to the scope of the duty to make accommodations, and the employee may challenge that decision through administrative and court proceedings.

The ADA does list the factors a court will use in making a determination of undue hardship, including:

- the nature and cost of the accommodation;

- the employer's overall financial resources of the facility, the number of persons employed, the effect on expenses and resources, or the impact otherwise of the accommodation upon the operation, the number, type and location of its facilities;
- the type of operation of the covered entity, including composition, structure, and functions of the work force of the employer, geographic separateness, administrative or fiscal relationship of the facility in question to the employer.

42 U.S.C. § 12111(10). ADA and Section 504 litigation regarding reasonable accommodations may serve as a guide to the courts interpreting this provision of the ADA. However, these cases are fact-specific, and it is impossible to know with assurance the precise scope of the employer's obligations in a particular case.

The ADA does diverge somewhat from Section 504 in the area of medical exams and inquiries. Under Section 504, physical exams for applicants and workers were not prohibited as long as they were consistently applied. Under the ADA, however, all traditional pre-employment physical examinations and inquiries are prohibited before an offer of employment. 42 U.S.C. § 12112(d)(2). In addition, confidential medical records should not be commingled with non-confidential personnel information. 42 U.S.C. § 12112(d)(4)(C). School boards may, therefore, need to revise job application forms requesting health and medical history information and should assure that they maintain medical records in accordance with ADA requirements.

The prohibition against requiring pre-employment physical examinations is based on the premise that obtaining disability information as part of the hiring process could permit an employer to use that information improperly. By contrast, a post-offer, pre-employment examination is permitted. If there were then an adverse employment decision based on the medical examination, that action could be considered on its merits.

Timing is essential under the ADA. After a school board has made an offer of employment and before the individual begins work, the ADA allows the school board to require an employment entrance physical examination and to condition an offer of employment on that examination if:

- all entering employees are subject to such an exam regardless of disability;

- information obtained regarding the medical condition or history of the applicant is collected and maintained on separate forms and in separate medical files and is treated as confidential medical records; and
- the results of the exam are used only in accordance with the ADA.

42 U.S.C. § 12112(3). If a school board withdraws an offer of employment based on the results of this physical, the school board must be able to show that the criterion is job-related and consistent with business necessity, and does not disproportionately screen out persons with disabilities.

An employer may require independent medical examinations for current employees as long as they are job-related and consistent with business necessity. 42 U.S.C. § 12112(d); 29 C.F.R. § 1630.14(c). In *Sullivan v. River Valley School District*, 197 F.3d 804 (6th Cir. 1999), for example, the court ruled that the superintendent's order that a teacher undergo physical and psychological examinations was permissible because the teacher's behavior would have made a reasonable person question whether the teacher was still capable of performing his job. *See also Tice v. Centre Area Transportation Authority*, 247 F.3d 506 (3d Cir. 2001).

Finally, caution is advised whenever an employer seeks information concerning a potential disability. The key is to limit the inquiry to the information that is *required*; the ADA prohibits employers from asking whether an employee has a disability or as to the nature or severity of the disability unless the inquiry is job-related and consistent with business necessity. 42 U.S.C. § 12112(d)(4)(A). In *Conroy et al. v. New York State Department of Correctional Services*, 333 F.3d 88 (2d Cir. 2003), the Second Circuit considered a challenge to the employer's practice of requiring a doctor's note with a general diagnosis after an absence (generally) of five or more days. The court remanded the matter to the district court, but it cautioned that "business necessity" is more than "mere expediency," but rather must be an interest "vital to the business." Sometimes less is more, and employers should generally limit their inquiries to whether the employee is able to perform the essential job functions with or without accommodation.

e. Religious discrimination

Both state and federal law prohibit discrimination against employees on the basis of religion. Conn. Gen. Stat. § 46a-60; Title VII of the Civil Rights Act of 1964, 42 U.S.C. § 2000e(j). Clearly, an employer may not make adverse decisions against an applicant or employee on the basis of religion. In addition, however, employers have an affirmative duty to make "reasonable accommodation" to their employees' religious beliefs and practices, unless they can show that such accommodation would be an "undue hardship." *Trans World Airlines, Inc. v. Hardison*, 432 U.S. 63 (1977) *See also* Conn. Gen. Stat. § 46a-51(18). Unpaid leave for religious observance has been considered a reasonable accommodation. *See Ansonia Board of Education v. Philbrook*, 479 U.S. 60 (1986), discussed in Chapter Two, Section B.

2. Enforcement of discrimination laws

Employees or applicants who believe they have been discriminated against have a choice of remedies. If a collective bargaining agreement establishes a grievance-arbitration process and prohibits employment discrimination, employees may file a grievance claiming discrimination. Employees may also file a complaint with the Connecticut Commission on Human Rights and Opportunities (CHRO) and/or the federal Equal Employment Opportunity Commission. Employees may appeal an unfavorable decision to court. Alternatively, the CHRO may permit an employee to bypass the CHRO proceedings and file a private lawsuit in state court immediately if the employee has filed a timely discrimination complaint with the CHRO. Conn. Gen. Stat. § 46a-100.

a. Grievance procedure

If an employee is governed by a collective bargaining agreement that prohibits employment discrimination, the employee may file a grievance claiming violation of the agreement, and that grievance may eventually result in arbitration. The agreement must contain either explicit anti-discrimination language or a general statement binding the school board to follow state and federal law. Filing a grievance, however, does not bar the employee from also filing a complaint with the CHRO or the EEOC. Conn. Gen. Stat. § 46a-85(a); *Alexander v. Gardner-Denver Co.*, 415 U.S. 36 (1974). If an arbitration decision has been reached, the CHRO may admit that decision as evidence. Conn. Gen. Stat. § 46a-85(b). The employee may seek review of both decisions in court.

b. CHRO proceedings

The CHRO administers and enforces Connecticut's fair employment laws. For employees not covered by a collective bargaining agreement that includes anti-discrimination language, filing a complaint is the only avenue for redress. The complaint must be filed in writing and under oath within 180 days after the alleged act of discrimination. Conn. Gen. Stat. § 46a-82(a), (e). If the basis of the alleged discrimination is an employee's prior criminal record, the complaint must be filed within 30 days. If an employee waits for resolution of the grievance arbitration process, the CHRO filing deadline may have already passed. Therefore, simultaneous filing is often recommended to the employee.

The complaint must include the name and address of the person alleged to have discriminated, and must describe the alleged discriminatory acts. Conn. Gen. Stat. § 46a-82(a). The CHRO will serve the employer with a copy of the complaint to which the employer must file a written answer under oath within thirty days or request a time extension upon a showing of good cause. Conn. Gen. Stat. § 46a-83(a); Conn. St. Reg. § 46a-54-63. Failure to file a timely answer under oath may result in a default judgment against the employer.

The statutes set forth a settlement option to parties involved in a complaint filed with the CHRO. Conn. Gen. Stat. § 46a-83b. The Alternative Dispute Resolution (ADR) process allows the parties to select a neutral third party to mediate and/or arbitrate their dispute. If the parties elect this option, the CHRO is required to suspend its investigation into the complaint for ninety days.

If the parties do not choose the ADR option, the CHRO will conduct a ninety day merit assessment review based on the complaint, the school board's answers, and the employee's comments. Conn. Gen. Stat. § 46a-83(b). The CHRO may summarily dismiss a complaint if it finds that it (1) fails to state a claim for relief; (2) is frivolous on its face; or (3) poses no reasonable possibility that further investigation will result in a finding of reasonable cause. The employee may request reconsideration of this dismissal or may instead file a lawsuit in state court. Conn. Gen. Stat. § 46a-83a. If the complaint is not dismissed, the CHRO will determine how best to process it further.

The CHRO may require the parties to participate in mandatory mediation in an attempt to reach a voluntary resolution. Both parties have a duty to attend and participate in this mediation. Conn. Gen. Stat. § 46a-83(c). A dismissal of the complaint or default judgment may be entered for failure to attend.

If a complaint is retained after the initial merit assessment review, the CHRO generally conducts fact finding conferences in order to determine if there is "reasonable cause" to believe discrimination has occurred, but alternatively may conduct a "full investigation," including subpoenaing documents and issuing interrogatories. Conn. Gen. Stat. § 46a-83(c), (h). "Reasonable cause" means a bona fide belief that the material issues of fact are such that a person of ordinary caution, prudence and judgment could believe the facts alleged in the complaint. *Id.* If an employer fails to respond to subpoenas or interrogatories, the CHRO may enter a default judgment against it. Conn. Gen. Stat. § 46a-83(i). Both the employer and the employee, and their representatives, may provide written and oral comments on all evidence, and may inspect and copy documents, statements of witnesses and other pertinent evidence. Conn. Gen. Stat. § 46a-83(g).

The CHRO must make its reasonable cause decision within 190 days from the date of the CHRO's merit assessment review of the complaint. The finding must be in writing listing the factual findings on which it is based. If the investigation reveals no reasonable cause to believe that discrimination occurred, the employee has the right to ask CHRO to reconsider or to appeal the decision to court. *See* Conn. Gen. Stat. § 46a-83(d) and (e) and Conn. St. Reg. § 46a-54-79; Conn. Gen. Stat. § 46a-94a and Conn. Gen. Stat. § 4-183.

If the CHRO finds reasonable cause, it must attempt to resolve the matter within the next fifty days by conference, conciliation and persuasion. Conn. Gen. Stat. § 46a-83(f). The employee has a duty to accept a "make whole relief offer" at any stage of the proceedings. A make whole relief offer is one where the school board has eliminated the discriminatory practice complained of, taken steps to prevent a like occurrence in the future and offered full relief to the employee. The CHRO has the option of closing its investigation into a complaint whenever the school board has made a "make whole relief offer." Conn. Gen. Stat. § 46a-83(c).

If conciliation fails, a formal hearing must be commenced by the convening of an initial hearing conference. This conference must be held within forty-five days of the date that the investigator certifies that the complaint was not resolved through conciliation. Conn. Gen. Stat. § 46a-84(b). Following this initial conference, the presiding hearing officer may conduct settlement negotiations. The CHRO may seek an injunction prohibiting the school board from continuing the allegedly discriminatory conduct until the hearing is concluded. Conn. Gen. Stat. § 46a-89; Conn. Gen. Stat. § 46a-95. If an injunction is issued, the hearing must be scheduled within forty-five days from the granting of the injunction. Conn. Gen. Stat. § 46a-90a.

A CHRO member or a hearing examiner conducts the hearing. CHRO counsel or a member of the Attorney General's office presents the employee's case, although the employee may also retain a private attorney. The school board may answer the charges in writing but almost always presents live witness testimony at the hearing, again with counsel. The hearing officer may subpoena witnesses and documents. All witnesses testify under oath, and either party may request that a record of the hearing be made. An arbitration decision may be entered as evidence if the award does not dispose of the CHRO proceeding.

The hearing officer then makes a decision either to dismiss the complaint or to order an appropriate remedy. If discrimination is found, the hearing officer may order the school board to stop discriminating, and to hire or reinstate the employee with or without back pay, restoration of seniority and other benefits. Conn. Gen. Stat. § 46a-86. For example, finding race discrimination in a decision adverse to an administrative candidate, a CHRO hearing officer awarded a school employee in Norwalk $56,390 in back pay and another $18,797 in "front pay." *CHRO ex rel. Saunders v. Norwalk Board of Education*, 6 Conn. Ops. 1161 (CHRO Doc. No. 9820124) (October 16, 2000), *affirmed Board of Education of the City of Norwalk v. CHRO*, 266 Conn. 492 (2003).

If no suitable position is available, the hearing officer may award "front pay" or prospective damages. A new employee will not be "bumped" in favor of the victim of discrimination. *See Civil Service Commission v. CHRO ex rel Trainor,* 195 Conn. 533 (1979). There is no express statutory authority for the CHRO to award compensatory or punitive damages or attorney's fees in employment cases.

In 1995, the Connecticut Supreme Court ruled that the CHRO does not have the right to award compensatory damages or attorney's fees under Conn. Gen. Stat. § 46a-86. *Bridgeport Hospital v. Commission on Human Rights and Opportunities,* 232 Conn. 91 (1995). Since that decision, however, hearing officers of the CHRO have occasionally awarded damages for emotional distress, relying on a different provision of the statutes, Conn. Gen. Stat. § 46a-58. Further litigation on this point, therefore, appears inevitable. *See, e.g., CHRO v. Truelove and Maclean*, 238 Conn. 337 (1996) (award of damages for emotional distress arising from discriminatory employment practice cannot be based on violation of general statutory prohibition against discrimination); *Thames Talent. Ltd. v. CHRO*, 265 Conn. 127 (2003) (back pay can be awarded without reinstatement).

The school board, the employee, or the CHRO may appeal the hearing officer's decision. However, factual findings, if "supported by substantial and competent evidence," are conclusive in any appeal, and the decision will be overturned only if it is determined to be arbitrary. *See Board of Education v. CHRO*, 176 Conn. 533 (1979). The school board can also "appeal" by objecting to the CHRO's request for court enforcement of its hearing officer's decision. Conn. Gen. Stat. § 46a-95.

c. Private lawsuits

Any employee who has filed a timely administrative complaint of employment discrimination under the Connecticut Fair Employment Practices Act (FEPA) with the CHRO and whose complaint has been pending for more than two hundred ten days, may request a release from the CHRO proceedings permitting him or her to file a private civil lawsuit in state or federal court against the school board. Conn. Gen. Stat. § 46a-100, Conn. Gen. Stat. § 46a-101. The executive director of the CHRO must grant the release within ten business days of the receipt of the request, unless the complaint has been scheduled for a CHRO hearing, or unless the executive director certifies that she or he has reason to believe the pending CHRO complaint may be resolved within the next thirty days. There is a similar process for requesting a right to sue letter from the EEOC after one hundred eighty days. 29 C.F.R. § 1601.28.

The employee must file the lawsuit within ninety days of receipt of the CHRO or EEOC release. However, the lawsuit will be barred if the complaint has been pending before the CHRO for more than two years. The CHRO has the right to intervene in any private lawsuit brought under the Fair Employment Practices Act by an employee.

The liability risk for the school board in a private lawsuit is significantly higher than in a CHRO hearing. The court may grant a successful employee damages for loss of back pay, fringe benefits and retirement benefits, and for front pay, as well as additional compensation for pain and suffering and for any other monetary loss incurred because of a discriminatory employment practice. The court may also grant the employee injunctive relief, attorney's fees and costs. Consequently, some employees simply wait out the CHRO process and go to court with their claims.

C. Other Employer Responsibilities

School districts in Connecticut face a host of other duties in their role as employers. While not an exhaustive review, the following identifies and briefly reviews some of the important responsibilities.

1. The employment relationship

A threshold question in considering the obligations of school districts as employers is whether a person is an employee or an independent contractor. This question is significant, because the answer determines whether the individual will be protected by the various laws that regulate the employment relationship, including workers' compensation, unemployment compensation, social security and state and federal income tax withholding. Given these obligations, it is important to be clear on whether a person is, or is not, an independent contractor. In considering this issue, the critical fact is the nature of the relationship, not how the parties themselves describe it.

Recently, in distinguishing between employees and independent contractors, courts and the IRS have focused on the "three categories of evidence test," which considers (1) behavioral control, (2) financial control, and (3) relationship of the parties. "Behavioral control" considers whether the employer has a right to direct and control how the work is done, through instruction, training and other means. "Financial control" considers whether the employer or business has a right to control the business aspects of the worker's job. This includes the extent the worker has reimbursed business expenses, the extent of the worker's investment in the business, the extent the worker makes services available to the relevant market, how the worker is paid by the business, and the extent to which the worker may realize a profit or loss. "Relationship of the parties" considers issues such as: (1) is there a contract describing the relationship between the worker and the business; if so, what type of relationship did the parties intend to make?; (2) is the worker available to perform services for other similar businesses?; (3) does the business provide the worker with employee-type benefits, such as insurance, a pension plan, vacation pay or sick pay?; and (4) is the relationship permanent? This "three categories of evidence test" is illustrated in IRS Form SS-8 "Determination of Worker Status." In summary, the person will be considered an employee if the employer has the right to control and direct the means and details of work. *Tianti v. William Raveis Real Estate, Inc.*, 231 Conn. 690, 696-97 (1995). *See also* Revenue Ruling 87-41.

A second basic question concerning the employment relationship is how it may be terminated. The vast majority of school district employees are in bargaining units, and such employees typically are subject to "just cause" provisions in collective bargaining agreements. *See* Chapter Six, Section A(7). In addition, certified staff members below the rank of superintendent are subject to the provisions of the Teacher Tenure Act. For non-union employees, however, the situation is very different. The general rule of employment is "employment-at-will," which means that the employment may be terminated by either party at any time. *D'Ulisse-Cupo v. Board of Directors of Notre Dame High School*, 202 Conn. 206 (1987), *Thibodeau v. Design Group One Architects, LLC*, 260 Conn. 691 (2002). When an employee is "at will," the employer may simply notify him or her that the employment has ended. Such action may be taken for any reason, or for no reason at all, as long as it is not taken for the wrong reason.

There are, of course, exceptions to this rule when the action is taken for an improper reason. First, an employee who is otherwise "at will" may claim that his/her termination should not be allowed because such action is against public policy. These claims arise, for example, if an employee is allegedly terminated for exercising a statutory right or for taking action that is in the public interest. In 1980, the Connecticut Supreme Court recognized that employees at will may make such claims. *Sheets v. Teddy's Frosted Foods*, 179 Conn. 471 (1980).

Second, since school districts are public employers, their actions against employees are subject to constitutional limitations. The United States Supreme Court has recognized that even public employees can be "at will." As described above in Section A(1), however, when employees have an expectation of continued employment, they have a property interest, the deprivation of which requires due process. Also, public employees have a liberty interest in their reputation and their ability to obtain other employment. Accordingly, they have a right to due process before the public employer makes public findings (or statements) that harm that liberty interest. Absent either a public policy or constitutional concern, however, employees at will are subject to termination in the discretion of school authorities.

Sometimes, school officials give employees who would otherwise be at will a contract of employment for a specified term. Also, employee handbooks can create a contract for continued employment, subject to the terms set forth in the handbook. Such contracts are enforceable, and they create a property interest that then may trigger due process rights. Typically, however, such contracts can be terminated for "just cause" in accordance with their terms, which may include positions elimination. *Rivers v. Milford Mental Health Clinic*, 2002 Conn. Super. LEXIS 1764 (Conn. Super. Ct. 2002). Moreover, the employers may terminate the contract if the employee commits serious misconduct, a commonsense right that employers have whether stated in the contract or not.

2. Wage and hour requirements

Connecticut public schools must adhere to both federal and state wage and hour laws. The Fair Labor Standards Act (the FLSA) is the federal statute regulating the wages and hours of employees. 29 U.S.C. § 201 *et seq.* The FLSA explicitly provides that states may establish stricter wage and hour standards for employers that fall within the FLSA's coverage. 29 U.S.C. § 218(a). Connecticut has adopted stricter standards, including a higher minimum wage, conditions for overtime pay, guidelines for determining the hours employees work, and certain child labor protections. *See* Conn. Gen. Stat. § 31-12 *et seq.*

Non-certified employees, such as custodians and school secretaries, are typically subject to all provisions of these laws. Both laws, however, exempt certain employees from the minimum wage and overtime provisions. Administrative, professional, and executive employees who meet certain tests set out in the statutes and regulations are exempt. Teachers and administrators are such exempt employees, since they are professional salaried employees.

The regulations specifically provide that deductions can be taken from the salary of exempt employees for absence of less than one day for leave under the Family and Medical Leave Act, 29 U.S.C. § 2601 *et seq.* Deductions are also permitted for absences of a day or more for sickness or disability after sick leave is exhausted pursuant to a policy or practice of providing sick leave. 29 C.F.R. § 541.118; Conn. St. Reg. § 31-60-16. There is question, however, over whether salary deductions of less than one week for disciplinary purposes will cause the employee to lose the exemption. In *Auer v. Robbins,* 519 U.S. 452 (1997), the United States Supreme Court held that, if the exemption is lost, it can be restored under certain circumstances by repayment of the deduction taken for disciplinary reasons. The new federal regulations clarify this issue by permitting deduction of one or more full days for violation of workplace rules, but it is not clear whether Connecticut will follow suit. *See* Conn. St. Reg. § 31-60-16(b)(4).

a. Hours of work

An employee is entitled to be paid for all hours during which he or she is working, is on duty, or is at the work place at the employer's request even though no work is provided. An employee must be paid for on-call time if he or she is required to be at a location designated by the school board. Conn. St. Reg. § 31-60-11. However, the employer is not responsible for paying on-call time when the employee is merely subject to call and need not be at any particular location. *Id.* In addition, travel time that occurs during the employee's normally scheduled working hours is included within the statutory definition of hours worked, Conn. Gen. Stat. § 31-76b(2), but travel time to and from work is normally not included unless the employee is called to work outside his or her normally scheduled hours.

Given these requirements, it is important that employers maintain accurate time records. When such records are not maintained, the employer is in violation of the law. Moreover, the lack of records can make it difficult or impossible to rebut a claim by an employee that he or she worked certain hours and is therefore entitled to pay for those hours.

b. Time off from work

Connecticut law requires employers to allow employees one day off each calendar week, effectively prohibiting more than twelve days of mandatory labor in a row. Conn. Gen. Stat. § 53-303e(a). The employee is not entitled to overtime pay for hours worked on Saturday or Sunday unless it constitutes overtime as defined under the statute, *i.e.* hours in excess of forty per workweek. *See* Conn. Gen. Stat. § 31-76c. State law does not require school boards or other employers to grant paid holidays, close on holidays, or to pay employees extra for working on holidays. Similarly, there is no statutory requirement that vacation be provided. However, these issues are often addressed in collective bargaining agreements and/or board policy. It is advisable to do so to avoid any disputes over whether an employee is or is not entitled to payment for such time.

Connecticut law requires the employer to give employees who work for seven and one-half or more consecutive hours at least a thirty minute meal break. Conn. Gen. Stat. § 31-51ii(a). It does not, however, require payment for these meal periods. Conn. Gen. Stat. § 31-76b(2)(A). Short rest breaks (up to twenty minutes) are normally considered working time for which employees must be paid.

c. Required overtime pay

State law requires overtime payment to employees who work more than 40 hours in a single workweek. Holidays and other days that are paid for but not worked do not count toward overtime. The overtime rate must be at least 150 percent of the employee's regular rate. Conn. Gen. Stat. § 31-76c. A normal workweek is seven consecutive days. The school board may not average hours worked over a two week period to avoid the overtime rate. Weekends, holidays, or hours in excess of the eight hour day do not qualify for the overtime rate unless the above criteria have been met. Teachers and administrators are exempt from this requirement. Conn. Gen. Stat. § 31-76i.

As an employer, the school board should be forewarned that an employee who is entitled to but not paid overtime wages may bring a civil action to recover twice the wages due and attorney's fees. Conn. Gen. Stat. § 31-68. School officials who violate these statutory provisions may also be fined or imprisoned for such failure to comply with these requirements. Conn. Gen. Stat. § 31-76a.

d. Minimum wage and wage payment laws

Under federal law, states may increase the federal minimum wage. 29 U.S.C. § 218(a). The Connecticut General Assembly has specified that the state minimum wage must always be at least one-half of one percent above the federal minimum wage. Conn. Gen. Stat. § 31-58(j). Once again, teachers and superintendents are exempt from this requirement.

State and federal law require that employees be paid for all hours worked during the pay period. Consequently, employees who are not otherwise exempt from the minimum wage provisions are to be paid for all hours worked within eight days of the close of the pay period. Conn. Gen. Stat. § 31-71b. Also, the pay period for non-exempt employees is generally weekly unless the employer has obtained a waiver from the Commissioner of Labor. Conn. Gen. Stat. § 31-71b and Conn. Gen. Stat. § 31-71i. These requirements do not apply to certified and non-certified unionized board employees, however, if it has negotiated an alternative payment schedule with the exclusive bargaining representative. Conn. Gen. Stat. § 31-71b(c).

There are special rules that apply to compensatory time for public employees. Under federal law, public employees can be scheduled so that they are forced to take compensatory time off rather than be paid for accrued compensatory time. *Christensen v. Harris County*, 529 U.S. 576 (2000).

As with overtime payments, employees paid less than the applicable minimum wage may bring a civil action to recover twice the wages due plus attorneys' fees. Conn. Gen. Stat. § 31-68. Similarly, employers who do not comply with these requirements may also face fines and imprisonment. Conn. Gen. Stat. § 31-69(b).

e. Written employer policies

Employers must maintain written policies or post a notice in a place accessible to employees concerning wages, vacation pay, sick leave, health and welfare benefits and comparable matters. Conn. Gen. Stat. § 31-71f. Also, new employees must be advised in writing of their pay rate, hours of employment and wage payment schedule. Employers may be subject to fines and imprisonment for any violation of such written policies. Conn. Gen. Stat. § 31-71g.

3. Workers' Compensation

The Connecticut Workers' Compensation Act guarantees medical care and protection against income loss for employees who suffer work-related injury, illness or death. Conn. Gen. Stat. § 31-275 *et seq.* While the Act grants benefits to an injured employee without regard for the fault or negligence of the employer, the benefits are generally the exclusive remedy for on-the-job injury or occupational disease. *See Davey v. Pepperidge Farms, Inc.*, 180 Conn. 469 (1980). While these laws impose significant costs on employers, they provide a mechanism for resolving issues relating to on-the-job injuries and permit employers to avoid expensive litigation and potentially large damage awards.

At the outset, we note that Connecticut law requires that employers with more than twenty-five employees establish health and safety committees to monitor work-place safety. These committees have significant responsibilities under state law, including "(A) establishing procedures for workplace safety inspections by the committee, (B) establishing procedures for investigating all safety incidents, accidents, illnesses and deaths, (C) evaluating accident and illness prevention programs, (D) establishing training programs for the identification and reduction of hazards in the workplace which damage the reproductive systems of employees, and (E) establishing training programs to assist committee members in understanding and identifying the effects of employee substance abuse on workplace accidents and safety." Conn. Gen. Stat. § 31-40v. The law also requires that employers maintain reports of the meetings of such committees. The operation of such committees is subject to regulations issued by the Workers' Compensation Commissioner.

Most school districts purchase insurance to cover their workers' compensation liability. However, school boards must assure that they provide insurance companies with the necessary information in a timely fashion, and meet the obligations that are not covered by insurance, such as the non-discrimination or anti-retaliation provision discussed below. Conn. Gen. Stat. § 31-290a.

The school district may, with the approval of the Workers' Compensation Commissioner, establish a preferred provider plan for injured employees. Conn. St. Reg. § 31-279-10. Each approved plan, along with any proposed changes, must be resubmitted to the chairman every two years for reapproval.

a. Employer obligations

Employers are responsible for ensuring that all of the Act's benefits are available to an employee who suffers a compensable injury. An employer must insure against its liability for weekly compensation payments, medical treatment for the injury, and payment for permanent functional loss. An employer can choose to self-insure, purchase this insurance from a company authorized in Connecticut, or combine the two methods. Any substitute forms of compensation are permitted only with the approval of the Insurance Commissioner. Conn. Gen. Stat. § 31-285 and Conn. Gen. Stat. § 31-286.

When an employee is receiving workers' compensation indemnity benefits, the municipal employer must continue to provide accident and health insurance and life insurance coverage, or make contributions to an employee welfare fund equivalent to those provided prior to the employee's injury. Conn. Gen. Stat. § 31-284b. The employer must inform the insurance commissioner of the extent of this coverage or contribution. School districts can insure this obligation; however, most choose to simply continue existing group insurance coverage.

When an employee is not totally incapacitated by the job-related injury, the employer is obligated to try to accommodate the employee by finding work that the employee can perform given the injury. The employer must, whenever possible, transfer the employee to "light duty" or "restricted work," suitable to the physical condition. Conn. Gen. Stat. § 31-313.

However, there is no statutory duty to create a light duty assignment if none exists.

Employers must post notices in visible locations informing employees that workers' compensation is available and provide the name of the insurance carrier and district compensation commissioner. Conn. Gen. Stat. § 31-279(a); Conn. Gen. Stat. § 31-284(f). A form for such notice is available from the Workers' Compensation Commission or the insurance carrier.

Finally, employers must keep a record of all work-related injuries that result in any employee being unable to work for one day or more. This record must be submitted weekly, in duplicate, to the commissioner, together with notices of claims that have been given to the employer. Conn. Gen. Stat. § 31-316.

b. Covered injuries

The Workers' Compensation Act covers injuries "arising out of and in the course of employment." Conn. Gen. Stat. § 31-284. There must be a causal connection between the injury and the job. *Farnham v. Labutis*, 147 Conn. 267 (1960). An employee must prove that the injury:

- occurred within the time period of employment;
- at a place where the employee may reasonably be; and
- while the employee was fulfilling the duties of employment or doing something incidental to it.

McNamara v. Town of Hamden, 176 Conn. 547 (1979); *Stakonis v. United Advertising Corp.*, 110 Conn. 384 (1930). Such injuries are called "compensable injuries," and are covered by the Act.

c. Injuries not covered

The employee will not be eligible for workers' compensation if the employer can prove that:

- the injury was caused by willful misconduct or intoxication; Conn. Gen. Stat. § 31-284(a) and Conn. Gen. Stat. § 31-275(1)(C); or
- the only injury attributable to the employee's work is weakened resistance (unless that condition was caused

by a work related injury) or lowered vitality; Conn. Gen. Stat. § 31-275(1)(B); or

- the injury was the result of "horseplay" or assaults (unless the employer was aware of such conduct and allowed it to continue). *See Shedlock v. Cudahy Packing Co.*, 134 Conn. 672 (1948).; or
- the claim is based on a mental or emotional impairment unless the impairment arises from a physical injury or occupational disease. Conn. Gen. Stat. § 31-275(16)(B)(ii). *See Gartrell v. Department of Correction*, 259 Conn. 29 (2002).

d. Employer liability

An employee must notify the employer of an injury as soon as possible after it occurs. Within one year from the date of an accident or three years from the first manifestation of an occupational disease, the employee must give written notice to the employer or the commissioner. Conn. Gen. Stat. § 31-294c. The employer can contest any workers' compensation claim by filing a notice to that effect (on Form 43) within twenty-eight days of receiving the employee's written notice of claim. Conn. Gen. Stat. § 31-294c. A copy of the notice must be sent to the employee. Prompt action in sending such a notice is crucial, because the employer will most likely lose the right to contest the claim if it fails to file Form 43 in time. *See Bush v. Quality Bakers of America*, 2 Conn. App. 363, *cert. denied*, 194 Conn. 804 (1984). The form of the notice must comply with the guidelines set out by the commissioner and must include specific reasons for denying compensation. *Id.* A general or vague denial will be considered invalid. *See Menzies v. Fisher*, 165 Conn. 338 (1973).

The employer and the employee may also choose to enter into a voluntary agreement concerning the compensation due. Any such agreement must be submitted in writing to the commissioner for approval. Conn. Gen. Stat. § 31-296. Once so approved, such agreements are binding. *Id.*

If the employer does not have enough information to either contest the claim or enter a voluntary agreement, it has the option of paying the employee benefits without prejudice and without admitting liability. The employer must notify the commissioner by letter of such an arrangement. The employer will then have six weeks to investigate the claim and decide whether to offer a voluntary agreement or promptly request an informal hearing. Conn. Gen. Stat. § 31-294c.

During this six week investigation period or when the claim is contested, the employer has the right to request that the employee submit to a physical examination conducted by a physician it selects and pays for. This examination will provide the employer with an objective determination of the nature of the injury and extent of the resulting incapacity. If the employee refuses to submit to a reasonable examination, that employee will lose the right to compensation during that period. Conn. Gen. Stat. § 31-294f.

Contested claims will first be reviewed in an informal hearing, often a conference with the commissioner to discuss any disputes in a case. If no agreement is reached, a formal hearing will be held at which both parties may appear and be represented by attorneys. Conn. Gen. Stat. § 31-297(a). Within 120 days after a formal hearing, the commissioner will send a written copy of his/her findings to both parties. Conn. Gen. Stat. § 31-300.

Either party may appeal the award to the Compensation Review Board by filing an appeal petition within twenty days from the date of the award. Conn. Gen. Stat. § 31-301. Appeals from the Compensation Review Board must be made to the appellate court within twenty days of the issuance of the decision. Conn. Gen. Stat. § 31-301a and Conn. Gen. Stat. § 31-301b . Appeals at this level, however, are limited to questions of law. Disagreements with the factual findings of the commissioners will not be heard. Conn. Gen. Stat. § 31-301b.

In general, workers' compensation is the employee's exclusive remedy against the employer for personal injury or death arising out of and in the course of employment. Conn. Gen. Stat. § 31-284(a); *Jett v. Dunlap*, 179 Conn. 215 (1979). This protection against negligence suits is the major benefit to employers under this Act. In addition, an employer may seek reimbursement from a negligent third party that caused the injury to recover any amounts paid or owed by the employer. Conn. Gen. Stat. § 31-293. However, in rare situations, the employer can be liable beyond workers' compensation obligations if the employer's intentional tort injures an employee or when the employer has engaged in wilful or serious misconduct. *Suarez* v. *Dickmont Plastics Corp.*, 229 Conn. 99 (1994).

Finally, employees are also restricted from suing their fellow employees except when they are injured by a co-worker's wilful or malicious misconduct or negligent operation of a motor vehicle. Conn. Gen. Stat. § 31-293a. This provision of the workers' compensation law significantly reduces the likelihood of litigation over workplace injuries.

4. Unemployment compensation

The Connecticut Unemployment Compensation Act provides financial benefits to workers who become partially or fully unemployed. Conn. Gen. Stat. § 31-222 *et seq*. Benefits are financed by employers, usually through quarterly payroll taxes. However, public agencies such as boards of education may decline to pay such taxes and bear the expenses of any claims directly. Conn. Gen. Sta. § 31-225(d). The Act is administered by the Employment Security Division of the State Department of Labor.

As with the workers' compensation act, employees must be made aware of the unemployment benefits available to them. Employers, including school boards, are required to display a poster stating that they are covered by the act. Conn. St. Reg. § 31-222-10.

a. Eligibility for benefits

In general, to be eligible for benefits, an individual must file the claim according to the procedures of the Employment Security Division, be physically and mentally able to work, and be available for and make reasonable efforts to obtain work. Employees need not be permanently laid off; an individual temporarily unemployed may still qualify. Conn. Gen. Stat. § 31-225a.

Otherwise eligible employees may be disqualified from receiving benefits if their employment ended for one of the following reasons:

- failure to apply for or accept suitable work;
- leaving suitable work voluntarily and without sufficient cause;
- discharge for felonious or larcenous conduct, willful misconduct, or participation in an illegal strike;
- termination as a result of a labor dispute; or
- lack of work between academic terms.

Each of these disqualifying circumstances merits brief review.

1. Availability of suitable work

Claimants must apply for available suitable work and accept it when offered. Conn. Gen. Stat. § 31-236(a)(1). However, employees are not required to accept any available work. Employees are permitted a reasonable period of time to look for "suitable" work at their present wage and skill level before being required to accept a less skilled or lower-paying job. *DaSilva v. Administrator*, 175 Conn. 562 (1978). The statute enumerates factors involved in determining whether or nor work is suitable including "the degree of risk involved to . . . health, safety and morals, physical fitness, prior training and experience, skills, previous wage level and length of unemployment."

2. Leaving work voluntarily

An employee who leaves work voluntarily and without sufficient cause connected to work is not eligible for benefits. Conn. Gen. Stat. § 31-236(a)(2)(A). However, the law provides that leaving a job as a result of changes in conditions created by the employer may be "sufficient cause" connected to work.

The Employment Security Division has interpreted this provision broadly in favor of employees. However, if an employer has not been given the opportunity to alleviate a work-related problem, it can challenge an employee who claims that he or she left work "involuntarily" because of that problem. Failure to notify the employer of the problem in an effort to explore all reasonable alternatives may disqualify the employee from receiving benefits. Conn. Gen. Stat. § 31-236(a)(2)(A)(iii). Employers are well-advised to adopt a policy to ensure that employee requests for assistance or accommodation are documented to establish whether an individual did explore alternatives before quitting. Similarly, to ensure that employees who leave voluntarily do not receive benefits, employers should adopt a procedure for documenting voluntary resignations. The employee should sign a severance form or other document (such as a letter of resignation) stating the reason for leaving, or participate in a documented exit interview.

3. Discharge, suspension and willful misconduct

An employee who is discharged or suspended for engaging in conduct that could constitute a felony or larceny, *i.e.* the intentional taking of property or services, is disqualified from receiving benefits. The employee need not be convicted or even formally charged, but the employer must be able to show that the employee has engaged in the conduct in the course of employment. Conn. Gen. Stat. § 31-236(a)(2)(B).

Employees are also ineligible for unemployment compensation if they are dismissed for willful misconduct. "Willful misconduct" is defined by statute as deliberate misconduct in willful disregard of the employer's interest, or a single knowing violation of a reasonable and uniformly enforced rule or policy of the employer, when reasonably applied, provided such violation is not a result of the employee's incompetence and provided further, in the case of absence from work, "willful misconduct" means an employee must be absent without either good cause for the absence or notice to the employer which the employee could reasonably have provided under the circumstances for three separate instances within a twelve-month period. Each consecutive one or two day period may be considered a separate instance. Conn. Gen. Stat. § 31-236(a)(16)

Repeated absence, tardiness or violation of a reasonable work rule, if not for good reason, may thus constitute willful misconduct. However, the employer must be sure that the employee is aware of its policies and must warn the employee that such conduct will not be tolerated. In any case of willful misconduct, the employer should ensure that the unacceptable behavior is documented over a period of time to show repeated offenses. Also, there are special rules with regard to absenteeism. To cause a claimant to be ineligible, the employee must be absent without notice on three separate instances in an twelve month period.

4. Labor disputes

If an individual's unemployment is due to the existence of a labor dispute at his or her place of work, the individual will be ineligible for benefits unless:

- the individual is not participating in or financing or directly interested in the labor dispute; and
- the individual is not a member of a trade, class or organization of workers whose members were employed at the premises of the dispute immediately before its commencement and are participating, financing or directly interested in the dispute; or
- the unemployment is due to a lockout.

Conn. Gen. Stat. § 31-236(a)(3). However, since it is illegal for school board employees to strike in Connecticut, this exclusion will not usually apply. Conn. Gen. Stat. § 7-475 and Conn. Gen Stat. § 10-153e.

5. Lack of work between academic terms

Given the unique schedule of school district employees, there is a specific disqualification applicable to such employees between semesters or academic years. The law provides that teachers and other persons employed in an instructional or principal administrative responsibility are not eligible for benefits between two successive academic years or during a similar period between two academic terms, or during a paid sabbatical leave provided for in the individual's contract. However, this disqualification is based on two requirements. First, the teacher or other employee must provide services in the first year or academic term before the break. Second, the employee must have a contract or a "reasonable assurance" that he or she will be employed in the second year or term. Other employees of boards of education are subject to a similar provision, except that the law also states that they will be entitled to benefits retroactively if they are not employed during the next year or academic term. Conn. Gen. Stat. § 31-227(d). Finally, the law also makes similar provision concerning "an established and customary vacation period or holiday recess." School employees are not entitled to benefits if they worked in the period immediately before the break and have a reasonable assurance that they will perform services immediately following the break. *Id.*

These provisions of the unemployment law can cause a strange result. Under certain circumstances, a teacher or other school employee can be fully paid during one year, be employed in the next year, and collect unemployment over the summer. This situation arises when a board of education anticipates reductions in force and notifies certain employees that they will not have a job in the next year. At that point, such employees no longer have a "reasonable assurance" that they will be employed in the following academic year, and the general disqualification for school employees between school years is not applicable.

b. Processing claims and appeals

The employer must fill out an unemployment notice (form UC-61), stating the reason for the unemployment, and give it to the employee upon termination, whether the employee resigns or is discharged. Failure to give this form to the employee can result in charges for retroactive benefit claims. Conn. State Regulations, § 31-222-9(1). If the employer indicates "lack of work" as the reason for unemployment, the Employment Security Division will normally pay benefits without further investigation.

Each claim is initially reviewed by an examiner in a fact-finding interview. Neither party needs to attend this interview, but may submit written evidence. Conn. Gen. Stat. § 31-241. It is imperative that the employer submit at least the written form provided by the Employment Security Division. Failure of the employer to appear or to submit this completed form may result in a permanent charge for benefits paid to the employee for up to six weeks even after a successful appeal. Notice of the decision will be sent to the employee and the employer, and appeals must be made within twenty-one days of the mailing date.

An appeal is first heard by a referee in a fairly formal hearing. Conn. Gen. Stat. § 31-242. All parties are required to appear, although the referee will issue a decision even when one party is absent. Conn. State Regulations, § 31-237g-26. The referee will issue a written decision including findings of fact and conclusions of law. It is very important for the employer to participate in the process at this point if there is any question as to eligibility for benefits. This appeal stage is usually the last opportunity for the employer, as a matter of right, to provide information, and all the relevant facts must be presented at this stage. The parties have twenty-one days to request reconsideration by the referee or appeal the referee's decision to the Board of Review. Conn. Gen. Stat. § 31-248 and Conn. Gen. Stat. § 31-249.

The Board of Review decides appeals on the basis of the record of the hearings at prior levels, except under circumstances justifying a further hearing. Conn. Gen. Stat. § 31-249. The decision of the Board of Review will become final on the thirty-first calendar day after the date on which it was mailed, unless one of the parties requests reconsideration or appeals to Superior Court. Review by the Superior Court is limited to a determination of whether the Board of Review acted illegally or abused its discretion. Either party may then appeal the ruling of the Superior Court to the Appellate Court or the Connecticut Supreme Court.

5. Other statutory provisions

Finally, school districts are subject to a variety of other laws regulating employer conduct or providing particular benefits to employees. Some of the more important provisions of state and federal law follow.

a. Criminal records check

School districts in Connecticut must require that each applicant for employment state whether he or she has ever been convicted of a crime and whether criminal charges are pending against him or her at the time of application. Conn. Gen. Stat. § 10-221d. Given potential confusion as to convictions that were later erased, employers, including boards of education, must include on the job application (1) a statement that prospective employees are not required to disclose convictions that have been erased pursuant to specific statutes, (2) an explanation of those statutes, and (3) a statement that a person whose arrest or conviction records have been erased may swear under oath that s/he has never been arrested. Conn. Gen. Stat. § 31-51i. This statute now also specifies that an employer may not discriminate against any applicant or employee on the basis of arrest/conviction records that have been erased.

Section 31-51i also appears to create a statutory exemption from disclosure that would otherwise be required under the Freedom of Information Act. The statute provides that the portion of the job application that elicits information regarding criminal conviction information must not be disclosed beyond those agents of the employer responsible for personnel. Therefore, such conviction information should not be released pursuant to a Freedom of Information Act request unless the employee authorizes the disclosure of the information or the Commission orders disclosure pursuant to Conn. Gen. Stat. § 1-214.

Within thirty days of employment, employees must submit fingerprint information for state and national criminal history records checks. Students in the district who are also employed by the school district are exempt from this requirement. Included, however, are workers with direct contact with students who (1) are placed within a school under a public assistance employment contract, or (2) provide supplemental services in accordance with the No Child Left Behind Act, P.L. 110-107. For substitutes, there are special provisions: (1) after the initial check, substitutes need not submit further to such a records check if they are "continuously employed," *i.e.* employed at least one day each school year, and (2) a records check submitted to another board of education within one calendar year of employment satisfies the requirement. Conn. Gen. Stat. § 10-221d.

The applicant may be charged for the actual cost of the records check, currently $26.00. The board of education is further authorized to dismiss any employee who has not previously disclosed a conviction of a crime, provided that termination of a certified employee is subject to the procedures of the Teacher Tenure Act, and that a non-certified employee must be notified of the reason for the termination and must have an opportunity to file an answer to the criminal conviction. Conn. Gen. Stat. § 10-221d. Regional educational service centers are now required to make fingerprint information available to boards of education at the request of the person fingerprinted. *Id.*

Section 10-221d also requires school districts to notify the Commissioner of Education if they receive notification that a person holding a certification, authorization or permit has been convicted of a crime (with no minimum threshold, *i.e.* misdemeanor *vs.* felony). In addition, boards of education are now required to make a documented good faith effort to contact previous employers of any applicant "in order to obtain information and recommendations which may be relevant to the person's fitness for employment." Conn. Gen. Stat. § 10-222c. Significantly, these requirements apply to all applicants, not just teachers.

These requirements can present legal issues after an employee has departed. If a former employee seeks employment with another district, that district should check the employee's references and may be calling. Negative comment can raise issues of defamation, as described in Chapter One, Section G(2), but school officials may be candid about the employee, as long as they act in good faith. Of course, a release from the employee may be advisable before one is too candid, to avoid a claim of defamation, even unfounded. In any event, school officials should take care not to whitewash a bad situation. In one infamous case, a school district was held liable for the misconduct of a former employee because it recommended him without disclosing material information bearing on his fitness. *Randi W. v. Muroc Joint Unified School District*, 929 P.2d 582 (Ca. 1997).

Finally, Connecticut has adopted a "Megan's law" (Conn. Gen. Stat. §§ 54-250 et seq.) that requires sexual offenders to register. In 2003, the United States Supreme Court upheld this requirement, ruling that it did not deny registrants due process. *Department of Public Safety v. Doe*, 538 U.S. 1. It is therefore advisable that school districts check this registry before hiring an employee or accepting a volunteer.

b. Employee qualifications

Establishing the qualifications for particular positions has traditionally been an employer prerogative. The No Child Left Behind Act, however, imposes new requirements concerning teachers and paraprofessionals. As to teachers, Section 1119 of the Act provides that all teachers hired after the date of its enactment (January 8, 2002) to teach in a core academic area in a program supported by Title I funds must be "highly qualified." Moreover, the State is required to assure that within four years of the Act's effective date (by January 8, 2006) *all* teachers must be "highly qualified" if they teach in core academic areas, *i.e.*, English, mathematics, reading/language arts, sciences, world languages, arts (including music), history, geography, civics and government, and economics. While it first appeared that only fully certified teachers would be considered "highly qualified," the State Department of Education has clarified that any teacher who has a proper credential to teach, including a durational shortage area permit or a temporary authorization to teach a minor assignment, is considered "highly qualified." Series 2003-2004, Circular Letter C-15 (October 20, 2003). Subsequently, the United States Department of Education announced additional flexibility in this regard for teachers of science, "multi-subject teachers," and teachers in certain rural communities, which include some Connecticut towns. Series 2003-2004, Circular Letter C-23 (May 17, 2004).

The No Child Left Behind Act also imposes obligations with respect to paraprofessionals. As with teachers prior to January 8, 2006, paraprofessionals will be subject to these requirements only if they are assigned to a program supported by Title I funds. If funds are targeted specifically to programs within a school, these requirements apply only to those programs, Section 1115, but if funds support the activities of a Title I school generally, all teaching and paraprofessional staff may be subject to these requirements. Section 1114. Paraprofessionals subject to No Child Left Behind Act requirements must either (1) have two years of college study and/or an associate's degree or (2) have a high school diploma *and* meet a "rigorous standard of quality," including passing a test to demonstrate knowledge of, and the ability to assist in instructing, reading, writing, and mathematics; or of related readiness skills, as appropriate. In 2002 the State Board of Education adopted as its standard a grade of 457 on the *ParaPro Assessment* published by ETS. Series 2003-2004, Circular Letter C-10 (October 29, 2003).

School districts receiving Title I funds must also notify parents of their right to request certain information concerning their teachers. Specifically, Section 1111(h)(6)(A) provides that such notification should set forth information concerning their child's classroom teacher and, if applicable, paraprofessional. In addition, the No Child Left Behind Act provides that, upon request, parents are entitled to (i) information on the level of achievement of the parent's child in each of the State academic assessments as required under this part; and (ii) timely notice that the parent's child has been assigned, or has been taught for four or more consecutive weeks by, a teacher who is not "highly qualified." These obligations are described in Series 2003-2004, Circular Letter C-10 (October 29, 2003).

c. Coaches

All coaches of interscholastic athletics must have a coaching permit as issued by the State Department of Education. A certified teacher or administrator is eligible for a coaching permit if he/she has completed a course on first aid within the preceding three years and has CPR certification. Conn. St. Reg. § 10-145d-423. Persons who do not have teacher or administrator certification may be employed as a coach, provided that they are a high school graduate at least 18 years of age, and have taken at least three semester hours or at least forty-five clock hours of instruction on the educational, legal, medical and safety aspects of coaching. *Id.* To retain a coaching permit, a coach must participate in at least fifteen clock hours of approved training every five years. *Id.*

Salary for coaching positions is often negotiated by the exclusive bargaining representative for teachers, because many teachers serve in such roles. Coaches do not achieve tenure in their positions as coach, however, whether or not they are otherwise certified employees of the district. *Dietter v. City of New Milford*, No. CV960070416, 1996 Conn. Super. LEXIS 1634 (Conn. Super. Ct. 1996); *Talmadge v. Bristol Board of Education*, No. 312200 (Conn. Super. Ct. 1986).

Even though coaches do not achieve tenure, they were given other statutory rights in 2004. All athletic coaches must be evaluated on an annual basis, and the school district must provide such coaches with copies of these evaluations. An "athletic coach" is defined as "any person holding a coaching permit who is hired by a local or regional board of education to coach for a sport season," and the term apparently does not include volunteer coaches. If such a coach has been employed in the same coaching assignment for at least three years, he or she must be notified that he/she will not be reappointed within ninety days after the end of the applicable athletic season. If that happens, such coaches now have the right to appeal that decision to the board of education in accordance with procedures that the board is obligated to establish. P.A. 04-243. The statute does not specify what happens if a district fails to give notice of at least ninety days. It provides, however, that the employment of a coach may be terminated at any time "(1) for reasons of moral misconduct, insubordination or a violation of the rules of the board of education, or (2) because a sport has been cancelled by the board of education." *Id.*

d. Indemnity

The statutes indemnify school district employees against economic loss in two very different ways. First, as described in Chapter One, Section G(3), school districts are required to hold school employees harmless when they are sued for alleged negligence or other actions taken in the course of their employment as long as such actions are not wanton, reckless or malicious. Conn. Gen. Stat. § 10-235. This right of indemnification includes the right to have counsel provided or to be reimbursed for reasonable attorney's fees incurred in defending against such claims. However, this right applies only to civil actions against a school employee, and school districts are not legally obligated to provide such representation when a teacher is a criminal defendant unless the district has independently promised to provide such representation through collective bargaining or otherwise.

Second, school district employees who are assaulted in the course of their employment are entitled to full payment for any medical or other services necessary as a result of that assault, to the extent that their individual insurance, workers' compensation or other source does not pay the bill. Conn. Gen. Stat. § 10-236a. In addition, such employees are entitled to continue to receive their full pay during any absence caused by an assault, less any amounts received from workers' compensation. Any such absence may not be charged against the employee's sick leave, vacation time or personal leave days. In 2004, the Superior Court ruled that a non-certified employee injured through student horseplay was not entitled to the benefits of Conn. Gen. Stat. § 10-236a. The court based its ruling on its definition of an "assault" as "an intentionally violent and hostile attack on another person." *Patrie v. Area Cooperative Educational Services*, No. CV000440418S, 2004 Conn. Super. LEXIS 1595 (Conn. Super. Ct. 2004).

e. Residency requirements

In general, a public employer in Connecticut may impose a residency requirement for its employees if that requirement is based on important municipal interests. *Bruno v. Civil Service Commission of Bridgeport*, 192 Conn. 335 (1984). After the *Bruno* case was decided, however, the General Assembly amended the statutes to provide that municipal employees who are subject to the terms of a collective bargaining agreement may not be required as a condition of employment to reside in the municipality where they are employed. Conn. Gen. Stat. § 7-460b. *See also* Conn. Gen. Stat. § 10-155f (residency requirements may not be imposed on teachers). Other employees of the school district, however, may be subject to residency requirements, and such is often the case with the superintendent.

f. Family and Medical Leave Act

In 1993, Congress enacted the Family and Medical Leave Act, 29 U.S.C. § 2601 *et seq.*, some three years after Connecticut passed a similar law. While the Connecticut law applies only to private employers and thus does not affect school district employees, the federal law does apply. It provides that employees meeting the eligibility requirements (*i.e.* employment for at least one year for at least 1250 hours actually worked in the twelve month period preceding the leave) are eligible for unpaid leave for specified purposes. Such leave may extend up to twelve weeks in a twelve month period, and during the leave period, the employer is obligated to maintain health insurance benefits on the same basis as is provided to other similarly situated employees.

Leave under the Act is available for (1) the birth and care of the employee's child, (2) the placement of a child with the employee for adoption or foster care, (3) the care of a spouse, child or parent of the employee who has a serious health condition, or (4) for the serious health condition of the employee that makes the employee unable to perform the function of his or her job.

It is important to note that the leave available for eligible employees under the Act is not intended to supplement leave otherwise provided to such employees. An employer may require that the employee substitute any accrued vacation or sick leave for any part of the twelve week period that may be taken for the serious health condition of a spouse, child or parent, or for the serious health condition of the employee him- or herself.

For the leave to count against the employee's FMLA entitlement, the employer should designate the leave in writing as FMLA-qualifying. In 2002, on a 5-4 vote, the United States Supreme Court struck down a United States Department of Labor regulation providing that leave would not count for FMLA purposes until such notification. *Ragsdale v. Wolverine World Wide, Inc.*, 535 U.S. 81 (2002). Holding that the statute did not authorize a categorical penalty for a failure to designate leave as FMLA leave, the Court directed the Labor Department to formulate a different approach as to notification. It is still advisable, however, to assure that FMLA-qualifying leave is so designated as soon as the facts are known.

The request for any such leave must be made at least thirty days in advance when the need for such leave is foreseeable. However, when the date of birth, placement (of a child), or date of treatment requires that the leave begin in less than thirty days, the employee must provide such advance notice of the requested leave as is practicable.

An employee returning from leave is entitled to return to the same position he or she left or to any equivalent position with equivalent benefits, pay and other conditions of employment. Decisions on the return to an "equivalent" position are controlled by the established school board policies and collective bargaining agreements. Employees are not entitled to accrue seniority during any such leave, but taking the leave may not result in the loss of any benefit that was accrued prior to the leave. When an employee is returning from leave due to a serious health condition, the employer may require certification from a health care provider that the employee is able to resume work if the employer has a uniform policy of requiring such certification from employees returning from medical leave.

Some provisions of the law are of particular interest to boards of education. For example, where spouses are employed by the same employer, the total amount of leave granted to both employees may be limited to twelve weeks in any twelve month period if the leave is taken for the birth, foster care placement or adoption of a child, or for the serious health condition of a parent. Otherwise, each employee is entitled to the full twelve weeks of leave.

There are two special provisions with respect to instructional employees. First, when an instructional employee requests intermittent leave due to the need for foreseeable, planned, medical treatment of the employee, or the employee's spouse, child or parent, and the employee would be on such intermittent leave for greater than twenty percent of the working days during the leave period, the school district may require that the employee choose either to (1) take leave for periods of a particular duration (not to exceed the duration of the planned medical treatment), or (2) transfer to an available alternate position for which the employee is qualified that is equivalent in pay and benefits, and that better accommodates the recurring periods of leave.

Second, when an eligible instructional employee begins leave close to the end of an academic term, the school district may restrict the return of the employee to the end of the term under the following circumstances: (1) more than five weeks before the end of the term, the employee begins a leave of at least three weeks and would return during the last three weeks of the term; (2) less than five weeks before the end of the term, the employee begins a leave of at least three weeks and would return during the last three weeks of the term, and (3) less than three weeks before the end of the term, the employee begins a leave of longer than five working days for a reason other than his or her own serious health condition.

g. Polygraph, electronic eavesdropping and electronic monitoring

Connecticut law generally prohibits school boards (or any other employer) from requiring any employee or applicant to submit to a lie detector test as a condition of obtaining or continuing employment. Conn. Gen. Stat. § 31-51g(b)(1). Violations of this provision are punishable by fines up to $1000.

The law appears to permit polygraph testing on a voluntary basis. The employer must be prepared, however, to demonstrate that the test was entirely voluntary. Before administering such a test, the employer should obtain a written statement from the employee stating that the test is completely voluntary.

Employers are also prohibited from operating a closed circuit television or any other audio or video surveillance system for the purpose of monitoring activities of employees in rest rooms, locker rooms, lounges, or other areas designed for the health or comfort of employees. Conn. Gen. Stat. § 31-48b(b). Furthermore, employers, unions and employees are all prohibited from eavesdropping or recording discussions pertaining to contract negotiations, unless all parties to the discussions have consented. Conn. Gen. Stat. § 31-48b(d). Violations of either of these provisions are punishable by fines of up to $1,000, imprisonment of up to one year or both.

In 1998, the General Assembly imposed new obligations on employers who conduct "electronic monitoring," which is defined as collection of information on the employer's premises by electronic means, including surveillance cameras (excluding those for security purposes in common areas open to public use), review of e-mail, voice mail, and possibly even magnetic access cards. Conn. Gen. Stat. § 31-48d requires that employers provide prior written notice of such monitoring to employees, and to post notice of such monitoring in a conspicuous place. The posting may serve as the prior written notice, but employers may wish to include such information in the employee handbook, if one exists.

There is an express exception to the requirement for prior written notice when the employer has reasonable grounds to believe employees are violating the law, violating the employer's or co-employees' legal rights or creating a hostile workplace environment, and monitoring may produce evidence of such misconduct. Similarly, criminal investigations are also exempt from the prior written notice requirement, and the employer may use information gathered in such an investigation.

h. Political activity and leave for public office

In the past, charter provisions in some towns have placed restrictions upon the rights of teachers and others to serve in town government. *See Cheshire v. McKenney*, 182 Conn. 253 (1980). However, in 1981 the General Assembly invalidated any such restrictions with regard to school district employees. Conn. Gen. Stat. § 10-156e provides that teachers and other school employees may serve on any governmental body of the town in which he or she resides, except of course their employing board of education. By contrast, Conn. Gen. Stat § 10-232 provides that a person cannot serve as a member of the board of education and be employed for compensation by that board of education.

The Connecticut General Assembly has protected the right of an employee to run for elective municipal or state office in various other ways as well. Any employer with twenty-five or more employees, including school districts, must grant a leave of absence to any individual who accepts full-time elective office with the state or municipal government for up to two consecutive terms of such office. Conn. Gen. Stat. § 31-51l. The employee is required to give the employer notice of his or her candidacy within thirty days of nomination. Upon expiration of the term of office and reapplication, the employer is obligated to reinstate the employee to the same or similar position with equivalent pay and benefits, unless it can show that employment circumstances have so changed as to make it "impossible or unreasonable to do so."

A special law protects persons who are candidates for the General Assembly. Candidates are protected from discrimination against them because they are running for such office. For persons who are elected to the General Assembly, the law further provides that they may not be discriminated against because they lose time from work to perform the duties of their office. However, the law does not prohibit the employer from refusing to pay the employee for any such time lost. The law provides that persons who violate these provisions may be subject to civil actions to recover costs and reasonable attorneys' fees. Conn. Gen. Stat. § 2-3a.

Similar provisions apply specifically to municipal employees. However, the law does not specifically define the term "municipal employees" in this context, and it is simply not clear whether these provisions apply to board of education employees. In any event, Conn. Gen. Stat. § 7-421 provides that any municipal employee may be a candidate for a federal, state or municipal office in a partisan election. However, the law states that any such candidate may not engage in political activity while on duty or otherwise during the time he or she is expected to perform the duties of his or her job. *Id.* The law also specifies that a municipal employee may serve on any town board or commission except the body directly responsible for supervising the employee. In addition, service on the board of finance, or a zoning or other land use planning body is not permitted unless the local charter or home rule ordinance authorizes such service. *Id.*

Any municipal employee who is elected to a full-time elective municipal office is entitled to a personal leave without pay for up to two terms or four years, whichever is shorter. Upon the expiration of the leave, the employee is entitled to reinstatement to the same or a similar position if it is available. If it is not, the employee is to be placed on all applicable reemployment lists. The employer is not required to pay wages or salary for any time lost by those running for or serving in the legislature. *Id.*

i. Jury duty

An employer may not discharge, threaten or coerce employees who are summoned for jury duty. Conn. Gen. Stat. § 51-247a. Employees who are discharged in violation of this section may seek reinstatement, lost wages, and attorney's fees. Employers must pay full-time employees serving as jurors their regular wages for the first five days of jury service. Failure to do so could result in treble damages and attorney's fees.

Many school districts have addressed the question of jury duty through collective bargaining, and some contract provisions require that employees receive full pay for the full period of any jury duty. In any event, the statutory exemption for teachers during the school year has been eliminated. Teachers can ask to be excluded for hardship reasons, as can others, but excusal is not automatic.

j. Military leave

Connecticut law provides that teachers have the right to leaves of absence for military service, and further that they shall be credited for any such service in the same way as if they had been employed during that period. Conn. Gen. Stat. § 10-156d. State law makes similar provision for non-certified employees of boards of education (and other municipal employees). Conn. Gen. Stat. § 7-462. More generally, any employee has the right to a leave of absence from his or her employer so that he or she may participate in military reserve and national guard meetings and drills. Conn. Gen. Stat. § 27-33, Conn. Gen. Stat. § 27-33a. Under the Teacher Retirement Act, teachers who enter military service while employed as teachers may continue to participate in the Teacher Retirement System, either by continuing payments themselves or by their employing board of education, or by purchasing the credit when they return to employment. *Letter from Sudol*, Teachers' Retirement Board (September 26, 2001).

Federal law provides similar protections and further provides that persons returning from military service shall be reemployed in similar positions, if such positions are available. Uniformed Services Employment and Reemployment Rights Act, 38 U.S.C. § 2024 *et seq.*

k. Whistle blower law

The General Assembly passed a "whistle blower law" in 1982 in response to a Connecticut Supreme Court ruling that disciplining an employee for disclosing illegal activities constitutes a violation of public policy. Conn. Gen. Stat. § 31-51m. *See also Sheets v. Teddy's Frosted Foods*, 179 Conn. 471 (1980).

The law prohibits discharge or any other penalty against an employee because the employee or anyone acting on the employee's behalf reports a violation or suspected violation of local, state or federal law to a public body, or because a public body requests an employee to participate in an investigation, hearing or court action. Conn. Gen. Stat. § 31-51m(b). An employer violating this law may face court orders granting the employee reinstatement, back pay, benefits, as well as attorney's fees and costs. Generally, an employer may impose disciplinary sanctions, up to and including dismissal, on employees who have falsely accused it of illegal action. Conn. Gen. Stat. § 31-51m(c). However, with public employees, caution is warranted, because such action may violate the First Amendment rights of such employees.

INDEX

385613 v.01